"The Gift of Dhamma Excels All Other Gifts"

— The Lord Buddha

Venerable Ācariya Mun Bhūridatta Thera

— A Spiritual Biography —

Ācariya Mahā Boowa Ñāṇasampanno

Translated by Bhikkhu Dick Sīlaratano

A Forest Dhamma Publication

Venerable Ācariya Mun Bhūridatta Thera

A Forest Dhamma Publication / January 2010

Author: Ācariya Mahā Boowa Ñāṇasampanno
Translator: Bhikkhu Dick Sīlaratano

ISBN 974-92007-4-8
U.S. Copyright Office Registration Number TX 5-864-808
Fourth Printing: January 2010

Printed in Thailand by:
Silpa Siam Packaging and Printing Co., Ltd.
Tel. (662) 444-3351-9
silpa@ksc.th.com

Published by:
Forest Dhamma Books
Baan Taad Forest Monastery
Udon Thani 41000, Thailand
fdbooks@gmail.com, fdbooks@hotmail.com
www.ForestDhammaBooks.com

Contents

Translator's Introduction — vii

About the Author — xv

Author's Preface — 1

1. The Early Years — 3

The Prophecy — 4

The Sign — 8

Ācariya Sao Kantasīlo — 16

Sarika Cave — 24

The Sāvaka Arahants — 41

2. The Middle Years — 55

The Dhutanga Practices — 59

A Monk's Fear of Ghosts — 68

Local Customs and Beliefs — 79

Hardship and Deprivation — 92

Graduated Teaching — 102

The Difference is in the Heart — 113

The Well-digging Incident — 118

An Impeccable Human Being — 129

3. A Heart Released — 143

The Spiritual Partner — 162

The Most Exalted Appreciation — 170

4. The Chiang Mai Years — 181

The Boxer — 191

Tigers in Disguise — 196

Powerful Magic — 210

Big Brother Elephant 220

Youthful Exuberance 226

The Mysterious Effects of Kamma 233

Hungry Ghosts 241

The Hypercritical Nāga 253

The Death of the Arahant 262

The Spiritual Warrior 266

5. Unusual Questions, Enlightening Answers 283

Complete Self-assurance 286

Past Lives 294

6. The Final Years 313

Fellowship with Pigs 320

Harsh Training Methods 331

The Therapeutic Qualities of Dhamma 343

Tigers Make the Best Teachers 352

His Final Illness 365

The Funeral 383

7. The Legacy 399

Relics Transformed 401

Other Mysteries 410

The Adventures of Ācariya Chob 426

Conclusion 438

Appendix I 451

Appendix II 455

Acknowledgements 465

Notes 467

Glossary 487

About the Translator 497

Venereable Ācariya Mun Bhūridatta Thera

Bone fragments collected after the cremation of Ācariya
Mun's body have since transformed into crystal-like
relics in various hues of translucency and opacity.

Translator's Introduction

Venerable Ācariya Mun Bhūridatta Thera is a towering figure in contemporary Thai Buddhism. He was widely revered and respected during his lifetime for the extraordinary courage and determination he displayed in practicing the ascetic way of life and for his uncompromising strictness in teaching his many disciples. During the 50 years since his death, he has assumed an exalted status in Buddhist circles and thus remains an overshadowing presence whose life and teachings have become synonymous with the Buddha's noble quest for self-transformation.

Although Ācariya Mun (pronounced to rhyme with "sun") left no written record of his own, this biography, compiled by one of his close disciples some 20 years after his death, is largely responsible for introducing his life, his achievements, and his teachings to a broad section of Buddhist society. Through the widespread popularity of this book, many Thai Buddhists have been given fresh hope that the spiritual liberation which the Buddha proclaimed to the world over 2,500 years ago, and which has been attained by so many aspirants over the succeeding centuries, is still accessible in today's modern age. Many Thais have expressed the view that they had lost confidence that *magga*, *phala*, and Nibbāna were still relevant today. But, by reading Ācariya Mun's biography, they realized that accounts of these exalted attainments are not mere fragments of ancient history, dead and dry — but a living, luminous legacy of self-transcendence accessible to any individual who is willing and able to put forth the effort needed to achieve them. They have come to understand that Buddhist monks, with their distinctive robes and monastic vocation, are not merely clerical figures representing the Buddha, Dhamma, and Sangha: some of them are indeed living proof of the Truth presented in the Buddha's teaching.

The noble aim of spiritual liberation must be accomplished by the appropriate means: the Middle Way as taught by the Lord Buddha.

Although the Buddha forbade the use of self-mortification as a means to gain enlightenment, he nevertheless authorized and encouraged those specialized ascetic practices, known as *dhutangas*, that harmonize effectively with this noble effort. The true Middle Way is not the smooth path of least resistance negotiated with easy compromises and happy mediums; but rather, it is that path of practice which most effectively counters the mental defilements that impede progress by resisting the aspirant every step of the way. The spiritual path is often arduous, being full of hardship and discomfort, while the inner forces opposed to success are formidable, and even intimidating. Thus the work of the spiritual warrior requires potent counter measures to subvert the inertial powers of laziness, craving, pride, and self-importance. So the Buddha encouraged monks, who were truly keen on extricating their hearts from the subtlest manifestations of these insidious defilements, to practice the *dhutangas*. Such ascetic observances are specifically designed to promote simplicity, humility, self-restraint, vigilance, and introspection in a monk's everyday life, and the Buddha was known to praise those monks who undertook their practice.

For this reason, the lifestyle of a Buddhist monk is founded on the ideal of life as a homeless wanderer who, having renounced the world and gone forth from the household, dresses in robes made from discarded cloth, depends on alms for a living, and takes the forest as his dwelling place. This ideal of the wandering forest monk intent on the Buddha's traditional spiritual quest is epitomized by the *dhutanga kammaṭṭhāna* way of life.

Like *dhutanga*, *kammaṭṭhāna* is a term designating a specific orientation shared by Buddhist monks who are dedicated to maintaining an austere meditative lifestyle. *Kammaṭṭhāna* (lit. "basis of work") denotes an approach to meditation practice that is directed toward uprooting every aspect of greed, hatred, and delusion from the heart and thus demolishing all bridges linking the mind to the cycle of repeated birth and death. *Kammaṭṭhāna*, with its emphasis on meditative development, and *dhutanga*, with its emphasis on the ascetic way of life conducive to intensive meditation, compliment each other perfectly in the noble effort to transcend the cycle of rebirth. They, along with the code of monastic discipline, are the cornerstones on which the edifice of a monk's practice is erected.

Both the letter and the spirit of this ascetic life of meditation can be found embodied in the life and teaching of Ācariya Mun. From the day he first ordained until the day he passed away, his entire way of life, and the example he set for his disciples, were modeled on the principles incorporated in these practices. He is credited with reviving, revitalizing, and eventually popularizing the *dhutanga kammaṭṭhāna* tradition in Thailand. Through his life-long efforts, *dhutanga* monks (or *kammaṭṭhāna* monks, the two are used interchangeably) and the mode of practice they espouse became, and still remain, a prominent feature of the Buddhist landscape there.

Ācariya Mun was especially gifted as a motivator and teacher. Many of the monks who trained directly under his tutelage have distinguished themselves by their spiritual achievements, becoming well-known teachers in their own right. They have passed on his distinctive teaching methods to their disciples in a spiritual lineage that extends to the present day. As a result, the *dhutanga kammaṭṭhāna* mode of practice gradually spread throughout the country, along with Ācariya Mun's exalted reputation. This nationwide acclaim began to escalate during the last years of his life and continued to grow after his death until he came to be considered a national "saint" by almost unanimous consent. In recent decades, he has gained recognition beyond the confines of his native land as one of the 20th century's truly great religious figures.

Ācariya Mun's life epitomized the Buddhist ideal of the wandering monk intent on renunciation and solitude, walking alone through forests and mountains in search of secluded places that offer body and mind a calm, quiet environment in which to practice meditation for the purpose of transcending all suffering. His was a life lived entirely out of doors at the mercy of the elements and the vagaries of weather. In such an environment, a *dhutanga* monk developed a deep appreciation of nature. His daily life was full of forests and mountains, rivers and streams, caves, overhanging cliffs, and wild creatures large and small. He moved from place to place by hiking along lonely wilderness trails in remote frontier regions where the population was sparse and village communities far apart. Since his livelihood depended on the alms food he collected from those small settlements, a *dhutanga* monk never knew where his next meal would come from, or whether he would get any food at all.

Despite the hardships and the uncertainties, the forest was a home to the wandering monk: it was his school, his training ground, and his sanctuary; and life there was safe provided that he remained vigilant and faithful to the principles of the Buddha's teaching. Living and practicing in the relatively uncultivated, undomesticated rural backwater that comprised most of Thailand at the turn of the 20th century, a *dhutanga* monk like Ācariya Mun found himself wandering through a centuries-old setting little changed from the time of the Buddha 2,500 years ago.

It is helpful to understand the temporal and cultural background to Ācariya Mun's wandering lifestyle. Thailand in the late 19th and early 20th centuries was a loose confederation of principalities that were largely inaccessible to the central authority because most of the land was densely forested and paved roads were almost nonexistent. During that period, 80% of Thailand's landmass was blanketed with pristine forests of mostly deciduous hardwoods and thick sub-tropical undergrowth. The lives of people in the hinterland areas were sustained by subsistence farming and the hunting of wild animals. Teeming with tigers and elephants, the vast forests were seen as being dangerous and frightening places, so the inhabitants banded together in village communities for the safety and companionship they provided. In the more remote frontier regions, such settlements were often a day's walk from one another following trails that made their way through uninterrupted woodland.

Forests and the rhythms of nature were defining features of the folklore and culture of those hardy people. To the villagers living together in isolated communities, the vast tracts of wilderness were forbidding, inhospitable territory where wild animals roamed freely and malevolent spirits were said to hold sway. The huge Bengal tigers indigenous to that part of the world were especially fearsome. Such creatures ruled not only the forests but the fears and fantasies of local people and monks alike.

Popular fear of those impenetrable forest areas turned them into places of isolation and solitude where no one dared to venture alone. It was in this remote wilderness environment that Ācariya Mun and his *dhutanga* monks lived and wandered, practicing the ascetic way of life. Their meditation practice and the mental fortitude it instilled in them were their only defences against the hardships and potential dangers they faced every day. Forests and mountains were proven training grounds for such monks, who saw themselves as spiritual warriors battling their own mental defilements for the sake of ultimate victory.

The story of Ācariya Mun's life is a vivid portrait of a consummate spiritual warrior unrivaled in modern times who practiced the Buddha's path to freedom with such perfection that he left those who knew and revered him in no doubt that he truly was a Noble disciple. A beautiful story from beginning to end, his life is reminiscent of those famed accounts of the Buddha's great disciples chronicled in the ancient texts. Like theirs, his life shows us that the spiritual ideals taught by the Buddha are achieved by real human beings struggling against the same fundamental hindrances that we find within ourselves. Thus we are made to feel that the Buddha's "ancient" path to spiritual liberation is as wholly relevant today as it was 2,500 years ago.

To this end, this biography of Ācariya Mun is less concerned with a precise account of events as they unfolded in Ācariya Mun's life and career than it is with providing a source of inspiration and edification for those devoted to Buddhist ideals. The author's perspective is that of an affirmative witness and advocate rather than an impartial observer chronicling events. Being a spiritual biography, it is intended to give us an insight into a model spiritual life. As such, this book should be viewed above all as an exercise in contemplation.

One aspect of Ācariya Mun's teaching career deserves special mention as it surfaces time and again in the course of his biography. Ācariya Mun possessed a unique ability to communicate directly with nonhuman beings from many different realms of existence. He was continually in contact with beings in the higher and lower celestial realms, spirits of the terrestrial realms, *nāgas*, *yakkhas*, ghosts of many sorts, and even the denizens of the hell realms — all of whom are invisible to the human eye and inaudible to the human ear but clearly known by the inner psychic faculties of divine sight and divine hearing.

The comprehensive worldview underlying Buddhist cosmology differs significantly from the view of the gross physical universe presented to us by contemporary science. In the traditional Buddhist worldview, the universe is inhabited not only by the gross physical beings that comprise the human and animal worlds but also by various classes of nonphysical, divine beings, called *devas*, that exist in a hierarchy of increasing subtlety and refinement, and by numerous classes of lower beings living in the sub-human realms of existence. Only the human and animal worlds are discernible to normal human sense faculties. The others dwell in a spiritual dimension that exists outside the range of human concepts of space and time, and therefore, beyond the sphere of the material universe as we perceive it.

It was Ācariya Mun's remarkable, inherent capacity for communicating with many classes of living beings that made him a teacher of truly universal significance. Knowing that living beings throughout the sentient universe share a common heritage of repeated existence and a common desire to avoid suffering and gain happiness, a great teacher realizes their common need to understand the way of Dhamma in order to fulfil their spiritual potential and attain enduring happiness. Having the eye of wisdom, he made no fundamental distinction between the hearts of people and the hearts of *devas*, but tailored his teaching to fit their specific circumstances and levels of understanding. Although the message was essentially the same, the medium of communication was different. He communicated with human beings through the medium of verbal expression, while he used non-verbal, telepathic communication with all classes of nonhuman beings.

To appreciate Ācariya Mun's extraordinary abilities we must be prepared to accept that the world we perceive through our senses constitutes only a small portion of experiential reality; that there exists this spiritual universe of *devas* and *brahmas* which is beyond the range of our limited sense faculties. For in truth, the universe of the wise is much more vast than the one perceived by the average person. The wise can know and understand dimensions of reality that others do not even suspect exist, and their knowledge of the principles underlying all existence gives them an insight into the phenomenal world that defies conventional limits.

Ācariya Mun's finely-tuned powers of perception contacted an immense variety of external phenomena, and in the best Buddhist tradition he spent a considerable amount of time and energy engaged in teaching them Dhamma. Such beings were as much a part of his personal world experience as the wild animals in the forest and the monks he trained so tirelessly. By virtue of his unparalleled expertise in these matters, he always felt a special obligation toward their spiritual welfare.

Such phenomena are what Ācariya Mun called "mysteries of the heart"; for they are conscious, living beings dwelling in spiritual dimensions that are just as real as the one we inhabit, even though those spheres lie outside the realm of human existential concepts. The words "heart" and "mind" are used interchangeably in Thai vernacular. "Heart" is often the preferred term, as "mind" tends to exclude the emotional and spiritual dimensions associated with the heart. The heart is the essential knowing nature that forms the basic foundation of the entire sentient universe. It is the fundamental awareness underlying all conscious existence and the very basis of all mental and emotional processes. The heart forms the core within the bodies of all living beings. It is the center, the substance, the primary essence within the body. Constantly emphasizing its paramount significance, Ācariya Mun always claimed that *the heart is the most important thing in the world.* For this reason, the story of Ācariya Mun's life and teachings is a story of the heart's struggle for spiritual transcendence, and a revelation of the ineffable mystery of the heart's pure essence.

The Pāli term *"citta"* is a word that Ācariya Mun often used when referring to this essential knowing nature, commonly known as heart and mind. Like so many words in the Buddhist lexicon, it is essentially a technical term used specifically in the science of Buddhist theory and practice. Since such terms represent salient aspects of the subject matter of this book, some of them have been kept in their original form. Generally, in cases where a suitably accurate English translation exists, that word has been substituted, with the Pāli term in question being annotated in an explanatory note. There are, however, certain terms for which, due to the complex and comprehensive nature of the truths they represent, no truly adequate English word exists. Those specialized terms have largely been left in the original Pāli. They may be found explained in the Notes and Glossary sections at the back of the book, and the reader is encouraged to take full advantage of these reference materials.

The author, Ācariya Mahā Boowa Ñāṇasampanno

Ācariya Mahā Boowa (circa 1962)

About the Author

Venerable Ācariya Mahā Boowa Ñāṇasampanno is himself an outstanding and distinguished figure in contemporary Thai Buddhism. He is well-known and respected by people from all walks of life for his impeccable wisdom and his brilliant expository skills. By aptitude and temperament, he is the ideal person to record for posterity Ācariya Mun's life and teachings. Spiritually, he is one of Ācariya Mun's exceptionally gifted disciples; didactically, he is one of the *dhutanga* tradition's truly masterful spokesmen. His no-nonsense, resolute character, his extraordinary charisma, and his rhetorical skills have established him as Ācariya Mun's natural successor.

Born in 1913 in the northeastern province of Udon Thani, Ācariya Mahā Boowa was ordained as a Buddhist monk in 1934. Having spent the first 7 years of his monastic career studying the Buddhist canonical texts, for which he earned a degree in Pāli studies and the title "Mahā", he adopted the wandering lifestyle of a *dhutanga* monk and set out to search for Ācariya Mun. Finally meeting up with him in 1942, he was accepted as a disciple and remained living under his tutelage until his death in 1949.

In the period following Ācariya Mun's death, Ācariya Mahā Boowa, by then fully accomplished himself, soon became a central figure in efforts to maintain continuity within the *dhutanga kammaṭṭhāna* fraternity and so preserve Ācariya Mun's unique mode of practice for future generations. He helped to spearhead a concerted attempt to present Ācariya Mun's life and teachings to an increasingly wider audience of Buddhist faithful. Eventually, in 1971, he authored this biography to showcase the principles and ideals that underpin *dhutanga kammaṭṭhāna* training methods and inform their proper practice.

By 1960, the world outside the forest came to exert a significant impact on the *dhutanga* tradition. The rapid deforestation of that period caused *dhutanga* monks to modify, and eventually curtail, their wandering lifestyle. As the geographic environment changed, teachers like Ācariya Mahā Boowa began establishing permanent monastic communities where *dhutanga* monks could conveniently carry on Ācariya Mun's lineage, striving to maintain the virtues of renunciation, strict discipline, and intensive meditation. Practicing monks gravitated to these forest monasteries in large numbers and transformed them into great centers of Buddhist practice. At Wat Pa Baan Taad, Ācariya Mahā Boowa's forest monastery in Udon Thani, a religious center arose spontaneously, created by the students themselves, who came for purely spiritual motives in hopes of receiving instruction from a genuine master. In the years that followed, the many Western monks who came to Ācariya Mahā Boowa were able to share wholeheartedly in this unique religious experience. Some have lived there practicing under his tutelage ever since, helping to spawn an international following which today spans the globe.

Highly revered at home and abroad, Ācariya Mahā Boowa remains to this day actively engaged in teaching both monks and laity, elucidating for them the fundamental principles of Buddhism and encouraging them to practice those bold and incisive techniques that Ācariya Mun used so effectively. Like Ācariya Mun, he stresses a mode of practice in which wisdom remains a priority at all times. Although ultimately pointing to the ineffable mysteries of the mind's pure essence, the teaching he presents for us is a system of instruction that is full of down-to-earth, practical methods suitable for everyone desiring to succeed at meditation. Studied carefully, it may well offer direction to persons who otherwise have no idea where their practice is taking them.

Ācariya Mun Bhūridatto (1870-1949)

Ācariya Sao Kantasīlo (1859-1942)

Chao Khun Upāli Guṇūpamācariya (1856-1932)

Ācariya Mun (second from right) with a group of his disciples

Monk's identification certificate of Ācariya Mun

Author's Preface

The life story that you are about to read of Ācariya Mun Bhūridatta Thera, his way of practice and his moral goodness, is the result of extensive research which I conducted in consultation with many *ācariyas* of his discipleship who lived with him throughout various periods of his monastic life.

I sought out these *ācariyas*, recorded their memories of him, and compiled their recollections to write this biography. This account is not as completely accurate as I wished, because it was virtually impossible for the monks to remember all the many experiences that Ācariya Mun conveyed to them about his life as a wandering forest monk. But, if I were to wait for every detail to be recalled before writing this biography, it would only be a matter of time before all information is forgotten and forever lost. All hope of recording his story for the edification of interested readers would then be surely lost as well. With great difficulty, I composed this biography; and, although it is incomplete, my hope is that it will prove to be of some benefit to the reader.

I shall attempt to depict the many aspects of Ācariya Mun's daily conduct, as well as the knowledge and insights he attained and elucidated to his disciples. I intend to illustrate his Noble life in the style of the Venerable Ācariyas of antiquity who transcribed the essence of the lives of the Buddha's Arahant disciples into ancient texts, ensuring that all future generations will have some understanding of the results that are possible when the Dhamma is practiced sincerely. May the reader forgive me if my presentation of Ācariya Mun's life appears inappropriate in any way. Yet the truth is that it is a factual account, representing the memories of Ācariya Mun Bhūridatta Thera's life as he himself conveyed them to us. Although I am not wholly comfortable with the book, I have decided to publish it anyway, because I feel that readers interested in Dhamma may gain some valuable insight.

1

The Early Years

The Venerable Ācariya Mun Bhūridatta Thera was a *vipassanā*
meditation master of the highest caliber of this present age; one
who is truly worthy of the eminent praise and admiration
accorded to him by his close disciples. He taught the profound nature
of Dhamma with such authority and persuasion that he left no doubts
among his students about the exalted level of his spiritual attainment.
His devoted followers consist of numerous monks and laity from
virtually every region of Thailand. Besides these, he has many more
devotees in Laos, where both monks and lay people feel a deep reverence for him.

His story is truly a magnificent one throughout: from his early years
in lay life through his long endeavor as a Buddhist monk to the day
he finally passed away. Nowadays, a life of such unblemished excellence
is harder to come by than a lode of precious gemstones.

Ācariya Mun was born into a traditional Buddhist family on Thurs-
day, January 20, 1870, the Year of the Goat. His birthplace was the
village of Ban Khambong in the Khongjiam district of Ubon Ratchathani province.

His father's name was Khamduang; his mother's Jun; and his family
surname Kaenkaew. He was the eldest child of eight siblings, though
only two of them were still alive when he passed away. A child of small
stature with a fair complexion, he was naturally quick, energetic,
intelligent, and resourceful.

At the age of fifteen he ordained as a novice[1] in his village monastery where he developed an enthusiasm for the study of Dhamma, memorizing the texts with exceptional speed. A young novice of affable character, he never caused his teachers or fellows any trouble.

Two years into his new way of life his father requested him to give up the robes, and he was required to return to lay life in order to help out at home. However, his fondness for the monk's life was so pronounced that he was certain he would ordain again some day. His good memories of life in a monk's robes never faded. Thus, he resolved to enter the monkhood again as soon as possible. This strong sense of purpose was due, no doubt, to the power of that indomitable faith, known as *saddhā*, which was such an integral part of his character.

When he reached age twenty-two, he felt an urge to ordain as a monk. So, for that purpose, he took leave of his parents. Not wanting to discourage his aspirations and having also kept the hope that their son would ordain again someday, they gave their permission. To this end, they provided him with a complete set of a monk's basic requisites for his ordination. On June 12, 1893,[2] he received his *Bhikkhu* ordination at Wat Liap monastery in the provincial town of Ubon Ratchathani.

His *upajjhāya* was the Venerable Ariyakawi; his *kammavācariya* was Phra Khru Sitha; and his *anusāsanācariya* was Phra Khru Prajuk Ubonkhun.[3] He was given the monastic name "Bhūridatta".[4] After his ordination, he took residence at Wat Liap in Ācariya Sao's *vipassanā* meditation center.

The Prophecy

When Ācariya Mun first began practicing *vipassanā* at Ācariya Sao's center, he meditated constantly, internally repeating the word "*buddho*", the recollection of the Buddha, as he preferred this preparatory Dhamma theme above all others. In the beginning, he failed to experience the degree of calm and happiness that he expected, which caused him to doubt whether he was practicing correctly. Despite his doubt he didn't flag in his persistent use of the word "*buddho*", and eventually his heart developed a certain measure of calm.

One night he had a dream:

He walked out of a village and entered a large, dense jungle over-grown with tangled undergrowth. He could hardly find a way to penetrate it. He struggled to find his way through this vast thicket until he finally emerged safe at the other end. When he came out, he found himself at the edge of an immense field that stretched as far as the eye could see. He set out resolutely, walking across this field until he happened to come across a huge fallen *jāti* tree.[5]

Felled long ago, its trunk was partially embedded in the ground, and most of its bark and sapwood had already rotted away. He climbed upon this giant *jāti* log and walked along its full length. As he walked, he reflected inwardly. He realized that this tree would never sprout and grow again. He compared this with his own life which would certainly not rise again in any future existence. He identified the dead *jāti* tree with his own life in *saṁsāra*. Seeing that the tree had rotted away, never to root and spring to life again, he reckoned that, by keeping up his diligent practice, he would surely find a way to reach a definite conclusion to his own life in this very existence. The vast expanse of open field symbolized the nature of the never-ending cycle of birth and death.

As he stood on the log contemplating this, a broad white stallion trotted up and stood next to the fallen *jāti* tree. As it stood there, Ācariya Mun felt an urge to ride it. So, he mounted the mysterious horse which immediately raced off at full gallop. He had no idea where he was being taken or why. The horse just continued gallop-ing at full speed without showing any obvious sign of direction or purpose. The distance it traveled across the vast field seemed immeasurable. As they strode along, Ācariya Mun saw a beautiful *Tipiṭika* cabinet[6] in the distance, adorned with exquisite silver trim. Without guidance, the horse led him directly to the enclosed bookcase, and came to a halt right in front of it. The moment Ācariya Mun dismounted with the aim of opening the cabinet, the white stallion vanished without a trace. As he stepped towards the bookcase, he noticed that it was standing at the very edge of the field with nothing in the background but more of the dense jungle, entangled and smothered with undergrowth. He saw no way of pen-etrating it. When he came to the *Tipiṭika* cabinet, he reached out to open it; but, before he had a chance to discover the contents inside, he woke up.

This was a dream *nimitta,* an omen confirming his belief that if he persevered in his efforts, he would undoubtedly discover a path for attaining what he sought. From then on, with renewed determination Ācariya Mun meditated intensively, unrelenting in his efforts to constantly repeat *"buddho"* as he conducted all his daily affairs. At the same time, he very carefully observed the austere *dhutanga* practices which he undertook at the time of his ordination, and continued to practice for the rest of his life.[7] The *dhutangas* he voluntarily undertook were: wearing only robes made from discarded cloth — not accepting robes directly offered by lay supporters; going on almsround every day without fail — except those days when he decided to fast; accepting and eating only food received in his alms bowl — never receiving food offered after his almsround; eating only one meal a day — never eating food after the one meal; eating only out of the alms bowl — never eating food that is not inside the one vessel; living in the forest — which means wandering through forested terrain, living and sleeping in the wilds, in the mountains or in the valleys; some time spent living under a canopy of trees, in a cave, or under an overhanging cliff; and wearing only his three principal robes — the outer robe, the upper robe, and the lower robe,[8] with the addition of a bathing cloth which is necessary to have nowadays.

Ācariya Mun also observed the remainder of the thirteen *dhutanga* practices when circumstances were convenient; but, he upheld the above seven routinely until they became integrated into his character. They became so much a part of him that it would be difficult to find one who is his equal these days.

On his own accord, he showed earnestness in finding meaning in everything he did. He never approached his duties halfheartedly. His sincere aim, always, was to transcend the world. Everything he did was directed toward the noble effort of destroying the *kilesas*[9] within himself. Due to this sense of purpose, he allowed no hiding room in his heart for arrogance and conceit, despite being exposed to the same defiling influences as was everyone else. In one respect he differed markedly from the average person: instead of allowing his mind free reign for the *kilesas* to trample all over, he always put up a fight, attacking them at every opportunity.

Later, when he felt confident that he had developed a sufficiently solid foundation in his meditation, he investigated the dream *nimitta*. Turning his attention to the dream, he analyzed it until he gradually comprehended its full meaning. He saw that ordaining as a monk and practicing the Dhamma properly was equivalent to raising the level of the *citta* beyond the poisons of the world. The dense, entangled jungle, where dangers of every kind await to ambush, was the analogy for the *citta*, a repository of pain and misery. The *citta* must be lifted until it reaches the vast, wide open expanse — a sphere of Ultimate Happiness, and freedom from all fear and concern.[10]

The majestic white stallion symbolized the path of practicing Dhamma. He rode the horse as the means of transport to the realm of complete contentment, where he encountered the beautiful *Tipiṭika* cabinet with an exquisite design. Able only to look upon it, he lacked the spiritual perfection necessary to secure the cabinet's opening and admire its library to his heart's content — a feat accomplished only by one who has acquired *catu paṭisambhidāñāṇa*. A person endowed with this four-fold knowledge is renown throughout the three worlds for his brilliant wisdom and his comprehensive knowledge of teaching methods, extensive as the sea and sky. Such a one is never at a loss when teaching *devas* and humans.

Because Ācariya Mun lacked a sufficiently high level of spiritual perfection, he was denied the opportunity to open the cabinet, and had to be content with simply admiring its beauty. Consequently, he would attain only the level of *paṭisambhidānusāsana*, meaning that he had sufficient wisdom and expository skills to elucidate to others the basic path of Buddhist practice, but not its entire breadth and depth. Although he humbly stated that his teaching was merely sufficient to show the way, those who witnessed his practice and heard the profound Dhamma that he taught throughout his life were so deeply impressed that no words can describe it. It would certainly be difficult to witness or hear anything comparable in this day and age — an age much in need of such a noble person.

The Sign

At one point during his meditation training at Wat Liap, Ācariya Mun's *citta* 'converged' into a state of calm[11] and a vision arose spontaneously. The mental image[12] was of a dead body laid out before him, bloated, oozing pus, and seeping with bodily fluids. Vultures and dogs were fighting over the corpse, tearing into the rotting flesh and flinging it around, until what remained was all scattered about. The whole scene was unimaginably disgusting, and he was appalled.

From then on, Ācariya Mun constantly used this image as a mental object to contemplate at all times — whether sitting in *samādhi*, walking in meditation, or engaging in other daily activities. He continued in this manner until, one day, the image of the corpse changed into a translucent disk that appeared suspended before him. The more he focused intensely on the disk, the more it changed its appearance without pause. The more he tried to follow, the more it altered its form so that he found it impossible to tell where the series of images would end. The more he investigated the visions, the more they continued to change in character — *ad infinitum*. For example, the disk became a tall mountain range where Ācariya Mun found himself walking, brandishing a sharp sword and wearing shoes. Then, a massive wall with a gate appeared. He opened the gate to look inside and saw a monastery where several monks were sitting in meditation. Near the wall he saw a steep cliff with a cave where a hermit was living. He noticed a conveyance, shaped like a cradle and hanging down the face of the cliff by a rope. Climbing into the cradle-like conveyance, he was drawn up to the mountain peak. At the summit, he found a large Chinese junk with a square table inside, and a hanging lantern that cast a luminescent glow upon the whole mountain terrain. He found himself eating a meal on the mountain peak ... and so on, and so forth, until it was impossible to see an end to it all. Ācariya Mun said that all the images he experienced in this manner were far too numerous to recall.

For a full three months, Ācariya Mun continued to meditate in this way. Each time when he dropped into *samādhi*, he withdrew from it to continue his investigation of the translucent disk which just kept giving him a seemingly endless series of images. However, he did not receive enough beneficial results from this to be convinced that this was the correct method. For after practicing in this manner, he was over-

8

sensitive to the common sights and sounds around him. Pleased by this and disappointed by that, he liked some things and hated others. It seemed that he could never find a stable sense of balance.

Because of this sensitivity, he came to believe that the *samādhi* which he practiced was definitely the wrong path to follow. If it were really correct, why did he fail to experience peace and calm consistently in his practice? On the contrary, his mind felt distracted and unsettled, influenced by many sense objects that it encountered — much like a person who had never undergone any meditation training at all. Perhaps the practice of directing his attention outwards towards external phenomena violated the fundamental principles of meditation. Maybe this was the reason he failed to gain the promised benefits of inner peace and happiness.

Thus, Ācariya Mun came to a new understanding about himself. Instead of focusing his mind on external matters, he brought his *citta* back inside, within the confines of his own physical body. From then on, his investigations were centered only on his own body.

Keeping a sharp mindfulness, he examined the body from top to bottom, side to side, inside out and throughout; every body part and every aspect. In the beginning, he preferred to conduct his examinations while walking in meditation, pacing back and forth in deep thought. Sometimes he needed to rest his body from these exertions. So, he sat in *samādhi* for awhile, though he absolutely refused to let his *citta* 'converge' into its habitual state of calm. Rather, he forced it to stay put within the body's domain. The *citta* had no other choice but to travel around the many parts of the body and probe into them. When it was time for him to lie down, the investigation continued inside his mind until he fell asleep.

He meditated like this for several days until he felt ready to sit in *samādhi* and try to attain a state of calm with his newly discovered method. He challenged himself to find out what state of calm the *citta* could attain. Deprived of peace for many days now, and having begun the intense training associated with body contemplation, his *citta* 'converged' rapidly into a calm state with unprecedented ease. He knew with certainty that he had the correct method: for, when his *citta* 'converged' this time, his body appeared to be separated from himself. It seemed to split into two at that moment. Mindfulness was in force during the entire time, right to the moment that the *citta* dropped into *samādhi*. It didn't wander and waver about as it had previously. Thus,

Ācariya Mun was convinced that his newfound method was the right one for the preliminary work of meditation practice.

From then on, he continued to religiously practice body contemplation until he could attain a state of calm whenever he wanted. With persistence, he gradually became more and more skilled in this method, until the *citta* was firmly anchored in *samādhi*. He had wasted three whole months chasing the disk and its illusions. But now, his mindfulness no longer abandoned him, and therefore, he was no longer adversely affected by the influences around him. This whole episode clearly shows the disadvantages of not having a wise teacher to guide one. Misjudgments occur without timely advice and direction in meditation. Ācariya Mun was a perfect example of this. Having no teacher can lead to costly mistakes that can easily harm the meditator, or, at the very least, delay his progress.

DURING ĀCARIYA MUN'S early years as a wandering monk, people showed little interest in the practice of *kammaṭṭhāna* meditation. Many regarded it as something strange, even alien to Buddhism, having no legitimate place in the life of a monk. Back then, a *dhutanga* monk, walking in the distance on the far side of a field, was enough to send country folk into a panic. Being fearful, those still close to the village quickly ran home. Those walking near the forest ran into the thick foliage to hide, being too scared to stand their ground or greet the monks. Thus, *dhutanga* monks, wandering in unfamiliar regions during their travels, seldom had a chance to ask the locals for much needed directions.

Women from the countryside often took their small children on excursions into the surrounding hills to pick wild herbs and edible plants, or to fish in outlying ponds. Suddenly spotting a party of *dhutanga* monks walking toward them, they would yell to each other in alarm, "Dhamma monks! Dhamma monks are coming!" With that they threw their baskets and other gear to the ground with a thud, and frantically rushed to find a safe hiding-place. Their discarded belongings could have been damaged or broken when flung to the ground, but they took no notice; everyone simply fled into the nearby forest, or if close by, to their village homes.

Meanwhile the children, who had no idea what was happening, started crying and pleading for help when they saw their mothers scream and run away. Too slow to keep pace with the adults, the little ones

10

raced around in confusion. Stranded, they ran back and forth in the open field while their mothers remained in the forest, too frightened to emerge and retrieve them. An amusing scene of needless panic, but at the same time pitiful: to see innocent children so frightened, running in circles, desperately crying in search of their mothers.

Obviously the situation didn't look good, so the *dhutanga* monks hurried past lest their prolonged presence provoke even more hysteria. Had they made any attempt to approach the children, the incident might have gotten out of control with terrified kids frantically scattering in all directions, their shrill screams ringing through the forest. In the meantime, their anxious mothers huddled, trembling, behind the trees, afraid of the 'Dhamma monks' and, at the same time, afraid that their children might flee in all directions. They watched nervously until the monks were out of sight.

When the monks finally disappeared, a big commotion erupted as mothers and children dashed excitedly about, trying to find one another. By the time the whole group was safely reunited, it seemed as though the entire village had disbanded for awhile. The reunion was accompanied by a hubbub of chatter, everybody laughing about the sudden appearance of the 'Dhamma monks' and the chaos that followed.

Such occurrences were common in those early years: women and children were terrified because they had never before seen *dhutanga kammaṭṭhāna* monks. Ordinarily people knew nothing about them and showed little interest, except to flee at their sight. There are several possible reasons for this. Firstly, their appearance was rather austere and reserved. They were unlikely to show much familiarity with anyone they hadn't personally known for a long time; someone who knew their habits well. Also, their robes and other requisites were an ochre color from dye made from the heartwood of the jackfruit tree — a color that was striking but had a tendency to inspire more fear than devotion.

These jackfruit-colored robes were worn by *dhutanga* monks as they wandered from place to place practicing the ascetic way of life. They carried their umbrella-tents,[13] which were considerably larger than ordinary umbrellas, slung over one shoulder. Over the other shoulder they carried their alms bowls. Walking in single file and dressed in their yellowish-brown robes, they were an eye-catching sight to those as yet unfamiliar with their mode of practice. Finding a quiet spot, conducive to meditation, *dhutanga* monks settled for a while in the outlying forests of rural communities, allowing the locals a chance to get better acquainted with them. By listening to their teachings, questioning them, and receiving their advice, people's lives benefited in so many ways. Gradually over time, their hearts grew to accept the reasonable explanations they heard, and faith issued naturally on its own. With a belief in Dhamma thus instilled in their hearts, old suspicions died away to be replaced by a reverence for the monks whose teachings made such an impression. Then, to those well acquainted with their peaceful temperament and exemplary conduct, the mere sight of monks walking across the countryside inspired devotion. During that early period, such enlightening experiences were shared by country people all over Thailand.

Traveling far and wide, and determined to practice correctly for the sake of Dhamma, *dhutanga* monks always managed to impress people and do them great service. They didn't depend on publicity to get out their message. They relied instead on their exemplary behavior[14] as a natural means of gaining public interest.

A *dhutanga* monk who is concentrated on Dhamma considers wandering in search of seclusion to be an indispensable part of his personal practice. Secluded places offer his mind and body a calm, quiet environment. So it was with Ācariya Mun. Each year at the end of the rainy season retreat he started traveling, hiking through forests and mountains in locales where he found just enough small villages to support his daily almsround. More than any other part of the country, he enjoyed wandering in Thailand's Northeast region. Among his favorites were the vast forests and mountain ranges in the provinces of Nakhon Phanom, Sakon Nakhon, Udon Thani, Nong Khai, Loei, and Lom Sak; or on the Laotian side of the Mekong River in such places as Tha Khek, Vientiane, and Luang Prabang. Those locations with their huge tracts of forest and mountainous terrain were ideally suited to practicing the ascetic way of life.

Wherever he was, whatever the time of day, Ācariya Mun's primary focus remained the same: working tirelessly to improve his meditation practice. He knew that this was his most important task in life. By nature, he disliked involvement in monastic building projects. He preferred to concentrate exclusively on the inner work of meditative development. He avoided socializing with fellow monks and remained aloof from civil society, much preferring life alone — a style of living that allowed him the freedom to focus all his attention and energy on one main task: transcending *dukkha*.[15] Earnestness and sincerity characterized everything he did: never deceiving himself, he never misled others.

The incredible energy, endurance, and circumspection that he put into his practice were truly amazing. Qualities such as these helped to ensure that *samādhi* and wisdom steadily progressed, never showing any signs of decline. Since the day he first discovered body contemplation to be the right method for the preliminary work of meditation, he kept that contemplation always in mind. Assiduously maintaining that method, repeatedly investigating his body, over and over again, he became very skilled at mentally dissecting the various body parts, large and small, and then breaking them apart with wisdom. Eventually, he could dissect his entire body at will and then reduce the whole lot to its constituent elements.

Through perseverance, Ācariya Mun steadily and increasingly attained more peaceful and calmer states of mind. He wandered through forests and over mountains, stopping at suitable locations to intensify his practice; but, never did he relax the persistent effort he put into all his activities. Whether walking for alms, sweeping the grounds, washing a spittoon, sewing or dying his robes, eating a meal, or simply stretching his legs, he was aware of striving to perfect himself at every waking moment and in all activities, without exception. Only when the time came to sleep did he relent. Even then, he resolved to get up immediately, without hesitation, as soon as he awoke. He made sure that this habit became ingrained in his character. The moment he was conscious of being awake, he rose quickly, washed his face, and resumed his meditation practice. If he still felt sleepy, he refused to sit in meditation right away for fear of nodding off to sleep again. Instead, he practiced walking meditation, striding back and forth to dispel the drowsiness that threatened to overtake him at the slightest lapse in vigilance. If walking slowly proved ineffective, he sought to invigorate himself by quickening his pace. Only when all drowsiness disappeared and he began to feel tired did he leave his meditation track to sit down to continue meditating until dawn.

Shortly after dawn, he prepared to go on his almsround. Wearing his lower robe, placing his under and upper robes together and wrapped about him, his alms bowl hanging from his shoulder by a strap, he walked to the nearest village in a self-composed manner, careful to maintain mindfulness the entire way. Considering his hike to and from the village a form of walking meditation, he focused his attention inward every step of the way, insuring that his mind did not venture out to become involved with any emotionally-charged sense object along the route. Returning to his campsite, or the monastery where he resided, he arranged the food he had received in his alms bowl. As a matter of principle, he ate only the food he was offered in the village, refusing to accept any food brought to him afterward. Only much later, in his very old age, did he relax this practice somewhat, agreeing to accept food that the faithful offered him in the monastery. During his early years, he ate only the food he had received in his alms bowl.

With everything to be eaten placed in the bowl, he sat contemplating the true purpose of the food[16] he was about to eat as a means of dousing the inner fires of hell; that is to say, any craving for food that might arise due to hunger. Otherwise, the mind might succumb to the power of craving and indulge in the fine taste of food, when in fact, it should be reflecting on food's essential qualities: how all food, being simply a composition of gross elements, is inherently disgusting by its very nature.[17] With this thought firmly fixed in his mind, he chewed his food mindfully to deny any opening to craving until he had finished the meal. Afterwards, he washed the bowl, wiped it dry, exposed it to direct sunlight for a few minutes, then replaced it in its cloth covering and put it neatly away in its proper place. Then, it was time once again to resume the task of battling the *kilesas*, with the aim of destroying them gradually until they were thoroughly defeated and unable ever again to trouble his mind.

It must be understood, however, that the business of destroying *kilesas* is an inexpressibly difficult task to accomplish. For though we may be determined to burn the *kilesas* to ashes, what invariably tends to happen is that the *kilesas* turn around and burn us, causing us so much hardship that we quickly abandon those same virtuous qualities that we meant to develop. We clearly see this negative impact and want to get rid of the *kilesas*; but then, we undermine our noble purpose by failing to act decisively against them, fearing that the difficulties of such action will prove too painful. Unopposed, the *kilesas* become lord masters of our hearts, pushing their way in and claiming our hearts as their exclusive domain. Sadly, very few people in this world possess the knowledge and understanding to counteract these defilements. Hence, living beings throughout the three worlds of

14

existence are forever surrendering to their dominance. Only the Lord Buddha discovered the way to completely cleanse his heart of them: never again did they defeat him.

After achieving that comprehensive victory, the Lord Buddha compassionately turned his attention to teaching the way, proclaiming the Dhamma to his disciples and inspiring them to resolutely follow the same Noble Path that he had taken. Practicing thus, they were able to emulate his supreme achievement, reaching the very end of the Noble Path, the highest attainment: Nibbāna. Dealing the all- powerful *kilesas* a fatal blow, these Noble individuals eradicated them from their hearts forever. Having extinguished their *kilesas*, they became those Arahant disciples that people the world over have worshipped with such devotion ever since.

Ācariya Mun was another Noble individual following in the footsteps of the Lord Buddha. He truly possessed unshakable faith and uncompromising resolve — he didn't merely talk about them. When the morning meal was over, he immediately entered the forest to begin walking meditation in those peaceful surroundings that were so conducive to calm and inner happiness. First walking, later sitting, he pursued his meditation until he felt the time was right to take a short rest. His strength renewed, he resumed his attack on the *kilesas*, creators of the endless cycle of existence. With such determination and steadfast application to the task, the *kilesas* were never given reason to scoff at Ācariya Mun's efforts. While practicing *samādhi* intensively, he also worked tirelessly to develop insight, his wisdom revolving relentlessly around whatever object he was investigating. In that way, *samādhi* and *vipassanā* were developed in tandem, neither one lagging behind the other; and his heart remained peaceful and contented in his practice.

Still, periods of slow progress were inevitable, for he had no one to advise him when he got stuck. Often he spent many days working his way through a specific problem, painstakingly figuring out the solution for himself. He was obliged to exhaustively investigate these stumbling blocks in his practice, examining every facet carefully, because they were a hindrance to his progress and also potentially dangerous. In such situations, the advice of a good teacher can be invaluable, helping the meditator to advance quickly and confidently without wasting time. For this reason, it's very important that meditators have a *kalyāṇamitta*. Ācariya Mun personally experienced the drawbacks of not having such a wise friend to give him timely advice, insisting that it was a definite disadvantage.

Ācariya Sao Kantasīlo

In his early years of practice, Ācariya Mun often wandered *dhutanga* in the company of Ācariya Sao,[18] comforted in the knowledge that he had a good, experienced teacher to lend him support. But when he asked his teacher to advise him on specific problems arising in his meditation, Ācariya Sao invariably replied: "My experiences in meditation are quite different from yours. Your *citta* is so adventurous, tending always toward extremes. One moment it soars into the sky, only to plunge deep into the earth the next. Then, after diving to the ocean floor, it again soars up to walk meditation high in the sky. Who could possibly keep up with your *citta* long enough to find a solution? I advise you to investigate these matters for yourself and find your own solutions." Ācariya Sao never gave him enough concrete advice to really help him, so Ācariya Mun was forced to solve his own problems. Sometimes, he nearly died before discovering a way past some of the more intractable problems he faced.

Ācariya Mun described his teacher as someone with a smooth, serene temperament who inspired deep devotion. A rather strange feature of Ācariya Sao's practice was his tendency to levitate while in *samādhi*, his body hovering quite noticeably above the floor. At first, doubtful that his body was indeed floating, he opened his eyes to see for himself. As soon as his eyes opened, concern about the condition of his body caused his *citta* to withdraw from *samādhi*. He promptly fell back to the floor, landing hard on his buttocks which was sore and bruised for many days. In truth, his body did float about three feet above the floor. But by opening his eyes to check, he lost the mindfulness needed to maintain his *citta* in *samādhi*. Withdrawing suddenly from *samādhi* caused him to come crashing to the floor, like any other object dropped from a height. Practicing *samādhi* later and feeling his body levitate again, he kept mindfulness firmly focused within that state of *samādhi*, and then, carefully opened his eyes to look at himself. It was obvious to him then that he did levitate. This time, however, he didn't fall back to the floor, for mindfulness was present to maintain total concentration.

This experience taught Ācariya Sao a valuable lesson about himself. Yet being an exceptionally careful, meticulous person, he wasn't entirely convinced. So he took a small object, inserted it into the underside of the thatched roof in his hut, and continued to meditate. When he felt his body beginning to float again, he firmly focused his *citta* in *samādhi*, and he was able to float upward until he reached that small object in the thatch. Drawing level with it, he slowly reached out and very mindfully took it in his hand so that he could bring it back down by means of *samādhi*. This meant that once he had it in his grasp, he gradually withdrew from *samādhi* to the point where his body could slowly, and safely, descend to the floor — a point still short of complete withdrawal from *samādhi*. Experimenting like this, he became convinced of his ability to levitate, though this did not occur every time he entered *samādhi*.

From the beginning of his practice to the end of his life, Ācariya Sao's *citta* tended to have this smooth, imperturbable quality; in sharp contrast to the wholly adventurous nature that characterized Ācariya Mun's *citta*. Unlike him, Ācariya Sao was not so motivated to live dangerously, seeking adventure; nor did he tend to perceive the variety of unusual phenomena that Ācariya Mun invariably did.

Ācariya Mun told us that, once, in ages past, Ācariya Sao had resolved to become a Paccekabuddha.[19] Intensifying his efforts at meditation caused him to recollect his longtime resolution, and his lingering attachment to that goal made him reluctant to strive for Nibbāna in the present. It soon became apparent that this vow would block any attempt to realize Nibbāna in his lifetime; therefore, he immediately decided to renounce the old vow. In its place, he resolved to attain Nibbāna as soon as possible. He became determined to reach this goal within his present lifetime in order to avoid the misery of being reborn in the future.

Having forsaken his original vow, and thus, unhindered by previous commitments, his meditation practice progressed smoothly until one day he finally reached the Land of Ultimate Happiness that he had been aiming for. However, his teaching skill was very limited, probably due to a natural predisposition toward becoming a Paccekabuddha: someone who has no inclination to teach others although he is able to fully enlighten himself. Furthermore, the fact that he could so easily give up his original resolve and then achieve his new goal meant that his previous vow had not yet matured to the stage of being irreversible.

Ācariya Mun related that in ages past he had made a similar resolution — in his case, a solemn vow to become a Buddha. As with Ācariya Sao, intensifying his efforts at meditation caused Ācariya Mun to recollect this long-standing intention, and this underlying attachment made him reluctant to strive for the attainment of Nibbāna in his present life. Ācariya Mun renounced his vow to be a Buddha only after he began practicing *dhutanga kammaṭṭhāna*, for he then realized that its fulfillment would take far too long. It required eons of traversing the round of *saṁsāra*: being born, growing old, becoming ill, and dying over and over again, enduring misery and pain indefinitely.

Renouncing the original vow relieved Ācariya Mun of this concern, opening the way for his meditation to progress smoothly. The fact that he could so easily abandon the original vow indicates that it was not yet so firmly fixed in his conscious being that he couldn't detach himself from it.

Ācariya Mun often accompanied Ācariya Sao on his excursions wandering *dhutanga* across the provinces of the Northeast region. Due to differences in personality, their meditation experiences varied in some respects; but each very much enjoyed the other's company. By nature, Ācariya Sao preferred to say very little. He was a reluctant teacher, especially of the laity. Occasionally obliged to give instruction to lay supporters, he was always very frugal with words. The little he did say could be summed up like this:

"You should renounce evil and cultivate goodness. Being fortunate enough to be born human, don't waste this good opportunity now. Our status as human beings is a very noble one; so, avoid all animal-like behavior. Otherwise, you'll sink below the animals, and be much more wretched as well. When you eventually fall into hell, your tortuous existence there will be far more grievous than that of any animal. So don't do evil!"

That said, he left his seat and returned to his hut, taking no further interest in anyone.

He always spoke very sparingly. In an entire day he might say only a few sentences. On the other hand, he could endure many hours of sitting and walking in meditation. He had a remarkably dignified, noble appearance that inspired respect and devotion. Just a glimpse of his serene, peaceful countenance made a lasting impression. He was greatly revered by monks and laity alike and, like Ācariya Mun, he had many devoted disciples.

It was well known that these two *ācariyas* shared immense love and respect for each other. In the early years, they enjoyed traveling in each other's company. They spent most of the year living together, both during and after the annual rainy season retreat. In the middle years, they normally spent these retreats in separate locations but close enough to each other to make visiting easy. Very seldom, then, did they spend a retreat together, for each had an increasingly large following of disciples, making it difficult to find enough space to accommodate them all at one location. Living separately eliminated the burden of having to arrange living quarters for so many monks.

Even when living apart, they often thought of each other with genuine concern. On occasions when Ācariya Sao's disciples visited Ācariya Mun, the first question he asked concerned the health and well-being of Ācariya Sao, who in turn invariably reciprocated by inquiring about Ācariya Mun's well-being when one of his disciples paid a visit. Through such messengers, each then conveyed his respectful greeting to the other, maintaining contact in this way at every opportunity. Each of these great *ācariyas* had enormous respect for the other's spiritual achievements. Both used words full of praise and admiration when speaking to their disciples about each other. Their comments never contained a hint of criticism.

ĀCARIYA MUN WHOLEHEARTEDLY agreed with Ācariya Sao's comment about his *citta* being adventurous, and tending to go to extremes: soaring high in the sky one moment, then plunging into the earth before diving to the ocean floor. His *citta* truly did have such mercurial characteristics. Dropping into *samādhi* in the early stages of his practice, his *citta* tended to focus outward then, perceiving all manner of unusual phenomena — things he had never dreamed of seeing. For example, he saw a bloated corpse laid out before him. As I have mentioned before, when he concentrated his attention on this image, it soon changed into a translucent disc which in turn altered its form, creating an endless series of images.

Even after discovering the correct method of practice, when his *citta* 'converged' into calm it was still inclined to focus outward, perceiving countless types of phenomena. Sometimes, he felt his body soaring high into the sky where he traveled around for many hours, looking at celestial mansions before coming back down. At other times, he burrowed deep beneath the earth to visit various regions in hell. There he felt profound pity for its unfortunate inhabitants, all experiencing the grievous consequences of their previous actions. Watching these events unfold, he often lost all perspective of the passage of time. In those days, he was still uncertain whether these scenes were real or imaginary. He said that it was only later on, when his spiritual faculties were more mature, that he was able to investigate these matters and understand clearly the definite moral and psychological causes underlying them. Any lapse in concentration as his *citta* 'converged' into calm created an opening through which it could again focus outward to perceive such phenomena. His newfound proficiency notwithstanding, if his attention turned outward, his *citta* would be off in a flash.

Ācariya Mun told us that early on, due to inexperience with the mercurial nature of his own mind, when focusing his *citta* to examine the lower half of his body, instead of following the various parts down to the soles of his feet, it would shoot out through his lower torso and penetrate deep into the earth — just as Ācariya Sao had so astutely remarked. No sooner had he hurriedly withdrawn the *citta* back into his body than it would fly through the top of his head, soaring high into the sky where it paced back and forth contentedly, showing no interest in returning to his body. Concentrating with intense mindfulness, he had to force the *citta* to reenter the body and perform the work he wanted it to do.

In those early days his mind developed a tendency to drop so speedily into a state of calm — like falling from a cliff, or down a well — that his mindfulness couldn't keep up with it. Resting only briefly in complete stillness before withdrawing slightly to the level of *upacāra samādhi,*[20] his *citta* tended to venture out so often, and experienced such a variety of strange things, that he became very frustrated. He tried to force it to remain inside the confines of his body, but often to no avail. His *citta* was far too fleeting for mindfulness and wisdom to keep pace.

Still too inexperienced to work out an effective solution, he felt uneasy about the direction of his meditation. Yet, being a strictly internal matter, he couldn't mention his predicament to anyone else. So, with an intense degree of mindfulness and wisdom to guide his efforts, he experimented with many different techniques, suffering considerable mental strain before finding a viable means of controlling his adventuresome *citta*. Once he clearly understood the correct method of taming his dynamic mind, he found that it was versatile, energetic, and extremely quick in all circumstance. Eventually working in unison, mindfulness and wisdom blended so well with the *citta* that they merged to become one with it. Thus strengthened, the *citta* functioned like a magic crystal ball; and he was fully capable of keeping pace with all the myriad phenomena arising within it.

Ācariya Mun possessed a bold, fearless character. He was also extremely intelligent. Because his rigorous training methods differed significantly from ones practiced by other monks, his style of practice was unique – and incredibly difficult to imitate. From my own observations, I can unequivocally state: *He was a truly noble character with a quick, adventurous mind who trained himself with uncompromising resolve. His harsh training methods were often quite unique. He had an ingenious way of mixing coercive pressure and gentle persuasion to tame a dynamic mind that, at the least lapse of concentration, ventured out to find things that could easily cause him problems.*

Struggling desperately on his own to find ways to control his unruly mind, practicing without a dependable guide and enduring difficulties, Ācariya Mun sometimes felt that he was beating his head against a mountain. Unlike so many others, he had to manage without the aid of a wise teacher's proven meditation methods – a disadvantage he often warned others against later on. To his own students he always emphasized his readiness to clarify any problems they experienced in meditation, thus saving them the difficulty of having to waste time as he had in his early years.

SHORTLY AFTER HIS ORDINATION, Ācariya Mun began wandering *dhutanga* in Nakhon Phanom province, and eventually crossed the Mekong River to enter Laos, where he contentedly practiced the ascetic way of life

21

in the mountainous district of Tha Khek. This area of Laos abounded in large, ferocious tigers — huge beasts that were considered far more vicious than tigers on the Thai side of the river. Repeatedly they attacked and killed the local inhabitants and then feasted on their flesh. Despite such brutality, those people, mostly of Vietnamese descent, weren't nearly as afraid of tigers as were their Lao and Thai neighbors. Time and again they watched these terrible beasts attack and kill friends and relatives; yet, they seemed indifferent to the carnage. Having seen a friend killed right in front of them, the flesh torn from the body by a hungry tiger, the people would casually venture back into that same tiger-infested forest the next day, as though nothing had happened. The Lao and Thai communities would have been extremely upset, but the Vietnamese seemed strangely unmoved by such occurrences. Perhaps they were so accustomed to seeing such things that it no longer affected them.

The Vietnamese had another strange habit: When they saw a man-eating tiger suddenly leap out to attack one of their companions, no one in the group made any effort to save their friend's life. They simply abandoned their friend to his fate and ran for their lives. Suppose a group were sleeping in the forest overnight. If a huge tiger leaped into the campsite and dragged one of them away, the others, awakened by the noise, would jump up and run away; and then, calmly find another place close by to sleep. Like children, they acted without much rhyme or reason in these matters. They behaved as though those huge beasts, which had already shown themselves to be so adept at devouring human flesh, were somehow too stupid to do the same to them.

I am also familiar with people who have no proper fear of tigers. When coming to live in our country, they like to settle in dense, over-grown jungle areas abounding in tigers and other wild animal. Venturing deep into the forest in search of timber, they then spend the night there far from the village, showing no signs of fear at all. Even alone, these people can sleep deep in the forest at night without fear. If they wish to return to the village late at night, they have no qualms about walking alone through the dense undergrowth, and back if necessary. If asked why they aren't afraid of tigers, their response is that, while the huge tigers in their own country have a taste for human flesh, Thai tigers don't; and that they're even scared of people. Conditions can be so dangerous in their homeland that people staying overnight in the forest must build an enclosure to sleep in that resembles a pigsty;

otherwise, they might never return home. Even within the precincts of some village communities, prowling tigers can be so fierce that no one dares leave home after dark, fearing an attack by a tiger leaping out of the shadows. The Vietnamese even chide the Thais for being such cowardly people, always entering the forest in groups, never daring to venture out alone. For these reasons, Ācariya Mun claimed that the Vietnamese lacked an instinctive fear of tigers.

When Ācariya Mun crossed into their country, however, the tigers there never bothered him. Camped in the forest, he often saw their tracks and heard their roars echoing through the trees at night. However, he never felt personally threatened by such things; they were simply natural aspects of forest life. In any case, Ācariya Mun wasn't worried about tigers so much as he was worried about the possibility that he might not transcend *dukkha* and realize the Supreme Happiness of Nibbāna in his lifetime.

When speaking of his excursions crossing the Mekong River, he never mentioned being afraid. He obviously considered such dangers to be a normal part of trekking through the wilds. If I had been faced with those same dangers instead of Ācariya Mun, surely the local villagers would have had to form a posse to rescue this cowardly *dhutanga* monk. When I'm walking in meditation in the forest at night, just the occasional roar of a tiger so unsettles me that I can barely manage to keep walking to the end of the track. I fear coming face to face with one of those beasts — and losing my wits. You see, since becoming old enough to understand such things, I always heard my parents and their neighbors vociferously proclaim that tigers are very fierce animals, and extremely dangerous. This notion has stuck with me ever since, making it impossible not to be terrified of tigers. I must confess that I've never found a way to counteract this tendency.

ĀCARIYA MUN SPENT most of the earlier years of his monastic career traveling at length through the various provinces of Thailand's Northeast region. Later, as he developed enough inner stability to withstand both external distractions and those mercurial mental traits that were so much a part of his character, he walked down into the central provinces, wandering contentedly across the Central Plains region, living the *dhutanga* lifestyle until eventually he reached the capital, Bangkok. Arriving shortly before the rainy season, he went to Wat

Pathumwan monastery and entered the retreat there. During the rains retreat he made a point of regularly going to seek advice from Chao Khun Upāli Guṇūpamācariya[21] at Wat Boromaniwat monastery to gain more extensive techniques for developing wisdom.

Ācariya Mun left Bangkok following the rains retreat, hiking to Lopburi province to stay awhile at Phai Khwang Cave in the Phra Ngam mountain range before moving on to Singto Cave. Life in such favorable locations gave him an excellent, uninterrupted opportunity to fully intensify his spiritual practice. In doing so, he developed a fearless attitude toward his mind and the things with which it came in contact. By then, his *samādhi* was rock-solid. Using it as the firm basis for his practice, he examined everything from the perspective of Dhamma, continually uncovering new techniques for developing wisdom. After a suitable interval, he returned to Bangkok, once again visiting Chao Khun Upāli at Wat Boromaniwat. He informed his mentor of developments in his meditation practice, questioning him about doubts he still had concerning the practice of wisdom. Satisfied that the new investigative techniques he had learned were sufficient to further his progress, he finally took leave of Chao Khun Upāli and left to seek seclusion at Sarika Cave in the Khaw Yai mountains of Nakhon Nayok province.

Sarika Cave

Ācariya Mun spent three years living and practicing in Sarika Cave. His entire stay there was filled with the most unusual experiences, making it a memorable episode in his life. To the best of my recollection, he first arrived at Ban Gluay village, the village nearest the cave and thus close enough to be convenient for almsround. Unfamiliar with the area, he asked the villagers to take him to Sarika Cave. Straightaway they warned him that it was a very special cave possessing numerous supernatural powers, insisting that no monk could possibly live there unless his virtue was pure. Other monks who had tried to live there quickly fell ill with a variety of painful symptoms — many had even died before they could be brought down for treatment. They told him that the cave was the domain of a spirit of immense size possessing many magical powers. It also had a very foul temper. This giant spirit guarded

24

the cave from all intruders — monks being no exception. Unexpected occurrences awaited all intruders into the cave, many of whom ended up dead. The spirit delighted in testing any monk who came bragging about his mastery of magic spells for warding off spirits. Invariably, the monk would suddenly fall ill and die a premature death. Fearing that Ācariya Mun might die likewise, the villagers pleaded with him not to go.

Curious about the talk of a huge, malevolent spirit with supernatural powers, Ācariya Mun asked and was told that a trespasser usually saw some sign of those powers on the very first night. An ominous dream often accompanied fitful sleep: An enormous black spirit, towering overhead, threatened to drag the dreamer to his death, shouting that it had long been the cave's guardian exercising absolute authority over the whole area, and would allow no one to trespass. So any trespasser was immediately chased away, for it accepted no authority greater than its own, except that of a person of impeccable virtue and a loving, compassionate heart, who extended these noble qualities to all living beings. A person of such nobility was allowed to live in the cave. The spirit would even protect him and pay him homage, but it did not tolerate narrow-minded, selfish, ill-behaved intruders.

Finding life in the cave a very uncomfortable experience, most monks refused to remain for long; and fearing death, they made a hurried departure. Generally, no one managed a long stay — only one or two days at most, and they were quickly on their way. Trembling and almost out of their minds with fear as they climbed back down, they blurted out something about a fierce, demonic spirit. Scared and chastened, they fled, never to return. Worse still, some who went up to the cave never came down again. Thus, the villagers worried about the fate that awaited Ācariya Mun, not wanting him to become the next victim.

Ācariya Mun asked what they meant by saying that some monks went up there never to return. Why hadn't they come down again? He was told that, having died there, they couldn't possibly come back down. They recounted a story of four seemingly competent monks who had died in the cave not long before. Prior to entering the cave, one of them had assured the villagers that he was impervious to fear, for he knew a potent spell that protected him against ghosts and other spirits, plus many other potent spells as well. He was convinced no spirit could threaten him. Warning him repeatedly about the dangers, the villagers

25

tried to discourage his intentions, but he reiterated that he had no fear and insisted on being taken to the cave. The villagers were left with no other choice, so they showed him the way. Once there, he came down with a variety of afflictions, including high fevers, pounding headaches, and terrible stomach pains. Sleeping fitfully, he dreamt that he was being taken away to his death.

Over the years, many different monks had tried to live there, but their experiences were strikingly similar. Some died, others quickly fled. The four most recent monks died within a relatively short period. The villagers couldn't guarantee that their deaths were caused by a malevolent spirit; perhaps there was another reason. But they had always noticed a powerful presence connected with the cave. Local people weren't so bold as to challenge its power, for they were wary of it and envisioned themselves being carried back down in critical condition — or as corpses.

Ācariya Mun questioned them further to satisfy himself that they were telling the truth. They assured him that such things happened so often it frightened them to think about it. For this reason, they warned any monk or lay person who came to search the cave for magical objects or sacred amulets. Whether the cave actually contained such things is another matter; but, the fact that some people liked to claim their existence meant that those with a penchant for sacred objects inevitably went there to search for them. The villagers themselves had never seen such objects in the cave; nor had they seen those seeking them encounter anything but death, or narrow escapes from death. Thus, fearing for Ācariya Mun's safety, they begged him not to go.

Ācariya Mun gave the villagers a sympathetic hearing, but in the end he was still curious to see the cave. Live or die, he wanted to put himself to the test, and so discover the truth of those stories. The scary tales he heard didn't frighten him in the least. In truth, he saw this adventure as a means to arouse mindfulness, an opportunity to acquire many new ideas for contemplation. He possessed the courage to face whatever was to happen, as befits someone genuinely interested in seeking the truth. So in his own unassuming way, he informed the villagers that, although the stories were very frightening, he still would like to spend some time in the cave. Assuring them that he would hurry back down at the first sign of trouble, he asked to be escorted to the cave, which they obligingly did.

FOR SEVERAL DAYS, Ācariya Mun's physical condition remained normal, his heart calm and serene. The environment around the cave was secluded and very quiet, disturbed only by the natural sounds of wild animals foraging for food in the forest. He passed the first few nights contentedly; but on subsequent nights he began to suffer stomach pains. Although such pains were nothing new, this time the condition grew steadily worse, eventually becoming so severe that he sometimes passed blood in his stool. Before long his stomach refused to digest food properly — it simply passed straight through. This made him reflect on what the villagers had said about four monks dying there recently. If his condition didn't improve, perhaps he would be the fifth.

When lay people came to see him at the cave one morning, he sent them to look in the forest for certain medicinal plants that he had previously found beneficial. They gathered various roots and wood essences which he boiled into a potion and drank, or else ground into powder, drinking it dissolved in water. He tried several different combinations of herbs, but none relieved his symptoms. They worsened with each passing day. His body was extremely weak; and though his mental resolve was not greatly affected, it was clearly weaker than normal.

As he sat drinking the medicine one day, a thought arose which, prompting a self-critical examination, reinforced his resolve:

I've been taking this medicine now for many days. If it really is an effective stomach cure, then I should see some positive results by now. But every day my condition worsens. Why isn't this medicine having the desired effect? Perhaps it's not helping at all. Instead, it may be aggravating the symptoms and so causing the steady deterioration. If so, why continue taking it?

Once he became fully aware of his predicament, he made an emphatic decision. From that day on he would treat his stomach disorder using only 'the therapeutic properties of Dhamma'. If he lived, so much the better; if he died, then so be it. Conventional types of treatment proving ineffective, he determined to stop taking all medicines until he was cured by Dhamma's therapeutic powers, or else died there in the cave. With this firm resolution in mind, he reminded himself:

I am a Buddhist monk. I have certainly practiced meditation long enough to recognize the correct path leading to magga, phala, and Nibbāna. By now my practice should be firmly anchored in this conviction. So why am I so weak and cowardly when faced with a small degree of pain? It's only a slight

27

pain, after all, yet I can't seem to come to grips with it. Becoming weak all of a sudden, I now feel defeated. Later, when life reaches a critical juncture — at the moment of death as the body begins to break up and disintegrate — the onslaught of pain will then crush down mercilessly on body and mind. Where shall I find the strength to fight it so I can transcend this world and avoid being outdone in death's struggle?

With this solemn determination, he stopped taking all medicines and began earnestly focusing on meditation as the sole remedy for all spiritual and bodily ailments. Discarding concern for his life, he let his body follow its own natural course, turning his attention to probing the *citta* — that essential 'knowing nature' which never dies, yet has death as its constant companion. He set to work examining the *citta*, using the full powers of mindfulness, wisdom, faith and perseverance that he had been developing within himself for so long. The seriousness of his physical condition ceased to interest him; concerns about death no longer arose. He directed mindfulness and wisdom to investigate the painful feelings he experienced, making them separate the body into its constituent elements, and then thoroughly analyzing each one. He examined the physical components of the body and the feelings of pain within it. He analyzed the function of memory which presumes that one or another part of the body is in pain.[22] And he analyzed the thought processes which conceive the body as being in pain.[23] All such vital aspects were targeted in the investigation conducted by mindfulness and wisdom as they continued to probe into the body, the pain, and the *citta*, relentlessly exploring their connections from dusk until midnight. Through this process, he succeeded in fully disengaging the body from the severe pain caused by his stomach disorder until he understood, with absolute clarity, just how they are interrelated. At that moment of realization, his *citta* 'converged' into complete calm — a moment that saw his spiritual resolve immeasurably strengthened, and his bodily illness totally vanish. The illness, the pain, the mind's preoccupations — all disappeared simultaneously.

Remaining only briefly in complete stillness, his *citta* withdrew slightly, reaching the level of *upacāra samādhi*. This 'luminous' *citta* then left the confines of his body and immediately encountered an enormous, black man standing fully thirty feet tall. The towering figure carried a huge metal club — twelve feet long and thick as a man's leg. Walking up to Ācariya Mun, he announced in a menacing voice that he was about to pound him right into the ground. He warned Ācariya

Mun to flee that very instant if he wished to remain alive. The metal club resting on his shoulder was so huge that a single blow from it would have been enough to pound a large bull elephant into the earth.

Ācariya Mun focused his *citta* on the giant spirit, asking why he wanted to club to death someone who had done nothing to warrant such brutal treatment. He reminded the giant that he had harmed no one while living there; that he had caused no trouble deserving of such deadly punishment. The giant replied by saying that he had long been the sole authority guarding that mountain and would never allow anyone to usurp that authority. He felt compelled to take decisive action against all intruders.

Ācariya Mun's response was reproachful: "I did not come here to usurp anyone's authority. I came to carry on the noble work of spiritual development, for I aim to usurp the authority that the *kilesas* exercise over my heart. Harming a virtuous monk in any way is an absolutely despicable act. I am a disciple of the Lord Buddha, that supremely pure individual whose all-powerful loving compassion encompasses the whole of the sentient universe. Does the great authority you boast give you power to override the authority of Dhamma, and of *kamma* — those immutable laws that govern the existence of all living beings?"

The creature replied: "No, sir."

Ācariya Mun then said: "The Lord Buddha possessed the skill and the courage to destroy those insidious mental defilements that like boasting of power and authority. Thus, he banished from his heart all thoughts of beating or killing other people. You think you're so smart, have you ever given any thought to taking decisive action against the *kilesas* in your heart?"

The creature admitted: "Not yet, sir."

"In that case, such overbearing authority will just make you a cruel, savage individual, resulting in very grave consequences for you. You don't possess the authority needed to rid yourself of evil, so you use the fires of magic against others, unaware that you're actually burning yourself. You are creating very grave *kamma* indeed. As though that weren't bad enough, you want to attack and kill someone who represents the virtues of Dhamma which are central to the world's well-being. How can you ever hope to lay claim to laudable virtues, when you insist on engaging in evil behavior of such unparalleled brutality?

"I am a man of virtue. I have come here with the purest intentions — to practice Dhamma for my own spiritual benefit, and the benefit of others. Despite that, you threaten to pound me into the ground, giving no thought to the consequences of such an evil deed. Don't you realize that it will drag you into hell where you will reap the terrible misery you have sown? Rather than feel concerned for myself, I feel very sorry for you — you've become so obsessed with your own authority that it's now burning you alive. Can your potent powers withstand the effect of the grave act you are about to commit? You say you exercise sovereign authority over this mountain, but can your magic powers override Dhamma and the laws of *kamma*? If your powers really are superior to Dhamma, then go ahead — pound me to death! I'm not afraid to die. Even if I don't die today, my death remains inevitable. For the world is a place where all who are born must die — even you, blinded as you are by your own self-importance. You are not above death, or the laws of *kamma* that govern all living beings."

The mysterious being stood listening, rigid as a statue, the deadly metal club resting on his shoulder as Ācariya Mun admonished him by means of *samādhi* meditation. He stood so completely still that if he were a human being we would say that he was so frightened and ashamed he could scarcely breath. But this was a special nonhuman being, so he didn't in fact breathe. Yet his whole manner clearly showed him to be so ashamed and fearful of Ācariya Mun that he could barely restrain his emotions, which he still managed to do quite admirably.

Ācariya Mun had finished speaking. Suddenly, the contrite spirit flung the metal club down from his shoulder and spontaneously trans-formed his appearance from a huge, black creature into a devout Buddhist gentleman with a mild, courteous demeanor. Approaching Ācariya Mun with heartfelt respect, the gentleman then asked his forgiveness, expressing deep remorse. Here is the gist of what he said:

"I was surprised, and felt somewhat frightened, the first moment I saw you. I immediately noticed a strange and amazing radiance extending out all around you, a brilliance unlike anything I had ever seen. It created such a profound impact that in your presence I felt weak and numb. I couldn't do anything — so captivated was I by that radiant glow. Still, I didn't know what it was, for I had never before experienced anything like it.

"My threats to kill you a moment ago didn't come from my heart's true feelings. Rather, they stemmed from a long-held belief that I possess unrivaled authority over nonhuman beings, as well as humans with evil intent who lack moral principles. Such authority can be imposed on anyone, at any time; and that person will be powerless to resist. This arrogant sense of self-importance led me to confront you. Feeling vulnerable, I didn't want to lose face. Even as I threatened you, I felt nervous and hesitant, unable to act on my threat. It was merely the stance of someone accustomed to wielding power over others. Please be compassionate enough to forgive my rude, distasteful behavior today. I don't wish to suffer the consequences of evil anymore. As it is now, I suffer enough. Any more, and I won't have the strength to bear it."

Ācariya Mun was curious about this: "You are a prominent individual with enormous power and prestige. You have an nonphysical body, so you needn't experience the human hardships of hunger and fatigue. You aren't burdened having to make a living as people here on earth are, so why do you complain about suffering? If a celestial existence isn't happiness, then which type of existence is?"

The spirit replied: "On a superficial level, perhaps, celestial beings with their ethereal bodies do actually experience more happiness than humans, whose bodies are much grosser. But speaking strictly in spiritual terms, a celestial being's ethereal body still suffers a degree of discomfort proportionate to the refined nature of that state of existence."

This discussion between spirit and monk was far too profound and complex for me to capture its every detail here, so I hope the reader will forgive me for this shortcoming.

As a result of the discussion, the mysterious celestial being, showing great respect for the Dhamma he heard, affirmed his devotion to the three refuges: Buddha, Dhamma, and Sangha. He let it be known that he considered Ācariya Mun to be one of his refuges as well, asking Ācariya Mun to bear witness to his faith. At the same time, he offered Ācariya Mun his full protection, inviting him to remain in the cave indefinitely. Had his wish been granted, Ācariya Mun would have spent the rest of his life there. This being cherished the opportunity to take care of him — he wanted to ensure that nothing whatsoever disturbed Ācariya Mun's meditation. In truth, he was not some mysterious being with a huge, black body — that was merely a guise. He was the chief leader of all the terrestrial *devas* living in that region.[24] His large entourage lived in an area that centered in the mountains of Nakhon Nayok and extended over many of the surrounding provinces as well.

Ācariya Mun's *citta* had 'converged' into calm at midnight, after which he met the terrestrial *deva*, communicating by means of *samādhi* meditation until four a.m., when his *citta* withdrew to normal consciousness. The stomach disorder that was troubling him so much when he sat down at dusk had completely disappeared by that time. The therapeutic power of Dhamma, administered by means of meditation, was the only remedy he needed to effect a decisive cure – an experience that Ācariya Mun found incredibly amazing. Forgoing sleep, he continued striving in his practice until dawn. Instead of feeling tired after a night of exertion, his body was more energetic than ever.

He had passed a night full of many amazing experiences: He witnessed Dhamma's powerful ability to tame an unruly spirit, transforming arrogance into faith; his *citta* remained in a serenely calm state for many hours, savoring that wonderful sense of happiness; a chronic illness was completely cured, his digestion returning to normal; he was satisfied that his mind had acquired a solid spiritual basis – one he could trust, thus dispelling many of his lingering doubts; he realized many unusual insights he had never before attained, both those that removed defilements and those that enhanced the special understanding which formed an intrinsic part of his character.

During the months that followed, his meditation practice progressed smoothly, accompanied always by indescribable peace and tranquillity. With his health back to normal, physical discomforts no longer troubled him. Sometimes, late at night, he met with gatherings of terrestrial *devas* who came from various places to visit him. *Devas* from the surrounding area had all heard of Ācariya Mun, for the mysterious *deva* who had engaged him in a war of words was now announcing his presence to others, and escorting groups of them to meet him. On nights when no visitors came, he enjoyed himself practicing meditation.

ONE AFTERNOON HE LEFT his meditation seat to sit in the open air not far from the cave, reflecting on the Dhamma that the Lord Buddha had so compassionately given to mankind. He felt this Dhamma to be so very profound that he understood how difficult it was going to be to practice it to perfection, and to fully realize its essential truths. He felt a sense of satisfaction, thinking how fortunate he was to be able to practice Dhamma and realize its many insights and truths — an amazing feeling. Even though he had yet to reach the ultimate realization, a dream he'd long desired to fulfill, still the spiritual contentment he experienced was very rewarding. He was sure now that, unless death intervened, his hopes would surely be realized one day. Savoring his contentment, he reflected on the path he took to practice Dhamma and the results he hoped to achieve, proceeding step by step, until he reached a complete cessation of *dukkha*, eliminating all traces of discontent still existing within his heart.

Just then, a large troop of monkeys came foraging for food in front of the cave. The leader of the troop arrived first, a good distance in front of the rest. Reaching the area in front of the cave, it spotted Ācariya Mun who sat very still with eyes open, glancing silently at the approaching monkey. The monkey immediately became suspicious of his presence. Nervous, worried about the safety of its troop, it ran back and forth along the branch of a tree, looking warily at him. Ācariya Mun understood its anxiety, and sympathized with it, sending out benevolent thoughts of loving kindness: *I've come here to practice Dhamma, not to mistreat or harm anyone; so there's no need to fear me. Keep searching for food as you please. You can come foraging around here every day if you like.*

In a flash, the lead monkey ran back to its troop, which Ācariya Mun could see approaching in the distance. He watched what happened next with a sense of great amusement, combined with sincere compassion. As soon as the leader reached the others, it quickly called out: *Goke, hey not so fast! There's something over there. It may be dangerous!* Hearing this, all the other monkeys began asking at once: *Goke, goke? Where, where?* And simultaneously, the leader turned his head toward Ācariya Mun's direction as if to say: *Sitting over there — can you see?* Or something like that, but in the language of animals, which is an unfathomable mystery to most human beings. Ācariya Mun, however, understood every word they spoke.

Once it had signaled Ācariya Mun's presence to the group, the lead monkey warned them to proceed slowly and cautiously until they could determine exactly what was up ahead. It then hurried off ahead of the group, warily approaching the front of the cave where Ācariya Mun was seated. Being concerned for the safety of those following behind, it was apprehensive, but also curious to find out what was there. It cautiously snuck up close to Ācariya Mun, jumping up and jumping down from branch to branch, as monkeys tend to do, for they are quite restless as everybody knows. The lead monkey watched Ācariya Mun constantly until it was sure that he posed no danger. Then, it ran back and informed its friends: *Goke*, we can go. *Goke*, there's no danger.

During this time, Ācariya Mun sat perfectly still, constantly gauging the lead monkey's inner feelings to judge its reaction to him. The way it ran back to speak to its friends was quite comic; yet, knowing exactly what they said, Ācariya Mun couldn't help feeling sorry for them. For those of us who don't understand their language, the calls they send back and forth to one another are merely sounds in the forest, much like the bird calls we hear every day. But when the lead monkey ran back, calling out to its troop, Ācariya Mun understood the meaning of what was said as clearly as if they had been conversing in human language.

In the beginning when the lead monkey first spotted him, it hurried back to its troop, warning its friends to take care and pay careful attention to what it had to say. Although it communicated this message in the *goke goke* sounds that monkeys make, the essential meaning was clear to the others: Hey, stop! Not so fast! There's danger up ahead. Hearing the warning, the others began wondering what danger there was. First, one asked: *Goke*, what is it? Then, another asked: *Goke*, what's the matter? The lead monkey answered: *Goke gake*, there's something up there — it may be dangerous. The others asked: *Goke*, where is it? The leader replied: *Goke*, right over there.

The sounds made by this large troop of monkeys, as they questioned and answered one another, reverberated through the whole forest. First, one called out in alarm; then another, until monkeys, large and small, ran frantically back and forth, seeking answers about their situation. Fearful of the possible danger they all faced, they yelled excitedly to one another in a state of general confusion — just as we people tend to do when confronted with an emergency. Their leader was obliged to speak up and to try to clarify the situation, cautioning them: *Goke gake*, everyone wait here first while I go back and check to make sure. With these parting instructions, it hurried back to look again. Approaching Ācariya Mun who was seated in front of the cave, it looked warily at him while scurrying to and fro through the branches of the trees. Its eyes examined him with intense interest until it was satisfied that Ācariya Mun wasn't an adversary. Then, it hurriedly returned to its troop and announced: *Goke gake*, we can go now, it's not dangerous.

There's no need to be afraid. So the whole troop moved forward until it reached the spot where Ācariya Mun was seated, all of them cautiously peering at him in a way that signaled their continuing mistrust. As monkeys tend to do when their curiosity is aroused, the troop was jumping about through the trees. The *goke gake* sounds of their queries echoed through the forest: What is it? What's it doing here? The sounds of their replies reverberated in the agitated tone of animals needing to find out what's going on.

This narration has a repetitive quality, for this is the narrative style that Ācariya Mun himself used when telling this story. He wanted to emphasize the points of interest for his audience, and thus clearly indicate their significance. He said that wild monkeys tend to panic when sensing danger because, for ages, human beings have used various brutal methods to kill these animals in countless numbers. So monkeys are instinctively very distrustful of people.

The flow of an animal's consciousness infuses the different sounds it makes with the appropriate meaning — just as human verbal expressions are determined by the flow of human consciousness. So, it is just as easy for monkeys to understand the meaning of their common sounds, as it is for people to understand the same language. Each sound that issues from an animal's flow of consciousness is attuned to a specific meaning and purpose. These sounds communicate a clear message, and those who are listening invariably comprehend their precise meaning. So, even though it has no discernible meaning for human beings, when monkeys emit a sound like *goke*, they all understand its intended meaning, since this is the language monkeys use to communicate. Much the same applies to people of different nationalities, each speaking their own native language. Just as most nations around the world have their own specific language, so too each species of animal has its own distinct means of communication. Whether animals and humans can comprehend each others' language ceases to be an issue when we accept that each group has the prerogative to decide on the parameters of its speech and the manner in which it is conducted.

Finally overcoming their fears, the monkeys roamed freely in the area around the cave, foraging for food as they pleased. No longer were they on guard, wary of the threat of danger. From that day on, they felt right at home there, showing no interest in Ācariya Mun; and he paid no special attention to them as he and they both went about their daily lives.

Ācariya Mun said that all the animals foraging for food in the area where he lived did so contentedly, without fear. Ordinarily, animals of all kinds feel comfortable living in places where monks have taken up residence, for animals are quite similar to human beings in emotion. They simply lack the same predominant authority and intelligence that humans possess. Their level of intelligence extends only to the tasks of searching for food and finding a place to hide in order to survive from day to day.

ONE EVENING ĀCARIYA MUN felt so moved by a profound sense of sadness that tears came to his eyes. Seated in meditation focusing on body contemplation, his *citta* 'converged' into a state of such total calm that it appeared completely empty. At that moment, he felt as though the whole universe had ceased to exist. Only emptiness remained – the emptiness of his *citta*. Emerging from this profound state, he contemplated the teaching of the Lord Buddha which prescribed the means for removing the defiling pollutants that exist in the hearts of all living beings – a knowledge arising from the incisive genius of the Lord Buddha's wisdom. The more he contemplated this matter, the more he understood the amazing sagacity of the Buddha – and the more profoundly saddened he was by his own ignorance. He realized the paramount importance of proper training and instruction. Even such common bodily functions as eating food and relieving ourselves must be taught to us. We learn to perform them properly by undergoing training and instruction. Washing and dressing ourselves, in fact all of our daily activities, must be learned through education – otherwise, they will never be done correctly. Worse than doing them incorrectly, we may end up doing something seriously wrong, which could have grievous moral consequences. Just as it's necessary to receive training in how to take care of our bodies, so it is essential to receive proper guidance in how to take care of our minds. If our minds don't undergo the appropriate training, then we're bound to make serious mistakes, regardless of our age, gender, or position in society.

The average person in this world resembles a young child who needs adult guidance and constant attention to safely grow to maturity. Most of us tend to grow up only in appearance. Our titles, our status, and our self-importance tend to increase ever more; but the knowledge and wisdom of the right way to achieve peace and happiness for ourselves and others, don't grow to maturity with them; nor do we show an interest in developing these. Consequently, we always experience difficulties wherever we go. These were the thoughts that moved Ācariya Mun to such a profound sense of sadness that evening.

AT THE FOOT OF THE MOUNTAIN, where the path to the Sarika Cave began, stood a *vipassanā* meditation center, the residence of an elderly monk who was ordained late in life, after having had a wife and family. Thinking of this monk one evening, Ācariya Mun wondered what he was doing, and so, he sent out his flow of consciousness to take a look. At that moment, the old monk's mind was completely distracted by thoughts of the past concerning the affairs of his home and family. Again, sending out his flow of consciousness to observe him later that same night, Ācariya Mun encountered the same situation. Just before dawn, he focused his *citta* once again, only to find the old monk still busy making plans for his children and grandchildren. Each time he sent out the flow of his *citta* to check, he found the monk thinking incessantly about matters concerned with building a worldly life now, and untold rounds of existence in the future.

On the way back from his almsround that morning, he stopped to visit the elderly monk and immediately put him on the spot: "How is it going, old fellow? Building a new house and getting married to your wife all over again? You couldn't sleep at all last night. I suppose everything is all arranged now so you can relax in the evenings, without having to get so worked up planning what you'll say to your children and grandchildren. I suspect you were so distracted by all that business last night you hardly slept a wink, am I right?"

Embarrassed, the elderly monk asked with a sheepish smile: "You knew about last night? You're incredible, Ācariya Mun."

Ācariya Mun smiled in reply, and added: "I'm sure you know yourself much better than I do, so why ask me? I'm convinced you were thinking about those things quite deliberately, so preoccupied with your thoughts you neglected to lie down and sleep all night. Even now you continue to shamelessly enjoy thinking about such matters and you don't have the mindfulness to stop yourself. You're still determined to act upon those thoughts, aren't you?"

As he finished speaking, Ācariya Mun noticed the elderly monk looking very pale, as though about to faint from shock, or embarrassment. He mumbled something incoherent in a faltering, ghostly sounding voice bordering on madness. Seeing his condition, Ācariya Mun instinctively knew that any further discussion would have serious consequences. So he found an excuse to change the subject, talking about other matters for a while to calm him down, then he returned to the cave.

Three days later one of the old monk's lay supporters came to the cave, so Ācariya Mun asked him about the monk. The layman said that he had abruptly left the previous morning, with no intention of returning. The layman had asked him why he was in such a hurry to leave, and he replied: "How can I stay here any longer? The other morning Ācariya Mun stopped by and lectured me so poignantly that I almost fainted right there in front of him. Had he continued lecturing me like that much longer, I'd surely have passed out and died there on the spot. As it was, he stopped and changed the subject, so I managed to survive somehow. How can you expect me to remain here now, after that? I'm leaving today."

The layman asked him: "Did Ācariya Mun scold you harshly? Is that why you nearly died, and now feel you can no longer stay here?"

"He didn't scold me at all, but his astute questions were far worse than a tongue-lashing."

"He asked you some questions, is that it? Can you tell me what they were? Perhaps I can learn a lesson from them."

"Please don't ask me to tell you what he said, I'm embarrassed to death as it is. Should anyone ever know, I'd sink into the ground. Without getting specific, I can tell you this much: he knows everything we're thinking. No scolding could possibly be as bad as that. It's quite natural for people to think both good thoughts and bad thoughts. Who can control them? But when I discover that Ācariya Mun knows all about my private thoughts — that's too much. I know I can't stay on here. Better to go off and die somewhere else than to stay here and disturb him with my wayward thinking. I mustn't stay here, further disgracing myself. Last night I couldn't sleep at all — I just can't get this matter out of my mind."

But the layman begged to differ: "Why should Ācariya Mun be disturbed by what you think? He's not the one at fault. The person at fault is the one who should be disturbed by what he's done, and then make a sincere effort to rectify it. That, Ācariya Mun would certainly appreciate. So please stay on here for awhile — in that way, when those thoughts arise, you can benefit from Ācariya Mun's advice. Then you can develop the mindfulness needed to solve this problem, which is much better than running away from it. What do you say to that?"

"I can't stay. The prospect of my developing mindfulness to improve myself can't begin to rival my fear of Ācariya Mun: it's like pitting a cat against an elephant! Just thinking that he knows all about me is enough to make me shiver, so how could I possibly maintain any degree of mindfulness? I'm leaving today. If I remain here any longer, I'll die for sure. Please believe me."

The layman told Ācariya Mun that he felt very sorry for that old monk, but he didn't know what to say to prevent him leaving: "His face was so pale it was obvious he was frightened, so I had to let him go. Before he left, I asked him where he'd be going. He said he didn't know for sure, but that if he didn't die first, we'd probably meet again someday — then he left. I had a boy send him off. When the boy returned I asked him, but he didn't know, for the elderly monk hadn't told him where he was going. I feel really sorry for him. An old man like that, he shouldn't have taken it so personally."

Ācariya Mun was deeply dismayed to see his benevolent intentions producing such negative results, his compassion being the cause of such unfortunate consequences. In truth, seeing the elderly monk's stunned reaction that very first day, he had suspected then that this might happen. After that day he was disinclined to send out the flow of his *citta* to investigate, fearing he might again meet with the same situation. In the end, his suspicions were confirmed. He told the layman that he'd spoken with the old monk in the familiar way that friends normally do: playful one minute, serious the next. He never imagined it becoming such a big issue that the elderly monk would feel compelled to abandon his monastery and flee like that.

This incident became an important lesson determining how Ācariya Mun behaved toward all the many people he met throughout his life. He was concerned that such an incident might be repeated should he fail to make a point of carefully considering the circumstances before speaking. From that day on, he never cautioned people directly about the specific content of their thoughts. He merely alluded indirectly to certain types of thinking as a means of helping people become aware of the nature of their thoughts, but without upsetting their feelings. People's minds are like small children tottering uncertainly as they learn to walk. An adult's job is to merely watch them carefully so they come to no harm. There's no need to be overly protective all the time. The same applies to people's minds: they should be allowed to learn by their own experiences. Sometimes their thinking will be right, sometimes wrong, sometimes good, sometimes bad – this is only natural. It's unreasonable to expect them to be perfectly good and correct every time.

THE YEARS ĀCARIYA MUN spent living in Sarika Cave were fruitful. He gained many enlightening ideas to deepen his understanding of the exclusively internal aspects of his meditation practice and many unusual insights concerning the great variety of external phenomena he encountered in his meditation. He became so pleasantly absorbed in his practice that he forgot about time: he hardly noticed the days, the months, or the years as they passed. Intuitive insights arose in his mind continuously – like water gently flowing along in the rainy season. On afternoons when the weather was clear, he walked through the forest admiring the trees and the mountains, meditating as he went, absorbed in the natural scenery all around him. As evening fell, he gradually made his way back to the cave.

The cave's surrounding area abounded in countless species of wild animals, the abundant variety of wild plants and fruits being a rich, natural source of sustenance. Animals such as monkeys, languars, flying squirrels, and gibbons, which depend on wild fruits, came and went contentedly. Preoccupied with their own affairs, they showed no fear in Ācariya Mun's presence. As he watched them foraging for food he became engrossed in their playful antics. He felt a genuine spirit of camaraderie with those creatures, considering them his companions in birth, ageing, sickness, and death. In this respect, animals are on an equal footing with people. For though animals and people differ in the extent of their accumulated merit and goodness, animals nonetheless possess these wholesome qualities in some measure as well. In fact, degrees of accumulated merit may vary significantly among individual members of both groups. Moreover, many animals may actually possess greater stores of merit than do certain people, but having been unfortunate enough to be reborn into an animal existence, they must endure the consequences for the time being. Human beings face the same dilemma: for although human existence is considered a higher birth than that of an animal, a person falling on hard times and into poverty must endure that misfortune until it passes — or until the results of that unfortunate *kamma* are exhausted. Only then can a better state arise in its place. In this way the effects of *kamma* continue to unfold, indefinitely. For precisely this reason, Ācariya Mun always insisted that we should never be contemptuous of another being's lowly status or state of birth. He always taught us that the good and the bad *kamma,* created by each living being, are that being's only true inheritance.

Each afternoon Ācariya Mun swept the area clean in front of the cave. Then for the rest of the evening he concentrated on his meditation practice, alternating between walking and sitting meditation. His *samādhi* practice steadily progressed, infusing his heart with tranquillity. At the same time, he intensified the development of wisdom by mentally dissecting the different parts of the body, while analyzing them in terms of the three universal characteristics of existence: that is to say, all are impermanent, bound up with suffering, and void of any self. In this manner, his confidence grew with each passing day.

The Sāvaka Arahants

Living in Sarika Cave, Ācariya Mun was occasionally visited by *sāvaka* Arahants,[25] who appeared to him by means of *samādhi nimitta*.[26] Each *sāvaka* Arahant delivered for his benefit a discourse on Dhamma, elucidating the traditional practices of the Noble Ones. Here is the substance of what was expressed:

Walking meditation must be practiced in a calm, self-composed manner. Use mindfulness to focus your attention directly on the task you have set for yourself. If you're investigating the nature of the *khandhas* or the conditions of the body, or simply concentrating on a specific Dhamma theme, then make sure mindfulness is firmly fixed on that object. Don't allow your attention to drift elsewhere. Such negligence is characteristic of one having no solid spiritual basis to anchor him, and thus lacking a reliable inner refuge. Mindful awareness should attend each and every movement in all your daily activities. Don't perform these actions as though you are so sound asleep that you have no mindful awareness of how your body tosses about, or how prolifically your sleeping mind dreams. Going on your morning almsround, eating your food, and relieving yourself: in all such basic duties you should adhere strictly to the traditional practices of the Lord Buddha's Noble disciples. Never behave as though you lack proper training in the Teaching and the Discipline. Always conduct yourself in the manner of a true *samaṇa*[27] with the calm, peaceful demeanor expected of one who ordains as a disciple of the Lord Buddha. This means maintaining mindfulness and wisdom in every posture as a way of eliminating the poisons buried deep within your heart. Thoroughly investigate all the food you eat. Don't allow those foods that taste good to add poison to your mind. Even though the body may be strengthened by food that's eaten without proper investigation, the mind will be weakened by its damaging effects. By nourishing your body with food that is eaten unmindfully, you will, in effect, be destroying yourself with nourishment that depletes your mental vitality.

A *samaṇa* must never endanger his own well-being or the well-being of others by shamefully accumulating *kilesas*; for, not only do they harm him, but they can easily mushroom and spread harm to others as well. In the view of the Buddha's Noble disciples, all mental defilements are to be greatly feared. Utmost care should be taken to ensure that the mind does not neglect to check any outflow of the *kilesas*, for each one acts like a sheet of fire destroying everything in its path. The Noble Dhamma, practiced by all of the Lord Buddha's Noble disciples, emphasizes scrupulous self-discipline at all times and under all conditions — whether walking, standing, sitting, lying down, eating or relieving oneself; and in all of one's conversations and social interactions. Inattentive, undisciplined behavior is a habit of the *kilesas*, leading to unwholesome thoughts, and thus, perpetuating the cycle of birth and death. Those wishing to escape from the cycle of rebirth should avoid such deplorable habits. They merely lead deeper into the abyss, eventually causing one to become that most undesirable of persons — a wretched *samaṇa*. No one wishes to partake of wretched food; no one wishes to reside in a wretched house; and no one wishes to dress in wretched clothes, or even look at them. Generally, people detest and shun wretched things — how much more so a wretched person with a wretched mind. But the most abhorrent thing in the world is a wretched *samaṇa* who is ordained as a Buddhist monk. His wretchedness pierces the hearts of good and bad people alike. It pierces the hearts of all *devas* and *brahmas* without exception. For this reason, one should strive to be a true *samaṇa* exercising extreme care to remain mindful and self-disciplined at all times.

Of all the many things that people value and care for in the world, a person's mind is the most precious. In fact, the mind is the foremost treasure in the whole world, so be sure to look after it well. To realize the mind's true nature is to realize Dhamma. Understanding the mind is the same as understanding Dhamma. Once the mind is known, then Dhamma in its entirety is known. Arriving at the truth about one's mind is the attainment of Nibbāna. Clearly, the mind is a priceless possession that should never be overlooked. Those who neglect to nurture the special status that the mind has within their bodies will always be born flawed, no matter how many hundreds or thousands of times they are reborn. Once we realize the precious nature of our own minds, we should not be remiss, knowing full well that we are certain to regret it later. Such remorse being avoidable, we should never allow it to occur.

Human beings are the most intelligent form of life on earth. As such, they should not wallow in ignorance. Otherwise, they will live an insufferably wretched existence, never finding any measure of happiness. The manner in which a true *samaṇa* conducts all his affairs, both temporal and spiritual, sets a trustworthy example to be followed by the rest of the world. He engages in work that is pure and blameless; his actions are both righteous and dispassionate. So, endeavor to cultivate within yourself the exemplary work of a *samaṇa*, making it flourish steadily, so that wherever you go, your practice will always prosper accordingly. A *samaṇa* who cherishes moral virtue, cherishes concentration, cherishes mindfulness, cherishes wisdom and cherishes diligent effort, is sure to achieve that exalted status of a full-fledged *samaṇa* now, and to maintain it in the future.

The teaching that I give you is the dispensation of a man of diligence and perseverance, a spiritual warrior who emerged victorious, a pre-eminent individual who completely transcended *dukkha*, freeing himself of all fetters. He attained absolute freedom, becoming the Lord Buddha, the supreme guide and teacher of the three worlds of existence. If you can understand the special value this teaching holds for you, before long you too will have rid yourself of *kilesas*. I entrust this Dhamma teaching to you in the hope that you will give it the most careful consideration. In that way, you will experience incredible wonders arising within your mind, which by its very nature is a superb and wonderful thing.

A *sāvaka* Arahant having delivered such a discourse and departed, Ācariya Mun humbly received that Dhamma teaching. He carefully contemplated every aspect of it, isolating each individual point, and then thoroughly analyzed them all, one by one. As more and more *sāvaka* Arahants came to teach him in this way, he gained many new insights into the practice just by listening to their expositions. Hearing their wonderful discourses increased his enthusiasm for meditation, thus greatly enhancing his understanding of Dhamma.

Ācariya Mun said that listening to a discourse delivered by one of the Buddha's Arahant disciples made him feel as if he was in the presence of the Lord Buddha himself, though he had no prior recollection of meeting the Buddha. Listening intently, his heart completely full, he became so absorbed in Dhamma that the entire physical world, including his own body, ceased to exist for him then. The *citta* alone existed, its awareness shining brightly with the radiance of Dhamma. It was only later, when he withdrew from that state, that he realized the oppressive burden he still carried with him: for he became conscious again of his physical body — the focal point where the other four *khandhas* come together, each one a heavy mass of suffering on its own.

During his lengthy sojourn at Sarika Cave, Ācariya Mun entertained many *sāvaka* Arahants and heeded their words of advice, making this cave unique among all the places where he had ever stayed. While living there, the Dhamma of unimpeachable certainty arose in his heart; that is, he attained the fruition of Anāgāmī.[28] According to Buddhist scripture, the Anāgāmī has abandoned the five lower fetters that bind living beings to the round of repeated existence: *sakkāyadiṭṭhi*, *vicikicchā*, *sīlabbataparāmāsa*, *kāmarāga*, and *paṭigha*. Someone reaching this level of attainment is assured of never being reborn in the human realm, or in any other realm of existence where bodies are composed of the four gross physical elements: earth, water, fire, and air. Should that individual fail to ascend to the level of Arahant before dying, at the moment of death he will be reborn into one of the five Pure Abodes of the *brahma* world. An Anāgāmī is reborn in the abode of *aviha, atappa, sudassa, sudassī* or *akaniṭṭha*, depending on the individual's level of advancement along the Arahant path.

Ācariya Mun revealed that he attained the stage of Anāgāmī in Sarika Cave exclusively to his close disciples; but, I have decided to declare it publicly here for the reader's consideration. Should this disclosure be considered in any way inappropriate, I deserve the blame for not being more circumspect.

ONE NIGHT, HAVING CONTINUED to practice peacefully for many months, Ācariya Mun experienced an unusually strong feeling of compassion for his fellow monks. By that time, amazing insights surfaced nightly in his meditation practice. He became keenly aware of many strange, wonderful things — things he had never dreamed of seeing in his life. On the night that he thought about his fellow monks, his meditation had an exceptionally unusual quality to it. His *citta* had attained an especially ethereal refinement in *samādhi*, resulting in many extraordinary insights. Fully realizing the harmful effects that his own past ignorance had caused him, he was moved to tears. At the same time, he understood the value of the effort he had struggled so diligently to maintain until he could reap the amazing fruits of that diligence. A deep appreciation for the Lord Buddha's supreme importance arose in his heart; for, it was he who compassionately proclaimed the Dhamma so that others could follow in his footsteps, thus allowing them to understand the complex nature of their own *kamma*, and that of all other living beings as well. Thus the vital significance of the Dhamma verse: *All beings are born of their kamma and kamma is their one true possession*, which succinctly sums up practically all the Buddha's teachings.

Those insights notwithstanding, Ācariya Mun continued to remind himself that despite their truly amazing character he had yet to reach the end of the path and the cessation of *dukkha*. To accomplish that he would need to pour all his energy into the practice — with unstinting resolve. In the meantime, he was pleased to see that the chronic stomach ailment which he had suffered so long was now completely cured.

More than that, his mind was now firmly anchored to a solid spiritual basis. Although he had yet to totally eradicate his *kilesas*, he was sure of being on the right path. His meditation practice, now progressing smoothly, had none of the fluctuations he had experienced earlier. Unlike in the past, when he was groping in the dark, feeling his way along, he now felt certain of the path leading to the highest Dhamma. He was absolutely convinced that one day he would transcend *dukkha*.

His mindfulness and wisdom had reached a stage where they worked ceaselessly in perfect concert. He never needed to urge them into action. Day and night, knowledge and understanding arose continuously – both internal spiritual insights and awareness of countless external phenomena. The more his mind delighted in such amazing Dhamma, the more compassion he felt for his fellow monks: he was eager to share with them these wondrous insights. In the end, this profound feeling of compassion precipitated his departure from that auspicious cave. With some reluctance, he eventually left to search out the *dhutanga* monks he had known previously, when he was living in the Northeast.

Several days prior to his departure from Sarika Cave, a group of terrestrial *devas*, led by the mysterious being he first encountered there, came to hear a discourse on Dhamma. After finishing his discourse, Ācariya Mun informed them of his decision, saying he would soon take leave of them. Unwilling to see him depart, the large company of *devas* who were gathered there beseeched him to stay on for the sake of their long-term happiness and prosperity. Ācariya Mun explained that, just as he had come to that cave for a reason, so too he had a reason for moving on – he didn't come and go slavishly, following his desires. Asking for their understanding, he cautioned them against feeling disappointed. He promised that, if the opportunity presented itself in the future, he would return. The *devas* expressed their sincere regrets, showing the genuine affection and respect for him they'd always felt.

At about ten p. m. on the night before his departure, Ācariya Mun thought of Chao Khun Upāli at Wat Boromaniwat monastery, wondering what was on his mind. So he focused his *citta* and sent the flow of his consciousness out to observe him. He found that Chao Khun Upāli was at that moment contemplating *avijjā* in relation to *paticca-samuppāda*.[29] Ācariya Mun took note of the time and the date. When eventually he arrived in Bangkok, he asked Chao Khun Upāli about

46

what he'd observed. With a hearty laugh Chao Khun Upāli immediately acknowledged it to be true, saying this in praise of Ācariya Mun:

"You are truly masterful. I myself am a respected teacher, yet I'm inept compared to you — and I feel embarrassed. You truly are a master. This is exactly how a genuine disciple of the Lord Buddha follows in the footsteps of the Supreme Teacher. We can't all be incompetent in the practice of the Lord Buddha's teaching — somebody has to maintain this exalted Dhamma in the spirit that it was originally taught. By not allowing the modern age we live in to foster a lazy, defeatist attitude toward the highest attainments, you have demonstrated the timeless quality of the Buddha's teaching. Otherwise, the true Dhamma will no longer arise in the world, despite the fact that the Buddha proclaimed it for the benefit of all mankind. The special knowledge you have just displayed to me is most admirable. This is the way the Lord's teaching should be developed and put into practice."

Ācariya Mun stated that Chao Khun Upāli had the utmost admiration and respect for him. There were certain occasions when he sent for Ācariya Mun to help him solve certain problems he was unable to resolve to his own satisfaction. Eventually when the time was right, Ācariya Mun left Bangkok and returned directly to the Northeast.

IN THE YEARS PRIOR to his sojourn at Sarika Cave, Ācariya Mun traveled into the neighboring country of Burma, later returning by way of the northern Thai province of Chiang Mai. Continuing on into Laos, he practiced the ascetic way of life for some time in the area around Luang Prabang, eventually returning to Thailand to spend the rains retreat near the village of Ban Khok in Loei province, quite close to Pha Pu Cave. The following rains retreat was spent at Pha Bing Cave, also in Loei province. Back then, these places were all wilderness areas, teeming with wild animals where village communities were located far and few between: one could walk all day without coming across a single settlement. A person losing his way in that vast wilderness could find himself in the precarious situation of having to sleep overnight in an inhospitable environment at the mercy of tigers and other wild beasts.

On one occasion Ācariya Mun crossed the Mekong River and settled in a large tract of mountainous forest on the Laotian side. While he camped there, a huge Bengal tiger often wandered into his living area. Always coming at night, it stood some distance away watching him pace back and forth in meditation. It never displayed threatening behavior, but it did roar occasionally as it wandered freely around the area. Being well accustomed to living in close proximity to wild animals, Ācariya Mun paid little attention to the tiger.

During that excursion he was accompanied by another monk, Ācariya Sitha, who had been ordained slightly longer than he had. A contemporary of Ācariya Mun, Ācariya Sitha excelled in the practice of meditation. He liked the type of seclusion that the wilderness offered, preferring to live in the mountains stretching along the Laotian side of the Mekong River. Only occasionally did he cross the river into Thailand, and then never for very long.

On that occasion, Ācariya Mun and Ācariya Sitha were camped some distance apart, each depending on a separate village for his daily alms food. One night while walking in meditation, Ācariya Sitha was visited by a huge Bengal tiger. The tiger crept in and quietly crouched forward to about six feet from his meditation track, right in between the lighted candles at each end of the track that allowed him to see as he paced back and forth in the dark. Facing the meditation track while remaining motionless, it sat there calmly like a house pet watching Ācariya Sitha intently as he paced back and forth. Reaching that place on the track opposite which the tiger was crouched, Ācariya Sitha sensed something out of place. At once he became suspicious, for normally nothing was at the side of his track. Glancing over he saw the huge Bengal tiger crouched there, staring back at him — since when he couldn't tell. Still, he felt no fear. He merely watched the tiger as it sat motionless, looking back at him like a enormous stuffed animal. After a moment he continued pacing back and forth, passing each time in front of the tiger — but thoughts of fear never crossed his mind. He noticed, though, that it remained crouched there for an unusually long time. Feeling sorry for it, he directed this train of thought at the tiger: *Why not go off and find something to eat? Why just sit there watching me?* No sooner had this thought arisen, than the tiger let out a deafening roar that resounded through the whole forest. The sound of its roar left Ācariya Sitha in no doubt that it intended to stay, so he quickly changed tack, thinking: *I thought that only because I felt sorry for you — I was afraid you might get hungry sitting there so long. After all, you have a mouth and a stomach to fill, just like all other creatures. But if you don't feel hungry and want to sit there watching over me, that's fine, I don't mind.*

The tiger showed no reaction to Ācariya Sitha's change of heart — it just crouched by the path and continued to watch him. He then resumed his meditation, taking no further interest in it. Some time later he left the meditation track and walked to a small bamboo platform situated close by to take a rest. He chanted *suttas* there for awhile then sat peacefully in meditation until time to go to sleep, which he did lying on the bamboo platform. During that entire time the tiger remained crouched in its original position, not far away. But when he awoke at three a.m. to resume his walking meditation, he saw no sign of the tiger anywhere — he had no idea where it had gone. As it happened, he saw it only that once; from then on until he left that place, it never appeared again.

This incident intrigued Ācariya Sitha, so when he met with Ācariya Mun he described to him how the tiger had crouched there watching him. He told Ācariya Mun the tiger had roared at the precise moment the thought arose wishing it to go away. He recounted how, although he wasn't conscious of any fear, his hair stood on end and his scalp went numb, as if he were wearing a cap. But soon he again felt quite normal, resuming his walking meditation as though nothing had happened. Actually, there probably was a subtle measure of fear buried deep inside that he was incapable of perceiving at the time. Although the tiger never returned to his campsite, he often heard the sound of its roars echoing through the nearby forest. Still, Ācariya Sitha's mind remained resolute and he continued to practice contentedly, as he always had.

Ācariya Mun (circa 1930)

Ācariya Thet Thesarangsī (1902-1994)

Ācariya Fan Ajāro (1898-1977)

Ācariya Khao Anālayo (1888-1983)

2

The Middle Years

In the early years when Ācariya Mun first began wandering *dhutanga*, he started in the northeastern province of Nakhon Phanom. From there he traveled across the provinces of Sakon Nakhon and Udon Thani, finally reaching Burma, where he stayed for awhile before returning to Thailand by way of the northern province of Chiang Mai. Staying briefly there he then traveled into Laos, practicing the ascetic way of life in Luang Prabang and later Vientiane before eventually returning to Loei province. From this northeastern locale, he wandered by stages down to Bangkok, spending a rains retreat at Wat Pathumwan monastery. Following that retreat period, he took up residence in Sarika Cave, remaining there for several years. Only upon leaving Sarika Cave did he return to the Northeast region.

During all those years of extensive wandering, he almost always traveled alone. On only a few occasions was he accompanied by another monk, and even then they soon parted company. Ācariya Mun always practiced with a single-minded resolve, which kept him aloof from his fellow monks. He invariably felt it more convenient to wander *dhutanga* alone, practicing the ascetic way of life on his own. Only after his heart had been sufficiently strengthened by higher spiritual attainment did the compassion arise which made teaching his fellow monks a priority. Such compassionate considerations were the reason why he left the peace and tranquillity of Sarika Cave to journey back to the Northeast.

Previously, his early years of wandering *dhutanga* in the northeastern provinces had given him an opportunity to instruct some of the *kammaṭṭhāna* monks he met there. In those days, he had found a large number of *dhutanga* monks practicing in various locations throughout the Northeast. In making this return trip, Ācariya Mun was determined to teach the monks and laity who trusted his guidance, putting all his energy into the task. Returning to the same provinces he had once wandered through, he found that monks and lay people everywhere soon gained faith in him. Many of them, inspired by his teaching, ordained as monks to practice the way he did. Even some senior *ācariyas*, teachers in their own right, discarded their pride and renounced their obligations to practice under his tutelage, their minds eventually becoming so firmly established in meditation that they were fully confident of their ability to teach others.

Monks among the first generation of Ācariya Mun's disciples included Ācariya Suwan, the former abbot of Wat Aranyikawat monastery in the Tha Bo district of Nong Khai province; Ācariya Singh Khantayākhamo,[1] the former abbot of Wat Pa Salawan monastery in Nakhon Ratchasima; and Ācariya Mahā Pin Paññāphalo,[2] the former abbot of Wat Saddharam monastery in Nakhon Ratchasima. All three of these venerable *ācariyas* came originally from the province of Ubon Ratchathani — all have now passed away. They were influential disciples whose teaching careers helped to perpetuate Ācariya Mun's legacy for the benefit of future generations. Ācariya Singh and Ācariya Mahā Pin were brothers. Before taking up the way of practice, they thoroughly studied the Buddhist canonical texts. They were two of the senior *ācariyas* who gained faith in Ācariya Mun, discarding their pride and renouncing their obligations in order to follow the practice as he taught it. Eventually, through their teaching efforts they were able to assist many people from all walks of life.

Next in order of seniority was Ācariya Thet Thesarangsī[3] who presently resides at Wat Hin Mak Peng monastery in the Sri Chiangmai district of Nong Khai province. He is a senior disciple of Ācariya Mun whose exemplary mode of practice is so inspiring that he is highly revered by monks and laity in almost all parts of the country. His manner is always simple and down-to-earth, as one would expect with his exceptionally gentle, gracious, unassuming character. He conducts himself with perfect dignity, while people from all levels of society are captivated by his eloquent discourse.

When it comes to temperament, or personal behavior, senior *ācariyas* differ in their natural qualities of mind and character. There are *ācariyas* whose personal behavior is an excellent example for everyone to emulate: those emulating them are bound to behave in a pleasing, amicable manner that's in no way offensive to other people. The personal behavior of some other *ācariyas*, however, is pleasing and appropriate only when practiced by them personally. Should others adopt the same style of behavior it's bound to appear false, immediately offending anyone exposed to it. So it is inadvisable for most people to imitate the idiosyncratic behavior of these *ācariyas*.

The personal conduct of Ācariya Thet, however, is unimpeachable in this regard. Following his sterling example, one is bound to develop the kind of pleasing, amicable demeanor appreciated by people everywhere. He has such a gentle, kindly disposition that it can be easily emulated without the risk of offending others. His example is especially appropriate for Buddhist monks, whose personal behavior should always reflect a truly calm and peaceful frame of mind. Ācariya Thet is one of Ācariya Mun's senior disciples who I believe deserves the highest respect. For as long as I have known him, I have always considered him to be an eminent teacher.

Next in line is Ācariya Fan Ajāro[4] who now resides at Wat Udomsomphon near the village of Na Hua Chang in the Pannanikhom district of Sakhon Nakhon province. He is widely known and lauded throughout the country for his excellent spiritual practice and his virtuous conduct. His mind excels in noble qualities, the most prominent being his immense loving kindness for people of all classes. He is a monk truly worthy of the enthusiastic devotion he receives from people of every region of our country. He genuinely puts his heart into helping people in any way he can, whether materially or spiritually — like one whose benevolence knows no bounds.

The next senior disciple I shall mention is Ācariya Khao Anālyo[5] who presently resides at Wat Tham Klong Phen monastery in the Nong Bua Lamphu district of Udon Thani province. As he is one of the foremost meditation masters of our time, it's very likely that the reader is already familiar with his outstanding reputation. Both his mode of practice and his level of spiritual attainment are worthy of the utmost respect. He has always preferred to practice in remote, secluded locations with such single-minded resolve that his diligence in this respect is unrivaled among his peers in the circle of *dhutanga* monks. Even today, at the age of 82, he still refuses to allow his declining health to curtail his customary zeal. Some people have asked me, out of concern for his failing health, why he continues to put such strenuous effort into practice when in truth he has nothing further to accomplish. They can't figure out why he remains so active and energetic. I try to explain to them that someone, who has completely eliminated the contentious factors that exploit every weakness to sap energy and hinder progress, has no debilitating lethargy left to entrap his mind in a web of delusion. Meanwhile the rest of us have amassed such a debilitating mountain of laziness that it virtually obscures us from view. As soon as we get started on some worthwhile endeavor, we become apprehensive lest the fruits of our efforts overload our capacity to store them. We worry ahead of time about how exhausted we'll be when the work becomes difficult. In the end having failed to gather those wholesome fruits, we are left with an empty basket, that is, an empty joyless heart, drifting aimlessly with no hard-earned store of merit to fall back on. Instead, we fill our empty hearts with complaints about all the difficulties we face. So laziness, this blight in our hearts, keeps throwing up obstacles to block our way. Those who have cleansed this blight from their hearts remain persistent, persevering in times of hardship. They never worry about overloading their capacity to store the fruits of their efforts. Those individuals whose hearts are pure, unblemished Dhamma, cleared of all worldly defilements, stand out majestically in all situation. Somber, sullen moods never arise in their hearts, making them perfect examples for the world to follow.

Each of the above-mentioned disciples of Ācariya Mun has certain brilliant qualities buried deep within his heart, shining there like precious gems. People having the good fortune to meet such noble teachers are bound to be rewarded with amazing insights to gladden their hearts — an experience they will cherish forever.

Ācariya Mun taught several different generations of disciples, many of whom have become important teachers in their own right. Being a meditation master of great stature rich in noble virtues, he was wonderfully clever in the way he elucidated the path of practice and its fruits. It was as though he had a miniature *Tipiṭaka* etched into his heart, as was so accurately prophesied by the initial *samādhi nimitta* he saw when he first began to practice. Traveling to many regions of the country during the course of his teaching career, he instructed large numbers of monks and lay supporters, who in turn developed a deep devotion for him and a genuine fondness for the edifying Dhamma he taught. His spiritual impact was a direct result of having realized within himself the true nature of that Dhamma. His words thus represented that Truth which he had fully comprehended — not mere guesswork, or conjecture about what the truth should be or might be. Being absolutely certain about the Truth arising in his own heart, he taught this same Truth to others. When Ācariya Mun left Sarika Cave to return to the Northeast for the second time, he was fully determined to teach the way to as many monks and laity as possible — both his previous acquaintances who had already undergone some training, as well as those who were just beginning to establish themselves in the practice.

The Dhutanga Practices

Ācariya Mun strongly believed that the observance of *dhutanga* practices truly exemplified the spirit of the ascetic way of life. He strictly adhered to these ascetic practices throughout his life, and always urged those monks studying under his tutelage to adopt them in their own practice.

Going on almsround every day without fail, excepting only those days when a monk is deliberately abstaining from food. Ācariya Mun taught his disciples that, when walking to the village for alms, they should always have mindfulness present and remain properly restrained in body, speech, and mind. A monk should never permit his mind to accidentally become prey to the various tempting sense objects contacting his eyes, ears, nose, tongue, body, or mind while walking to and from the village on almsround. He stressed that mindfulness should bring their every movement, every thought, at every step of the route, under vigilant scrutiny. This should be treated as a sacred duty requiring reflection of the utmost seriousness each time a monk prepares to go on his morning almsround.

Eating only that food which has been accepted in the alms bowl on almsround. A monk should consider the quantity of food he receives in his bowl each day to be sufficient for his needs, as befits one who is content with little, and thus easily satisfied. For him it's counterproductive to expect extra food by accepting the generous offerings that are made later inside the monastery. Such practices easily encourage the insatiable greed of his *kilesas*, allowing them to gain the strength to become so domineering that they're almost impossible to counteract. A monk eats whatever food is offered into his bowl, never feeling anxious or upset should it fail to meet his expectations. Anxiety about food is a characteristic of hungry ghosts – beings tormented by the results of their own bad *kamma*. Never receiving enough food to satisfy their desires, they run madly around, desperately trying to fill their mouths and stomachs, always preferring the prospect of food to the practice of Dhamma. The ascetic practice of refusing to accept any food offered after almsround is an excellent way of contravening the tendency to be greedy for food. It is also the best method to cut off all expectancy concerning food, and the anxiety that it creates.

Eating only one meal per day is just right for the meditative lifestyle of a *dhutanga* monk, since he needn't worry about food at all hours of the day. Otherwise, he could easily become more worried about his stomach than he is about Dhamma – a most undignified attitude for one sincerely seeking a way to transcend *dukkha*. Even when eating only once a day, there are times when a monk should reduce his consumption, eating much less than he normally would at that one meal. This practice helps facilitate the work of meditation, for eating too much food can make the mental faculties sluggish and unresponsive. In addition, a monk whose temperament is suited to this practice can be expected to experience results invaluable to his spiritual development. This particular *dhutanga* observance is a useful tool for eliminating the greedy mentality of practicing monks who tend to be infatuated with food.

In this respect, the safeguards of Dhamma operate in much the same manner as the safeguards that society has introduced to protect itself. Enemies of society are confronted and subdued wherever they pose a threat to wealth, property, life and limb, or peace of mind. Whether it be fierce animals, such as wild dogs, snakes, elephants and tigers, or pestilent diseases, or simply pugnacious individuals, societies all over the world possess appropriate corrective measures, or medicines, to effectively subdue and protect themselves against these threats. A *dhutanga* monk whose mind displays pugnacious tendencies in its desire for food, or any other unwholesome qualities deemed distasteful, needs to have effective measures for correcting these threatening tendencies. Thus, he will always possess the kind of admirable self-restraint which is a blessing for him and a pleasing sight for those with whom he associates. Eating only one meal per day is an excellent way to restrain unwieldy mental states.

Eating all food directly from the alms bowl without using any other utensils is a practice eminently suited to the lifestyle of a *dhutanga* monk who strives to be satisfied with little while wandering from place to place. Using just his alms bowl means there's no need to be loaded down with a lot of cumbersome accessories as he travels from one location to another, practicing the ascetic way of life. At the same time, it is an expedient practice for monks wishing to unburden themselves of mental clutter; for each extra item they carry and look after, is just one more concern that weighs on their minds. For this reason, *dhutanga* monks should pay special attention to the practice of eating exclusively from the alms bowl. In truth, it gives rise to many unique benefits. Mixing all types of food together in the bowl is a way of reminding a monk to be attentive to the food he eats, and to investigate its true nature using mindfulness and wisdom to gain a clear insight into the truth about food.

Ācariya Mun said that, for him, eating from the bowl was just as important as any other *dhutanga* practice. He gained numerous insights while contemplating the food he was eating each day. Throughout his life he strictly observed this ascetic practice.

Investigating the true nature of food mixed together in the bowl is an effective means of cutting off strong desire for the taste of food. This investigation is a technique used to remove greed from a monk's mind as he eats his meal. Greed for food is thus replaced by a distinct awareness of the truth concerning that food: food's only true purpose is to nourish the body, allowing it to remain alive from one day to the next. In this way, neither the pleasant flavor of good foods, nor the unpleasant flavor of disagreeable foods, will cause any mental disturbance that might prompt the mind to waver. If a monk employs skillful investigative techniques each time he begins to eat, his mind will remain steadfast, dispassionate, and contented – unmoved by excitement or disappointment over the taste of the food he is offered. Consequently, eating directly from the alms bowl is an excellent practice for getting rid of infatuation with the taste of food.

Wearing only robes made from discarded cloth is another *dhutanga* observance that Ācariya Mun practiced religiously. This ascetic practice is designed to forestall the temptation to give in to the heart's natural inclination to desire nice, attractive-looking robes and other requisites. It entails searching in places, like cemeteries, for discarded pieces of cloth, collecting them little by little, then stitching the pieces together to make a usable garment, such as an upper robe, a lower robe, an outer robe, a bathing cloth, or any other requisite. There were times, when the dead person's relatives were agreeable, that Ācariya Mun collected the shroud used to wrap a corpse laid out in a charnel ground. Whenever he found discarded pieces of cloth on the ground while on almsround, he would pick them up and use them for making robes — regardless of the type of cloth or where it came from. Returning to the monastery, he washed them, and then used them to patch a torn robe, or to make a bathing cloth. This he routinely did wherever he stayed. Later as more and more faithful supporters learned of his practice, they offered him robe material by intentionally discarding pieces of cloth in charnel grounds, or along the route he took for almsround, or around the area where he stayed, or even at the hut where he lived. Thus his original practice of strictly taking only pieces of old, discarded cloth was altered somewhat according to circumstances: he was obliged to accept cloth the faithful had placed as offerings in strategic locations. Be that as it may, he continued to wear robes made from discarded cloth until the day he died.

Ācariya Mun insisted that in order to live in comfort a monk must comport himself like a worthless old rag. If he can rid himself of the conceit that his virtuous calling makes him somebody special, then he will feel at ease in all of his daily activities and personal associations, for genuine virtue does not arise from such assumptions. Genuine virtue arises from the self-effacing humility and forthright integrity of one who is always morally and spiritually conscientious. Such is the nature of genuine virtue: without hidden harmful pride, that person is at peace with himself and at peace with the rest of the world wherever he goes. The ascetic practice of wearing only robes made from discarded cloth serves as an exceptionally good antidote to thoughts of pride and self-importance.

A practicing monk should understand the relationship between himself and the virtuous qualities he aspires to attain. He must never permit pride to grab possession of the moral and spiritual virtues he cultivates within his heart. Otherwise, dangerous fangs and daggers will spring up in the midst of those virtuous qualities — even though intrinsically they're a source of peace and tranquillity. He should train himself to adopt the self-effacing attitude of being a worthless old rag until it becomes habitual, while never allowing conceit about his worthiness to come to the surface. A monk must cultivate this noble quality and ingrain it deeply in his personality, making it an intrinsic character trait as steadfast as the earth. He will thus remain unaffected by words of praise, or of criticism. Moreover, a mind totally devoid of conceit is a mind imperturbable in all circumstances. Ācariya Mun believed that the practice of wearing robes made from discarded cloth was one sure way to help attenuate feelings of self-importance buried deep within the heart.

Living in the forest. Realizing the value of this *dhutanga* observance from the very beginning, Ācariya Mun found forest dwelling conducive to the eerie, secluded feeling associated with genuine solitude. Living and meditating in the natural surroundings of a forest environment awakens the senses and encourages mindfulness for remaining vigilant in all of one's daily activities: mindfulness accompanying every waking moment, every waking thought. The heart feels buoyant and carefree, unconstrained by worldly responsibilities. The mind is constantly on the alert, earnestly focusing on its primary objective — the transcendence of *dukkha*. Such a sense of urgency becomes especially poignant when living far from the nearest settlement, at locations deep in remote forest areas teeming with all kinds of wild animals. In a constant state of readiness, the mind feels as though it's about to soar up and out of the deep abyss of the *kilesas* at any moment — like a bird taking flight. In truth, the *kilesas* remain ensconced there in the heart as always. It is the evocative forest atmosphere that tends to inspire this sense of liberation. Sometimes, due to the power of this favorable environment, a monk becomes convinced that his *kilesas* are diminishing rapidly with each passing day, while those remaining appear to be ever more scarce. This unfettered feeling is a constant source of support for the practice of meditation.

A monk living deep in the forest tends to consider the wild animals living around him — both those inherently dangerous and those that are harmless — with compassion, rather than with fear or apathy. He realizes that all animals, dangerous and harmless, are his equals in birth, ageing, sickness, and death. We human beings are superior to animals merely by virtue of our moral awareness: our ability to understand difference between good and evil. Lacking this basic moral judgment, we are no better than common animals. Unknown to them we label these creatures 'animals', even though the human species is itself a type of animal. The human animal is fond of labeling other species, but we have no idea what kind of label other animals have given to us. Who knows? Perhaps they have secretly labeled human beings 'ogres',[6] since we're so fond of mistreating them, slaughtering them for their meat — or just for sport. It's a terrible shame the way we humans habitually exploit these creatures; our treatment of them can be quite merciless. Even among our own kind, we humans can't avoid hating and harassing each other, constantly molesting or killing one another. The human world is troubled because people tend to molest and kill each other, while the animal world is troubled because humans tend to do the same to them. Consequently, animals are instinctively wary of human beings.

Ācariya Mun claimed that life in the forest provides unlimited opportunities for thought and reflection about one's own heart, and its relation to many natural phenomena in the external environment. Anyone earnestly desiring to go beyond *dukkha* can find plenty of inspiration in the forest, plenty of incentive to intensify his efforts — constantly.

At times, groups of wild boars wandered into the area where Ācariya Mun was walking in meditation. Instead of running away in panic when they saw him, they continued casually foraging for food in their usual way. He said they seemed to be able to differentiate between him and all the merciless 'ogres' of this world, which is why they kept rooting around for food so casually, instead of running for their lives.

Here I would like to digress from the main story a little to elaborate on this subject. You might be tempted to think that wild boars were unafraid of Ācariya Mun because he was a lone individual living deep in the forest. But, when my own monastery, Wat Pa Baan Taad, was first established[7] and many monks were living together there, herds of wild boars took refuge inside the monastery, wandering freely through the area where the monks had their living quarters. At night they moved around unafraid, only a few yards from the monks' meditation tracks — so close that they could be heard snorting and thumping as they rooted in the ground. Even the sound of the monks calling to one another to come and see this sight for themselves failed to alarm the wild boars. Continuing to wander freely through the monastery grounds every night, boars and monks soon became thoroughly accustomed to each other. Nowadays, wild boars only infrequently wander into the monastery because ogres, as animals refer to us humans – according to Ācariya Mun – have since killed and eaten almost all the wild animals in the area. In another few years, they probably will have all disappeared.

Living in the forest, Ācariya Mun met the same situation: almost every species of animal likes to seek refuge in the areas where monks live. Wherever monks take up residence, there are always a lot of animals present. Even within the monastery compounds of large metropolitan areas, animals – especially dogs – constantly find shelter. Some city monasteries are home to hundreds of dogs, for monks never harm them in any way. This small example is enough to demonstrate the cool, peaceful nature of Dhamma, a spirit of harmlessness that's offensive to no living creature in this world – except, perhaps, the most hard-hearted individuals.

Ācariya Mun's experience of living in the forest convinced him just how supportive that environment is to meditation practice. The forest environment is ideal for those wishing to transcend *dukkha*. It is without a doubt the most appropriate battlefield to choose in one's struggle to attain all levels of Dhamma, as evidenced by the preceptor's first instructions to a newly ordained monk: Go look for a suitable forest location in which to do your practice. Ācariya Mun maintained this ascetic observance to the end of his life, except on infrequent occasions when circumstances mitigated against it. A monk living in the forest is constantly reminded of how isolated and vulnerable he is. He can't afford to be unmindful. As a result of such vigilance, the spiritual benefits of this practice soon become obvious.

Dwelling at the foot of a tree is a *dhutanga* observance that closely resembles living in the forest. Ācariya Mun said that he was dwelling under the shade of a solitary tree the day his *citta* completely transcended the world – an event that will be fully dealt with later on. A lifestyle that depends on the shade of a tree for a roof and the only protection against the elements is a lifestyle conducive to constant introspection. A mind possessing such constant inner focus is always prepared to tackle the *kilesas*, for its attention is firmly centered on the Four Foundations of Mindfulness[8] – *rūpa, vedanā, citta,* and *dhamma* – and The Four Noble Truths[9] – *dukkha, samudaya, nirodha,* and *magga.* Together, these factors constitute the mind's most effective defense, protecting it during its all-out assault on the *kilesas.* In the eerie solitude of living in the forest, the constant fear of danger can motivate the mind to focus undivided attention on the Foundations of Mindfulness, or the Noble Truths. In doing so, it acquires a solid basis for achieving victory in its battle with the *kilesas* — such is the true path leading to the Noble Dhamma. A monk who wishes to thoroughly understand himself, using a safe and correct method, should find an appropriate meditation subject and a suitable location that are conducive for him to exert a maximum effort. These combined elements will help to expedite his meditation progress immeasurably. Used as an excellent means for destroying *kilesas* since the Buddha's time, the *dhutanga* observance of dwelling at the foot of a tree is another practice meriting special attention.

Staying in a cemetery is an ascetic practice which reminds monks and lay people alike not to be neglectful while they are still alive, believing that they themselves will never die. The truth of the matter is: we are all in the process of dying, little by little, every moment of every day. The people who died and were relocated to the cemetery — where their numbers are so great there's scarcely any room left to cremate or bury them — are the very same people who were dying little by little before; just as we are now. Who in this world seriously believes himself to be so unique that he can claim immunity from death?

We are taught to visit cemeteries so that we won't forget the countless relatives with whom we share birth, ageing, sickness, and death; so as to constantly remind ourselves that we too live daily in the shadow of birth, ageing, sickness, and death. Certainly no one who still wanders aimlessly through the endless round of birth and death would be so uncommonly bold as to presume that he will never be born, grow old, become sick, or die. Since they are predisposed toward the attainment of freedom from this cycle by their very vocation, monks should study the root causes of the continuum of suffering within themselves. They should educate themselves by visiting a cemetery where cremations are performed, and by reflecting inwardly on the crowded cemetery within themselves where untold numbers of corpses are brought for burial all the time: such a profusion of old and new corpses are buried within their bodies that it's impossible to count them all.[10] By contemplating the truly grievous nature of life in this world, they use mindfulness and wisdom to diligently probe, explore, and analyze the basic principles underlying the truth of life and death.

Everyone who regularly visits a cemetery — be it an outdoor cemetery or the inner cemetery within their bodies — and uses death as the object of contemplation, can greatly reduce their smug sense of pride in being young, in being alive, in being successful. Unlike most people, those who regularly contemplate death don't delight in feeling self-important. Rather, they tend to see their own faults, and gradually try to correct them, instead of merely looking for and criticizing other people's faults — a bad habit that brings unpleasant consequences. This habit resembles a chronic disease that appears to be virtually incurable, or perhaps it could be remedied if people weren't more interested in aggravating the infection than they are in curing it.

Cemeteries offer those interested in investigating these matters an opportunity to develop a comprehensive knowledge and understanding of the nature of death. Cemeteries are the great gathering places of the world. All people without exception must eventually meet there. Death is no small hurdle to be easily stepped over before a thorough investigation of the issue. Before they finally crossed over, the Lord Buddha and his Arahant disciples had to study in the 'great academy' of birth, ageing, sickness, and death until they had mastered the entire curricula. Only then were they able to cross over with ease. They had escaped the snares of Māra,[11] unlike those who, forgetting themselves, disregard death and take no interest in contemplating its inevitability; even as it stares them in the face.

Visiting cemeteries to contemplate death is an effective method for completely overcoming the fear of dying; so that, when death seems imminent, courage alone arises despite the fact that death is the most terrifying thing in the world. It would seem an almost impossible feat, but it has been accomplished by those who practice meditation — the Lord Buddha and his Arahant disciples being the supreme examples. Having accomplished this feat themselves, they taught others to thoroughly investigate every aspect of birth, ageing, sickness, and death so that people wanting to take responsibility for their own well-being can use this practice to correct their misconceptions before it becomes too late. If they reach that 'great academy' only when their last breath is taken, it will then be too late for remedial action: the only remaining options will be cremation and burial. Observing moral precepts, making merit, and practicing meditation will no longer be possible.

Ācariya Mun well understood the value of a visit to the cemetery, for a cemetery has always been the kind of place that encourages introspection. He always showed a keen interest in visiting cemeteries — both the external variety and the internal one. One of his disciples, being terrified of ghosts, made a valiant effort to follow his example in this. We don't normally expect monks to be afraid of ghosts, which is equivalent to Dhamma being afraid of the world — but this monk was one such case.

A Monk's Fear of Ghosts

Ācariya Mun related the story of a *dhutanga* monk who inadvertently went to stay in a forest located next to a charnel ground.[12] He arrived on foot at a certain village late one afternoon and, being unfamiliar with the area, asked the villagers where he could find a wooded area suitable for meditation. They pointed to a tract of forest, claiming it was suitable, but neglected to tell him that it was situated right on the edge of a charnel ground. They then guided him to the forest, where he passed the first night peacefully. On the following day he saw the villagers pass by carrying a corpse, which they soon cremated only a short distance from where he was staying. As he looked on, he could clearly see the burning corpse. He started to grow apprehensive the moment he saw the coffin being carried past, but he assumed that they were on their way to cremate the body somewhere else. Still, the mere sight of the coffin caused him considerable consternation, as he thought ahead to the coming night. He was worried that the image of the coffin would haunt him after dark, making it impossible for him to sleep. As it turned out he had camped on the edge of a charnel ground, so he was obliged to watch as the corpse was burned right in front of him. This sight upset him even more, causing him severe discomfort as he contemplated the prospect of having to spend the night there. Feeling very uneasy from the first sight of the corpse passing by, the feeling gradually intensified until he was so terrified that, by nightfall, he could hardly breathe.

It's pitiful to think that a monk can be so terrified of ghosts. I am recording this incident here so that those of my readers having a similar fear of ghosts may reflect on the tenacity with which this monk strove to confront his fear head on, and so take a valuable lesson from the past.

Once all the villagers had gone home, leaving him alone, his torment began in earnest. He could not keep his mind focused on meditation because whenever he closed his eyes to meditate, he saw a long line of ghosts moving toward him. Before long ghosts hovered around him in groups, an image which frightened him so much that all presence of mind deserted him, throwing him into a panic. His fear began in mid-afternoon, at the first sight of the corpse. By the time darkness fell all around, his fear had become so intense he was just barely able to cope.

Since ordaining as a monk, he had never experienced anything like this long struggle with visions of ghosts. At least he was mindful enough to begin reflecting: *The fear, the ghosts — all of it may simply be a delusion. It is more likely that these haunting images of ghosts are creations of my own mind.*

As a *dhutanga* monk he was expected to be steadfast and fearless when facing death, ghosts, or any other danger. So he reminded himself: *People everywhere praise the fearless courage of dhutanga monks, yet here I am shamelessly afraid of ghosts. I'm acting like a total failure, as though I've ordained just to live in fear of ghosts and goblins without any rhyme or reason. I'm a disgrace to my fellow monks in the dhutanga tradition. I am unworthy of the admiration of people who believe we are noble warriors fearing nothing. How could I let this happen?*

Having reminded himself of the noble virtues expected of a *dhutanga* monk, and roundly criticizing himself for failing to live up to these high standards, he resolved that he would force himself to face the fear directly from then on. The corpse that smoldered before him on the funeral pyre being the cause of his fear, he decided to go there immediately. Putting on his robe, he started walking straight for the funeral pyre, which he saw clearly glowing in the darkness. But after a few steps his legs tensed up, and he could hardly move. His heart pounded and his body began to perspire profusely, as though exposed to the midday sun. Seeing that this was not going to work, he quickly adjusted his tack. Starting with small, deliberate steps, he placed one foot just in front of the other, not allowing his forward motion to stop. By that time, he was relying on sheer strength of will to push his body forward. Frightened to death and shaking uncontrollably, he nevertheless kept his resolve to walk on — as though his life depended on it.

Struggling the entire way, he eventually reached the burning corpse. But instead of feeling relieved that he had achieved his objective, he felt so faint he could barely stand. About to go crazy with fear, he forced himself to look at the partially burned corpse. Then, seeing the skull burned white from long exposure to the fire, he got such a fright that he nearly fainted straightaway. Bravely suppressing his fear, he sat down to meditate just a short distance from the burning pyre. He focused on the corpse, using it as the object of his meditation, while forcing his terrified heart to mentally recite continuously: *I'm going to die — just like this corpse, there's no need to be afraid. I'm going to die someday too — there's no point in being afraid.*

Sitting there grappling with his fear of ghosts and forcing his heart to repeat this meditation on death, he heard a strange sound just behind him — the sound of approaching footsteps! The footsteps stopped, then started again, slow and cautious as if someone were sneaking up to pounce on him from behind — or so he imagined at the time. His fear now reaching its peak, he was poised to jump up and run away, crying "Ghosts! Help!" But he managed to control this impulse and waited, listening nervously as the footsteps slowly drew nearer then stopped a few yards away. Poised to run, he heard a strange sound — like someone chewing, loud and crunchy. This sent his imagination racing: *What's it chewing on around here? Next, it'll be chewing on my head! This cruel, heartless ghost is sure to mean the end of me.*

Unable to stand the suspense any longer, he decided to open his eyes. Should the situation look drastic, he was prepared to run for his life — a far better option than just letting some terrible ghost devour him. *Escaping death now,* he reasoned, *will give me the chance to resume my practice later with renewed diligence, whereas I gain nothing by sacrificing my life to this ghost.* With that he opened his eyes and turned to look in the direction of the chewing, crunching sounds, all set to make a dash for his life. Peering through the darkness to catch a glimpse of the terrible ghost he had imagined, he saw instead a village dog, casually eating the scraps of food left by the villagers as offerings to the spirits as part of the local custom. It had come scrounging for something to fill its stomach, as hungry animals are wont to do; and it wasn't the least bit interested in him sitting there.

Suddenly realizing that it was only a dog, the monk laughed at his own folly. Turning his attention to the dog, which showed no interest in him whatsoever, he thought: *So! You're the almighty specter that nearly drove me crazy. You've taught me the lesson of my life!* At the same time, he was deeply dismayed by his own cowardice:

"Despite my determination to confront my fears like a warrior, I was thrown into a panic as soon as I heard the sound of this dog scrounging for food — a mad *dhutanga* monk fleeing frantically for his life! It's a good thing I had enough mindfulness to wait that fraction of a second longer to discover the real cause of my fear. Otherwise, it would probably have driven me mad. Gosh! Am I really so grossly stupid as that? If so, do I deserve to continue wearing the yellow robes, the emblem of courage; for it denotes a disciple of the Lord Buddha, whose superior courage transcends all comparison? Being this useless, should I still walk for alms, and thus desecrate the food that the faithful offer with such respect? What can I do now to redeem myself after such a despicable display of cowardice? Surely no other disciple of the Buddha is as pathetic as I am. Just one inept disciple like myself is enough to weigh heavily on the *sāsana* — should there be any more, the burden would be enormous. How am I going to tackle this fear of ghosts that's just made me look so foolish? Hurry up! Take a stand, right this minute! It is better to die now than to postpone this decision any longer. Never again can I allow this fear of ghosts to trample on my heart. This world has no place for a monk who disgraces himself and the religion he represents."

With this self-admonition fresh in his mind, the monk made a solemn vow:

"I will not leave this place until I've overcome my fear of ghosts. If I have to die trying, then so be it! If I can't defeat this fear, then I don't deserve to continue living in such disgrace. Others might follow my bad example, becoming useless people themselves, thus further increasing the burden on the *sāsana*."

So he vowed to himself that, from that moment on, he would remain in that cemetery day and night as a way of dealing sternly with his fear. He focused on the corpse before him, comparing it with his own body, seeing that they were both composed of the same basic elements. As long as consciousness is there in the heart to hold everything together, then that person, or that animal, continues to live. But as soon as consciousness departs, the whole combination of elements begins to disintegrate, and is then referred to as a corpse.

It was clear that his notion about the dog being a ghost was shamefully absurd; so he resolved that he would never again lend any credence to thoughts of being haunted by ghosts. As this incident clearly showed, his mind simply haunted itself with ghostly apparitions, and his fear was the outcome of this self-deception. The misery he suffered arose from such faith in this delusion that a mere dog, harmlessly scrounging for food, almost became a matter of life and death.

Recalling how deluded he had been for so long, trusting the self-deceptions that his mind constantly churned out, he thought:

"Although they've always been at work, this is the first time they have brought me so close to catastrophe. Dhamma teaches us that *saññā* is the master of deception,[13] but until now I've never clearly understood what that means. Only now, inhaling the stench of my own living death, do I understand its significance: My fear of ghosts is nothing more than *saññā's* deceptive trickery. From now on, *saññā* will never again trick me as it has in the past. I must stay put here in this cemetery until the 'master of deception' is dead and buried, so that the specter of ghosts will not continue to haunt me in the future. Only then will I agree to leave here. Now it's my turn to torture to death this cunning, deceitful conjurer, then cremate its stinking corpse like that fleshly corpse I've just seen cremated here. Dealing a decisive blow to *saññā's* insidious trickery — this is the only pressing matter in my life right now."

The monk took up this challenge with such earnest resolve that whenever *saññā* caused him to suspect a ghost was lurking somewhere around him, he immediately went to that spot, exposing the deception. Forgoing sleep, he kept up this vigil throughout the night, until finally *saññā* no longer had the strength to assert its assumptions. In the early hours of the evening, he had been engaged in a struggle with external ghosts, in the guise of the village dog which had nearly been his undoing. Later, when he understood the situation and became conscious of his error, he turned his attention inward, battling his inner ghosts into submission. Beginning the moment he became aware of his folly, his fear of ghosts subsided and ceased to trouble him for the rest of the night. On subsequent nights, he remained alert, ready to confront any hint of fear using the same uncompromising stance. Eventually he transformed himself into a monk of incredible courage – in all circumstances. This whole experience had a profound and lasting impact on his spiritual development. His fear of ghosts gave rise to an outstanding lesson in Dhamma, thus converting him into a truly authentic monk.

I include this story in the biography of Ācariya Mun in the hope that the reader will gain some valuable insights from it, just as I trust the story of Ācariya Mun's life will prove to be of great benefit to people everywhere. As can be seen from the above story, visiting cemeteries has always been an essential *dhutanga* practice.

WEARING ONLY THE THREE PRINCIPAL ROBES is another *dhutanga* observance that Ācariya Mun followed religiously from the day he first ordained until old age and declining health eventually forced him to relax his strict adherence somewhat. In those days, *dhutanga* monks rarely settled in one location for very long, except during the three months of the rainy season retreat. They wandered through forests and mountains, traveling by foot the whole way since there were no automobiles back then. Each monk had to carry his own belongings – he could expect no help from others. For this reason, each monk took with him only as much as he could conveniently manage. Since it was awkward to be loaded down with too many things, only absolute essentials were taken. As time went on, this frugal attitude became an integral part of a monk's character. Should someone give him something extra, he would simply give it away to another monk to avoid accumulating unnecessary possessions.

The true beauty of a *dhutanga* monk lies with the quality of his practice and the simplicity of his life. When he dies, he leaves behind only his eight basic requisites[14] – the only true necessities of his magnificent way of life. While he's alive, he lives majestically in poverty – the poverty of a monk. Upon death, he is well-gone with no attachments whatsoever. Human beings and *devas* alike sing praises to the monk who dies in honorable poverty, free of all worldly attachments. So the ascetic practice of wearing only the three principal robes will always be a badge of honor complementing *dhutanga* monks.

Ācariya Mun was conscientious in the way he practiced all the *dhutanga* observances mentioned above. He became so skillful and proficient with them that it would be hard to find anyone of his equal today. He also made a point of teaching the monks under his tutelage to train themselves using these same ascetic methods. He directed them to live in remote wilderness areas, places that were lonely and frightening: for example, at the foot of a tree, high in the mountains, in caves, under overhanging rocks, and in cemeteries. He took the lead in teaching them to consider their daily almsround a solemn duty, advising them to eschew food offered later. Once lay devotees in the village became familiar with his strict observance of this practice, they would put all their food offerings into the monks' bowls, making it unnecessary to offer additional food at the monastery. He advised his disciples to eat all food mixed together in their bowls, and to avoid eating from other containers. And he showed them the way by eating only one meal each day until the very last day of his life.

WANDERING BY STAGES across the Northeast, Ācariya Mun gradually attracted increasing numbers of disciples at every new location along the way. When he stopped to settle in one place for some time, scores of monks gravitated to that area to live with him. Having set up a temporary monastic community in the forest, sixty to seventy monks would gather there, while many more stayed close by in the surrounding area. Ācariya Mun always tried to keep his disciples spread apart, living in separate locations that were not too close to one another, yet close enough to his residence so that they could easily seek his advice when they encountered problems in their meditation. This arrangement was convenient for all, for when too many monks are living in close proximity, it can become a hindrance to meditation.

On the *uposatha* observance days, when the *Pāṭimokkha*[15] was recited, *dhutanga* monks came from various locations in his vicinity to assemble at his residence. After the recitation of the *Pāṭimokkha,* Ācariya Mun addressed the whole assembly with a discourse on Dhamma, and then answered the monks' questions, one by one, until their doubts cleared up and everyone was satisfied. Each monk then returned to his own separate location, buoyed by the exposition of Dhamma he had just heard, and resumed his meditation practice with renewed enthusiasm.

Although he sometimes had large groups of monks staying to train with him, he found them easy to supervise because they were all prepared to put what he taught into practice for their own spiritual benefit. Monastic life under his tutelage was so orderly and quiet that the monastery often appeared deserted. Excepting mealtimes and times when the monks assembled for meetings, a visitor coming at any other hour wouldn't have seen the monks. The place would have looked deserted with each monk having slipped into the dense forest to diligently pursue walking or sitting meditation in his own secluded spot, day and night.

Ācariya Mun often assembled the monks in the evenings at about dusk to give a discourse on Dhamma. As the monks sat together quietly listening, Ācariya Mun's voice was the only sound they heard. The rhythm of his voice articulating the essence of Dhamma was at once lyrical and captivating. Carried along by the flow of his teaching, his audience completely forgot themselves, their weariness, and the time that passed. Listening, they were aware only of the flow of Dhamma having an impact on their hearts, creating such a pleasant feeling that they could never get enough of it. Each of these meetings lasted many hours.

Within the circle of *dhutanga* monks, listening to a Dhamma discourse in this way is considered another form of meditation practice. *Dhutanga* monks have an especially high regard for their teacher and his verbal instructions. He constantly guides and admonishes them to such good effect that they tend to view his teachings as the lifeblood of their meditation practice. Showing the utmost respect and affection for their teacher, they are even willing to sacrifice their lives for him. The Venerable Ananda is an excellent case in point: He had such unwavering affection for the Buddha that he was willing to sacrifice his life by throwing himself into the path of the wild, charging elephant that Devadatta had let loose in an attempt to kill the Buddha.

In Ācariya Mun's case, *dhutanga* monks listened to his instructions with great reverence, enthusiastically taking them to heart. This was especially evident when he advised one of his monks to go live in a certain cave in order to give his practice new impetus. Monks, singled out in this manner, never objected, but faithfully followed his recommendations with genuine conviction, refusing to allow fear or concern for their safety to become an issue. Instead they were pleased, feeling that their practice was bound to be strengthened by living in the locations he recommended. This in turn infused them with determination to strive relentlessly both day and night. They were convinced that, if Ācariya Mun suggested a certain location to them, then their efforts there were sure to be rewarded with good results – as though they had received an assurance of success from him in advance. This could be likened to the assurance that the Lord Buddha gave to the Venerable Ananda, just prior to his *Parinibbāna*, when he told him that in three months time his heart would be free from all *kilesas*. He was predicting that the Venerable Ananda was certain to attain enlightenment, becoming an Arahant on the opening day of the First Sangha Council.[16] It's obvious that devout obedience to the teacher is vitally important. It engenders an unwavering interest in practice, guards against carelessness and apathy, and so helps to anchor the basic principles of Dhamma in the disciple's heart. It facilitates the establishment of a common understanding between teacher and disciple so that instructions need not be repeated over and over until it becomes annoying and tiresome for both parties.

ĀCARIYA MUN'S SECOND TRIP to the Northeast was a cause for much interest and excitement among monks and lay supporters throughout the region. During that period, he traveled extensively teaching in almost all the northeastern provinces. He passed initially through Nakhon Ratchasima; then through Si Saket, Ubon Ratchathani, Nakhon Phanom, Sakon Nakhon, Udon Thani, Nong Khai, Loei, Lom Sak, and Phetchabun, and occasionally crossed the Mekong River into Laos to visit Vientiane and Tha Khek. He crisscrossed these areas many times in those days, but he preferred to remain longer in provinces that were mountainous and thickly forested because they were especially suitable for meditation. For instance, south and southwest of the town of Sakon Nakhon there were many forest-covered mountain ranges where he spent the rains retreat near the village of Phon Sawang in the district of Sawang Dan Din. The mountainous terrain in this area is so conducive to the ascetic way of life that it is still frequented by *dhutanga* monks today.

Monks wandering in such areas during the dry season usually slept out in the forest on small bamboo platforms. They were made by splitting sections of bamboo lengthwise, spreading them out flat, then securing them to a bamboo frame with legs, making a raised sleeping surface of about six feet long, three or four feet wide, and about one and a half feet above the ground. One platform was constructed for each monk and was spaced as far apart from another as the living area of the forest would allow. A large tract of forest allowed spacing of at least 120 feet with the thick foliage in between each platform acting as a natural screen. If the area was relatively small, or a large group of monks lived together in an area, then the spacing might be reduced to 90 feet intervals, though the minimum distance was usually 120 feet. The fewer the number of monks living in a particular area, the farther apart they were individually — being close enough to one another only to hear the distant sound of a cough or a sneeze. Local villagers helped each monk to clear a walking meditation track approximately 60 feet in length, which was located beside his sleeping platform. These tracks were used day and night for practicing meditation in a walking mode.

When monks fearful of ghost or tigers came to train under Ācariya Mun, he usually made them stay alone, far from the rest of the monks — a severe training method designed to draw attention to the fear so that the monk could learn to come to grips with it. He was required to remain there until he became accustomed to the wilderness environment, and inured to the tigers and ghosts that his mind conjured up to deceive him. The expectation was that, in the end, he would achieve the same good results as others who had trained themselves in this way. Then he wouldn't have to carry such a burden of fear indefinitely. Ācariya Mun believed this method accomplished better results than simply leaving a monk to his own devices, and to the very real prospect that he might never find the courage to face his fears.

Upon arriving in a new location, a *dhutanga* monk had to first sleep on the ground, collecting various kinds of leaves, or in some places straw, to make a crude mattress. Ācariya Mun said that the months of December and January were especially difficult due to the prevailing seasonal weather patterns, as the approaching cold weather met and mixed with the outgoing rainy weather. When it did rain during the winter months, a monk inevitably got drenched. Sometimes it rained continuously all night, and the umbrella-tent he used as shelter was no match for the driving rain and high winds. Still, he had no choice but to sit shivering under this makeshift shelter, enduring the dank cold and unable to move for it was impossible to see in the dark. A downpour during the daylight hours was not quite so bad. A monk still got wet, but at least he could see his surroundings and search for things in the forest to help shelter him from the elements without feeling totally blind. Essential items like his outer robe and his matches had to be kept in his alms bowl with the lid tightly secured. Folding his upper robe in half, he draped it around himself to keep out the cold and damp. The cloth mosquito net that hung from the suspended umbrella down to the ground formed a tent-like shelter that was indispensable for blocking out the windswept rain. Otherwise, everything got soaked and he had to endure the discomfort of having no dry robe to wear in the morning for almsround.

The months of February, March, and April saw the weather change again, as it began to heat up. Normally *dhutanga* monks then moved up into the mountains, seeking out caves or overhanging cliffs to shelter them from the sun and the rain. Had they gone to these mountainous locations in December and January, the ground would still have been saturated from the rainy season, exposing them to the risk of malarial infection. Malarial fever was never easy to cure. Many months could pass before the symptoms finally went away. It could easily develop into a chronic condition, the fever recurring at regular intervals. This kind of chronic malaria was locally referred to as 'the fever the in-laws despise', for its victims can eat well enough but they can't do any work because the fever is so debilitating. In such cases, not only the in-laws but also everyone else became fed up. No effective remedies for malaria existed then; so those who caught it had to just let it run its course. I myself quite often suffered from such chastening fevers, and I too had let them run their course as we had no medicines to treat malaria in those days. Ācariya Mun used to say that most of the *dhutanga* monks he knew during that period had been infected with malaria, including himself and many of his disciples. Some even died of it. Listening to those accounts, one couldn't help feeling a profound sympathy for him and his monks: he nearly died before gaining the necessary understanding to teach the way of Dhamma to his disciples, so they too could practice following his example.

Local Customs and Beliefs

Earlier, before Ācariya Mun and Ācariya Sao began wandering through the region to enlighten people about the nature of moral virtue and to explain the consequences of their actions and beliefs, the worship of spirits and ghosts had become endemic in the Northeast and a common aspect of everyday village life. Whether it was planting the rice, putting in a garden, building a house, or making a shed, an auspicious day, month, and year had to be determined for the start of every endeavor. Before any type of work could begin, propitiatory offerings were routinely made to placate the local spirits. Should those ritual offerings be neglected, then the least untoward thing — a common cold or a sneeze — was attributed to incurring the disfavor of the spirits. A local spirit doctor was then called in to divine the cause and pacify the offended spirit. Doctors in those days were much smarter than they are today: they unhesitatingly declared that this spirit, or that ghost, had been wronged, claiming that a certain offering or sacrifice would cure everything. Even if the supplicant was hacking and sneezing long after offering the prescribed oblation, it made no difference. Back then, if the doctor declared you cured, you were, and you felt relieved despite the symptoms. This is the reason I can so boldly assert that both the doctors and the patients of that era were very smart: whatever the doctor declared was final, and the patient accepted it without reservation. It was unnecessary to search for medical cures, since the spirit doctor and his ghosts could cure everything.

Later when Ācariya Mun and Ācariya Sao passed through these areas, reasoning with local inhabitants, and explaining the principles of truth, their preoccupation with the power of spirits and the agency of spirit doctors gradually waned. Today it has virtually disappeared. Even many of the spirit doctors themselves began taking refuge in the Buddha, Dhamma, and Sangha in place of the various spirits and ghosts they had been worshipping. Nowadays, hardly anyone engages in such occult practices. Traveling from village to village in the Northeast today, we no longer have to tread our way through offerings laid out for the spirits as we did in the past. Except for the odd group here or there, spirit worship is no longer an issue in people's lives. It's truly a blessing for this region that people no longer have to live their whole lives clinging to these beliefs. The people of the Northeast have long since transferred their faith and allegiance to the Buddha, Dhamma and Sangha, thanks largely to the compassionate efforts of Ācariya Mun and Ācariya Sao to whom we all owe an immense debt of gratitude.

DURING HIS TIME IN THE REGION, Ācariya Mun taught the local people, applying all his strength and ability to render them as decent human beings. He passed through some villages where the local 'wise men' asked him questions. They asked questions such as: Do ghosts really exist? Where do human beings come from? What is it that causes sexual attraction between men and women, since they've never been taught this? Why are male and female animals of the same species attracted to one another? From where did humans and animals learn this mutual attraction? Though I can't recall all the questions he was asked, these I do remember. I accept blame for any inaccuracies in what is recorded here as my memory has always been somewhat faulty. Even recalling my own words and other personal matters, I cannot avoid making mistakes; so my recollection of Ācariya Mun's stories is bound to be incomplete.

To the question *"Do ghosts really exist?"* Ācariya Mun's reply was:

"If something truly exists in the world, whether a spirit or anything else, it simply exists as it is. Its existence does not depend on the belief or disbelief of anyone. People may say that something exists or doesn't exist, but whether that thing actually exists or not is dependent entirely on its own nature. Its state does not alter according to what people imagine it to be. The same principle applies to ghosts, which people everywhere are skeptical about. In reality, those ghosts that frighten and torment people are actually creations of their own minds. They've come to believe that, here and there, dwell ghosts that will harm them. This in turn causes fear and discomfort to arise in them. Ordinarily, if a person doesn't mentally conjure up the idea of ghosts, he doesn't suffer from a fear of them. In a majority of cases, ghosts are just mental images created by those who tend to be afraid of them. As to whether there really are such things as ghosts in the world — even if I were to say that they do exist, there is still not enough proof to make skeptics into believers, since people have a natural tendency to deny the truth. Even when a thief is caught red-handed with stolen articles, he will often refuse to admit the truth. More than that, he'll fabricate an alibi to get himself off the hook and deny any wrongdoing. He may be forced to accept punishment due to the weight of the evidence against him; but, he will still continue to protest his innocence. When he is imprisoned and someone asks him what he did wrong to deserve that punishment, he will quickly answer that he was accused of stealing, but insist that he never did it. It is rare for such a person to own up to the truth. Generally speaking, people everywhere have much the same attitude."

To the question *"Where do human beings come from?"* Ācariya Mun's reply was:

"All human beings have a mother and father who gave birth to them. Even you yourself were not born miraculously from a hollow tree. We all obviously have parents who gave birth to us and raised us, so this question is hardly an appropriate one. Were I to say that human beings are born of ignorance and craving, this would cause more confusion and misunderstanding than if I gave no answer at all. People have no knowledge whatsoever of what ignorance and craving are, although they are present there in everyone — except, of course, in the Arahants. The trouble is people are not interested enough to make the necessary effort for understanding these things, so that leaves the obvious answer: we are born of our parents. This then opens me up to the criticism that I've answered too briefly. But it is hard to give a reply which goes to the truth of the matter, when the one asking the question is not really much interested in the truth to begin with. The Lord Buddha taught that both people and animals are born of *avijjā paccaya sankhāra... samudayo hoti.*[17] The ceasing of birth, which is the cessation of all *dukkha*, stems from *avijjāya tveva asesavirāga nirodhā sankhārā nirodho ... nirodho hoti.*[18] This condition is inherent within the heart of each and every person who has *kilesas*. Once the truth has been accepted, it becomes clear that it's just this which leads to birth as a human being or an animal until the world becomes so crowded one can hardly find a place to live. The primary cause is just this ignorance and insatiable craving. Though we haven't even died yet, we are already searching for a place to be born into where we can carry on living — an attitude of mind that leads human beings and animals all over the world to birth and constant suffering. Anyone wishing to know the truth should take a look at the *citta* that's full of the kind of *kilesas* which are frantically looking to affirm birth and life at all times. That person will undoubtedly find what he's looking for without having to ask anyone else. Such questions merely display a level of ignorance that indicates the inquirer is still spiritually inadequate. The *citta* tends to be the most unruly, conceited thing in the world. If no interest is taken in reigning it in, we will never become aware of how really stubborn it is, and all our noble hopes and aspirations will come to nothing."

What is it that causes the sexual attraction between men and women and animals of the same species, since they've never been taught this? Ācariya Mun replied:

"Rāgataṇhā[19] is not to be found in any book, nor is it learned in school from a teacher. Rather, *rāgataṇhā* is a stubbornly shameless condition that arises and exists in the hearts of men and women, causing those who have this vulgar condition to come under its spell and become vulgar themselves without ever realizing what's happening. *Rāgataṇhā* makes no distinction between man, woman, or animal, nationality, social status or age group. If it is strong it can easily cause disaster in the world. If there is insufficient presence of mind to restrain it and keep it within acceptable limits, sexual craving will become like runaway floodwater, overflowing the banks of the heart and spreading out to flood towns and cities, leaving ruin everywhere in its wake. Such a condition has always been able to thrive within the hearts of all living beings precisely because it receives constant nourishment and support — things which give it the strength to assert its suffocating influence continuously, sowing havoc and causing misery throughout the world. We hear only about floods occurring in towns and cities, and how they cause destruction to people and their belongings. No one is interested in noticing the flood of *rāgataṇhā* engulfing the hearts of people who are quite content to let themselves and their belongings be ravaged by those surging floodwaters all year round. Consequently, no one understands the real reason for the on-going deterioration of world affairs because each and every person is contributing to and encouraging this situation by failing to recognize that *rāgataṇhā* is directly responsible for the worsening situation. If we do not focus our attention on the real cause, it will be impossible for us to find any genuine sense of contentment."

The original question asked only about that aspect of *rāgataṇhā* concerning the attraction between people, completely ignoring the destruction instigated by *rāgataṇhā* through hatred and anger. But in his explanation Ācariya Mun touched on the full range of detrimental results stemming from *rāgataṇhā*. He said that it is *rāgataṇhā* which dictates the passionate urges of men, women, and all the animals, facilitating the pleasure they find in each others company — this is a principle of nature. Nothing other than this gives rise to mutual affection and mutual animosity. When *rāgataṇhā* uses its deceptive tricks for passionate ends, people fall in love. When it uses its deceptive tricks to bring forth hatred and anger, they inevitably hate, get angry, and harm each other. Should it wish to control people using love as a means, then people become so attracted to one another that there's no separating them. Should it wish those same people to fall under the influence of hatred and anger, then they'll feel an irresistible urge to do just that.

Ācariya Mun asked the lay people present: "Haven't you ever quarreled among yourselves? You husbands and wives who have been in love since before you were married? You asked me about it, but you should know a lot more about this matter than a monk does." To this they replied: "Yes, we've quarreled until we are sick of it and never want to again, but still we have another argument."

Ācariya Mun then continued: "You see, this is the very nature of the world: one moment there's affection, another moment there's friction, anger, and hatred. Even though you know it to be wrong, it's hard to correct. Have you ever seriously tried to correct this problem? If so, it shouldn't happen very often. Even a minimum effort should be enough to keep it under control. Otherwise, it's like eating three meals a day: in the morning you quarrel, in the afternoon you quarrel, and in the evening you quarrel — regularly around the clock. Some people even end up in divorce, allowing their children to become caught up in the conflagration as well. They are innocent, yet they too must bear the burden of that bad *kamma*. Everyone is affected by this blazing fire: friends and acquaintances keep their distance due to the shame of it all. Assuming both parties are interested in settling the issue, they should be aware that an argument is a bad thing, stop as soon as it starts, and make an effort to correct it at that point. The matter can then sort itself out so that in the future such problems don't recur. For instance, when anger or aversion arises, first, think of the past you have shared together; and then, think of the future you will share living together for the rest of your lives. Now compare this to the malice that's just arisen. That should be enough to lay the matter to rest.

"Mostly, people who go astray do so because they insist on having their own way. Without considering whether they're right or wrong, they want to personally dominate everybody else in the family — something which just isn't possible to achieve. Such arrogance spreads and rages, singeing others until everyone is scarred. Even worse, they want to exert their influence over everyone else in the world, which is as impossible as trying to hold back the ocean with your hands. Such thoughts and actions should be strictly avoided. If you persist in them, they will bring your own downfall. People living together must adhere to and be guided by equitable standards of behavior when dealing with their husbands, wives, children, servants, or co-workers. This means interacting with them in a reasonable, harmonious way. Should others not accept the truth, it is they who are at fault for being so unreasonable, and it is they who will pay the price — not those who adhere firmly to guiding principles."

ON THOSE OCCASIONS when Ācariya Mun had to teach large numbers of lay supporters, as well as the monks living with him, he would allot separate times for giving instructions. He instructed the laity from four to five p.m. He taught the monks and novices from seven p.m. onwards, at the end of which they returned to their huts to practice meditation. He tended to follow this routine on his first and second tours of the Northeast. On his third and final trip, after returning from Chiang Mai to Udon Thani, he changed this routine considerably. Rather than disrupt the sequence of events, I shall explain the adjustments he made later.

Ācariya Mun's chief concern was teaching monks and novices. He took a special interest in those students experiencing various insights in their meditation by calling them in for a personal interview. It's quite normal for those practicing meditation to have varying characters and temperaments, so the types of insights arising from their practice will vary accordingly — although the resulting cool, calm sense of happiness will be the same. Differences occur in the practical methods they employ and in the nature of insights that arise during meditation. Some meditators are inclined to know only things existing exclusively within their own minds. Others tend to know things of a more external nature — such as visions of ghosts or *devas*, or visions of people and animals dying right in front of them. They may see a corpse carried along and then dumped right in front of them or they may have a vision of their own body lying dead before them. All such experiences are beyond the capability of beginning meditators to handle correctly with any certainty, since the beginner is unable to distinguish between what is real and what is not. People who are not inclined to analyze their experiences carefully may come to a wrong understanding, believing what they see to be genuine. This could increase the likelihood of psychological damage in the future. The type of person whose *citta* tends to go out to perceive external phenomena when it 'converges' into a state of calm is quite rare — at most, about one in twenty people. But, there will always be someone in whom this occurs. It is crucial that they receive advice from a meditation master with expertise in these matters.

Listening to *dhutanga* monks as they relate their meditation results to Ācariya Mun, and hearing him give advice on ways to deal with their experiences was so moving and inspirational that everyone present became thoroughly absorbed in it. In explaining the proper method for dealing with visions, Ācariya Mun categorized different types of *nimittas* and explained in great detail how each type should be handled. The monks who listened were delighted by the Dhamma he presented, and so gained confidence, resolving to develop themselves even further. Even those who did not experience external visions were encouraged by what they heard. Sometimes the monks told Ācariya Mun how they had achieved a state of serene happiness when their hearts 'converged' into a state of calm, explaining the methods they had used. Even those who were as yet unable to attain such levels became motivated to try — or to even surpass them. Hearing these discussions was a joyous experience, both for those who were already well developed and those who were still struggling in their practice.

When the *citta* 'converged' into calm, some monks traveled psychically to the heavenly realms, touring celestial mansions until dawn; and only then did the *citta* return to the physical body and regain normal consciousness. Others traveled to the realms of hell and were dismayed by the pitiful condition of the beings they saw, enduring the results of their *kamma*. Some visited both the heavenly abodes and the hells to observe the great differences between them: one realm was blessed with joy and bliss while the other was in the depths of despair, the beings there tormented by a punishment that seemed to have no end. Some monks received visits from ethereal beings from various planes of existence — the heavens, for instance, or the terrestrial *devas*. Others simply experienced the varying degrees of calm and happiness coming from the attainment of *samādhi*. Some investigated, using wisdom to divide the body into different sections, dissecting each section to bits, piece by piece, then reducing the whole lot to its original elemental state. There were those who were just beginning their training, struggling as a child does when it first learns to walk. Some could not make the *citta* attain the concentrated state of calm they desired and wept at their own incompetence; and some wept from deep joy and wonder upon hearing Ācariya Mun discuss states of Dhamma they themselves had experienced. There were also those who were simply like a ladle in a pot of stew: although submerged there, it doesn't know the taste of the stew, and even manages to get in the cook's way. This is quite normal when many different people are living together. Inevitably, both the good and the bad are mixed in together. A person having effective mindfulness and wisdom will choose to keep only those lessons which are deemed to be really useful — lessons essential to skillful practice. I regret I cannot guarantee my own skillfulness in this matter. In fact, it's a problem we all face occasionally, so let's pass on and not worry about it.

On his second trip, Ācariya Mun remained teaching in the North-east for many years. Normally, he did not remain in the same place for more than a single rains retreat. When the rainy season was over, he wandered freely in the mountains and forests like a bird burdened only by its wings, contented to fly wherever it wishes. No matter where it lands in its search for food — a tree, a pond, or a marsh — it is satisfied and simply leaves all behind to fly off with no lingering attachment. It doesn't think that the trees, bark, fruit, ponds, or marshes belong to it. Like a bird, the monk who practices Dhamma, living in the forest, leads a life of contentment. But it's not easy to do, for people are social animals who enjoy living together and are attached to their homes and property. Initially, he feels a lot of resistance going out and living alone as Ācariya Mun did all his life. It is sort of like a land animal being dragged into the water. Once his heart has become closely integrated with Dhamma, however, the opposite is true: he enjoys traveling by himself and living alone. His daily routine in every posture remains entirely his own, his heart unencumbered by disturbing preoccupations. That leaves Dhamma as his preoccupation — and Dhamma promotes only contentment. The monk who is occupied solely with Dhamma has a heart that's cheerful and wonderfully content. He is free from the kind of hindrances which cause dullness or confusion; he is empty of all defiling preoccupations. He basks in a full-fledged, natural inner peace, never having to worry that it might alter or diminish in any way. This is known as *akālika* Dhamma: Dhamma which exists beyond space and time. It exists in the heart that has completely transcended conventional reality,[20] the source of all deception. Ācariya Mun was one well-gone;[21] one completely contented in all his activities. Coming and going, sitting, standing, walking, or lying down – he remained completely contented. Although he led his disciples along this path, relatively few of the monks reached a high level of Dhamma. Yet even this small number is of great benefit to people everywhere.

WHEN ĀCARIYA MUN led his disciples on almsround he took various animals along the way as objects of contemplation, and combining them with his inner Dhamma, he skillfully taught the monks who were with him. They clearly heard his every word. This was his way of teaching his disciples to be aware about the laws of *kamma*, in that even animals must receive the results of their actions. He would just point out an animal they came across as an example. Ācariya Mun insisted that animals should not be looked down upon for their lowly birth. In truth, animals have reached their time in the perpetual cycle of birth and death, experiencing the results of a past *kamma*. So it is with human birth as well. In fact, both animal life and human life consist of a mixture of pleasure and pain, each living according to the consequences of their own individual *kamma*. In one respect, Ācariya Mun brought up the subject of animals such as chickens, dogs, or cattle simply out of compassion for their plight. In another respect, he wanted to make others understand the variations in the consequences of *kamma*, indicating that – just as we have been brought to human birth by certain types of *kamma* – we too have passed through uncountable previous births of all sorts. Finally, he reflected aloud upon the very mysterious nature of those things that are responsible for birth as an animal – things that are difficult to fathom despite their presence in everyone. If we are unskillful in solving these problems, they will always be a danger to us, and we will never find a way to go beyond them. On almost every almsround Ācariya Mun spoke in this manner about the animals or the people whom he encountered along the way. Those who were interested in investigating these themes stimulated their mindfulness and wisdom, gaining useful ideas from him in this way. As to those who were not interested, they did not gain any benefit. Some probably wondered who he was talking about, since the monks had moved on by then and the animals he spoke about were no longer present.

IN SOME OF THE NORTHEAST PROVINCES, Ācariya Mun would give Dhamma instructions to the monks late at night on special occasions. Visible to Ācariya Mun, terrestrial *devas* gathered at a respectful distance and listened to his talks. Once he became aware of them he called off the meeting and quickly entered *samādhi*, where he talked privately to the *devas*. Their reticence on those occasions was due to the profound respect they had for monks. Ācariya Mun explained that *devas* of all levels were careful to avoid passing by the monks' dwellings on the way to see him late at night. Upon arriving they circled around Ācariya Mun three times before sitting down in an orderly fashion. Then the leader – *devas* of every plane have a leader whom they obey with great deference – would announce the realm from which they came and the aspect of Dhamma to which they wished to listen. Ācariya Mun would return their greetings and then focus his *citta* on that aspect of Dhamma requested by the *devas*. As this Dhamma arose within, he began the talk. When they had comprehended the Dhamma that he delivered, they all said "*sādhu*" three times, a sound that echoed throughout the spiritual universe.[22] This exclamation was heard by everyone with celestial hearing, but not by those whose ears were like the 'handles on a pot of soup'.

When his discourse on Dhamma ended, the *devas* again circumambulated him three times, keeping him on their right, and then returned to their realms in an elegant fashion – very different from we humans. Not even Ācariya Mun and his monks could emulate their graceful movements; for there's a great difference between the grossness of our bodies and the subtle refinement of theirs. As soon as the *deva* guests retreated to the edge of the monks' area, they floated up into the air like pieces of fluff blown by the wind. On each visit they descended in the same manner, arriving outside the monks' living area and then walking the remainder of the way. Always very graceful in their movements, they never spoke making a lot of noise the way humans do when going to see an *ācariya* they revere. This is probably due to the refined nature of their celestial bodies, which restrict them from behaving in such a gross manner. Here is an area in which human beings can be considered superior to *devas* — talking loudly. *Devas* are always very composed when listening to Dhamma, never fidgeting restlessly or showing any conceit that could disturb the speaking monk.

Ācariya Mun usually knew beforehand when the *devas* would be arriving. For instance, if they were planning to come at midnight, by early evening he was aware of it. On some occasions he had to cancel a scheduled meeting with the monks for that evening. At the appropriate hour Ācariya Mun left his walking meditation path and sat entering *samādhi* until the time approached for the *devas* to come. He then withdrew his *citta* up to the access level,[23] sending out the flow of his *citta* to see if they had arrived. If they had yet to arrive, he continued with his *samādhi* practice before sending his *citta* out again to check. Sometimes, the *devas* had already arrived or were just in the process of arriving. At other times, he had to wait, continuing his *samādhi* practice for some time before they came. On rare occasions, when he knew that they would be arriving late — like at one, two, or three a.m. — he would practice for a while and then take a rest, getting up to ready himself just before the *devas* were expected to arrive.

Gatherings of *devas* who came to see Ācariya Mun did not happen very often nor in very large numbers while he lived in the Northeast. They came only infrequently to listen in on his talks to the monks. But when they did, he would dismiss the monks as soon as he became aware of their presence, entering quickly into *samādhi* to expound on Dhamma for the *devas'* benefit. After he finished and the *devas* had departed, he would lie down to rest, arising in the morning as usual to continue his normal routine of practice. Ācariya Mun considered receiving *devas* a special responsibility. Since honoring one's promises is very important to them, he was always careful to be punctual. They were likely to be critical of a monk who missed an appointment unnecessarily.

Discussions between *devas* and monks are carried on entirely in the universal language of the heart, bypassing the multitude of conventional languages used by human beings and other types of animals. Arising from the *citta*, the substance of the inquiries turns into questions in the language of the heart which the inquiring individual clearly understands as if they were words in conventional language. Each word or phrase of the respondent emanates directly from the heart, so the questioner in turn understands the reply perfectly well. In fact, the language of the heart directly conveys the true feelings of the speaker, eliminating the need for explanations to clarify further, as might be required in conventional languages. Verbal communication is also a mechanism of the heart; but, its nature is such that spoken words often do not reflect the heart's true feelings, so mistakes are easily made in communicating its true intent. This incongruity will remain so long as conventional language is used as a surrogate medium for the heart's expression. Since people are unfamiliar with the language of the heart, their hearts cannot avoid using normal speech as a mechanism to facilitate communication, even though it's not very accurate in expressing the heart's true meaning. There is no possible way to solve this common dilemma — unless people learn the heart's own language and expose its mysteries.[24]

Ācariya Mun was extremely proficient in all matters pertaining to the heart, including the skills needed to train others to become good people. The rest of us, though we are quite capable of thinking of these things for ourselves, insist on going around borrowing from others. That is, we tend to constantly travel from place to place studying under one teacher and then another. Even then, we fail to properly safeguard what we've learned, letting it slip through our grasp by forgetting what the teacher said. Thus we are left virtually empty-handed. The things we do not forget or let drop are our habitual failings: a lack of mindfulness, wisdom, and contemplative skill. Lacking the very qualities of Dhamma which instill a sense of hope in our lives, we are constantly disappointed in whatever we do in life.

ĀCARIYA MUN'S OWN MEDITATION practice, as well as his teaching duties, continued to progress smoothly, any undue disturbances having long since passed. Wherever he went he brought a refreshing calm and serenity with him. Monks and novices everywhere respected and revered him. As soon as the laity in an area heard of his arrival, they were delighted and rushed to pay him their respects with heartfelt devotion. A case in point is Ban Thum village in the district of Tha Khek where both Ācariya Mun and Ācariya Sao resided at one time or another.

Shortly before Ācariya Mun arrived, the entire village began suffering from smallpox. The villagers were overcome with joy at the sight of Ācariya Mun's arrival, running out of their homes to welcome him and begging him to remain as their refuge. So in place of the spirits the whole village had been worshipping, Ācariya Mun had them take refuge in the Buddha, Dhamma, and Sangha. He guided them in the correct way to practice, such as paying daily homage to the Buddha and performing morning and evening chanting, and they gladly followed his instructions. As for Ācariya Mun, he performed a kind of internal spiritual blessing to help them; and the results were strange and marvelous to witness. Before his arrival, many people died each day from the smallpox. But from his arrival onwards, no one else died; and those who were infected quickly recovered. More than that, no new instances of the disease occurred, which astounded the villagers who had never seen or imagined such a miraculous reversal of circumstances. As a result, the community developed enormous faith in and devotion to Ācariya Mun which have persisted undiminished through each generation to the present day. This includes the local monastery's present-day abbot, who has a deep respect for Ācariya Mun. He always raises his joined palms in homage before beginning to speak about him.

Incidents such as this were made possible by the power of Dhamma in Ācariya Mun's heart which radiated forth to give comfort and happiness to the world. Ācariya Mun said that he set aside three times each day to extend loving kindness to all living beings. He would do this while sitting in meditation at midday, before retiring in the evening, and after rising in the morning. In addition to that, there were many times during the day when he sent loving kindness out specifically to certain individuals. When radiating all-encompassing loving kindness, he did so by focusing his *citta* exclusively inward and then directing the flow of his *citta* to permeate throughout all the worlds, both above and below, in all directions without interruption. At that time his *citta* had the power to extend its aura of brilliance to all worlds: limitless, all-pervasive, and brighter than a thousand suns – for there is nothing brighter than a heart that's entirely pure. The unique properties emanating from a *citta* of such purity brighten the world and imbue it with peacefulness in an indescribable and wondrous way. A *citta* having absolutely no impurities possesses only the cool, peaceful qualities of Dhamma. A compassionate, kindhearted monk with an absolutely pure heart can expect protection and reverential devotion from people and *devas* wherever he stays, while members of the animal kingdom feel no fear or danger in his presence. His *citta* constantly sends forth a gentle compassion to all beings everywhere without bias — much like rain falling evenly over hills and valleys alike.

Hardship and Deprivation

Upon leaving the province of Ubon Ratchathani, Ācariya Mun spent the next rainy season retreat at the village of Ban Nong Lat in the Warichabhum district of Sakon Nakhon province accompanied by the many monks and novices under his guidance. The lay men and women there reacted as if a truly auspicious person had arrived. They were all very excited — not in a frenzied way, but in an anticipatory way — at the prospect of doing good and abandoning evil. They abandoned their worship of spirits and ghosts to pay homage to the Buddha, Dhamma, and Sangha. At the end of the rains, Ācariya Mun went wandering again until he arrived in the province of Udon Thani where he traveled to the districts of Nong Bua Lamphu and Ban Pheu. He stayed at the village of Ban Kho for the rains retreat while spending the following rains in the Tha Bo district of Nong Khai province. He remained practicing for some time in both these provinces.

As mentioned previously, Ācariya Mun lived mostly in wilderness areas where villages were spaced far apart. Since the countryside was relatively unpopulated then, he could easily put the teaching into practice. Virgin forests abounded, full of great, tall trees which were still uncut. Wild animals were everywhere. As soon as night fell, their myriad calls could be heard echoing through the forest. Listening to such sounds, one is carried away by a sense of camaraderie and friendliness. The natural sounds of wild animals are not a hindrance to meditation practice, for they carry no specific meaning. The same cannot be said for human sounds. Be it chatting, singing, shouting, or laughing, the specific meaning is immediately obvious; and it is this significance that makes human sounds a hindrance to meditation practice. Monks are especially vulnerable to the sounds of the opposite sex. If their *samādhi* is not strong enough, concentration can easily be destroyed. I must apologize to women everywhere because my intention here is not to criticize women in any way. It is the unsuccessful meditator that I am addressing here so that he may arouse mindfulness as an antidote to counter these influences and not merely surrender meekly to them. It's possible that one reason monks prefer to live in mountains and forests is that it allows them to avoid such things in order to relentlessly pursue the perfection of spiritual qualities until they reach the ultimate goal of the holy life.[25] Ācariya Mun enjoyed living in forests and mountains right up until the day he passed away, a preference which helped him to attain the Dhamma he has so generously shared with all of us.

Ācariya Mun said that if his meditation practice were compared to an illness, it would be a near-fatal one, since the training he undertook resembled physical and mental torture. There was hardly a single day when he could just relax, look around, and enjoy himself as other monks seemed to do. This was because the *kilesas* became tangled up with his heart so quickly that he barely had a chance to catch them. Should his mind wander for only a moment, the *kilesas* immediately gave him trouble. Once they had established a hold on his heart, their grip became ever tighter until he found it difficult to dislodge them. Consequently, he could never let his guard down. He had to remain totally alert, always ready to pounce on the *kilesas,* so they couldn't gain the strength to bind him into submission. He practiced diligently in this manner until he had gained sufficient contentment to be able to relax somewhat. Only then did he develop the strength of heart and ease of body necessary to teach others. From that time forward — monks, novices, and lay people from all over the Northeast sought him out. Ācariya Mun understood their situation and was very sympathetic toward them all. At certain times, so many people came to see him that there wasn't enough room for them to stay. He also had to consider the safety of others, such as the women and nuns who came to visit him. For in those days, many tigers and other wild animals were in the outlying areas, but there were very few people.

Ācariya Mun once stayed in a cave near Ban Namee Nayung village in the Ban Pheu district of Udon Thani province. Since many large tigers frequented the area around the cave, it was definitely not a safe place for visitors to remain overnight. When visitors came, Ācariya Mun had the villagers build a very high bamboo platform — high enough to be beyond the reach of any hungry tiger which might try to pounce upon the sleeping person. Ācariya Mun forbade the visitors to come down to the ground after dark, fearing that a tiger would carry them off and devour them. He told them to carry up containers for their toilet needs during the night. With so many vicious tigers there at night, Ācariya Mun refused to allow visitors to stay long. He sent them away after a few days. These tigers were not afraid of people — especially not of women — and would attack if given the opportunity. On some nights when Ācariya Mun was walking in meditation by the light of candle lanterns, he saw a large tiger boldly stalk a buffalo herd as it went past his area. The tiger had no fear of Ācariya Mun as he paced back and forth. Sensing the tiger, the buffaloes instinctively headed for the village. Nevertheless, the tiger was still bold enough that it continued to follow them, even while a monk walked close by.

Monks who trained under Ācariya Mun had to be prepared for anything, including the possibility of death, for danger was all around the various places where they practiced. They also had to give up any pride in their own self-worth and any sense of superiority regarding their fellow monks, thus allowing for a harmonious living situation as if they were different limbs on the same body. Their hearts then experienced a measure of contentment and, untroubled by mental hindrances, their *samādhi* quickly developed. When a monk is constrained by living under certain restrictions — for example, living in a frightening place where the food is limited and the basic requisites are scarce — his mental activity tends to be supervised by mindfulness, which continuously restricts the thinking processes to the matter at hand. The *citta* is usually able to attain *samādhi* faster than would normally be expected. Outside there is danger and hardship; inside mindfulness is firmly in control. In such circumstances the *citta* might be compared to a prisoner who submits willingly to his fate. In addition to these factors, the teacher is also there to straighten him out should he go astray. The monk who practices while hemmed in by hardship on all sides will see an improvement in his *citta* that exceeds all expectations.

Nighttime in the forest is a frightening time, so a monk forces himself to go out and do walking meditation to fight that fear. Who will win and who will lose? If fear loses, then the *citta* becomes courageous and 'converges' into a state of calm. If the heart loses, then the only thing that emerges is intense fear. The effect of intense fear in such a situation is a sensation of simultaneously being both hot and cold, of needing to urinate and defecate, of feeling breathless and being on the verge of death. The thing that encourages fear is the sound of a tiger's roar. The sound of roaring may come from anywhere — from the foot of the mountain, from up on the ridge, or from out on the plains — but the monk will pay no attention to the direction. He will think only: "A tiger is coming here to devour me!" Walking all alone in meditation and so afraid that he's shaking and useless, he is sure that it's coming specifically for him. Not considering the broad terrain, it doesn't occur to him that the tiger has four feet and might just be going somewhere else. His only thought is that the tiger is coming straight for his tiny plot of land — straight for this cowardly monk who is shaken by fear. Having completely forgotten his meditation practice, he has only one thought in mind which he repeats over and over again like a mantra: "The tiger's coming here, the tiger's coming here." This negative train of thought merely intensifies his fear. The Dhamma in his heart is ready to disintegrate, and if, perchance, the tiger really were to wander accidentally into that place, he'd stand there mindlessly scared stiff at best; and at worst, something very unfortunate could happen.

It's wrong to establish the *citta* with such a negative attitude. The ensuing results are bound to be harmful in some way. The correct approach is to focus the *citta* firmly on some aspects of Dhamma, either the recollection of death or some other Dhamma theme. Under such circumstances, one should never allow the mind to focus outward to imagined external threats and then bring those notions back in to deceive oneself. Whatever happens, life or death, one's attention must be kept squarely on the meditation subject that one normally uses. A *citta* having Dhamma as its mainstay doesn't lose its balance. More-over, despite experiencing intense fear the *citta* is clearly strengthened, becoming courageous in a way that's amazing beyond description.

Ācariya Mun taught his disciples that becoming firmly established in the practice means putting everything on the line — both body and mind. Everything must be sacrificed except that aspect of Dhamma which is the fundamental object of attention. Whatever occurs, allow nature to take its course. Everyone who is born must die — such is the nature of this world. There's no point in trying to resist it. Truth can not be found by denying the natural order of things. Ācariya Mun taught that a monk must be resolute and brave in the face of death. He was particularly interested in having his disciples live in isolated wilderness areas infested with wild animals so that they could discover the virtues of meditation. Such places encourage the development of *samādhi* and intuitive wisdom. Tigers can definitely help to stimulate Dhamma in our hearts — especially if we don't stand in awe of the

Lord Buddha because we fail to trust his teaching, but we do stand in awe of tigers because we are convinced how vicious they can be. This conviction is a very effective aid for corralling the mind and focusing it on Dhamma, using fear as an incentive to meditate until Dhamma arises within. Consequently, when that inner Dhamma is finally realized, belief in the Lord Buddha and the Dhamma he taught will arise naturally. At that critical moment, when one is alone in the wilderness, dormant faculties of *samādhi* and wisdom will be stirred into action. If there is nothing to put pressure on the *citta*, it tends to become lazy and amass *kilesas* until it can barely function. A tiger can help to remove those *kilesas* which foster such a lazy and easy-going attitude that we forget ourselves and our own mortality. Once those insidious defilements disappear, we feel a sense of genuine relief whatever we do, for our hearts no longer shoulder that heavy burden.

Ācariya Mun emphasized that monks should go to practice meditation in places that arouse fear and avoid places that do not; otherwise, they were unlikely to achieve any strange and marvelous results. More than that, the *kilesas* might well lead them so far astray that they end up losing sight of the spiritual path, which would be regrettable. He assured his monks that unless they lived in an environment which forced them to focus internally on themselves they would find it difficult to attain a stable state of calm and their meditation practice would suffer accordingly. On the other hand, the results were bound to be good in places where they were always alert to the possibility of danger, since mindfulness — the skillful means for directing the effort — was inevitably close at hand. No one who genuinely hopes to transcend *dukkha* should succumb to the fear of death while living in what are imagined to be frightening places — like remote wilderness areas. When faced with a real crisis situation, the focus of attention should be kept on Dhamma and not sent outside of the sphere of one's own body and mind, which are the dwelling-place of Dhamma. Then the meditator can expect to experience a pervading sense of security and an inspired mental fortitude that are incontrovertible. In any case, unless that person's *kamma* dictates that his time is up, he will not die at that time — no matter what he thinks.

Ācariya Mun said that his inspiration for meditation was derived almost exclusively from living in dangerous environments, which is why he liked to teach his disciples to be resolute in threatening situations. Instead of merely relying on something vague like 'inherent virtuous tendencies' — which are usually more a convenient fiction than a reality — in this way, they had a chance to realize their aspirations in the shortest possible time. Relying on the rather vague concept of virtuous tendencies from the past is usually a sign of weakness and resignation — an attitude more likely to suppress mindfulness and wisdom than to promote them.[26]

To say a monk has confidence that Dhamma is the basic guarantor of his life and practice means that he sincerely hopes to live and die by Dhamma. It is imperative that he not panic under any circumstance. He must be brave enough to accept death while practicing diligently in fearful places. When a crisis looms — no matter how serious it seems — mindfulness should be in continuous control of his heart so that it stays steadfastly firm and fully integrated with the object of meditation. Suppose an elephant, a tiger, or a snake threatens him: if he sincerely resolves to sacrifice his life for the sake of Dhamma those things won't dare to cause him any harm. Having no fear of death, he will experience the courageous feeling that he can walk right up to those animals. Instead of feeling threatened, he will feel deep within his heart a profound friendship toward them which dispels any sense of danger.

As human beings we possess Dhamma in our hearts, in a way that animals do not. For this reason, our hearts exert a powerful influence over animals of all types. It makes no difference that animals are incapable of knowing this fact; there exists in our hearts a mysterious quality that has a soothing effect on them. This quality is the potent, protective power of Dhamma which softens their hearts to the point where they don't dare act threateningly. This mysterious power of the heart is something experienced internally by the individual. Others can be aware of it only if they have special intuitive knowledge. Even though Dhamma is taught and studied all over the world, it still remains a mystery if the heart has yet to attain any level of understanding in Dhamma. When the heart and Dhamma truly become one, all doubts concerning the heart and Dhamma disappear on their own because the nature of the heart and the nature of Dhamma share the same exquisite, subtle qualities. Once that state is reached, it is correct to say that the heart is Dhamma and Dhamma is the heart. In other words, all contradictions cease once the *kilesas* have been eliminated.

Normally the heart has become such an extension of the *kilesas* that we are unaware of its intrinsic value. This happens because the heart is so thoroughly impregnated with *kilesas* that the two become indistinguishable. The heart's real value is then obscured from view. If we allow this condition to continue indefinitely because we are indifferent about finding a solution, neither our hearts nor Dhamma will have any actual value for us. Even were we to be born and die hundreds of times, it would simply be a matter of exchanging one set of dirty clothes for another set of dirty clothes. No matter how many times we change in and out of dirty clothes we cannot escape the fact that we remain filthy. Which is certainly very different from someone who takes off his dirty clothes and exchanges them for nice clean ones. Similarly, the interchange between good and evil within the heart is an important problem that each of us should take personal responsibility for and investigate within ourselves. No one else can carry this burden for us and so give us peace of mind. It's extremely important that each and every one of us be aware that, in both the present and the future, we alone are responsible always for our own progress. The only exceptions are those, like the Lord Buddha and the Arahant disciples, who carefully developed themselves spiritually until they attained a state of total security. For them the job is completed, the ultimate goal secure. These are the Noble individuals that the rest of us take as our refuge, providing us hope for the future. Even miscreants who still understand the difference between right and wrong will take the Buddha, Dhamma, and Sangha as their refuge. They at least have enough sense to feel some remorse. Just as good people and bad people alike feel a natural dependence on their parents, so people of all kinds instinctively look to the Buddha as a dependable refuge.

ĀCARIYA MUN EMPLOYED many training methods with his monks to ensure that they saw clear results in their practice. Those who practiced with unwavering faith in his instructions were able to achieve such results to their own satisfaction. By following the power of his example, they became knowledgeable, respected teachers themselves. They in turn have passed on these training methods to their own disciples, so that they too can witness for themselves, through their own efforts, that the paths and fruits of the Buddha's teaching are still attainable today; that they have not completely disappeared. When looking at the life he lived and the methods he employed in training others, it is fair to say that Ācariya Mun followed a *practice of deprivation.* He and his disciples lived in conditions of virtual poverty in places where even the basic necessities were lacking. The simple daily requisites they depended on were usually in short supply. Encountering such an uncertain existence, those accustomed to living in carefree abundance would probably be utterly dismayed. There being nothing in this difficult lifestyle to attract them, they would surely find it most disagreeable. But the monks themselves, though they lived like prison inmates, did so voluntarily for the sake of Dhamma. They lived for Dhamma, and accepted the inconvenience and hardship associated with its practice. These conditions, which are seen as torture by people who have never submitted to them, were actually a convenient spiritual training ground for the monks who practiced in this way. Due to their determination to endure hardship and poverty it is appropriate to call this the *practice of deprivation*; for such living conditions naturally go against the grain. Monks had to literally force themselves to live in this way. During all their normal daily activities, they were required to resist the physical and mental pressure to simply follow their natural inclinations.

Sometimes it was necessary to endure days of fasting and hunger for the purpose of accelerating the practice of meditation. These periods, when monks abstain from food altogether despite their hunger, are days of uninterrupted dedication to the practice. The physical discomfort at such times is obvious, but the purpose of enduring hunger is to increase mental vigilance. In truth, fasting is a very suitable method for certain temperaments. Some types of people find that if they eat food every day their bodies tend to be vigorous but the mental endeavor — meditation — fails to progress. Their minds remain sluggish, dull and timid, so a solution is needed. One solution is to try either reducing the intake of food each day or going without food altogether, fasting — sometimes for a few days, sometimes for a longer period — and carefully observing all the while the method that gives the best results. Once it becomes apparent that a certain method is suitable, that method should be pursued intensively. For instance, should a monk discover that fasting for many days at a stretch is suitable to his temperament, then it's imperative that he accept the necessity of following that path. Though it may well be difficult, he must put up with it because he inevitably wants to gain the appropriate knowledge and skill to go beyond *dukkha*.

A person whose temperament is suited to long-term fasting will notice that the more he fasts the more prominent and courageous his heart is in confronting the various objects of the senses that were once its enemies. His mental attitude is bold, his focus sharp. While sitting in *samādhi* his heart can become so absorbed in Dhamma that it forgets the time of day; for when the heart contacts Dhamma there is no longer any concern with the passage of time or pangs of hunger. At that time, he is aware only of the delight experienced at that level of Dhamma which he has achieved. In this frame of mind, the conditions are right for catching up with *kilesas*, such as laziness, complacency, and restlessness, since they are inactive enough then for the meditator to get the better of them for the time being. If we hesitate, waiting around for a more auspicious time to tackle them, the *kilesas* will awaken first and give us more trouble. It's quite likely we'd be unable to handle them then. We could easily end up being 'elephants' for the *kilesas*, as they mount us, straddle our necks, and beat us — our hearts — into submission. For in truth our hearts have been the 'elephants' and the *kilesas* the 'mahouts' for an infinitely long time. A deep-rooted fear of this master makes us so apprehensive that we never really dare to fight back with the best of our abilities.

From the Buddha's perspective, the *kilesas* are the enemies of Dhamma; yet, from the vantage point of the world, the *kilesas* are considered our hearts' inseparable companions. It is incumbent upon us, who practice the Buddha's teaching, to battle the thoughts and deeds that are known to be our enemies, so that we can survive their onslaught, and thus become free of their insidious control. On the other hand, those who are satisfied to follow the *kilesas* have no choice but to pamper them, dutifully obeying their every command. The repercussions of such slavery are all too obvious in the mental and emotional agitation affecting those people and everyone around them. Inevitably, the *kilesas* cause people to suffer in a multitude of harmful ways, making it imperative for someone sincerely caring about his own well-being to fight back diligently using every available means. If this means abstaining from eating food and suffering accordingly, then so be it; one has no regrets. If necessary, even life itself will be sacrificed to honor the Buddha's teaching, and the *kilesas* will have no share in the triumph.

In his teachings, Ācariya Mun encouraged his monks to be courageous in their efforts to transcend the *dukkha* oppressing their hearts.

He himself had thoroughly investigated the *kilesas* and Dhamma, testing both in a most comprehensive fashion before he finally saw the results emerge clearly in his own heart. Only after this attainment did he return to the Northeast to teach the incomparable Dhamma that he then understood so well.

ONE PROMINENT ASPECT of Ācariya Mun's teaching, which he stressed continuously during his career, was the Dhamma of the *five powers*: faith, diligent effort, mindfulness, concentration, and wisdom. He said the reason for emphasizing these five factors was that a person who possessed them would always have something worthwhile to count on, no matter where he went; and, therefore, he could always expect to make steady progress in his practice. Ācariya Mun separated them according to their specific functions, using them to inspire an indomitable spirit in his disciples. He gave them his own heartfelt interpretation as follows:

Saddhā is faith in the Dhamma that the Lord Buddha presented to the world. There's no doubt that each of us in this world is perfectly capable of receiving the light of Dhamma – provided we practice the way in earnest. We all accept the fact that we will have to die some day. The key issue is: will we die defeated by the cycle of *kilesas* and the cycle of *kamma* and its results? Or, will we overcome them, defeating them all before we die? No one wants to be defeated. Even children who compete at sports are keen on winning. So we should rouse ourselves and not act as if defeated already. The defeated must always endure suffering and anguish, accumulating so much *dukkha* that they cannot find a way out. When they do seek escape from their misery, the only viable solution seems to be: It's better to die. Death under those conditions is precisely defeat at the hands of one's enemy. It is a result of piling up so much *dukkha* inside that there's no room for anything else. Positive results cannot be gained from abject defeat.

If we are to die victorious, like the Lord Buddha and the Arahants, then we must practice with the same faith, effort, and forbearance as they did. We must be mindful in all our bodily and mental activities, as they were. We must take our task very seriously and not waver uncertainly like someone facing a crisis without mindfulness to anchor him. We should establish our hearts firmly in those causes that give rise to the satisfactory results that the Buddha himself attained. The *sāsana* is the teaching of a great sage who taught people that they too can develop wisdom in all its many aspects. So we should reflect on what he taught. We should not wallow in stupidity, living our whole lives in ignorance. No one considers the word 'stupid' to be a compliment. Stupid people are no use. Adults, children, even animals — if they are stupid, they are hardly any use at all. So if we remain stupid, who's going to admire us for it? We should all analyze this matter thoroughly to avoid remaining bogged down in ignorance. Wallowing in ignorance is not the way to overcome *dukkha*, and it is definitely not becoming for a *dhutanga* monk — who is expected to skillfully analyze everything.

This was Ācariya Mun's own personal interpretation of the *five powers*. He used it effectively in his own practice and taught it to his disciples as well. It is excellent instruction for inspiring mindfulness and wisdom, and an uncompromising attitude towards practice. It is highly suitable for *dhutanga* monks who are fully prepared to compete for the ultimate victory in the contest between Dhamma and the *kilesas*. This ultimate attainment is the freedom of Nibbāna, the long-wished-for supreme victory.[27]

Graduated Teaching

Once a senior disciple of Ācariya Mun recalled that the many monks and novices living under his guidance tended to behave as though free from *kilesas*. Although they lived together in a large group, no one behaved in an unseemly manner. Whether they were on their own, in the company of others performing their duties, or attending a meeting, all were calm and composed. Those, who had never heard the monks discuss their levels of meditation with Ācariya Mun, might well suspect from observing them that they were all full-fledged Arahants. The truth became apparent only when he advised the monks on how to solve specific problems in their meditation. Each monk was advised according to his level of achievement: from basic concentration and wisdom techniques to the higher levels of concentration and insight.

Whether addressing the problems of individual disciples or instructing the whole assembly, Ācariya Mun always displayed the same uncompromising self-assurance. His audience was fully aware that the Dhamma he expounded was something he had actually realized within himself. He never relied on speculative assessments, such as, 'it could be like this' or 'it might be like that'. Those listening were also fully convinced that the Dhamma he taught existed potentially within all of them. Even though they had not achieved it yet, surely they would realize it for themselves one day, provided they did not falter in their efforts.

Ācariya Mun modified his talks according to the character and the level of his listeners' understanding, so that everyone who was present gained some benefit from the assembly. He was careful in explaining the teaching in all its stages, ensuring that listeners at different levels of meditation were able to understand and apply it to their individual practice in order to attain satisfactory results. When teaching lay people, he usually emphasized aspects of Dhamma that were suitable to their situation — such as, generosity, moral virtue, and meditative development — as the basis for their practice. He explained that these three *dhammas* are the basic criteria needed for birth in the human world and so are the foundation of the *sāsana*. Someone born as a human being must necessarily have cultivated these three *dhammas* in the past. At least one of them must have been previously developed to serve as a catalyst for being born fully human.[28]

Generosity is a means of demonstrating one's goodwill. People, who are noble-hearted and considerate toward fellow human beings and animals in-need, sacrifice and share some of their own good fortune according to their means. Whether it's a gift of material goods, a gift of Dhamma, or a gift of knowledge of any sort, it is a gift freely given to benefit others without expectation of anything in return, except the good results of the act of giving itself. This also includes the generous gesture of forgiving those who behave wrongly or offensively. Those who are benevolent and prone to selfless giving are bound to be gracious people who stand out among their peers, irrespective of their physical appearance. *Devas*, humans, and animals all revere and cherish them. Wherever they go there will always be someone willing to help them. They never suffer acute poverty and hardship. Quite clearly, philanthropists in society are never out of fashion and rarely disliked. Even a wealthy, but stingy person looks forward to gifts from others — not to mention the hapless poor who have little hope of someone helping them. Due to the power of generosity, those who have developed a habit of giving will never be born into a world where they must live in hardship. Donors and their generosity have always served to maintain balance and prosperity in the world. As long as people still value self-sacrifice and extend a helping hand to one another, life on this earth will always have meaning. Generous people are inevitably hospitable and supportive, which makes the world a better place to live. In this sense, generosity is absolutely essential for us all. Without it, life in this world would be a parched and barren existence.

Moral virtue is effectively a barrier that prevents people from abusing or destroying each other's material and spiritual wealth. It's the very basis of those special good qualities that every human being should have, and should never let slip away. People who do not have moral virtue to protect and maintain their inner wealth are like a fire raging through human society. Without morality's protective restraint, mistreatment and destruction would run rampant in the world to the point where there would hardly be an island of security left where a person could rest in peace. As long as people believe that material wealth is more valuable than moral virtue, they will have no real security. In such a case, even if the world economy were to flourish until material wealth was piled as high as the sun, the sun's heat would be no match for the scorching heat of an immoral world.

Moral virtue is the true foundation of human perfection that was personified by the Lord Buddha. He uncovered this truth, presenting it as a means by which a world confused and fearful of *dukkha* might rely on its restraining power to live in the cool, soothing glow of trust. Left to their own devices, people with *kilesas* will tend to think in ways that make the world oppressively hot. If these thoughts are allowed free rein, powered by the *kilesas* and untempered by even a hint of moral virtue, they will surely create innumerable poisonous 'monsters' that will spread throughout the world to devour everything in their path. The thoughts of a supremely virtuous person like the Lord Buddha, who totally eliminated the *kilesas* from his heart, produce only welcome peace and happiness in the world. Compare this with the thought patterns instigated by the *kilesas* that cause us, and everyone else, unimaginable trouble. The difference is obvious enough that we should want to search for a way to resolve this problem and stem the tide of such thoughts before it is too late. Moral virtue is like a medicine that counteracts infectious diseases as well as chronic ones. At the very least, a patient who is sick with the 'kilesa-fever' can find some measure of relief and hope of recovery in the practice of moral virtue. More than that, it may just effect a complete cure.

Out of his compassion, Ãcariya Mun used to instruct lay people on both the merits of moral virtue and the faults of having no moral standard. These instructions went straight to the heart and were so impressive that, in hearing his advice to lay people, I found myself thinking that I too would like to keep the five moral precepts — forgetting that, as a monk, I was already observing 227 monastic rules! I was overcome with enthusiasm to hear him talk and lost my mindfulness for a moment. When I finally came to my senses, I was rather embarrassed, and did not mention it to anyone for fear that other monks might think me a bit crazy. In fact, I was a little bit crazy at that time since I forgot my own shaved head and thought about keeping the layman's five precepts. This is a problem we all face: when thinking in ways that are wrong, we end up acting wrongly in that manner as well. Therefore, we should be aware of our thoughts at all times — aware of whether they are good or bad, right or wrong. We must constantly rein in our own thoughts; otherwise, they can easily spin out of control.

Meditative development means training the mind to be clever and unbiased with respect to basic principles of cause and effect, so that we can effectively come to terms with our own inner processes, and all other related matters as well. Instead of abandoning the mind to unbridled exuberance, we rely on meditation to rein in our unruly thoughts and bring them into line with what is reasonable — which is the path to calm and contentment. The mind that has yet to undergo meditation training is similar to an untrained animal that cannot yet properly perform its appointed tasks and is, therefore, not as useful as it might be. It must be trained to do those jobs in order to gain maximum benefit from its work. Likewise, our minds should undergo training as a means of understanding ourselves as we carry out all our daily tasks, be they mental or physical, significant or trivial, gross or subtle.

Those who develop meditation as a solid anchor for the mind enjoy reflecting carefully on whatever they do. They are not likely to take unnecessary chances in a situation they are unsure of, when a mistake could hurt them or someone else who is involved. Meditative development brings definite benefits, both immediately and in the future, but the most significant are those we experience here and now in the present. People who develop an aptitude for meditation will be successful at whatever they put their minds to. Their affairs are not conducted halfheartedly, but are well thought out with an eye to the expected benefits of a job well-done. In this way, people can always look back with satisfaction on the fruits of their labor. Since they are firmly grounded in reason, people who meditate have no difficulty controlling themselves. They adhere to Truth as the guiding principle for all they do, say, and think. They are mindful not to leave themselves open to the myriad temptations that habitually arise from the *kilesa* of craving – wanting to go there, wanting to come here, wanting to do this, wanting to say this or think that – which give no guidance whatsoever to right and wrong, good and bad. Craving is a very destructive defilement that tends to lead us repeatedly into misery in countless ways. In truth, we have no one to blame but ourselves, so we are left to accept the consequences as something regrettable, trying to do better the next time. When sufficient mindfulness is maintained we can reverse this trend. But if we do not have enough mindfulness to reflect prudently on these matters, everything we do will have adverse effects, sometimes irrevocably so. This is the real crux of the *kilesas* – they inevitably lead us toward misfortune.

Meditation is a good means for making a clean break with the unseemly business of the *kilesas*. Meditation techniques are arguably somewhat difficult to practice, but that's because they are designed to put pressure on the mind and bring it under control, much like trying to bring a monkey under control in order to tame it. Meditation techniques are actually methods for developing self-awareness. This means observing the mind which is not content to just remain still but tends instead to jump about like someone who's been scalded with hot water. Observing the mind requires mindfulness to keep us aware of its movement. This is aided by using one of a number of Dhamma themes as an object of attention to keep the mind stable and calm during meditation. A very popular method and one that gives good results is mindfulness of breathing.[29] Other popular themes include the use of a word such as *"buddho"*, *"dhammo"*, *"sangho"*,[30] or *kesā, lomā, nakhā, dantā, taco* in forward and reverse order,[31] or meditation on death,[32] or whatever theme seems most suitable. The mind must be forced to stay exclusively with that object during meditation. Calm and happiness are bound to arise when the mind depends on a particular Dhamma theme as a good and safe object of attention.

What is commonly referred to as a 'calm *citta*' or a '*citta* integrated in *samādhi*' is a state of inner stability that is no longer associated with the initial object of attention, which merely prepared the *citta* by holding it steady. Once the *citta* has entered into *samādhi*, there exists enough momentum for the *citta* to remain in this state of calm, independent of the preparatory object, whose function is temporarily discontinued while the *citta* rests peacefully. Later when the *citta* withdraws from *samādhi*, if time permits, attention is refocused on the initial Dhamma theme. When this is practiced consistently with dedication and sustained effort, a mind long steeped in *dukkha* will gradually awaken to its own potential and abandon its unskillful ways. The struggle to control the mind, which one experiences in the beginning stages of training, will be replaced by a keen interest in the task at hand.

The *citta* becomes unforgettably calm and peaceful once it enters *samādhi*. Even if this happens only once, it will be an invigorating and indelible experience. Should it fail to occur again in subsequent attempts at meditation, an indescribable sense of loss and longing will linger in the *citta* for a long time. Only with further progress, as one becomes more and more absorbed in increasingly subtler states of calm, will the frustration of losing the initial state of calm be forgotten.

WHEN HEARING ABOUT MEDITATION, you may fret and feel mentally and physically inadequate to the task, and be reluctant to try. You may be tempted to think:

Fate has surely conspired against me. I can't possibly manage it. My duties and responsibilities both at home and at work make it difficult. There are all the social obligations, raising children and looking after grandchildren. If I waste time sitting with eyes closed in meditation, I'll never be able to keep up and make ends meet and I'll probably end up starving to death!

Thus, you become discouraged and miss a good opportunity. This way of thinking is buried deep within everyone's psyche. It may be just the sort of thinking that has prevented you from ridding yourself of *dukkha* all along; and it will continue to do so if you don't try to remedy it now.

Meditation is actually a way to counteract and alleviate all the mental irritations and difficulties that have plagued us for so long. Meditation is not unlike other methods used in the world to relieve pain and discomfort; like bathing when we feel hot, and putting on warm clothes or lighting a fire when we feel cold. When hungry, we eat and drink; when ill, we take medicine to relieve the symptoms. All these are methods that the world has used to relieve pain and discomfort over the ages without anyone ever dismissing them as being too burdensome or too difficult to do. People of every ethnic and social group are obliged to look after themselves in this way. Even animals have to take care of themselves by searching for food to alleviate their discomfort and survive from day to day. Similarly, mental development through meditation is a very important means of taking care of ourselves. It is work that we should be especially interested in because it deals directly with the mind, which is the central coordinator for all our actions.

The mind is in the front line when it comes to anything relating to ourselves. In other words, the *citta* is absolutely essential in everything. It has no choice but to accept the burden of responsibility in all circumstances without discrimination or hesitation. Whatever happens, the mind feels compelled to step in and immediately take charge, unfazed by ideas of good and bad or right and wrong. Although some situations are so depressing they're nearly unbearable, the mind still boldly rushes in to shoulder the burden, heedless of the risks and its own inherent limitations. More than that, it recites its litany of thoughts over and over again until eating and sleeping become almost impossible at times. Still, the mind charges ahead refusing to admit failure. When engaging in physical activity, we know our relative strengths and when the time is right to take a rest. But our mental activities never take a break — except briefly when we fall asleep. Even then, the mind insists on remaining active, subconsciously churning out countless dream images that continue overloading its capacity to cope. So the mind lives with a sense of intolerable dissatisfaction, never realizing that this dissatisfaction arises in direct relationship to its heavy work load and the unbearable mental aggravation it generates.

Because it is always embattled, the mind could well be called a 'warrior'. It struggles with what is good and it struggles with what is bad. Never pausing to reflect, it engages everything that comes along. Whatever preoccupations arise, it insists on confronting them all

108

without exception, unwilling to let anything pass unchallenged. So it's appropriate to call the mind a 'warrior', since it recklessly confronts everything that comes across its path. If the mind does not come to terms with this dilemma while the body is still alive, it will keep on fighting these battles indefinitely, unable to extricate itself. Should the heart's endless desires be indulged in without Dhamma to act as a moderating influence, real happiness will always be out of reach, regardless of how abundant material wealth may be. Material wealth itself is not a true source of happiness, and can readily become a source of discontent for the heart lacking inner Dhamma to serve as an oasis of rest.

The wise have assured us that Dhamma is the power which oversees both material wealth and spiritual well-being. Regardless of how much or how little wealth we acquire, we will enjoy a sufficient measure of happiness if we possess some measure of Dhamma in our hearts. Unsupported by Dhamma and left to its own desires, the heart will be incapable of finding genuine happiness, even with a mountain of valuable possessions on hand. These are merely physical and emotional supports that intelligent people can use wisely for their own pleasure. If the heart is not intelligent in the way of Dhamma, or Dhamma is absent altogether, the place where we live will resemble a wasteland, no matter what our choice. The heart and all its wealth will then end up as just so much accumulated waste — stuff that is useless for our spiritual development.

When it comes to being stoic in the face of adversity, nothing is as tough and resilient as the heart. Receiving proper assistance, it becomes something marvelous in which we can take pride and satisfaction under all circumstances. From the time of birth to the present moment, we have exploited our hearts and minds — mercilessly. Were we to treat a car like we treat our minds, it would be pointless to take to a garage for repairs, for it would have become a pile of scrap metal long ago. Everything that we utilize must receive some sort of upkeep and repair to ensure that it continues providing useful service. The mind is no exception. It's an extremely important resource that should be well looked after and maintained, just as we do with all our other possessions.

Meditation is a therapy designed exclusively for the mind. All of us who are truly interested in taking responsibility for our minds — which, after all, are our most priceless possessions — should care for them in the correct and proper way. This means training our minds with suitable meditation techniques. To use the car comparison: it means examining the mind's various component parts to see if anything is defective or damaged; and then taking it into the garage for a spiritual overhaul. This entails sitting in meditation, examining the mental components, or *sankhāras*, that make up our thoughts; then determining whether the thoughts that surface are fundamentally good or harmful, adding fuel to the fires of pain and suffering. Thus, an investigation is undertaken to ascertain which thoughts have value and which are flawed. Then we should turn our attention to the physical components; that is, our bodies. Do our bodies keep improving with age or are they deteriorating as time goes by — the old year inevitably turning into a new one, over and over again? Does the body continue regenerating or does it inevitably wear down and grow older with each successive day? Should we be complacent about this by failing to mentally prepare ourselves while there's still time? Once we are dead, it will be too late to act. This is what meditation is all about: cautioning and instructing ourselves by examining our shortcomings to determine what areas need improvement. When we investigate constantly in this manner, either while sitting in meditation or while going about our daily tasks, the mind will remain calm and unperturbed. We will learn not to be arrogantly overconfident about life, and thus avoid fueling the flames of discontent. And we will know how to exercise proper moderation in our thoughts and deeds so that we don't forget ourselves and get caught up in things which may have disastrous consequences.

The benefits of meditation are too numerous to address, so Ācariya Mun kept his explanations to the lay audience at a level appropriate to their practice. His explanations to monks and novices were of a very different caliber. I have written down just enough here to give the flavor of his teaching. Some people may find that I've included certain things that seem excessive, or even distasteful; but the account would be incomplete if I did not convey all aspects of his teaching. I have made the effort to compile these teachings in the hope that the readers will encourage me with the benefit of their criticism. So you are welcome to criticize me for whatever you find to be inappropriate; but, please do not blame Ācariya Mun because he had no part in writing the book.

Ācariya Mun conducted higher Dhamma teaching only within the circle of his close disciples. But the author has somewhat of an irrepressible nature and cannot sit still; so, I have gone around, collecting oral accounts from all the *ācariyas* today who lived with Ācariya Mun in the past and are his disciples. I've recorded this information so that the reader may know something of his practice, even though it is not a complete account. Ācariya Mun's mode of practice was so uniquely resolute and uncompromising that one could surely say that none of his disciples can match him in the austerities he performed, the noble virtues he perfected, and the inner knowledge he so skillfully mastered. To this day he remains unexcelled.

ĀCARIYA MUN SAID that when he stayed in the forests and mountains of Udon Thani and Nong Khai, *devas* from the upper and lower realms occasionally came to hear Dhamma from him. Some groups came regularly every two weeks, others only once a month. *Devas* from that area did not come to see him nearly as often as those from Chiang Mai province. I shall relate those experiences in due course; but, for now, let me continue following the sequence of events so as not to confuse matters.

Ācariya Mun spoke of a huge city of *nāgas*, located under the mountain west of the Laotian city of Luang Prabang. While he lived there, the chief of those *nāgas* regularly brought his followers to hear Dhamma, occasionally in large numbers. The *nāgas* tended to ask far fewer questions of him than the *devas* of the upper and lower realms, who always had many questions for him. All these groups, however, listened to what he had to say with equal respect. During the time Ācariya Mun lived at the base of that mountain, the chief *nāga* came almost every night to visit him. Only on special occasions did he bring a large following; and in that case, Ācariya Mun always knew of their arrival in advance. Due to the remote location, he had little contact with people at that time, so he was able to be of particular service to the *nāgas* and *devas*. The *nāgas* did not visit very late at night — they came at maybe ten or eleven p.m. — which was probably due to his remote location. As a sign of their profound respect, the *nāgas* invited Ācariya Mun to remain living there out of compassion for them. They even arranged to protect him both day and night, taking turns to keep watch. They never came too close, maintaining a convenient distance always, yet close enough to observe anything that might happen. The *devas*, on the other hand, usually came later than the *nāgas* — at about one or two a.m. If he was living in the mountains, far from a village, the *devas* sometimes came earlier, say ten or eleven p.m. There was never a sure time, but normally the *devas* came after midnight.

DURING MIDDLE AGE, Ācariya Mun's normal daily routine was as follows: After the meal he walked meditation until noon and then took a short rest. Rested, he sat in meditation for an hour and a half before continuing his walking meditation until four p.m. After that, he swept the area around his dwelling, bathed, and again practiced walking meditation until about seven or eight p.m., when he entered his hut to sit again. If it did not rain after seated meditation, he walked again, until late at night. Or, if it was already very late, he retired for the night. He normally retired at eleven p.m. and awoke at three a.m. Ācariya Mun usually knew in advance when the *devas* would visit. If they were going to arrive later than midnight, he rested before receiving them. If they were expected to arrive between eleven p.m. and midnight, he first entered into *samādhi* and waited there for them. This is the daily routine that he maintained throughout that period of his life.

WHEN BOTH HEAVENLY and terrestrial *devas* wished to come on the same night, Ācariya Mun would receive the first group, give them a Dhamma talk, answer their questions, and then tell them that another group was soon coming. The first group then left in a timely manner and the other *devas* entered from where they'd been respectfully waiting at a distance. He then began speaking to the second group, discoursing on a Dhamma theme he deemed suitable for their temperament and level of understanding. Sometimes the chief of the *deva* group requested a certain topic. Ācariya Mun then focused his attention on that specific Dhamma theme. When he felt his heart in possession of this knowledge, he began his discourse. Sometimes the *deva* leader requested a discourse on a *sutta*, using an archaic title with which Ācariya Mun was unfamiliar. So Ācariya Mun asked and was told the present-day title. Usually Ācariya Mun could figure out for himself the *suttas* that were being requested; but occasionally he had to ask for clarification. At other times, the *devas* requested a *sutta* by a title of which he felt certain. But, as soon as he began to elucidate it, they informed him that he had made a mistake; that it was not the one they requested. To refresh his memory, they recited some verses from the *sutta*. After one or two verses he could usually remember it correctly. He began his discourse only when he was sure he had the right topic.

On rare occasions, the *devas* from the upper and lower realms all came to listen to Dhamma at the same time as the *nāgas*. This is not unlike various groups of humans all showing up to visit a teacher simultaneously. When this happened often, he scheduled their arrivals at different times for the convenience of all concerned. According to Ācariya Mun, even though he lived deep in the forests and mountains, he did not have much free time because he had to deal with so many groups of *devas* from different realms of existence. If on a particular night no *devas* from the celestial realms came to see him, then there were bound to be terrestrial *devas* from one location or another; so, he had little free time at night. Fortunately, there were few human visitors in those remote places. If he stayed near a village or a town, however, then human inhabitants from the area came to see him. He received these people in the afternoon or early evening, teaching the monks and novices afterwards.

The Difference is in the Heart

Having written about the *devas*, I shall now write about the human visitors who came to see Ācariya Mun. Being human, I am also included in this matter; but I still wish to apologize to the reader if there is anything unappealing or inappropriate in what follows. In some ways I have an incurably roguish character, as you will no doubt notice. However, I feel it necessary to record truthfully what Ācariya Mun told his disciples privately. I ask for your forgiveness, but I include this so that you may compare humans and *devas* and learn something from it.

Ācariya Mun said there was a great difference between humans and *devas* in the way they communicated with him and listened to his discourses on Dhamma. *Devas* of every realm, from the highest to the lowest, are able to comprehend the meaning in a discussion of Dhamma much more easily than their human counterparts. And when the discussion is over, their exclamations of approval — "*sādhu, sādhu, sādhu*" — echo throughout the spiritual universe. *Devas* of every realm have enormous respect for monks; not one of them shows any sign of impropriety. When coming to listen to a monk discourse on Dhamma, their comportment is always calm, orderly, and exquisitely graceful. Human beings, on the other hand, never really understand the meaning of a Dhamma discourse — even after repeated explanations. Not only do they fail to grasp the meaning, but some are even critical of the speaker, thinking: What is he talking about? I can't understand a thing. He's not as good as that other monk. Some who themselves have previously ordained as monks cannot keep their gross *kilesas* from surfacing, boasting: When I was ordained I could give a much better talk than this. I made those listening laugh a lot so they didn't get tired and sleepy. I had a special rapport with the audience which kept them howling with laughter. Still others think: It's rumored that this monk knows the thoughts of others. So whatever we think, he knows immediately. Why, then, doesn't he know what I'm thinking right now? If he knows, he should give some sign — at least indirectly, by saying that this or that person shouldn't think in such and such a way because it's wrong. Then we would know if he deserves his reputation. Some people come ready to find fault so they can show off their own cleverness. These types are not interested in Dhamma at all. Expounding Dhamma in their presence is like pouring water on a dog's back — they immediately shake it all off, leaving not a drop behind.

Ācariya Mun would often laugh when talking about this type of person, probably because he was amused by his occasional encounters with such 'clever' people. He said that some people who came to see him were so opinionated they could barely walk, the burden of their conceit being much heavier than that which an ordinary mortal could carry. Their conceit was so enormous that he was more inclined to feel trepidation than pity for them, which made him disinclined to talk to them about Dhamma. Still, there were certain social situations where this was unavoidable, so he struggled to say something. But as he was about to speak, the Dhamma seemed to vanish and he could think of nothing to say. It was as if Dhamma could not compete with such overbearing conceit — and so, it fled. All that remained was his body, sitting like a lifeless doll, being stuck with pins, and ignored by everyone as though he had no feelings. At such times, no Dhamma arose for discourse, and he simply sat like a tree stump. In cases like that, where would the Dhamma come from?

Ācariya Mun used to laugh as he described those situations to his disciples, but there were some in his audience who actually trembled. Since they weren't feverish and the weather wasn't cold, we can only

114

assume that they were shuddering from feelings of trepidation. Ācariya Mun said that he would not teach very conceited individuals unless absolutely necessary because his discourse could actually turn into something toxic for the heart of someone who listened without any feeling of respect. The Dhamma that Ācariya Mun possessed was truly of the highest order and of enormous value to those who established their hearts in the principle of goodwill, not considering themselves superior to Dhamma in any way. This is a very important point to keep in mind. Every effect has its cause. When many people sit together listening to a Dhamma talk, there will be some who feel so uncomfortably hot they almost melt and there will be others who are so cool they feel as if they are floating in the air. The difference, the cause, is right there in the heart. Everything else is inconsequential. There was simply no way he could help lighten the burden of someone whose heart refused to accept Dhamma. One might think that if teaching them doesn't actually do any good, it also would not do any harm. But that's not really the case, for such people will always persist in doing things which have harmful repercussions — regardless of what anyone says. So it's not easy to teach human beings. Even with a small group of people, invariably there were just enough noxious characters among them to be a nuisance. But rather than feel annoyed like most people, Ācariya Mun would simply drop the matter and leave them to their fate. When no way could be found to help reform such people, Ācariya Mun regarded it simply as the nature of their *kamma*.

There were those who came to him with the virtuous intention of searching for Dhamma, trusting in the good consequences of their actions — and these he greatly sympathized with — though they were far and few between. However, those who were not looking for anything useful and had no restraint were legion, so Ācariya Mun preferred to live in the forests and mountains where the environment was pleasant and his heart was at ease. In those places he could practice to the limit without being concerned with external disturbances. Wherever he cast his glance, whatever he thought about, Dhamma was involved, bringing a clear sense of relief. Watching the forest animals, such as monkeys, languars, and gibbons, swinging and playing through the trees and listening to them call to one another across the forest gave rise to a pleasant inner peacefulness. He need not be concerned with their attitude toward him as they ran about in search of food. In this deep solitude, he felt refreshed and cheerful in every aspect of his life. Had he died then, he would have been perfectly comfortable and contented. This is dying the truly natural way: having come alone, he would depart alone. Invariably all the Arahants pass into Nibbāna in this way, as their hearts do not retain any confusion or agitation. They have only the one body, the one *citta*, and a single focus of attention. They don't rush out looking for *dukkha* and they don't accumulate emotional attachments to weigh them down. They live as Noble Ones and they depart as Noble Ones. They never get entangled with things that cause anxiety and sorrow in the present. Being spotlessly pure, they maintain a detachment from all emotional objects. Which stands in sharp contrast to the way people act in the world: the heavier their heart's burden, the more they add and increase their load. As for Noble Ones, the lighter their load, the more they relinquish, until there's nothing left to unload. They then dwell in that emptiness, even though the heart that knows that emptiness remains — there is simply no more loading and unloading to be done. This is known as attaining the status of someone who is 'out of work', meaning that the heart has no more work left to do in the *sāsana*. Being 'out of work' in this way is actually the highest form of happiness. This is quite different from worldly affairs, where unemployment for someone with no means of making a living signifies increased misery.

Ācariya Mun related many differences between *devas* and humans, but I've recorded here only those which I remember and those which I think would benefit the discerning reader. Perhaps these asides, such as the *deva* episodes, should all be presented together in one section according to the subject matter. But Ācariya Mun's encounters with such phenomena stretched over a long period of time and I feel it necessary to follow his life story as sequentially as possible. There will be more accounts about *devas* later; but I dare not combine the different episodes because the object is to have the parallel threads of the story converge at the same point. I ask forgiveness if the reader suffers any inconvenience.

What Ācariya Mun said about *devas* and humans refers to these groups as they existed many years before, since Ācariya Mun, whose reflections are recorded here, died over 20 years ago. The *devas* and humans of that age have most probably changed following the universal law of impermanence. There remains only the 'modern' generation who have probably received some mental training and improved their conduct accordingly. As for the contentious people whom Ācariya Mun encountered in his life, probably such people no longer exist to clutter up the nation and the religion. Since then, there has been so much improvement in the education system; and well-educated people aren't likely to harbor such vulgar ambitions. This affords people today some relief.

AFTER LIVING AND TEACHING the monks and the local population in the Udon Thani and Nong Khai areas for a considerable time, Ācariya Mun moved eastward to the province of Sakon Nakhon. He traveled through the small villages in the forests and mountains of the Warichabhum, Phang Khon, Sawang Dan Din, Wanon Niwat, and Akat Amnuay districts. He then wandered to Nakhon Phanom through the district of Sri Songkhram, passing through the villages of Ban Sam Phong, Ban Non Daeng, Ban Dong Noi, and Ban Kham Nokkok. All these places were deep in the wilderness and infested with malaria, which, when caught, was very difficult to cure: a person could be infected the better part of a year and still not fully recover. Assuming one did not die, living through it was still a torment. As I've already mentioned, malaria was called 'the fever the in-laws despise', because those who suffered chronically from this illness were still able to walk around and eat, but unable to do any work. Some became permanent invalids. The villagers in that area, as well as the monks and novices who lived in the same forests, were frequently victims of malaria. Some even died from it. For three years Ācariya Mun spent successive rains retreats in the area around Ban Sam Phong village. During that time quite a few monks died of the illness. Generally, those monks were from cultivated areas where there was little malaria — such as the provinces of Ubon, Roy Et, and Sarakham — so they were not used to the forests and mountains. They could not live easily in those forests with Ācariya Mun because they couldn't tolerate the malaria. They had to leave during the rainy season, spending their retreat near villages that were surrounded by fields.

Ācariya Mun recounted that when he gave evening Dhamma talks to the monks and novices near the village of Sam Phong, a *nāga* from the Songkhran River came to listen almost every time. If he failed to arrive at the hour when the discourse took place, he would come later when Ācariya Mun sat in *samādhi*. The *devas* from the upper and lower realms came only periodically, and not as often as they did when he stayed in the provinces of Udon Thani or Nong Khai. They were always particular about coming on the three holiest observance days of the rains retreat — the first, the middle and the last day. No matter where Ācariya Mun lived, whether in towns or cities, the *devas* always came from one realm or another to hear his Dhamma. This was true in the city of Chiang Mai while he was staying at Wat Chedi Luang monastery.

The Well-digging Incident

A strange incident occurred while he was staying near the village of Ban Sam Phong. It was the dry season. About 60 to 70 monks and novices were living there, and there was not enough clean water available. The monks held a meeting with the villagers and decided that they would have to dig the existing well deeper in order to acquire a clean, adequate supply. After the decision was made, a senior monk requested permission from Ācariya Mun to proceed with the work. After listening to the request, Ācariya Mun remained quiet for a moment before he answered sternly in a rough voice, "No, it could be dangerous." That was all he said. The senior monk was puzzled by the words "it could be dangerous." After paying his respects to Ācariya Mun, he related the conversation to the monks and the lay people. Instead of agreeing with Ācariya Mun, they decided to proceed secretly with the plan.

The well was some distance from the monastery. At noon, when they thought Ācariya Mun was resting, they quietly went out to dig. They had not dug very deep when the earth around the top edge gave way and collapsed into the well, leaving a gaping hole at ground level and ruining the well with loose earth. Everyone was terrified: Having disrespectfully ignored Ācariya Mun's warning, and showing a lack of mindfulness by failing to call off the project, they had caused the earth to cave in, almost killing someone in the process. They were afraid he would find out what they had done against his express wishes. They were extremely worried and felt chastened by their error. Together they quickly gathered wood to repair the mouth of the well, praying all the while for Ācariya Mun's assistance in their efforts to dig out the loose earth and restore the well for use again. Fortunately, once they appealed for Ācariya Mun's help, everything was put into good order with amazing ease so that some of them even ended up smiling.

As soon as the work was completed everyone fled the scene, afraid that Ācariya Mun might suddenly show up. Back in the monastery the monks and novices remained in a state of constant anxiety about what they had done. The closer it came to the evening meeting, the more apprehensive they became. They could all vividly remember Ācariya Mun's scoldings in the past when something of this nature had happened. Sometimes when they did something inappropriate and then forgot, Ācariya Mun knew and eventually brought it up as a way of teaching a lesson. The well incident was a serious misdeed that was committed by the whole monastery behind his back. How could he possibly have not known about it? They were all certain that he knew and that he was bound to mention it that evening, or at the latest, the very next morning. They were preoccupied with these uncomfortable feelings for the rest of the day.

As it turned out, when the time arrived no meeting was called. Instead of scolding them, Ācariya Mun mentioned nothing about the incident. Ācariya Mun was very astute in teaching his disciples. He knew very well about the incident and about many other mistakes made by the monks and novices. But he also knew about their anxiety. Since they obviously realized their mistake, scolding them at this point would have needlessly increased their deep remorse.

Ācariya Mun's early morning routine was to rise from seated meditation at dawn, then do walking meditation until it was time to put on his robes at the meeting hall before going for alms. The next morning, when Ācariya Mun left his walking path and entered the meeting hall, the monks were still worried about how he would deal with them. While they waited in anxious anticipation, Ācariya Mun turned the whole affair around by speaking gently and in a comforting manner designed to relieve their distress:

"We came here to study Dhamma. We should not be unreasonably audacious, nor should we be excessively afraid. Anyone can make a mistake — the value lies in recognizing our mistakes. The Lord Buddha made mistakes before us. He realized where he had gone wrong and strove to correct his errors as soon as he became aware of them. This kind of intention is noble, but still through ignorance mistakes can happen. From now on you should all take care to control yourselves under all circumstances. Using mindfulness at all times to watch out for oneself is the way of the wise."

That was all he said. He just smiled broadly at the monks in a disarming way and took them on almsround as usual. There was no meeting later that evening, Ācariya Mun merely told everyone to be diligent in their practice. Three nights passed without a meeting. All during that time the monks and novices were still scared he would scold them about the well-digging incident. On the fourth night a meeting was called. But again, no mention was made of the incident, as though he knew nothing about it.

A long time later, after everyone had forgotten about the matter, it quite unexpectedly cropped up. No one had ever told him about the mishap, for the whole affair had been hushed up. Ācariya Mun himself never went to the well, which was quite a distance from the monastery. He began a Dhamma discourse as he usually did, speaking about various aspects of a monk's practice, about being reasonable and about having respect for the teacher and Dhamma. These, he said, led to the correct behavior of those coming to train and practice under a teacher. He stressed that they should especially take the issue of cause and effect very seriously, for this was the true Dhamma:

"Although you're constantly under pressure from your desires, you shouldn't allow them to surface and intrude into the sphere of practice. Otherwise, they will destroy Dhamma, the tried and true way to go beyond *dukkha*, gradually spoiling all of your hopes. Never should you go against Dhamma, the monastic discipline, or the word of a respected teacher, as this is equivalent to destroying yourselves. Disobedience merely gives impetus to those bad habits which are destructive to you and others as well. The earth around that well was more than just clay. There was also sand underneath. Digging too deeply can cause the sand, then the clay to collapse into the well, possibly burying and killing someone. That was why I forbade it. I thoroughly investigate everything before giving or refusing permission for any type of work. Those who are here for training should consider this. Some matters are exclusively internal, and I don't feel it necessary to reveal every aspect of them.

"What I did reveal was clear enough for you to understand; so why did you behave as if you didn't? When I forbid something, you go ahead and do it anyway. If I tell you to do something, you do the opposite. This was not a matter of misunderstanding — you understood perfectly well. Being contrary like this displays the stubborn side of your character, dating from the time you lived with your parents who tolerated it just to keep you happy. It has now become an ingrained characteristic, buried deep inside monks who are now adults. To make matters worse, you flaunt it in the face of your teacher and the spiritual life you lead. Stubbornness in a monk of your age is unforgivable and cannot be tolerated as mere childish behavior. It deserves a stern reprimand. If you persist in being stubborn, it will further entrench this unfortunate trait in you, so that you will be appropriately branded as 'obstinate *dhutanga* monks'. Thus all your requisites should be labeled 'the belongings of an obstinate monk.' This monk is stubborn, that monk is shameless, the monk over there is dazed — until the whole monastery ends up doggedly disobedient. And I end up with nothing but hardheaded students. Once obstinacy becomes the norm, the world will break up from the strain and the *sāsana* will surely be reduced to ruin. Which of you still want to be a hardheaded monk? Is there anyone here who wants me to be a teacher of hardheaded monks? If so, go back tomorrow and dig out that well again, so the earth can collapse and bury you there. Then you will be reborn in a hardheaded heavenly paradise where the *devas* can all come and admire your true greatness. Surely no group of *devas*, including those in the *brahma* realms, have ever seen or lived in such a peculiar paradise."

After that the tone of his voice became gentler, as did the theme of his talk, enabling his audience to wholeheartedly reflect on the error of their stubborn disobedience. During the talk, it seemed as if everyone had forgotten to breathe. Once the talk was over and the meeting adjourned, the monks excitedly questioned one another to find out who might have dared inform Ācariya Mun of the incident, prompting this severe scolding which nearly made them faint. Everyone denied informing him, as each dreaded a scolding as much as another. The incident passed without a definitive answer to how Ācariya Mun knew.

SINCE HIS TIME AT SARIKA CAVE, Ācariya Mun possessed a mastery of psychic skills concerning all sorts of phenomena. Over the years, his proficiency grew to such an extent that there seemed to be no limit to his abilities. As the monks living with him were well aware of these abilities, they took strict care to be mentally self-controlled at all times.

They couldn't afford to let their minds wander carelessly because their errant thoughts could become the subject of a Dhamma talk they might receive at the evening meeting. They needed to be especially vigilant during the meeting when Ācariya Mun was actually speaking to them. In those brief moments when he stopped speaking — perhaps to catch his breath, perhaps to observe something — if he detected any stray thought among the monks, he immediately made an issue of it. The tone of his voice changed dramatically as he mimicked the unmindful thoughts of one of those present. Although Ācariya Mun did not mention anyone by name, his tone immediately startled that individual who became quite frightened to ever dare think like that again.

Another time to be careful was when they followed him on alms-round. Those who were unmindful then were bound to hear about their wayward thoughts at the next meeting. Sometimes it was very embarrassing to have to listen to a talk on one's own wayward thoughts as other monks cast sidelong glances around the assembly, not knowing who among them was being reprimanded. But once discovered, all the monks and novices tended to react similarly in a positive manner. Instead of feeling angry or disappointed after leaving the meeting, all would appear cheerful and content; some even laughed as they inquired of each other: "Who was it today? Who got caught today?" It's remarkable how honest they were with their fellow monks about their errant thoughts. Instead of trying to keep his indiscretion a secret, the guilty monk would confess as soon as someone asked: "I'm really stubborn and I couldn't help thinking about … even though I knew I was bound to get told off for thinking like that. When those thoughts came up, I forgot all about my fear of Ācariya Mun and just felt full of myself thinking such crazy thoughts. I deserved exactly what I got. It will teach me a good lesson about losing my self-control."

I would like to apologize to the reader because I don't feel very comfortable about writing down some of these matters. But these stories are factual — they actually happened. The decision to include them was a difficult one to make. But if what I recount is the truth, it should be all right. It could be compared to a situation in which a monk confesses to a disciplinary offense as a means of eliminating any sense of guilt or anxiety about its recurrence in the future. Thus, I would like to relate a few incidents from the past to serve as food for thought for all of you whose thoughts may cause you similar problems.

 In most cases, practicing monks received a severe rebuke from Ācariya Mun because of affairs pertaining to external sense objects. For example, sights and sounds are the most likely sense impressions to cause trouble. And the most likely occasion for monks to be scolded was the morning almsround. Walking to the village for alms is an essential duty of every monk. On these occasions, monks encounter sights and sounds, and are bound to think about them. Some become so infatuated with what they encounter that their thoughts swirl into disarray without their actual knowledge. These are the primary causes of mental distraction, enticing the mind even when one has no desire to think about them. By the time a monk regained mindfulness, it was time for the evening meeting and the tongue-lashing he received would prompt him to try to be more controlled. After a time, he again encountered the same enticing objects and reopened the sore. Upon returning to the monastery, he would receive another dose of 'strong medicine', in the form of another scolding, to apply to his sore. A great many monks and novices lived with Ācariya Mun and most of them had such festering sores. If one monk didn't get a dose of his medicine then another did. They went to the village and were confronted by attractive sights and sounds until they were unable to stay out of trouble. Consequently, upon their return to the monastery, when the opportunity arose, Ācariya Mun would have another go at them. It's natural for someone with *kilesas* to have a mixture of good and bad thoughts. Ācariya Mun did not give a lecture for every bad thought. What he criticized was the tendency to think in harmful ways. He wanted them to think in terms of Dhamma, using mindfulness and wisdom, so that they could free themselves from *dukkha*. He found that, instead of easing their teacher's burden with rightful thinking, monks preferred to think in ways that troubled him. Since many such monks lived with him, there were scoldings nearly every evening.

 All of this serves to illustrate that Ācariya Mun's subtle ability to know the thoughts of others was very real.[33] As for those reprehensible thoughts, they did not arise intentionally but accidentally, due to occasional lapses in mindfulness. Nevertheless, as a teacher imparting knowledge and skill to his students, Ācariya Mun quickly sounded a warning when he noticed something inappropriate, so that the perpetrator could become conscious of his lapse and learn to be more self-controlled in the future. He did not want his students to get trapped into such thinking again, for it promotes habitual thought patterns that lead directly to misfortune.

Ācariya Mun's teaching for the monks was thoroughly meticulous, showing great attention to detail. The rules of monastic discipline were taught in detail and *samādhi* and wisdom, belonging to the higher Dhamma, were taught in even greater depth. During the time he lived in Sarika Cave, he had already begun to master all levels of *samādhi* and all intermediate levels of wisdom. As for the highest levels of wisdom, I shall write about them later in the story when Ācariya Mun's practice finally reached that stage. After continuing his training in the Northeast region for a while longer, he became even more proficient. This enabled him to use his expertise to teach the monks about all levels of *samādhi*, plus the intermediate levels of wisdom. They in turn listened intently to his expositions, which never deviated from the authentic principles of *samādhi* and wisdom.

Ācariya Mun's *samādhi* was strange and quite extraordinary, whether it was *khaṇika samādhi*, *upacāra samādhi* or *appanā samādhi*.[34] When his *citta* entered into *khaṇika samādhi*, it remained only for a moment, and instead of returning to its normal state, it then withdrew and entered *upacāra samādhi*. In that state, he came into contact with a countless variety of external phenomena. Sometimes he was involved with ghosts, sometimes *devas*, sometimes *nāgas* — innumerable worlds of existence were contacted by this type of *samādhi*. It was this access level *samādhi* that Ācariya Mun used to receive visitors whose forms were invisible to normal sight and whose voices were inaudible to normal hearing. Sometimes his *citta* floated up out of his body and went off to look at the heavenly realms and the different levels of the *brahma* world; then, it traveled down into the regions of hell to look at the multitude of beings tormented by the results of their own *kamma*.

The terms 'going up' and 'going down' are relative, conventional figures of speech, referring to the behavior of gross physical bodies. They have very little in common with the behavior of the *citta*, which is something so subtle that it is beyond temporal comparison. In terms of the physical body, going up and going down require a degree of earnest effort, but in terms of the *citta*, they are merely figures of speech with no degree of effort involved. When we say that the heavens, the *brahma* realms, and Nibbāna are progressively 'higher' and more refined levels of existence or that the realms of hell consist of progressively 'lower' levels of existence, we are in fact using a physical, material

124

standard to measure that which exists in a spiritual, psychic dimension. We might say that hell and heaven, which are considered to be lower and higher respectively, are in some respects analogous to hardened criminals and petty offenders who live together in the same prison, which itself is located in a community of law-abiding citizens. There's no distinction in kind between the two types of prisoners because they all live together in the same prison. And there's no distinction in kind between them and law-abiding citizens because they are all human beings living on the same land in the same country. What distinguishes them is the fact that they've been kept separated.

At least the prison inmates and the general public can use their normal sense faculties to be aware of each other. But beings in the different spheres of existence are unaware of each other. Those living in the hell realms are unable to perceive those who are in the heavenly realms; and vice versa. Both groups are unable to perceive the *brahma* world. And human beings, in turn, are unaware of all who are in these different realms of existence. Even though the flows of consciousness from each of these beings intermingle constantly as they pass through one another's sphere of existence, they are as oblivious of others as if theirs is the only group in existence.

Ordinarily, our minds are unable to know the thoughts of others. Because of this inability, we might then reason that they do not really exist. No matter how persistent these denials might be, we would be wrong because all living beings possess a mind. Even though we are not aware of the thoughts of other beings, we have no right to deny that they exist simply because we can't perceive them. We cannot afford to hold hostage within the limitations of our sense faculties the existence of things which are too subtle to see and hear . If we do, we are just fooling ourselves.

When we say that the heavens and the *brahma* worlds are arranged vertically in a series of realms, one shouldn't understand this in the gross material sense — such as, a house with many stories requiring the use of stairs or an elevator. These realms exist in a spiritual dimension and they are ascended in the spiritual sense by spiritual means: that is, by the heart which has developed this sort of capability through the practice of virtue. When we say that hell is 'down below', this does not mean descending into an abyss. Rather, it refers to descent by spiritual means to a spiritual destination. And those who are able to observe the hell realms do so by virtue of their own internal psychic faculties. But those beings who 'fall' into these realms do so through the power of their own evil *kamma*. They remain there, experiencing whatever torment and agony is imposed on them by their own misdeeds, until they have completed their punishment and are released, in the same way that prison inmates are released at the end of their sentences.

From the very beginning of Ācariya Mun's practice, *upacāra samādhi* and *khaṇika samādhi* were bound together because the nature of his *citta* was inherently active and adventurous. As soon as his *citta* entered *khaṇika samādhi*, it instantly began to roam and experience the different phenomena existing in the sphere of *upacāra*. So he trained himself in *samādhi* until he was proficient enough to make his *citta* stay still or go out to experience various phenomena as he wished. From then on it was easy for him to practice the *samādhi* of his choice. For instance, he could enter momentarily into *khaṇika samādhi* and then move out to access *samādhi* in order to experience various phenomena, or he could focus intensively and enter into the full absorption of *appanā samādhi*, where he would rest for as long as necessary. *Appanā samādhi* is a state of perfect calm that's absolutely serene and peaceful. Because of this, meditators may become attached to it. Ācariya Mun said that he was attached to this type of *samādhi* for awhile, but not for long, since he was by nature inclined toward wisdom. So he was able to resolve this matter himself and find a way out before complacency set in.

Anyone who is transfixed in *appanā samādhi* will make slow progress if they do not try to apply wisdom to examine it. Because it fills one with such happiness, many meditators are held fast by this kind of *samādhi*. A strong, lingering attachment forms, and the meditator yearns for more, overwhelming any inclination to examine things with wisdom, which is the way to eradicate all *kilesas*. Meditators who fail to receive timely advice from a wise person will be reluctant to disengage themselves and realize the path of wisdom. When the *citta* remains attached for a long time in such *samādhi*, conceits of various kinds may develop; such as, believing that this calm and happy state is none other than Nibbāna, the end of *dukkha*. In truth, when the *citta* 'converges' into the one-pointedness of *appanā samādhi* so that its focal point is experienced with the utmost clarity, it dwells fully absorbed in serene happiness. But, the *kilesas* that cause birth in all realms of existence simultaneously converge at the same focal point as well. If wisdom is not used to penetrate and destroy those *kilesas*, there is no doubt that future rebirths will take place. Therefore, regardless of the level of *samādhi* one practices, wisdom should be incorporated into the practice as well. This is especially true of *appanā samādhi*. Otherwise, the *citta* will only experience tranquility without evincing a capacity for resourcefulness and discernment.

By THE TIME OF HIS SECOND TRIP to the Northeast, Ācariya Mun was well-experienced in the intermediate level of wisdom, since sufficient wisdom is necessary for having advanced to the Anāgāmī level of Dhamma. Otherwise, he would not have been capable of effective investigation at that level. Before reaching that level, one must employ wisdom to successfully pass through body contemplation. This requires seeing the attractive as well as the repulsive aspects of the body without getting caught up in either extreme.[35] The *citta* uses wisdom to isolate the attractive and repulsive aspects and then passes through the midpoint where these two extremes meet, having resolved all doubt and attachment concerning the body. This passage, however, is nothing more than a transitional stage along the way. It is analogous to taking an examination and passing with the minimum requirement, necessitating further study to achieve the maximum grade. Those who have penetrated to the Anāgāmī level of understanding must still train their wisdom until it reaches an even more refined degree of expertise before it can be said that they are full-fledged Anāgāmīs. Should such a person then die, he would immediately be reborn in the fifth or *akaniṭṭha* plane of the *brahma* world without having to pass through the four lower *brahma* planes.

Ācariya Mun recounted how he was delayed at that level for quite some time because he had no one to advise him. As he struggled to familiarize himself with the Anāgāmī level of practice, he had to be very careful not to make any mistakes. He knew from his experience in analyzing subtle aspects of Dhamma that the *kilesas* might undermine his efforts, for they were as equally subtle as the mindfulness and wisdom he was using to counter them. This made it very difficult to penetrate each successive level of Dhamma. He said it was absolutely incredible how hard he struggled to negotiate that dense, thorny thicket. Before he made his way through to come and kindly teach the rest of us, he suffered great hardship, making the arduous journey all alone.

When the occasion was right, he used to describe this part of his practice to us. I myself was moved to tears in two instances while listening to his description of the terrible ordeal he faced at that time, and the amazingly subtle and profound nature of the Dhamma he attained. I wondered whether I had enough inherent virtue to enable me to crawl along in his footsteps, or whether I was destined to go the way of ordinary people in the world. But his words were very encouraging and always helped to sustain my resolve to persevere. Acariya Mun said that whenever he accelerated his efforts to apply wisdom, his *citta* became weary of association with others and he became even more committed to his meditation practice. He knew at that stage that his practice still needed strengthening; yet he felt obliged to stay and train his disciples so that they might also develop some Dhamma principles in their hearts.

ĀCARIYA MUN LIVED for three or four years in the area of Ban Sam Phong village in Sri Songkhram district, Nakhon Phanom province. He spent one year at Ban Huay Sai village in Kham Cha-ee district of the same province, as well as the villages of Nong Sung and Khok Klang. He particularly liked staying in those places since they were all very mountainous. Nearby in the Pak Kut mountains were many *devas* — and tigers there were particularly abundant. When night descended, tigers would wander around his living area while the *devas* came to rejoice in hearing the Dhamma.

In the middle of the night, the roars of huge tigers echoed through the forest close to where he lived. On some nights a whole host of them roared together, much like a crowd of people yelling back and forth to one another. When the terrifying sounds of those enormous cats resounded through the darkness, the effect was indeed very frightening. There were nights when the monks and novices failed to get any sleep, fearing that the tigers would come to snatch and devour them. Acariya Mun cleverly found ways to use their fear of tigers to spur the monks to practice diligently. Rather enigmatically, he would say: "Anyone who's efforts are lazy — watch out! The tigers in this mountain range really love lazy monks. They find them especially tasty eating! So if you want to avoid becoming a tasty meal for a tiger, you had better be diligent. You see, tigers are actually afraid of anyone who's diligently striving, so they won't eat that person." After hearing this, all the monks redoubled their efforts as though their very lives depended on it. They forced themselves to go out and do walking meditation, despite the roar of tigers all around the vicinity. Although they remained afraid, they believed what Ācariya Mun told them: that lazy monks could expect to be a tiger's next meal.

Their precarious situation was made even worse by the fact that they didn't have huts as they would in a monastery – only small platforms just big enough to sleep on which were very low to the ground. If a tiger became hungry there'd be no contest. Ācariya Mun related that on some nights huge tigers wandered into the monk's area, but then simply walked harmlessly past. He knew that tigers normally would not dare do anything for the *devas* were always on guard. When *devas* came for a Dhamma talk, they mentioned to him that they were protecting the area and would not let anything trouble the monks or cause them harm. Those *devas* also invited Ācariya Mun to remain in the area for a long time.

In truth, Ācariya Mun's admonition to the monks was simply a means of arousing fear so that they would take an increased interest in their practice. As for the tigers, they seemed to know that the monks' living area was a safe haven. Various kinds of wild animals, too, felt no need to be wary of hunters entering the monks' vicinity, for when the villagers knew where Ācariya Mun was staying, they rarely dared to hunt the area. They were concerned about the dreadful moral consequences. They were terrified that if anyone shot a gun in that area it would explode in his hands and kill him. Strangely enough, whenever he went to stay in an area teeming with tigers, those beasts would stop killing the domesticated cows and buffaloes around the local villages. Nobody knew where they went to obtain their food. These remarkable incidents were related by Ācariya Mun himself and later confirmed by many villagers in those localities where he had stayed.

An Impeccable Human Being

Another mysterious incident happened when a gathering of *devas* visited Ācariya Mun. Their leader began a conversation with him, stating:

"Your stay here has caused much delight in all the *devas*. We all enjoy an extraordinary sense of happiness due to your all-embracing aura of compassionate love that permeates through the heavens and spreads across the earth. This aura that radiates from you is indescribable and wonderful beyond compare. Because of it, we always know where you are. This aura of Dhamma emanates from you and streams out in all directions. When you are teaching Dhamma to the monks, novices and lay people, even the sound of your voice resonates unbounded through the higher and lower realms. Wherever *devas* live they hear your voice – only the dead are deaf to it."

I would like to write a bit more about this conversation between Ācariya Mun and the *deva*. Although I cannot vouch for its accuracy, I heard it from a reliable source. Ācariya Mun took up the conversation with this question: "If my voice really resonates as you say, why don't human beings hear it as well?"

The leader of the *devas* replied:

"What would humans know about moral virtue? They couldn't care less. They use their six senses to make evil *kamma* and create the conditions for hell within themselves all the time. They do this from the day they are born until the day they die. They are not nearly as concerned about moral issues as they ought to be, given their status as human beings. There are very few indeed who are interested in using their senses in any morally beneficial way. The amount of moral virtue in their lives is really quite limited. By way of comparison: in the time that it takes one human being to die and be reborn, repeatedly ten or even one hundred times, the average *deva* has yet to pass away even once—not to mention the *brahma devas* who have exceptionally long lives. The population of humankind is vast, and this in turn means a vast amount of negligence, for those who are heedful are few and far between. Mankind is supposed to safeguard the *sāsana*, and yet people themselves know precious little about the *sāsana* or moral excellence.

"Bad people know only evil. Their sole claim to being human comes from the fact that they are breathing. As soon as their breathing stops, they are immediately buried under the weight of their own wickedness. The *devas* know about this. Why shouldn't they? It's no secret. When a person dies, monks are invited to chant auspicious verses of Dhamma for the deceased. Why would an evil person listen then? From the initial moment of death, his consciousness is completely bound up by his evil *kamma*. So what chance would he have to come and listen to

Dhamma? Even while alive he wasn't interested. Only the living can hear Dhamma — if they have the interest and desire. But it's obvious that they're not really interested. Haven't you noticed them? When have they ever shown an interest when the monks chant Dhamma verses? Because they show no interest, it's obvious that the *sāsana* is not truly embedded in their hearts. The things that they're most infatuated with are sordid and disliked even by some animals. These are just the kinds of things that immoral people have always enjoyed more than anything else; and they never ever grow tired of them. Even when they are near death they still hanker after such things. We *devas* know much more about humans than humans know about *devas*. You, venerable sir, are a very special monk. You are quite familiar with humans, *devas*, creatures of hell, and beings of all sorts. That is why *devas* everywhere pay homage to you."

When the *deva* had finished speaking, Ācariya Mun asked him for clarification: "*Devas* possess divine sight and divine hearing, enabling them to see and hear over great distances. They know about the good and bad of human affairs better than do humans themselves. Couldn't you find a way to make humans more aware of right and wrong? I feel that you are more capable of it than we human teachers are. Is there any way you could do this?"

The *deva* replied:

"We *devas* have seen many humans, but we have never seen one as impeccable as you, sir. You have always extended loving kindness to *devas* and humans alike while acquainting them simultaneously with the great variety of beings in existence, from the grossest to the most refined. You have tried to teach them to accept the fact that *devas*, and countless other spheres of existence, really do exist in this world. But still, generation after generation, from birth to death, people have never actually seen these beings. So what interest would they have in *devas*? At most, they may catch a glimpse of something strange, and, without considering the matter carefully, claim they have seen a ghost. How could they possibly hope to receive any advice about matters of good and bad from us *devas*? Although *devas* are constantly aware of them, humans aren't the least interested in knowing anything about us. By what means would you have us teach people? It's really a hopeless situation. We just have to let *kamma* and its results take their course. Even the *devas* themselves constantly receive the results of their *kamma.* Were we free from it, we would all attain Nibbāna. Then we wouldn't have to remain in this difficult situation so long."

"You say that one may attain Nibbāna when one's *kamma* is exhausted. Do *devas* know about Nibbāna? Do they experience pain and suffering like other beings?"

"Why shouldn't we, venerable sir? All the Buddhas who have come to teach the world have taught without exception that we should transcend *dukkha.* They never instructed us to remain mired in suffering. But worldly beings are far more interested in their favorite playthings than they are in Nibbāna. Consequently, not one of them ever considers attaining Nibbāna. All *devas* remember and are very impressed by the concept of Nibbāna as it was taught by each and every Buddha to living beings everywhere. But *devas* still have a dense web of *kamma* to work through before they can move clear of their celestial existence and go the way of Nibbāna. Only then will all problems cease and this oppressive, repetitive cycle of birth, death and rebirth finally come to a halt. But as long as some *kamma* remains in an individual – be it good *kamma* or bad *kamma* – regardless of his realm of existence, *dukkha* will be present as well."

"Are many monks able to communicate with *devas?*"

"There are a few but not many. Mostly, they are monks who like to practice living in the forests and mountains as you do"

"Are there any lay people with this ability?"

"There are some, but very few. They must be people who desire the way of Dhamma and who have practiced the way until their hearts are bright and clear. Only then can they have knowledge of us. The bodily form of celestial beings appears relatively gross to those beings themselves, but is far too subtle for the average human being to perceive. So only people whose hearts are bright and clear can perceive *devas* without difficulty."

"In the scriptures it says that *devas* do not like to be near humans because of their repugnant smell. What is this repugnant odor? If there is such an odor, why do you all come to visit me so often?"

"Human beings who have a high standard of morality are not repugnant to us. Such people have a fragrance which inspires us to venerate them; so we never tire of coming to hear you discourse on Dhamma. Those, exuding a repulsive odor, are people whose morality stinks, for they have developed an aversion to moral virtue even though it is considered to be something exceptionally good through-out the three worlds. Instead, they prefer things that are repugnant to everyone with high moral standards. We have no desire to approach such people. They are really offensive and their stench spreads far and wide. It's not that *devas* dislike humans; but this is what *devas* encounter and have always experienced with humans."

When Ācariya Mun told stories about *devas* and other kinds of spirits, the monks were mesmerized: They forgot all about themselves, the passing time, and their feelings of fatigue. They wished that, someday, they also would come to know about such things; and this hope made them happy to practice. This was also the case when Ācariya Mun thought it necessary to speak of his past lives or the past lives of others. His audience became eager to know about their own past lives and forgot about overcoming *dukkha* and attaining Nibbāna. Sometimes a monk was startled to find his mind wandering in this way and admonished himself: *Hey, I'm starting to get crazy. Instead of thinking about freedom from dukkha, here I am chasing after shadows of a past that's long gone.* In this way he regained his mindfulness for a while, but as soon as it slipped again he would revisit those same thoughts. For this reason, many monks found it necessary to censure themselves on a regular basis.

ĀCARIYA MUN'S STORIES about the *devas* and other visiting spirits were quite fascinating. In particular, he spoke about how the ghost world has its share of hooligans just like we do. Bad characters, who cause disturbances, are rounded up and imprisoned in a place which we humans would call a jail. Different types of offenders are imprisoned in different cell blocks, and all the cells are full. There are male hooligan ghosts and female hooligan ghosts. And then there are the very brutal types, again either male or female. Ācariya Mun said that it was clear from the cruelty in their eyes that they would not respond to kindness and compassion.

Ghosts live in cities, just as we humans do. They have huge cities with leaders who supervise and govern them. Quite a few ghosts are inclined to be virtuous and thus earn high respect from both the ordinary ghosts and the hooligans. It's natural for all ghosts to stand in genuine awe of those among them who tend to possess great power and authority. This is not merely a matter of flattery. Ācariya Mun always claimed that the effects of evil are less powerful than the effects of goodness; and what he himself encountered in the ghost cities was further evidence of this. There are beings with accumulated merit who are nonetheless born into the ghost state as a result of their *kamma*, but, their virtuous characters never change, so they exercise great authority. One such individual is even capable of governing a large community. These ghost communities do not segregate into groups or castes as humans do. Instead, they adhere strictly to the authority of Dhamma principles. The effects of their *kamma* make it impossible for them to hold the kind of prejudice that people do. The nature of their existence is governed by the nature of their *kamma* – this is a fixed principle. The way we use authority in this world cannot, therefore, be applied in the world hereafter. Ācariya Mun explained this matter in great detail but, I'm sorry to say, I can remember only a little of it.

Ācariya Mun's visits to the ghosts were done psychically through *samādhi* meditation. As soon as they saw him they hurried to tell everyone to come and pay their respects to him, just as we humans would do. The chief ghost, who was very respectful of Ācariya Mun and had great faith in him, guided him on a tour past the many places where the ghosts lived, including the 'jail' where the male and female hooligans were kept. The chief ghost explained to Ācariya Mun the living conditions of the different types of ghosts, pointing out that the imprisoned ghosts were mean-hearted types who had unduly disturbed the peace of the others. They were sentenced and jailed according to the severity of their offense. The word 'ghost' is a designation given to them by humans; but actually they are just one type of living being among others in the universe who exist according to their own natural conditions.

Ācariya Mun invariably liked to remain in and around mountains and forests for long periods of time. After having been in Nakhon Phanom for quite a while instructing the monks, he began to necessarily consider his own position. He often reflected on the nature of his own practice. He knew that he still lacked sufficient strength of purpose to finish the ultimate task before him. It became clear that as long as he continued to resist this call and remain teaching his disciples, his own personal striving would be delayed. He said that ever since he had returned from the Central Plains in order to instruct monks in the Northeast, he felt that his *citta* had not advanced as fast as when he was living alone. He felt that he had to accelerate his efforts once more before he could achieve the final goal and be free of all concerns about himself. At that time, Ācariya Mun's mother had been living with him for six years as an *upāsikā*.[36] His concern for her made it inconvenient for him to go anywhere. So, having secured her agreement, he decided to escort her to Ubon Ratchathani. He then left Nakhon Phanom with his mother and a large following of monks and novices, cutting straight across the Nong Sung mountains, through Kham Cha-ee, and coming out at the district of Lerng Nok Tha in the province of Ubon Ratchathani. That year he spent the rains retreat at Ban Nong Khon in the Amnat Charoen district of Ubon Ratchathani province. Many monks and novices stayed there with him, and he trained them vigorously. While he was there the number of monks and lay devotees, who gained faith and came to train under him, steadily increased.

LATE ONE EVENING Ācariya Mun sat in meditation and as soon as his *citta* dropped into calm a vision appeared of many monks and novices walking respectfully behind him in a nice, orderly fashion which inspired devotion. Yet, there were other monks who hurried past, walking ahead of him without respect or self-control. Others looked for an opportunity to pass him in a completely undisciplined manner. And finally, there were some who held pieces of split bamboo, using them to pinch his chest so that he could hardly breath. When he saw these different monks display such disrespect — even cruelly tormenting him — he focused his *citta* carefully to look into events of the future. Immediately, he understood that those, who walked respectfully behind him in a nice, orderly fashion which inspired devotion, were the monks who would conduct themselves properly, faithfully putting his teaching into practice. These were the monks who would revere him and uphold the *sāsana*, assuring that it would flourish in the future. They would be able to make themselves useful to the *sāsana* and to people everywhere by maintaining the continuity of traditional Buddhist customs and practices into the future. Honored and respected by people on earth and beings throughout the celestial realms, they would uphold the integrity of the *sāsana* following the tradition of the Noble Ones, so that it did not decline and disappear.

Walking past him carelessly without respect were the pretentious ones who thought they already knew it all. They considered their own meditation to be even superior to that of their teacher, disregarding the fact that he had previously guided them all in its proper practice. They were not the least bit interested in showing gratitude for his tutelage in matters of Dhamma because they already considered themselves to be clever experts in everything. And thus they behaved accordingly, which was ruinous not only to themselves, but also to the entire *sāsana*, including all the people who might come to them for guidance. Their minds poisoned by the errors of such monks, these people would in turn harm themselves and others, including future generations, without discovering whether they were on the right path or not.

The next group consisted of those who waited for the chance to pass him, signaling the start of a bad attitude that would develop and have repercussions for the future *sāsana*. Much like the previous group, they held a variety of erroneous views, causing harm to themselves and the religion as a whole. Together, they were a menace to the *sāsana*, the spiritual focus of all Buddhists. Because they failed to rightly consider the consequences of their actions, the *sāsana* was in danger of being utterly destroyed.

The monks who pinched Ācariya Mun's chest with pieces of split bamboo considered themselves to be astutely well-informed and acted accordingly. Despite their wrongful actions, they did not take right and wrong into consideration in thinking about their behavior. On top of that, they were bound to cause Buddhist circles and their teacher a great deal of discomfort. Ācariya Mun said that he knew exactly who were among this last group of monks, and that they would cause him trouble before long. He was saddened that they would do such a thing since they were his former disciples who had his consent and blessing to spend the rains retreat nearby. Rather than treating him with all the respect he deserved, they planned to return and bother him.

A few days later, the provincial governor and a group of government officials came to visit his monastery. The delegation was accompanied by the very same disciples who had led the assault on him in his vision. Without revealing his vision to them, he carefully observed their actions. Together they requested his support in soliciting money from the local people in order to build several schools in the area. They explained that this would help the government. They had all agreed to approach Ācariya Mun for assistance since he was highly revered by the people. They felt that the project would surely be a success if he were involved. As soon as he knew the reason for their visit, Ācariya Mun immediately understood that these two monks were the principle instigators of this troublesome business. It was represented in his vision of the assault. Later, he asked both monks to come to him and instructed them in appropriate behavior for a practicing Buddhist monk — someone who's way of life is rooted in self-restraint and tranquillity.

This story is recounted here to help the reader understand the mysterious nature of the *citta*: how it is quite capable of knowing things both apparent and hidden, including knowledge of things past and future, as well as of the present. Ācariya Mun exemplified this ability on numerous occasions. He conducted himself with total detachment. His thoughts never concealed any ulterior, worldly motives. Whatever he said stemmed from his knowledge and insights and was purposefully spoken to make people think. His intention was never to fool credulous people or to cause harm.

What is recorded here was told to his close inner circle of disciples — not just anyone. Thus the writer might be showing bad judgment in exposing Ācariya Mun's affairs. But I think this account offers those who are interested something useful to dwell upon.

Among present-day *kammaṭṭhāna* monks, Ācariya Mun's experiences stand out for being uniquely broad in scope and truly amazing — both in the sphere of his meditation practice and the insights derived from his psychic knowledge. Sometimes, when the circumstances were appropriate, he spoke directly and specifically about his intuitive knowledge. Yet at other times, he referred only indirectly to what he knew and used it for general teaching purposes. Following his experience with the elderly monk, whose thoughts he read during his stay at Sarika Cave, he was extremely cautious about disclosing his insights to others despite his earnest desire to help his students see the errors in their thinking.

When he pointed out candidly that this monk was thinking in the wrong way, or that that monk was thinking in the right way, his listeners were adversely affected by his frankness. They invariably misunderstood his charitable intent instead of benefiting from it as was his purpose. Taking offense at his words could easily lead to harmful consequences. Thus, most of the time Ācariya Mun admonished monks indirectly for he was concerned that the culprits would feel embarrassed and frightened in front of their fellows. Without identifying anyone by name, he merely gave a warning in order to foster self-awareness. Even so, the culprit sometimes became terribly distressed, finding himself rebuked amidst the assembled monks. Ācariya Mun was very well aware of this, as he was of the most expedient method to use in any given circumstance.

Some readers may feel uncomfortable with some of the things that are written here. I apologize for this; but I have accurately recorded everything that Ācariya Mun related himself. Many senior disciples, who lived under his tutelage, have confirmed and elaborated on these accounts, leaving us with a vast array of stories.

GENERALLY SPEAKING, external sense objects pose the greatest danger to practicing monks. They enjoy thinking about sights, sounds, smells, tastes, bodily contact and mental images concerning the opposite sex. Though this is unintended, the tendency to do it is deeply ingrained in their personalities. Inevitably these were the primary subjects of Ācariya Mun's admonitions, whether given directly or indirectly. Monks had other kinds of thoughts of course, but unless they were particularly serious he wouldn't take much notice.

The evening meeting was the most important time by far. Ācariya Mun wanted the members of his audience to be both physically and mentally calm. He didn't want anything to disturb them, or himself, while he was speaking, ensuring that his disciples received maximum benefit from listening. If someone allowed wild, unwholesome thoughts to arise at that time, he was usually struck by a bolt of lightning — right in the middle of the thoughts that absorbed him, right in the middle of the meeting. This made the monk, who dared to think so recklessly, tremble and almost faint on the spot. Although no name was mentioned, Ācariya Mun's disclosure of the content of the offensive thoughts was enough to send a shock through the guilty one. Other monks were also alarmed, fearing that in a moment of carelessness they themselves might fall prey to similar thoughts. When lightning struck continuously during the course of a Dhamma talk, his audience succumbed to the pressure and sat very attentively on guard. Some monks actually entered into a meditative state of complete tranquillity at that time. Those who did not attain such a state were still able to stay calm and cautious from fear that lightning might strike again if their thoughts strayed — or perhaps the hawk they feared was swooping down to snatch their heads!

For this reason, those monks residing with Ācariya Mun gradually developed a solid foundation for centering their hearts. The longer they remained with him, the more their inner and outer demeanors harmonized with his. Those who committed to stay with him for a long time submitted willingly to his vigorous teaching methods. With patience, they came to understand all the skillful means he used, whether in the daily routine or during a discourse on Dhamma. They observed him tirelessly, trying to thoroughly follow his example as best they could. Their tendency to desire Dhamma and be serious about all aspects of daily practice increased their inner fortitude little by little each day, until they eventually stood on their own.

Those monks who never achieved positive results from living with him usually paid more attention to external matters than to internal ones. For instance, they were afraid that Ācariya Mun would berate them whenever their thoughts foolishly strayed. When he did rebuke them for this, they became too scared to think of solving the problem themselves, as would befit monks who were training under Ācariya Mun. It made no sense at all to go to an excellent teacher only to continue following the same old tendencies. They went there, lived there, and remained unchanged: they listened with the same prefixed attitudes, and indulged in the same old patterns of thought. Everything was done in an habitual manner, laden with *kilesas*, so that there was no room for Ācariya Mun's way to penetrate. When they left him, they went as they had come; they remained unchanged. You can be sure that there was little change in their personal virtue to warrant mentioning, and that the vices that engulfed them continued to accumulate, unabated. Since they never tired of this, they simply remained as so many unfortunate people without effective means to oppose this tendency and reverse their course. No matter how long they lived with Ācariya Mun, they were no different than a ladle in a pot of delicious stew: never knowing the taste of the stew, the ladle merely moves repeatedly out of one pot and into another.

Similarly, the *kilesas* that amass immeasurable evil, pick us up and throw us into this pot of pain, that pot of suffering. No doubt, I myself am one of those who gets picked up and thrown into one pot and then into another. I like to be diligent and apply myself, but something keeps whispering at me to be lazy. I like to follow Ācariya Mun's example; and I like to listen and think in the way of Dhamma as he has taught. But again, that something whispers at me to go and live and think in my old habitual way. It doesn't want me to change in any way whatsoever. In the end, we trust the *kilesas* until we fall fast asleep and submit to doing everything in the old habitual way. Thus, we remain just our old habitual selves, without changes or improvements to inspire self-esteem or admiration from others. Habitual tendencies are an extremely important issue for every one of us. Their roots are buried deep inside. If we don't really apply ourselves conscientiously, observing and questioning everything, then these roots are terribly difficult to pull out.

ĀCARIYA MUN DEPARTED from Ban Nong Khon with his mother at the beginning of the dry season. They stayed one or two nights at each village until they arrived at his home village, where Ācariya Mun resided for a time. He instructed his mother and the villagers until they all felt reassured. Then he took leave of his family to go wandering in the direction of the Central Plains region.

He traveled leisurely, in the style of a *dhutanga* monk: he was in no particular hurry. If he came upon a village or a place with an adequate supply of water, he hung up his umbrella-tent and peacefully practiced, continuing his journey only when he regained strength of body and mind. Back then, everyone traveled by foot, since there were no cars. Still, he said that he wasn't pressed for time; that his main purpose was the practice of meditation. Wandering all day on foot was the same as walking meditation for the same duration of time. Leaving his disciples behind to walk alone to Bangkok was like a lead elephant withdrawing from its herd to search alone for food in the forest. He experienced a sense of physical and mental relief, as though he had removed a vexatious thorn from his chest that had severely oppressed him for a long time. Light in body and light in heart, he walked through broad, sectioned paddy fields, absorbed in meditation. There was very little shade, but he paid no attention to the sun's searing heat. The environment truly seemed to make the long journey easier for him. On his shoulders he carried his bowl and umbrella-tent, the personal requisites of a *dhutanga* monk. Although they appeared cumbersome, he didn't feel them to be burdensome in any way. In truth, he felt as though he were floating on air, having relieved himself of all concern about the monks he left behind. His sense of detachment was complete. His mother was no longer a concern for him, for he had taught her to the best of his ability until she developed a reliable, inner stability. From then on, he was responsible for himself alone. He walked on as he pondered over these thoughts, reminding himself not to be heedless.

He walked meditation in this manner along paths free of human traffic. By midday the sun was extremely hot, so he would look for a pleasant, shady tree at the edge of a forest to rest for awhile. He would sit there peacefully, doing his meditation practice under the shade of a tree. When late afternoon came and the heat had relented somewhat, he moved on with the composure of one who realized the dangers inherent within all conditioned things, thus cultivating a clear, comprehending mind. All he needed were small villages with just enough houses to support his daily almsround and, at intervals along his journey, suitable places for him to conveniently stay to practice that were far enough from the villages. He resided in one of the more suitable places for quite some time before moving along.

Ācariya Mun said that upon reaching Dong Phaya Yen forest between the Saraburi and Nakhon Ratchasima provinces, he discovered many forested mountain ranges that brought special joy to his heart. He felt inclined to extend his stay in the area in order to strengthen his heart, for it had long been thirsting to live again in the solitude of the mountains and forests. Upon coming across a suitable location, he would decide to remain awhile and practice meditation until the time came to move on again. Steadily he wandered through the area in this way. He would tell of the region's forests and mountains abounding in many different kinds of animals, and of his delight in watching the barking deer, wild pigs, sambor deer, flying lemurs, gibbons, tigers, elephants, monkeys, languars, civets, jungle fowl, pheasants, bear, porcupine, tree shrews, ground squirrels, and the many other small species of animals. The animals showed little fear of him when he crossed paths with them during the day when they were out searching for food.

Those days, the forested terrain didn't really contain any villages. What few there were consisted of isolated settlements of three or four houses bunched together for livelihood. The inhabitants hunted the many wild animals and planted rice and other crops along the edge of the mountains where Ācariya Mun passed. Villagers there had great faith in *dhutanga* monks, and so he could depend on them for alms food. When he stayed among them, his practice went very smoothly. They never bothered him or wasted his time. They kept to themselves and worked on their own so his journey progressed trouble-free, both physically and mentally, until he arrived safely in Bangkok.

3

A Heart Released

Venerable Ācariya Mun said that he often traveled back and forth from the Northeast to Bangkok, sometimes taking the train to 'the end of the line', which extended only part of the distance in those days. All other times he walked *dhutanga*. Upon arriving in Bangkok on this trip, he went to Wat Pathumwan monastery, and stayed there through the rains retreat. During the rains he frequently studied Dhamma texts with the Venerable Chao Khun Upāli Guṇūpamācariya at his monastery, Wat Boromaniwat.[1] Chao Khun Upāli invited Ācariya Mun to accompany him to Chiang Mai after the rains. So, during the dry season, they went to Chiang Mai by train. On the train Ācariya Mun remained in *samādhi* almost the whole time. Between Bangkok and Lopburi he laid down to rest; but after the train departed Lopburi and reached the foothills of Uttaradit, he entered *samādhi* and remained there for the duration of the trip to Chiang Mai. At the start of his meditation, he made a decision to withdraw from it only upon arrival at Chiang Mai, and then focused exclusively on his meditation. After approximately twenty minutes, his *citta* completely 'converged' into the very base of *samādhi*. From that moment on, he was no longer aware of whether the train was moving or not. Absolute stillness was all that his heart knew; all awareness of external phenomena, including his body, completely ceased. Any perception, that might have disturbed it, vanished from the *citta*, as though the world no longer existed, having disappeared along with all thoughts and inner sensations. The noise of the train, the other passengers, and all the things that were associated with the *citta* earlier were extinguished from his awareness. All that remained was his state of *samādhi*. The external environment faded out of consciousness from the moment his *citta* first 'converged' until he arrived in Chiang Mai, where his previous determination restored him to his normal state of consciousness.

When he opened his eyes to look around, he saw the surrounding buildings and houses of the city. As he began collecting his things in preparation for leaving the train, he noticed that the passengers and railway officials around him were staring at him in astonishment. When it was time to disembark, the railway officials approached him and, smiling cheerfully, helped him with his things, while everyone else in the passenger carriage stared curiously at him. Even before he had stepped off the train, he was asked what monastery he was from and where he was going. He replied that he was a forest-dwelling monk without a fixed residence, and that he intended to go wandering alone in the remote mountains of the North. Inspired by faith in him, some of them asked where he would stay and whether anyone had agreed to take him there. He thanked them, replying that there was someone to receive him since his traveling companion was Chao Khun Upāli, a very senior monk and one who was highly respected by all in Chiang Mai, from the governor to the merchants and the general public. So it happened that a crowd of monks, novices, and lay supporters awaited to receive Chao Khun Upāli. There were even automobiles in waiting, which were quite rare in those days. Official government cars as well as private ones were there to escort them to Wat Chedi Luang monastery.

Once people learned that Chao Khun Upāli had returned to reside at Wat Chedi Luang, they came to pay their respects and hear him expound the Dhamma. Chao Khun Upāli took advantage of the many people present to invite Ācariya Mun to give a discourse on Dhamma. Speaking eloquently, Ācariya Mun enthralled the large audience so much that they wished it would not end. Starting from the basics, he gradually climbed step by step to the higher levels of Dhamma, where he ended his discourse to the sincere regret of all who were absorbed in his presentation. He then paid his respects to Chao Khun Upāli before he left center stage to find a place to relax by himself. Meanwhile, Chao Khun Upāli praised his talk before the whole assembly:

144

A Heart Released

"Ācariya Mun expounds Dhamma so eloquently that it is difficult to find anyone to equal him. He clarifies *muttodaya* — the heart released, the land of absolute freedom — in a way that leaves no room for doubt. Everything is so precisely illustrated that I myself couldn't possibly match his unique, engrossing style. The rhetorical fluency of this *dhutanga* monk is most extraordinary. Listening to him is a pleasurable, learning experience. His discourses never become stale or boring. He speaks of common, everyday things — things we see and hear all the time but never pay attention to utilize. We recall their significance only after he mentions them. Ācariya Mun is an important *kammaṭṭhāna* monk who uses mindfulness and wisdom to faithfully follow the path taught by the Buddha. He never tramples upon it in an unseemly, worldly manner. His talks employ a full range of expression: sometimes casual, sometimes serious, sometimes emphatic, stressing specific points. He elaborates the profound complexities of Dhamma in a way the rest of us are hard pressed to do so candidly. He is quite capable of analyzing the disparate aspects of Dhamma and articulates them in a way that deeply affects our hearts. His commentary is so brilliant that it's hard to keep up with him. I myself have needed to ask him questions about problems I couldn't solve on my own, and he quickly and adeptly solved those problems with his wisdom. I have benefited in innumerable ways from his counsel.

"Since I was coming to Chiang Mai I wanted Ācariya Mun to accompany me, and he readily agreed. Although he did not specifically mention this to me, he probably agreed to come here because he knows Chiang Mai abounds in mountains and forests suitable for the spiritual life. Monks like Ācariya Mun are extremely hard to find. Even though I am his senior, I wholly revere the Dhamma within him — and yet, he is still so humble and gracious towards me that I sometimes feel embarrassed. He has intended to stay here for only a short while before going off in search of seclusion. I must allow my friend to follow his inclinations as I dare not contradict them, for it is rare indeed to find such a monk. With his intentions being solely focused on Dhamma, we should wish him the best as he strives to improve himself. He can then be of greater benefit to us all in the near future.

"Those of you who have problems with your meditation practice, please go to him and seek his advice. You certainly won't be disappointed. But please don't ask him for powerful amulets, magic spells, or lucky charms to ward off danger, for they are all outside the way of practice.

You will just make yourself a nuisance to him for no good reason. You may well receive a reprimand – don't say I never warned you! Ācariya Mun is not that kind of monk. He is a genuine monk, sincerely teaching people to know the difference between right and wrong, good and bad, virtue and evil. His teaching never deviates from the path of Dhamma. His way of practice and knowledge of Dhamma are true to the teachings of the Lord Buddha. No one else nowadays can convey such incredible ideas as he has presented me from our discussions on Dhamma. That has been my experience. I hold an immense respect for him in my heart, but, I have never told him this. Nevertheless, he may already know of it from his powers of intuition.

"Ācariya Mun is a monk truly worthy of the highest respect, and is unquestionably 'an incomparable field of merit for the world'. He himself never makes claims of noble attainments, though they are apparent to me when we discuss Dhamma in private. I am wholly convinced that he is firmly established in the third level of the Noble Dhamma. It is obvious from the way he expresses himself. Although he has never made statements of his specific level of attainment, I know for certain what it is: for the knowledge of Dhamma he has conveyed to me is absolutely consistent with that level as described in the Buddhist texts. He has shown me nothing but loyalty and respect, and I have never known him to be in any way stubborn or disdainful. He conducts himself with such humility that I cannot help but admire him from the bottom of my heart."

These were the words of praise that Chao Khun Upāli addressed to the lay followers, monks, and novices after Ācariya Mun gave his Dhamma talk and returned to his hut. Afterwards, monks who were present reported this speech to Ācariya Mun, who later recounted the story to his disciples when a good opportunity arose. The term *muttodaya* means "a heart released". Its mention in the short biographical sketch distributed at Ācariya Mun's cremation stems from that occasion in Chiang Mai when Chao Khun Upāli praised his noble virtues. The name stuck and was then passed down to future generations by word of mouth. According to Chao Khun Dhammachedi of Wat Bodhisomphon monastery in Udon Thani, Ācariya Mun remained practicing in Chiang Mai from 1929 to 1940 when he left for the province of Udon Thani. More will be written later concerning his stay in Udon Thani.

HAVING LIVED AT Wat Chedi Luang monastery for some time, Ācariya Mun paid his respects to Chao Khun Upāli and took leave to wander in search of solitude in the remote wilderness areas of the North. Chao Khun Upāli readily gave his permission; and so Ācariya Mun departed alone from Chiang Mai, beginning another journey. He had eagerly awaited the ideal seclusion he needed for a long time, and the perfect opportunity finally arose. Having been long involved in teaching others, it was the first time in many years that he had time alone. Initially, he wandered through the Mae Rim district in Chiang Dao, staying in the forested mountains there throughout the dry and rainy seasons.

His efforts had reached the crucial, final stage. He exhorted himself to strive earnestly to reach the final goal, whatever happened — live or die. Nothing whatsoever would be allowed to interfere. Out of compassion he had taught his fellow monks to the best of his ability — of this he had no doubt. The results of his guidance had already begun to show in some of his disciples. Now it was time to have compassion for himself, to educate and lift himself above and beyond those obscuring inner factors which still needed to be overcome.

The life of someone with social obligations and responsibilities is a life of distraction and of almost unbearable stress, never allowing adequate time for being alone. One must admit that this kind of life is a perpetual struggle to be endured, even though a person may have enough mindfulness and wisdom to avoid this burden somewhat and alleviate the stress so that it doesn't overwhelm him. The opportunities to practice meditation are limited; the results are likely to be minimal and not worth all the disappointments and difficulties.

This solitary excursion into the untamed wilderness was an ideal opportunity for him to disengage and live alone, aloof from all entanglements. Wild, remote forests are just the right kinds of places to live and practice for someone aiming to sever all residual attachments, both internal and external, from his heart. He can discard all the remaining concerns that might form the seeds of future existence — the source of all forms of *dukkha* that brings menace in its wake and causes endless suffering. Remote forests are the right environment in which a persistent and diligent person can zero in on the fundamental causes of existence—the great internal masters of deception leading us astray—and excise them quickly from his heart. While one is still far from reaching the shores of Nibbāna, little benefit can be gained from involvement in other people's affairs; for that is comparable to overloading a barge that is ready to sink even before it starts going. When the coveted goal of the holy life seemed within reach, Ācariya Mun's compassionate concern for others dropped away, replaced by motivations of a more personal nature. He was no longer considering the suffering of others. His resolve was focused firmly on the realm of purity and he was concerned, lest he not reach it this time. Thus he reflected:

"Now I must worry about myself – pity myself – so that as a diligent disciple of the Tathāgata, I can live up to his exalted virtue of unwavering perseverance. Am I fully aware that I have come here striving to cross beyond the world of *saṁsāra* and attain the goal of Nibbāna – the freedom from all anxiety and *dukkha*? If so, what methods should be used by someone attempting to cross beyond the conventional world? The Lord Buddha first led the way and then taught us the Dhamma – what kind of guidance did he give? Did he teach us to forget our purpose and start worrying about this and that as soon as we have gained a modest understanding of Dhamma?

"In the beginning, the Lord Buddha publicly proclaimed the *sāsana* with the help of a small number of Arahants, getting his message rapidly spread far and wide – most properly so. But I am not in the same exalted position, so I must view my own development as paramount right now. When I have perfected myself, then benefits to others will inevitably follow. This view befits one who is circumspect and reluctant to waste time. I must reflect on this carefully, so I can learn a lesson from it.

"Right now, I am striving for victory in a battle between the *kilesas* and *magga*, the way of Dhamma, in order to win freedom for the *citta*. Until now its loyalties have been divided between these two rivals, but I aim to make Dhamma its undisputed master. If my persistence slackens and my powers of discernment are inadequate, the *citta* will slip from my grasp and fall under the ignoble influence of the *kilesas*; and they will ensure that the *citta* keeps turning in a never-ending cycle of birth and despair. But if I can keep up my persistence and keep my wisdom sharp, the *citta* will come under my control and be my own priceless treasure for the taking.

"The time has come for me to put my life on the line and engage the *kilesas* in a fierce all out assault, showing no hesitation or weakness. If I lose, then let me die while battling it out. I will not allow myself to retreat in disarray so that the *kilesas* can ridicule me — that will be a lasting disgrace. If I am victorious, I shall remain perfectly free for all eternity. So now, there is only one path for me to take: I must fight to the death with all my might for the sake of this victory. There is no other choice."

This is the kind of exhortation that Ācariya Mun used to embolden himself for the impending realization of the goal he had set for himself. It reflected his uncompromising decision to accept the obligation of striving for Nibbāna steadfastly both day and night — whether standing, walking, sitting, or lying down. Except when he rested to sleep, his time was wholly devoted to diligent effort. His mindfulness and wisdom circled around all external sensations and all internal thought processes, meticulously investigating everything without leaving any aspect unexplored. At this level of practice, mindfulness and wisdom act in unison like a Wheel of Dhamma, turning continuously in motion, irrespective of the body's action.

Later, when Ācariya Mun described his tremendous efforts during that time, his audience was so awe-struck by his Dhamma exploits that they sat motionless with bated breath. It was as though Ācariya Mun had opened the door to Nibbāna, allowing them a glimpse inside, without their having ever experienced Nibbāna before. In truth, Ācariya Mun was then in the process of accelerating his efforts toward the realization of Nibbāna. Although only a stage in the course of his development, it nevertheless moved those who had never before heard of such a thing, and they were always carried away by the awesome power of his achievement.

ĀCARIYA MUN SAID that his *citta* had long attained the third *ariya* level of Anāgāmī; but, because of his continual obligations to his followers, he had no time to speed up his efforts as he wished. Only when he had the opportunity to go to Chiang Mai was he able to maximize his practice and accomplish his objective.

Chiang Mai's environment was conducive and his *citta* was well prepared. Physically, he was in excellent shape, fit to exert himself in every activity. His fervent hope was like the radiant sun, streaming forth continuously to reach the shore free of *dukkha* in the shortest possible time. He compared his inner struggle between Dhamma and the *kilesas* to a hunting dog, which, at full run, corners its prey; and it is only a matter of time before the prey is torn to shreds in the jaws of the chasing hound. There could be no other ending, for the *citta* was armed with *mahāsati* and *mahāpaññā* – supreme-mindfulness and supreme-wisdom. They never lapse for a single moment, even when one has no intent to be vigilant. At this level, mindfulness and wisdom are fully present, reacting automatically to all matters arising within oneself. As soon as their cause is known and their true nature is clearly understood, one simply lets go of them. It is not necessary then to be in command, giving orders, as is the case in the initial stages of practice. When equipped with habitual mindfulness and wisdom, there is no need for specific directions and calculated decisions to practice this or to investigate that, while having to simultaneously guard against lapses in attention. "Reason and result" are integrated into the nature of automatic mindfulness and automatic wisdom; so, it is unnecessary to search on one's own for reasons and skillful methods to encourage their operation. With the exception of sleep, all daily activities are the working arenas for this level of *mahāsati* and *mahāpaññā*. Just like spring water that flows steadily out of the ground all year round, they work ceaselessly.

The thinking process is taken as the focal point of the investigation, in order to find the true source of these thoughts. The four *nāma khandhas* – *vedanā, saññā, sankhāra,* and *viññāna* – are the appropriate battleground for this superior degree of mindfulness and wisdom. As for the *rūpa khandha* – the physical body – it ceased to be a problem when one achieved the intermediate level of wisdom. This form of wisdom performs the tasks necessary for realizing the Anāgāmī stage of the Noble Path. To attain this exalted level, one must focus on the physical body, investigating it scrupulously in every detail until all mis-understandings and concerns about the body are forever banished.

When one comes to the final stage – the path to Arahantship, it is absolutely essential to investigate the *nāma khandhas* so that one gains a deep and clear understanding about how all phenomena arise, briefly exist, and then vanish. These three aspects of the investigation converge in the truth of *anattā*. This means examining all phenomena as being empty of a permanent self: empty of being a man or woman, empty of being me or them. No self-entity — whatsoever — exists anywhere within mental phenomena.[2] To comprehend the true nature of the *nāma khandhas*, one must discover the fundamental principles underlying them and understand them deeply and clearly with wisdom. It's not enough that we anticipate results or speculate about their nature, as is the common tendency of most people — people who just prefer to do guesswork.

A theoretical understanding, acquired from learning, differs from a genuine understanding based on wisdom as the earth differs from the sky. People whose understanding is founded upon knowledge gained through memorization are very preoccupied with their own ideas, always assuming that they are highly intelligent. In truth, they are completely deluded. Consequently, they become overly conceited and are reluctant to accept help and advice from anyone.[3]

This arrogant tendency is quite apparent when a group of scholars discusses Dhamma, each one constantly trying to champion his own intellectual theories. These meetings usually degenerate into verbal sparring matches, spurred on by this common attitude of self-importance, until everyone — regardless of age, race, gender, or clan — forgets to observe the proper etiquette expected of such 'civilized' people.

Understanding, based on wisdom, is ready to uproot all types of speculative views that continually manifest our conceit. Wisdom is prepared to ferret out and expose these erroneous views, penetrating every niche until the whole edifice of these *kilesas* comes crashing down. There is not one *kilesa* that can successfully withstand the penetration of the highest degree of mindfulness and wisdom.

In the Dhamma's arsenal, mindfulness and wisdom are the foremost weapons. Never have the *kilesas* been intrepid enough to defeat them. The Lord Buddha became the Supreme Teacher because of mindfulness and wisdom. His disciples became Arahants because of mindfulness and wisdom. Because of mindfulness and wisdom, they were able to see with insight into the true nature of things. They didn't uproot their *kilesas* by using learning, supposition, or mere guesswork. In the initial stages of practice, concepts recalled from memory can be used to delineate the boundaries of the way forward; but, one must exercise great caution lest this kind of conjecture cause delusion appearing in the guise of genuine truth.

When the Lord Buddha and his Arahant disciples proclaimed the Truth of his teaching to the world, they were proclaiming the way of wisdom — the way that brings us to see the true nature of all phenomena. We practitioners of meditation must be extremely careful that the master of speculation doesn't sneak in and conjure up his tricks in place of wisdom. If we aren't, we will be led to mistake mere concepts for true understanding, without ever removing a single *kilesa* from our hearts. We may find ourselves inundated with knowledge about salvation, yet unable to save ourselves. This is exactly what the Lord Buddha meant when he advised the people of Kālāma not to believe in speculation or conjecture, and not to believe teachings handed down from the past or teachers who are considered to be reliable; but to believe that the principles of truth can be discovered within themselves — by the wisdom within themselves. This is the surest kind of knowledge there is. The Lord Buddha and his Arahant disciples didn't need anyone to validate the authenticity of their attainment, for *sandiṭṭhiko* is there within everyone who practices the Buddha's teaching in the right way.[4]

Ācariya Mun said that when he came to this last level of advanced practice, he became so intrigued with it that he lost all sense of time. He completely forgot the time of day, forgot to sleep, and then forgot how tired he was. Fearless and unshakable, his *citta* was constantly in position to oppose every type of *kilesa*, ready to excise them by their roots. From the time he left Wat Chedi Luang in Chiang Mai, he did not allow a single day to pass in vain. And before long, he reached the point of ultimate understanding.[5]

At the moment he set off alone, his *citta* began to express the dynamic characteristics of a daring thoroughbred stallion. It wanted to soar high and glide through the air, dive underground and then shoot up into the sky again. It felt inclined to venture out to experience the many countless variety of phenomena in the universe. He felt as if his *citta* was about to dig up and remove all of the *kilesas* in a single instant. The adventurous nature of his mindfulness and wisdom had long been hemmed in by social obligations. They were unable to move freely about in their preferred domain — the observation and analysis of just those things Ācariya Mun had wanted to know about for such a long time. Now he was blessed — blessed with the opportunity of leaping away and vanishing, finally able to give mindfulness and wisdom the chance to display their considerable prowess as they explored throughout the three worlds of existence.

Ācariya Mun investigated thoroughly, internally and externally. His mindfulness and wisdom penetrated all around — constantly moving in and out, up and down — all the while resolving issues, detaching himself, and then letting go as he cut, slashed, and pulverized every manner of falsehood with all the strength he could muster. Feeling unbound as a giant fish swimming happily in the ocean, he looked back on his entire past and saw only dark obstructive times lurking there, fraught with all kinds of dangerous, inevitable consequences. His heart beat faster at the prospect of finding a way to save himself. Looking to the future, he saw before him only a majestic, empty expanse of brilliant illumination — a view that completely surpasses any conventional understanding and is utterly beyond all description. So much so, that I find it difficult to elaborate any further for the benefit of the reader. I sincerely regret that I am unable to do justice to all the inspiring things Ācariya Mun said.

Ācariya Mun sat in meditation late that night, not too long after supreme-mindfulness and supreme-wisdom had reached the peak of their performance. Like a Wheel of Dhamma, they moved in unison as they rotated non-stop around the *citta* and everything related to it. He was residing at the base of a mountain, in a broad, open area covered with enormous flat rocks. Clear, open space surrounded him as he sat at the foot of a solitary tree — the only tree in that entire area. This tree had abundant cool shade during the day, so he sometimes went to meditate under it.

I regret that I cannot recall what type of tree it was, or its exact location. As Ācariya Mun described this amazing event, I was so thoroughly overwhelmed by the magnitude of his achievement that I failed to remember any of the pertinent details — what district and township he was in, or even the name of the mountain range. Hearing him talk of his great victory, I couldn't help thinking about myself. Was I going to simply waste my birth as a human being, carelessly throwing away the wonderful opportunity it gave me? Did I have enough spiritual potential to one day succeed in realizing that same Supreme Dhamma? Reflecting in this manner, I forgot everything else. I had no idea that, someday, I would be writing his biography.

At dusk Ācariya Mun began walking meditation, focusing on *paṭiccasamuppāda*, as the theme of primary relevance to this level of contemplation.[6] Starting with *avijjā paccaya saṅkhāra*, he became so intrigued by the subject of 'dependent origination' that he was soon investigating it to the exclusion of all else. By the time he sat down at about nine o'clock, his mind was concentrated solely on scrutinizing *avijjā,* examining each of the interdependent conditions through to the logical conclusion, then reversing the order to arrive back at *avijjā.* Contemplating thus, he deliberated back and forth, over and over — inside the *citta* — the focal point where birth, death, and *kilesas* converge with the principal cause — *avijjā.*

Seated in meditation late that night, the crucial moment had arrived. The battle lines were drawn: supreme-mindfulness and supreme-wisdom — the razor sharp weapons — against *avijjā,* an enemy especially adroit at repulsing their advances then counterattacking, leaving its opponents in total disarray. Since time immemorial no one has dared to challenge its might, allowing *avijjā* to reign supreme and unopposed over the 'kingdom of birth and death' inside the hearts of all living beings. But at three a. m. that night when Ācariya Mun launched his final, all out assault, *the result was the total destruction of the king's mighty throne and the complete overthrow of his reign in the kingdom of birth and death. Suddenly impotent and deprived of room to maneuver, the king could not maintain his sovereignty. At that moment avijjā perished, victim to a lightning strike of magnificent brilliance.*

Ācariya Mun described how that fateful moment was accompanied by a tremor that appeared to shake the entire universe. Celestial beings throughout this vast expanse immediately paid tribute to his supreme accomplishment, roaring an exclamation of approval that reverberated across the sentient universe, and proclaimed the appearance of another disciple of the Tathāgata in the world. Overjoyed to have witnessed this event, they were eager to offer their congratulations. Human beings, however, were unaware of the momentous event that had just taken place. Occupied with worldly pleasures, they were too oblivious to care that, only a moment before, the Supreme Dhamma had arisen in the heart of a fellow human being.

When the awesome moment passed, what remained was *visuddhi-dhamma.*[7] This pure Dhamma — the true, natural state of the *citta* — suffused Ācariya Mun's body and mind, and extended its light in all directions. The experience aroused an indescribable feeling of great awe and wonder. His customary compassion for the world virtually disappeared, and with it, his interest in teaching other people. He was convinced that this Supreme Dhamma was far too profound and overwhelming in its greatness for people to ever truly understand. So he became disheartened in this respect, feeling disinclined to teach others. He felt it was enough to simply enjoy this wonderful Dhamma alone while still living in the midst of the conventional world.

Ācariya Mun reflected at length that night on the beneficence of the Lord Buddha. This Supreme Teacher, having fully realized the Truth, taught people who were receptive to his message so that they too could attain genuine deliverance. It was obvious that not a single falsehood was concealed anywhere within the Buddha's teaching. He spent the rest of that night tirelessly paying homage to the supreme virtues of the Lord Buddha.

Ācariya Mun had always been compassionate – he was deeply sympathetic to the spiritual state of fellow human beings. But his *citta* had just attained a clarity that was so extraordinary in its brilliance and purity that he felt he could not possibly explain the true nature of this Dhamma to others. Even if he tried, ordinary people with *kilesas* could never hope to attain this exalted state of mind. More than that, hearing him speak in such superlatives, they could accuse him of insanity for daring to teach the world something that no good, sane person would ever discuss. He believed it unlikely that there would be enough sympathetic people to generate his enthusiasm for teaching. He was free to live a life of solitude for the remainder of his years. It was sufficient that he had fully realized his life-long ambition. He saw no reason to burden himself with difficult teaching responsibilities. It could end up being an example of good causes with bad effects: that is, his compassionate intentions could well turn into harmful results for contemptuous people.

Such was Ācariya Mun's frame of mind shortly after attaining the Supreme Dhamma – a time when he had yet to focus on the wider picture. Eventually, his thoughts gathered on the Lord Buddha's guiding role in revealing the correct path of practice. Reviewing his attainment of Dhamma and the path he took, he saw that he, too, was a human being in the world just like everyone else, and undistinguished from others by any special characteristic that would make him the only person capable of understanding this Dhamma. Certainly, others with strong spiritual tendencies were capable of this understanding. By failing to broaden his perspective, his initial outlook had tended to disparage the spiritual tendencies of his fellow human beings – which was unfair.

The Lord Buddha did not reveal the path of practice leading to *magga, phala* and Nibbāna for the benefit of only one individual. This revelation was a gift for the whole world, both his contemporaries and succeeding generations. In total, the number of those who have reached *magga, phala* and Nibbāna, following the Buddha's teaching, is enormous beyond reckoning. In this respect, Ācariya Mun's achievement was definitely not unique, though he initially overlooked the capacity of others for similar achievement.

Carefully reviewing all aspects of the Buddha's teaching, he saw its relevance for people the world over, and its accessibility to anyone willing to practice correctly. These thoughts gave him a renewed desire to help others. Once again, he felt comfortable with the idea of teaching people who came to him for guidance, provided they were receptive to his instructions. For in teaching Dhamma, the teacher has an obligation to treat Dhamma with respect by refusing to instruct anyone who is disrespectful or indifferent to what is being taught.

Some people can't help making noise while listening to Dhamma: they are obviously apathetic to the value of the Dhamma and the opportunity they have for hearing it. They appear oblivious to where they are or how they are expected to behave at that time. Such people see Dhamma as something quite ordinary. They have adopted a typically worldly attitude of being thoroughly indifferent to Dhamma, to the monastery, and to the monks. They see the whole lot as just commonplace. Under such circumstances, it is unconscionable to teach Dhamma: the teacher is then censurable and the audience fails to gain any real benefit.

Before he realized the Supreme Dhamma and then made it available to others, Ācariya Mun nearly gave up his life in the forests and mountains as he struggled relentlessly with every ounce of strength. After such heroic effort, the notion of bringing this precious Dhamma and having it simply dissipate in the ocean was inconceivable. When has that ever happened? After all, a monk is the type of person who considers everything scrupulously before he acts. Dhamma exists in a class by itself, so special attention must be paid to when and how it is presented to a public audience. Should these considerations be neglected in the presentation of Dhamma, the outcome might well prove harmful.

Dhamma is taught for the purpose of helping people in the world — much like a doctor, desiring the well-being of his patients, prescribes medications to cure sickness and relieve pain. But when people are unwilling to accept help, why should a monk worry about teaching them? If he really has true Dhamma in his heart, he is perfectly content

156

to live in solitude. It's unnecessary for him to seek students in order to alleviate the discomfort and stress caused by an irrepressible urge to teach others the way — an urge which merely adds to a person's sense of discontent, anyway. Lacking sincerity in the Dhamma that the Lord Buddha strove so earnestly to realize, such a person, though he calls himself a teacher, is one only in name.

Ācariya Mun said he had complete confidence that he was mentally and physically attuned to living alone because his heart was supremely tranquil, possessing genuine Dhamma. Dhamma means tranquillity. A heart filled with Dhamma is a heart whose serenity transcends everything. Ācariya Mun naturally preferred living in forested mountain areas since these places were conducive to dwelling sublimely with Dhamma.[8] He considered teaching others to be a special situation. It was an obligation he performed occasionally and not an actual necessity as was living by Dhamma— an essential aspect of his life to the very end. Otherwise, he would not have enjoyed a convenient daily existence.

When we possess Dhamma, understand Dhamma, and abide in Dhamma, we are unperturbed by things in the world, and so do not go searching for *dukkha*. Where Dhamma abides, there is happiness and tranquility. According to natural principles, Dhamma abides in the hearts of those who practice it; so happiness and tranquility arise in the hearts of those practitioners. It cannot arise in any other place.

Ācariya Mun was always extremely circumspect when teaching Dhamma. He never taught indiscriminately, for Dhamma itself is never indiscriminate. He never practiced Dhamma in a random fashion but always followed well-established principles, practicing within the confines of the Noble tradition recorded in the Buddhist scriptures. Understanding did not arise in him in a random fashion either — it arose in progressive stages following the principles of truth. Ācariya Mun advised practicing monks to guard against being indiscriminate by always keeping the strictures of the Teaching and the Discipline in mind, since they represent the Buddha and the path of practice he followed. He stressed that the monk who maintains *magga* and *phala* — and maintains the Teaching and the Discipline — is one who is humble and unassuming, and always careful not to let his actions, his speech, or his thoughts go astray. Practicing thus, he will be able to stand on his own — indefinitely.

Having addressed the issue of teaching Dhamma to others, Ācariya Mun again turned his attention to the nature of his inner Dhamma. He said that the moment of realization, when Dhamma arises in all its glory within the *citta*, is a moment that's completely unimaginable. Dhamma's true nature reveals itself in a totally unexpected manner, as it is inconceivable and impossible to speculate about beforehand. At that moment, he felt as though he had died and been born again into a new life — a uniquely amazing death and rebirth. The quality of awareness, intrinsic to this transformation, was a state of knowing that he had never before experienced, even though it had always been there, unchanging. Suddenly, then, it became apparent — spectacular, and inconceivably amazing. It was this quintessential quality that caused Ācariya Mun to consider — somewhat unconventionally — that it would not be possible to teach others this Dhamma because they would never be able to truly understand it.

Since his early days of practice, Ācariya Mun always possessed a very dynamic character. That distinguishing characteristic was evident at the moment of his final attainment, which was so unforgettable for him that he would later tell this story to inspire his disciples. Once his *citta* had completely overthrown the cycle of repeated birth and death, it appeared to make three revolutions, circling around the newly-arisen *vivaṭṭa-citta.*[9] Upon conclusion of the first revolution, the Pāli term *lopo* — cutting off — arose together with its essential meaning: at that moment the *citta* had completed the function of totally excluding all vestiges of relative, conventional reality. Upon conclusion of the second revolution, the Pāli term *vimutti* — absolute freedom — arose together with its essential meaning: at that moment the *citta* had completed the function of attaining total release. Upon conclusion of the third revolution, the Pāli term *anālayo* — total detachment — arose together with its essential meaning: at that moment the *citta* had completed the function of wholly severing all attachments. *Citta* and Dhamma were then one and the same — *ekacitta ekadhamma*. The true nature of the *citta* is synonymous with the true nature of Dhamma. Unlike relative, conventional reality, there is no duality. This is *vimuttidhamma* pure and simple.[10] It is absolute in its singularity and devoid of any trace of relative, conventional reality within. This pure Dhamma is fully realized only once. It never requires further perfection.

The Lord Buddha and the Arahants become fully enlightened only once: the *citta* and Dhamma being exactly of the same nature, they have no need to search further. The *khandhas*, that make up their conventional existence, are then just *khandhas* pure and simple — they contain no defiling elements. The *khandhas* of an Arahant remain the same as before, for the attainment of Nibbāna does not alter them in any way. For example, those *khandhas* responsible for thought processes continue to perform this function at the behest of their boss, the *citta*. By nature, the release of *vimutti* is already freed of any intermingling with the *khandhas*, the *citta* and the *khandhas* each existing as separate, distinct phenomena, each one true within its own natural state. They no longer seek to deceive or disrupt one another. Both sides exist peacefully in their distinct natural states, performing their specific functions until, at death, each constituent element goes its own separate way.[11]

When the body finally dies, the purified *citta* attains *yathādīpo ca nibbuto:* just as the flame in a lamp is extinguished when all of the fuel is exhausted, so too goes the *citta* according to its true nature.[12] Relative, conventional realities like the *khandhas* are no longer involved with the purified *citta* beyond that point. In truth, nothing of the relative, conventional world accompanies this *citta* to create a cause for coming to birth in the future. Such was the essence of Dhamma that arose in Ācariya Mun's *citta* at the moment it completed the three revolutions expressing its dynamic character. That was the final occasion when the relative reality of the *khandhas* and the absolute freedom of the *citta* joined forces before finally separating to go their separate ways — forever.[13]

Throughout the remainder of that night Ācariya Mun considered with a sense of dismay how pathetically ignorant he had been in the past, being dragged endlessly from one existence to another — like a puppet. He wept as he thought of how he finally came upon a pool of crystal-clear, wondrous-tasting water. He had reached Nong Aw,[14] that sparkling pool of pure Dhamma that the Lord Buddha and his Arahant disciples encountered and then proclaimed to the world over 2500 years ago. Having at long last encountered it himself, he tirelessly paid heartfelt homage, prostrating himself over and over again to the Buddha, the Dhamma, and the Sangha. Should people have seen him then, tears streaming down his face as he prostrated over and over again, surely they would have assumed that this monk was suffering immensely, shedding tears so profusely. They probably would have suspected him of beseeching the guardian spirits, living in all directions, to help ease his pain; or else of being on the verge of madness, for his behavior was extremely unusual. In fact, he had just arrived at the truth of the Buddha, Dhamma, and Sangha with utmost clarity, as epitomized in the maxim: *He who sees the Dhamma, sees the Tathāgata, and thus abides in the presence of the Buddha, the Dhamma, and the Sangha.* Ācariya Mun was simply engaged in the kind of conduct befitting someone who is overwhelmed by a sincere sense of gratitude.

That night celestial *devas* of all realms and terrestrial *devas* from every direction, paid tribute in a resounding exclamation of approval that reverberated throughout the world systems, and then gathered to listen to Ācariya Mun expound the Dhamma. But being still fully engaged in his immediate commitment to the Supreme Dhamma, he was not yet ready to receive visitors. So, he signaled to the assembled *devas* that he was occupied, indicating they should return on a later occasion. The *devas* then left, thoroughly delighted that they had seen a *visuddhi-deva* on the very night when he attained Nibbāna.[15]

At dawn, Ācariya Mun rose from his meditation seat, reflecting still on the unforgettably amazing Dhamma. Thinking back to the moment of final release, he recalled the three revolutions together with the profound subtlety of their essential meanings. He also reflected with appreciation on the tree that had sheltered him as he sat in meditation, and the local villagers who had always supported him with food and other basic needs.

At first, Ācariya Mun considered foregoing his morning almsround that day. He reckoned that the happiness he felt from his attainment was all that he needed for sustenance. But he could not help feeling compassion for the local villagers who had done so much for him. So, while he had no desire to eat, he nevertheless went on almsround. Entering the village that morning he fixed his gaze firmly on the people, having paid little attention to them before. As he gazed intently at the people who came forward to put food in his bowl, and at those milling around the houses with children at play in the dirt, he experienced an extraordinary sense of love and compassion for them all. The whole village appeared to be especially bright and cheerful that day, with smiling faces beaming at him as people saw him come.

A Heart Released

Upon return at his mountain retreat, his heart felt replete with Dhamma, while his body felt fully satisfied even though he had yet to eat. Neither body nor *citta* was the least bit hungry. Nonetheless, he forced himself to eat for the body's sake, since it requires nourishment to sustain its life. The food, however, appeared to have no taste. The taste of Dhamma alone permeated the whole of his body — and his heart. As the Buddha said: *The taste of Dhamma surpasses all other tastes.*[16]

Eager to hear Dhamma, all the *devas* came to visit Ācariya Mun the following night. Both terrestrial *devas* and celestial *devas* arrived in groups, hailing from nearly every direction. Each group described the amazing radiance caused by the incredible power of his Dhamma the previous night. They compared it to a magnificent tremor that passed through all the celestial abodes in the vast realms of all the world systems. This tremor was accompanied by a fantastic incandescence that rendered the length and breadth of the upper and lower realms ineffably translucent. They told him:

"Those of us with intuitive knowledge were able to see unobstructed throughout the entire universe due to the luminous quality of the Dhamma pouring forth from your person, venerable sir. Its brilliance was far more radiant than the light of a hundred or even a thousand suns. It is truly unbearable to think that there were those who missed seeing such a wonder. Only humans and animals, living futile earthbound existences, could be so incredibly blind and unperceptive as to have been unaware of last night's splendor. *Devas* everywhere were so stunned, astonished, and utterly amazed that they let out an emphatic exclamation of approval to express their exultation at the perfection of your achievement. If it were not such an absolutely amazing achievement, how could knowledge of it have been so widespread?

"You, venerable sir, are a person of saintly virtue, majestic power, and vast influence, capable of being a refuge to a great number of beings in numerous realms of existence. All will be able to find blessed comfort in the shadow of your greatness. Beings of every class — be they humans, *devas*, or *brahmas*, living underwater, on land, or in the air — are rarely fortunate enough to encounter such perfection. We *devas* consider ourselves especially blessed to have met you, venerable sir, having the precious opportunity to pay our respects to you and to receive your beneficent teaching. We are grateful to you for expounding the Dhamma to brighten our hearts, leading us on the path of practice so that we can gradually become aware of how to improve ourselves."

When the assemblies of *devas* finally returned to their respective realms, Ācariya Mun began to reflect on the tremendous difficulties he had experienced in his effort to realize this Dhamma. Because his practice had entailed such exceptional hardship, he regarded it as *Dhamma at the threshold of death.* Had he not come so close to death, while struggling to reach freedom from *dukkha*, then surely he would never have attained that freedom.

The Spiritual Partner

Sitting in meditation after his final attainment, Ācariya Mun recalled a certain personal matter from his past — one which he had not taken much interest in before. Here I would like to tell a story relevant to Ācariya Mun's past. I feel it would be a shame to leave out such an intriguing story, especially as this type of relationship may be following every one of you like a shadow, even though you are unaware of it. Should the story be deemed in any way unseemly, please blame the author for not being properly circumspect. As you may already have guessed, this is a private matter that was discussed only by Ācariya Mun and his inner circle of disciples. I have tried to suppress the urge to write about it here, but the more I tried to suppress it, the stronger this urge became. So I finally gave in and, after writing it down, the urge gradually subsided. I must confess that I'm at fault here, but I hope the reader forgives me. Hopefully, it will provide everyone, caught in the perpetual cycle of birth and death, something worthwhile to think about.

This story concerns Ācariya Mun's longtime spiritual partner.[17] Ācariya Mun said that in previous lives he and his spiritual partner had both made a solemn vow to work together toward the attainment of Buddhahood. During the years prior to his final attainment, she occasionally came to visit him while he was in *samādhi*. On those occasions, he gave her a brief Dhamma talk, then sent her away. She always appeared to him as a disembodied consciousness. Unlike beings from most realms of existence, she had no discernible form. When he inquired about her formless state, she replied that she was so worried about him she had not yet decided to take up existence in any specific realm. She feared that he would forget their relationship — their mutual resolve to attain Buddhahood in the future. So out of concern, and a sense of disappointment, she felt compelled to come and check on him from time to time. Ācariya Mun told her then that he had already given up that vow, resolving instead to practice for Nibbāna in this lifetime. He had no wish to be born again, which was equivalent to carrying all the misery he had suffered in past lives indefinitely into the future.

Although she had never revealed her feelings, she remained worried about their relationship, and her longing for him never waned. So once in a long while she paid him a visit. But on this occasion, it was Ācariya Mun who thought of her, being concerned about her plight, since they had gone through so many hardships together in previous lives. Contemplating this affair after his attainment, it occurred to him that he would like to meet her so they could reach a new understanding. He wanted to explain matters to her, and thus remove any lingering doubts or anxieties regarding their former partnership. Late that very night and soon after this thought occurred to him, his spiritual partner arrived in her familiar formless state.

Ācariya Mun began by asking her about her present realm of existence. He wanted to know why she had no discernible form like beings from other celestial realms, and what exactly was her present condition. The formless being answered that she lived in one of the minor ethereal states of being in the vast sentient universe. She reiterated that she was waiting in that realm because of anxiety concerning him. Having become aware of his desire to meet her, she came to him that night.

Ordinarily, she didn't dare to visit him very often. Though sincerely wanting to see him, she always felt shy and hesitant. In truth, her visits were in no way damaging to either of them for they were not of such a nature as to be harmful. But still, her long-standing affection for him made her hesitant about coming. Ācariya Mun had also told her not to visit too often, for although not harmful, such visits could nevertheless become an emotional impediment, thus slowing his progress. The heart being very sensitive by nature, it could well be affected by subtle emotional attachments, which could then interfere with the practice of meditation. Convinced that this was true, she seldom came to visit him.

She was quite aware that he had severed his connection to birth and death, including former friends and relatives — and of course the spiritual partner who was counting on him — with no lingering regrets whatsoever. After all, it was an event that had a dramatic effect throughout the world systems. But rather than rejoice with delight, as she would have done in the past when they were together, this time she felt slighted, prompting an unorthodox reaction. She thought instead that he was being irresponsible, neglecting to consider the loyal spiritual companion who had shared his suffering, struggling together with him through so many lifetimes. She felt devastated now, left alone in misfortune, clutching *dukkha* but unable to let go. He had already gone beyond *dukkha*, leaving her behind to endure the burden of suffering. The more she thought about it, the more she felt like one bereft of wisdom who, nonetheless, wanted to reach up to touch the moon and the stars. In the end, she fell back to earth clutching her misery, unable to find a way out of such grievous misfortune.

Despondent, hapless being that she was, and struggling to endure her misery, she pleaded with him for assistance: "I am desperately disappointed. Where can I possibly find happiness? I so want to reach up and touch the moon and the stars in the sky! It's just terrible, and so painful. You yourself are like the moon and the stars up in the sky shining brightly in every direction. Having established yourself in Dhamma, your existence is never bleak, never dreary. You're so completely content and your aura radiates throughout every part of the universe. If I am still fortunate enough, please kindly show me the way of Dhamma. Please help me bring forth the bright, pure knowledge of wisdom,[18] releasing me quickly from the cycle of repeated birth and death, to follow you in the attainment of Nibbāna so that I will not have to endure this agony much longer. May this vow be strong enough to produce the results my heart desires, allowing me to attain the grace of enlightenment as soon as possible."

Convulsed with sobs of anguish, such was the fervent plea of that sorrowful formless being as she expressed her hopes of gaining enlightenment.

Ācariya Mun replied that his intention in wishing to see her was not to elicit regrets about the past: "People who wish each other well should not think in that way. Haven't you practiced the four *brahma-vihāras: mettā, karuṇā, muditā,* and *upekkhā?*[19]

The formless spirit replied: "I have practiced them for so long that I can't help thinking about the closeness we once shared practicing them together. When a person saves only himself, as you have, it is quite natural for those left behind to be disappointed. I'm in misery because I have been abandoned without any concern for my welfare. I still can't see any possibility of easing my pain."

He cautioned her: "Whether practicing on your own or in concert with others, goodness is developed for the purpose of reducing anxiety and suffering within yourself, not for increasing them until, being agitated, you become all upset. Isn't that right?"

"Yes, but the tendency of people with *kilesas* is to somehow muddle through, not knowing which path is the right one for a smooth, safe passage. We don't know if what we are doing is right or wrong, or whether the result will be happiness or suffering. We know the pain in our hearts, but we don't know the way out of it. So we are left to fret about our misfortune, as you see me doing now."

Ācariya Mun said that the formless spirit was adamant in her complaints about him. She accused him of making his escape alone, showing no pity for her — she who for so long had struggled together with him to go beyond *dukkha.* She complained that he had made no effort to assist her so that she too could gain release from suffering.

He tried to console her: "When two people eat food together at the same table, inevitably one will be full before the other. It's not possible for both to be fully satiated at the same moment. Take the case of the Lord Buddha and his former spouse, Yasodharā. Although for many ages they had jointly developed goodness of all kinds, the Lord Buddha was the first to transcend *dukkha,* returning then to teach his former spouse so that later she also crossed over to the other shore. You should consider this lesson carefully and learn from it, instead of complaining about the person who's right now trying his best to find a way to help you. I am earnestly searching for a means to help you cross over, yet you accuse me of being heartless and irresponsible. Such thoughts are very inappropriate. They will merely increase the discomfort for both of us. You should change your attitude, following the example of the Lord Buddha's former spouse — an excellent example for everyone, and one giving rise to true happiness.

"My reason for meeting you is to assist you, not to drive you away. I have always supported your development in Dhamma. To say that I have abandoned you and no longer care for your welfare is simply not true. My advice to you emanates from a heart whose loving kindness and compassion are absolutely pure. If you follow this advice, practicing it to the best of your ability, I will rejoice in your progress. And should you receive completely satisfactory results, I will rest contented in equanimity.[20]

"Our original aspiration to achieve Buddhahood was made for the express purpose of crossing beyond the cycle of rebirth. My subsequent desire to attain the status of *sāvaka*[21] instead, was actually a desire aimed toward the same goal: a state free of *kilesas* and *āsava*,[22] free of all *dukkha*, the Supreme Happiness, Nibbāna. As I've followed the righteous path through many different lives, including my present status as a Buddhist monk, I have always done my utmost to keep in touch with you. Throughout this time, I have taught you as best I could with the immense loving compassion that I feel for you. Never was there a moment when I thought of forsaking you to seek only my own salvation – my thoughts were constantly full of concern, full of sympathy for you. I have always hoped to free you from the misery of birth in *saṁsāra*, leading you in the direction of Nibbāna.

"Your abnormal reaction – feeling offended because you suppose that I've abandoned you without any concern for your well-being – is of no benefit to either of us. From now on, you should refrain from such thinking. Don't allow these thoughts to arise and trample all over your heart, for they will bring only endless misery in their wake – a result incompatible with my objective, as I strive with heartfelt compassion to help you out.

"Escaping without a care? Where have I escaped to? And who is it I don't care about? At this moment I am doing my utmost to give you every possible assistance. Doesn't everything I've taught you arise solely out of such compassionate concern as I am showing you right now? The constant encouragement I have provided comes straight from a heart full to the brim with a compassion that exceeds all the water in the great oceans, a compassion that pours forth unsparingly, without concern that it might run dry. Please understand that helping you has always been my intention and accept this Dhamma teaching that I offer. If you just trust me and practice accordingly, you will experience the fruits of inner happiness for yourself.

"From the day I first ordained as a monk, I have sincerely practiced the way of Dhamma — never for a moment have I thought ill of anyone. My motive in wanting to meet with you was not to deceive you, or cause you harm, but to assist you as best I can with all my heart. If you refuse to trust me, it will be difficult for you to find anyone else so worthy of your complete faith. You said you were aware of the universe trembling that night. That trembling, do you think it was caused by the 'Dhamma of deception' arising in the world? Is that why you're so hesitant about taking to heart the advice I have so graciously offered you? If you understand that Dhamma is indeed the Dhamma of Truth, then you should consider the trembling of the universe that night as a decisive factor in your faith, and take comfort in the fact that you still have great resources of merit. You are still able to listen to a timely exposition of Dhamma, even though your birth in that formless realm of existence should render such a thing impossible. I consider it my good fortune to be able to teach you now. You should feel proud of your own good fortune in having someone to come and rescue you from the hopeless gloom that your misguided thinking has caused. If you can think positively like this, I shall be very pleased. Such thinking will not allow *dukkha* to bind you so tightly that you can't find a way out. It won't allow Dhamma to be seen as something mundane, or compassionate concern to be seen as something malevolent."

As she listened to Ācariya Mun present these reasoned arguments with such loving compassion, his spiritual partner felt as though she was being bathed in a stream of celestial water. Gradually she regained her composure. Enchanted by his discourse, her mind soon became calm, her manner respectful.

When he finished speaking, she admitted her mistake: "My affection and my hopeless yearning for you have caused so much trouble. I believed that you had discarded me, going your own way, which left me feeling neglected. I became terribly disappointed. I couldn't stop thinking how useless and rejected I felt, with no one to turn to. But now that I have received the light of Dhamma, my heart is cool and contented. I can now put down the burden of misery that I've been carrying, for your Dhamma is like a divine nectar washing over my heart, cleansing it and making it bright. Please forgive me whatever wrong I have done to you through my ignorance. I am determined to be more careful in the future — never shall I make such a mistake again."

When she finished speaking, Ācariya Mun advised her to take birth in a more appropriate realm of existence, telling her to cease worrying about the past. Respectfully, she promised to follow his advice, then made one final request: "Once I have taken birth in a suitable realm, may I come and listen to your advice as before? Please give me your blessing for this." Once Ācariya Mun had granted her request, she immediately vanished.

The formless spirit having departed, Ācariya Mun's *citta* withdrew from *samādhi*. It was nearly five a.m. and almost light. He had not rested the entire night. Having begun sitting in *samādhi* at around eight p.m., he had spoken with the formless spirit for many hours into the night.

Not long afterwards, the same spirit came to visit him again. This time she came in the bodily form of a beautiful *deva*, although in deference to the especially revered monk she was visiting, she was not adorned in the ornamental style customary of the *devas*.

Upon arriving, she explained to him her new situation: "After listening to your explanation, which removed all my doubts and relieved me of the misery that was tormenting me, I came to birth in the *Tāvatiṁsa* heavenly realm — a celestial sphere full of delightful pleasures, all of which I now enjoy as a result of the goodness we performed together as human beings. Although I experience this pleasant existence as a consequence of my own good deeds, I can't help remembering that you, venerable sir, were the one who initially encouraged me to do good. On my own, I would never have had the wisdom capable of accomplishing this to my complete satisfaction.

"Feeling fortunate enough to be reborn in heavenly splendor, I am wholly contented, and no longer angry or resentful. As I reflect back on the immense kindness you've always shown me, it becomes apparent to me how important it is for us to choose discretely in our lives — concerning everything from our work to our food to our friends and companions, both male and female. Such discretion is crucial for leading a smooth, untroubled existence. This is especially true when choosing a spouse to depend on, for better or for worse. Choosing a spouse merits special attention, for we share everything with that person — even our very breath. Every happiness and every sorrow along the way will necessarily affect both parties.

"Those who have a good partner, even though they may be inadequate in terms of their intelligence, their temperament, or their behavior, are still blest to have someone who can guide and encourage them in dealing with all their affairs — both their secular affairs, which promote peace and stability in the family, and their spiritual affairs, which nourish the heart. All other matters will benefit as well, so they won't feel they are groping blindly in the dark, never certain how these matters will turn out. Each partner being a good person, they compliment each other to create a virtual paradise within the family, allowing everyone to remain peaceful, contented, and free from strife at all times. Always cheerful, such a household is undisturbed by temperamental outbursts. All members contribute in creating this atmosphere: each is calm and composed, firmly established in the principles of reason — instead of just doing whatever they like, which is contrary to the very moral principles that insure their continued peace and contentment. Married couples work together to construct their own future. Together they create good and bad *kamma*. They create happiness and misery, virtue and evil, heaven and hell, from the very beginning of their relationship onwards to the present and into the future — an unbroken continuum.

"Being blessed with the chance to accompany you through many lives, I've come to realize this in my own situation. By your guidance, venerable sir, I have made goodness an integral part of my character. You have always steered me safely through every danger, never letting me stray in the direction of evil or disgrace. Consequently, I've remained a good person during all those lifetimes. I cannot tell you how deeply moved I am by all the kindness you've shown me. I now realize the harm caused by my past mistakes. Please kindly forgive my transgressions so that no lingering animosity remains between us."

Assenting to the *deva's* request, Ācariya Mun forgave her. He then gave her an inspiring talk, encouraging her to perfect herself spiritually. When he had finished, she paid him her respects, moved off a short distance, and floated blissfully up into the sky.

Some of the resentful comments she made when she was still a formless spirit were too strange to record here, so I've been unable to recount every detail of their conversation; and for that I ask your forgiveness. I am not really that satisfied with what has been written here either, but I feel that without it a thought-provoking story would have been left out.

The Most Exalted Appreciation

On the nights subsequent to Ācariya Mun's attainment of *vimutti*, a number of Buddhas, accompanied by their Arahant disciples, came to congratulate him on his *vimuttidhamma*. One night, a certain Buddha, accompanied by tens of thousands of Arahant disciples, came to visit; the next night, he was visited by another Buddha who was accompanied by hundreds of thousands of Arahant disciples. Each night a different Buddha came to express his appreciation, accompanied by a different number of Arahant disciples. Ācariya Mun stated that the number of accompanying Arahant disciples varied according to each Buddha's relative accumulation of merit — a factor that differed from one Buddha to the next. The actual number of Arahant disciples accompanying each Buddha did not represent the total number of his Arahant disciples; they merely demonstrated the relative levels of accumulated merit and perfection that each individual Buddha possessed. Among the Arahant disciples accompanying each of those Buddhas were quite a few young novices.[23] Ācariya Mun was skeptical about this, so he reflected on it and realized that the term "Arahant" does not apply exclusively to monks. Novices whose hearts are completely pure are also Arahant disciples, so their presence did not raise issue with the term in any way.

Most of the Buddhas who came to show their appreciation to Ācariya Mun addressed him in much the following manner:

"I, the Tathāgata, am aware that you have escaped from the harmful effects of that monstrous suffering which you endured in the prison of saṁsāra,[24] so I have come to express my appreciation. This prison is enormous, and quite impregnable. It is full of seductive temptations which so enslave those who are unwary that it is extremely difficult for anyone to break free. Of the vast number of people living in the world, hardly anyone is concerned enough to think of looking for a way out of dukkha that perpetually torments their bodies and minds. They are like sick people who cannot be bothered to take medicine. Even though medicines are plentiful, they are of no use to a person who refuses to take them.

"Buddha-Dhamma is like medicine. Beings in saṁsāra are afflicted with the painful, oppressive disease of kilesas, which causes endless suffering. Inevitably, this disease can be cured only by the medicine of Dhamma. Left

uncured, it will drag living beings through an endless succession of births and deaths, all of them bound up with physical and mental pain. Although Dhamma exists everywhere throughout the whole universe, those who are not really interested in properly availing themselves of its healing qualities are unable to take advantage of it.

"Dhamma exists in its own natural way. Beings in saṁsāra spin around, like wheels, through the pain and suffering of each successive life — in the natural way of saṁsāra. They have no real prospect of ever seeing an end to dukkha. And there is no way to help them unless they are willing to help themselves by holding firmly to the principles of Dhamma, earnestly trying to put them into practice. No matter how many Buddhas become enlightened, or how extensive their teachings are, only those willing to take the prescribed medicine will benefit.

"The Dhamma, taught by all the Buddhas, is invariably the same: to renounce evil and do good. There exists no Dhamma teaching more exceptional than this: For even the most exceptional kilesas in the hearts of living beings are not so exceptional that they can transcend the power of Dhamma taught by all the Buddhas. This Dhamma in itself is sufficient to eradicate every kind of kilesa there is — unless, of course, those practicing it allow themselves to be defeated by their kilesas, and so conclude that Dhamma must be worthless.

"By nature, kilesas have always resisted the power of Dhamma. Consequently, people who defer to the kilesas are people who disregard Dhamma. They are unwilling to practice the way, for they view it as something difficult to do, a waste of the time they could otherwise spend enjoying themselves — despite the harm such pleasures cause them. A wise, far-sighted person should not retreat into a shell, like a turtle in a pot of boiling water — it is sure to die because it can't find a way to escape. The world is a cauldron, boiling with the consuming heat of the kilesas. Earthly beings of every description, every where, must endure this torment, for there is no safe place to hide, no way to elude this conflagration burning in their own hearts — right there where the dukkha is.

"You have seen the truly genuine Tathāgata, haven't you? What is the genuine Tathāgata? The genuine Tathāgata is simply that purity of heart you have just realized. The bodily form in which I now appear is merely a manifestation of relative, conventional reality.[25] This form does not represent the true Buddha, or the true Arahant; it is just our conventional bodily appearance."

Ācariya Mun replied that he had no doubts about the true nature of the Buddha and the Arahants. What still puzzled him was: how could the Buddha and the Arahants, having attained *anupādisesa-nibbāna*[26] without any remaining trace of relative, conventional reality, still appear in bodily form. The Buddha explained this matter to him:

"*If those who have attained anupādisesa-nibbāna wish to interact with other Arahants who have purified their hearts but still possess a physical, mundane body, they must temporarily assume a mundane form in order to make contact. However, if all concerned have already attained anupādisesa-nibbāna without any remaining trace of relative, conventional reality, then the use of conventional constructs is completely unnecessary. So it is necessary to appear in a conventional form when dealing with conventional reality, but when the conventional world has been completely transcended, no such problem exists.*

"*All Buddhas know events concerning the past and the future through nimittas that symbolize for them the original conventional realities of the occurrences in question.*[27] *For instance, when a Buddha wishes to know about the lives of the Buddhas who preceded him, he must take the nimitta of each Buddha, and the particular circumstances in which he lived, as a device leading directly to that knowledge. If something exists beyond the relative world of conventional reality, that being vimutti, then there can be no symbol representing it. Because of that, knowledge about past Buddhas depends on mundane conventions to serve as a common basis for understanding, as my present visit illustrates. It is necessary that I and all of my Arahant disciples appear in our original mundane forms so that others, like yourself, have a means of determining what our appearance was like. If we did not appear in this form, no one would be able to perceive us.*[28]

"*On occasions when it is necessary to interact with conventional reality, vimutti must be made manifest by the use of suitable conventional means. In the case of pure vimutti, as when two purified cittas interact with one another, there exists only the essential quality of knowing — which is impossible to elaborate on in any way. So when we want to reveal the nature of complete purity, we have to bring in conventional devices to help us portray the experience of vimutti. We can say that vimutti is a 'self-luminous state devoid of all nimittas representing the ultimate happiness', for instance, but these are just widely-used, conventional metaphors. One who clearly knows it in his heart cannot possibly have doubts about vimutti. Since its true characteristics are impossible to convey, vimutti is inconceivable in a relative,* conventional sense. *Vimutti manifesting conventionally and vimutti existing in its original state are, however, both known with absolute certainty by the Arahant. This includes both vimutti manifesting itself by means of conventional constructs under certain circumstances, and vimutti existing in its original, unconditioned state. Did you ask me about this matter because you were in doubt, or simply as a point of conversation?"*

"I have no doubts about the conventional aspects of all the Buddhas, or the unconditioned aspects. My inquiry was a conventional way of showing respect. Even without a visit from you and your Arahant disciples, I would have no doubts as to where the true Buddha, Dhamma, and Sangha lie. It is my clear conviction that *whoever sees the Dhamma sees the Tathāgata.* This means that the Lord Buddha, the Dhamma, and the Sangha each denote the very same natural state of absolute purity, completely free of conventional reality, collectively known as the Three Jewels."

"*I, the Tathāgata, did not ask you that question thinking you were in doubt, but rather as a friendly greeting.*" [29]

On those occasions when the Buddhas and their Arahant disciples came to visit, only the Buddhas addressed Ācariya Mun. None of the disciples accompanying them spoke a word as they sat quietly composed, listening in a manner worthy of the highest respect. Even the small novices, looking more adorable than venerable, showed the same quiet composure. Some of them were quite young, between the ages of nine and twelve, and Ācariya Mun found them truly endearing.

Ordinarily, the average person would see only bright-eyed, adorable children. Being unaware that they were Arahants, one would most probably be tempted to fool around, reaching out playfully to stroke their heads, without realizing the impertinence of doing so. When Ācariya Mun spoke about this, I thought mischievously that I would probably be the first to succumb to the urge to reach out and play with them, despite the consequences. Afterwards, I could always beg their forgiveness.

Ācariya Mun said that, although they were young novices, their behavior was very mature. They were as calm, composed, and impressive to see as all the other Arahant disciples. In short, all the Arahant monks and novices who accompanied each Buddha exhibited impeccable behavior worthy of the highest respect. They were neat, orderly, and pleasing to the eye — like immaculately folded robes.

Ācariya Mun had always been curious to know how walking and sitting meditation were practiced at the time of the Buddha. He also had questions about the proper etiquette to be used between junior and senior monks, and whether it was necessary for a monk to wear his formal robes while doing meditation. When such questions arose in his mind, invariably one of the Buddhas, or an Arahant disciple, appeared to him in *samādhi* and demonstrated how these practices were originally performed in the Buddha's day. For example, Ācariya Mun was curious to know the correct manner of practicing walking meditation so as to show proper respect for Dhamma. A Buddha or an Arahant then appeared, demonstrating in detail how to place the hands, how to walk, and how to remain self-composed. Sometimes, these demonstrations included explicit instructions; at other times, the methods were demonstrated by example. They also showed him such things as the proper way to sit in *samādhi*, including the most suitable direction to face and the best seated posture to assume.

Ācariya Mun had some strange things to say about how junior and senior monks showed their respect for each other. Ācariya Mun wanted to know how monks at the time of the Buddha conducted themselves with appropriate respect toward one another.[30] Shortly after this thought arose, the vision of a Buddha and many Arahant disciples appeared to him. The Arahants were of all different ages — some were young, others older, a few being so old that their hair had turned completely white. A considerable number of small novices of all ages accompanied them. However, the Buddha and his disciples did not arrive together — each Arahant arrived individually. Those arriving first sat in the front, while those arriving later sat further away — without regard for seniority. Even those novices who arrived earlier sat ahead of the monks who arrived later. Finally the last monk, a very elderly man, arrived to take the last available seat — way in the back; but the others showed no sign of shame or embarrassment. Even the Buddha himself sat down in whichever seat was available at the time he arrived.

Seeing this, Ācariya Mun was somewhat incredulous. Could it be that the monks at the time of the Buddha did not respect seniority? It was definitely not an inspiring sight. How could the Buddha and his disciples proclaim the *sāsana* and then expect people to have faith in it when the *sāsana's* leader and his closest disciples behaved in such an indiscriminate fashion? Instantly, the answer arose in his heart without the Buddha and his disciples having offered any comment: This was an instance of pure *vimuttidhamma* devoid of any trace of relative, conventional reality — so there was no fixed order of propriety. They were demonstrating the true nature of Absolute Purity,[31] being perfectly equal for all, irrespective of conventional designations such as young and old, or high and low. From the Lord Buddha on down to the youngest Arahant novice, all were equal with respect to their state of purity. What Ācariya Mun had witnessed was a conclusive indicator that all the Arahant monks and novices were equally pure.

This having been made clear to him, he wondered how they deferred to each other in the conventional world. No sooner had this thought arisen, than the vision of the Buddha and the Arahants seated before him changed. Whereas before they had been sitting together in no special order, now the Buddha sat at the head of the assembly, while the small novices, previously in the front, sat in the last seats. It was an impressive sight — worthy of the highest respect. At that moment Ācariya Mun clearly understood that this image represented the traditional way in which monks at the time of the Buddha showed each other respect. Even Arahants who were junior in rank were obliged to respect those of their seniors who were practicing correctly but still had *kilesas* in their hearts.[32] The Buddha then elaborated on this theme:

"The Tathāgata's monks must live in mutual respect and friendship, as though they were all one single entity. This does not mean that they are friendly in a worldly way, but rather that they are friendly in the equal, unbiased way of Dhamma. When my monks live together, even in large numbers, they never quarrel or display arrogance. Monks who do not respect their fellows according to the principles of the Teaching and the Discipline of the Buddha, are not worthy of being called the Tathāgata's monks. Even though those monks may imitate the disciples of the Buddha, they are merely impostors making false claims. As long as monks respect each other according to the principles of the Teaching and the Discipline — which substitute for the Buddha himself — and never violate these principles, then wherever those monks live, whenever they were ordained, whatever their race, status, or nationality, they remain true disciples of the Tathāgata. And whoever is a true follower of the Tathāgata must surely see the end of dukkha one day."

The Buddha and all his disciples vanished instantly the moment he finished speaking. As for Ācariya Mun, all his doubts had vanished the moment that vision appeared to him so clearly.

Concerning Ācariya Mun's doubts about the necessity of wearing the formal robes when doing meditation: one of the Arahant disciples appeared to him, demonstrating how it was unnecessary to wear them every time. He personally demonstrated when and how sitting and walking meditation should be practiced while wearing the formal robes, as well as the instances when it was unnecessary to wear them. Every aspect of a monk's robes was made clear to him, including the correct color for a monk's three principal robes. He showed Ācariya Mun ochre-colored robes that were dyed from the heartwood of the jackfruit tree in three different shades — light, medium, and dark brown.[33]

Careful consideration of these episodes is enough to convince us that Ācariya Mun always had sound, acknowledged precedents for the way he practiced. He never jeopardized his vocation by merely guessing about things he was unsure of. Consequently, his practice was always smooth, consistent, and irreproachable from beginning to end. Certainly, it would be hard to find his equal nowadays. Those adopting his mode of practice are bound to exhibit a gracefulness befitting disciples of such a fine teacher, and their own practice is sure to progress very smoothly. However, those who prefer to flout convention are like ghosts without a cemetery, or orphans without a family. Having forsaken their teacher they may well modify the practice to suit their own opinions. Ācariya Mun possessed a mysterious, ineffable inner compass to direct him in these matters, one which none of his disciples could ever match.

Ācariya Mun

Dhutanga ācariyas of Ācariya Mun's lineage; including, on the top row
from left to right: Ācariya Fan, Ācariya Khao, Chao Khun Dhammachedi,
Ācariya Awn, and Ācariya Mahā Boowa.

From left to right: Ācariya Fan, Ācariya Mahā Pin, and Ācariya Singh.

Chao Khun Dhammachedi (seated center), Ācariya Khao and Ācariya Fan
(seated left on second row), Ācariya Mahā Thong Sak and Ācariya Kongma
(seated right on second row), Ācariya Mahā Boowa (standing far right).

First and second generation disciples of Ācariya Mun

4

The Chiang Mai Years

Venerable Ācariya Mun wandered *dhutanga* in the northern province of Chiang Mai for many years, spending the annual rains retreat in a different location each year. He spent one rains retreat in each of the following places: Ban Chom Taeng in the Mae Rim district, Ban Pong in the Mae Taeng district, Ban Kloi in the Phrao district, Ban Pu Phraya in the Mae Suai district, and Mae Thong Thip in the Mae Sai district of Chiang Rai province. He also spent rains retreats at Wat Chedi Luang in the city of Chiang Mai; in the mountains of Mae Suai district; and in the neighboring province of Uttaradit. Outside of the retreat period, he wandered extensively through the provinces of Chiang Mai and Chiang Rai for a total of eleven years, making it impossible to give a strict chronological account of all the village communities he passed through on his travels. In the following account, I shall mention by name only those villages having a direct bearing on the story as it unfolds.

Except for his stay at Wat Chedi Luang monastery, Ācariya Mun always wandered in solitude, staying in the wilderness, mountainous areas where danger was ever-present. It is the exceptional nature of his wandering *dhutanga* practice and the many insights into Dhamma, that arose along the way, which make Ācariya Mun's life story so significant. This strange and wonderful tale is unique among the stories of all the *dhutanga* monks who wandered alone. Ordinarily, such a lifestyle is believed to be bleak and lonely. Living in an inhospitable environment, oppressed by danger, and unable to eat or sleep normally, the sense of fear can be stifling. But Ācariya Mun was perfectly content living a solitary existence. He found it conducive to his efforts to remove the *kilesas* from his heart, having always relied on the method of striving in seclusion to accomplish that goal.

It was only later that other monks began to seek him out. For example, Ācariya Thet of Tha Bo district in the province of Nong Khai, Ācariya Saan, and Ācariya Khao of Wat Tham Klong Phen monastery lived with him for short periods of time. After training them for a while in the way of practice, he sent them off alone to find secluded places in sparsely populated forests where villages were far apart — perhaps at the foot of a mountain, perhaps on a mountain ridge. Villages in that region were quite small, some consisting of only 4 or 5 houses, others 9 to 10 houses — just enough to support an almsround from one day to the next.

The *kammaṭṭhāna* monks who followed Ācariya Mun during that period were extremely resolute, fearless individuals. They constantly showed a willingness to put their lives on the line in their search for Dhamma. Therefore, Ācariya Mun preferred to send them to live in places teeming with wild animals, such as tigers, for such places tended to automatically dispel complacency and stimulate mindfulness and wisdom, boosting the strength of the *citta* faster than could otherwise be expected.

Ācariya Mun himself thrived comfortably in the peace and quiet of these virtually unpopulated mountain regions. Though human contact was scarce, communication with *devas*, *brahmas*, *nāgas*, and other spirits from various realms of existence was normal for him — much in the same way that a person knowing foreign languages regularly communicates with people from other countries. Due to his long-standing fluency in this type of communication, his time spent living in mountainous regions was of special benefit to celestial beings.

It was also beneficial to the local hill tribes, who tended to be straightforward, honest, even-tempered people. Once they came to know his character and to appreciate his Dhamma, they revered him so much that they were willing to sacrifice their lives for him. Hill tribes and forest peoples such as the Ekor, Khamu, Museur, and Hmong are generally considered to be rather scruffy, unattractive, primitive people. But Ācariya Mun found them to be handsome, clean-looking people who were courteous and well-behaved, always treating their elders and local leaders with great respect. They maintained a good community spirit, and there were hardly any troublemakers in their villages back then. They placed so much trust in their elders, especially the village headman, that when he spoke everyone paid attention and obediently complied with his wishes. And they were not opinionated, making them easy to teach.

Those so-called wild, uncivilized jungles were actually inhabited by good, honest, moral people. There, unlike in the jungles of human civilization, theft and robbery were virtually unknown. Jungles consisting of trees and wild animals aren't nearly so dangerous as the civilized jungles of human society — places teeming with all kinds of perilous *kilesas* where greed, hatred, and delusion are constantly on the assault. They inflict deep internal wounds, gradually eroding a person's physical and mental health until the damage becomes acute. Such wounds are extremely difficult to treat. In any case, most people can't even be bothered to look for suitable care. Though such *kilesa*-inflicted wounds tend to fester menacingly, those who are afflicted usually neglect their injuries, hoping they will somehow heal by themselves.

This sort of *kilesa*-infested jungle exists in the hearts of all human beings — men, women, monks, and novices — without distinction. Ācariya Mun said that he used life in the wilds as a means of cutting back this wild inner jungle, which otherwise could be so savage and disturbing that the heart never experienced any peace and quiet. At least by living alone in the wilderness he could quell the *kilesas* enough to feel comfortable and relaxed. He felt that this was the only sensible way to use our natural human intelligence, and thus not squander the good fortune inherent in human birth.

Monks who sought out Ācariya Mun in the wilderness tended to be especially courageous and self-sacrificing, so he trained them in ways that suited their uncompromising attitude and the harshness of their environment. Training methods that he found appropriate for himself were suitable for them as well. If necessary, they were willing to die to achieve their goal. As long as they lived, they were dedicated to the struggle for Dhamma in order to transcend the world and end the perpetual cycle of birth and suffering.

The training methods that Ācariya Mun employed with the monks he encountered in Chiang Mai differed from those he previously used. They were far more rigorous and uncompromising. The monks who came to train under his guidance were mostly resolute individuals. They paid scrupulous attention to the *kilesas* arising within themselves in an attempt to reduce their strength and choke them off. They were not concerned that his admonitions might be too harsh or too intense. In fact, the intensity of his tone increased as the Dhamma under discussion became more profound. Those focusing on a certain level of tranquility were reinforced in that calm state, while those concentrating on investigative analysis followed every nuance of his reasoning to discover new techniques for developing wisdom.

The discourses that Ācariya Mun delivered to his students in Chiang Mai were especially profound because his knowledge of Dhamma was by then complete. Another factor was the high degree of understanding that the monks who sought his guidance already possessed. They were absolutely determined to strive for higher and higher levels of Dhamma until they reached the ultimate goal. Besides his usual admonitions, Ācariya Mun also had some very unusual techniques for thwarting the monks whose thoughts tended to go astray. He used these techniques to trap 'thieves' and catch them in the act. But these were no ordinary thieves. The thieves that Ācariya Mun caught lurked inside the hearts of monks whose thoughts liked to steal away to everything imaginable — in the usual way of the *kilesas*.

A STRANGE INCIDENT occurred while Ācariya Mun was staying in the mountains of Chiang Mai — an incident that should never have happened in the circle of *kammaṭṭhāna* monks. I hope you will forgive me for recounting what I heard. I feel it may be a thought-provoking lesson for anyone who finds himself in a similar situation. This story was known exclusively within the inner circle of Ācariya Mun's senior disciples, and Ācariya Mun's own assessment of the whole matter was crucial. A certain senior monk living with him at the time related the story as follows:

One afternoon he and another monk went to bathe in a rock pool located near a path leading to the fields of the local village, which was quite a long distance away. While they were bathing, a group of young women happened to pass by on their way to work in the fields — something that had never before occurred while they were bathing. When the other monk spied them walking past, his mind immediately wobbled, his mindfulness failing him as the fires of lust flared up and began smoldering inside him. Try as he might, he couldn't manage to reverse this situation. While fearful that Ācariya Mun might become aware of his predicament, he was equally afraid that he might disgrace himself. From that moment on, his mind was constantly fluctuating as he desperately tried to come to grips with the problem. Nothing like this had ever happened to him before, and he felt miserable about it.

That same night Ācariya Mun, investigating on his own, became aware that this monk had encountered something unexpected and was consequently very distraught, caught between feelings of infatuation and apprehension. The monk struggled through a sleepless night, trying to resolve the dilemma. The next morning Ācariya Mun did not say anything about it, for he knew that the monk was already fearful of him; confronting him would only make matters worse. When they met, the monk was so ashamed and apprehensive he was almost trembling; but Ācariya Mun just smiled amicably as though he didn't know what had happened. When it came time to go on almsround, Ācariya Mun found an excuse to address the monk.

"I can see how earnest you are in pressing on with your meditation practice, so you needn't go on almsround today. The rest of us will go, and we will share our food with you when we return. Providing food for one extra monk is hardly a problem. Go and continue your mediation practice so that the rest of us may share the merit you make as well."

He said this without looking directly at the monk, for Ācariya Mun understood the monk better than the monk understood himself. Ācariya Mun then led the others on almsround while the monk forced himself to do walking meditation. Since the problem arose due to a chance encounter and not an intentional one, it had been impossible to prevent. Realizing that, Ācariya Mun did what he could to assist him. He was well aware that the monk was doing his utmost to solve the problem; so, he was obliged to find a clever means of helping him without further upsetting his mental state.

When they returned from almsround, the monks shared their food with the monk, each putting some in his bowl. Ācariya Mun sent someone to inform the monk that he could take his meal with them or alone in his hut, whichever he preferred. Upon hearing this, the monk quickly went to eat with his fellow monks. Ācariya Mun ignored him when he arrived, but, later spoke gently to him in order to soothe his injured psyche and mitigate his sense of remorse. Although he sat with the other monks, he ate only a token amount of food so as not to appear impolite.

185

Later that day, the other monk, who had also bathed at the rock pool – the one who would later tell this story – became suspicious, being as yet unaware of the whole story. He wondered why Ācariya Mun treated that monk with a deference he had never seen before. He figured that since Ācariya Mun was being so supportive, his friend's meditation practice was undoubtedly very good. When he found the opportunity, he went to ask about his meditation. "Ācariya Mun said that you didn't have to go on almsround because you're intensifying your efforts, but he didn't indicate how good your meditation is. So, how is your meditation going? Please tell me about it."

The monk gave a wry smile. "How could my meditation be good? Ācariya Mun saw a poor, miserable soul and he's just trying to help, using his own skillful methods. That's all."

His friend persisted in attempting to get to the truth, but the monk continued to deflect his questions. Finally his friend confronted him directly. He asked, "What did you mean when you said that Ācariya Mun saw a poor, miserable soul? And how is it that he's trying to help?" Exasperated, the monk relented. "There is no need to tell Ācariya Mun about this. Anyway, he already knows me better than I know myself, so I feel fearful and ashamed in his presence. Did you notice anything unusual when we were bathing together at the rock pool yesterday?"

The other monk said that he hadn't noticed anything, except for a group of women passing by. So, the monk confessed, "That's just it. That's why I'm so miserable right now, and why Ācariya Mun wouldn't let me go on almsround this morning. He was afraid I would pass out and die right there in the village should I happened to see her again. How could my meditation be any good? Do you understand now how good the meditation of this miserable fellow is?"

The other monk was stunned. "Oh, my gosh! What is it between you and those women?"

"Nothing," answered the monk, "except blindly falling in love with one of them and having my meditation going to pieces. What appeared in its place was a beautiful image – a crazy infatuation crushing down on my heart all night long. Even now this madness continues unabated, and I just don't know what to do about it. Please, can you do something to help me?"

"You mean it still isn't any better?"

"No." The monk's voice sounded wretchedly pathetic.

"In that case, I have a suggestion. If you can't suppress this thing, then it is not prudent for you to stay here any longer — things will only get worse. I think it's better that you move away from here and find another place to do your practice. If you don't feel up to asking Ācariya Mun about this, then I will speak to him for you. I'll inform him that you wish to go look for another secluded place because you don't feel so well here. I'm sure he will immediately give his permission because he is well aware of what's happening to you. He just hasn't said anything about it yet for fear of shaming you."

The monk readily agreed. That evening his companion went to speak with Ācariya Mun, who immediately gave his consent. But there was a caustic element latent here. Ācariya Mun said rather cryptically: "A disease arising from karmic attraction is hard to cure. Contagions spread quickly when their original cause still remains." And that was all he would say on the matter. Even the monk who went to speak with him didn't understand his connotation.

Everyone kept quiet about this matter. The monk never spoke directly to Ācariya Mun about it; his friend never mentioned it to anyone else; and Ācariya Mun kept the whole thing to himself. Although fully aware of the truth of the matter they all behaved as if nothing had happened. No one spoke openly about it.

The next day the monk went to take leave of Ācariya Mun, who consented without mentioning the matter. The monk then left and went to stay near another village quite a distance away. Had this not been a true case of karmic attraction, as Ācariya Mun had hinted, then surely the monk would have been well out of danger there. But, alas for the uncertainty of karmic consequences: things turned out exactly as Ācariya Mun had suggested. Shortly after the monk left Ācariya Mun, the young woman, who shared the same karmic connection, ended up moving to the other village by a fortuitous coincidence, and their paths crossed again. This itself is very interesting, since it was most unusual for hill tribe women to stray so far from home.

Later, after Ācariya Mun and his group of monks had departed from the first village, they heard that the monk had disrobed, returning to lay life because he couldn't put up with the constant strain. His *kamma* had come full circle: he married the pretty Museur woman and settled in that village.

This was a genuine case of mutual *kamma*. Without such a karmic connection, how could it have been possible? The monk who told this story insisted that his friend became infatuated the moment he saw the woman, having never seen or spoken with her before. This was confirmed by the other monks who were living there. They lived together in the monastery the whole time, never having any occasion to get involved with the villagers. Besides that, they were living with Ācariya Mun in a place safe from such liaisons. There can be no doubt that an enduring karmic bond existed between them. The monk once told his friend that mere eye contact with her was enough to make him feel giddy and lose all presence of mind, and an irresistible passion gripped his heart so tightly he could scarcely breath. Those powerful emotions plagued him relentlessly, leaving him in such an emotional quandary that he felt completely demoralized. Realizing his predicament, he tried to escape. But fate pursued him, again casting its spell over him. And that was it – he succumbed.

Those who have never had such an experience may smile; but others who have, know that we cannot all imitate the Arahant Sundara Samudda by simply floating up and out to safety.[1] Normally, hill tribe people are not overly familiar with monks; but if *kamma* is involved, then such incidents can happen. No one is exempt from *kamma*, for *kamma* has jurisdiction over those who create it. Ācariya Mun was fully aware of this truth. Although he tried using skillful means to help the monk, the outcome was probably inevitable. For this reason, he didn't make any direct attempt to intervene. In the final analysis, in a world where everyone lives under the authority of *kamma*, matters must be allowed to take their natural course. I have included this story in the hope that it may serve as a timely reminder for anyone finding himself in a similar situation. As always, I trust you will forgive any indiscretion on my part.

PREVIOUSLY I MENTIONED Ācariya Mun's special talent for catching 'thieves', a technique for reading minds and catching stray thoughts that kept his students watchful and alert. When a *kammaṭṭhāna* monk with an especially bold, resolute character came to see him in Chiang Mai, Ācariya Mun used this teaching technique to good advantage. Unlike those less earnestly committed, these monks were not apt to react in a negative way. Being fully dedicated to the cause of Dhamma, as soon as Ācariya Mun admonished them about their faults, they were willing to do their best to rectify them. No matter how pointedly he admonished them, they did not feel ashamed or apprehensive when their mistakes were exposed.

Ācariya Mun was a consummate teacher and his message went straight to the heart of his listeners. Whether sharing his own personal knowledge or pointing out the shortcomings of his students, he was always frank and outspoken. He remained candid and impartial in his criticism with the intention of giving as much help as he possibly could. His students were in no way contemptuous. They never refused to accept the truth; nor were they conceited about their own achievements, as often happens in a group of meditators.

His Dhamma explanations were invariably adapted to the individual needs of his students, touching only on the points that were essential to the individual's level of practice. When he determined that a student was practicing correctly, he encouraged him to step up his efforts. But when he felt that someone's meditation was faulty or potentially dangerous, he pointed this out as a way of encouraging the student to abandon that practice.

For monks who went to him with doubts or questions, his explanations were unerringly right to the point; and, as far as I know, his students were never disappointed. It's safe to say that everyone who went to him with a question about meditation practice, could have expected to receive expert advice, for meditation was his field of greatest expertise. His knowledge and understanding of every aspect of meditation were unparalleled. Every facet of his Dhamma teaching benefited from his lyrical presentation, captivating the listener and demonstrating an eloquence which no one today can equal. His comments on moral virtue were engrossing to his listeners, while his discourses on the different levels of *samādhi* and wisdom were exceptional. His audience became so absorbed that, being satiated in the Dhamma they heard, their feeling of satisfaction often lasted for days thereafter.

DURING THE PERIOD when Ācariya Mun pushed himself relentlessly toward realization of the Supreme Dhamma, he lived alone in mountain caves or forest retreats. As he waged an all out assault on the *kilesas*, his efforts were directed inward at all times. Only during hours of sleep did he relax this persistent introspection. Mindfulness and wisdom were his constant companions throughout that exhaustive investigation to uproot the *kilesas*. He carried on a continuous dialogue with the *kilesas*, mentally attacking and counterattacking them with mindfulness and wisdom. His sheer determination to go beyond *dukkha* was the catalyst for these conversations, which were not rhetorical encounters. Rather, they were internal contemplations using mindfulness and wisdom to rebut the *kilesas*. No matter how they tried to evade him, no matter what tricks they used to rebuff or entangle him, Ācariya Mun used mindfulness and wisdom at each step of the way to follow their movements, and to corner and crush them into submission – until, finally, he emerged victorious. Wherever he found the *kilesas* still having the upper hand, he made an effort to upgrade his arsenal – mindfulness, wisdom, faith, and perseverance – increasing their strength with each new challenge until it exceeded that of his archenemy. Triumphant at last, as we already know, the world inside his heart shook – *maggañāṇa* had destroyed the king of the *vaṭṭa-citta*.[2]

This was how Ācariya Mun applied himself in the ultimate battle. He did not place any time constraints on his walking and sitting meditation as he strove day and night, wielding mindfulness and wisdom to secure victory. Having finally cleared through the dense jungle of *kilesas*, supreme-mindfulness and supreme-wisdom, that were his weapons of choice in this campaign, ceased to be meaningful or relevant. Mindfulness and wisdom became routine faculties to be engaged in normal mental processes. He used them to think about one of the many aspects of Dhamma or to engage in other mental activities, letting them fade away when their services were no longer required. Previously, they needed to be in a constant state of alert to combat the *kilesas*. Once victory was achieved, if nothing came along to stimulate his thoughts, he existed much as though he were mentally idle – a simpleton. Mindfulness and wisdom, which for so long had been caught up in the heat of intense struggle, were nowhere to be found. All that remained was a timeless tranquillity that nothing could disturb, eclipsing everything else in his heart. Left totally to itself, free of all external influences, his heart did not think about affairs of the past or the future. It was as though everything had disappeared along with the *kilesas* – only emptiness remained.

The Boxer

When Ācariya Mun accepted a group of monks as his students, he held regular meetings where he instructed them in the way of practice. If he noticed that a monk's attitude was unbecoming, or his behavior offensive, he took the opportunity to openly rebuke him. While in meditation, knowledge about the unseemly behavior of his students might arise in his mind as visual images, or else he might psychically read their errant thoughts. He then devised some cunning method to bring this to the culprit's attention, assuring that greater care and restraint was exercised in the future.

The visual *nimittas* that arose in Ācariya Mun's *citta* during meditation varied according to the overall situation of the person who was the principal cause of that vision. To give you an idea of the nature and the scope of his *nimittas*, there is the story of the monk who was a rather famous boxer as a layman. Giving up his profession to ordain as a monk, he developed a strong faith and decided to practice *kammaṭṭhāna*. Aware of Ācariya Mun's excellent reputation as a revered meditation master, he set out to find the place where Ācariya Mun was staying. But as he set off, he unwittingly carried in his bag ten pictures of boxers in various boxing poses. With these photos, he traveled from Bangkok to Chiang Mai, searching for Ācariya Mun in that mountainous region. Finally arriving at Ācariya Mun's wilderness retreat, he paid his respects and explained his reasons for coming. Ācariya Mun accepted him without offering any comments.

During the night Ācariya Mun must have thoroughly investigated this monk; for, the following morning, when all the monks gathered to eat, he came in and immediately began speaking about the new arrival.

"This monk came here for the express purpose of learning about Dhamma. Looking at his behavior, I can find nothing offensive — it's commendable. Why then did he exhibit such dreadful conduct last night? As I sat in meditation, he approached and stood right in front of me, just a few feet away. He then proceeded at some length to assume various boxing poses, before gradually backing away. As he slowly faded from my view, he continued to shadow box, kicking first right and then left as he went.[3] What's the story with this monk? Was he a boxer before he ordained as a monk? Is that the reason he gave me a lengthy boxing exhibition?"

While he spoke, all the monks, including the former boxer, sat motionless in bewildered silence. Ācariya Mun turned to the former boxer, whose face had gone pale.

"What do you have to say for yourself? What did you have in mind, behaving in such a manner? At least you didn't take a punch at me!"

As it was time to go on almsround, Ācariya Mun said nothing more that morning. Nor did he bring the matter up later, when instructing the monks at the evening meeting. But during the night he was again confronted with the same problem. So, he brought it up again the following morning.

"What's your real purpose for coming to me? Last night, there you were again, displaying your boxing skills, jumping and kicking all over the place. It lasted nearly all night. Such behavior is not normal for someone whose intentions are noble. What did you have in mind before you came to see me? And what are your thoughts now that you are here? Please tell me the truth, or else I won't be able to let you stay on here. I've never experienced anything quite like the events of the last two nights."

The monk sat trembling, his face ashen, as though he was ready to faint. One of the other monks, noticing his worsening condition, requested an opportunity to speak privately with him.

"Please be forthcoming and tell Ācariya Mun your true feelings about this matter. He's asking you about it only because he wants to ascertain the truth, not because he has any intention to hurt you. None of us, who are living here with him, are saints, free of *kilesas*. We are bound to make mistakes and so must accept his admonitions. All of us live here as his disciples. Being our teacher, he's like a father and a mother to us. As a teacher, he has an obligation to reprimand anyone who does something noticeably wrong. A teacher must keep an eye on his students — for their own sake, educating them by questioning and criticizing them as circumstances require. I myself have been subjected to many such castigations; some even more severe than the one you received. Ācariya Mun has even ordered some monks to leave the premises immediately, only to relent and allow them to stay on when they realized their faults and accepted the blame. Please think carefully about what he just said to you. My own feeling is that you shouldn't be unreasonably afraid. If you have anything on your mind, just express it truthfully. If you feel you have done nothing wrong, or you cannot recall where you made a mistake, tell him straight out that you cannot seem to recollect your past errors. Then put your fate in his hands, letting him take what action he sees fit, and accept the consequences. The matter will then resolve itself."

When the other monk finished speaking Ācariya Mun continued: "So what do you have to say for yourself? It's not that I want to find fault with you for no good reason. But as soon as I close my eyes I have to watch your antics blocking my view for the rest of the night. Why would a monk behave like that? It dismays me to see it every night. I want to know what kind of sinister motives you may have for persisting in such conduct. Or do you think that my own intuition, which has always been reliable in the past, is now playing tricks on me, and contaminating you in the process? I want you to tell me the truth. If it turns out that you're innocent, my intuition being at fault, then that means I'm just a crazy old monk who doesn't deserve to live with a group of students like this — I will only lead them astray. I'll have to run off and hide myself away like some lunatic, and immediately stop teaching others. Should I persist in teaching such crazy knowledge to the world, the consequences would be disastrous."

The other monk again encouraged his friend to speak up. Finally, the former boxer moved to answer Ācariya Mun. In a ghostly, trembling voice, he blurted out, "I'm a boxer", and then fell silent.

Ācariya Mun sought confirmation: "You're a boxer, is that right?"

"Yes." And that was all he said.

"Right now you're a monk; so, how can you also be a boxer? Do you mean you traveled here boxing for money along the way, or what?"

By this time, the monk's mind was in a daze. He could offer no coherent response to Ācariya Mun's inquiries. The other monk took up the questioning in an effort to help him regain his mental focus: "Don't you mean that you were a boxer in lay life, but now that you are a monk you no longer do that?"

"Yes. As a layman I was a boxer, but after ordaining as a monk I stopped boxing."

Ācariya Mun saw that his condition didn't look very good, so he changed the subject, saying it was time to go on almsround. Later, he told the other monk to go and question him privately, since his fear of Ācariya Mun prevented him from being coherent. After the meal this monk found an opportunity to put his questions in private. He discovered that the new monk had previously been a well-known boxer in the Suan Kulap boxing camp. Becoming disillusioned with lay life, he ordained as a monk and set off to find Ācariya Mun.

Once he had the whole story, the monk related it to Ācariya Mun, who made no further comment. It was assumed that this would be the end of the matter, especially since Ācariya Mun spoke directly to the former boxer during the evening meeting. But that wasn't to be the case. That night, Ācariya Mun again investigated the matter for himself. In the morning, he confronted the former boxer once more in front of everyone.

"It's not merely that you were once a boxer — something else is hidden there as well. You should go and carefully reconsider this whole affair. If it was simply a matter of being a boxer in lay life, the matter should have been settled by now. It should not keep recurring in this way."

That was all he said.

Later, the monk who had become familiar with the former boxer went to see him. After further questioning he discovered that the new monk had the ten pictures of boxers in his possession. After looking at them, his friend became convinced that they were the cause of all the trouble. He advised him to either throw them away, or burn them. The boxer monk agreed, and together they burned the whole lot. After that, everything returned to normal and this matter never surfaced again.

The former boxer was diligent in his practice, always conducting himself admirably. He lived contentedly with Ācariya Mun from then on. Ācariya Mun was always especially kind to him — never again did he allude to his past. Afterwards, when the opportunity arose, his fellow monks teased him about that incident. Referring to his scolding from Ācariya Mun, he said, "I was half-dead and in such a daze I didn't know what was what, so I answered him like a half-dead idiot." Addressing the monk who helped him, he continued, "If you hadn't been so kind, I'd probably have gone hopelessly mad. But Ācariya Mun was remarkably clever — as soon as he saw I was losing my wits, he quickly put a stop to the whole affair, acting as though nothing had ever happened."

This is an example of the type of visual *nimitta* that might arise in Ācariya Mun's meditation. He regularly used the knowledge he gained from such visions to teach his students — a means no less significant than his ability to read the thoughts of others.[4]

ĀCARIYA MUN HAD MORE sensational experiences while living in Chiang Mai than during any other period of his life. Some of these phenomena appeared exclusively within his *citta*; others surfaced in the world around him. They included many amazing, stimulating insights — knowledge of a kind never occurring to him before. Living alone in particular, he encountered a myriad of mysterious phenomena far too numerous to mention. The *citta* in its natural state of knowing is like that: knowledge and understanding arise continuously, both during meditation and in engagement with normal daily activities. It's strange, and truly wondrous, considering that the *citta* had previously been blind and ignorant, never imagining it possessed the ability to perceive the phenomena that arise each moment. It was as if such phenomena just came into being, even though they have actually existed since time immemorial.

Only when the *citta* enters into a state of total calm do these functions cease. All manner of phenomena are excluded from the *samādhi* state, so nothing arises to affect the *citta* in any way. As the *citta* rests with Dhamma, Dhamma and the *citta* merge. The *citta* is Dhamma, Dhamma is the *citta*. This is a state of complete unity where the *citta* and Dhamma are one and the same, without any trace of duality. Conceptual reality does not exist: all concepts of time and space are transcended. There is no awareness of the body, or the mind, and concepts of pain and pleasure do not arise. As long as the *citta* remains there and doesn't withdraw from that state — whether it's for a period of days, months, years, or eons — then conventional realities such as *anicca*, *dukkha*, and *anattā* will not disturb it, for it is a state in which all duality ceases — entirely. If, for instance, the mundane physical body were to break up and disintegrate while the *citta* remained quiescent in *nirodhadhamma* — meaning the cessation of conventional reality — the *citta* in that state would be completely unaware of what was happening.[5]

In truth, the state of *nirodha* is one in which the cessation of conceptual reality is only temporary — not lasting for years, as that is highly unlikely. It may be compared to a deep, dreamless sleep. During that time, the sleeper is completely unaware of body and mind. No matter how long he remains in deep, dreamless sleep, that condition stays the same. Only after waking up does one become aware of normal physical and mental sensations.

Deep states of *samādhi,* including *nirodhasamāpatti,* all exist within the realm of relative, conventional reality, however. Only the *vimutticitta* has gone completely beyond it. And if the *citta* entering into these *samādhi* states is already liberated from every aspect of relative, conventional reality, then that pure *visuddhi-citta* is in no way affected by such conventional levels of attainment. It remains *vimutticitta,* free from all constraints of time and space — *akāliko.* It's absolutely impossible to conceptualize the nature of *vimutti-citta,* so any attempt to speculate about its qualities is only a waste of time and effort. The *citta* that enters into a state of total quiescence, free from all conceptual reality, simply ceases to function, as those conditioned phenomena — that would ordinarily be involved with the *citta* — temporarily disappear. Later when the *citta* has withdrawn from deep *samādhi* into *upacāra samādhi,* or back into the normal state of *visuddhi-citta,* it functions normally, receiving and processing sense data as it sees fit.[6]

Whether in *upacāra samādhi,* or in its normal waking state, Ācariya Mun's *citta* was always receptive to a multitude of phenomena. The difference was in the depth, scope, and quality of the experience. If wishing to investigate something thoroughly, he would enter into *upacāra samādhi* to get a more extensive view. Clairvoyance and clairaudience, for example, require a state of *upacāra samādhi.* In this calm state one can perceive whatever one wishes to know about the forms and sounds of people and animals — and much, much more. Fundamentally, it's no different from seeing with the physical eyes and hearing with the physical ears.

Tigers in Disguise

Ācariya Mun said that, excepting the few who had visited large towns in the region, most of the hill tribe people in Chiang Mai had never seen monks before. Early in his travels, Ācariya Mun and another monk went to live in the mountains about a mile and a half from a hill tribe village. They camped in the forest, taking shelter under the trees. In the morning, when they went to the village for alms food, the villagers asked why they had come. Ācariya Mun said they had come to collect alms. Puzzled, the villagers asked him what that meant. Ācariya Mun explained that they had come to collect offerings of rice. They asked him if he wanted cooked rice or uncooked rice. When he said cooked rice, they got some and put a little in each of their alms bowls. The two monks then returned to their camp and ate the plain rice.

Lacking faith from the very beginning, the villagers were very suspicious of the monks. That evening the village headman sounded the bamboo clapper to call everyone to a meeting. Referring to Ācariya Mun and his disciple, he announced that there were now two 'tigers in disguise' staying in the nearby forest. He said that he had yet to determine what kind of tigers they were, but they weren't to be trusted. He forbade the women and children to enter the forest in that area; and men who went were warned to go armed and in groups lest they should be attacked by the two tigers.

As it happened, Ācariya Mun was beginning his evening meditation at precisely the time the announcement was made to the village community. So, Ācariya Mun, who was the object of this warning, was also privy to the whole affair. He was deeply saddened by the senseless accusations; but, instead of feeling angry or discouraged, he felt only ineffable loving compassion for the local villagers. He was concerned that the majority might naively believe such slanderous talk and, therefore, be burdened by its dreadful moral consequences until they died – at which time they might well be reborn as tigers. Early the next morning, he informed his disciple of what he had seen.

"Last night the village headman assembled everyone and announced that we are 'tigers in disguise'. We were both accused of being tigers who are disguised as monks in order to deceive them into trusting us so that we can then destroy both their persons and their properties. Because of this, they have no faith in us at all. If we were to leave here now while they still harbor these negative thoughts, they may all be reborn as tigers when they die – a grievous *kamma* indeed. So for their benefit, I think it's incumbent on us as monks to remain here and put up with the situation for a while. We must endure the ensuing hardships until they've changed their attitude before we move to another location."

Not only did the villagers distrust them, but groups of three or four armed men often came to keep an eye on them. Sometimes, they stood watching from a distance. But at other times, seeing Ācariya Mun walking meditation, they came closer and stared at him from the end of his walking path, or from the side of it, or even stood right in the middle of it. They glanced around, surveying the whole area for about 10 to 15 minutes, then left. This surveillance routine continued day after day for many weeks.

The villagers showed no concern whatsoever about the personal welfare of these two 'tigers'. They were not interested in whether or not they had enough food and other necessities to survive. Thus, the living conditions of these two tigers were difficult in the extreme. The most they received on almsround was plain rice. On some days, it was just barely enough to satisfy them; on other days, it wasn't nearly enough, even though they drank a lot of water with it as well.

Since there was no cave or cliff overhang in which they could take shelter, they lived and slept under the trees, putting up with exposure to the sun and the rain. When it rained in that area, it tended to rain all day. After the rain abated and things dried out a bit, they went looking for dry leaves and grasses to construct a make-shift thatched roof, giving them some limited protection against the weather. It provided enough cover to survive from day to day, albeit with much discomfort. When it rained heavily, they sheltered under their tent-umbrellas with the cloth sheeting hanging down around them as protection against the cold wind.[7] Often the rain was accompanied by strong winds that came howling down out of the mountains, blowing their umbrellas, soaking their belongings, and leaving both monks drenched and shivering. If it happened during the daytime, they could at least see what they were doing while collecting their requisites to look for some cover. But when it occurred at night, the situation was extremely trying. They were unable to see even as the rain poured down and the cold wind blasted through the trees, causing branches to break off and crash down around them. They were never sure of surviving this onslaught of rain, wind, cold, and loose debris flying at them from all directions. During such hardships, they just endured the best they could. They had to abide the heat, the cold, the hunger, the thirst, and the uncertainty of their existence while they waited for the villagers' mistrust to subside. Even though they received only plain rice, their supply was, at best, erratic. Drinking water was hard to come by; so they had to walk down to the foot of the mountain to fill their kettles, carrying the water back up to serve their daily needs. Despite such an impoverished existence, the villagers showed no sympathy for their plight.

In spite of the hardships, Ācariya Mun felt free of anxieties and responsibilities as his meditation practice progressed unhindered. He took great pleasure from listening to the calls of the various wild animals in the surrounding forest. Seated in meditation under the trees late at night, he constantly heard the sounds of tigers roaring close by. Curiously, those huge tigers rarely ventured into the area where he was seated. Occasionally, a tiger did approach Ācariya Mun. Perhaps suspecting him to be wild game, it snuck in to have a look. But as soon as the tiger saw him make a move, it leapt off into the forest in alarm, and was never seen again.

Nearly every afternoon, three or four men came to check them out. They stood around whispering among themselves without a word to Ācariya Mun, who, in turn, ignored their presence. When they arrived, Ācariya Mun focused his *citta* on their thoughts. They, of course, never suspected that he knew what they were thinking or what they were whispering about. It's unlikely they even considered the possibility that someone could be privy to their thoughts, which they indulged in unrestrainedly. Ācariya Mun focused his attention on everyone who came. As was to be expected of a reconnaissance party, he discovered that they were primarily looking to find fault with him in some way. Instead of taking precautions against such findings, Ācariya Mun responded with great compassion. He knew that a majority of the villagers were subject to the corrupting influence of a small minority.

Ācariya Mun remained at this site for many months; yet, the villagers persisted in trying to catch him at suspicious doings. Their sole purpose was to find him doing something that would confirm their worst fears. Although they were sincerely committed to this, they never tried to chase him away: they merely took turns spying on him. The villagers must have been surprised that despite many months of continuous surveillance, they still couldn't catch him doing anything wrong.

One evening while sitting in meditation, Ācariya Mun became psychically aware that the villagers were assembled for a meeting concerning his case. He could hear the village headman questioning the others about the results of their surveillance: What had they been able to determine so far? Those, who had taken turns observing the two monks, said the same thing: they could find no evidence to confirm their suspicions. They were worried that their suspicious attitude might be doing them more harm than good.

"Why do you say that?" The headman wanted to know.

They replied: "As far as we can tell, there's nothing in their conduct to confirm our assumptions about them. Whenever we go to check them out, either they are sitting still with their eyes closed, or they're calmly pacing back and forth, not looking here and there like most people do. People who are tigers in disguise, poised to attack their prey, would hardly behave like that. These two monks should have exhibited some sort of incriminating behavior by now, but we've seen nothing so far. If we keep treating them like this, we may suffer the consequences. The correct approach would be to speak with them to find out about their motives. Presuming their motives to be sinister may well reflect badly on us all.

"Good monks are hard to find. We have enough experience to tell good monks from bad ones. These monks deserve our respect. Let's not hastily accuse them of treachery. To find out the whole story, let's go speak with them. Let's ask them why they sit still with their eyes closed, and why they pace back and forth — what are they searching for?"

A decision was reached at the meeting to send a representative to question the monks. In the morning, Ācariya Mun spoke to his companion: "The villagers are beginning to have a change of heart. Last night they held a meeting about their surveillance of us. They have decided to send someone here to question us about their suspicions."

Just as Ācariya Mun foresaw, a village representative arrived that very afternoon to question him: "What are you searching for when you sit still with your eyes closed, or pace back and forth?"

Ācariya Mun replied, "I've lost my *buddho*. I'm searching for *buddho* while sitting and walking."

"What is this *buddho*? Can we help you find it?"

"*Buddho* is the most precious gem in the three worlds of existence — a jewel of all-pervading knowledge. If you help me find it, that'll be excellent. Then we will all see *buddho* quickly and easily."

"Has your *buddho* been missing long?"

"Not long. With your help we'll find it a lot faster than if I look for it alone."

"Is *buddho* something large?"

"Neither large nor small, it's just the right size for all of us. Whoever finds *buddho* will become a superior person, able to perceive anything he wishes."

"Will we be able to see the heavens and the hells?"

"Of course. Otherwise, how could we call it superior."

"What about our dead children, and our dead spouses, can they be seen?"

"You can see anything you want once buddho is yours."

"Is it very bright?"

"It's much brighter than hundreds, even thousands, of suns. The sun is not able to illuminate heaven and hell, but buddho can penetrate everywhere, illuminating everything."

"Can woman and children help search for it too?"

"Everyone can help — men, women, young and old, all can join in the search."

"This superior buddho, can it protect us from ghosts?"

"Buddho is superior in countless ways. It is superior in the three worlds — *kāma-loka, rūpa-loka, arūpa-loka*. All three of them must pay homage to *buddho*. No being anywhere is greater than *buddho*. Ghosts are very afraid of *buddho* — they must bow down and worship it. Ghosts are frightened of people who search for *buddho* too, even though they haven't found it yet."

"This buddho jewel, what color is it?"

"It's a bright, sparkling jewel with countless colors. *Buddho* is a special asset of the Lord Buddha — a gleaming aggregate of knowledge, not a material thing. The Lord Buddha bequeathed it to us many years ago, but since then it's gone missing and we no longer know how to find it. But it's location is not so important. If you're trying to find it, what's important is to sit and walk thinking "*buddho, buddho, buddho*" exclusively within your heart. Keep your attention focused within your body, not letting it wander outside. Fix your awareness firmly on the repetition of *"buddho, buddho"*. If you can manage to do this, you may even come across buddho before I do."

"How long must we to sit and walk searching for *buddho* before we find it?"

"To begin with, sit or walk for about 15 to 20 minutes at a time. *Buddho* doesn't want you to spend too much time searching for it yet. It's afraid you'll grow tired and so be unable to keep up with it. Losing interest, you will not want to search anymore. Then you'll miss it altogether. This is enough to get you started. If I elaborate any further, you won't remember it all, thus jeopardizing your chances of meeting *buddho*."

With these instructions in mind, the villager returned home. He didn't take leave of Ācariya Mun in any special way, because that was not the hill tribe custom. Deciding that it was time to go, he simply got up and left. As soon as he arrived at the village, everyone gathered around to hear what had taken place. He explained why Ācariya Mun sat still with his eyes closed and why he paced back and forth: he was searching for the precious gem *buddho* and not, as they had presumed, because he was a 'tiger in disguise'. He then explained Ācariya Mun's brief instructions on how to find buddho. Once the villagers knew the method, everyone — from the headman on down to the women and older children — began to practice, mentally repeating *"buddho"*.

Several days later, something truly amazing happened. The Dhamma of the Lord Buddha arose clearly in the heart of one of the villagers. While mentally repeating the word *"buddho"* over and over again as Ācariya Mun had suggested, one man in the village found Dhamma: his heart attained a state of peace and calm. A few days earlier, the man had dreamed that Ācariya Mun was placing a very large, bright-shining candle on top of his head. The moment Ācariya Mun set the candle on his head, his whole body, from the head on down, was brightly illuminated. He felt overjoyed as the radiance, spreading out around him, illuminated the surrounding area as well. Soon after he attained this state of tranquility, he went to tell Ācariya Mun about his achievement, and about the amazing dream he had prior to it. Ācariya Mun then gave him additional instructions on how to proceed with his practice. As it turned out, his progress was very quick: he was soon able to psychically know other people's thoughts. He informed Ācariya Mun of this very matter-of-factly in the forthright manner typical of forest people.

Sometime later, this man declared to Ācariya Mun that he had examined Ācariya Mun's *citta* and had clearly seen its characteristics. Playfully, Ācariya Mun asked if he could see much evil in his *citta*. The man answered without hesitation, "Your *citta* has no focal point whatsoever – only an absolutely incredible radiance shining within. Your preeminence is unrivaled anywhere in the world. I've never seen anything like it. You've been here about a year now, why didn't you teach me about this right from the beginning?"

"How could I teach you? You never came to ask me any questions."

"I didn't know you were a supreme master. Had I known, I'd have come for sure. Now we all know you're an extremely clever person. When we came asking you why you sat still with your eyes closed and what you were looking for as you paced back and forth, you told us your *buddho* was lost and asked us to help you find it. When asked to describe it, you said *buddho* is a bright, sparkling jewel, but in truth the real *buddho* is your heart. The missing *buddho* was simply a clever ploy to persuade us to meditate on *buddho* so that our hearts could become bright like yours. Now we realize that you're a supremely wise person whose only desire was for us to discover the supreme *buddho* in our own hearts, thus ensuring our long-term welfare and happiness."

The news of this man's attainment of Dhamma spread rapidly through the community, further arousing everyone's interest in *buddho* meditation so that even small children took it up. Their faith in Ācariya Mun thus reinforced, their reverence for his teaching steadily increased. No one ever mentioned 'tigers in disguise' again.

From that time on, the man who had learned to meditate carried Ācariya Mun's alms bowl back to his forest retreat every day after the almsround. After Ācariya Mun finished eating, he would then seek advice on his practice. On the days when he had business to attend to, he told someone to inform Ācariya Mun that he wouldn't be available to carry the alms bowl. Although quite a few men and women in the village learned to meditate, this first man was the most accomplished.

When people are satisfied, everything else naturally falls into place. For instance, previously these people were not the least bit interested in how Ācariya Mun ate or slept, or even whether he lived or died. But later when faith and respect arose in them, those things that pre viously were scarce soon became plentiful. Without having to be asked, the villagers joined forces to make him a walking path. They also built him a hut and a platform on which to sit and have his meal. When they came to help, they disguised their praises of him in reproachful tones.

"Look at that walking meditation path. It's all overgrown with vegetation. You'd have to be a wild boar to penetrate that thicket. And yet, you still insist on walking there. You're really weird, you know. When we ask you what the path is for, you say it's a place to search for *buddho* — I've lost my *buddho*. When asked why you sit still with your eyes closed, again you say you're looking for *buddho*. Here you are a supreme master, yet you don't tell anyone about it. You're the strangest person we've ever known, but we like you just the way you are. Your bed is a carpet of moldy smelling leaves strewn over the ground. How could you stand it all these months? It looks like a pig's lair. Looking at it now, we feel so sorry for you we could cry. We were very stupid, all of us. We didn't realize what a wonderful person you are. Worse than that, a few of us accused you of having sinister motives, convincing the rest to dislike and distrust you. Finally now the whole village trusts and reveres you."

Ācariya Mun said that, when hill tribe people decided to trust and respect someone, their belief was heartfelt and unequivocal. Their loyalty was unconditional — they would sacrifice their lives if they had to. They took what they were taught to heart, conducting themselves accordingly. As they became more familiar with the method and more proficient in their practice, Ācariya Mun taught them to steadily increase the amount of time they spent doing *buddho* meditation.

Ācariya Mun stayed with those people for over a year — from February of one year to April of the following year — until he finally left. However, because of his great compassion for them, taking leave of them was very difficult for him. They were very reluctant to see him go. They assured him that, were he to remain there until he died, the whole community would arrange for his cremation. Those people were willing to put their complete trust in him out of a deep sense of love and devotion. Unmistakably, they had seen for themselves the good results of his teaching. And to their credit, they were smart enough to see their own faults as well. Once they came to know him as a truly virtuous, highly respected monk, they realized their mistake and so begged his forgiveness. He forgave them, later telling his disciple that their amends were complete. This meant that the two of them were then free to go somewhere else.

But taking leave of them was no simple matter. Ācariya Mun said that it was moving beyond description to witness their affection and deep devotion as they beseeched him to stay. Having heard that he was preparing to leave, the whole village came out, weeping and pleading with him until the entire forest was disturbed by the commotion. It sounded as though they were mourning the dead. While explaining his reasons for leaving, he tried to comfort them, assuring them that such distress was unwarranted. He counseled self-restraint, which is the way of Dhamma.

When they calmed down, seemingly resigned to his departure, he began to leave his forest retreat. Then, something totally unexpected happened. All the villagers, including the children, ran after him. Surrounding him on the path, they proceeded to snatch away his requisites. Some grabbed his umbrella, his bowl, and his water kettle, while others clutched at the robes he wore or clung to his arms and legs, trying to pull him back again — acting just like children. They were determined to not let him go.

Ācariya Mun was obliged once again to explain his reasons for leaving, consoling them until they calmed down. Finally they agreed. But no sooner had he started walking off than the crying began and they rushed to drag him back again. Several hours passed before he eventually got away. Meanwhile, the whole forest was disturbed by noisy scenes of hysteria that were heartrending to watch. The initial epithet 'tigers in disguise' meant nothing to them then. In its place had arisen deep reverence and attachment for a man of supreme virtue. In the end, these hill tribe people couldn't hold back their emotions. As they gathered around him crying and pleading, their many voices merged into a crescendo: "Hurry back to visit us again. Please don't be gone long, we miss you so much already it's breaking our hearts."

Having arrived in the area surrounded by suspicion and dissatisfaction, Ācariya Mun departed amid emotional scenes of affection and attachment. He had managed to turn something unseemly into something beautiful, so enhancing its value immensely — as befits one ordained as a disciple of the Buddha. The Buddha's disciples never hold grudges or look to blame others. Should anyone dislike them, they will try to help that person with loving compassion. They never take offense at other people's misbehavior nor do they harbor feelings of animosity that could lead to mutual recriminations. A heart full to overflowing with loving compassion inspires faith in those ablaze with *kilesas* by providing them with a peaceful, dependable refuge. A heart of such loving grace possesses virtuous qualities that are unparalleled in the world.

Later when listening to Ācariya Mun tell this story, we couldn't help sympathizing with the hill tribe people. We formed in our minds a clear image of those chaotic scenes in the forest – as though we were watching a movie. We could imagine the villagers' potent faith, ready to sacrifice anything for this man of supreme virtue. All they asked was a chance to bask in his aura of loving kindness, thus continuing to enjoy a life of prosperity. So they cried and pleaded with him, clutching at his arms and legs, pulling on his robes and other requisites, until he returned to the small eating platform with the thatched roof that had been a source of such contentment. Though an incredibly moving occasion, the time had come for him to move on. No one can possibly negate the transient nature of the world. The driving principle of constant change keeps everything moving – nothing can halt its progress. For this reason, when the right time came, Ācariya Mun had to leave, though he fully understood the position of those faithful villagers who were so emotionally attached to him.

Although Ācariya Mun was once labeled a 'tiger in disguise' by the hill tribe people, it is well known that he was, in truth, a 'pure one' who existed as 'an incomparable field of merit for the world'.[8] Ācariya Mun left that mountain community in order to follow his natural inclination – to be of the most benefit to the greatest number of people.

Buddhism is a priceless inheritance that has always been an integral part of our very existence. But, perhaps it too could fall prey to insidious accusations of being a 'tiger in disguise' much in the same manner that Ācariya Mun did. It could end up being severely damaged by people whose views are hostile to Buddhist principles and traditions. In truth, this process has already begun, so we should not be complacent. If we fail to fulfill our obligations, we may forfeit this inheritance, only to regret it later.

Ācariya Mun followed the way of *sugato*.[9] When living deep in the forests and mountains he was constantly of service to the hill tribesmen, or else the *devas*, *brahmas*, ghosts, *nāgas*, and *garudas*. He was always compassionately assisting the world in some way or other. In human society he taught monks, novices, nuns, and lay people from all walks of life without exception. People everywhere sought him out to hear his instructions. They all gained an enormous benefit from his teachings, always delivered in a thorough, coherent manner that would be hard for anyone else to equal.

While he lived in the mountains of Chiang Mai, the hill tribe people received great joy, listening to his Dhamma discourses in the late afternoons. Later at night, he taught Dhamma to *devas* from various levels of existence, always responding to their many inquiries. Teaching *devas* was a heavy responsibility, since it was difficult to find another monk with the same psychic skills to stand in for him. Teaching people was a responsibility that could be delegated to others — at least the people listening would gain enough understanding to derive some benefit if they made the effort. Acariya Mun's relationship with *devas* of all realms was of primary importance to him. So his biography is interspersed with stories about them at different times in different places, right to the very end.

Not so long ago I went to pay my respects to a *vipassanā kammaṭṭhāna ācariya* of the highest caliber, a senior monk with an exceptionally kind, gentle disposition who is greatly revered by monks and lay people all over Thailand.[10] When I arrived he was discussing Dhamma with several of his close disciples, so I took the opportunity to join them. We began by discussing various practical aspects of Dhamma, eventually coming around to the subject of Acariya Mun, who had been his teacher. In the past, he lived under Acariya Mun's tutelage in the remote mountains of Chiang Mai, training with him at a forest retreat that was several days walk from the nearest town. It's hard to find words to describe the many remarkable, amazing stories he told me that day. I shall relate the ones I feel are appropriate here, while the others I shall skip, for reasons I explained earlier.

This *ācariya* said that, besides his undoubted purity of heart, Acariya Mun also possessed many unique abilities that inspired awe in his students and assured their vigilance at all times. He said he couldn't possibly remember all of the strange, unusual stories he had heard from Acariya Mun; so, I urged him to tell me what he could remember. His words would serve as a memorial — a source of inspiration for future generations. This is what he said:

"Acariya Mun knew everything I was thinking — what more can I say? I felt as though I were on a tight leash day and night, such was the vigilance I applied to observing my mind. Despite my best efforts, he could still catch my errant thoughts, publicly exposing them for everyone to hear. My meditation was actually quite good while staying with him, but I couldn't always prevent stray thoughts from arising. We should never underestimate the mind's ability to think incessantly, day and night — non-stop. How many of us can catch up with our thoughts long enough to restrain them effectively? So I was constantly on guard, for he was better at catching my thoughts than I was! Sometimes he brought up thoughts that I'd forgotten having. Suddenly, I was made to recall thoughts that had long since past."

I asked the *ācariya* if Ācariya Mun had ever scolded him. He told me:

"Occasionally he did; but, more often he read my thoughts, then used them as a way of teaching me Dhamma. Sometimes other monks were listening as well, which really embarrassed me. Fortunately, if other monks sat listening, Ācariya Mun never revealed the name of the offender — he merely spoke about the relative merits of the thoughts in question."

I wanted to know why he thought Ācariya Mun scolded him sometimes. He said:

"Do you know the word *puthujjana?*[11] It means a mind denser than a mountain of stone, careening out of control. It doesn't consider whether thoughts are good or bad, right or wrong — which was a sufficient reason for him to give a scolding."

I asked him if he felt afraid when Ācariya Mun scolded him.

"Why shouldn't I have been afraid? My body may not have been shaking, but my mind certainly was. I almost forgot to breathe at times. I have no doubt that Ācariya Mun truly did know the minds of others — I experienced it myself. He could literally collect all my thoughts, then confront me with them later. For example, from time to time I rather foolishly thought about going off on my own. If such a thought occurred to me at night, early the next morning, as soon as I encountered him, Ācariya Mun immediately started lecturing me: 'Just where do you think you're going? It's far better here than anywhere else. It's best that you stay here with me …' and so on. He never let these thoughts pass undetected. 'It's more enjoyable here. Staying here and listening to the Dhamma is better than going off on your own.' He never would consent to my going. I believe he was worried that my meditation practice might deteriorate, so he tried to keep me under his tutelage the whole time.

"The thing that terrified me about him was, day or night, whenever I decided to focus my *citta's* attention on him, I saw him staring back at me. It seemed he never took a rest! There were nights when I didn't dare lie down because I could visualize him sitting right in front of me, scrutinizing me every moment. Whenever I focused my *citta* on external objects, I invariably found him there looking at me. Because of this, my mindfulness was constantly alert.

"As his students, we were forced to be mindful. Following him on almsround, we carefully kept our thoughts under control, restraining our minds from straying beyond the confines of our bodies. Were we careless, we could expect to hear about it — sometimes immediately. Consequently, we exerted mindfulness over our thoughts — at all times. Even then, he could usually find something to lecture us about, and always with good reason. Inevitably, at least one monk among us gave Ācariya Mun cause to speak out. During the evening meeting, Ācariya Mun might speak in a scolding tone about some rather strange affair that seemed to make no sense. As soon as the meeting adjourned, the monks would quietly ask around to find out whose thoughts he was censuring that day. Eventually one of the monks confessed that, as strange as it might seem, he actually had been thinking such nonsense. Living with Ācariya Mun was a wonderful experience, for fear of him always promoted a mindful attitude within each of us."

This *ācariya* told me that when he first arrived in Chiang Mai, he went to stay at one of the local monasteries. Having been there less than an hour, he saw a car pull into the monastery grounds and come to a stop right in front of the hut he had just moved into.

"When I looked out to see who had come, there was Ācariya Mun! Hurrying down to receive him, I respectfully asked why he had come. He replied without hesitation that he came to pick me up. He said that he knew the night before that I would be coming. I asked if someone had informed him that I would be arriving in Chiang Mai. He replied that it was beside the point how he learned of it — he knew about it and wanted to be here, so he just came on his own. Hearing that, I became apprehensive. And the more I considered the implications, the more apprehensive I grew. Later, when I was living with him, all my fears were confirmed.

"If our minds were free of conceited opinions when we received his Dhamma discourse, then we became pleasantly absorbed in listening. His entire discourse was Dhamma — pure and simple; and it engaged our full attention more than anything else we had ever heard. On the other hand, if a monk listened halfheartedly, burdened by the weight of worldly thoughts, then we soon perceived fire in his discourse, and the offending monk would promptly feel the heat. In giving a talk, Ācariya Mun was not concerned about whose *kilesas* his words might disturb — his Dhamma rushed to confront the *kilesas* at just that point where they were most prolific.

"Occasionally, he did identify a monk by name, confronting him directly. 'Why were you meditating like that last night? That's not the right way to meditate, you must do it this way' Or, 'Why were you thinking like that this morning? If you want to avoid being ruined by such harmful thinking, then don't think like that again. Why don't you think and act in ways that the Lord Buddha has taught us? What's the matter with you? We're here to train ourselves in the way of Dhamma in order to get rid of wrong attitudes and erroneous thinking. We are not here to indulge our thoughts, burning ourselves with them the way you've been doing.' Those who wholeheartedly accepted the truth, lived contentedly with him, and he didn't say much to them. But any furtiveness caused him deep misgivings, as though the offending thoughts were fire burning him, and he would suddenly make a surprising comment about it. If, however, the monk realized his mistake and changed his attitude, then nothing further was said and the matter rested there."

Powerful Magic

One evening, a group of hill tribesmen from a village near Ācariya Mun's residence began wondering among themselves whether Ācariya Mun had any magic formulas to ward off and chase away ghosts. So they decided to go the next day to ask if he had anything he could give them. Early the next morning, Ācariya Mun related this incident to the monks living with him:

"Last night while sitting in meditation I overheard a group of hill tribesmen in the village wondering if we monks might have some magic formula for warding off and chasing away ghosts . They intend to come here today to ask us about it. Should they come, give them the formula "*buddho, dhammo, sangho*" to meditate on. It's an excellent formula

210

against ghosts, for the only things that ghosts fear in this world are the Buddha, the Dhamma, and the Sangha. Not a single ghost would dare stand against them."

That morning, just as Ācariya Mun had foreseen, the hill tribesmen came to request a magic formula against ghosts. Ācariya Mun gave them the formula *"buddho, dhammo, sangho"* as well as the method for using it. Assuring them that ghosts were terrified of this formula, he told them to mentally recite *"buddho"*, *"dhammo"*, *or "sangho"*, whichever they preferred.

With Ācariya Mun's instructions fresh in their minds, they began what they thought to be a ritual for warding off ghosts, unaware that, in truth, he had given them a meditation subject. Using this method, they attained *samādhi* before long. The next morning they rushed off to see Ācariya Mun and told him what had happened. He assured them that they were practicing the formula correctly, and because of that, ghosts in the area were terrified and bound to run away. Now protected by the power of Dhamma, they no longer had to fear ghosts. In fact, ghosts had already begun to fear even those people in the village who couldn't yet meditate.

Being inherently good, honest folks, hill tribe people were easy to teach. When Ācariya Mun instructed them to meditate each day, they took up the practice with such sincerity that before long some of them were getting exceptionally good results. Their hearts became brightly illuminated and they were able to know the minds of other people, including those of the monks in the monastery, just like the man in the previous story about 'tigers in disguise'.

On visits to the monastery they spoke to Ācariya Mun about their meditation practice, describing their extraordinary perceptual abilities. Some of the monks were astonished, and worried that these people might be able to read their thoughts. Though timid by nature, they nonetheless wanted to find out what the people knew. They couldn't resist the temptation of asking for specific information about their own thoughts. The hill tribesmen told them the truth. Still unconvinced, the monks challenged them. Unfazed by a display of their own ignorance, they cross-examined the hill tribesmen closely to find out if they truly could read thoughts. It was as though they believed that their minds were tightly sealed by hundreds of impenetrable layers. The hill tribesmen answered with the customary frankness of forest people who are uninhibited by social formalities — answers which left the monks feeling very vulnerable. After that, they remained apprehensive that these people might have access to everything they were thinking.

These same hill tribesmen casually informed Ācariya Mun that they knew about the state of his *citta*, having checked it out first, before checking on that of the other monks.

"What's my *citta* like – is it afraid of ghosts?"

"Your *citta* is devoid of all traces of conventional reality. All that's left is Nibbāna in a human body. Your *citta* is absolutely supreme – it fears nothing."

After that, the villagers made no further mention of ghosts. Those accomplished in meditation informed the others who gradually came to have faith in Ācariya Mun and the Buddhasāsana, thus losing interest in the business of ghosts. Every morning they gathered together in the village center to offer alms to the monks. Having placed some food in each monk's bowl, they received a blessing from Ācariya Mun. He taught them to show their appreciation by exclaiming *"sādhu"* together in a loud voice, allowing the *devas* to rejoice in their offerings and receive a portion of the merit as well. Each day the villagers responded faithfully by loudly calling out *"sādhu"*. Ācariya Mun had them exclaim *"sādhu"*, for he knew from the *devas*, who came to hear his Dhamma talks every night, that this sound reached them in the realms where they lived. Hearing this sound, they knew that Ācariya Mun was living in the area.

DEVAS WHO VISITED Ācariya Mun were invariably escorted by a leader who was in charge of the group. These groups represented many different realms of existence. Some were terrestrial *devas* from near and far. Many were from the various celestial realms mentioned in the Buddhist texts. When a group of *devas* intended to pay Ācariya Mun a visit, he always knew their time of arrival in advance. If he knew, for instance, that a group intended to arrive at two or three a.m., he would take some rest beforehand, getting up to enter *samādhi* only when the time approached to receive them. If, however, they were scheduled to arrive around midnight, he would first enter and then wait for them in *samādhi*. This was accomplished in two stages. First, he practiced normal meditation until he attained a deep state of calm, where he rested for a while. Then, as the time approached, he withdrew to just the right meditative level to receive his intended visitors. There, he knew intuitively whether or not they had arrived, or whether they were still on their way. Having acknowledged their arrival, he then discussed with them whatever seemed appropriate for their particular circumstances. Had he remained in a deep state of *samādhi*, his visitors would not have been able to have access to him. In normal waking consciousness, on the other hand, one would have to be a very skilled person indeed to be able to acknowledge and interact with beings from other realms. Even were he able to acknowledge them, it would still be easier to accomplish this at the appropriate level of *samādhi*. For this reason, *upacāra samādhi* — the access gate — is a level suitable to nearly every eventuality.

Ācariya Mun became an expert in these matters during his sojourn at Sarika Cave many years before. At that time, he had been an ordained monk for twenty-two years. By the time he passed away, after spending a total of sixty years in the robes, he had become a true master of these matters. Everyone in the world has the same potential for perceiving such phenomena as Ācariya Mun had — they need only to develop it. But, very few can develop his exceptional skills. However, even though they fell short of his total mastery, if people could develop at least some skill, it would be sufficient for witnessing such things. Instead, being unable to see them, people tend to believe that such phenomena do not actually exist in the world around them.

It's difficult to convince people who lack sufficient knowledge of Dhamma for endowing their hearts with a strong spiritual basis. Should our hearts develop the principles of Dhamma — principles certifying the true nature of all phenomena — and gain the necessary skills, then no amount of denial could possibly negate what we clearly see for ourselves. Even if everyone on earth insisted on denying the existence of such things, it would merely be an empty denial. The true nature of what we perceive remains unchanged — nothing can possibly alter it. Truth does not depend on beliefs or opinions of any kind. It is true according to immutable natural principles.

Ācariya Mun wandered far and wide throughout most of the remote and mountainous districts of Chiang Mai province, traveling more extensively there than in any other province. He remained in Chiang Mai much longer than he did in other places, largely because it was suitable for meditation. It was conducive to the many kinds of insights that were a unique feature of his practice. He claimed there were many reasons for his long sojourn there. First of all, the environment was suitable to meditation. Secondly, he felt sorry for the hill tribes people who needed his assistance, and was reluctant to abandon them. Although it was sparsely populated, many extraordinary individuals lived in that area. They needed proper training and encouragement to insure their steady progress and to avert disappointment and reversal to their old ways. And then there were all the *devas* whom he was determined to assist.

Groups of *devas* and *nāgas* usually came to ask questions and listen to his discourses at least twice a month. He said that, at night, he was always busy receiving visitors from all over the celestial and terrestrial realms. Before speaking with Ācariya Mun, the leader of each group would announce the approximate number of *devas* present on that occasion: for instance, ten or a hundred thousand celestial *devas* are here today, or one to ten thousand terrestrial *devas*, or five hundred to a thousand *nāgas*.

Almost daily, when he walked meditation in the late afternoon, Ācariya Mun would be informed of the hour of arrival of one group or another from these different realms. Occasionally, he received the information later on during seated meditation. There were nights when several different groups announced their impending visit; and he had to arrange specific times for each group so that their visits did not overlap. He did not have them come simultaneously, because relative spiritual development varied among the different realms and his Dhamma teaching had to vary accordingly to be appropriate for each group. Since one group preferred hearing a certain aspect of Dhamma, while another group preferred something different, Ācariya Mun arranged separate visits to ensure that his discourse was suitable to everyone present. This was done for his own convenience, as well as that of his visitors. Such obligations were a major part of the reason for his long stay in Chiang Mai. As a matter of fact, the number of *devas* of all types who visited him there well exceeded the number of people, *nāgas*, *garuḍas*, and other spirits combined. In reality, very few individuals can achieve telepathic communication with *devas*, which is essential for teaching them.

Devas often complained to Ācariya Mun that, unaware of the existence of *devas*, human beings have no understanding about *devas* and are not interested in knowing that devic existence is another state of sentient existence adhering to the principles of *kamma*. Devic existence is irrelevant to most human beings, who fail to recognize that *devas* also have hopes and aspirations, just like everyone else. Rarely did *devas* encounter a man of supreme virtue, like Ācariya Mun— a man who possessed the intuitive insight to realize that animals, humans, *devas*, and all other forms of existence are undeniably real and should be honored as such. They could not help feeling an overwhelming sense of joy upon meeting him. They so enjoyed coming to pay him their respects, ask him questions and listen to his teaching. They wanted to imbibe his exquisite Dhamma to nourish their hearts, thus increasing their happiness and well-being and sustaining their whole existence. For this reason, *devas* everywhere venerate anyone possessing extremely high virtue.

Relating that *devas* are just as important as all other living beings, Ācariya Mun understood their intentions and sympathized with their meritorious aspirations. He stated that, intent on improving themselves, the *devas* who came to him for assistance greatly outnumbered the human beings who visited him. Still, they remain a mystery to people who lack the proper psychic skills. Though appearing on the surface to be an insoluble problem for human society, it need not be an insurmountable obstacle for a person wishing to truly know and understand these things. For those skilled in the ways of the *citta*, psychic communication is just as normal as any other aspect of human experience. Certainly Ācariya Mun considered it commonplace, allowing him to function effectively with *devas* throughout his life. Regardless of where he lived, he always remained in contact with *devas* requiring his assistance. This was especially true in Chiang Mai province, because such beings preferred to contact him when he was living in remote, isolated places, free from human congestion. The forests and mountains of Chiang Mai were ideal in this respect. Ācariya Mun had few social obligations there, so he could devote more time to his *deva* visitors.

A STRANGE INCIDENT occurred while he was living among the Museur people deep in the mountains near Ikaw Village. A group of *devas* from Germany came to visit him. They wished to hear a discourse that would give them a 'victory formula'. Focusing his *citta* on their request, an appropriate Dhamma verse arose: *"akkodhena jine kodhaṁ."* It means *conquer anger with lack of anger.*[12] Ācariya Mun elaborated on this theme with the assembled *devas*.

"Conquer anger with lack of anger, remember this. For anyone hoping to achieve victory, this is the most important Dhamma to practice. Consider it well — it is the main source of peace and happiness in the world. Love and kindness — these are an effective deterrence against an evil such as anger. By helping to reduce anger's power to destroy human and devic societies alike, loving kindness fosters peace and prosperity everywhere. Thus, this loving attitude is a prerequisite for social harmony— one we should all strive to develop. In a world lacking this victory formula, dissatisfaction and unrest will arise at the very least. At the extreme, the world will be consumed by mortal strife. Anger and resentment can never defeat our enemies, for they are evils that succeed only in indiscriminately destroying us and everyone close to us. The more anger is used, the more the world we live in becomes a sea of flames, burning uncontrollably toward total annihilation.

"Anger is actually a type of fire that's inherent in the nature of this world. Although it has no physical properties, it does succeed in creating havoc in its wake. So anyone desiring a stable, sensible world — a place worth living in — should realize the disastrous harm that the fires of anger and resentment can cause; and refrain from ever using them. Starting a fire like this merely causes oneself and everyone else to suffer. Mutual feelings of affection and loving kindness among all living beings maintain the world in its proper equilibrium. Oppressive forces of unrestrained anger and selfish pride should never be allowed to run rampant, causing a never-ending cycle of destruction.

"With his acute wisdom, the Lord Buddha realized the indisputable harm caused by anger. He saw the value of loving kindness as a gentle force that can spontaneously join all living beings in a sense of mutual harmony and goodwill, for all share a common desire for happiness and a common dislike of pain. For this reason, he taught that love and kindness were powerful means of maintaining peace and security in the world. So long as living beings still have loving kindness in their hearts, there's every chance that their desire for happiness will be fulfilled. But should their hearts become estranged from thoughts of loving kindness, then even with all the material comforts, their lives will still be devoid of genuine peace and happiness. Angry, hateful people tend to encounter only trouble, feeling resentful and annoyed wherever they go.

"Once we know with certainty that Dhamma is something truly beneficial to us, we can clearly see that a heart full of brutality is like a blazing fire gradually destroying everything in its path. We must then urgently strive to overcome these dangers as best we can. You may never again get such a good opportunity; so, take advantage of it now and avoid regrets in the future. The world is in a constant state of change and that changing world is situated right here in the bodies and minds of us all."

Such was the essence of the 'victory formula' that Ācariya Mun gave to the *devas* from Germany. As soon as Ācariya Mun finished speaking, they gave a thunderous "*sādhu*" in unison that echoed throughout the world systems. Ācariya Mun asked how they knew where he was staying since, in human terms, they lived so far away. They replied that they always knew precisely where he was staying. More than that, *devas* from Thailand regularly visit the *devas* of Germany. In truth, *devas* don't consider the distance between countries like Thailand and Germany to be very great, the way human beings do. They simply think of it as an area through which they can easily and naturally pass back and forth. Whereas humans travel by foot or by vehicle, *devas* transport themselves by means of a supernormal power that is equivalent to transfering consciousness to a particular destination — it arrives there instantly. So *devas* can move around much more easily than human beings.

Ācariya Mun said that the *devas* from Germany regularly came to listen to his Dhamma talks, much in the same way that terrestrial *devas* came from all over Thailand to hear him. Both celestial and terrestrial *devas* tended to show their respect for him in a similar fashion. If Ācariya Mun was living with a group of monks, *devas* who came to see him never passed through the area where the monks had their living quarters. Besides that, they tended to arrive very late at night when all the monks were asleep. Upon arrival, they circumambulated Ācariya Mun clockwise, three times in a calm, composed manner. When they departed — again circumambulating him clockwise three times — they first withdrew to a respectful distance. When they reached the edge of his living area, they simply floated into the air like puffs of cotton. All types of *devas* demonstrated their respect for him in this fashion.

Ācariya Mun found the mountains of Chiang Mai to be an ideal environment for meditation. Heart free and mind unencumbered, he lived a life of complete ease, abiding sublimely in Dhamma — Dhamma was the enduring source of comfort in his life. With no intrusions taking up his time, he was free to meditate whenever he wished. He lived a very healthy, contented life there. As for his teaching obligations, the *devas*, who came only at night, were beings of a refined nature, so they were hardly a burden. Sometimes in the afternoon or early evening he gave helpful advice to the local lay community. The monks living under his tutelage assembled for instruction in the evening, at about seven p.m. Most of his students had already achieved a certain level of proficiency in the practice of *samādhi* and in the various stages of wisdom. Being wholly committed to the practice, they listened to his teaching, striving to attain *magga*, *phala*, and Nibbāna.

When Ācariya Mun taught a group of monks, whose individual levels of mental development varied, he always structured his discourses to encompass all levels of practice, from basic *samādhi* through the higher levels of wisdom to the most subtle level of all — the realization of Nibbāna. Monks, skilled in meditation, became so absorbed in the successive stages of his discourse that they lost all sense of time and place. Practicing monks were usually given a talk lasting for at least two hours. But the monks were less interested in the time than they were in the flow of his Dhamma discourse, as they were able to gradually increase their own understanding with each successive stage. Consequently, listening to Dhamma in an attentive, thoughtful manner is itself a valuable meditation practice, one that is equally as important as other methods. For his part, the teacher is determined that his audience realize the truth of what he teaches — every step of the way. He points out the kind of thoughts that are truly harmful, as well as those that are truly beneficial; so, his students will understand which thinking is faulty and should be abandoned, and which has merit and should be developed further. More than at any comparable time, those focusing their undivided attention on the *citta* — the focal point of

Dhamma — can expect to attain some degree of calm in *samādhi*; or receive various techniques for investigating with wisdom, while they listen to the teacher discuss these topics. Thus, the diligent meditator can progress step by step while listening to his teacher's instructions. Receiving an insight into one aspect of Dhamma today, another aspect of Dhamma tomorrow, students manage to strengthen their mindfulness and wisdom every time they listen. Since the teacher has realized the Truth of Dhamma within himself, he can point directly to that same Truth existing within his students. Listening to his detailed explanations, they can progressively develop their skills in all aspects of *samādhi* and wisdom, allowing them to successfully pass through each level of meditation practice until they reach the highest Dhamma.

Dhutanga monks have always considered hearing Dhamma an essential part of their practice, one they seek to maintain as long as there is a skilled teacher to whom they can listen. For this reason, truly dedicated *dhutanga* monks like to search out a teacher who can guide them in their meditation practice. They cherish and revere a teacher in whom they feel they can put their complete trust. His advice is sincerely taken to heart, carefully contemplated, and wholeheartedly put into practice. They routinely consult with him, asking for specific advice on any doubtful points arising in their practice, then adjust their practice according to his recommendations. For this reason, *dhutanga* monks have always preferred to gather around eminently qualified meditation masters, such as Ācariya Mun and Ācariya Sao. Both of those great teachers had unusually large numbers of disciples among the *dhutanga* monks of Thailand's Northeast region.

But in Ācariya Mun's case, once he moved to Chiang Mai he resolved to avoid his fellow monks and practice deliberately on his own, without the added burden of responsibility that teaching entails. In the beginning, he wanted to accelerate his drive for the ultimate goal. Later, he found it conducive to living in comfort. All the same, he had to accept certain obligations to teach monks as well as lay people, and it's well known that he had many disciples all over Thailand. In the period before Ācariya Mun went off alone to make his decisive push in the wilds of Chiang Mai, he often mentioned that, spiritually, he still was not strong enough — either in his own practice, or in his ability to teach others. So he resolved to go away and practice with the utmost diligence until no doubts — of any kind — remained in his heart. From that time on, he never mentioned anything about lacking sufficient strength.

Big Brother Elephant

Once Ācariya Mun was wandering *dhutanga* in the Chiang Mai mountains with two other monks, Ācariya Khao of Wat Tham Klong Phen monastery in Udon Thani province and Ācariya Mahā Thongsak of Wat Suddhawat monastery in Sakon Nakhon province. As they reached a narrow gap in the path leading up the mountain, they chanced upon a large, solitary elephant whose owner had released it and then wandered off someplace. All they could see there was a gigantic elephant with huge six-foot tusks searching for food — quite a fearsome sight. They conferred among themselves about how to proceed. This was the only path up the mountain, and it allowed no room for going around the elephant. Ācariya Mun told Ācariya Khao to speak with the elephant, which was eating bamboo leaves at the side of the path. Standing about twenty yards away with its back to them, it had yet to notice their approach. Ācariya Khao addressed the elephant:

"Big brother elephant, we wish to speak with you."

At first, the elephant didn't clearly hear his voice, but it did stop chewing the bamboo leaves.

"Big brother elephant, we wish to speak with you."

Clearly hearing this, the elephant suddenly swung around to face the monks. It stood stock-still, its ears fully extended.

"Big brother elephant, we wish to speak with you. You are so very big and strong. We're just a group of monks, so weak and so very frightened of you, big brother. We would like to walk past where you're standing. Would big brother please move over a bit so that we have room to pass by? If you keep standing there, it really frightens us, so we don't dare walk past."

As soon as he finished speaking, the elephant immediately turned to the side and thrust its tusks into the middle of a clump of bamboo, signaling its intention to let them pass, unharmed. Seeing it facing the clump of bamboo, Ācariya Mun told the others that they could continue on as it would not bother them now. The two monks invited

Ācariya Mun to walk between them, Ācariya Khao walking in front and Ācariya Mahā Thong Sak following behind. They walked past in single file only six feet from the elephant's rear end, without incident. But as they were walking away, the hook on Ācariya Mahā Thong Sak's umbrella got tangled by chance in some bamboo just a few yards past the elephant. It defied all attempts to extricate it, so he was forced to struggle with it for quite some time. Terrified of the elephant — which was now looking right at him — he was soon drenched in sweat. Fighting desperately to disentangle the hook, he glanced up at the eyes of the elephant, which stood there like a huge stuffed animal. He could see that its eyes were bright and clear. In truth, its countenance inspired affection rather than fear, but at that moment his fear remained strong. When he finally did get free, his fear subsided, and he realized that this elephant was a very endearing animal. Seeing that they were all safely past, Ācariya Khao turned to the elephant.

"Hey, big brother, we've all passed by now. Please relax and eat in peace."

As soon as he finished speaking, the sound of crunching, breaking bamboo filled the air.

Later the monks praised this intelligent elephant, agreeing it was an animal that inspired affection and sympathy. The only faculty it lacked was the ability to speak. As they were discussing this, Ācariya Mahā Thong Sak was curious to hear Ācariya Mun's reaction, so he asked:

"Were you able to read that elephant's mind the whole time, from the moment we spoke to it until we passed clear of it? Since it was so endearing, I'd really like to know. When it first heard us call out, suddenly turning around to face us in an agitated fashion, I was sure it was about to charge and crush us to pieces right then and there. But as soon as it understood the situation, it had a change of heart — almost like a person in an animal's body — and quickly thrust its tusks into the middle of that clump of bamboo and stood very still. Clearly it seemed to be telling us: 'You little brothers can come now. Big brother won't do anything. Big brother has put away his weapons. Believe me, come along.' "

Ācariya Mahā Thong Sak then teased Ācariya Khao:

"Ācariya Khao is really amazing, speaking with an animal as though it was just another human being: 'Big brother, your little brothers are frightened and dare not pass. Please make way so that we can go by without fearing big brother.' As soon as it received this bit of flattery, it was so pleased that it immediately prepared to make way for us. But this little brother was really clumsy. I got past big brother only to get my umbrella hook caught up in the bamboo. Try as I might I couldn't get it free. It was determined to keep me there with big brother. My heart sank at that moment — I was afraid that big brother wouldn't play fair."

Ācariya Mun laughed heartily hearing Ācariya Mahā Thong Sak teasing Ācariya Khao about being clever enough to talk to an elephant. He assured them that he had been paying attention to the elephant's mental state.

"Of course I was focusing my attention there. I've read the minds of birds and monkeys with far less reason than this. This was a matter of life and death, how could I avoid it?"

Ācariya Mahā Thong Sak wanted to know what the elephant was thinking when Ācariya Mun focused on it.

"When it first heard us, it was startled — that's why it turned around so quickly. It thought only of preparing to fight. But seeing us dressed in yellow robes, it knew instinctively that we could be trusted, for it's quite used to seeing monks. Its owner has long since trained it not to endanger them. So when Ācariya Khao addressed it in a pleasant tone, calling it 'big brother', it was hugely pleased and immediately got out of the way."

"Did it understand every word that Ācariya Khao said to it?"

"Of course it did. Otherwise, how could it be trained to haul logs down from the mountains? If it couldn't understand, it would probably have been disposed of as useless long ago. This kind of animal must be trained until it knows man's language well before it can be made to perform various tasks. This particular elephant is over a hundred years old. Look at its tusks — they're almost six feet long. It must have lived among people for a long time. Its owner is relatively young, yet he's still able to drive it to work. How could it not understand human speech? It's certain to have no problem."

"What was it thinking when it turned and stuck its tusks into the clump of bamboo?"

"Well, it understood the situation, as I said, and so was giving way to us. It didn't think of doing anything else."

"Did you focus on its mind the whole time we were walking past it? What was it thinking just as we walked by?"

"All I saw was the elephant giving way. It wasn't thinking about anything else."

"The reason I asked: I was worried that as we were walking past it might have thought it would like to attack us — just for sport, as animals sometimes do."

"You have an uncommonly prolific imagination, Mahā Thong Sak. If you enjoyed thinking and asking probing questions like this about matters of substance then you could certainly expect to transcend *dukkha* one day. But you're like most people — you insist on wasting your time thinking about inane matters instead of useful ones, and you probably don't care to change. Are you going to keep pondering this matter, asking about that elephant all night without the slightest regard for Dhamma?"

With this warning, Ācariya Mahā Thong Sak dropped the whole affair. He was afraid that pressing the matter further would result in an even more severe rebuke.[13]

MANY MONKS WERE REBUKED for speaking carelessly to Ācariya Mun or speaking without good reason. Some even went mad afterwards. One rather obtrusive monk lived with Ācariya Mun for a short while. When Ācariya Mun made a comment, this monk liked to chime in expressing his own views. When he first arrived, Ācariya Mun frequently warned him to mind his own business. He advised him to keep a close watch on his thoughts and restrain the impulse to speak out. Monks dedicated to the practice must know how to properly conduct themselves. Those who are mindful will see the inadequacies of a mind that wants to flow out. But it seems that this monk was not as interested as he should have been in Ācariya Mun's teaching.

Ācariya Mun had a unique habit of taking the animals, or the people, that he encountered on almsround as objects of contemplation, using them to teach the monks walking behind him. He commented out loud on what he observed, as though speaking to no one in particular. One day, he spied a cute little calf playfully running around its mother. At first it didn't see the monks approaching; but as they came abreast, it looked around startled and raced to its mother's side, nuzzling in under her neck, then peering out to look at the monks with fear in its eyes. Seeing the calf run up to her, the cow quickly turned her head to look in the direction of the monks, then remained impassive, as animals do when they are accustomed to seeing monks daily. But the calf remained under her chin, staring out distrustfully. Observing them,

Ācariya Mun commented in a general way about the difference between the reaction of the calf and that of its mother.

"That cow is quite unperturbed, but its calf is so frightened it looks like it wants to pick her up and flee.[14] As soon as it got a glimpse of us, it ran bawling to its mother for help. People are just the same — they rush to find a reliable refuge. If they are near their mother, they will run to her. If they are near their father, they will rush to him. People invariably lean on family and friends for support. Rarely do they think about relying on themselves. When we are young, we expect to rely on other people in one way; when we grow up, we expect to rely on them in another way; and when we grow old, we still expect to rely on others in yet a different way. Very few of us turn inward, looking for support within ourselves. By constantly looking for someone else to lean on, we tend to foster our own weakness and so never allow ourselves to become truly self-reliant.

"We monks are the same as lay people. Having ordained, we become lazy about studying. Worrying that it will be painful and difficult, we become lazy about practicing the way. We never seem to finish what we start, for no sooner do we have a good idea and begin to put it into practice than laziness creeps in, blocking our progress. Lacking the ability to help ourselves, we have to look to others for support. Otherwise, we couldn't carry on in this life. The maxim: *attāhi attano nātho* — oneself is one's own refuge — is meaningless for us if we cannot breath through our own noses. *Dhutanga* monks who are dedicated to the practice shouldn't always have to depend on others for life and breath.

"Listen to your teacher, think about what he teaches, and commit yourselves to attaining it. Don't let his teaching just slip through your grasp to no avail. Be persistent. Consider what he says and follow his example until you see the benefits within yourselves. Then you no longer need to lean on him for support. You'll be breathing through your own noses, meaning you will have developed the knowledge and wisdom needed to rid yourselves of *dukkha*. Gradually, you will become more confident, more self-reliant, until finally you become full-fledged, fully-independent monks in your own right."

Ācariya Mun brought up this matter to give the monks on almsround with him something to contemplate. As he paused for a moment, the rather obtrusive monk began to prattle away on his own without considering the impropriety of such an intrusion. Perhaps this monk's idiocy struck a dissonant chord deep within Ācariya Mun, for he turned around and gave him a severe rebuke that took the other monks aback, making them all somewhat apprehensive.

"You must be mad! You're like a rabid dog that pounces and chews furiously on any old piece of wood tossed at it. Why don't you look inside yourself where this madness arises. You'll go crazy if you don't curtail this sort of mindless prattle."

Ācariya Mun then turned around and walked back to the monastery without another word. Arriving at the monastery, the monks noticed something peculiar about the obtrusive monk — he seemed stunned, eating very little. Seeing his odd behavior, the monks kept quiet, as if nothing had happened. They were afraid he would feel embarrassed. For the rest of the day life in the monastery continued as normal, each monk applying himself to his meditation. But later, during the night when all was quiet, they heard someone cry out in a deranged, incoherent voice. They immediately rushed over to find the monk lying in his hut, tossing deliriously about, mumbling something about being sorry for offending Ācariya Mun so rudely. Shocked by this sight, some of them hurried off to get the local villagers to help take care of him. They brought some herbal remedies for him to take, then massaged his limbs for a while until he finally calmed down and fell asleep for the rest of the night. The next morning someone took him to a doctor for treatment. His condition soon improved, though he did have occasional relapses. When he was well enough to travel, they sent him home. There was no further news about his condition after that.

Ācariya Mun's reprimands varied with circumstances. A mild scolding was usually sufficient to promote mindfulness in the present and increase vigilance in the future. However, if someone did something that prompted a severe reprimand, but lacked the good judgment to make use of it, then it could well be damaging, as we have seen. So monks living with Ācariya Mun tended to be exceedingly vigilant and always self-controlled. Just because they had lived with him for a long time didn't mean they could expect to get overly familiar with him, for he was the type of person who didn't readily countenance familiarity

in anyone. His students could never afford to be complacent —
sometimes even the deer that's wary of hunters gets shot.

Youthful Exuberance

Occasionally, when the monks living with him were highly attained
individuals, Ācariya Mun conducted himself in a naturally easy-going
and relaxed manner, as one would expect among people of equal
status who are all well-acquainted. He was not so stern and strict at
such times. But his whole demeanor could change dramatically
according to the situation. He behaved quite differently in one set of
circumstances than he did in another, treating each individual as a
separate case. His disciples were constantly amazed at the quickness
and novelty of his responses to the situations that emerged around him.

Ācariya Mun used to tell the monks an amusing story about his
youth that illustrates his dynamic character. I shall retell it here for it
demonstrates the incredible changes that a person can go through.

Back in the days when Ācariya Mun was still a young layman, he
used to compete in local folk singing contests known as *maw lam*.[15]
One day he attended a large fair in a neighboring village where
thousands of people had gathered. Suddenly, he felt emboldened to
get up on stage and sing in competition with a talented young woman
who was a renowned folk singer in those parts. Perhaps he thought it
would be fun to have a go at her on stage, or perhaps he felt a little bit
in love — who knows? At any rate, jumping up on stage, he found the
young woman quite willing to accept his challenge. By the time they
sang through several sets of verses, it became clear that young Mun
was losing the contest. As it happened, a savior appeared just in time.
Chao Khun Upāli,[16] who was then a young man several years older
than young Mun, had come to the same fair and was in the audience
at the competition. Obviously his friend was losing badly, and things
were getting worse with each new set of verses. Continued much
longer, the girl would probably have driven him off the stage in
disgrace, for she was a seasoned performer and young Mun was a mere
novice. Acting on a bold impulse, Mun had leapt up on the stage only
to meet a ferocious tigress, her mouth full of fangs, while he was just a
pup sporting a few baby teeth. Jan, as Chao Khun Upāli was called

then, anxiously thought that if his friend persisted, she would skin him alive, then sell his hide. He thought to himself: *Mun doesn't know a tiger when he sees one. He just sees a young lady — he doesn't realize he's about to be slaughtered. I'll have to do something now to save his hide. If I don't, it'll be on sale in the market for sure.* Having thought this, Jan jumped up on the stage and began shouting:

"Damn it Mun! I've been looking for you all over the place! Your mother fell from the top of the house — I'm not sure if she's still alive or not. I saw her lying there in a heap on the ground and tried to help, but she insisted I go look for you. I've been running around all day trying to find you. I haven't eaten a thing and I'm worn out."

Both Mun and the young lady were stunned into silence by this ruse. Mun immediately asked about his mother's condition.

"Jan, how is my mother?"

Jan pretended to be so exhausted he could hardly speak.

"I think she's probably dead by now. I'm about to die myself now from hunger and exhaustion."

With that he grabbed Mun's arm, dragging him from the stage before a crowd of thousands of shocked onlookers, and ran with him as fast as possible. By the time they reached the village outskirts, Mun was desperate to find out more about his mother.

"What was my mother doing on the top of the house to make her fall?"

"I don't really know what caused her to fall. Seeing her lying there on the ground, I rushed to help. But she sent me right off to look for you, so I came straight away. I didn't have a chance to get the full story."

"As far as you could tell, was my mother going to die?"

"We're on our way now to find that out for ourselves."

When they had walked sufficiently far from the village that Jan reckoned Mun wouldn't dare go back alone at such a late hour[17] his whole demeanor abruptly changed as he frankly told Mun that nothing had happened to his mother.

"I put on that act because I couldn't bear to see your old lady mop the floor with you. I was afraid she'd skin your hide and sell it in the market. That would have been humiliating for me, and for our whole village. She was about to emasculate you there just for the fun of it. So I tricked you both into believing this story, at the same time convincing the crowd that you had to flee the scene because of a real emergency — not because you'd lost the will to fight. I rushed you away before anyone had a chance to catch on to my ruse. Even that feisty old lady of yours couldn't help being overwhelmed by my ingenious scheme. Did you see how taken in she was? Alarmed by what I said, she watched us leave with heartfelt sympathy for you and your mother. I saved you from the hell she had in store for you. Now what do you think, wasn't that an ingenious scheme?"

"Oh no! What a shame! Damn you Jan, look what you've done to me! I was having a great time chopping her to pieces! By dragging me away, you spoiled my fun. I never imagined you'd do this to me. I'd like to have another go at her right now. I'd be the one sending her hide to the market!"

"Ha! You were being slaughtered, and I saved your life! And now you're bragging about how good you were. Maybe I should take you back right now so your old lady can put you on the chopping block again."

"Look, seeing she was a woman, I figured I'd go easy on her at first, hoping she'd get overconfident. When I had her where I wanted her, I planned to tie her up, throw her in a sack, and sell her to the highest bidder. You failed to understand my strategy — I was baiting her, like a tiger luring a monkey."

"If you're so smart then how come you fell for my little sham to pull you away from her devilish clutches. You were so shocked you almost started crying shamelessly right in front of your lady friend. Who'd have ever considered you capable of bagging the old girl? It was obvious — she was about to tie you up and throw you off the stage in full view of thousands of people. Stop bragging so much Mun! You should appreciate my brotherly efforts to save you from defeat at the hands of that woman."

That night Mun and Jan both ended up missing the fair they had so looked forward to attending.

ALTHOUGH THEY WERE STILL in lay life at the time, such stories about these two sages matching wits were fascinating to hear. Despite the worldly nature of the conversation, it demonstrates how clever people converse — each new retort captures the imagination. When Ācariya Mun related stories about the two of them, we became so absorbed listening that we could almost visualize them as they spoke. There are lots of stories about these two men matching wits, but a few examples should be enough to give the reader an idea of what I mean. The clever ploys they used as young men gave an early indication of their intelligence. Eventually entering the monkhood, both became great sages. Chao Khun Upāli Guṇūpamācariya and Ācariya Mun Bhūridatta Thera are renowned throughout Thailand as present day sages of the highest caliber.

I have used the diminutives Jan and Mun because that's how Ācariya Mun himself told the story to his students during relaxed moments when there was a break in the usual tense, guarded atmosphere the monks felt when they were around him. I sincerely apologize to both of these esteemed venerables, and to the readers as well, if anything I've written is deemed inappropriate. Had I written the story in a more formal style, the meaning would not have come across so effectively. Such familiarity implies a mutual respect among peers and is commonly used between close friends of all ages. Moreover, I find it convenient to write the story the way I originally heard it. It allows us a glimpse of these two renowned elders as high-spirited youths having a good time, which we can then compare with our usual image of them as absolutely amazing monks who completely renounced the world.

Although Ācariya Mun preferred to keep to the present, rarely speaking about the past, he liked to sing the praises of Chao Khun Upāli's cleverness from time to time. On one occasion, when they were discussing the story of Lord Vessantara,[18] he asked Chao Khun Upāli about the mother of Lady Madrī, a character in the story. He hadn't seen her name mentioned in the scriptures, and thought perhaps he had missed it. Chao Khun Upāli's response was immediate:

"What, you've never seen or heard of Madrī's mother? Everyone in town knows about her. Where've you been looking that you haven't come across her yet?"

Admitting that he hadn't come across her name in the scriptures, Ācariya Mun wondered where it was mentioned.

"Scriptures? What scriptures? What about that loudmouth Mrs. Op who lives in the big house at the crossroads on the way to the monastery?"

Ācariya Mun was puzzled. He couldn't recall any mention of a monastery in the story. Which crossroads and what monastery was he referring to.

"You know, Madrī's mother whose house is right next to yours. How could you not know Madrī and her mother? How pitiful — Madrī and her mother live in your own home village and you don't even recognize them. Instead, you go searching in the scriptures. I feel embarrassed for you."

The moment Chao Khun Upāli said that Madrī and her mother lived in his home village, Ācariya Mun caught on and was able to recollect them. Prior to that he was puzzled, for he kept thinking of the *Vessantara Jātaka* story. He said that Chao Khun Upāli was very clever at skillfully matching wits, using wordplay and riposte in unexpected ways to keep his listeners off balance, thus making them use their intelligence. Ācariya Mun used to laugh when he told us about falling victim to Chao Khun Upāli's little artifice.

ĀCARIYA MUN SPENT one rains retreat near the village of Ban Nam Mao in the Mae Pang district of Chiang Mai province. Sakka, the heavenly *devarāja*, frequently came to visit, bringing a large retinue with him. Even in the dry season, when he went off into the mountains alone and stayed in Dok Kham Cave, Sakka brought his followers to visit him there. Usually numbering well over one hundred thousand on those occasions, they came more often and in larger numbers than other groups of *devas*. If some in his retinue had never come before, Sakka first explained to them the proper way to listen to Dhamma. Ācariya Mun usually took *mettā appamaññā brahmavihāra*[19] as the theme of his discourse because these *devas* were especially fond of that subject.

Being very isolated, tranquil places, Ban Nam Mao and Dok Khan Cave brought more groups of *devas* from many different realms to visit Ācariya Mun than did any of his other locations. These beings showed great respect for Ācariya Mun, and for the place where he lived. Upon entering the area, they were always careful to bypass his walking meditation path which the villagers had smoothed out with sand: it was sacrosanct. *Nāgas*, too, avoided passage across the path when arriving for a visit. On occasions when their leader had to pass through that area, he always circled around the head of the meditation path. Sometimes the *nāgas* sent a messenger to invite Ācariya Mun to attend a function, much as humans do when they invite monks to local functions. The messengers always avoided crossing his meditation path. Occasionally, when they were unable to avoid crossing over some of the sand that the villagers had scattered around that area, they would first sweep the sand away with their hands, and then crawl across. Standing up again, they walked to Ācariya Mun's residence. Their behavior was always wonderfully composed.

Ācariya Mun believed that if human beings, the custodians of the *sāsana*, have a true interest in Dhamma and a deeply-rooted feeling of genuine self-respect, they should exhibit the same reverential behavior toward the *sāsana* as *devas* and *nāgas* do. Although we're unable to see for ourselves how those beings show their respect, the teachings of Buddhism address all such matters in full. Unfortunately, we humans are not as interested in them as we should be. We seem more intent on creating a stifling, negligent attitude within ourselves, thus failing to experience the kind of happiness we could otherwise expect. In truth, the *sāsana* is the wellspring of all virtuous conduct, which assures happiness to those adhering to the venerable principles of Buddhism.

Ācariya Mun continually emphasized that the heart is the most important thing in the world. A heart that is vulgar ends up vulgarizing everything with which it comes into contact. Much like a filthy body, it soils whatever it touches — no matter how nice and clean it may initially be — making it filthy too in the end. So Dhamma cannot escape being tainted by a vulgar heart. Even though Dhamma itself is perfectly pure, it becomes tarnished as soon as it's embraced by someone with a corrupt heart — like a clean cloth being rubbed in the dirt. For example, when a wicked person tries to impress others with his knowledge of the Buddhist scriptures, nothing good ever comes of it. Vulgar people who are stubborn and unyielding about religious matters are just the same; and no matter how extraordinary Buddhism is, they are unable to derive any of its benefits. They merely proclaim themselves to be Buddhists but they never understand the real significance of Buddhism and how it applies to them personally.

The actual truth about the *sāsana* is this: we ourselves are the *sāsana*. No matter how good or bad our actions are, whatever subsequent degree of happiness or suffering we experience — all directly affect the *sāsana*. The word "*sāsana*" means the correct way of living as practiced by each individual. If we think the *sāsana* exists outside of ourselves, then our understanding is wrong, and so our practice too is bound to be wrong. Anything which is wrong is more or less useless. It can be made useful only at the expense of the righteousness, dignity, and integrity of each individual. Put simply and clearly: if we are wrong in our hearts, then whatever we do turns out wrong. For instance, calculations don't add up; clothes don't fit properly; traffic regulations are ignored; married couples deviate from accepted norms, failing to honor their vows; parents and children are at logger-heads; wealth is ill-gotten, its distribution inequitable; the authorities flout the laws of the land which are designed to keep peace; rulers and their constituents cannot seem to work together for the common good according to the law, and so become distrustful, behaving like enemies.

Regardless of how we experience the harmful consequences, the disappointment and misfortune that result from wrong actions will inevitably arise right where they are committed — in the heart. The cause being wrong, the effect is bound to be harmful. When we wrong someone, the harmful consequences from that action are unavoidable, even in cases where we are unaware of having wronged that person. The wrongdoer must necessarily receive the full results of his actions. It's no use thinking that we can somehow avoid the unpleasant consequences — whatever they are, they will definitely manifest themselves someday. By remaining indifferent or negligent about wrongdoing, we face the clear prospect of personal misfortune here and now in this lifetime. Looking any further ahead than this would merely amount to grasping at shadows and missing the real issue. The *sāsana* is not a shadowy specter, deluding people into ignorance. It's a path that unerringly reveals the Truth in all its many aspects. Followers of the *sāsana,* who deviate from the path and then unfairly accuse it of having failed them, are inextricably compounding their own miserable predicament. The *sāsana,* as always, remains pure and unperturbed.

Ācariya Mun always stressed that people who accept the Truth, embodied in Buddhist principles, receive the blessings of Dhamma. Being cool and calm themselves, all their relationships tend to be the same as well. The world they live in is a peaceful place where they are unlikely to suffer the kind of contentious bickering that causes acrimony and engulfs both parties in heated recriminations. The reason people never experience the happiness they long for is that they allow a fiery, inflamed mentality to dictate their attitude in everything from business dealings to workplace, from legal proceedings to marketplace. Wherever they go, whatever they do — they are as hot as fire, so they find it hard to maintain a balance in their lives. Such people never seem to consider dousing the bonfire they constantly carry in their hearts so as to gain enough breathing room to relax, balance themselves, and find some measure of happiness.

Ācariya Mun said that during his whole life as a Buddhist monk he enjoyed investigating the Dhamma taught by the Lord Buddha, whose incomparable breadth and depth are infinitely greater than those of the vast oceans. In all truth, the *sāsana* is so inconceivably profound and subtle that it's virtually impossible to investigate every aspect of it; and the results attained from each successive stage of the practice are so amazing that they defy description. He insisted that only his concern that others would think him crazy kept him from continuously prostrating himself to the Buddha, Dhamma, and Sangha. He would consider it his occupation otherwise, performing it easily and joyfully without ever experiencing fatigue or boredom. He was absolutely certain that, whatever happened, he would always be inseparable from the Buddha, Dhamma, and Sangha — *akāliko*. In stark contrast, the world of *anicca*, *dukkha*, and *anattā* constantly smothers the hearts of living beings, leaving them forever distressed and resentful.

The Mysterious Effects of Kamma

Once while he was meditating, deep in the Chiang Mai mountains, Ācariya Mun saw a vision of a woman and a small novice walking back and forth through the area, nearly every night in the late hours. Becoming suspicious after a while, he asked why they were there. They told him that they were worried about the fate of an unfinished *stupa*[20] which they were building together when they died. The small novice was the woman's younger brother, and they had worked together to construct the *stupa*. Their concern about the *stupa* and their regrets at having died before its completion made them feel a strong, persistent obligation to it. Although reborn into a state of anxiety, they were not as tormented by it as might be expected. Still, they could not feel decisive about being reborn into another realm of existence.

So Ācariya Mun advised them: "You should not be concerned about things that have already come and gone, for they are truly irredeemable. No matter how convinced you may be that you can turn back the clock — it's just not possible. Anyone supposing they can will experience nothing but frustration when their hopes fail to materialize. The future, having yet to come, shouldn't be clung to either. What has already happened should be let go of as being past. What has yet to arrive should be let go of as its time is not yet ripe. Only in the present is it possible to accomplish something meaningful.

"If your dream of building that *stupa* were meant to come true, then you would have had a chance to finish it first instead of dying unexpectedly. Now you are trying to deny death. Not only that, you still long to complete the *stupa* even though it is now wholly impossible. So, now you have erred twice in your thinking. If you continue on hoping to fulfill this wish, you will compound your mistake yet a third time. Not only is your thinking affected by this, but your future state of birth and your well-being in that state will also be adversely affected. Such an unreasonable aspiration should not be allowed to continue.

"In building a *stupa*, we hope to acquire merit and goodness — not bricks and mortar. The value you obtain from building a *stupa* is the merit that you gain from this action — merit which results from your efforts and which rightly belongs to you. You shouldn't worry about gross material things like bricks and mortar that can never fulfill your desires anyway. People everywhere who gain merit by doing good deeds take with them only the merit they've thus acquired, not the material things they gave away as donations. For example, contributing to the construction of a monastery, a monk's residence, an assembly hall, a road, a water tank, a public building, or any other offering of material goods, are simply the outward manifestations of the good intentions of those wishing to be generous. They are not the actual rewards of generosity, meaning that material offerings themselves are not merit or goodness or heaven or Nibbāna, nor are they the recipient of such rewards. For, over time, all material things disintegrate and fall apart.

"The spiritual qualities that are gained from the effort and the generosity required to do charitable works are experienced internally as merit and goodness. The inspiration behind the good intentions to make such donations is the heart of each individual donor. *The heart itself is virtuous. The heart itself is meritorious. It is the heart that exists as heaven or magga, phala and Nibbāna, and the heart that achieves these attainments. Nothing else could possibly achieve them.*

"The unfinished *stupa* that you two were building lacked the conscious capacity to have good intentions for its own spiritual

234

improvement. Your concern for it stems from a covetous mentality that is a hindrance to you even though it is directed at holding on to something good. Clinging to it is not in your best interest. Your procrastination here is retarding your progress to a favorable rebirth. Instead of trying to take the whole thing with you, had you two been satisfied with the merit you made from working on that *stupa*, you would both have comfortably gone on to a favorable existence long ago — for merit is the mainstay of a good rebirth. And merit is never transformed into something bad. It remains virtuous forever — *akāliko*.

"It's a mistake to be unduly concerned for things past. There is no way you can possibly finish that *stupa* now, so you shouldn't set your hearts on such a hopeless endeavor. The power of the merit you have made impacts you here in the present. So, don't waste your time thinking about the past or the future when now you should be reaping the good results of what you've already done. Correct your thinking and soon you will be able to pass on, free of anxiety. Turn your attention to the present. It contains all the virtues necessary for *magga*, *phala*, and Nibbāna. The past and the future are impediments you must overcome without wasting any more time.

"I feel really sorry for you two. You've done some very meritorious work for the sake of a happy future, only to get so bogged down in your attachment to mere bricks and mortar that you can't freely move on. If you both make the effort to cut these attachments from your hearts, before long you will be free of all binding ties. The strength of your accumulated merit is ready and waiting to take you to the rebirth of your choice."

Ācariya Mun then explained to them the essential meaning of the five moral precepts, a code of conduct applying equally to all living beings.

§   First: Every living being values its own life, so no one should destroy that intrinsic value by taking someone else's life. This results in very bad *kamma*.

§   Second: All beings cherish their own possessions. Even if they don't appear to have much value, the owner values them nonetheless. Regardless of its worth, nothing belonging to another person should be debased by theft or robbery. For such actions debase not only their possessions, but their hearts as well. Stealing is a terrible act — so never steal.

§   Third: Husbands and wives, children and grandchildren, all love each other dearly. They do not want to see anyone taking liberties with their loved ones. Their personal rights should be respected and their private space should be off limits to others. Spousal infringement is extremely damaging to people's hearts, and as such is an act of incalculable evil.

§   Fourth: Lies and prevarication destroy other people's trust, causing them to lose all respect. Even animals abhor deceit, so one should never hurt others by using false, deceitful language.

§   Fifth: Alcohol is by its very nature intoxicating and immensely harmful. Drinking it can cause a perfectly normal person to go crazy and steadily waste away. Anyone wishing to remain a normal, sane human being should refrain from drinking any form of liquor because it damages physical and mental health, eventually destroying people and everyone else around them.

Each of these five moral precepts has its own special benefits. By maintaining the first one, we can expect to enjoy good health and longevity. By the second, our wealth and property will be safe from criminal attack or other misfortune. By the third, family members will keep faith with each other, and live contentedly without unwanted interference. With the fourth, we will be trusted because of our integrity. When our speech is charming and pleasant, humans and *devas* alike will respect and cherish us. Honest people pose no threat to themselves or anyone else. And by maintaining the fifth precept, we will be clever, intelligent people who are not easily misguided nor readily thrown into confusion.

People who maintain moral virtue tend to reassure living beings everywhere by promoting a sense of satisfaction and mutual trust. Immoral people, on the other hand, cause untold suffering by harming people and animals all over the world. Those who value their own existence should understand that all people value themselves similarly, and should, therefore, refrain from harming others in any manner. Due to the supportive, protective power of moral virtue, honest, virtuous people can expect to be reborn into an elevated, heavenly existence. Thus it is vital to maintain high moral standards — the result will surely be a heavenly destination in the next life. Remember this Dhamma teaching, practice it diligently, and your future prosperity is assured.

By the time Ācariya Mun finished advising the small novice and his sister, both were delighted by his teaching and requested the five moral precepts from him, which he gave them. Having received the moral precepts, they respectfully took leave of Ācariya Mun, and immediately vanished. The power of their accumulated merit and the goodness they cultivated from attending to his discourse and taking the five precepts, led the two to be quickly reborn in the *Tāvatiṁsa* heavenly realm.

They then regularly visited Ācariya Mun to hear his teaching. On their first visit they thanked him for his kind assistance in illuminating the way out of the vicious cycle they were in, allowing them to finally enjoy the pleasure of the heavenly existence they had anticipated for so long. They told him that they now realized the great danger that attachments pose to the heart, and the delay they can cause in moving on to a favorable birth. Having received his compassionate advice, they were able to transcend all their concerns and be reborn in a heavenly realm.

Ācariya Mun explained the nature of emotional attachments to them, pointing out that they are a hindrance in many different ways. The wise always teach us that at the moment of death we should be careful not to have emotional attachments to anything whatsoever. The danger is that we may recall, then, an infatuation of some kind, or even worse, angry, revengeful thoughts about a particular person. The moment when the *citta* is about to leave the physical body is crucial. If at that moment the *citta* latches on to a pernicious thought, it may get burned and end up being reborn into a realm of misery, such as one of the hells, or a world of demons, ghosts, or animals — all miserable, unfavorable existences.

So when we're in a good position to train the *citta* — when we are in human birth and fully cognizant of ourselves — we must take decisive advantage of it. As human beings, we can realize our shortcomings and quickly act to correct them, so that, later, when our backs are against the wall — at the time of death — we will be fully prepared to fend for ourselves. We need not be worried about falling prey to the destructive forces of evil. The more we train ourselves to sever all emotional attachments, both good and bad, the better our position will be.

The wise know that the heart is the most important thing in the whole universe, for material and spiritual welfare are dependent upon the heart. So, they make a point of training their hearts in the correct way and then teach others to do the same. We live by means of the heart, and experience contentment and dissatisfaction by means of the heart. When we die, we depart by means of the heart. We are then born again according to our *kamma* — with the heart as the sole cause. As it is the sole source of everything that befalls us, we should train our hearts in the right way so that we can conduct ourselves properly now and in the future.

When Ācariya Mun finished speaking the newly reborn *devas* were overjoyed by his teaching. Praising it highly, they said they had never heard anything quite like it before. Upon their departure, they circumambulated him three times, then withdrew to the edge of his living area before floating up into the air like wisps of cotton borne by the wind.

ONCE, WHILE LIVING in a deep mountainous region of Chiang Mai, far from the nearest village, Ācariya Mun saw an extraordinary *nimitta* arise in his meditation. The hour was three a.m., a time when the body elements are especially subtle. He had just awoken from sleep and was sitting in meditation when he noticed that his *citta* wanted to rest in complete tranquility. So, he entered into a deep state of *samādhi* where he remained for about two hours. Then, his *citta* began withdrawing gradually from that state and paused at the level of *upacāra samādhi* instead of returning to normal, waking consciousness. Immediately, he became aware of certain events.

A huge elephant appeared. Walking up to Ācariya Mun, it knelt before him, indicating that it wanted him to mount. Ācariya Mun promptly climbed up onto its back and sat straddling its neck. Once he was settled on the elephant, he noticed two young monks following behind him, both riding on elephants. Their elephants were also very large, though slightly smaller than the one he was riding. The three elephants appeared very handsome and majestic, like royal elephants that possess human-like intelligence and know their master's wishes. When the two elephants reached him, he led them toward a mountain range that was visible directly ahead, about half a mile away.

Ācariya Mun felt the whole scene to be exceptionally majestic, as though he were escorting the two young monks away from the world of conventional reality forever. Upon reaching the mountain range, his elephant led them all to the entrance of a cave that was situated on a hill a short distance up the mountainside. As soon as they arrived, it turned around, placing its rear to the entrance. With Ācariya Mun still straddling its neck, it backed into the cave until its rear was touching the back wall. The other two elephants with the two young monks astride walked forward into the cave and each took a place on either side of Ācariya Mun's elephant, facing inward as he faced outward. Ācariya Mun then spoke to the two monks as if he were giving them his final, parting instructions.

"I have reached my final hour of birth in a human body. Having been completely cut off, perpetual existence in the conventional world will soon cease altogether for me. Never again shall I return to the world of birth and death. I want you both to return and fully develop yourselves first; then, before long, you will follow in my footsteps, departing this world in the same manner as I am preparing to do now. Escaping from the world, with its multitude of lingering attachments and all of its debilitating pain and suffering, is an extremely difficult task that demands unwavering commitment. You must exert yourselves and pour every ounce of energy into the struggle for this righteous cause — including crossing the very threshold of death — before you can expect to attain freedom from danger and anxiety. Once freed, you will never again have to deplore death and grasp at birth in the future.

"Having completely transcended every residual attachment, I shall depart this world unperturbed, much like a prisoner released from prison. I have absolutely no lingering regrets about losing this physical body — unlike most people whose desperate clinging causes them immense suffering at the time of death. So you should not mourn my passing in any way, for nothing good will come of it. Such grief merely promotes the *kilesas*, so the wise have never encouraged it."

When he finished speaking, Ācariya Mun told the two young monks to back their elephants out of the cave. Both elephants had been standing perfectly still, one on either side, as though they too were listening to Ācariya Mun's parting words and mourning his imminent departure. At that moment, all three elephants resembled real, living animals, rather than mere psychic images. At his command, the two elephants, carrying the young monks, slowly backed out of the cave, facing Ācariya Mun with an imperiously calm demeanor all the while.

Then, as Ācariya Mun sat astride its neck, the hindquarters of Ācariya Mun's elephant began to bore its way into the cave wall. When half of the elephant's body had penetrated the wall of the cave, Ācariya Mun's *citta* began to withdraw from *samādhi*. The *nimitta* ended at that point.

Having never experienced such an unusual *nimitta* before, Ācariya Mun analyzed it and understood its meaning as being twofold. Firstly, when he died, two young monks would attain Dhamma after him, though he didn't specify who they were. Secondly, *samatha* and *vipassanā* are valuable assets for an Arahant to have from the time of his initial attainment until the time he passes away. During this whole period, he must rely on *samatha* and *vipassanā* to be his 'Dhamma abodes',[21] easing the discomfort that is experienced between the *citta* and the five *khandhas,* which remain interdependent until that moment — popularly known as 'death' — when the mundane *khandhas* and the transcendent *citta*[22] go their separate ways. At death, *samatha* and *vipassanā* cease to function, disappearing like all other mundane phenomena. Following that, nothing further can be said.

Most people would have been terrified to see the elephant they were riding bore its rear end into the wall of a cave. But in the event, Ācariya Mun felt unperturbed — he simply allowed the elephant to complete its appointed task. At the same time, it was heartening for him to know that two young monks would realize Dhamma around the time of his death, either just before or soon after. He said it was very strange that, in his parting instructions to them, he spoke about his own impending death as though his time had already come.

Unfortunately, Ācariya Mun never revealed the names of those two monks. Hearing this story from him, I was so eager to find out their names that I completely neglected to consider my own shortcomings. I kept trying to imagine which of my fellow monks they might be. I've kept an eye on this matter ever since Ācariya Mun passed away. But even as I write his biography I still don't have a clue who these auspicious monks might be. The more I think about it, the more I see the folly of jumping to conclusions.[23]

No one has admitted to being one of those monks — which is understandable. Who would publicize their attainments like that? Such achievements are not rotten fish to be peddled about merely to attract a swarm of flies. Anyone attaining that level of Dhamma must possess a very high degree of intelligence and propriety. Would he then be so stupid as to broadcast his achievements so that fools could laugh at him while the wise deplore it? Only the gullible would get excited about such news — like those in the story of the panic-stricken rabbit who, hearing a loud thud, imagined the sky was caving in.[24]

My own foolishness about this matter has eventually subsided, so I have written it down for your consideration. I deserve blame for any impropriety here, for such stories are usually shared only between a teacher and his inner circle of disciples so that no one is adversely affected. I know I deserve the criticism, and I hope, as always, that you will be kind enough to forgive me.

Hungry Ghosts

Giving helpful advice to nonphysical beings from many diverse realms of existence was a serious responsibility that Ācariya Mun continued to fulfill right up to the time of his death. He was in constant communication with such beings wherever he lived, but more so in the mountain regions. There, in remote wilderness areas, far from human habitation, one group or another visited with him almost every night. Even hungry ghosts, awaiting offerings of merit dedicated to them by their living relatives, came to seek his assistance. It was impossible to tell how long they had been dead, what family or nationality they had once belonged to, or even whether or not those ghosts had any living relatives left at all. In contacting Ācariya Mun they hoped that, out of compassion, he would assist them by finding their living relatives and telling them to make donations, dedicating a portion of the merit to the dead to help lessen their torment and suffering and make their lives more bearable. Many of them had already suffered unspeakable miseries in hell for such a long time that it was impossible to calculate the length of their stay in terms of human existence. When they were finally able to rise clear of the hell realms, they still could not evade such misfortune sufficiently to experience some measure of comfort; instead, their suffering continued unabated. For beings who are stuck with the consequences of their evil *kamma*, it matters little which state of existence they are born into, since very little changes to help alleviate their suffering.

Hungry ghosts used to tell Ācariya Mun they had no idea how long it would take them to work their way through the consequences of their evil deeds. They clung to one desperate hope: if he could kindly inform living relatives of their plight, those relatives might be willing to share the merit of their good deeds with them, allowing them to escape from such unbearable torment. When he questioned the hungry ghosts about their relatives, they talked about another world altogether, one that was incomprehensible to him. Having died and been reborn in one of the realms of hell, some had remained there for tens or even hundreds of thousands of years in nonphysical existence before being released into another lesser state where they had to work through the remainder of their evil *kamma*. Their ghost-like existence then lasted another five hundred to a thousand nonphysical years, so it was quite impossible to trace their family lineage. Such was the cruel irony of their karmic dilemma: by the time that the most severe consequences of their *kamma* were exhausted and only the lesser aspects remained — a state where they could finally receive assistance from their relatives — they had lost all track of their families. So they had no choice but to suffer that karmic misery indefinitely, without any idea when it would end. Such ghosts resembled stray animals who have no owners to care for them.

Other hungry ghosts could be helped somewhat, for they died only recently and their *kamma* was not so severe — meaning that they were in a position to receive merit dedicated to them by their relatives. Since they had living relatives whose names and addresses they could recall, Ācariya Mun was able to give them some assistance as long as their families lived in the vicinity where he was residing. Once he knew who they were, he looked for an opportunity to speak with them. He advised them to dedicate to their dead relatives, who awaited, the merit they made by performing special religious functions — or more commonly, by daily offerings of food to the monks. Some ghosts are able to receive a portion of the merit made by generous people everywhere even though it is not specifically dedicated to them. Therefore, Ācariya Mun always made such dedications while extending loving kindness to all living beings. According to the specific nature of their *kamma*, some ghosts can receive merit dedicated by anyone, while others can receive only the merit that is personally dedicated to them by their relatives.

Ācariya Mun said that ghosts live a very peculiar type of existence. From his extensive experience with them, he always found ghosts far more bothersome than any other class of nonphysical beings. Having no recourse to merit of their own, ghosts depend on and always feel indebted to others for their survival. Should these others fail them, the ghosts are left completely destitute. Their dependence on others puts them in the extremely difficult position of never being able to stand on their own.

Generosity and other forms of merit-making are vitally important as the key elements for laying a foundation of individual self-reliance in this and in all future lives. All living beings are the product of their *kamma*. They themselves must take full responsibility for the consequences they encounter. No one else can accept that responsibility because no one can experience the *kamma* generated by another. Births, both good and bad, and the relative degrees of comfort and pain one experiences therein, are the sole responsibility of the individual who created the circumstances that produced these outcomes. No being can substitute for another in this regard. Even those who expect no benefit from their actions still receive the karmic credit for them.

Ācariya Mun was an expert in matters concerning ghosts, *devas*, *brahmas*, *yakkhas*, *nāgas*, and *garuḍas*. Although he did not always reveal the extent of his knowledge, he had the ability to explore endless varieties of phenomena within the many gross and refined nonphysical states of existence that lie beyond the range of human perception. His stories about ghosts were quite hair-raising — even those without fear of ghosts couldn't help but feel trepidation about the mysterious powers of *kamma*. He said that if only people could see their own and other people's good and bad *kamma* in the way they see substantive things, like water and fire, no one would dare do evil anymore than they would dare walk into a blazing fire. Instead, they would be eager to do only good — which has the cool, refreshing quality of water. Trouble would gradually diminish in the world as each person worked to guard himself against the dangers of evil.

ONCE WHEN ĀCARIYA MUN was explaining about heaven, hell, and the ghost realms to the monks, one of his senior disciples spoke up: "Since people cannot actually see heaven and hell or the various nonphysical beings like ghosts, *devas*, *garuḍas*, and *nāgas*, they can't fully understand the ultimate consequences of their actions. But you can see all those things, so wouldn't it be a good idea for you to elucidate them for the benefit of people everywhere? All are natural phenomena which were clearly understood by the Lord Buddha and his Arahant disciples. No one has ever faulted the Buddha and his disciples for teaching people about them, so I don't see why anyone should object to your doing so. People are likely to show the same appreciation for your amazing talents as we, your disciples, do."

Ācariya Mun was adamant in his response:

"The kind of craziness that you suggest will destroy us both. I have never considered speaking out publicly about this matter. Should I do so, you and I and the rest of the monks sitting here would end up being a bunch of lunatics. And once the whole monastery has gone mad, what kind of monastic asylum do you think would accept us all? The *sāsana* was proclaimed and taught with discretion – to be practiced, understood, and spoken about with discretion. This nonsense you suggest – is it really a matter of discretion, or is it something foolhardy? Think about it. In my opinion, the very thought of it is crazy, let alone actually suggesting it. Even though people might survive listening to us talk about it, we ourselves would surely be doomed. So why bring it up?

"If you consider the tangible, visible things all around us, people everywhere are quite capable of dealing with them in an appropriate, reasonable manner. Although Dhamma is the Supreme Truth, it still counts on the involvement of people in the world, so we should always work to harmonize the proprieties of society with the Truth of Dhamma. The Buddha was the first to clearly know and understand the true nature of all phenomena. He spoke about them with absolute assurance, but he was always impeccably discreet in the way he handled these issues. Speaking publicly about any of them, he invariably took the specific circumstances and the people he was addressing into consideration. He spoke then only with the utmost discernment and discretion.

"Knowledge and understanding about the diverse nature of non-physical phenomena is a prerogative of the one who has attained that kind of perception. But talking away indiscriminately about such knowledge is quite abnormal, so normal people are reluctant to listen. This is not intended to be a criticism of anyone. Rather, what's important to keep in mind here is that those who do possess such

244

knowledge should act properly according to the principles of Dhamma – for their own benefit and for the benefit of everyone associating with them. Being convinced of the amazing nature of what we have perceived is not sufficient reason to speak out about things which may encourage others to go mad. Those people, who are keen on listening to such talk simply because their religious conviction is dependent on hearing about amazing phenomena, are already on the road to madness. So I don't approve of conviction and amazement of this kind. I'd prefer that the kind of discernment the Lord Buddha taught us be used by people in their convictions, and in their sense of amazement. Even though we aren't all exceptionally wise, at least there's hope that enough good judgment will be shown to maintain the *sāsana*, preserving it for the future.

"Let me ask you this: Suppose you had a certain amount of money which could be useful to you if you were clever, but harmful to you if you weren't. How would you handle it when going into a crowd of people to insure that both you and your money were safe?"

The senior disciple replied: "I'd take every reasonable precaution to look after my money."

"How exactly would you go about looking after it in a large crowd of people to avoid any possible danger?"

"If I felt it was appropriate to spend some of my money there, I'd take care to count out and hand over the necessary amount without allowing anyone to see the larger amount that I still had with me. That amount I'd keep well hidden from view to avoid any possible danger."

Ācariya Mun then said: "Okay now, let's suppose that you possess a certain knowledge and understanding about ghosts and other nonphysical beings. How would you handle that knowledge discreetly in relation to others so that it would be of some benefit to them without becoming an issue of widespread, public notoriety, which could be harmful to both you and the *sāsana*?"

"I'd have to use the same kind of care in handling such knowledge that I'd use in handling my money."

"Just a moment ago, you implied that I should broadcast my knowledge about such phenomena to the general public without ever considering the consequences. Why was that? I figure that the average discriminating person would never suggest what you just did, and yet you spoke right up. If you don't even have the common sense of the average person, what will anyone find to admire in you? I fail to see anything at all admirable in your thinking. Should someone reproach you for lacking judgment, how would you defend yourself when confronted with the truth of this accusation? Think about it: Which are the greater in this world, the wise or the foolish? And how would anyone be able to reasonably maintain the *sāsana* and preserve its continued welfare by following the suggestion you made to me just now?"

His disciple replied: "Thinking about it now, I feel that what I suggested was totally wrong. I spoke up because hearing about such amazing things has so inspired me that I wanted to share this knowledge with people everywhere. I assumed they would probably be inspired as well and so benefit enormously from it. But I never considered the obvious adverse consequences that such a disclosure would have for the whole *sāsana*. Please be kind enough to forgive me — I don't want to see this tendency to be indiscreet become ingrained in my character. I shall try to be more circumspect in the future so that it doesn't happen again.

"If someone reproaches me for lacking judgment, I will gladly admit my mistake for I clearly deserve the criticism. Until you asked me just now, I had never really considered whether or not the fools outnumber the wise. Now I realize that there must be many more fools in this world, since in our village communities there are very few wise people who care about moral issues. Mostly, people don't seem to know what they're here for and where they are going. They aren't very interested in thinking about why they do things and whether they do right or wrong, good or bad. Being satisfied with whatever is easy and convenient at the moment, they simply let fate decide their future. I understand all this a lot better now. Those people who are capable of reasonably maintaining the *sāsana* and preserving its continued welfare must be wise and discerning people who lead others in an even, harmonious manner so that everyone can benefit from their example. A wise, discerning teacher is the cornerstone of success in the same way that a capable leader is essential to all affairs in all walks of life."

Ācariya Mun took up the discussion at this point:

"Since you're capable of understanding that a wise person is essential to the success of every endeavor, why don't you think about what's important in your own endeavors as a practicing monk? Spiritual endeavors, being very subtle, are difficult to fully understand. For this reason, only clever, discerning people can uphold the *sāsana* to perfection. Here I'm not referring to the kind of cleverness that causes

246

destruction in the world and damage to the *sāsana*, but cleverness that discriminates wisely, making decisions favorable to one's material and spiritual prosperity. It's this type of cleverness that's implicit in the first two factors of the Noble Eightfold Path: *Sammā-diṭṭhi* and *Sammā-sankappo* — Right View and Right Thought. And these factors are personified by someone whose words and actions always follow the principles of wisdom.

"Even Right *Samādhi* is dependent on the analytical, probing wisdom of Right View to avoid becoming 'comatose *samādhi'*. When the *citta* converges into a state of calm, wisdom should always be there, playing a supportive role. Otherwise, how could those dedicated to understanding the true nature of all phenomena deal correctly with the knowledge arising within the *citta*, or the external phenomena with which it comes into contact? If wisdom is not there to help, one is bound to make mistakes in judgment.

"The diversity of internal and external phenomena that can become involved with *samādhi* is limitless, the perception of them being limited only by each individual's natural inclinations. Those so inclined will naturally perceive such phenomena and nothing can prevent them from doing so. But the key factor here is wisdom. Wisdom analyzes arising phenomena and then chooses the ones that are suitable to focus on, so that the rest can be allowed to pass by without causing trouble. Those lacking wisdom will even have a hard time successfully getting through the *samādhi* practice: they will find themselves being pleased with this perception or displeased with that one, ecstatic about this, despondent about that — all are emotional reactions impinging on the heart, causing it to become attached. Unless wisdom is present to effectively deal with them, such disturbing emotional attachments can never be eliminated. Wisdom can be selective, ignoring what is superfluous to focus on what is essential thus indicating the direction in which one's practice should proceed.

"Our purpose in being ordained as Buddhist monks is to search for knowledge and wisdom so that we can develop those virtuous qualities admired by people everywhere. We aren't here to parade our ineptitude in front of the *kilesas* by succumbing to their devious tricks, but rather to develop clever tactics of our own to outmaneuver the *kilesas*, thus countering their tricks. Living without an adequate means of protection, we leave ourselves in a very precarious position.

The principles of Dhamma and the monastic discipline are a monk's protective armor, while mindfulness and wisdom are his preferred weapons. If we want to remain steady in our practice and be constant in all situations, we must maintain mindfulness and wisdom in all our daily activities. Mindfulness and wisdom must permeate all that we think, say, and do — without exception. Only then can we be certain of our mode of practice.

"I'd really like to see all my students display uncompromising diligence in their efforts to transcend *dukkha*, using mindfulness and wisdom to oversee this work. You will thus make yourselves worthy recipients of the Buddha's outstanding teaching which stresses the importance of using skillful means in all circumstances. I have no desire to see my students floundering foolishly in a state of confusion about emotional attachments because complacency and laziness keep them from doing the work necessary to carry them beyond these dangers. So don't be indifferent to the work at hand.

"A practicing monk who is striving to cross beyond the world of *saṁsāra* is engaged in the noblest form of endeavor. No other kind of work is more demanding than the task of lifting the heart beyond the pain and suffering experienced in *saṁsāra*.[25] It requires unstinting effort on all fronts — including a willingness to sacrifice your life. Entrust your life to your own diligent efforts as they attempt to pull you from the abyss of the *kilesas*. Unlike other types of work, there is no room for ambiguity here. If you want to realize the wondrous results that you have yet to experience, you must persist in putting your life on the line for the sake of Dhamma. No other method can be expected to achieve the right result. You must be willing to give your life to transcend the world of *saṁsāra*. Only then will you be free of the burden of *dukkha* in future births.

"I myself never expected to survive and become a teacher, for my determination to transcend *saṁsāra* was much stronger than my concern for staying alive. All my efforts in all circumstances were directed toward a goal beyond life. I never allowed regrets about losing my life to distract me from my purpose. The desire to maintain my course on the path to liberation kept me under constant pressure and directed my every move. I resolved that if my body could not withstand the pressure, I would just have to die. I had already died so many countless times in the past that I was fed up with dying anyway. But were I to live, I desired only to realize the same Dhamma that the

Buddha had attained. I had no wish to achieve anything else, for I had had enough of every other type of accomplishment. At that time, my overriding desire was to avoid rebirth and being trapped once more in the cycle of birth and death.

"The effort that I put forth to attain Dhamma can be compared to a turbine, rotating non-stop, or to a 'Wheel of Dhamma' whirling ceaselessly day and night as it cuts its way through every last vestige of the *kilesas*. Only at sleep did I allow myself a temporary respite from this rigorous practice. As soon as I woke up, I was back at work, using mindfulness, wisdom, faith, and diligence to root out and destroy those persistent *kilesas* that still remained. I persevered in that pitched battle with the *kilesas* until mindfulness, wisdom, faith and diligence had utterly destroyed them all. Only then could I finally relax. From that moment on, I knew for certain that the *kilesas* had been vanquished — categorically, never to return and cause trouble again. But the body, not having disintegrated along with the *kilesas*, remained alive.

"This is something you should all think about carefully. Do you want to advance fearlessly in the face of death, and strive diligently to leave behind the misery that's been such a painful burden on your hearts for so long? Or do you want to persist in your regrets about having to die, and so be reborn into this miserable condition again? Hurry up and think about it! Don't allow yourselves to become trapped by *dukkha*, wasting this opportunity — you'll regret it for a long time to come.

"The battlefield for conquering the *kilesas* exists within each individual who practices with wisdom, faith, and perseverance as weapons for fighting his way to freedom. It is very counterproductive to believe that you have plenty of time left since you're still young and in good health. Practicing monks should decisively reject such thinking. It is the heart alone that engenders all misjudgment and all wisdom, so you should not focus your attention outside of yourself. Since they are constantly active, pay close attention to your actions, speech, and thoughts to determine the kind of results they produce. Are they producing Dhamma, which is an antidote to the poisons of apathy and self-indulgence; or are they producing a tonic that nourishes the delusions that cause *dukkha*, giving them strength to extend the cycle of existence indefinitely? Whatever they are, the results of your actions, speech, and thoughts should be thoroughly examined in every detail; or else, you'll encounter nothing but failure and never rise above the pain and misery that haunt this world."

Ācariya Mun's response to the monk, who suggested that he teach people indiscriminately about the unusual phenomena he experienced, was fierce and uncompromising. The gist of his reply makes for a remarkable Dhamma teaching — one that is seldom heard. It seems unlikely that the monk deserved a condemnation as strong as Ācariya Mun's stirring rebuke might have suggested. Perhaps speaking up was his way of prompting Ācariya Mun into giving us a talk. As far as I could tell, if nothing out of the ordinary happened to strike his heart and provoke a response, Ācariya Mun preferred to speak in a smooth, easy manner — especially when the subject was very profound. At such times, however, his listeners often felt something missing and were not fully satisfied with his teaching. But if someone started something by asking him a question, or if he became annoyed hearing some monks talk ambiguously about Dhamma, or if their discussion piqued his interest, then the Dhamma in his heart began to stir and stream forth, expressing itself in unusual ways that lent fire and excitement to our listening.

Each time Ācariya Mun delivered a declamation of this kind his audience felt deeply moved in a way that's difficult to describe. I myself, having a rather rough temperament, always preferred listening to his fiery exhortations since they fit so well with my natural disposition. For this reason, I reckon that those monks who employed various means to provoke Ācariya Mun into fiery talks were in fact using their ingenuity to come up with clever provocations. Since they probably intended to benefit from his response, they were not entirely in the wrong. The resolute Dhamma expositions that inspired me the most invariably occurred when I asked him probing, prodding questions. His explanations then were bound to be directed personally at me, unlike the general explanations meant for all the monks. Once I had lived with him for some time, I came to know many different ways of eliciting his comments without waiting for him to bring these matters up himself in a general monastic meeting.

ONCE ĀCARIYA MUN and three or four monks were living in a secluded cave in Chiang Dao district. After passing three nights there, Ācariya Mun told the monks that, in his meditation, he had seen a spacious, inviting cave situated high up a steep mountain slope in the area nearby. He told them that many Paccekabuddhas[26] had resided there in the past, but that nowadays monks couldn't live there: the ascent was too steep and the location too high for finding a place within walking distance where they could obtain alms food. He told the monks to climb up the mountain to look at the cave, and insisted they take a supply of food with them. Since there was no path leading up to the mountain, they would have to climb as best they could until they reached the summit. The cave was situated a short distance from the very top.

Taking several lay people along, the monks made the climb to the summit where they found a beautiful, spacious cave, exactly as Ācariya Mun had predicted. The air was clear and the ambiance pleasant and inviting. The monks were so pleased with their discovery that they didn't want to leave. They would have preferred to remain there indefinitely, practicing meditation. Unfortunately, the cave was so high up and so far from the nearest village that they had no place to go for almsround. When the food they brought was nearly exhausted, they had to come back down to the cave where Ācariya Mun resided. Upon their return, he asked them about their impressions.

"Well, how was the cave, nice and inviting? Seeing an image of it in my meditation, I felt it was so beautiful and spacious that I wanted you all to go up and take a look. I was sure you'd like it. When we first arrived, I didn't think to examine this mountain to see what's here. When investigating it a few days later, I discovered how many strange, amazing things it contains. That cave you went to is constantly protected by terrestrial *devas*. Anyone acting improperly there can expect to feel the consequences. When I sent you up there, I forgot to mention that the cave is protected by *devas* and to warn you to restrain yourselves and behave properly the whole time. I didn't want you to be loud and noisy, which is unacceptable behavior for a monk. I was afraid that if the *devas* protecting the cave were displeased, they might cause you discomfort by precipitating something unpleasant."

The monks informed Ācariya Mun that they'd prefer to spend a longer time in the cave; but he insisted that, no matter how attractive the place was, it would not be possible to live there because no food was available. Ācariya Mun spoke of the cave in a very matter-of-fact way, as though he had actually seen it many times. Of course, he had never gone up there, the climb being too steep and difficult. Nonetheless, he spoke about it with the assurance of someone who knew for certain that the knowledge arising in his meditation was no mere illusion.

Ācariya Mun constantly warned his monks to behave in a careful, restrained manner wherever they went, for the *devas* living in those remote places prefer everything to be orderly and very clean. When terrestrial *devas* witness such slovenly behavior as a monk sleeping carelessly, lying on his back spread-eagled like a corpse, tossing and mumbling in his sleep like an idiot, they feel quite disgusted — regardless of the fact that it's impossible for a sleeping person to control his actions. *Devas* often approached Ācariya Mun to explain how they felt about this matter.

"Monks occupy positions of reverence and esteem in the hearts and minds of living beings everywhere, so their deportment should be guarded and restrained at all times — even while sleeping. As far as possible, a monk's appearance should be attractive and pleasing, never disagreeable or offensive. We hate to see monks behaving intemperately — like ordinary lay people showing little concern for the consequences. Especially since the circumspection needed to act with restraint is well within their capabilities. It's not our intention to be critical of all monks. *Devas* everywhere are grateful for the opportunity to pay homage to those monks exhibiting exemplary behavior because we all appreciate virtue and dearly wish to uphold the *sāsana*. We mention this to you so you can warn your disciples to conduct themselves in a restrained manner that's appealing to human beings and *devas* alike. Monks, who are worthy of respect, will cause *devas* of all realms to feel an even deeper reverence for the *sāsana*."

In response to what the *devas* told him, Ācariya Mun always cautioned his disciples to keep all their requisites in a neat, orderly fashion when staying in remote mountainous areas favored by terrestrial *devas*. Even the foot-wiping rags had to be neatly folded and not just tossed in a heap. His monks were required to relieve themselves in appropriate places, and latrines were dug only after careful consideration of the surrounding area. Sometimes Ācariya Mun explicitly told the monks not to make a latrine under a certain tree, or in a certain area, because the *devas* residing there, or passing through on their way to visit him, would be displeased.

Monks who were already well acquainted with the *deva* world needed no such caution, for they were fully aware of the correct way to behave. Many of Ācariya Mun's disciples do possess this capability. However, because their proficiency in such matters is developed in the wilds, they are reluctant to speak about it openly, fearing that learned people everywhere will make fun of them. But within the circle of *kammaṭṭhāna* monks, it's easy to determine their identity simply by listening to their discussions about various *devas* who came to visit them and the nature of their conversations with these nonphysical beings. At the same time, we can get an insight into each monk's level of spiritual attainment.

The Hypercritical Nāga

At one point Ācariya Mun spent some time living in Chiang Dao Cave — not the long cave in the middle of the mountain that has become popular with tourists, but one higher up the mountain. This cave was home to a great *nāga*[27] who had kept guard over it for a very long time. Apparently this *nāga* was rather conceited and had a tendency to be overly critical of monks. During his stay in the cave, Ācariya Mun became the object of this *nāga's* constant criticism. It found fault with nearly everything he did. It appeared incapable of accepting Ācariya Mun's thoughts of loving kindness, probably as a consequence of its long-standing enmity toward monks.

At night when Ācariya Mun wore his sandals to do walking meditation, the *nāga* complained about the sound of his footsteps: "What kind of a monk are you, stomping around like an unbridled race horse? The sound of your sandals striking the earth shakes the whole mountain. Did you ever think you might be annoying somebody with all that noise?"

It raised these complaints despite Ācariya Mun's composed manner of pacing softly back and forth. Hearing the criticisms, he took care to walk even more softly than before; but still, the *nāga* wasn't satisfied: "What kind of a monk are you, walking meditation like somebody sneaking around hunting birds?" Occasionally, Ācariya Mun's foot would stumble on a stone in the meditation path, causing a slight thumping sound which elicited another reproach: "What kind of a monk are you, bucking up and down your meditation path like a chorus dancer?"

There were times when Ācariya Mun leveled out the surface of his meditation path to facilitate smooth, easy walking. As he moved stones around and put them neatly into place, the *nāga* complained: "What kind of a monk are you, always moving things around – you're never satisfied. Don't you realize that all your fussing about gives others a splitting headache?"

Ācariya Mun had to exercise special care with whatever he did at that cave. Even then, this opinionated *nāga* would find an excuse to criticize him. Should his body move slightly while he slept at night, he could sense psychically upon awakening that the *nāga* had been criticizing him for tossing, turning, wheezing, snoring, and so on. Focusing his attention on this angry, hypercritical *nāga*, Ācariya Mun always found its head sticking out, peering at him intently, as though it never took its eyes off him. Vicious-looking and mean-spirited, it refused to accept any merit dedicated to it and was determined to indulge in feelings of anger that burned like a fire inside its heart. Seeing that it compounded its evil *kamma* all the time, Ācariya Mun felt truly sorry for the *nāga*. But as long as it showed no interest in reasonable discourse, it was impossible for him to help in any way. All it could think about was fault-finding.

On one occasion, Ācariya Mun explained the general principles underlying a monk's life, specifically mentioning his own purpose and intentions:

"My purpose for being here is not to cause trouble to somebody else, but rather to work as best I can for my own benefit and the benefit of others. So you should not entertain ignoble thoughts, thinking that I'm here to cause you harm or discomfort. I am here consciously trying to do good so that I can share the merit of my actions with all living beings without exception. That includes you as well, so you needn't be upset thinking that I've come just to annoy you.

"Physical activity is a normal feature of people's everyday life. Comings and goings are part of living in this world – only the dead cease to move about. Although as a monk I am always self-composed,

254

I'm not a corpse in repose: I have to inhale and exhale, and the force of my breathing varies from one posture to another. My breathing continues to function while I sleep, as does my whole body; so, naturally, there will be some sounds emitted. The same is true when I awaken and begin walking-meditation, or perform chores. There is some sound, but always within the bounds of moderation. When have you ever seen a monk standing frozen stiff like a corpse, never moving a muscle? Human beings don't behave like that.

"I try hard to walk as carefully and softly as possible, but still you complain that I walk like a race horse. In truth, an animal like a race horse and a virtuous monk mindfully walking meditation could not be more different, one from the other. You should avoid making such comparisons. Otherwise, you become a wretched individual aiming for a berth in hell. It's impossible for me to satisfy all your unreasonable whims. If, like everyone else, you expect to find happiness and prosperity, then consider your own faults for awhile and stop lugging the fires of hell around in your heart all the time. Only then will you find a way out.

"Criticizing other people's faults, even when they really are wrong, merely serves to increase your own irritation and put you in a bad mood. My behavior here is in no way improper for a monk, yet you keep carping about it constantly. If you were a human being, you'd probably be incapable of living in normal society: you'd see the world as one big garbage dump and yourself as pure solid gold. Such feelings of alienation are due to emotional turmoil caused by your hypercritical attitude — which gives you no peace. The wise have always condemned unjustified criticism of others, saying it brings terrible moral consequences. So why do you enjoy doing it with such a vengeance, and such indifference to the painful consequences? I'm not the one who suffers from your criticism — it is your own emotional health that's adversely affected. Such ill effects are quite obvious, so how can you be unaware that your whole attitude is wrong? I'm fully cognizant of everything you are thinking, and at the same time, I have always forgiven you. You concentrate on doing terrible things that consume your mind and ravage your heart as though you can't get enough of doing evil. Were your condition a disease, it would be an untreatable one.

"I have been trying to change your mental attitude, just as I've long been trying to help many other living beings. Human beings, ghosts, *devas, brahmas, yakkhas,* and even great *nāgas* far more powerful than yourself, have all accepted the truth of the Lord Buddha's teaching on *kamma.* None, except you, have angrily criticized the value of Dhamma, which is revered throughout the world systems. And you're so peculiar that you won't accept the truth of anything at all. The only pleasure you take is in making derogatory remarks and angrily censuring people who have done nothing wrong. You devote yourself to these as though they were propitious actions. But the wise have never thought that such actions foster peace and security. When you finally slough off the skin of this ill-fated existence, you won't then encounter a pleasant, pain-free existence, unaffected by the evil consequences of your actions.

"I apologize for speaking so candidly about the principles of Dhamma, but my intentions are good. Nothing malicious is intended in my remarks, regardless of what misconceptions you may have. Since the very beginning of my stay here, I have tried to do everything in a careful, restrained manner, for I know that this is your home and I'm concerned that my presence here may inconvenience you. Although I am well aware that you're an individual who delights in looking for things to criticize, I still can't seem to avoid being seen in a disparaging light. I myself experience genuine contentment, unaffected even by constant criticism. But, I worry that the repercussions of your dogged pursuit of evil will be extremely unpleasant for you. I did not come here in search of wickedness or evil. Being quite sure that everything I do and say emanates from a pure heart, I have no fear that my actions will incur any unpleasant moral consequences.

"As soon as intelligent people begin to understand the difference between secular matters and spiritual ones, they tend to appreciate virtuous conduct, admiring all wholesome, meritorious actions performed for the sake of peace and happiness. From ages past, the wise have always taught living beings to feel good about being virtuous. So why do you adhere to the maverick notion that it's all right to strip yourself of virtue and wallow in evil? You seem to detest virtue so dreadfully much that you can't be bothered to reflect on your own vices. Although I won't be experiencing the dire consequences that await you, still I fear for you in that miserable state. You must stop thinking in ways that are harmful, for the mean intent behind your actions has the power to deprive you of all moral value. Such undesirable consequences, bringing unimaginable torment, are what I fear more than anything else in the world. The whole world dreads old age, sickness, and death, but I don't fear them nearly so much as I fear evil and its attendant consequences.

"People with *kilesas* tend to eschew spiritual principles, preferring instead the things that religious tenets proscribe. So ordaining as a Buddhist monk to practice the Teaching and the Discipline requires us to undergo an agonizing character transformation. Even though I knew how difficult it would be to oppose the *kilesas*, I nonetheless felt compelled to join the monkhood and endure the severe hardship. The extreme discomfort caused by constantly opposing the *kilesas* — that's what makes the practice so difficult. But if we desire to transcend *kamma* and the defiling *kilesas* that create it, we must endure such torment — for *kilesas* always steadfastly resist the teachings of the Lord Buddha.

"I've come here to practice, living in this cave like a worthless social outcast, solely because I fear evil and its consequences. I did not come here to harm or trouble anyone. Nor do I feel contempt for any living being. I respect them all as friends whose lives are also subject to the law of *kamma*, and who are thus all of equal intrinsic value. I dedicate the merit of my actions equally to all beings with the hope that they may live in contentment wherever they may be. I have never taken the arrogant attitude that I'm a human being ordained as a Buddhist monk and therefore superior to my companions in birth, ageing, sickness, and death.

"You too exist within the sphere of *kamma*, so you ought to humbly reflect on how your own faults affect you. Criticizing others without proper consideration will never bring you good results — it merely piles up the ill effects of bad *kamma*, which then linger on indefinitely. You should feel dismayed by your errant behavior and drop this dangerous practice. Only then can you hope to become a good individual with a chance for a better, happier birth in the future. Then your mean, angry heart will soften, and you can avoid being engulfed in misery forever.

"All living beings in the universe — from humans and animals to *devas*, *brahmas*, and *yakkhas* — cherish happiness and loathe suffering. They do not have an aversion for Dhamma simply because they can't yet put it into practice. Dhamma has always been the quintessential nature of the universe. Those beings who are in a position to practice Dhamma find great satisfaction in it — for instance, human beings. Their state of birth makes them well suited to the practice of Dhamma.

"You yourself are a living being who's fully capable of distinguishing between good and bad, and thus choosing what's most beneficial for you. So why do you do just the opposite? I'm puzzled that you seem content to revel in those things which the wise abhor while scorning those which the wise applaud. You know about *dukkha* and you hate it, yet you strive to produce the very causes that bring you great unhappiness and discomfort. The wise tell us that our efforts to find fault with others produce consequences that cause greater and greater unhappiness — exactly what you shamelessly do all the time. You may not be interested, but although I'm fully aware of your despicable thoughts, I've always forgiven you. I'm not angry or offended, but I do feel sorry for you. Thus, I have decided to tell you the plain truth. Should it prove useful to you, I shall be pleased for your sake. I receive no unpleasant consequences from your thoughts for I'm not the one who engages in them. All I experience are peace, serenity, and loving compassion that have long been my heart's abode."

The *nāga* didn't make any comment as Ācariya Mun explained these various aspects of Dhamma, but it did experience the rise of some salutary thoughts while listening: *This monk talks a lot of sense. But right now I'm unable to do as he says, being still too content with my old ways. Perhaps I'll have more interest in my next existence. This monk has many awesome qualities — he even perceives things that should be unknowable. How can he know my private thoughts? I live in a hidden world, yet somehow he sees me. Over the years, many monks have come to stay in this cave, but none have known about my existence, much less my thoughts. I've even forced some of them to flee because I couldn't stand having them around.*[28] *But this monk knows everything, including my thoughts. Even while sleeping he remains aware. Later, he can tell me exactly what I was thinking, as if he hadn't been asleep at all. Why am I so opinionated that I can't take what he teaches to heart and put it into practice? Like he said: I must surely have some very grave kamma. Despite knowing the despicable nature of my mind, he still makes an effort to explain how his daily activities are not intended to bother me. My present state of existence is certainly unfortunate. He's right when he says that I'm quite capable of distinguishing between good and bad. Yet I'm hampered by my wretched conceit, meaning that my next life will probably be just as unfortunate as this one — and so on indefinitely.*

After a short pause Ācariya Mun asked the *nāga* if it had managed to understand any of his explanations on Dhamma.

The *nāga* replied: "I understand everything you so kindly explained to me. But unfortunately, I'm burdened by some very grave *kamma* and I've yet to grow weary of my wretched condition. I'm still debating this matter with myself and I haven't come to any definite conclusions. My heart tends to gravitate toward a state of degradation, as it always has, so it balks at listening to the Dhamma you are teaching."

Ācariya Mun asked the *nāga* what it meant by saying that its heart liked to gravitate toward a state of degradation.

The *nāga* answered: "My heart enjoys finding fault with you all the time, even though you've done nothing wrong — that's just the way my heart is. I don't know how to convince myself of the harmful effects of this tendency so that I can correct it and practice the way of virtue from now on."

Ācariya Mun offered some encouragement:

"Careful consideration will convince you that such bad tendencies are truly harmful. Once you are persuaded, then evil will naturally begin to fade from your heart, ceasing to be so conspicuous in the future. But by assuming that these tendencies are beneficial and then encouraging them, you will naturally tend to think in an endless variety of ways that are detrimental to you. Unless you hurry to improve things now, you'll keep on doing evil until you are completely beyond help. I cannot do this job for you. I can give some guidance, but it's up to you to make the necessary adjustments in your character. The onus is on you to press ahead, trying to accomplish this as best you can. Once you do, you will see the dangerous aspects of your character gradually diminish as beneficial qualities develop, displacing them until all that's left is pure, simple virtue, untainted by any form of evil. By placing your faith in the Dhamma of the Lord Buddha, which has always helped living beings to transcend *dukkha*, you will always be contented living under its protective influence. Never feeling distraught, never disturbed, you will remain even-tempered in every situation. You won't be moved to praise one thing as good or criticize another as bad, and so suffer the resulting consequences — conduct that's contrary to the way of the wise."

At the conclusion of these remarks, the *nāga* promised to make an effort to follow Ācariya Mun's advice. In the days that followed, Ācariya Mun kept an eye on it as he continued with his own practice. He noticed some improvement, as the *nāga* was able to restrict its hypercritical tendencies by exercising some measure of control over them. But he also noticed that this effort caused the *nāga* much consternation. So finding some excuse to leave the cave, he moved on – which pleased the *nāga*. His association with it ended there.

From that time on, Ācariya Mun alluded to the story of this *nāga* as a means of elaborating on various aspects of human nature, for the personal benefit of those listening. The gist of what he said is worth repeating here, hopefully so that the reader can learn some valuable lessons from his teaching.

Ācariya Mun explained that good and evil do not arise on their own but are dependent on habitual ways of behaving that gradually become part of one's character. If our tendency is to do evil, it is very difficult to remedy because everything we do tends to flow in that direction. If it is our tendency to do good, we become more and more skillful and assertive as we progress in that direction. For this reason, clever parents will try to train their children in the way of goodness from a very early age – before it becomes too late. When necessary they will entrust them to the care of someone who is suitably supportive so that their children's upbringing is not simply left to chance.

Children begin to learn about basic common principles from a very tender age. But unlike learning in the classroom, this learning process is not interrupted by time or season. Such basic common principles are more firmly implanted in children's characters than any of their school subjects, for these things exist all around them – at home, in school, and everywhere else. Children are constantly taking lessons from what they see, hear, taste, smell, and touch in the world, remembering well what they have learned. A child's senses are its natural blackboard. The impressions imprinted there are pregnant with moral significance; that is, matters of good and evil. They constantly pick up impressions from their playmates and the adults in their lives, as well as from movies and other entertainment that is normally available to them. Such everyday impressions are a child's true teachers; and children are all too willing to learn new ideas that are constantly conveyed to them. Contact with evil affairs can definitely induce a child to follow evil ways, while good influences can definitely induce a child to go the way of virtue. Children naturally take the things they see and hear as examples to emulate; and, over time, this establishes a pattern of behavior that defines a child's character. Once these patterns have become ingrained, the children will speak and act according to the good or evil orientation thus established.

The fact that some people readily take satisfaction in doing evil and are unwilling to change, while others just as readily take satisfaction in doing good and cherish moral virtue all their lives, indicates the fundamental importance of character development. Those left to their own devices easily abandon the effort to resist their bad tendencies — even before they have seen enough satisfactory results to encourage perseverance. Consequently, basic character development is absolutely essential for all people. This means that nothing should be done carelessly or thoughtlessly, for once such tendencies become habitual they are difficult to correct. The importance of this principle becomes apparent as we strive to develop positive character traits until they become part of our very nature; for instance: being reasonable about how and where we travel; being reasonable about how we spend our money so that everyone in the family benefits; and being reasonable in our eating and sleeping habits so that we do not overindulge in them. All such exemplary behavior patterns should be enthusiastically developed until they become instinctive. The inner resistance we meet in the early stages of training will naturally give way to a smooth, easy character transformation. This transformation itself is sufficient proof that character training is well within our capabilities. But we must be willing to persevere in the beginning.

Training is required to make any kind of work successful. Just as we must undergo training in order to succeed in our professions, so the heart and mind must be trained in order to obtain optimum results. Only after death are we beyond the need for training. Wishing to gain proficiency in something, we must work at it, practicing until we are well-skilled in it. Character training develops a skill which is synonymous with virtue. Take this message to heart, consider it well, and put it into practice — your efforts will surely be rewarded with a wealth of personal virtue. Such was the gist of Ācariya Mun's teaching on character training. I have included it here to help those who are developing Dhamma in this way.

The Death of the Arahant

While Ācariya Mun lived in Chiang Dao Cave, numerous *nimittas* appeared in his meditation, some of them quite extraordinary. Here I shall mention only a few. In the late hours of almost every night he received a wide range of *deva* visitors from the upper and lower celestial realms who arrived in groups of varying sizes at appointed times. Arahants also came regularly to hold inspirational conversations on Dhamma with Ācariya Mun. Each Arahant showed him the manner in which his passing away into total Nibbāna had occurred.[29] Some were Arahants who had passed away in the Chiang Dao Cave, while others had attained total Nibbāna elsewhere. Such demonstrations were accompanied by an inspiring explanation of the sequence of events that had taken place.

Hearing Ācariya Mun talk about those Arahants, I felt dismayed and somewhat discouraged by my own unfortunate circumstances. There I was a human being with eyes, ears, and mental faculties just like Ācariya Mun; yet, I couldn't accomplish the things that he did. On the one hand, I was elated to hear his stories; on the other, I felt disheartened. I found myself laughing and crying at the same time, but I kept my tears to myself for fear that my fellow monks would think I was mad. In fact, at that time, deep inside, I really was a bit mad.

The inspirational conversations that Ācariya Mun had with the Arahants were so captivating that it's hard to find anything else in the world that compares with them. I shall try to faithfully recreate the essence of those conversations here, though I fear I may not do them proper justice. Here is the gist of what the Arahants said to Ācariya Mun.

"All Arahants possess superb qualities within their hearts that are most amazing — intrinsic virtues unsurpassed in the human and *deva* worlds. Each Arahant who appears in the world following the Lord Buddha does so only with the greatest of difficulty. Each is like a goldmine cropping up spontaneously in the middle of an emperor's imperial city — a very rare occurrence indeed. An Arahant's lifestyle contrasts sharply with worldly lifestyles because an Arahant's life is invigorated by Dhamma. Although his body is composed of the same physical elements as those of everyone else, the heart maintaining that body is pure, and such purity of heart invigorates every aspect of the physical element.

"You yourself have now completed the task of filtering from your heart all possible causes of existence, thus becoming one of the Arahants. Being one whose heart will never again give rise to birth and existence, you have become another incomparable source of merit for the world to venerate. So we've come to visit you now to show our appreciation for your achievement, which because of its enormous difficulty, is seldom accomplished. Although many people desire to attain what you have, very few succeed when they are faced with the difficulties. People born into this world instinctively cling to their parents and relatives for support. Hardly any of them realize the importance of relying on their own hearts as their mainstay. The vast majority of people just drift aimlessly, accomplishing nothing of real value — their numbers are beyond reckoning. So the appearance in the world of a fully-enlightened Arahant is a remarkable event that benefits living beings throughout all the world systems. Your attainment of purity has made you an enormous boon for humans, *devas*, and *brahmas* alike. You are also well-versed in the universal language of the heart, which is far more important than any other form of communication. All the Buddhas, and certain categories of Arahants, use the language of the heart when giving assistance to living beings, for it is the universal language of sentient beings throughout the universe. Contacting and teaching nonphysical beings is achieved exclusively by means of this universal form of communication. Those communicating in the language of the heart can understand each other much more quickly and easily than would normally be the case."

———————⟨⦿⟩———————

After concluding his inspirational conversation with Ācariya Mun, each Arahant would then demonstrate the manner in which he had passed away into total Nibbāna. Nearly every Arahant who came allowed him to observe the posture in which this was achieved. Some Arahants demonstrated how they had died and passed into total Nibbāna while sitting cross-legged in *samādhi*. Some demonstrated how they were reclining on their right side in the 'lion's posture'[30] at that time. Others showed him how they were standing still in the middle of the meditation path; still others revealed how they were pacing back and forth in meditation at the time of their total Nibbāna. The sitting and reclining postures were the most common – relatively few Arahants passed into Nibbāna while walking or standing.

Their deaths were demonstrated in a precise manner, showing every detail right up to the final moment. As a seated Arahant passed away, he slumped over gently like soft cotton, while his body ceased to function and became perfectly still. It was more difficult to discern the exact moment when an Arahant reclining in the 'lion's posture' passed away. His breathing was the only visible sign of life and that became ever more refined as he lay quietly, as if asleep, without the slightest movement in any part of his body, until his breathing gradually ceased altogether. Those Arahants who demonstrated death in a standing posture stood erect, assuming a reflective pose with the right hand placed on the left hand, head slightly bowed and eyes firmly closed. They appeared to reflect momentarily before slowly slumping into a heap on the ground – first in a sitting position, then slumping gradually further, until, softly, like cotton wool, they lay on the ground. Arahants, who died while walking in meditation, paced back and forth about six or seven times before gently slumping to the ground where they lay perfectly still.

When giving these demonstrations, the Arahants came to within six feet of Ācariya Mun so he could clearly view every aspect of their passing away, which created a lasting impression in his heart. Listening to him recount those episodes, I felt the urge to shed tears. I had to turn my face to the wall as this strange feeling overcame me. Otherwise, I might have created a stir, which could have become an embarrassing epilogue to this story. The total Nibbāna of those Arahants was accomplished with a serene gracefulness that stands in marked contrast to the distress typically suffered by most people at the time of death. I was so moved by hearing how each Arahant passed away that I simply couldn't hold back my tears. Those amazing individuals were taking final leave of the world of conventional reality with all its chaos and confusion – which is an amazing thing to contemplate. I am sure that anyone else who listened would have been deeply affected in the same way.

Three Arahants attained total Nibbāna at the cave in Chiang Dao – two while reclining in the 'lion's posture' and one while walking meditation. Prior to giving Ācariya Mun a visual demonstration of how his death had occurred, each Arahant gave him a detailed explanation of why he had chosen to pass away in that posture. Very few died while standing or walking. Many more did so while sitting, but the majority passed away while reclining. On the basis of what he had seen, Ācariya Mun came to the conclusion that over the centuries many Arahants had passed away in Thailand. As far as I can remember, they included the three Arahants at the cave in Chiang Dao, one in the Wong Phra Chan mountains, one at Tago Cave in Lopburi province, one at Khow Yai in Nakhon Nayok province, and one at Wat Dhatuluang monastery of Ko Kha district in Lampang province. There were others as well, but unfortunately I can no longer recall them.

"Nibbāna" is a term used exclusively with reference to Buddhas, Paccekabuddhas, and Arahants, all of whom have expunged from their hearts every trace of the *kilesas* leading to future birth. It is not a term associated with living beings who still have *kilesas*, for those beings continue to accumulate the seeds of future births in their hearts constantly, thus making the designation "Nibbāna" entirely inappropriate for them. Having died here, they are reborn there; dying there, they're reborn somewhere else. Negligent human beings who've made no effort to develop virtuous qualities in this life so as to enhance their future lives, may well be reborn as animals after they die. The opportunities for birth as an animal are more numerous than those for birth in the much higher human, *deva*, and *brahma* realms. So those who prefer making bad *kamma* may be on one of the many paths to rebirth in the animal kingdom, which is far more diverse and extensive than the higher realms. But animals, humans, and *devas* all have one thing in common: the burden of emotional attachments that causes them to be reborn over and over again — indefinitely. Consequently, the term Nibbāna does not apply to them.

The only ones who deserve the designation "Nibbāna" are those individuals who have completely eradicated the *kilesas* from their hearts — extinguishing them forever, even while they are physically alive. At the moment of passing away, they have no lingering attachments that could bind them to the round of *saṁsāra* — not even to the body that's starting to decompose. Absolutely no attachment or concern for anything anywhere exist in their hearts. Thus they bid final farewell to the world with no trepidation, having no expectations of experiencing karmic consequences in another realm of existence — a source of endless frustration. The heart that has attained absolute freedom is constant, unchanging, and wholly contented. It harbors no expectations at all concerning conventional realities such as the body. Therefore, not even an atom of the conventional world could enter and affect the heart's state of total purity. The word "Nibbāna" refers to the total purity of one who is never agitated or melancholy — neither sorrowful in life nor regretful at death — but always imperturbably unchanging throughout.

Nibbāna is a special term used with reference to a special type of individual. No one who has yet to purify his heart would dare assume this title. Nibbāna is not a kind of personal property, like an orchard or a farm, which can be taken over by powerful interests even without the owner's consent. Whoever wants to take possession of Nibbāna must make the effort to develop it within the heart — there is no hope for those who merely lie around waiting for it to appear.

Ācariya Mun, the subject of this biography, received inspirational Dhamma from many Arahants. He has received national acclaim and respect from faithful Buddhists everywhere. He achieved this renown by faithfully practicing the Dhamma until he realized the Truth in his own heart, where nothing false existed. He was able to understand that things like organic life are inherently false; and as such, he let go of them so they no longer burdened his heart. The true Ācariya Mun, no longer subject to change, was the Truth of the Dhamma he realized. That Dhamma remains true — forever. Unlike all other things which are inherently unstable and so of limited duration, the passage of time has no effect whatsoever on it.

The Spiritual Warrior

Ācariya Mun became seriously ill on many occasions while living deep in the wilderness areas of Chiang Mai — sometimes he came very close to death. Had he been like most people, totally dependent on doctors and their medicines, he would probably have succumbed long before. But Ācariya Mun was able to survive by using the curative powers of Dhamma to treat himself. He said that as soon as the symptoms of illness began to appear the 'therapeutic qualities of Dhamma' immediately arose in response and began to effect a cure. Such was his temperament that normally he showed little interest in conventional medicines. Even in old age when his vitality was steadily declining, he continued to prefer the 'therapeutic qualities of Dhamma' to maintain well-being in his body elements.

Ācariya Mun once stayed with several other monks in a mountainous area full of malaria. One of the monks happened to contract the disease, but not a single medicine was available to treat it. When the fever was at its worst, it raged continuously all day. Ācariya Mun visited the monk every morning and evening to instruct him in the use of investigative techniques for reducing fever — meditation methods he himself always used with good results. But since their levels of spiritual attainment were so different, this monk was incapable of investigating in the same way as Ācariya Mun could. Each time his fever intensified, he had to simply wait for it to abate on its own. He had developed no effective methods for bringing it down himself. Eventually becoming rather exasperated, Ācariya Mun scolded him:

"It seems you're a Mahā[31] in name only, since the knowledge you have learned is obviously of no help when you really need it. What's the point of studying to be a Mahā if you're just going to waste a lot of paper and then come away empty-handed? The knowledge gained from studying should benefit you in some way, so I cannot figure out what you've been learning that's so completely useless. Here you are virtually dying of fever, but your learning can't help alleviate your condition even a little bit. What's the purpose of all that learning anyway? It doesn't make sense to me. I can't figure it out. I haven't learned any grade of Pāli studies — not one. I have learned only the five kammaṭṭhāna[32] that my preceptor gave me at my ordination, which I still have with me today. They are all I need to take care of myself. They don't make me weak like you — you're as weak as you are educated. In fact, you are weaker than a woman with no education at all! You're a man and a Mahā, so why all this weakness? When you get sick, you exhibit no manly characteristics, nor any indication of the Dhamma you learned. You should take all your masculine equipment and exchange it for a woman's, thus completing your metamorphosis. Maybe then the fever will abate a bit. Seeing that you're a woman, the fever may be reluctant to torture you so much.

"Instead of seeing some reassuring signs of defiance and courage when I visit you, all I see is a weak display of self-pity. Why don't you investigate those kammaṭṭhāna in the Pāli studies you've learned?

What does *dukkhaṁ ariyasaccaṁ* mean to you? Does it mean weakness? When having a fever, just cry and long for your parents, is that what it means? If you cannot bear even the painful feelings arising from a fever, in a truly life-threatening crisis you'll be overwhelmed and unable to cope. Even now you can't manage, so how can you ever hope to understand the true nature of the Noble Truth of *Dukkha*? Anyone wanting to transcend the mundane world must realize unequivocally the truth inherent in each of the Noble Truths. But as soon as the Truth of *Dukkha* awakens and begins to become a little active, you lie down and admit defeat. What do you expect to gain from that?"

Having given this fiery piece of advice to probe the monk's character, Ācariya Mun paused quietly for a moment. He then noticed that the monk was sobbing, tears streaming down his face. So Ācariya Mun quickly found an excuse to leave and return to his hut, telling the monk not to worry — he would soon get better. He assured him that he had only pretended to give him a hard time.

Reconsidering the matter that night, Ācariya Mun decided to try a different type of medicine, since the remedy he had just prescribed was probably too harsh for the patient — he just was not strong enough to take it. From the next morning onward, he changed his approach completely, never again displaying any fierceness with that monk. From then on he assumed a sympathetic, comforting attitude, pampering the monk in a way that was very uncharacteristic of him. His speech was sweet and gentle, like large quantities of molasses being poured out every morning and evening, until the whole area seemed sweet and fragrant, suiting that monk's outbreak of weakness perfectly. He watched over his patient's progress, giving him these sugarcoated pills every morning and evening until it was clear that both the patient and his fellow monks were contented. The patient continued to improve with each passing day until finally he made a complete recovery, a process that lasted many months. Obviously this particular medicine was effective beyond all expectations.

Such are the therapies of a clever doctor who always has the intelligence to adjust his treatments according to the circumstances and then administer them appropriately. Consequently, he is an excellent example for the rest of us who are searching for wisdom, which is why I have included the preceding incident. Those who are interested should be able to gain some benefit from reading it, for it concerns the skillful means of a clever man whose wisdom was so sharp that he was never stymied by any turn of events.

Rather than remaining passive in a critical situation, Ācariya Mun instinctively preferred to analyze the crisis with mindfulness and wisdom. When he was sick, or when his investigations uncovered some particularly insidious *kilesas* that he found to be especially obstructive — these constituted critical situations. Instead of feeling resigned, his *citta* responded by circling the problem day and night until he found an ingenious method to deal with the crisis, allowing him to overcome it gradually and move on unhindered. From the beginning stages of his practice to the very end, he invariably experienced good results from this approach.

When the monks living with him became ill, he usually advised them to develop meditative techniques for relieving the symptoms so they would not become overly dependent on medications. At the same time, he wanted them to develop those techniques into methods for investigating Dhamma. Ācariya Mun believed that physical and mental pain are direct manifestations of the Truth of *Dukkha*; and as such, they should be investigated until that Truth is understood. He did not expect his monks to simply succumb to pain as though they had never before received training in Dhamma.

Ācariya Mun acquired many techniques from the illnesses he suffered. He never let the pain of his illness subdue him without probing into the nature of that pain as best he could. At such times, he believed it imperative to investigate pain to the very limit of one's ability in order to determine whether or not mindfulness and wisdom can cope with the task at hand. When found to be deficient, they could be modified and improved until their performance is deemed satisfactory. When the highly trained forces of mindfulness and wisdom enter into combat with feelings of severe pain, the heart will not be apprehensive as it confronts the Truth of *Dukkha* — which is a genuine Truth. Mindfulness and wisdom are then fully up to the task. They remain unshakable while being buffeted on all sides by an onslaught of pain coming from every conceivable direction. In the midst of this intense pain, they are able to narrow down the scope of their investigation until it focuses sharply on the very principles of Truth. Such mental training employs the factors of mindfulness, wisdom, faith, and effort, instilling them with greater strength and courage. For precisely this reason, Ācariya Mun liked to emphasize the investigation of painful feelings to his disciples. When the moment of truth arrives and the body is about to break up, one should experience no fear of the agonizing pain that emerges at that moment. Investigating as prescribed, the meditator clearly perceives the true nature of both body and feelings, meaning that he lives in comfort and dies triumphant. Such is the path of the warrior who emerges truly victorious to become a superior individual. He conquers himself, becomes superior within himself – and is fully contented.

Ācariya Mun was an exemplary teacher in every aspect of his practice. His persistence, fortitude, courage, frugality, and all-round ingenuity were outstanding qualities that put him in a class of his own in the present day and age. It would be very difficult for any of his disciples to surpass him. He possessed celestial hearing and celestial sight, as well as *paracittavijjā*: the ability to communicate psychically with beings as diverse as animals, humans, ghosts, *devas, brahmas, yamas,* and *nāgas.*[33] He could see not only animals and humans with their gross physical bodies, but also the subtle nonphysical forms of ghosts and *devas.* He knew the intimate joys and sorrows of human beings and could read their innermost thoughts.

Monks who lacked mindfulness to supervise their thoughts, letting their minds wander constantly, often became aware of those thoughts only when they heard Ācariya Mun give voice to them. Some of the more pathetic ones were so bemused that they did not realize Ācariya Mun was referring to them. It wasn't necessary to be in his presence – just living together with him in the same monastic community was sufficient reason for caution. Any monk mindlessly giving rein to wild thoughts was sure to hear something unusual from Ācariya Mun when eventually they met. But especially at risk were those who dared to let their minds wander in his presence. It didn't matter what he was doing at the time – he might be instructing the monks, or having a conversation, or whatever. He would give the culprit a tongue-lashing or use some unusual ploy to get his attention. Only when he felt disinclined to respond did he allow such thoughts to pass unchallenged.

According to the accounts of many senior disciples who lived with him in Chiang Mai, Ācariya Mun's mastery of such faculties as celestial hearing, celestial seeing, and thought reading, was so amazing it could be frightening. His ability to read thoughts was so lightning quick that those entertaining unwholesome thoughts almost invariably heard about it. Consequently, monks who lived with him needed to guard their sense faculties very carefully. If not, they certainly got caught for they could not elude his penetrating genius and find a safe way to hide.

Once, due to his fear of Ācariya Mun, a monk thought about the ferocity of Ācariya Mun's admonitions. When the monk next saw him, Ācariya Mun immediately addressed the question.

"Almost everything we use — from our food to our requisites to the robes we wear — must pass through various stages of preparation before being turned into useful items. Rice must be planted, harvested, and cooked; wood must be cut, sawed, and planed; and cloth must be woven and sewn into robes. Isn't that right? These things don't become finished products ready for use or consumption unless a lot of work is done on them. Food and shelter are the product of man's labor. They do not simply materialize from nowhere. Only corpses are totally inactive, lying lifeless and having no need to provide for their own livelihood. With no reason to adjust their behavior, they have no need for a teacher to scold them and give instructions. But you are alive and still seeking a teacher's guidance. Yet you're unreasonably afraid of your teacher, citing his fierce admonitions as a rationale. Then again, if your teacher simply kept his mouth shut, you would probably accuse him of failing to teach you and thus be even more upset. In the final analysis, nothing quite suits you. Your thoughts jump around like a monkey jumping up and down in the trees. If it keeps jumping about long enough, it will jump on a rotten branch and end up in a heap on the ground. Which do you want to be? Do you want to be a monkey jumping on a rotten branch, or a monk with a teacher to guide you?"

Sometimes, he confronted the culprit directly, motivating him to become more mindfully aware of his own thoughts. At other times, he simply made some oblique, sarcastic reference to a monk's thoughts. The objective in either case was to warn a student that his thoughts had not passed into oblivion, but could return again to haunt him. He was made aware of his mistake so that in the future he could exercise more restraint in his thinking.

Sometimes, in order to inspire his disciples in their practice, Ācariya Mun gave a fiery discourse in which he offered himself as living proof of what could be achieved through perseverance and courage in the face of death.

"If you allow the fear of death to stop you from practicing meditation with uncompromising diligence, you will be obliged to come back and die time and time again in future births. Those who can overcome their fear of death will be able to reduce the number of future births until eventually they transcend birth and death altogether. Never again will they return to bear the burden of *dukkha*. While persevering unflinchingly in the face of excruciating pain, I myself passed out three times — yet I did not die. I managed to survive and become your teacher. None of you have ever persisted in your efforts to the point where you passed out, unconscious. So, what makes you so afraid of dying? If you don't actually experience what it's like to die, it is unlikely you'll ever see the wonders of Dhamma. Whether you believe it or not, this is the method I used to realize Dhamma. So there is no way I can teach you to merely take it easy: Eat a lot, sleep a lot, and be lazy — then the *kilesas* will take fright. I cannot teach that because that's not the way to instill fear in the *kilesas*. Such an attitude will only amuse the *kilesas*: 'We thought these monks had come to be diligent, so why are they lying around like breathing corpses? These breathing dead are hardly worthy of admiration'."

After Ācariya Mun finished speaking, a certain monk in the audience thought to himself that persevering to the point of passing out was excessive: *If I have to reach the point where I pass out, unconscious, I don't want to go to Nibbāna yet. I'll just put up with the pain and suffering of this world like everyone else. I've got lots of company. If going to Nibbāna means pushing oneself to the extent of passing out, then whoever wants to go is welcome to do so, but I'm not going — that's for sure. Life in the world is surely painful, but not nearly as painful as being rendered unconscious. Besides, if we have to pass out before we can attain Nibbāna that means there's not much difference between Nibbāna and a drug-induced coma. Who wants that? I certainly don't. I have no desire to pass out. Just seeing someone else faint scares me to death, let alone having it happen to me.*

Before long Ācariya Mun began speaking again, this time in heated tones that penetrated forcibly into the monk's reverie.

"You don't believe me, huh? Do you think I'm lying to you just for fun, or what? If you do not trust me, please leave! Why stay here being a burden on this monastery? I did not invite you to come here — you came on your own, so you should leave on your own. Don't wait to be thrown out! It's useless for you to stay here anyway — the Buddha's teaching wasn't proclaimed for idiots like you! Your way of thinking is entirely inappropriate for a monk wearing the yellow robes. A Buddhist monk is one who puts his faith in Dhamma. But since your ideas contradict the Lord Buddha's path to liberation, it is obvious that you don't trust me or the Dhamma. You are welcome to go anywhere to eat and sleep in comfort without having to trouble yourself with meditation practice. If you come to realize the Truth of Dhamma using this method, please come back and have mercy on this stupid old monk. I shall raise my clasped hands to the heavens to honor your gracious majesty's benediction!

"I teach the truth when I say that anyone expecting to transcend *dukkha* must be fearless when facing death. But you don't believe it's true. You figure it is better to die and be reborn in this world so you can continue carrying your burden of misery wherever you go. If you want to go on like this, that's your business. But, don't come here and contradict the teaching of the Lord Buddha. If you do, you will be a thorn in the Buddha's side and an obstacle blocking the path of those truly wishing to follow him. Opinions like yours are not only wrong, but, should you decide to give voice to them, you will become an enemy of Buddhism and religious people everywhere. I assumed that you came here to develop yourself spiritually and so uphold the *sāsana*. I never imagined you were going to ruin yourself and then destroy the *sāsana* and devoted followers of the Lord Buddha as well. But now I realize that you have come like an executioner to destroy everything. You'd better change your attitude right away. Otherwise, you will certainly ruin yourself and take a lot of other people with you — and that would be a terrible shame.

"The Lord Buddha is said to have passed out unconscious three times as he strived to attain enlightenment. Don't you believe it is true? If you don't, perhaps you suppose the Buddha was lying to us. A person like you, who ordains as a *dhutanga* monk but still refuses to trust the Buddha and his Dhamma, is someone devoid of intrinsic human value. Your opinions make you no different than a breathing corpse — a living, stinking corpse that somehow manages to keep breathing from one day to the next. What do you say? Which path are you going to choose for your own safe passage? I have no better path to offer you than the one I have already specified. It is the path that the Lord Buddha and all the Arahants have taken. There is no easier, more esoteric path. I have followed this path from the time of my ordination up to the present, and it is the source of the Dhamma that I teach to all my disciples."

This was one of the most impassioned declamations ever given by Ācariya Mun — right to the point and full of fireworks. What I have recreated here is merely a sample, not the full substance of what he said by any means. Those listening were so shaken and intimidated they nearly sank through the floor. Never in their lives had they heard anything like it. By going straight to the point, these fiery expositions caused his audience to see the truth of his words, and thus submit to it, even as they felt frightened to death of him.

Realizing the truth of what he heard, the monk, whose thoughts provoked this barrage, gradually acquiesced until he accepted it totally and without reservations. As that happened, the intensity in Ācariya Mun's voice gradually subsided until he sounded quite conciliatory. When he was convinced that the monk had accepted the truth, he finished speaking and adjourned the meeting.

As it disbanded, there was a stir of excitement. The monks asked one another who had dared entertain thoughts so perverse to have elicited such a fierce response from Ācariya Mun that his voice raged furiously, like thunder and lightning. There must have been some provocation; otherwise, he would never have given a blazing admonition like that. Those thoughts must have affected him so acutely that he couldn't resist unleashing the full force of his reason. Eventually, the monk in question owned up to the thoughts that I have mentioned before.

Normally *dhutanga* monks did not conceal their thoughts and opinions from one another. If their thoughts became the subject of Ācariya Mun's rebuke, they invariably admitted their lapses in judgment when they were questioned later. Although the monks usually found it amusing when a fellow-monk was roasted by Ācariya

Mun, they also became conscious of their own shortcomings. Such shortcomings could be easily exposed on almsround, or on some other errand outside the monastery, where a monk encountered an emotionally stimulating object that stuck in his mind and became a preoccupation. Such indiscretion was likely to elicit the kind of fierce response that frightened everyone within earshot and prompted nervous glances all around. Terrified of Ācariya Mun, ashamed in front of his friends, the culprit was usually shaking as he sat, rooted to his seat, with his head bowed and not daring to look up. When the meeting was over, the monks would ask around and find out that, as always, there was indeed one in their group whose thoughts caused Ācariya Mun's rebuke. It was rather a pity, for those monks had no intention of offending Ācariya Mun. Like people everywhere with *kilesas*, they were emotionally susceptible to things in their environment. Their mindfulness was simply too slow in catching up with the lightning quickness of their minds — thus, Ācariya Mun's frequent scoldings.

Ācariya Mun was extremely quick at reading other people's thoughts. Monks who lived with him had no doubts whatsoever about this. He was able to read our errant thoughts and then caution us about them with unerring accuracy. Only on occasions, when he could not be bothered to say anything, did he remain quiet. Though his rebukes were frequent, he did relax occasionally to let us catch our breath. Otherwise, we'd probably have suffocated to death. Because of my incurable restlessness, I myself was chastised more often than most. But those of us who endured and lived patiently with him over a long period of time were usually energized in our meditation practice. We developed a firm anchor in our hearts as a result of his exhortations which constantly forged, tempered, and beat our practice into shape. Constant vigilance, and the restraint it fostered, made it possible to cultivate the mindfulness and wisdom necessary to resist incidental temptations. In the context of the art of magic, it can be compared to learning the necessary skills and then testing them out against the teacher until one is impervious to attack. Calm and secure in the knowledge that their harmful potential has been neutralized, one can withstand guns and swords, unperturbed.[34] In the context of Dhamma practice, it means one can stand firm in the face of evocative emotions and temptations that normally arouse desire, without fear of being influenced or seduced. In other words, remaining unperturbed in all situations.

The trouble is, most people react to talk about Nibbāna by feeling oddly dejected and dismayed. It doesn't put them in a good mood as does talk about worldly matters. Having no personal experience of Nibbāna, they probably think that it's not as enjoyable as the humdrum things they are accustomed to. Not only has the present generation lost interest in Nibbāna — even our parents and grandparents were not much interested, nor did they encourage others to take an interest. At most, they may have encouraged their family to go to the local monastery from time to time to take the precepts and hear Dhamma. Perhaps they sometimes encouraged their families to do meditation practice to calm them down a bit and keep their behavior within acceptable limits. Of course, one way or another they did manage to advise their family and friends to do just about everything else, until fed up with hearing their advice, most people no longer bothered to take it.

Undoubtedly, most people have already decided that Nibbāna must be a very silent place, there being no music or entertainment and no one to indulge them in their favorite pastimes. They probably see it as a place devoid of anything stimulating or exciting; and therefore, they don't want to go there. They fear dropping into a still, silent hell without a soul in sight: there would be no family, no friends, and no sounds, ever, of birds and cars, or laughter and crying. It appears to be a rather bleak, undesirable place in every way. So people who still harbor ambitions do not want to go to Nibbāna. And even if they did, they would be unable to go, for their ambitions would hold them back and make them hesitate.

People who can truly attain Nibbāna are those who have absolutely no worldly ambitions or involvements. Being neither passionate nor impassive, neither relaxed nor tense, but remaining perfectly balanced, they are naturally centered in the Middle Way. Having no desires, no expectations, and no longings, they take no enjoyment from worldly pleasures, which merely agitate the heart and cause frustration. Always imperturbable, they experience only an exquisite, serene happiness that contrasts sharply with the happiness of those whose hearts are corrupted by worldly concerns. Such mundane happiness, being ambiguous and fluctuating, is always fleeting, and unreliable. It resembles murky, muddy water. It's like food that's spicy, sour, bland,

and salty all at once: besides causing indigestion and uncomfortable drowsiness, it is not very appetizing. So people should carefully examine the things they encounter every day and test them to discover which ones are advantageous and which are not. Then they can filter out the unwholesome elements and prevent them from piling up in their hearts until their numbers overwhelm and there is no room to store them all. Otherwise, wherever they look, they will see only this accumulation of misery that they've collected.

When it comes to self-discipline, the wise are much more clever than we are. Everything they do, say, or think is directed precisely toward achieving their intended objective. They are not at odds with the Truth, nor arrogant and conceited about their achievements. When cautioned, they quickly take the warning to heart as a useful lesson, which is quite different from the way the rest of us react. By following the example of the wise, we will become reasonable, moderate people who refuse to follow those desires that have ruled over our hearts for so long. Our efforts to overcome those desires will thus transform our hearts in a way that definitely results in a degree of contentment that's clearly evident to us. Even without millions in the bank, our own exemplary conduct, plus what little wealth we do possess, will be sufficient to keep us happy.

Clever people manage their lives in a way that is conducive to peace and security. They don't feel the need to rush around trying to make vast sums of money in order to maintain a sense of happiness in their lives. Wealth may bring a measure of happiness, but those who enjoy a moderate amount of wealth, righteously acquired, will inevitably be far more contented than those who acquire their wealth by unscrupulous means. Though its actual ownership is not disputed, dubious wealth doesn't really belong to its owner in any genuine sense. For under the laws of true justice, *kamma* condemns such gains, bestowing fruits of misery as just rewards for the future. Wise people view this prospect with great trepidation; but we, of lesser intelligence, still prefer to scramble headlong after our desires, selfishly indulging in pleasures that come along without ever getting enough to satisfy our appetites. No matter how hard we try, we never seem to experience the kind of contentment that we long for.

DURING HIS YEARS in Chiang Mai, Ācariya Mun received numerous letters from Chao Khun Dhammachedi of Wat Bodhisomphon monastery in Udon Thani province. In his letters, Chao Khun Dhammachedi, who had been a disciple of Ācariya Mun since his youth, always invited him to return to Udon Thani. Ācariya Mun never replied to those letters, nor did he accept the invitation. Then in the year 1940, Chao Khun Dhammachedi traveled from Udon Thani all the way to the isolated region where Ācariya Mun lived to invite him personally, and thus gave him a chance to answer all the correspondence he had received. He told Chao Khun Dhammachedi that he had read all his letters, but he reckoned they were small and insignificant compared to the 'big letter' that had just arrived; so, now he was ready to reply. That said, both monks laughed heartily.

At the first opportunity, Chao Khun Dhammachedi personally invited Ācariya Mun to return to the province of Udon Thani where he once lived so many years before. Chao Khun Dhammachedi informed him that his disciples in Udon Thani, missing him very much, had asked him to invite Ācariya Mun on their behalf. This time he could not object — he had to accept. Chao Khun Dhammachedi suggested they work out a timetable for picking up Ācariya Mun and escorting him back to Udon Thani. They decided on the beginning of May 1940.

As his departure from the mountain retreat became imminent, large groups of terrestrial *devas* pleaded with him to stay. Being very reluctant to see him leave, they told him that *devas* from all realms experienced peace and contentment while he lived there, due to the power of loving kindness which emanated from him and issued in all directions — day and night. Feeling very happy in his presence, they all greatly revered him. They were unwilling to have him leave for they knew that their sense of contentment from his presence would soon fade. Even their social cohesion could be affected as a result.

Ācariya Mun told them that, having given his word, he must leave. He must honor his promise — he couldn't possibly renege on it. Unlike most people, a monk's word is a solemn covenant. A monk is a man of virtue so he must remain true to his word. If he goes back on a promise, his virtue immediately disappears and his worth as a monk is then devalued. So a monk must preserve his moral integrity.

When May arrived Ācariya Mun and the monks accompanying him to Udon Thani left their mountain retreat and began the long trek to the city of Chiang Mai where they stayed at Wat Chedi Luang monastery. Ācariya Oon of Wat Tipayaratananimit monastery arrived with some lay supporters at about the same time to receive Ācariya Mun and to escort him to Udon Thani. Ācariya Mun remained at Wat Chedi Luang monastery for about one week. During that time, a large group of his local devotees came to persuade him to extend his stay in Chiang Mai for the benefit of everyone there. But having accepted the invitation to Udon Thani, he could not delay his departure.

Before he left, Chao Khun Rājakawi asked him to give a special talk on the occasion of Visākha Pūjā[35] to serve as a remembrance for his many devotees. At that time, I had just myself arrived in Chiang Mai and so listened to this discourse with great interest. He spoke for exactly three hours that day; and what he said was so impressive that I have never forgotten it. Here is the essence of what he said:

"Today is Visākha Pūjā. It celebrates the day the Lord Buddha was born, the day he attained enlightenment, and the day he passed away into *Parinibbāna*. The birth of a Buddha stands in marked contrast to the births of all other beings. In being born, the Buddha did not succumb to worldly illusions about birth, life, or death. More than that, through the power of his all-encompassing wisdom, he was able to realize the true nature of birth, life, and death — attaining what we call 'enlightenment'. At the appropriate time he bid farewell to his *khandhas,* which were the tools he relied on to develop virtue to perfection; and then passed away — *sugato,* as befits a world teacher who is absolutely beyond reproach. Before departing his physical body, which had reached the end of its natural life, he bequeathed the Dhamma to the world, intending that it represent him and fulfill the role of teacher in his stead. Such a gift is worthy of our complete faith, and worthy of any sacrifice.

"As you know, we are born as human beings because we possess sufficient inherent goodness to make it possible. But we shouldn't take ourselves and our inherent goodness for granted by neglecting to develop virtuous qualities in this life to enhance our future lives. Otherwise, the human status we enjoy may disappear to be irrevocably eclipsed by a low, undesirable birth. Be it high status or low status — with happiness of every possible degree up to the Ultimate Happiness, or pain and suffering of every possible degree down to the most excruciating – we ourselves are responsible for our own life circumstances. Don't think that only those presently affected by adverse circumstances experience such things. As potential life situations, they are shared in common by everyone, becoming our own personal heritage if and when we create the conditions for them. For this reason, the Buddha taught that we should never look down on other people, holding them in contempt. Seeing someone living in misery or abject poverty, we should reflect on the possibility that one day we could also find ourselves in such a position, or one even worse. At the moment of reckoning, none of us has the power to avoid the consequences of our actions. All of us share the same capacity to make good and bad *kamma*, so it's possible that some day we will be in their position and they will be in ours. The *sāsana* is a doctrine that we can use to examine ourselves and others, enabling us to correctly choose the best possible way forward. In this respect it has no equal.

"Throughout my many years as a monk I have remained firmly committed to the practice of examining myself, striving always to discriminate between the good and the bad things arising within me from moment to moment. I now clearly realize that the heart is the principal instigator in the creation of *kamma*. In other words, our hearts are the source of all *kamma* – *kamma* that belongs solely to the one who makes it. There should be no doubt about this. Those doubting the existence of *kamma* – and so, disbelieving of its effects – blindly take their own situation for granted until they're beyond redemption. Although they've been born and raised by their parents, such people fail to see the value of the mother and father who gave them life and sustenance. They look no further than their own selfish existence, unaware of how awful it really is, for they care little that they were born and raised by parents who supported their growth and development in every way. A child's body is nourished by the food and drink its parents provide, allowing it to grow up strong and healthy. If such actions are not *kamma*, what then should they be called? And if the nourishment the body receives in this way is not the fruit of *kamma*, then what else, in truth, could it be?

"Obviously there is a root cause for all the goodness and evil, all the happiness and suffering experienced by people everywhere in the world. When someone's reckless thinking leads him to commit suicide – there's a reason behind it. The root cause, *kamma*, manifesting itself within the heart, can have such an impact on a person that he actually takes his own life without realizing that the *kamma* he has already created is playing a role. What is that but total blindness?

"*Kamma* exists as a part of our very being. We create *kamma* every moment, just as the results of our previous *kamma* arise to affect us every moment. If you insist on doubting the existence of *kamma* and its results, then you are stuck at a dead end. *Kamma* is not something that follows us like a dog following its master. On the contrary, our very thoughts, speech, and actions are *kamma*. The true results of *kamma* are the degrees of happiness and suffering experienced by all beings in the world, including those beings who live out their lives unaware of *kamma*. Such ignorance is also a karmic consequence."

I myself listened to this talk with heartfelt satisfaction as I had long been keenly interested in Ācariya Mun. I experienced such a deep sense of joy about him and his Dhamma that I felt as if I were floating on air. I felt that I simply couldn't hear enough. I have given you the gist of what he said so that all of you, who had no opportunity to hear him speak, may understand something about the nature of your *kamma*. *Kamma* being something common to us all, it is possible you may recognize you own *kamma* in his words.

When he finished speaking, Ācariya Mun rose from his seat and prostrated himself in front of the main Buddha image. Chao Khun Rājakawi told him how much everyone had enjoyed the outstanding discourse he had just delivered. Ācariya Mun replied that it might well be his "final encore" since he probably wouldn't return to give another talk due to his declining years. This was his way of telling everyone present that he would not return to Chiang Mai again before he died. As it turned out, this was true – Ācariya Mun never again returned to Chiang Mai.

After remaining several more days at Wat Chedi Luang monastery, Ācariya Mun finally left, heading first for Bangkok. Somdet Phra Mahā Wirawong and the other senior monks, together with scores of lay supporters, escorted him from the monastery to the train station. Also present was a host of *devas*. Ācariya Mun said that *devas* filled the sky around him in every direction as they, too, came to escort him to the station. They remained, hovering in the sky, even after he reached the station, waiting to send him off before returning to their respective realms. A chaotic scene ensued as he had to greet the scores of monks and lay people who were gathered there, while he simultaneously tried to psychically bestow his blessing upon all the *devas* who hovered in the air for a final blessing from him. In the end, he was able to turn his undivided attention to the *devas* and bestow his final blessing only after he had finished speaking to all the people and the train began pulling out of the station.

He said he truly felt sorry for those *devas* who held him in such high esteem that they were reluctant to see him leave. They showed all the same signs of distress and disappointment that human beings do. Some even continued to hover behind the train as it sped down the tracks, until finally Ācariya Mun felt it necessary to tell them to return to their respective realms. They departed reluctantly, wondering if he would ever come back to assist them again. In the end they were to be disappointed, for he never did return. He never mentioned whether the terrestrial *devas* of Chiang Mai came to visit him later on when he lived in the provinces of Udon Thani and Sakon Nakhon.

5

Unusual Questions,
Enlightening Answers

Upon arriving in Bangkok, Ācariya Mun went to stay at Wat
Boromaniwat monastery, following the instructions tele-
grammed from Somdet Phra Mahā Wirawong. Before he
departed for Udon Thani, many people came to see him at Wat
Boromaniwat with questions. Some of these questions were rather
unusual, so I have decided to include them.

Question: "I understand that you maintain only one rule instead of
the full 227 monastic rules that all other monks keep. Is that true?"

Ācariya Mun: "Yes, I maintain only the one rule."

Question: "Which one do you maintain?"

Ācariya Mun: "My mind."

Question: "So, you don't maintain all 227 rules?"

Ācariya Mun: "I maintain my mind by not allowing any wrong
thoughts, speech, or actions that would violate the prohibitions laid
down by the Buddha, be they 227 in number or even more than that.
Those who doubt whether or not I maintain the 227 monastic rules
can think and say what they please. As for me, from the day of my
ordination I have always maintained strict control over my mind, as it
is the master of body and speech."

Question: "You mean we have to maintain our minds in order to
maintain the moral precepts?"

Ācariya Mun: "What else would you maintain to develop good moral virtue, if not your mind? Only the dead have no need to look after their minds, much less their actions and speech. The wise have never claimed that dead people have a moral bias, it being impossible for corpses to show willful intent. If corpses did have morality, then it would be a dead and useless one. But I am not a corpse, so I cannot maintain a dead man's morality. I must do what befits one fully endowed with both good and evil tendencies — I must maintain my mind in moral virtue."

Question: "I've heard it said that keeping our actions and speech in good order is called morality, which lead me to understand that it's not really necessary to look after the mind. That's why I asked."

Ācariya Mun: "It is quite true that morality entails keeping our actions and speech in good order. But before we can put our actions and speech in good moral order, we must consider the source of moral virtue. It originates with the master of body and speech — the mind — which makes them behave properly. Once we have established that the mind is the determining factor, we must ascertain how it relates to action and speech so that they stay in good moral order that is a source of comfort to us and others alike. It's not only moral virtue that the mind must deal with. The mind supervises the performance of every activity we engage in, making sure that it's done in a proper, orderly fashion to produce excellent results each time.

"Treating an illness requires diagnosing its cause, then devising an effective cure before it develops into a chronic condition. Taking care of morality requires the mind to be in effective control. Otherwise, the result will be a tarnished morality that's patchy, and full of holes. Such splintered, inconsistent virtue is truly pitiful. It moves people to live an aimless existence and inevitably causes an adverse effect on the entire religion. Besides that, it's not a source of comfort to the person practicing it, nor is it admired by his peers.

"I have never done much studying. After I ordained, my teacher took me as a wandering monk into the mountains and forests. I learned Dhamma from the trees and grasses, the rivers and the streams, the cliffs and the caves. I learned it from the sounds of birds and wild animals, from the natural environment around me. I didn't study the scriptures long enough to become well-versed in the teaching on moral virtue; and my answers to your questions tend to reflect that primitive education. I feel rather inadequate for my inability to provide answers that would be suitably eloquent for your edification."

Question: "What is the nature of morality and what constitutes genuine moral virtue?"

Ācariya Mun: "Being mindfully aware of our thoughts; knowing which things are appropriate to think about and which are not; taking care how we express ourselves by way of body, speech, and mind; controlling these three factors so that they remain within the confines of what is morally acceptable. By properly adhering to these conditions we can be confident that the moral nature of our behavior is exemplary and we are never unruly or offensive. Apart from such exemplary conduct in body, speech, and mind, it's difficult to say what genuine moral virtue is, since it's impossible to separate its practice from the person who maintains it. They are not distinct entities, like a house and its owner — the house on one hand, the owner on another. Trying to distinguish between moral virtue and the person who maintains it is very problematic, so I wouldn't want to do it. Even the peace of mind resulting from the practice of moral virtue cannot actually be separated from that moral virtue. If morality could be isolated in this manner, it would probably have been on sale in the stores long ago. In such a case, people's moral virtue would probably become a lucrative target for thieves to steal and sell off to the highest bidder, leaving many people totally deprived. Like all other possessions, moral virtue would then become a source of anxiety. It would cause Buddhists to become weary of striving for it, and insecure about holding onto their acquisition. Consequently, the inability to know what precisely constitutes genuine moral virtue is a way to avoid the dangers arising from moral issues, thus allowing virtuous individuals a clever way to gain peace of mind. Being very wary of the inherent dangers, I have never thought of separating myself from the moral virtue that I practice. Those unwilling to make this separation remain content wherever they go, whatever they do, for they never have to worry about losing their moral virtue. Those who see it as something separate from themselves might worry so much that they end up coming back as ghosts after death to anxiously watch over their store of accumulated virtue. It would be like dying people who fret about their wealth, and therefore, get stuck in a frame of mind where they return as ghosts to keep anxious watch over their accumulated riches."

Complete Self-assurance

One day a prominent elder of Wat Boromaniwat invited Ācariya Mun for a private conversation with him.[1] He began with a question. "When you are living alone in the mountains and forests, preferring not to be bothered by monks or lay people, whom do you consult for solutions when a problem arises in your practice? Even though I live in the capitol, which is full of learned scholars who can help me clear up my doubts, still there are times when I find myself so completely baffled that no one is able to help me resolve those dilemmas. I know that you usually live alone; so when questions arise, who do you consult or how do you deal with them? Please explain this to me."

Boldly, Ācariya Mun replied:

"Please allow me to answer you with complete self-assurance which I gained from studying fundamental natural principles: I consult Dhamma, listening to it both day and night in all my daily activities, except in sleep. As soon as I wake up, my heart is immediately in contact with Dhamma. As for problems, my heart carries on a constant debate with them. As old problems are resolved, new ones arise. In resolving one problem, some of the *kilesas* are destroyed, while another that emerges starts another battle with the *kilesas* that remain. Every conceivable type of problem, from the grossest to the subtlest, from the most circumscribed to the most comprehensive, all of them arise and are fought within the heart. Consequently, the heart is the battleground where *kilesas* are confronted and then eliminated each time a problem is resolved.

"I am not so interested in thinking about whom I would consult if problems arise in the future. I'm much more interested in attacking the immediate ones that set the stage for the *kilesas* lurking in the background. By demolishing them at every turn, I gradually eliminate the *kilesas* from my heart. So, I do not concern myself with consulting other monks to help solve my problems and rid my *kilesas*, for it's much quicker to rely on the mindfulness and wisdom that arise continuously in my heart. Each time I'm faced with a problem, I am clearly conscious of the maxim *attāhi attano nātho*[2] — oneself is one's own refuge — so I use methods I devise from my own mindfulness and wisdom to immediately solve that problem. Instead of trying to glean answers from the scriptures, I depend on Dhamma, in the form of mindfulness and wisdom, that arise within me, to accept the challenge and find a solution that allows me to proceed, unimpeded. Although some problems are so profound and complex they require a sustained, meticulous investigative effort, they are no match for the proven effectiveness of mindfulness and wisdom in the end. So they too dissolve away.

"I have no desire to seek the companionship of my fellow monks just so they can help me solve my problems. I much prefer to live alone. Living all alone, solitary in body and mind, means contentment for me. When the time comes for me to die, I shall pass away unencumbered by concerns for the past or the future. At the moment my breath ceases, all other matters will cease with it. I apologize for answering your question so unintelligently. I'm afraid my reasoning wasn't very eloquent."

The elder, who had listened attentively, was so wholeheartedly convinced by what he heard that he complimented Ācariya Mun.

"You are an exceptional person, as befits one who truly likes living alone in the mountains and forests. The Dhamma that you have presented here cannot be found in the scriptures because the Dhamma recorded in the texts and the natural principles of Dhamma arising in the heart are really quite different. To the extent that the Dhamma in the texts was recorded directly from the mouth of the Lord Buddha by those possessing a level of purity equal to his, to that extent, it is pure and unadulterated. But transcribers of the texts in later generations may not have been so genuinely pure as the original ones, so the overall excellence of the Dhamma as subsequently recorded may have been moderated by its transcribers. For this reason, it is understandable that Dhamma arising fresh from the heart would be different from what is recorded in the scriptures, even though they are both within the scope of what we consider "Dhamma".

"I have no more doubts concerning the question I rather stupidly asked you. Still, such stupidity does have its own benefits, for had I not made a stupid inquiry, I would not have heard your sagacious reply. Not only have I sold my stupidity today, but I have also bought a lot of wisdom. You might also say that I've discharged a load of ignorance to acquire a wealth of wisdom.

"I do have one other question though. After the Lord Buddha's disciples took leave of him to go out and practice on their own, they returned to ask his advice when problems arose in the course of their practice. Once he helped clear up their doubts, they again returned to their respective locations. What was the nature of those problems that the Buddha's disciples sought his advice on?"

Ācariya Mun replied:

"When someone is available for help with quick, timely results, people, who by nature prefer to depend on others, will opt for the shortcut, certain that it is better than trying to go it alone. Except, of course, when the distances involved make traveling there and back entirely impractical. Then they are obliged to struggle as best they can, relying on the strength of their own mindfulness and wisdom, even if this does mean slower results.

"Being omniscient, the Lord Buddha could help solve people's problems and resolve their doubts much more clearly and quickly than they could expect to do on their own. Consequently, disciples of his, who experienced problems or had doubts, felt obliged to seek his advice in order to resolve them as quickly and decisively as possible. If the Lord Buddha were alive today and I was in a position to visit him, I too would go to ask him questions that I have never been able to resolve to my satisfaction. In that way I could avoid having to trudge along laboriously, wasting precious time as I've done in the past.

"Still, reaching definite conclusions on our own, while practicing alone, is a laborious task that we must all undertake, for, as I've mentioned, we must ultimately depend on ourselves. But having a teacher who elucidates the correct way of practice and then recommends the right methods to follow helps us see practical results quickly and easily. This contrasts sharply with results we achieve from guesswork when we are practicing alone. I have seen the disadvantages of such uncertainty in my own practice, but it was an unavoidable situation as I did not have a teacher to instruct me in those days. I had to make my way tentatively, stumbling and picking myself up, making numerous mistakes along the way. The crucial factor was my resolve, which remained single-minded and unyielding. Because it never lapsed, never waned, I was able to smooth out the rough patches in my practice, little by little, until I gradually achieved a true sense of satisfaction. That contentment gave me the opportunity to get my balance on the path of practice; and this, in turn, allowed me to look deeply into the nature of the world and the nature of Dhamma in the way I've already mentioned."

The elder asked many more questions of Ācariya Mun, but having covered the most important ones, I shall pass over the rest.

WHILE STAYING IN BANGKOK, Ācariya Mun was regularly invited out to eat in private homes, but he declined, for he found it difficult to take care of bodily necessities after he finished eating.

When he felt the time was appropriate, Ācariya Mun left Bangkok and headed for Korat where he had been invited to stay by devotees in Nakhon Ratchasima. Staying at Wat Pa Salawan monastery, he received numerous visitors who came to ask him questions. There was one which was especially interesting that Ācariya Mun himself recounted to me — one which I have never forgotten even though I tend to be forgetful. Perhaps I suspected it would one day form part of his biography! This question was asked as a means of discovering the true nature of Ācariya Mun's attainment, and whether he was actually worthy of the popular acclaim he received. The questioner was an ardent student of the way of *kammaṭṭhāna* who earnestly sought the truth.

Questioner: "When you accepted the invitation to come to Korat, was it simply because you want to help your devotees here, or have you also come hoping to strive for the attainment of *magga, phala,* and Nibbāna?"

Ācariya Mun: "Being neither hungry nor deluded, I am not searching for anything that would create *dukkha* and cause me trouble. Hungry people are never content as they are, so they run around searching here and there, latching on to whatever they find without considering if their behavior is right or not. In the end, their acquisitiveness scorches them like a blazing fire. Deluded people are always searching for something. But I have no delusion, so I am not searching. Those who are not deluded have no need to search. Everything is already perfect within their hearts, so why should they bother? Why should they get excited and grasp at shadows when they know perfectly well that shadows are not genuine truths. Genuine truths are the Four Noble Truths, and they are already present within the minds and bodies of all living beings. Having fully understood these truths, I am no longer deluded; so what else would you have me seek? I'm still alive and people need my help, so I assist them — it's as simple as that.

"It's much easier to find precious stones than it is to find good people with Dhamma in their hearts. One virtuous person is more valuable than all the money in the world, because all that money cannot bring the world the kind of genuine peace and happiness that a beneficent person can. Just one such individual is capable of bringing so much enduring peace and happiness to the world. The Lord Buddha and the

Arahants are excellent examples of this. Each virtuous person is more precious that any amount of wealth, and each realizes that good deeds have far greater value than money. As long as they remain virtuous and people around them are contented, they don't care if they are poor. But fools, preferring money over virtue and virtuous people, will do anything to get money. They can't be bothered about the consequences of their actions, no matter how wicked or depraved they may be. Even the devil is so disgusted and so fearful they will wreak havoc among the denizens of hell that he's reluctant to accept them as inmates. But such fools care about only one thing: getting their hands on some money, no matter how ill-gotten. Let evil settle the accounts, and to hell with the devil! Virtuous people versus wicked people, material wealth versus the virtues of Dhamma, this is how they differ. Sensible people should think about them right now before it's too late to choose the correct path.

"Ultimately the varying results that we experience depend on the *kamma* we make. We have no choice but to accept the consequences dictated by our *kamma* — remonstrations are of no avail. It's for this very reason that living beings differ so widely in everything from the type of existence they are born into, with their different bodily forms and emotional temperaments, to the degrees of pleasure and pain they experience. All such things form part of one's own personal makeup, a personal destiny for which each of us must take full responsibility. We must each bear our own burden. We must accept the good and the bad, the pleasant and the painful experiences that come our way, for no one has the power to disown these things. The karmic law of cause and effect is not a judicial law: it is the law of our very existence — a law which each one of us creates independently. Why have you asked me this question anyway?"

This remarkably robust response, which I heard about from Ācariya Mun as well as from a monk who accompanied him on that occasion, was so impressive that I have never forgotten it.

Questioner: "Please forgive me, but I have heard your excellent reputation praised far and wide for a long time now. Monks and lay people alike all say the same thing: Ācariya Mun is no ordinary monk. I have longed to hear your Dhamma myself, so I asked you that question with this desire in mind. Unfortunately, the lack of discretion in the way I asked may have disturbed you somewhat. I've had a keen interest in practice for many years, and my heart has definitely become more and more peaceful throughout that time. I feel that my life has not been wasted, for I have been fortunate enough to encounter the Buddhasāsana and now have paid homage to a renowned teacher revered for his excellent practice and superb virtue. The clear, precise answer you gave me a moment ago exceeded my expectations. Today my doubts have been allayed, at least as far as is possible for one still burdened with *kilesas*. It's now up to me to carry on with my own practice as best I can."

Ācariya Mun: "The way you phrased your question prompted me to answer as I did, for in truth I am neither hungry nor deluded. What else would you have me search for? I had enough of hunger and delusion back in the days when I was still inexperienced in the way of practice. Back then, no one was aware of how I nearly died striving in the mountains and forests before I felt secure in my practice. It was only later as people began to seek me out that my fame started to spread. But I didn't hear anyone praising me at the time when I passed out, unconscious, three times and barely survived to tell about it. This renown came only long after the event. Now everyone lauds my achievements, but what's the use in that?

"If you want to discover the superior qualities latent within yourself, then you must take the initiative and practice. It's no use waiting until you are dead and then invite monks to chant auspicious verses for your spiritual benefit. That's not what we call 'scratching the place that itches' — don't say I didn't warn you. If you want to get rid of that itch, you must hurry and immediately scratch the right place; that is, you must intensify your efforts to do good in order get rid of your attachment and concern for all material things of this world. Possessions like wealth and property do not really belong to us — we lay claim to them in name only. In doing so, we overlook our true worth. The wealth we accumulate in this world can be used wisely to bring us some measure of happiness. But if we're very stupid, it can soon become a blazing fire that completely destroys us.

"The venerable individuals who transcended *dukkha* in ages past did so by accumulating virtuous qualities within themselves until they became an important source of refuge for all of us. Perhaps you think they had no cherished possessions in those days. Do you honestly believe that wealth and beauty are something unique to the present day and age? Is that why you're so immoderate and self-indulgent? Is our country so lacking in cemeteries to cremate or bury the dead that you figure you won't have to die? Is that why you're so rashly overconfident? You are constantly worried about what you will eat and how you will sleep and how to keep yourself entertained, as if the world were about to vanish at any moment and take everything with it. So you rush around scooping up such a mass of useless stuff that you can hardly lug it all around. Even animals don't indulge themselves to that extent, so you shouldn't assume that you are so much more exalted and clever than they are. Such blind ignorance will only make matters much worse. Should you fall on hard times in the future, who knows? You may find yourself even more destitute than the animals you disparage. You should start laying the groundwork for a proper understanding of this matter right now, while you are still in a position to do so.

"I must apologize for speaking so harshly, but it is necessary to use harsh language to persuade people to abandon evil and do good. When nobody is willing to accept the truth, this world of ours will see the *sāsana* come to an end. Virtually everyone has done a certain amount of gross, evil *kamma* in the past for which they must inevitably suffer the consequences. People who still do not understand this are unlikely to see their own faults enough to remedy the situation. Instead, they tend to fault the Teaching for being too severe — and so the situation remains hopeless."

At this point the author would like to apologize to all you gentle readers for having been so presumptuous and indiscreet in what I've just written. My purpose was to preserve for posterity the way that Ācariya Mun taught Dhamma on certain occasions. I tried to present it in a manner that reflected his speech as accurately as possible. I wanted to record it for the sake of those wishing to contemplate the truth of his teaching. Being thus reluctant to reduce the forcefulness of his remarks, I tried to disregard any qualms I had and wrote precisely what he said.

Wherever Ācariya Mun sojourned, people constantly came to see him about Dhamma questions. Unfortunately, I cannot recall all the questions and answers that have been recounted to me over the years by monks who were present on those occasions. I noted down and remember only those answers which especially impressed me. I have forgotten those that failed to make a strong impression; and now they are gone.

AFTER A SUITABLE INTERVAL, Ācariya Mun left Nakhon Ratchasima to resume his journey to Udon Thani. When his train pulled into the station at Khon Kaen, a crowd of local people were waiting to invite him to break his journey there and stay in Khon Kaen for awhile. Since he was unable to accept the invitation, his devotees in Khon Kaen were disappointed at missing the opportunity to meet with him.

Finally arriving in Udon Thani, Ācariya Mun went to stay with Chao Khun Dhammachedi at Wat Bodhisomphon monastery. People from the provinces of Nong Khai and Sakon Nakhon, as well as Udon Thani, were waiting there to pay their respects. From there he proceeded to Wat Non Niwet monastery where he remained for the rainy season retreat. Once a week on observance day, during the rains retreat that year, Chao Khun Dhammachedi took a group of public officials and other lay supporters to hear Ācariya Mun's Dhamma talks in the evening. It was, of course, Chao Khun Dhammachedi himself who had taken so much trouble to invite Ācariya Mun to return to Udon Thani. He had trekked through the thick forests of Chiang Mai to personally offer that auspicious invitation. All of us, who met Ācariya Mun and heard his Dhamma after he arrived in Udon Thani, owe Chao Khun Dhammachedi a sincere debt of gratitude. Chao Khun Dhammachedi was always keenly interested in the way of practice. He never tired of talking about Dhamma, no matter how long the conversation lasted. He was especially appreciative when the Dhamma discussion dealt with meditation practice. He felt great respect and affection for Ācariya Mun. Therefore, he took a special interest in his well-being while he stayed in Udon Thani, constantly asking people who had seen Ācariya Mun recently how he was getting along. In addition, he always encouraged people to meet with Ācariya Mun and get to know him. He would even tirelessly escort those who did not dare go alone. His efforts in that respect were outstanding and truly admirable.

During the dry season following the rains retreat, Ācariya Mun preferred to wander off into the countryside, seeking seclusion where he could practice the way of Dhamma in a manner most suitable to his character. He liked to stay in the vicinity of Ban Nong Nam Khem village, which was located about seven miles from the town of Udon Thani. He lived for long periods in this area because it had pleasant forests that were conducive to meditation practice.

His presence in Udon Thani during the rains retreat greatly benefited both the monks and the general public from the town and surrounding districts. As news of his arrival spread, monks and lay people from the area gradually began to converge on the monastery where he resided in order to practice with him and hear his Dhamma. Most of these people had been disciples of his from the time he lived in the area before going to Chiang Mai. Upon receiving word that he had returned, they were overjoyed at the prospect of seeing him again, offering him alms, and hearing his advice. He was not very old yet, being only about 70 then. He was still able to get around without much trouble. By nature he tended to be quick and agile anyway, always ready to get up and move on, never staying too long in one place. He much preferred to wander with no specific destination, hiking through the mountains and forests where life was peaceful and undisturbed.

Past Lives

In Udon Thani, just as they had in other places, the local people often came to Ācariya Mun with questions. While some of their questions were very similar to the ones that he had received many times before, the more unusual ones arose from the views and opinions of certain individuals. Among the more commonly asked questions were those dealing with past-life associations[3] of living beings who have developed virtuous qualities together over a period of many lives, and how such inherent character traits have continuity in their present lives. Other questions dealt with past-life associations of husbands and wives who had lived together happily for many lifetimes. Ācariya Mun said that people had more doubts about these questions than any others.

As for the first question, Ācariya Mun did not specify the exact nature of what he was asked. He merely mentioned the question of past-life associations in a general way and gave this explanation:

"Things like this must originate with the establishment of volitional intent, for that determines the way the lives of specific individuals become interrelated."

The second question was more specific: How is it possible to determine whether the love between a man and a woman has been preordained by previous association in lives past? How can we distinguish between a loving relationship based on past-life connections and one which is not?

Ācariya Mun replied:

"It is very difficult to know with any certainty whether or not our love for this person or our relationship with that person has its roots in a mutual affinity developed over many lifetimes. For the most part, people fall in love and get married rather blindly. Feeling hungry, a person's tendency is to just reach out and grab some food to satisfy that hunger. They will eat whatever is available as long as it is sufficient for their day-to-day needs. The same can be applied to past-life associations as well. Although such relationships are a common feature of life in this world, it is not at all easy to find genuine cases of people who fall in love and get married simply due to a long-standing past-life association. The problem is, the *kilesas* that cause people to fall in love don't spare anyone's blushes, and they certainly don't wait patiently to give past-life affinities a chance to have a say in the matter first. All the *kilesas* ask is that there be someone of the opposite sex who suits their fancy — that's enough for passion to arise and impulsively grab a hold. Those *kilesas* that cause people to fall in love can turn ordinary people into 'fighters' who will battle desperately to the bitter end without respect for modesty or moderation, no matter what the consequences might be. Even if they see they have made a mistake, they will still refuse to admit defeat. Even the prospect of death cannot make them abandon their fighting style. This is what the *kilesas* that cause people to fall in love are all about. Displaying themselves conspicuously in people's hearts, they are extremely difficult to control.

"Anyone who wants to be a reasonable, responsible person should avoid giving these *kilesas* their head, never permitting them to charge on ahead unchecked. So you must exercise enough self-control to insure that, even if you know nothing about your past-life associations, you will still have an effective means of reining in your heart — a means of avoiding being dragged through the mire and down a steep, dark precipice. Unless you are an accomplished meditator with an aptitude for perceiving various types of phenomena, you will find it very difficult to access knowledge about your past lives. Whatever the case, you must always have enough presence of mind to maintain proper self-control. Don't let those offensive *kilesas* burst their banks, pouring out like flood waters with no levee to contain them. Thus you will be able to avoid sinking deep into the great quagmire of unbridled love."

Questioner: "What should a husband and wife, who have lived together happily in this life and wish to remain together in the next life, do to insure that they'll be reborn together in the future? Is it enough that they both hold the same desire for meeting again in future lives?"

Ācariya Mun: "That desire merely creates the prospect of achieving one's intended objective; but if that desire is not accompanied by concrete action it will not bring the expected results. Take the example of someone who desires to be rich. If that person is too lazy to go out and earn his wealth, then there is no way he'll ever be rich. To stand any chance of success, an intention must be supported by a concerted effort toward reaching that goal. It's the same with a husband and wife who wish to maintain their loving relationship, living together happily in each successive life. To avoid being separated, their viewpoints must be analogous, and they must remain faithful to each other. They must refrain from taking advantage of each other because this destroys their mutual trust and leads to dissatisfaction. They must cherish virtue, behave properly, and trust each other. By establishing a mutual understanding about their partnership and then making a sincere effort to foster their future together by doing what is beneficial to it, they can expect to fulfill that desire for it is well within their power to do so. On the other hand, should the opposite hold true — with either the husband being good while the wife is bad, or vice versa, with one or the other doing only that which pleases him or her — then no matter how many hundreds of resolutions they make together, they will all come to naught. Their very actions will perforce undermine their desire. And what about you? Do you cherish the desire to be together with your wife above all other wishes?"

Questioner: "I desire nothing more than the fulfillment of this wish. Wealth and all its trappings, rank, title, royal status, heavenly bliss, or spiritual attainment — none of these would mean anything without my wife, who is my one true love. This is the major focus of every person's desire, so we must wish for a loving mate first of all; then other desires can be considered in due course. That is why I had to ask you about this matter first, although I was embarrassed and afraid you might scold me. Such is the reality of the world we live in, though people are often too shy to speak about it."

Ācariya Mun laughed: "That being the case, you have to take your wife wherever you go, right?"

Questioner: "I'm ashamed to say that it's really concern about my wife that has prevented me from ordaining as a monk all this time. I am worried that she'd be awfully lonely with no one there to advise and reassure her. My children just bother her for money to buy things, making a nuisance of themselves all the time. I don't see how they can offer her any security or peace of mind. I can't help worrying about her.

"There's another thing I don't understand. The Dhamma teaches that the heavenly realms are inhabited by both male and female *devas*, much like the human world. Beings there live a blissfully happy existence, enjoying a variety of pleasures that make it a very inviting place to live. But, unlike here on earth or in the heavens, it seems that no distinction is made between male and female beings in the *brahma* realms. Doesn't it get kind of lonely there? I mean, they have no one to cheer them up or humor them when they get in a bad mood. And Nibbāna is even worse — there is no involvement with anything whatsoever. One is absolutely self-reliant in every way. Without the need to depend on anyone or anything for help, there is no need for one to become involved with others in anyway. One is truly independent. But how can one possibly take pride in anything there? Ordinarily, someone reaching an exalted state like Nibbāna should expect to be honored and praised by the other beings who live there. At least in the world, a prosperous person who has wealth and social status receives praise and admiration from his fellow human beings. But those going to Nibbāna find only silence — there's no question of receiving praise and admiration from their peers. Which makes me wonder how such total silence can truly be a state of happiness. Please forgive me for asking such a crazy, unorthodox question, but unless I find out from someone who really knows the answer, this dilemma will continue to trouble me to no end."

Ācariya Mun: "The heavenly realms, the *brahma* realms, and Nibbāna are not reserved for skeptics like you. They are reserved for those who can realize their own true inner worth. Only such people realize the value of the heavenly realms, the *brahma* realms, and Nibbāna because they understand that the value of each successive realm increases relative to the virtuous qualities inherent in those who would attain them. Somebody like you can hardly dream of attaining such states. Even if you wanted to, you wouldn't be able to go as long as your wife was still around. Were she to die, you would still be unable to stop yearning for her long enough to start wishing for a heavenly existence. The way you feel, even the exalted *brahma* realms and Nibbāna cannot compare with your wife, since those states cannot take care of you like she can. Thus, you don't want to go, because you are afraid that you will lose the one who takes care of all your needs."

Ācariya Mun and his questioner both laughed heartily, then Ācariya Mun continued: "Even the kinds of happiness we experience here in the human world vary widely according to individual preferences. It is comparable to the way our sense faculties, which coexist in the same physical body, deal with different types of sensations. For example, the eyes prefer to see forms, the ears prefer to hear sounds, the nose prefers smells, the tongue prefers tastes, the body prefers tactile sensations, while the mind prefers to perceive mental objects – each according to its own natural bias. They can't all be expected to have the same preference. Partaking of a good meal is one way to find pleasure. Living happily married together is yet another form of pleasure. The world has never been short of pleasant experiences, for they are an indispensable part of life that living beings everywhere feel obliged to pursue. There are forms of happiness experienced here on earth; there are others experienced in the heavenly realms, and still others in the *brahma* realms. Then there is the "happiness" of Nibbāna which is experienced by those who have totally eradicated the vexatious *kilesas* from their hearts. Their happiness is something entirely different from the worldly happiness of those with *kilesas*.

"If the happiness you receive from your wife's company is really all you need, then why bother looking at sights and listening to sounds? Why bother eating or sleeping? Why bother developing virtuous qualities by giving donations, maintaining morality, or doing meditation? All you need do is live with your wife and let that happiness be the sum of all happiness you would otherwise receive from these sources. You could save yourself a lot of trouble that way. But can you actually do it?"

Questioner:"Oh no, sir! How could I possibly do that? What about all those times when we quarrel with each other? How could I make all my happiness dependent on her alone? That would just complicate my life even more."

Ācariya Mun said this man had a rather bold, forthright character and, for a layman, he had a very keen interest in moral virtue. He was deeply devoted to Ācariya Mun who usually made an effort to give him special attention. This man used to come to see Ācariya Mun and casually start up a conversation when there were no other visitors around. Normally, other people could not bring themselves to ask Ācariya Mun the kinds of questions he did. He was extremely fond of his wife and children, while his fond devotion for Ācariya Mun made him a frequent visitor at the monastery. If he came and found Ācariya Mun with visitors, he would simply pay his respects, then go off to help the monks with the air of someone who feels quite at home in a monastery. He chose those occasions when no visitors were present to ask the questions that intrigued him. And Ācariya Mun was kind enough to oblige him nearly every time.

Ācariya Mun was exceptionally clever at recognizing a person's basic character traits; and treated each individual according to his assessment. Whether speaking casually or giving a discourse, he always tailored his remarks to fit the audience, as you can no doubt see from what I have written so far.

WHILE ĀCARIYA MUN lived at Wat Non Niwet monastery in Udon Thani, numerous monks came to seek his guidance, and many spent the rains retreat under his tutelage. In those days, Wat Non Niwet monastery was a much quieter place than it is today. There was very little traffic back then and very few people came to visit. By and large, people who did come to the monastery were those with a genuine interest in making merit and developing virtuous qualities — unlike nowadays when people tend to come and disturb the monks' peaceful environment whether they intend to or not. Back then, monks could practice as they pleased without disturbance. Consequently, many monks developed themselves spiritually, becoming a source of contentment not only to themselves, but also to the local people who looked to monks for refuge.

Ācariya Mun instructed the monks in the evening. He usually began with a general explanation of moral virtue, followed by *samādhi* and then wisdom, going briefly through them stage by stage until the highest level of absolute freedom — the essential goal of Dhamma. He then went back and gave a comprehensive exposition of how a monk should practice to attain the various stages of Dhamma that he had outlined. For monks engaged in meditation practice, he always emphasized the vital importance of mindful adherence to the monastic code of discipline.

"Only a monk who is firm in his discipline and respectful of all the training rules can be considered a full-fledged monk. He should not transgress the minor training rules merely because he considers them to be somehow insignificant. Such negligence indicates someone who feels no shame about immoral behavior, and it may eventually lead to more serious transgressions. A monk must strictly adhere to the monastic code of discipline to make sure that his moral behavior is not punctuated with unsightly blemishes or gaps. In that way, he feels comfortable and confident living among his peers. He need never be concerned that his teacher or his fellow monks will be critical or reproachful. For the inner monk in your heart to reach perfection, starting from Sotāpanna and progressing to Arahant, you must be steady and relentless in your effort to attain each successive level of both *samādhi* and wisdom. If you persevere in this manner, these faculties will arise and continue to develop until they are able to scrub clean that filthy mess of defilements in your heart.

"A monk's conduct and speech should be absolutely above reproach. His *citta* should be absolutely superb by virtue of the Dhamma qualities that he develops step by step: *samādhi, paññā, vimutti,* and *vimuttiñāṇadassana.*[4] A monk should never be dreary or sad. He should never appear undignified, shunning his fellows because a guilty conscience is eating away inside him, troubling his heart. This is contrary to the way of the Lord Buddha, whose splendid internal conduct and external behavior were irreproachable. Following in his footsteps, a monk must muster the resolute courage to abandon all evil and do only good. He must be a man of integrity who is honest with himself and his peers while being faithful to the Dhamma and the Discipline. He will thus be supported by his exemplary practice everywhere he goes. The brightness of his mindfulness and wisdom will light the way as his heart will be suffused with the taste of Dhamma. He will never find himself trapped in a state of delusion with no means of escape. Such are the characteristics inherent in a true disciple of the Lord Buddha.

Study them carefully and take them to heart. Adhere closely to them as the basis for a bright, trouble-free future when you can claim them as your own valuable, personal possessions."

This was how Ācariya Mun usually instructed practicing monks.

MONKS WHO HAD DOUBTS or questions about their practice could consult individually with Ācariya Mun during the day when the time did not conflict with his daily routine. His daily life had a regular pattern that he tended to follow without fail wherever he stayed. Rising from his meditation seat early in the morning, he walked meditation outside his hut until it was time to go on almsround. After collecting alms food in the village and eating his morning meal, he again walked meditation until noon and then took a short rest. Once rested, he sat in meditation for awhile before continuing his walking meditation until four p.m. At four, he swept the open areas around his residence. When he finished, he bathed, and again practiced walking meditation for many hours. Upon leaving his meditation track, he entered his hut to do several hours of chanting. Following that, he again sat in meditation late into the night. Normally, he slept no more than four hours a night. On special occasions he went entirely without sleep, sitting in meditation until dawn. When he was young, he displayed a diligence in his practice that none of his contemporaries could match. Even in old age he maintained his characteristic diligence, although he did relax a bit due to his strength, which declined with each passing day. But he differed significantly from the rest of us in that his mind showed no signs of weakness even as his health gradually deteriorated.

Such was the life of a great man who set a perfect example for us all. He never neglected his personal responsibilities, nor did he relax the relentless effort which had been such an important source of strength, spurring him on to that gratifying victory deep in the mountains of Chiang Mai, as we have seen. As human beings, we all possess attributes that should allow us to duplicate Ācariya Mun's achievement. In actual practice, those able to achieve the kind of unqualified success that he did are few and far between. Despite the fact that the world is now grossly overpopulated, very few people indeed will see their hopes fulfilled by attaining this exalted goal. In the present age, such an attainment is very rare.

The outstanding difference between someone like Ācariya Mun and the rest of us is the degree of diligence and determination he applied to the pursuit of knowledge and understanding, an effort firmly grounded in the four *iddhipāda: chanda, viriya, citta,* and *vimaṁsa.*[5] And when the causes are so different, the results are bound to be radically different as well — so much so that it's almost unbelievable how varied they can be from one person to the next. But the good and bad results that people receive from their actions are evident everywhere in the world around us, and they cannot be denied. We must acknowledge the obvious: that a mixture of goodness and evil, happiness and suffering arises in each and every one of us. There is no way we can divest ourselves of them.

Among modern-day *ācariyas,* Ācariya Mun's life story is splendidly unique. A rich story, it flowers and bears fruit from beginning to end. Magnificent every step of the way, it is a life worthy of everyone's heart-felt respect. He is now revered far and wide in places where people have heard about his excellent reputation. It's a great shame that so many Buddhists who were keenly interested in Dhamma never heard of him while he was still alive. Although they might have very much wanted to meet a man of such exceptional virtue, they never had a chance to do so. This was largely because he did not like to frequent crowded places like towns and cities. He found life in the mountains and forests far more satisfactory his entire life.

Many monks who were dedicated to the practice of Dhamma also experienced great difficulty in reaching him. The dirt roads were hardly passable in those days — and anyway, there were no vehicles. They had to hike for days in order to reach the places where he liked to stay. Those who were unaccustomed to hiking just couldn't manage it. Their excuses for not going varied. Some monks were simply not courageous enough to accept the plain truth about Dhamma that he taught. Some were afraid that food and other necessities would be in short supply and of poor quality. Some were afraid they could not eat just one meal a day as he did. Where Ācariya Mun was concerned, monks tended to create any number of obstacles for themselves, most of them appearing insurmountable. Although their aspirations were sincere, such concerns amounted to self-imposed barriers that prevented them from gaining the benefit of their good intentions. In the end, they realized the kind of monk he really was only long after he had passed away and they heard the story of his life. He epitomized the *sāsana* which has preserved *magga* and *phala* from Lord Buddha's initial attainment down through the countless number of Arahants who have maintained *magga* and *phala* to this day. The essence of the *sāsana* has been transmitted by means of *supaṭipanno, uju, ñāya, sāmīcipaṭipanno sāvakasangho*[6] as practiced by all those who have attained *magga, phala,* and Nibbāna. They are like a vast stream of the great deathless ocean of Nibbāna, shimmering forth from the pristine nature of those who have practiced to perfection what the Buddha taught.

Ācariya Mun was one of the Arahants of this present age. He passed away not so long ago on November 10, 1949, about 20 years ago.[7] The story of his passing away will be described later when we reach the final chapter of his life. In any case, physical death has existed since time immemorial and will continue to exist as long as some form of conventional reality still remains. What arises must pass away. What remains unconditionally is the prodigious wonder of the Lord Buddha's infinite compassion, wisdom, and absolute freedom, all of which are enshrined in the *sāsana*. Such intrinsic qualities being exactly the same, Ācariya Mun's unqualified compassion, wisdom, and absolute freedom remain unchanged in the same way as those of the Lord Buddha. For us, it is essential that we faithfully practice the way laid down by the Buddha — the degree of success we have will depend on the amount of time and effort we put into the practice. This is something we should all take an interest in while we are still alive. Without making an effort to practice, no results can be achieved, and the opportunity will be irrevocably lost.

ONE OF THE ANSWERS that Ācariya Mun gave to the people of Nakhon Ratchasima especially caught my attention. Here is a summary of what he said:

"Don't think and act as if you, your family and friends, and the society you live in will never have to face the cemetery. Otherwise, when death comes — as it does to everyone in the world — you will find yourself hopelessly unprepared and so risk sinking into the kind of unfavorable state no one would wish for. Whatever you think, say, or do should be accompanied by some recollection of the cemetery, which symbolizes death, for cemeteries and *kamma* go hand in hand. Reflection on death will encourage reflection on *kamma*, which in turn will cause you to reflect back on yourself.

"Don't get cocky, thinking you're so smart, when in truth you are always at the mercy of *kamma*. Such arrogance will merely lead to your own misfortune. You should never take the attitude that you are smarter than the Buddha — that great, all-knowing teacher who, unlike people with *kilesas* who feel very cocky, never relied on conjecture. In the end, such people become trapped in the bad *kamma* that their own arrogant assumptions have created for them."

Such straight talk can be quite startling in its effect, inducing the listener to submit wholeheartedly to the truth about *kamma*. It cuts through all the self-importance that causes us to overlook our true place in this world. I have revisited the subject of *kamma* here for I feel that what I previously wrote on the subject is inadequate, since it failed to capture the full impact of what Ācariya Mun taught. This oversight has just come to my attention, which shows just how unreliable our memories are. In fact, they easily mislead us, blocking the truth from view. So please forgive me for going over the same material again from time to time.

ĀCARIYA MUN HAD the knowledge and the ability to confer Dhamma excellence on his monk disciples. As a result, many of them developed into veritable Bodhi trees[8] in their own right. This type of Bodhi tree is extremely difficult to plant and nurture to maturity for it tends to be surrounded by hazards. Many disciples of his who became senior *ācariyas* are still alive today. Some of them I have already mentioned by name. Ācariya Mun's senior disciples include such well-known *ācariyas* as Ācariya Sing and Ācariya Mahā Pin from Ubon Ratchathani, Ācariya Thet from Tha Bo in Nong Khai, Ācariya Fan from Sakon Nakhon, Ācariya Khao of Wat Tham Klong Phen in Udon Thani, Ācariya Phrom from Dong Yen village of Nong Han district in Udon Thani, Ācariya Lee of Wat Asokaram in Samut Prakan, Ācariya Chob and Ācariya Lui from Loei province, Ācariya Sim and Ācariya Tei from Chiang Mai, and Ācariya Kongma from Sakon Nakhon.[9] There are still many others whose names I cannot recall. Each of these *ācariyas* possesses certain exceptional qualities setting him apart from the rest.

Each is outstanding in his own distinct way, and all are worthy of the highest respect. Some being quite famous, they are well-known to monks and lay people across the country. Some by nature prefer to live in quiet seclusion. There are senior disciples of Ācariya Mun possessing exceptionally virtuous qualities who remain virtually unknown because they naturally prefer to live in anonymity.

More than any other teacher in the Northeast region of Thailand Ācariya Mun was able to firmly establish monks in *bodhidhamma*. *Bodhi* means wisdom. The *Bodhi* of the Lord Buddha is called Enlightenment; but in the case of these *ācariyas* I would prefer to simply call it *bodhidhamma*, as befits their humble status and the forest tradition to which they belong. Establishing a monk in *bodhidhamma* is very similar to raising a child. First the monk is taught how to develop a firm basis in moral discipline. Then he's taught how to use that moral excellence as a basis for his meditation practice, focusing inward to develop sufficient knowledge and understanding that will allow him to safely look after himself. The spiritual development of each and every monk represents an extremely difficult challenge because implanting virtuous qualities deeply into the heart of someone who is oppressed by the *kilesas* is always a very demanding task. The teacher must be on his guard at all times, exercising complete mastery over every type of *kilesa* so that the student remains earnestly motivated to undergo the training. Persistent practice under a good teacher allows the student a chance to bring his own character into harmony with Dhamma and so steadily grow in confidence and determination.

On our own, we all suffer from *kilesas*. Everyone coming to train under a teacher is equally full of *kilesas*. So it is difficult for them to find the strength necessary to drag one another to safety. I believe the most difficult task any human being can undertake is that of trying to transform an ordinary monk into a monk who's truly worthy of the highest respect. That task is further complicated when the teacher tries to encourage the student to shift from his original, mundane position up to the transcendent levels of Sotāpanna, Sakadāgāmī, Anāgāmī and Arahant.[10] The degree of difficulty increases dramatically with each successive level of attainment. In all likelihood, insects will come along and chew at its roots, boring into them until the whole tree topples to the ground before the nascent Bodhi tree has a chance to sprout and branch out, developing into a useful specimen. This is what we usually see happen. Seldom do the roots grow deep enough to resist the ravages of wind, rain, and insects. When we plant an ordinary tree in the ground we can expect it to soon bear fruit. When, however, we try to establish a monk in Dhamma, he always appears on the verge of falling over. Even if no apparent dangers are on the horizon, he will go out looking for something to trouble him, thus causing himself a lot of harm. All of which makes developing a monk difficult indeed. If you don't believe me, just give it a try: ordain as a monk and try following the monastic discipline laid down by the Buddha. What's the bet you'll be hungry for supper before the sun has even set. Forgetting all about your newly-shaved head, you will be itching to travel about all the time, sight-seeing, listening to sounds, smelling this, tasting that, and touching things that are nice and soft. Morning, noon, and evening – never will there be enough to satisfy your appetite. Soon you'll forget all about your status as a monk. It's unlikely that you will ever take an interest in cultivating that inner Bodhi tree, for your heart will never accept reason and persevere with the monk's training long enough to gain genuine peace of mind.

Left unattended, the Bodhi tree of the heart will gradually wither and shrivel up. Harmful influences will then have the upper hand. What Bodhi tree could stand erect against such an onslaught? The *bodhi* of a monk is sensitive to those influences, so his heart may easily be swayed by such discordant elements. If his *bodhi* cannot withstand the pressure, it will topple hopelessly to the ground. Thus it is an extremely difficult task to establish *bodhi* properly. Those who have never tried to establish *bodhi* in their hearts don't know how potent those negative influences can be. They attempt to fertilize the nascent Bodhi tree with substances that only serve to stunt its growth, eventually ruining it altogether. Consequently, such Bodhi trees tend to have a dreary look about them, as if they were going to die at any moment from a profound shortage of noble virtue.

I have experience in planting such Bodhi trees and looking after them. And due to a lack of sound judgment, I've had my share of disappointments. So I am well aware of how difficult they are to establish and take care of. They always seem to be on the verge of withering up and dying. Even today I cannot say for sure whether or not this Bodhi tree of mine will grow and mature nicely, or simply deteriorate, since as a rule it threatens to take a turn for the worse. In fact, I haven't seen enough progress to be able to gauge the level of decline – steady decline seems to be the norm. Preferring to look for stimulation that is invariably harmful, this type of *bodhi* can easily destroy itself without any outside help.

Anyone who makes the agonizing effort to oppose his heart's natural inclinations until it submits to the authority of Dhamma is able to develop *bodhi* to perfection. Such a person is truly worthy of veneration. Ācariya Mun is a classic example of a teacher who develops *bodhi* so thoroughly that he becomes a reassuring source of comfort to all his disciples. Ācariya Mun carefully cultivated his Bodhi tree until the trunk was strong, the branches extensive, the foliage thick, and the fruits and flowers abundant. It was always a peaceful source of shade for those who sought to shelter there. Although he has already passed away, just reading the story of his life is enough to arouse faith in him and the Dhamma he practiced. It's almost as though he never passed away at all.

Ācariya Mun (circa 1940)

Ācariya Mun's residence at Wat Nong Pheu monastery.

The meeting hall at Wat Nong Pheu monastery where monks assembled for the morning meal and evening meetings.

Ācariya Mahā Boowa standing in front of a typical forest monk's hut.

The stretcher (covered with a white canopy) carrying Ācariya Mun's
dying body from Ban Nong Pheu to Ban Phu, accompanied by scores
of monks and lay supporters.

6

The Final Years

fter departing Chiang Mai, Ācariya Mun stayed two rains
retreats at Wat Non Niwet monastery in Udon Thani. Following the second retreat, a group of lay devotees from Sakon
Nakhon, headed by a longtime disciple, Khun Mae Num Chuwanon,
came and invited him to return with them for the spiritual benefit of
people there. When he readily agreed, all concerned were delighted,
and arrangements were made to escort him there. Upon arriving
in Sakon Nakhon in late 1941, Ācariya Mun first resided at Wat
Suddhawat monastery. Soon monks and laity were arriving daily to pay
their respects and seek his advice.

While at Wat Suddhawat, somebody came with a camera and asked
permission to take his photograph to keep as an object of worship. In
all, Ācariya Mun allowed his picture to be taken three times: on this
occasion in Sakon Nakhon; previously, when he was staying in Nakhon
Ratchasima; and later, at Ban Fang Daeng in That Phanom district of
Nakhon Phanom province on his return from Ācariya Sao's funeral.[1]
The photographic prints that his devotees collect as objects of worship
today are reproductions of pictures taken on these three occasions. But
for these, there would be no photographic images to remind us what
he looked like. It was not easy to get permission to take Ācariya Mun's
picture. Those who tried were on pins and needles, fidgeting nervously
as they waited drenched in sweat, looking for a good opportunity to
broach the subject with him. Well aware that he rarely gave permission

for such activities, they were afraid that if they did not handle the situation properly, then he might simply dismiss them with a curt retort.

Ācariya Mun stayed at Wat Suddhawat monastery for awhile before moving to a small forest monastery near the village of Ban Na Mon which, being very quiet and secluded both day and night, suited him perfectly. The monks and novices living with him were an impressive sight – they said very little, but packed quite a punch. That is to say, instead of chatting among themselves, they preferred to put effort into their practice, each monk sitting in his own hut or walking meditation out in the forest. At four o'clock in the afternoon they all emerged from their living quarters to sweep the grounds together. With the whole area swept clean, they drew water from the well and carried it around to fill up the water barrels used for cleaning their feet and washing their alms bowls. These chores completed, everyone bathed together at the well in an admirably quiet, composed manner. They performed each daily chore with a remarkable self-control, always applying mindfulness and wisdom to analyze the nature of the tasks at hand – no one absent-mindedly engaged in idle conversation. As soon as the day's duties were finished they separated, each monk returning to his hut to sit or walk in meditation as he saw fit.

When the monks returned to their huts, the monastery appeared deserted. A visitor happening to arrive then would not have seen a single monk simply standing around or sitting idly. Had the visitor ventured into the surrounding forest, he would have discovered some of the monks pacing back and forth on their meditation tracks, and others sitting peacefully in their small huts, all preferring to practice quietly, in solitude. They came together for almsround and the morning meal, or when there was an evening meeting, and only occasionally for other required duties. Even on almsround, each monk walked to and from the village with cautious restraint, mindfully intent on his meditation practice. They were not negligent, walking along casually gazing here and there, chatting with anyone who chanced to pass by. His monks truly were an inspirational sight to see as they walked for alms with such dignified composure.

Back in the monastery, the monks sat together investigating the food in their alms bowls as they prepared to eat. They reflected on the dangers inherent in attachment to food. Remaining mindful as they ate, they gave no indication that they were enjoying the food. With their attention focused on the contents of their alms bowls, they refrained from talking and did not allow their gaze to stray from the task of eating. They chewed their food carefully to avoid making loud, impolite noises that could disturb the others. The meal over, they helped each other put everything neatly away and swept the place clean. Each monk washed his alms bowl, dried it with a cloth, and carefully placed it in the sun for a few minutes. Only then did he put his alms bowl away in the appropriate place.

These duties completed, each monk returned to the seclusion of his own living quarters, turning his full attention to training his heart and mind in the manner of practice best suited to him. Sometimes a monk exerted himself to the limit; at other times, less so. In either case, he concentrated solely on his practice, unconcerned about how many hours passed or how much energy he expended. Basically, his objective was to make sure his mind remained focused on the meditation subject he had chosen to control it until that focus of attention became a mental object he could rely on to direct his heart toward peace and calm. Such calm, in turn, helped him to concentrate his mental focus on the cause and effect relationships inherent within whichever phenomena his wisdom then chose to investigate, allowing him to gradually attain increasingly more subtle levels of Dhamma as he progressed toward the ultimate goal. While applying himself assiduously, he always tried to make sure that his mode of practice was correct for the level of Dhamma he was working on.

It is extremely important that a monk have mindfulness at every stage of his practice. It is also essential that a monk use wisdom when his practice reaches those levels of Dhamma where wisdom is indispensable. Mindfulness, however, is always indispensable — at all times, in all activities. *Whenever mindfulness is missing, effort also is missing. Lacking mindfulness, walking and sitting meditation are just empty postures void of anything that could be called "right effort". For this very reason, Ācariya Mun stressed mindfulness more than any other aspect of a monk's practice. In fact, mindfulness is the principal foundation supporting every aspect on every level of meditation practice. Practiced continuously, it eventually develops into the kind of supreme-mindfulness that fosters the highest levels of wisdom. Mindfulness must be used intensively at the preliminary level of developing meditative calm and concentration. In all succeeding levels of practice, mindfulness and wisdom must be developed in tandem, working as a team.*

Ācariya Mun taught his monks to be very resolute and courageous in their practice. Anyone who was not earnestly committed to the practice was unlikely to remain with him for long. About once a week he called a meeting and gave a talk; on other nights he expected the monks to expedite their efforts on their own. Those with doubts or questions about their practice could consult him without having to wait for the next meeting. An aura of Dhamma pervaded the atmosphere around him, giving his students the feeling that *magga*, *phala*, and Nibbāna were truly within their reach. His reassuring presence gave them the determination and courage necessary to pursue their practice to the limit, conducting themselves in a manner that suggested they had the highest attainments in their sights. When meditating, they made little distinction between day and night; each monk strived in earnest regardless of the hour. On moonless nights, candle lanterns illuminated meditation tracks around the whole area. On moonlit nights, monks walked meditation by the light of the moon, each practicing with a sense of urgency that allowed him very little time for sleep.

ĀCARIYA MUN'S PROFICIENCY in chanting the *suttas* was unrivaled. He chanted *suttas* alone for many hours every night without fail. He would chant long discourses, like the *Dhamma-cakka-pavattana Sutta* and the *Mahā Samāya Sutta*, nearly every night. Occasionally, he translated the meaning of the *suttas* for our benefit, translations based on his own personal experience. He spoke directly to their essential meaning, often bypassing the strict rules of Pāli grammar normally used to maintain uniformity in translations. The undeniable clarity of his translations allowed his audience to glimpse the fundamental message of the ancient texts he quoted. Amazingly, he translated Pāli better than the accomplished scholars, though he had never studied Pāli in any formal way. No sooner had he mentioned a Pāli phrase than, without even a pause, he had translated it as well in a quick, fluent style that defied belief. For instance, when citing passages from the *Dhamma-cakka-pavattana Sutta* or the *Mahā Samāya Sutta* during the course of his talks, he gave fast, simultaneous translations worthy of a tenth grade Pāli scholar.[2] I say the tenth grade because I have heard ninth grade Pāli scholars translate and they tend to be slow and plodding. They deliberate quite a long time over each passage and even then they are not very sure of their translations.

Not only was Ācariya Mun quick, he also was boldly confident of the truth of his words. Having clearly experienced the truth of their essential meaning himself, he was certain of his translations. Pāli verses arose spontaneously in his heart, which he then elaborated on in a way that differed somewhat from classical interpretations. For example, *vātā rukkhā na pabbato*, which he translated as: "gale force winds can uproot whole trees, yet they can't move a mountain of stone." This is an example of one Dhamma verse that arose spontaneously in his heart, along with the translation, while he was giving a talk to the monks.

What I just wrote about the ninth and tenth grades of Pāli scholarship shouldn't be taken too seriously. It is merely a figure of speech used by monks in the forest tradition — no offense is intended. We forest monks tend to act a bit like monkeys that have grown accustomed to living in the wild: even if they are caught and raised as pets, they still retain their old habits. They can never really adapt to human behavior. Please excuse me for presuming to compare Ācariya Mun's translations with those of Pāli scholars. Some readers may feel that I have overstepped the mark here.

In due time Ācariya Mun left Ban Na Mon and moved to Ban Khok, just over a mile away, where he spent the rainy season retreat. Since it was difficult to find a better location, the monastery was located only half a mile from the village. Still, the place was very quiet. Not more than eleven or twelve monks stayed with him at any one time in either of those places due to the limited number of available huts. It was while he resided at Ban Khok that I arrived. He was kind enough to accept me as a student, although I was about as useful as an old log. I lived there like a ladle in a pot of stew. I feel ashamed just thinking about it now: this useless log of a monk staying with an absolutely brilliant sage of such universal renown.

All the same, I do feel easier about writing his story from this period onward. Up to this point in the story I have felt somewhat hampered, and not a little frustrated, by the fact that most of my information comes secondhand from senior disciples who lived with him in the early years. In preparation for writing this biography, I spent many years going around to meet those *ācariyas*, interviewing them and writing down their memories, or taping my conversations with them. All this material then needed to be carefully arranged in chronological order before it could be presented in a meaningful, readable format – a very demanding task. From now on I shall be writing about what I myself witnessed in the final years of Ācariya Mun's life. Although this part of the story may not impress the reader as much as what has gone before, as the author I feel relieved to be writing from personal experience.

ĀCARIYA MUN SPENT the rains retreat at the Ban Khok forest monastery with a small group of monks, all of whom remained healthy and contented throughout the three months. Ācariya Mun called a meeting about once a week, both during the retreat period and after it was over. Although his discourses usually lasted for two to four hours, his audience was so completely absorbed in meditation practice that thoughts of weariness and fatigue never crossed their minds. For his part, Ācariya Mun was completely absorbed in delivering the Dhamma, expounding the nature of cause and effect in a reasonable way that struck a chord with his listeners, all of whom were genuinely searching for Truth. The Dhamma he presented was delivered straight from a heart that had realized this Truth with absolute clarity – leaving no room for doubt. Only one doubt remained: Could the monks actually do the practice the way he described it?

He delivered his discourses in a manner reminiscent of times past when the Lord Buddha delivered a discourse to a gathering of monks. We can be sure that the Lord Buddha's discourses were concerned solely with the great treasures of Dhamma; that is, he spoke only on subjects directly related to *magga, phala,* and Nibbāna. Thus, monks listening to him were able to attain *magga, phala,* and Nibbāna one after another, in steady succession, right up until the day of his final passing away. Because the Buddha's teaching emanated directly from an absolutely pure heart, the Dhamma he delivered was incomparably superb. This was *magga* and *phala,* pure and simple, and his listeners were able to emulate his teaching to perfection.

The Dhamma that Ācariya Mun delivered was spontaneous Dhamma of the present moment – refined and purified in his heart. He did not theorize or speculate when he spoke. His audience already had their own doubts and uncertainties about the practice, and further speculation would only have served to increase those doubts. Instead, as they listened, his Dhamma gradually dispelled their doubts. Those who heard his wonderful expositions were able to use them as a way to significantly reduce their *kilesas*. Beyond that, they could be used to conclusively eliminate all doubts.

ĀCARIYA MUN CHANTED *suttas* every night for several hours. On a night when no meeting was held, he left his meditation track at about eight o'clock and entered his hut to quietly chant *suttas* at length before resuming seated meditation until it was time to retire. On meeting nights, his chanting began later, after the meeting was over. This meant that his normal schedule was delayed when there was a meeting so that he retired later than usual, at midnight or one a.m.

One evening, hearing him softly chanting in his hut, I had the mischievous urge to sneak up and listen. I wanted to find out what *suttas* he chanted at such length every night. As soon as I crept up close enough to hear him clearly, however, he stopped chanting and remained silent. This did not look good, so I quickly backed away and stood listening from a distance. No sooner had I backed away than the low cadence of his chanting started up again, now too faint to be heard clearly. So again I sneaked forward – and again he went silent. In the end, I never did find out what *suttas* he was chanting. I was afraid that if I stubbornly insisted on standing there eavesdropping, a bolt of lightning might strike and a sharp rebuke thunder out. Meeting him the next morning I glanced away. I did not dare to look him in the face. But he looked directly at me with a sharp, menacing glare. I learned my lesson the hard way: never again did I dare to sneak up and try to listen in on his chanting. I was afraid I would receive something severe for my trouble. From what I had observed of him, if I persisted there was a real chance I'd get just what I was asking for.

It was only later, after long association with him, that I clearly understood just how well he perceived everything going on around him. Thinking about it now, how could he possibly have been unaware that I was standing there like an idiot and listening so intently. It's obvious – he was fully aware. But before making any comment, he wanted first to wait and check out this stubborn, silly monk. Any further such behavior was bound to invoke a severe response. What amazed me was: each time I crept close to his hut he stopped chanting straight away. He obviously knew exactly what was going on.

319

Fellowship with Pigs

One day, shortly after my arrival – during a time when I was extremely wary of Ācariya Mun – I laid down in the middle of the day and dozed off. As I slept, Ācariya Mun appeared in my dream to scold me: "Why are you sleeping like a pig? This is no pig farm! I won't tolerate monks coming here to learn the art of being a pig. You'll turn this place into a pigsty!" His voice bellowed, fierce and menacing, frightening me and causing me to wake with a start. Dazed and trembling, I stuck my head out the door expecting to see him. I was generally very frightened of him anyway; but, I had forced myself to stay with him despite that. The reason was simple: it was the right thing to do. Besides, he had an effective antidote for pigs like me. So, I was in a panic. I stuck my head out, looking around in all directions, but I didn't see him anywhere. Only then did I begin to breathe a bit easier. Later when I had a chance, I told Ācariya Mun what happened. He very cleverly explained my dream in a way that relieved my discomfort – a tolerant approach that I don't always agree with, since soothing words can easily promote carelessness and complacency. He explained my dream like this:

"You've just recently come to live with a teacher and you are really determined to do well. Your dream simply mirrored your state of mind. That scolding you heard, reproaching you for acting like a pig, was the Dhamma warning you not to bring pig-like tendencies into the monkhood and the religion. Most people do only what they feel like doing, failing to take into account the value of their human birth and the consequences of their actions. This makes it difficult for them to fully realize their human potential. There's an old saying that someone is 'not all there'. It refers to a basic lack of human potential arising from callous insensitivity to the fact that human beings possess intrinsic qualities that are superior to those of animals. This attitude promotes such degrading behavior that some people end up damaged almost beyond repair – an empty human shell lacking all intrinsic goodness. Even then, they are unaware of what has happened to them, or why.

"If we possess sufficient mindfulness and wisdom, Dhamma can guide us in investigating this matter for ourselves. Your dream was a good, timely warning – learn from it. From now on, whenever you're feeling lazy you can use it as a means of stirring up the mindfulness necessary to overcome your indolence. This type of dream is exceptionally potent. Not everyone has a dream like this. I appreciate such dreams for they effectively stimulate mindfulness, keeping it constantly vigilant. This in turn accelerates progress in meditation, allowing the heart to attain calm with relative ease. If you take this lesson that Dhamma has provided and put it consistently into practice, you can expect to quickly achieve meditative calm. Who knows, you may even penetrate the true nature of Dhamma ahead of those who have been practicing meditation for many years. That dream of yours was very worthwhile. It wasn't a bad omen by any means.

"Don't be excessively frightened of your teacher — it will only cause you to feel uncomfortable all the time. Nothing of benefit can be gained from unreasonable fear of the teacher. He has a moral obligation to educate his students, using every means available to him. It's not your teacher you should fear, but evil, for evil leads directly to suffering. I don't accept monks as my students just so I can castigate them for no good reason. The training a monk undertakes is a stringent one, following principles laid down by the Buddha. A teacher's guidance must follow the strict logic of these principles. If he deviates from this path, neither he nor the student benefits in any way.

"So put your mind at ease and work hard at your practice. Effort is key — don't become discouraged and ease up. Dhamma belongs to everyone who truly desires it. The Buddha did not limit the possession of Dhamma to a particular individual. Everyone who practices in the right way enjoys the same right of ownership. Don't forget that auspicious dream. Reflect on it often, and all pig-like tendencies will fade into the background — as *magga*, *phala*, and Nibbāna draw ever closer. Then it's only a matter of time before the domain beyond *dukkha* appears. It's inevitable. I'm truly pleased about your dream. I have trained myself with a similar fiery intensity and I've always had good results. I found it imperative to use such methods throughout my years of practice, and now occasionally I must use similar methods to train my students."

Ācariya Mun used this interpretation of my dream to console a youngster who was new to the training. He was concerned this kid might lose heart and give up trying to make an effort, thus rejoining the fraternity of pigs. That's why he resorted to this method of teaching. His teaching methods always displayed an unparalleled ingenuity.

I often went to speak with him during that early period when my mental state was fluctuating between periods of progress and periods of decline – a time of particular stress and uneasiness for me – and he advised me in the same comforting manner. As soon as I paid my respect to him, he asked me how my *citta* was doing. If it happened to be a time when my meditation was progressing nicely, I told him so. He then voiced his approval and encouraged me to keep up the good work so that I could quickly transcend *dukkha*. If my meditation was deteriorating, I replied that my mind was so bad it seemed all traces of happiness had gone. He then adopted a sympathetic attitude:

"That's too bad. Where's it gone? Well, don't be discouraged. Just put maximum effort into your practice and it will reappear for sure. It has simply wandered off somewhere. If you accelerate your efforts it will come back on its own. The *citta* is like a dog: it inevitably follows its owner wherever he goes. It won't just run away. Intensify your practice and the *citta* is bound to return on its own. Don't waste time thinking about where it's gone to. Wherever it's gone, it can't possibly run away. If you want it to return quickly, concentrate your efforts. Any discouragement will only boost the *citta's* ego. Thinking you really miss it so much, it will play hard-to-get. So stop thinking about the *citta* you've lost. Instead, think *"buddho"*, repeating it continuously, over and over again. Once the word *"buddho"* has been mentally established by repeating it continuously in rapid succession, the *citta* will hurry back of its own accord. Even then, don't let go of *buddho*. *Buddho* is the *citta's* food – as long as there is food, it will always come running back. So repeat *"buddho"* constantly until the *citta* has eaten its fill, then it will have to take a rest. You too will feel satisfied while the *citta* rests calmly. When it's calm, it ceases to run madly about looking to cause you trouble. Keep this practice up until you cannot chase it away, even if you want to. This is the perfect method to use with a mind whose ravenous appetite is never satiated. As long as it has enough food, it will not leave even if you try to drive it away. Follow my advice and the state of your *citta* will never again deteriorate. *Buddho* is the key. So long as its food is there, it won't stray. Do as I say and you'll never again experience the disappointment of seeing your *citta* get worse time and time again."

This was yet another technique employed by Ācariya Mun to teach those of us who were really stupid. But at least I believed him – in my own stupid way. Otherwise, I would probably still be chasing after a mind in perpetual decline without any chance of ever catching it. I've written about this matter for the sake of those readers who may glean some useful ideas from the way a clever person teaches a stupid one. It is not my intention to glorify my own stupidity or the lenient treatment that I received from Ācariya Mun at that time.

FOLLOWING THE RAINS RETREAT, Ācariya Mun returned briefly to Ban Na Mon and then moved on to Ban Huay Kaen, settling in the nearby forest for awhile. From there he moved to an abandoned monastery at the base of a mountain near the village of Ban Na Sinuan, remaining there for several months. While he was there, he came down with a fever which lasted for days, curing himself as usual with the 'therapeutic power of Dhamma'.

In April 1942 he traveled to Ubon Ratchathani to attend the funeral of his teacher, Ācariya Sao. Once the cremation ceremony was completed, he returned to Ban Na Mon for the rains retreat. During that retreat Ācariya Mun employed a wide variety of methods to press his students to maximize their efforts, exhorting them to be diligent in their practice. He called a meeting once every four days throughout the entire rains period, helping many monks to develop in Dhamma and attain inner strength. Many experienced unusual insights which they reported to Ācariya Mun. I had the privilege of listening to those experiences, although I was not as accomplished in my practice as many of the others. Many memorable things occurred during that rains retreat — things that I have never forgotten. I will remember those outstanding experiences for the rest of my life.

During that retreat period Ācariya Mun began to use tough, coercive measures with us, treating us more like old footrags. Until then, he had used relatively gentle methods, turning a blind eye to our shortcomings. He probably decided that the time was right to get tough with us. If he continued to tolerate our lapses indefinitely, he would feel burdened all the time and his students would never awake from their slumber long enough to open their eyes and see the earth, the sky, the moon and the stars. As a result, all the monks were eager to do meditation practice and excited about the insights they gained from their efforts. Monks routinely described their inner experiences to Ācariya Mun so that he could help them to further their understanding. At the same time, he would point out how they could perfect those aspects of their practice that still needed improvement. He did his best to answer every question that was put to him. Those question-and-answer sessions, when he gave advice to specific individuals, were engrossing expositions on the practical aspects of Dhamma. His responses to the monks who approached him about their meditative experiences were never predictable, being dictated by the specific nature of the experience or the question under discussion. He always answered in the manner best suited to the individual student, elucidating points of practice and recommending techniques appropriate for his specific level of practice. Those of us, who had the privilege of listening in, especially enjoyed hearing about the meditation experiences and questions posed by monks whose practice had reached an advanced stage. We were truly captivated then, wishing for those discussions never to end. We were keen to hear such exchanges very often and so imbibe this Dhamma to our heart's content.

Ācariya Mun addressed many different topics during the course of a meeting. He told us about his past lives. He recounted the initial stages of his own practice, including insights into various phenomena arising in his meditation. He elaborated on the methods he used in his struggle to extricate himself from the quagmire of *saṁsāra* to the point where he verged on transcending the world of conventional reality, and how that final transcendence actually occurred. Talk of his supreme attainment made those of us, who yearned for this transcendent Dhamma, eager to attain it ourselves. This prompted some of us to feel a bit dejected, wondering if we really had enough inherent potential to successfully reach that sphere of Dhamma that he had realized to perfection. Perhaps we would remain stuck in this quagmire forever, unable to escape from the deep pit of *saṁsāra*. How is it he can attain freedom, yet we still cannot arouse ourselves from sleep? When will we be able to realize the same transcendent freedom he has? This sort of thinking had the advantage of awakening a persistent determination in us to tolerate the difficulties and press ahead with our efforts. This in turn facilitated every aspect of the practice. We were so inspired and energized by the Dhamma he so kindly elucidated for us that all sense of weariness and fatigue vanished. Our faith in him gave us the necessary strength to willingly shoulder the heaviest burdens.

The Lord Buddha taught us to associate with the wise. The truth of this is obvious to students living in the presence of a good teacher, listening day in and day out to his uplifting instructions. Their enthusiasm gains momentum as his teaching gradually permeates deep into the fabric of their being, and his virtuous qualities eventually infuse their characters. Although they cannot hope to match him in every respect, at least they exemplify their teacher's virtues. The opposite also holds true: the more we associate with fools, the worse off we are. These two teachings of the Buddha are equally valid: we can become good through association with good people, or we can suffer harm through association with bad people. If we observe someone who has spent a long time training under a good teacher, it is evident that he has gained some steadfast principles from that relationship. Conversely, it's obvious that those who get mixed up with fools will eventually display the same foolish characteristics — or perhaps worse ones.

Here I am referring to the external fools we meet in society. But you should understand that there are still other, internal fools buried deep within the personalities of each and every one of us — even well-mannered people like monks and nuns who wear the sacred Buddhist robes, openly proclaiming themselves to be disciples of the Lord Buddha. By inner fool, I mean the craven stupidity and timidness that makes us shrink from facing up to the mind's baser instincts, which are just waiting to express themselves in ignoble, degrading ways. Many people are unaware of the repugnant forces buried within their minds. But even people who are aware of them tend to believe that as long as those things remain hidden inside and do not express themselves in speech or actions, then their repugnance is not really an issue. In truth, all bad things, regardless of where they exist, are intrinsically repugnant by nature. It's not necessary for bad instincts to express themselves externally to be considered repugnant. They are already frightfully repugnant in and of themselves and must be dealt with as such.

That wisest of sages, the Lord Buddha, taught us to renounce all bad things and root them out, completely eradicating them from our hearts. The Lord Buddha and his Arahant disciples were perfect examples of this: Both their hearts and their conduct were free from blemish. Wherever they lived they always remained unperturbed and sublimely contented. In my opinion, based on personal observation,

Ācariya Mun was another monk free from blemish. I say this with complete confidence, accepting full responsibility, for I am certain that it is true. Any skepticism should be directed at me, not Ācariya Mun — his escape from the snares of Māra is already well completed.

AFTER THE RAINS RETREAT, Ācariya Mun continued living at Ban Na Mon for many months. Just prior to the next retreat he moved back to Ban Khok, but not to the same forest monastery where he previously lived. He stayed in a new monastery, built and offered to him by Ācariya Kongma Chirapuñño. He found the location quite suitable, comfortably spending the rains retreat there in good health. As usual, he held regular meetings to instruct the monks.

In summary, Ācariya Mun stayed continuously in the area around Ban Huay Kaen, Ban Na Sinuan, Ban Khok, and Ban Na Mon in the Tong Khop district of Sakon Nakhon province for three successive years, including three rainy season retreats. As usual he taught the nonphysical beings who contacted him, though fewer *devas* came in Sakon Nakhon and their visits were far less frequent than those of *devas* in Chiang Mai. It was probably because the region was less remote, and thus less secluded. They tended to come only on religious festival days, such as Māgha Pūjā, Visākha Pūjā and the observance days at the beginning, the middle, and the end of the rains retreat. Other than that, relatively few *devas* came to visit him.

Only a small group of monks actually spent these rains retreats with him due to a limited number of available huts. He could not accept new arrivals unless there were vacancies. The situation was different outside of the retreat period. Then monks from many different places came to train under him. Following the retreat, a steady flow of monks came and went at his monastery, and he always very kindly made a special effort to instruct them in their practice.

In the dry season, following the third rains retreat, a group of lay people from the village of Ban Nong Pheu Na Nai went to see Ācariya Mun, and invited him to return with them to live near their village. He accepted their offer, and was escorted to their village in the Na Nai sub-district of Phanna Nikhom in Sakon Nakhon province, where he spent the next rains retreat. He traveled the distance from Ban Khok to Ban Nong Pheu hiking through thick forest, camping out along the way each night. Making his way through rough, wooded terrain the entire way, he finally arrived several days later.

Soon after his arrival, he came down with a severe case of malaria. The symptoms of this strain of malaria alternate between bouts of very high fever and shivering cold chills. It's a punishing affliction that lasts for months. Anyone falling victim to such severe malaria lives to dread it because the fever never quite seems to go away. It may last for years, the symptoms returning again and again after apparently having been cured. The fever can disappear for fifteen days, or maybe a month; and then, just when one thinks it's finally cured, it resurfaces. Sometimes several months may elapse before it returns.

I previously described how malarial fever caused in-laws to lose patience with each other. If the son-in-law came down with it, his wife's parents soon became fed up with him. If one of his wife's parents had it, the son-in-law soon got fed up. The patient became a burden on the rest of the family because — although he couldn't do any heavy work — he still ate a lot, slept constantly, and then complained bitterly no end. Malaria is a most tiresome illness which tries everyone's patience. Its effect was compounded by the fact that in those days there were no effective medicines for curing malaria as there are today. A person contracting it just had to wait for it to disappear on its own. If it refused to go away, it could easily become a chronic condition, dragging on for years. Young children who became infected usually had swollen, distended bellies and pale, anemic complexions. Natives of the low-lying plains, who had moved to settle in forested areas, tended to be the worst victims of this strain of malaria. Indigenous forest inhabitants were not immune, though their symptoms were seldom so severe as those of people who came from open, lowland areas.

Malaria was also common among *dhutanga* monks, as they normally liked to wander extensively through forested mountain areas. Were this dreaded disease something valuable, something to boast about, then I myself could boast with the best of them, having suffered its devastating effects many times. It scares me just thinking about it now. I was hit with a case of malaria my very first year at Ban Nong Pheu, an ordeal that severely chastened me. Fever plagued me the entire rainy season, then lingered on intermittently into the dry season, refusing to completely go away. How could I fail to be chastened? Being fully sensitive to pleasure and pain like everybody else, monks naturally dread the thought of pain and discomfort.

Once Ācariya Mun became settled at Ban Nong Pheu, the number of monks coming to stay with him on a regular basis steadily increased. As many as twenty to thirty monks came each year to spend the rains retreat with him. In addition to the monks who lived in the monastery, many others stayed close by in the vicinity of other small villages. A few monks lived together in some locations, five or six in others, and occasionally nine or ten in some places. Each of these groups stayed in separate places, all within walking distance of Ācariya Mun's monastery. As many as thirty to forty monks from the surrounding area used to assemble at his monastery on *uposatha* observance days. Combined with resident monks, the total assembly easily reached fifty or sixty. Outside the retreat period, it sometimes exceeded that number, as monks continuously arrived at Ban Nong Pheu seeking Ācariya Mun's guidance. During the day they dispersed into the thick forest surrounding the monastery grounds to do their practice in solitude. The forest in this region was many tens of miles wide, while its length was almost unlimited as it extended along a series of overlapping mountain ranges that seemed to stretch on forever.

In those days, virtually the whole region from the district of Phanna Nikhom south to the province of Kalasin was blanketed by forests. For this reason, Ācariya Mun's monastery at Ban Nong Pheu proved to be an excellent central location for *dhutanga* monks of the *kammaṭṭhāna* tradition who were obliged to attend regular recitations of the *Pāṭimokkha*[3] and receive Dhamma instructions from their teacher. Those wanting to come with questions about their meditation practice could easily do so. During the dry season, his disciples wandered off into the surrounding mountains, living and practicing in the many caves and under the overhanging rocks scattered throughout the rugged terrain. Numerous small settlements of thatched huts dotted the mountain ridges where five or six families eked out a living, growing crops. Many *dhutanga* monks relied on those communities for their daily alms food. But they could live conveniently anywhere in the region's thick forests since small village communities of ten to thirty houses were scattered throughout.

The village of Ban Nong Pheu was situated in a rather broad valley completely surrounded by mountains. The villagers made a living by farming the land they could clear. Beyond that, forested mountain ranges stretched in every direction, making it an ideal place for *dhutanga* monks who easily found the kinds of secluded sites they preferred.

Consequently, large numbers of *dhutanga* monks lived throughout the region, in the rainy and the dry seasons alike. Many went to see Ācariya Mun regularly, and then wandered off again to practice in the mountains, walking down from there to hear his instructions, then returning to continue their practice. Some traveled from other provincial districts, or even other regions, to train with him at Ban Nong Pheu, especially in the dry season when travel was more convenient.

Lay people also made the arduous journey to pay their respects to him and hear his advice. They traveled by foot from locations all around the region, some, quite far away. Everyone came by foot, except for the elderly and women who, unaccustomed to hiking, hired ox carts to take them to the monastery. The dirt track extending from the main district of Phanna Nikhom to Ban Nong Pheu was about twelve miles long, following a path that cut straight up through the mountains. Following a more circuitous route around the base of the mountains, the distance was about fifteen miles. Those unaccustomed to hiking would never make it if they took the direct route, since there were no villages along the way where they could find food and shelter. The more circuitous route had only a few villages, spread far apart; so it wasn't very convenient either. Monks traveling to see Ācariya Mun went on foot, there being no road to Ban Nong Pheu that was suitable for motorized traffic. What public transport there was in those days went along the main provincial highways, and then only infrequently. Latecomers usually missed their ride and wasted a whole day waiting for the next one.

DHUTANGA MONKS PREFERRED traveling by foot. They found riding in vehicles inconvenient, since they were usually crowded with people. A *dhutanga* monk considered hiking from place to place simply another aspect of his meditation practice. Once he determined which mountain range or forest he wanted to head for, he focused on his practice and started his journey as though he were walking in meditation and the forest trails were his track. He did not fret about where the next village might be or whether he would reach it before dark. He resolved to walk until dusk, then look for a place to rest for the night. The next morning he walked on until he reached the nearest village. There he collected alms food from the local inhabitants as he passed through. He was satisfied to eat whatever they offered. The quality of the food was usually poor, but that didn't worry him — if it was sufficient to keep him going from one day to the next, he was contented. Having eaten his meal, he continued on his journey peacefully until he reached his destination. There he searched until he found a site in the forest that best suited his personal requirements. He paid special attention to the availability of water — a vital requisite when living in the wilds.

Having set up camp in a suitable location, the *dhutanga* monk turned his attention to the task of intensifying his efforts internally, alternating walking and sitting meditation around the clock, day and night. Bolstered by mindfulness and aided by the contemplative faculties of wisdom, he concentrated on a Dhamma theme that suited his temperament, thus inducing his heart to drop into the peaceful calm of *samādhi*. Withdrawing from *samādhi*, he focused on developing wisdom by investigating whichever phenomena arose in his field of awareness. Subjects included impressions from the external environment that constantly impinged on his sense faculties, and aspects of his internal environment, such as the physical elements and the sense organs, which continually fluctuate as they remain constantly in motion. He meditated on *viparināmadhamma* : that all things perpetually come and go, subject to the instability of constant change. He could not afford to be apathetic toward anything that might entangle his heart. He used wisdom to thoroughly analyze his body and mind to clearly understand their true nature, gradually letting go of any attachment to them. Wisdom was the tool he used to excavate the entire root system of the *kilesas*, relentlessly destroying them trunk, roots, and all. His mind was fixed on a single purpose: investigating all arising phenomena. Everything that made contact with the mind was scrutinized in terms of the *ti-lakkhana*[4] to gain insight into its true nature, thus eliminating the *kilesas* associated with it. Any *dhutanga* monk who felt uncertain about his mode of practice returned to Ācariya Mun as quickly as possible to ask him for clarification. As soon as his doubts were cleared up, he left, returning to the seclusion of the mountains to press ahead with his spiritual development.

Many *dhutanga* monks relied on Ācariya Mun to give them guidance in meditation. There was not sufficient room in his monastery to accommodate them all. So, after receiving his instructions, they went to live in the surrounding hills and forests. Spreading out in different directions, either alone or in pairs, each monk looked for a secluded place to set up camp that was within walking distance of Ācariya Mun's

330

monastery. In that way they could return to see him with minimum inconvenience. Depending on individual preferences, some monks lived three or four miles away, others between five to eight miles, while a few might have lived as far as twelve to fifteen miles from him. Monks traveling a distance of twelve miles or more to consult Ācariya Mun remained overnight in his monastery before walking back to their respective locations.

The trails that connected forest and mountain hamlets then were very different from the provincial roads seen everywhere today. They were mere dirt tracks that those communities had used for ages to keep in touch with one another; and all the local people were familiar with the routes. Since the villagers seldom made long treks to visit one another, the trails were often overgrown and obscured by undergrowth. Anyone unfamiliar with this network of trails had to be very careful not to take a wrong fork and get lost in the densely forested terrain. One might well end up in an area where there were no settlements at all. The distance between some communities could be twelve to fifteen miles of uninterrupted jungle. Such lengthy trails required special caution, for any traveler who lost his way would almost surely end up spending the night in the wilderness without any food. Besides that, he might never safely find his way out unless he chanced upon a hunter who pointed him in the right direction or conducted him back to the main trail to his destination.

Harsh Training Methods

Dhutanga kammaṭṭhāna monks were motivated by their great enthusiasm for Dhamma. They regularly endured many hardships: in their wandering lifestyle, in their living conditions, and in their mode of practice. It was difficult for them to find an excellent teacher like Ācariya Mun, a teacher capable of training them in the authentic way, thus bringing joy to their practice. Whenever they met him, they were as excited as small children greeting their parents. The devotion and affection they felt combined to give them a feeling of complete confidence in him. Their lives and well-being were placed solely in his hands. *Dhutanga* monks naturally tended to have immense faith in their teacher, revering him so much that they would willingly give up their lives for him without regrets. Even when living apart from him, they continued to feel an extraordinary sense of obligation to their teacher. No matter how much hardship they endured, or how difficult their training was, they were contented to persevere so long as their teacher was supportive. They could manage to put up with the deprivations they suffered daily – going without, as often as not – because they were convinced in their hearts that Dhamma was more important than anything else. There were times when they had to sleep in the pouring rain through the night, shivering like little birds. Still, their determination to endure adversity for the sake of Dhamma never wavered.

It was always very interesting to hear *dhutanga* monks discuss their experiences of wandering through remote forest areas. The way they practiced, the way they endured – it was pitiable how, due to extreme deprivations, they lived in the forest like wild animals, often sleeping on the ground without shelter. They used a variety of techniques to intensify their meditation, experimenting until they found the ones that best suited their character. They tried: going without sleep; reducing the amount of food they ate; fasting entirely for as many days as they could reasonably manage; walking in meditation all night, from dusk until dawn; sitting in *samādhi* for many hours at a stretch; sitting in *samādhi* all night, from dusk to dawn; sitting in *samādhi* on a trail used by tigers when entering their lair; sitting in *samādhi* at night on forest trails frequented by tigers; sitting in *samādhi* in a cemetery on the day a corpse was being cremated; sitting in *samādhi* at the edge of a precipice; venturing deep into the mountains at night looking for a particularly scary place to sit in *samādhi*; sitting in *samādhi* late at night at the foot of a tree in a tiger-infested area, relying on the threat of danger to help the *citta* attain calm. These methods were all practiced with the same aim in mind – to torment the *citta*, and so forcibly tame its unruly nature.

When a monk discovered that any one or more of these techniques matched his individual temperament, he used it to good effect, focusing his mind and strengthening his resolve, thus achieving his objective and learning many valuable lessons in the process. For this reason, *dhutanga* monks actually preferred such harrowing practices. Ācariya Mun himself had used them and so liked to encourage his monks to do likewise, insisting that this was the way clever people trained themselves. These techniques have never been abandoned – they are still being practiced by *dhutanga* monks today.

The training we undertake to develop our spiritual worth requires a fair amount of coercion to be successful. The hardships we experience are insignificant when compared with the good results we gain: virtue, contentment, discipline, and firm Dhamma principles to supervise and maintain our lives — all qualities that people highly value. Only useless junk and cadavers require no maintenance. The personal worth we hope to realize will only arise through conscientious self-improvement, so we should work to maintain this purpose in our lives. By this means, we will be good, happy, prosperous people now and in the future. *Dhutanga* monks therefore deserve a lot of respect for refusing to allow adversity and hardship to hinder their practice, thus clearing the way for Dhamma to develop in their hearts.

So long as people are interested in practicing Dhamma properly, the Buddha's *sāsana* will last indefinitely in the world. The *sāsana* rewards those truly desiring Dhamma who practice accordingly, giving excellent results at every step along the path. This principle was embodied in the Lord Buddha, who was earnest in his pursuit of Truth — a Truth that he fully realized and then taught to the world. Those who truly believe in Buddhism are those who earnestly pursue Truth. They never practice in a halfhearted, inept manner, thus impeding the *sāsana's* progress and devaluing it to the extent that non-Buddhists find cause to be contemptuous. The genuine *sāsana* are the very Noble Truths that deserve to be proclaimed and accepted throughout the universe without concern about their validity, since they are true natural principles emanating directly from the Buddha's absolute purity — unless, of course, one is uninterested in Truth or unable to understand it. In that case, the *sāsana* may simply be held hostage within the countless diverse opinions of people whose hearts are totally obscured by a mass of deep-rooted *kilesas* — a veil of defilements that the *sāsana* has long since thoroughly penetrated.

Please excuse me for this lengthy digression — it shows I lack the firm principles needed to restrain my wayward tendencies. I would like to continue discussing those harsh training methods that *dhutanga* monks tended to use until they became second nature. Diligently practiced, each of these methods produces clear-cut results. They help diminish the unruly, arrogant nature of the mind, a condition exacerbated by excessive physical vitality. Reducing the intake of food, fasting, going without sleep, or other harsh methods, such as walking or sitting in meditation continuously for long periods of time — all of these practices provide the heart with the strength required to advance easily on the path of Dhamma. Other practices are designed for those who are scared of tigers or ghosts, which when practiced unflinchingly, force the heart to turn inward where its true sanctuary lies, remaining there until calm and courage arise. Fears can be alleviated, or even banished, by such means. The *citta* then comes to realize its own strength and ability so that when it is driven into a corner at a truly critical juncture — for example, when the body is racked by excruciating pain — it has the means to emerge victorious, and survive. Normally, mindfulness and wisdom are fully aroused only when the *citta* is placed in a critical situation. Otherwise, they never have a chance to realize their full potential.

An excellent way to develop the capacity of mindfulness and wisdom to act boldly in full knowledge of their true potential is to use our basic ingenuity, experimenting with various forceful techniques until we find those that best suit us. Our hearts then remain unperturbed, regardless of what happens. Each of these methods brings its own distinct results. Those who have long suffered from fear of ghosts can rid themselves of this debilitating fear by forcing themselves to spend the night in a cemetery. Those who are terrified of wild animals, like tigers, can overcome this fear by forcing themselves to spend the night alone in terrifying wilderness. Those who have persistent craving for food can alleviate it, or even overcome it, by drastically reducing the amount they eat, or by going on fast.

We all appreciate good food. We tend to believe that eating a lot of good, tasty food will make us happy. The trouble is: greed never accepts that it's had enough. It always hankers for more. No matter how much discontent it causes us, we fail to consider that the dissatisfaction stems from our tendency to overindulge. So, those of us practicing Dhamma for the sake of understanding ourselves and our attachments must investigate such desires and exercise some forceful restraints on their excesses. In the case of *dhutanga* monks, this sometimes takes the form of self-imposed austerities. When a monk notices that a certain type of food kindles an unseemly craving in his heart, he punishes the craving by refusing to eat that food. Instead, he eats things that he feels no desire for. If he feels that he'd like to eat a lot, he eats only a little instead. Or he may eat only plain rice, even though there are plenty of other foods to choose from. Those foods which invigorate the body may hamper his *citta* by overwhelming its mental faculties, thus making meditation more difficult. His practice then fails to progress as it should, despite the fact that he is striving with the same intensity as ever. Once he realizes the cause of the problem, he strives to eliminate it by adamantly refusing to follow the greed in his heart. This is the attitude of a monk truly committed to training himself under the guidance of a good teacher: he resists any temptation to follow his usual self-indulgent tendencies.

Just as a *dhutanga* monk trains himself to be moderate and restrained in what he eats, so too, when he goes to sleep, he determines to awaken at a predetermined time. He doesn't just let sleep take its course, waking him up randomly whenever it so desires. He trains himself to carefully consider the appropriateness of his actions. He resists doing anything that may violate the ethical principles of Dhamma and therefore be inappropriate, even though it may not strictly be in violation of the disciplinary rules. He strives to inculcate Dhamma within his heart so that it steadily flourishes, never deteriorating – an extremely difficult task. So difficult, in fact, that no other endeavor can compare with it.

When, however, we inculcate the ways of the world in our hearts, defilements easily arise and flourish, then wait there ready to cause harm whenever we're off guard. We can never manage to bring them under control. In an instant, they furtively infiltrate our hearts and multiply until we cannot keep track of them all. We can be sure they will cause us nothing but trouble. They arise and flourish so quickly that, within the blink of an eye, they are everywhere, and we are helpless to catch them. Sexual craving[5] is one such defilement – very easy to arise but so difficult to purge. Sexual craving creates a destructive, offensive state of mind that tends to express itself with unrivaled audacity. Because everyone in the world is so fond of it, it becomes emboldened, causing destruction everywhere while ignoring the moral consequences. It does show some fear of people with Dhamma in their hearts. But, more than anything else, it is terrified of the Lord Buddha and the Arahants. Since these Noble Ones have completely demolished its normal playground, sexual craving does not dare enter their hearts to prowl around. But it still creates plenty of trouble for the rest of us who remain under its power.

Dhutanga monks are aware that these oppressive *kilesas* are obstructing their spiritual progress. That's the reason they torture themselves with such arduous training practices. For *kilesas* are not in the least disconcerted by the fact that monks have ordained into the holy life and wear the yellow robes: the distinctive 'badge of victory' for those who defeat the forces of Māra. They invariably try to convince monks to give up the yellow robes and the spiritual quest they symbolize, refusing to admit defeat regardless of a monk's age or seniority. For this reason, *dhutanga* monks feel compelled to use coercive methods in their struggle to eradicate the *kilesas* from their hearts. They endure and press ahead in spite of the difficulties, battling pain and discomfort but never reversing course. Otherwise, the *kilesas* will make fun of them as they disgrace themselves and the yellow robes they wear. Even more damaging is the discredit they do to the monkhood — an order of spiritual warriors who never accept defeat — and the *sāsana* which is the principal basis for all mankind. Better they sacrifice their lives to redeem themselves and the yellow robes, than allow themselves to perish in disgrace. In that way, they redeem the monkhood and the religion as well.

Dhutanga monks use such exhortations to embolden themselves to strive for victory, thus honoring the Dhamma that some day will undoubtedly lead them to that sublime domain beyond *dukkha*. Only the Dhamma of the Lord Buddha is capable of showing the way to that sublime transcendence. It is without a doubt the one straight path leading to the land beyond suffering. There is not a more esoteric way that can be taken to avoid the difficulty of putting maximum effort into the practice. Alternative paths are all littered with stumbling blocks that constantly thwart the wayfarer's hopes of success. They inevitably cause pain and frustration, leading to despair and a lack of confidence that the chosen way will ever lead to a state of total freedom.

Before emerging as a revered teacher of such renown, Ācariya Mun practiced with the attitude that cemeteries were irrelevant to him. That is, he was prepared to discard his body wherever he happened to be when he breathed his last breath. He felt no qualms about dying for the sake of Dhamma. Later, when instructing his students, he taught them in a forceful, dynamic fashion that stressed the sharp, incisive tactics he had honed to perfection in his own practice. His teaching was mentally stimulating, helping his students constantly develop new skills to see through the cunning tricks of the *kilesas* and thus uproot and destroy them once and for all. Only then would they be safely out of danger, living contentedly without *dukkha*. They would no longer meander through the round of *saṁsāra*, where one birth changes into another continuously, but the *dukkha,* that is carried around in the heart, remains unchanged — regardless of how many times one is reborn. Since each new life is merely a new instrument for one's own destruction, no one should be satisfied with birth in any realm of existence. It is equivalent to a prisoner changing cells within the same prison: as long as he remains imprisoned, there is no fundamental improvement. The wise well understand the dangers of the cycle of repeated birth and death. It's as though with each new birth the heart has moved into yet another house that is on fire: no matter where it's reborn it can never escape the threat of danger. This is but a small taste of how Ācariya Mun routinely taught his *dhutanga* disciples. Perhaps some of my readers will discover an affinity for his style of teaching.

ON UPOSATHA OBSERVANCE days, when as many as forty to fifty additional monks attended from various locations, Ācariya Mun gave discourses on Dhamma that generally differed from those he gave exclusively to. the monks who regularly lived with him. Although his *uposatha* discourses were often forceful and profound, they could not match the ones given regularly to the monks living in his monastery. Those talks were truly dynamic, and penetrating. Each time he spoke, the impact of his Dhamma was so powerful it seemed to dispel the *kilesas* from the hearts of his listeners, as if the whole world had momentarily vanished from their awareness. What remained was an awareness of the heart united in perfect harmony with Dhamma, an experience so amazing and gratifying it defies description. For days thereafter the dynamic power of his Dhamma seemed to subdue their *kilesas,* as though he had issued them all a defiant challenge. Inevitably, their *kilesas* gradually reemerged after several days, until they were finally back in full force. By then, another meeting had been scheduled where Ācariya Mun subdued them once more, giving the monks a few more days of relief.

All *dhutanga* monks earnestly striving to reach the Dhamma that transcends *dukkha* feel an exceptionally strong bond with their teacher. Eradicating the *kilesas* requires that individual effort be inextricably combined with the help and advice of a good teacher. When confronted with an intractable problem, a monk practicing on his own will hurry back to consult his teacher who clarifies the nature of the problem, allowing the student to understand its underlying causes and so overcome his doubts. Sometimes while a monk is struggling with a problem which is too complex for him to resolve on his own, his teacher unexpectedly explains the solution of that very problem to him, immediately eliminating that obstacle so his student can proceed unhindered.

Practicing monks are able to determine the precise levels of Dhamma that their fellows, and even their teacher, have attained by listening to their discussions about meditation practice. This knowledge helps to foster an atmosphere of mutual trust within the circle of practice. When a monk explains the nature of his experiences and the stages he has passed through, from that description it is possible to immediately determine the level of Dhamma he has realized. When a student tells the teacher about his experiences in meditation, or when he asks advice about a specific problem, he can assess his teacher's level of attainment at that time by gauging his responses. If the teacher has passed beyond that point himself, he is already familiar with those experiences, and he is able to use them as a starting point to advise his student on how to proceed. Or, in the case of a specific problem, he is able to pinpoint the nature of the problem in such a precise way that the student accepts his advice without reservation. Perhaps a student deludes himself into thinking he has reached the highest level of Dhamma, having completely transcended the different stages. But, the teacher, through his own experience, knows this to be untrue. The teacher must then explain to his student why he is wrong, pointing out exactly where his thinking went astray. Once he is willing to accept the validity of his teacher's reasoning, he can safely avoid such dangers.

Once *dhutanga* monks have discussed the various aspects of meditation practice among themselves and reach the point where they know and accept the truth of their respective levels of attainment, there is then no need for further confirmation. The principles of truth that have been discussed constitute their own proof. Practicing monks use this knowledge to determine one another's level of Dhamma. From the teacher on down to the junior monks, they all rely on evidence gathered in this way. As for intuitive knowledge of these matters, it requires an inner faculty to which I can lay no claim. I shall leave this matter to those with the appropriate expertise. It is a special case requiring individual skill.

The regular conversations on meditation that Ācariya Mun held with his disciples enabled them to develop close personal relationships with him. Due to the profound respect this tutelage inspired, they willingly entrusted their lives to his care. This deep faith induced them to unreservedly accept as true whatever he told them, for he always spoke about principles of truth, never presenting mere opinions or guesswork based on information from other sources.

I myself have always been someone with strong views, being reluctant to submit to anyone's judgment. So I liked to argue with him. In this respect, I admit to being one of Ācariya Mun's more annoying and contentious disciples. Sometimes I was so caught up in disputing an issue with him that I forgot I was a student seeking his guidance — not a teacher instructing him. I still pride myself on my audacity to speak up, having no sense of misgiving. Although he then slapped me down and chopped me to pieces, the important thing was: I was able to learn for myself whether the truth lay in my opinions, or in the wisdom of my teacher. When I argued with him, it sounded like a shouting match. The more I pressed my case, the more I realized that he had all the truth on his side. I had only my inane fallacies, piled up all around me. I always fought a losing battle. When the dust settled, I thought long and hard about what he said, respectfully accepting its truth with all my heart. At the same time, I made a mental note of my misconceptions. On occasions when I refused to yield to his reasoning because I still couldn't understand what he was getting at, I would wait for another opportunity to debate with him. But I always came away bruised and battered by the power of his reasoning, my opinions tied in knots. Still, I could not resist smiling to myself, delighted by the mighty power of his Dhamma.

Although Ācariya Mun realized full well that I was wildly opinionated, he did not scold me or try to force me to change my attitude. Instead, he could not help but smile when looking at me. He may have been thinking how insufferable I was; or he may have felt sorry for this idiot who liked fighting with such diehard assurance. I must admit: I was never a very fine person. Even today, I still shamelessly argue with senior *ācariyas*. But it's paid off for me in the sense that I've learned many unusual lessons this way which form a valuable part of my education to this day. These monks never seem to mind my intrusions; in fact, they are often amused by them. It's not so often that a stubborn old monk drops by to stir things up. Ordinarily, no one dares come and argue with one of these *ācariyas*. So when the monks in his monastery hear what's going on, they become rather puzzled — and more than a little alarmed.

AFTER LEAVING CHIANG MAI, where he passed beyond the thick jungle of repeated birth and death, he invariably had a profound reason in mind when he decided to live in any one place for a long time, although he kept these reasons to himself. Nakhon Ratchasima was a case in point. Many monks and lay people there had long developed a true devotion to Dhamma; so, many of them came to study with him as accomplished meditators. Later, some followed him to Udon Thani and Sakon Nakhon where they continued to study with him until he died. The monks and laity from Nakhon Ratchasima who kept in contact with him were all well established in meditation practice. Some of those monks have since become famous *ācariyas* who possess a firm basis of Dhamma in their hearts, and are still teaching monks and laity today. Many lay devotees have continued to see steady progress in meditation. Today, they show the way of generosity and spiritual development to other devotees in the area in a truly commendable fashion.

He next settled at Udon Thani, where he spent the rains retreat. Chao Khun Dhammachedi, the abbot of Wat Bodhisomphon monastery, was an influential monk with a large following of monks and lay supporters. He praised Ācariya Mun's preeminence, encouraging them all to make his acquaintance, offer donations and, above all, hear his teaching. Since his ordination, Chao Khun Dhammachedi had been a devoted disciple, and Ācariya Mun reciprocated by showing unusual kindness and affection toward him — thus, his willingness to stay several years in Udon Thani.

Later after moving to Sakon Nakhon and living at Ban Na Mon, Ācariya Mun met an elderly, white-robed nun who ran a small convent in the village. She was a major reason why he remained there as long as he did: her meditation was exceptionally good. She had developed a firm basis in Dhamma, so Ācariya Mun gave her regular instructions on practice. He said it was rare to find someone so accomplished.

Ācariya Mun's lengthy residence at Ban Nong Pheu was prompted by both the significance of the location and the people living in the village. The place was centrally situated in a very broad valley, completely surrounded by mountains, making it an ideal environment for the *dhutanga* life. Living in the village was an elderly white-robed lay woman who was approaching eighty. Much like the elderly nun at Ban Na Mon, she was an accomplished meditator who always received special attention from Ācariya Mun. She consulted him often, walking with difficulty from her home to the monastery. Shuffling slowly along, supported by a cane, she had to stop for rest three or four times before she finally arrived at the monastery, exhausted and out of breath. We all truly felt sorry for her. Seeing her struggle so painfully, Ācariya Mun would feign disapproval: "Why come all the way out here? Don't you realize how exhausted you are? Even children know when they're tired. Here you are eighty, ninety years old, yet you still don't know when you're worn out. Why do you take all the trouble to come here?"

Her reply was always characteristically straightforward and fearless. He then inquired about her meditation and explained various aspects of Dhamma relating to it. Not only had this woman developed a solid foundation for her meditation, she also possessed *paracittavijjā*, the psychic ability to know the fundamental moral bias of a person's heart. On top of that, she had a knack for perceiving unusual external phenomena. Addressing Ācariya Mun, she recounted these extra-ordinary perceptions with a daring self-assurance that amused him, causing him to laugh about her indomitable spirit.

"Your *citta* has long since gone beyond", she boldly declared. "I've been aware of your *citta* for a long time – it's absolutely without parallel. Since your *citta* is already so supreme, why do you continue to meditate?"

Ācariya Mun laughed. "I will resolutely continue meditating until the day I die. A disciple of the Buddha never allows his resolve to weaken."

To this she said: "If you still had more to accomplish, I could understand that. But your heart is already filled by an exceedingly luminous radiance. How can you go further than that with meditation? I look at your *citta* and see its radiance encompassing the whole world. Your awareness extends everywhere – nothing can possibly obstruct its scope. But my own *citta* sadly lacks such supreme qualities, which is why I must come to ask your help. Please tell me: how should I practice to attain the same preeminence you have?"

Hearing her discussions with Ācariya Mun, one sensed that her meditation was truly exceptional. Upon encountering a problem, she inevitably started dragging herself slowly down the path to the monastery, with her cane keeping her company. Ācariya Mun was especially kind to her: he made a point of advising her every time she came. On such occasions, the monks would sneak up to listen quietly at one side of the meeting hall where their discussions were held, eager to hear her questions and his answers. Because her questions arose directly from her own experiences in meditation, these exchanges fascinated the monks. Some of her doubts concerned internal matters, focusing on intrinsic Noble Truths; other questions related to external affairs and focused on the *deva* and *brahma* realms. If Ācariya Mun accepted her understanding of these matters as being correct, he encouraged her to continue her investigations. But if he did not agree with the course she was pursuing, he advised her to forgo that approach, explaining how she should adjust her practice to set it right.

Her claims to knowing their minds intrigued the monks who, though eager to hear her insights, were also rather apprehensive about what they might reveal. But she always described an impressive vision: radiant auras of increasing brilliance, from the young novices on up to Ācariya Mun, resembling the night sky's array of stars and planets: some were bright, some less so. It was a majestic sight, for not even the junior monks or young novices had somber, gloomy states of mind. Each being admirable, every monk was worthy of respect in his own way as he strove to improve and refine himself spiritually. Sometimes she recounted her visits to the *brahmaloka*, describing how she saw large numbers of monks, but no lay people. This puzzled her, so she asked Ācariya Mun to explain — which he did.

"The *brahmaloka* is mostly inhabited by monks who have already attained the level of Anāgāmī, that's why. When a monk who has attained Anāgāmī dies, he is reborn in the *brahmaloka*. Very few lay people develop themselves to that level, so they rarely gain access to the *brahma* realms. Thus you saw only monks there, but no lay people. Another thing: if you're so curious, why didn't you ask one of the monks you saw? Neglecting to ask them while you were there, you now want to come and ask me."

She laughed. "I forgot to ask them. I didn't think about it until I'd come back down, so I decided to ask you. If I remember, next time I go up I'll ask those monks."

Ācariya Mun's explanations usually had a dual purpose: to expound the truth of the matter, and then to clear up her doubts. Later he discouraged her from sending out her awareness to perceive external phenomena, for it used up the valuable time she needed to spend investigating internal phenomena and the basic principles underlying them — investigations leading directly to the realization of *magga* and *phala*. Obediently, she practiced as he advised. He often praised this woman's meditation practice, telling his monks of her high achievements in Dhamma – a level of success that many of them could not emulate.

Her practice, no doubt, was a factor in his decision to live so long at Ban Nong Pheu – the longest residence of his monastic life. Also, it was a convenient central location serving all the practicing monks living and wandering in the surrounding area. Well within walking distance of his monastery were many secluded places, suitable for practice. Monks had a choice of staying in wooded lowlands, high mountains, or caves – all being environments conducive to the ascetic way of life.

Ācariya Mun lived at Ban Nong Pheu monastery for five years. Because of his advanced age – he was seventy-five years old with failing health when he began staying there – he remained within the confines of the monastery all year, unable to wander extensively as he had in the past. He was content to provide sanctuary to all his disciples earnestly seeking Dhamma. While he was living there, the *devas* seldom contacted him, tending to visit only on certain special occasions. So he concentrated his efforts on assisting the monks and laity more than he had at other places.

The Therapeutic Qualities of Dhamma

Ban Nong Pheu monastery was situated in a dense forest, rife with malaria. As the rainy season approached, Ācariya Mun advised monks, who came simply to visit him, to hurry and leave before wet weather arrived. In the dry season they could stay without risk. Monks who fell victim to malaria just had to put up with the debilitating symptoms. They had no access to anti-malarial medicines, such medicines being scarce everywhere back then. So, they had to rely on the 'therapeutic qualities of Dhamma' instead. This meant investigating painful feelings as they arose with an intense, incisive degree of mindfulness and wisdom. Otherwise, they had no effective means of alleviating the pain. If successful, they reduced the fever, thus effecting a cure much quicker than could normally be expected.

A courageous monk who succeeds through the power of mindfulness and wisdom to overcome the painful feelings caused by illness, creates thereby a solid base of support that will serve him well in times of good health as well as in times of sickness. Ultimately, at the time when death is imminent, he will not feel weak and disheartened, and thus not be overwhelmed. Having succeeded in establishing total mastery of the truth about *dukkha*, he boldly faces the natural process we call 'death'. Mindfulness and wisdom have taught him to recognize *dukkha's* intrinsic nature, so he never again worries about pain. He always maintains the firm basis of truth he achieved through his investigations. Later, when a critical situation does arise, the mindfulness and wisdom that he has trained to proficiency will come to his rescue. He can utilize their investigative skills to override the pain, allowing him to immediately reach safety. Thus trained, mindfulness and wisdom will not abandon their duty, leaving him simply to wallow in misery as he did before he came to realize the true nature of *dukkha*. On the contrary, they will immediately engage the enemy. His external manifestations of illness will resemble those of any other sick person: that is, he will appear just as weak and exhausted as anyone else. But internally, mindfulness and wisdom will manifest within his heart like soldiers preparing to do battle. Then no amount of pain will affect his state of mind. His only consideration will be the inner search for the true causal basis of the physical body, the painful feelings, the *citta*, and the mental phenomena arising in conjunction with it;[6] for, this is precisely where the full intensity of *dukkha* will converge at that moment. Since his ability to confront the pain and endure its effects is no longer a concern, his confidence is unshakable. His primary concern is whether mindfulness and wisdom will successfully realize the entire truth of these phenomena in time.

Once a monk has investigated a Truth of Dhamma, like the Truth of *Dukkha*, until its true nature is fully understood, the next time he wishes to repeat that accomplishment, he does not allow the difficulties of the investigation to block his way and needlessly weaken his resolve. He simply considers what he previously did to enable him to see the truth so clearly, then reproduces that same effort in the present moment. In that way, a clear realization of the truth always lies within the powers of his mindfulness, his wisdom, his conviction, and his persistent effort. The truth is: pain, body, and *citta* all exist separately, each one being true within its own sphere. They in no way conflict or interfere with one another. By the power of this realization, *samudaya* — the cause of *dukkha* — is conquered, and all apprehension about the pain, the condition of the illness, or the prospect of dying is vanquished with it. Such fears are really emotional concerns that demoralize the spirit and lead to a debilitating sense of frustration. Once this decisive breakthrough is achieved, the illness is likely to subside as a result. But even if the symptoms don't entirely abate, they will not intensify to the point where the *citta* is overwhelmed by an onslaught of painful feelings, thus producing a twofold illness: one of an ailing body, the other of an ailing mind.

In times of severe illness, *dhutanga* monks are sure to examine the resultant pain. It's considered an essential means of sharpening up mindfulness and wisdom, thus honing their skills until they are quick enough to keep pace with all mental activity — thoughts that are inevitably bound up with physical and mental pain. Any monk showing signs of anxiety or uneasiness when ill is considered a failure within the circle of practicing monks. Mentally, his *samādhi* and wisdom are insufficient to sustain him in a time of crisis. Lacking mindfulness, his practice is unbecoming and unreliable. This doesn't fit with a monk's obligation to stockpile mindfulness and wisdom as the weapons of choice for protecting himself in his battles with pain of all kinds. Those who have developed the qualities needed to remain mindfully self-controlled, never showing signs of agitation, are considered truly praiseworthy examples of the warrior spirit typical of practicing monks. In critical situations, they stand their ground — and fight. The benefits of this to their meditation are self-evident. Those good results are also noticed by their fellow monks, all of whom greatly admire a fighting mentality. The others have faith that, no matter how overwhelming the pain is, a *dhutanga* monk will never be defeated — even in death. That is, his mindfulness and wisdom will never accept defeat, for they are the investigative tools he uses to search for a safe, trouble-free way to go beyond when it finally becomes impossible to keep body and soul together.

Anyone practicing Dhamma, who arrives at the Truth proclaimed by the Lord Buddha, is absolutely certain of its universal validity. Confronted with the enemy, he will never accept defeat and withdraw his forces. He is obligated to fight to the death. If it so happens that his body cannot withstand the pressure — he will let it die. But he will never relinquish his *citta*, or the mindfulness and wisdom which maintain and protect it. He is committed to fighting on to victory. Failure is never an option. He displays the attributes of a warrior who expects to be victorious, and thus reach a sanctuary that is truly safe and secure. Practicing with unwavering faith in the principles of Truth, he is certain to personify the maxim: *dhammo have rakkhati dammacāriṁ* – Dhamma protects those who practice it faithfully. If, however, he practices in a hesitant, halfhearted fashion, the outcome will only contradict the Truth, never validate it. It cannot be otherwise, because Dhamma, the *svākkhātadhamma*, requires that results be directly correlated with their causes.

Despite all the rewards the world seems to offer, a *dhutanga* monk prefers to concentrate on the immediate, inner rewards offered by the *sāsana*. For example, the peaceful calm of *samādhi* and the intuitive wisdom needed to extract the *kilesas* piercing his heart; both reward him with a steadily increasing sense of contentment that is clearly evident, moment by moment. These immediate, tangible results are the ones a *dhutanga* monk strives to realize. In doing so, he cuts through burdensome problems and unresolved doubts. If he truly has the capability to transcend the world in this lifetime – be it today, tomorrow, next month, or next year – this feat will be accomplished by means of his unflagging diligence at each and every moment.

Ācariya Mun employed inspirational teaching methods to reinforce this fighting spirit, regardless of whether his students were sick or not. He insisted his monks always be warriors fighting to rescue themselves from danger. But it was in times of illness that he placed special emphasis on being uncompromising. He worried they might become dispirited in the face of this challenge. A sick monk showing signs of weakness or anxiety, lacking the mindful self-control expected of him, was bound to be severely rebuked. Ācariya Mun might actually forbid the monks in his monastery to care for a sick monk, believing that weakness, anxiety, and a whining mentality were not the right way to deal with illness. Sick people react in that way all the time and never see it as a problem. But a monk, whose status demands that he put up with difficult situations and investigate them carefully, should never react like that. It creates a bad example. For if a monk brings this kind of defeatist attitude into the circle of practice, it may spread like a contagious disease, easily infecting others.

Think of the mess that might cause: Monks moaning and groaning, tossing and turning like dying animals. You are practicing monks, so don't adopt animal-like behavior. If you begin thinking and acting like animals, the religion will soon develop animal characteristics, spreading confusion everywhere – definitely not the way of the Buddha.

We have all been sick at one time or another, so we are well aware of what someone else feels like when sick. It isn't necessary for you to make a public display of your discomfort. If mental anguish and vociferous complaints were effective cures, then conventional medicines would not be needed. Whoever fell ill could just whine about his plight in a loud voice to make the illness go way — easy as that. There would be no need to spend a lot of time and trouble treating the patient. Can whining really cure your present illness? If it can't, why disgust everyone else with your useless whining? This is a sample of the lecture Ācariya Mun might give a monk whose inability to face hardship was an annoyance to the whole monastic community.

On the other hand, when he visited a sick monk, who maintained a strong, mindful calmness, showing no signs of agitation about his condition, Ācariya Mun invariably demonstrated his approval. He commended the monk for his fortitude and gave him some very inspiring words of encouragement. Even after his recovery, Ācariya Mun continued to praise that monk's mental toughness, holding him up as an excellent example for the others.

"That's how a true warrior in the battle with pain gets the job done. Don't complain about the enemy's overwhelming numbers. Just dig in and fight them all to the limit of your strength and ability without flinching. Never withdraw your forces, never accept defeat. Never let the enemy stomp on you while you're down. We within the circle of practice must be warriors. It is no use complaining how extremely painful an illness is — just focus on the pain as it arises and try to understand its true nature. Regardless of how much, or how little pain we experience, all pain is a manifestation of the Truth of *Dukkha*."

Any monk who was weak and submissive when faced with a painful affliction heard a different tune from Ācariya Mun.

"If you want the Truth, but refuse to investigate it because you are afraid of pain, how will you ever discover where the Truth lies? The Lord Buddha succeeded in realizing the Truth by thoroughly investigating everything, not by whining about everything like this useless monk now disgracing himself. Where did the Buddha ever state that reaching a true understanding requires moaning and groaning? I didn't study many books, so perhaps I missed it. Where in the *suttas* does it refer to moaning and groaning? If any of you who are well-versed in the scriptures comes across a passage where it states that the Buddha extolled the merits of moaning and groaning, please point it out to me. Then I won't have to teach monks to trouble themselves about investigating pain and putting up with difficulties. You can all just moan and groan until the Truth arises to fill the whole universe. We can then witness the appearance of wise, sagacious individuals who have succeeded in reaching *magga* and *phala* by the power of their loud moans and groans. They will be in a position to question the legitimacy, and the current relevance, of the Dhamma that Lord Buddha proclaimed over 2,500 years ago.

"The Dhamma of these latter-day sages will be a new, modern Dhamma whose attainment requires no troublesome investigations. All that's required to attain *magga* and *phala* is a chorus of moaning and groaning, a method suited to an age when people prefer to seek righteous results from unrighteous causes – a pernicious attitude consuming the whole world today. Before long there won't be enough room on the planet to hold all these modern-day sages. I myself have an old-fashioned mentality. I trust what the Lord Buddha taught and dare not take any shortcuts. I am afraid that, as soon as I put a foot forward, I would fall flat on my face – and die there in disgrace. That would be immensely heartbreaking for me."

Any monk who showed weakness when in pain could expect such uncompromising treatment. The same kind of punishing rebuke was meted out to a monk who succumbed to weakness or discouragement while undertaking any harsh training practice, since they were obstacles preventing him from making use of the various investigative techniques at his disposal. Ācariya Mun constantly urged his monks to display the fighting spirit necessary to overcome these impediments, so they very often heard this dynamic teaching. For them, seekers of the true Dhamma, his words were a kind of therapy which roused their courage, invigorated their practice, and kept their spirits high. Thus buoyed, they were ready to advance triumphantly, step by step, up the path to that sphere of blissful contentment the Dhamma promises to reveal. Inspiring commitment, his stimulating instruction dispelled tendencies toward weakness and laziness that prepare the way for the misery of *saṁsāra*.

WHILE ĀCARIYA MUN lived there, two monks died in the monastery at Ban Nong Pheu, and another one died close by, at Ban Na Nai. The first to die was a middle-aged monk who ordained specifically to practice meditation. Living in Chiang Mai as Ācariya Mun's disciple, he eventually followed his teacher to Udon Thani, and then Sakon Nakhon — sometimes staying with him, sometimes practicing alone, until he finally passed away at Ban Nong Pheu. He was very skilled in *samādhi* meditation, and, prompted by Ācariya Mun's constant tutoring, his wisdom practice had already developed a sense of urgency. He was a very devout, resolute character who gave wonderfully lyrical talks on Dhamma, in spite of being wholly illiterate. His talks, quick-witted and clever, were invariably illustrated with skillful similes, allowing his listeners to easily grasp his meaning. Unfortunately, he had tuberculosis. Long a chronic illness, it eventually reached a critical stage while he was living in the monastery. There, early one morning at about seven o'clock, he passed away in a calm, peaceful manner, befitting one who had been a genuine practicing monk for so long. Witnessing his final moments, and then the moment when his breathing stopped, I developed a deep respect for this monk and his proficiency in meditation.

At death, it is we who control our destiny. So we must take sole responsibility for our future. For no one else, no matter how close or dear, can intervene to affect the outcome. Before that moment arrives, we must develop a means of focusing all our strength and skill on facing this critical juncture wisely, so as to extricate ourselves from danger and safely move on. Our final moments will present us with a significant challenge. All of us, whether we are well-prepared or not, will eventually be confronted with this situation. Those of us who have devised clever means for helping ourselves will fare well. But those of us, who remain ignorant and confused, will founder helplessly, unable to salvage our fate.

The Lord Buddha declared: *"Kho nu hāsa kim ānando..."*.[7] It can be translated essentially as: *When the world is engulfed in lust, anger, and delusion — a blazing bonfire that rages day and night — how can you keep smiling and laughing all the time? Why don't you immediately search for a refuge you can depend on? Stop this negligence now! Don't carry on with it until the day you die, or else you will experience the painful consequences into the future — indefinitely.* The Buddha was cautioning people not to be unreasonably heedless in their lives. But when people hear the Buddha's words today, they feel so embarrassed, so ashamed of their wanton infatuation with sensual pleasures that they want to hide their faces. Despite their shame, they are still lured by their desires – loving this, hating that – for this kind of intransigence has always been an integral part of worldly attitudes. And they don't know how to stop themselves. So, sadly, their only response to the Buddha's warnings is shame.

The death of the monk at Ban Nong Pheu should prove a valuable lesson to all of you who are headed toward the same fate. Please consider the manner of his death carefully. Just as he was about to pass away, Ācariya Mun and the other monks, who were on their way for alms, stopped by to witness that sad event. Afterwards, Ācariya Mun stood in silent contemplation for a moment; then he spoke to everyone in a solemn tone of voice:

"There's no need to worry about him. He has already been reborn in *Abhassara*, the sixth *brahma* realm. He's all right for now. But it's a shame in one way, for had he lived longer and developed his insight with a little more intensity, he could well have been reborn in one of the five *suddhāvāsa brahma* realms.[8] There he would have progressed directly to the ultimate goal, destined never again to enter the cycle of rebirth. And what about the rest of you – what kind of rebirth are you preparing for yourselves? Will it be one in the animal world, the ghost world, or in the realms of hell? Or will it be as a human, a *deva*, or a *brahma*? Or will it be Nibbāna? Which will it be? If you want to know for sure, look closely at the compass bearing of your heart to see the direction in which you are headed. Examine yourselves now to find out whether your present course is a good one, or a bad one. Once you are dead, it will be too late to make adjustments. Everyone knows that death is final – nothing more can be done after that."

The second death was that of a monk from Ubon Ratchathani who came down with malaria and died a month later. Shortly before it happened, his death was foreseen in the meditation of another monk who was living there at the time. The monk went to speak with Ācariya Mun the next evening. After discussing various aspects of meditation practice for awhile, their conversation turned to the sick monk, and the monk informed Ācariya Mun about the vision that appeared in his meditation.

"Something odd occurred in my meditation last night. I was investigating in my normal way when I reached a state of calm and suddenly saw an image of you standing before a pile of firewood, saying, 'Cremate that monk right here. This is the best place to do it.' I don't fully understand the meaning of it. Will that sick monk die of malaria? His condition certainly doesn't appear to be that serious."

Ācariya Mun responded immediately.

"I have been investigating this matter for a long time now. He is bound to die, it cannot be avoided. Still, he won't have died in vain. I have seen his mental state: it's exceptional. So, he's sure to fare very well. But I strictly forbid you to mention anything about this to him. If he finds out that he's certain to die, he will feel very disappointed. Then his health will deteriorate even further, and his mental state could waver to the extent that he misses the excellent rebirth he can expect now. Disappointment is a very harmful emotion in this respect."

Several days later, that monk's condition suddenly took a turn for the worse. He died calmly at about three a.m. This prompted me to consider how Ācariya Mun must have investigated the circumstances that lay behind every incident that appeared to him during meditation, pursuing them all until he clearly understood their significance. Then he simply let go, allowing them to follow their natural course.

One morning, a disciple of Ācariya Mun, who was running a very high fever due to malarial infection, decided to forgo almsround and fast for the day. He used his investigative skills to battle the intense pain from early morning until three in the afternoon, when the fever began to abate. Feeling completely exhausted in the middle of the day, he drew his attention to and concentrated solely on those points where the pain was most intense, but without making an effort to probe and analyze the pain with wisdom. At midday, Ācariya Mun momentarily sent out the flow of his *citta* to check how the monk was coping with the pain. Later in the afternoon, while visiting Ācariya Mun, he was surprised to hear Ācariya Mun immediately question his mode of practice.

"Why were you investigating like that? How can you expect to understand the truth about the body, the pain, and the *citta*, if you merely concentrate your mind on a single point? Instead, use your intuitive wisdom to analyze all three of them. In that way, you discover the true nature of each. Yours is the kind of concentration one expects from a yogi; it has all the single-minded intensity of a dogfight! It is not the right practice for a monk wanting to discover the truth about pain. Don't do it again. It's the wrong way to go about realizing the many truths to be found within the body, the pain, and the *citta*. During the middle of the day I examined your practice to see how you were coping with the pain caused by your fever. I noticed you were just focusing your attention exclusively on the pain. You were not using mindfulness and wisdom to ease the problem by looking at all three aspects of it: body, pain, and *citta*. This is the only effective way to quell pain, and neutralize the symptoms, so that the fever subsides as well."

Tigers Make the Best Teachers

When Ācariya Mun believed that a specific kind of advice would help one of his students, he spoke to him directly about it. He could be very blunt in his advice to certain monks.

"You'd be better off going to meditate in that cave than you are living here in the monastery. Characters like yours prefer tough, coercive measures. Better still, find a tiger to be your teacher — fear of it will subdue your *citta*, forcing it to enter into calm. Realizing Dhamma in this way, you can gain some contentment. Living here in the monastery is not right for you. Stubborn people need hard things to soften them up and make them more pliable. Since tigers are such good tormentors, anyone fearing them should take one as a teacher. It's much better than having a teacher you don't fear. If you are afraid of ghosts, you should take ghosts as teachers to enforce mental discipline. Take as a teacher whatever your heart most fears. This is how a clever person forces himself to submit to the training."

Before ordaining, the monk he was addressing had been a real tough guy with a bold, no-nonsense sort of character. If he said he was going to do something, he did it. He was a rather stubborn person, but stubborn in the way of a monk. As soon as he heard Ācariya Mun's resolute advice, he immediately decided to follow it, reasoning something like this to himself: *Surely a monk of Ācariya Mun's caliber would never send me to be killed by a tiger. I must go and live in the cave he mentioned. If that means death, I'll just have to accept it. If I want to see for myself the truth of what he said, then I must have no qualms about dying. I've heard that he always has very sound reasons for what he says; and he's careful to thoroughly examine every situation before speaking. Anyone who can understand his teaching and put it into practice is bound to get good results. I must take what he just said very seriously — it came from an insight into my character, and a genuine concern for my well-being. It is as though he plucked out my heart and examined it, and has found out all about me. How can I doubt his advice? If I fail to act on it now, how can I call myself a monk? I might as well be a lay person. I'm going to live in that cave — whatever happens. If I die there — so be it. If I don't, then all I ask is a chance to realize some amazing Dhamma while I'm there. It's obvious that he was talking about me when he referred to being stubborn and recalcitrant. It's a true measure of his genius: he knows me better than I know myself. I know I'm that type of person, one hundred percent. For my own good, I can't afford to disregard his advice about tigers. I must do what he said and subject myself to this agonizing practice.*

This monk truly was a stubborn character, reluctant to accept advice from anyone, just as Ācariya Mun indicated. After considering Ācariya Mun's remarks and reaching a definite decision, he went to take his leave. As he approached, Ācariya Mun immediately asked him where he was going.

"Where are you off to? You look all dressed up, and ready to march earnestly into battle."

"I'm going off to die in that cave you told me about."

"What! What did I say to you: go die in that cave, or go meditate there?"

"Well, you told me to meditate there, not die there. But I know from the other monks that there's a tiger living in the cave above the one I'll be staying in. They say that the tiger's cave is just close by — it comes and goes there all the time. When it goes out to hunt for food, it will pass right in front of my cave, so I have my doubts about remaining alive there. I was simply voicing my apprehension."

"Many other monks have already stayed in that cave, on many different occasions, and none of them were devoured by tigers. So, why should a tiger suddenly decide to come gobble you up? What's the difference between your flesh and the flesh of those other monks that makes it so much more likely to whet a tiger's appetite? Where did you get this savory flesh tigers like so much that they are waiting to pounce on and devour only you and no one else?"

Ācariya Mun then explained about the deceptive nature of the mind that deludes people in ways that are far too numerous to easily keep up with.

"If you don't examine everything and test it out with a critical, discerning attitude, you will be tormented by the mind's myriad tricks and never learn to tame its unruly nature. You have yet to leave, but already you trust the whisperings of the *kilesas* more than the advice of your teacher. How will you ever manage? Although people the world over have yet to die, they are all terrified of death. But birth, the enticement luring them into death, is feared by no one — everyone craves birth. I cannot figure out why people are so infatuated with birth. Just one birth in a physical body means immense suffering and anxiety. Suppose human beings could send up shoots like a clump of bamboo: their eagerness for birth would increase rampantly. Each person desiring to branch out into hundreds, or thousands, of additional people, without giving thought to how the combined fear of so many people dying at once might affect them. The whole world would become tumultuous with the fear of death and there would be no safe place to live.

"You are a practicing monk, a trained spiritual warrior. Yet your fear of death surpasses that of the untrained laity. Why do you let the *kilesas* harass you in this way? You have the mindfulness and wisdom needed to defend yourself, so why don't you use them? Go on the offensive. Chase out the devious *kilesas* lurking there in your heart. Then you will realize how stupid you've been, blindly serving their interests, unaware of the power they have over you. A warrior's victory depends on his willingness to brave death on the battlefield. If you're not willing to die, then you shouldn't enter the battle zone. Only by braving death will you be able to defeat your enemies. If you are truly determined to transcend *dukkha*, by realizing its true nature, you must view your fear of death as one form of *dukkha* — a product of the *kilesas* stored in your heart. You can only resolve this matter by making a stand on a battlefield conducive to victory, like the one I just indicated. Persevere, and you will come to realize fear's harmful effects: it stirs the emotions and demoralizes the spirit, always giving rise to suffering. It is better to take a defiant stand now. Don't simply keep clinging to that fear, hugging it tightly to your chest and burning your heart until you cry out in agony. Fail to act decisively now and your suffering will continue indefinitely.

"Will you believe in the supreme sanctity of your teacher and the Dhamma? Or are you going to trust that fear the *kilesas* have released into your heart which is depriving you of the very mindfulness and wisdom you need to defeat it? Looking around, you seem to see only tigers, all coming to tear out your flesh and make a meal of you.

Why is that? Please reflect deeply on the matter. I assure you that I have used the same combative training method to good effect in my own practice."

Such was his delight in the Dhamma he heard that the monk said he felt his *citta* glowing bright with courage as he listened to Ācariya Mun's strong rebuke. When Ācariya Mun finished speaking, the monk took his leave and immediately prepared to go to the cave.

He arrived at the cave still buoyed by a sense of courage and rapturous delight. He put down the belongings he carried with him and began to survey the surrounding area. Then, by some mischance, the thought arose in his mind that the cave was home to a tiger. With this thought in mind and his eyes scanning the ground in front of the cave, he spied a tiger's paw-print in the dirt. Never considering that it was probably made long before, the sight of it sent shock waves of fear through him, nearly scaring him out of his wits. In that instant, he completely forgot his teacher and the sense of courage that glowed so brightly while he sat listening to him in the monastery. Fear overwhelmed his heart and he was helpless to prevent it. He walked over and erased all traces of the paw-print with his foot, but the fear persisted. Still, he did feel a little better not having to look at it anymore.

From the moment he glanced down to discover the tiger's paw-print, he was terrified – a paralyzing fear lasting all night. Even during the day, his fear remained; but it became especially intense once night fell, as he imagined the whole area around his cave to be teeming with huge tigers. To make matters even worse, he had a sudden recurrence of malaria, with fever and chills. He felt as though he had fallen into a living hell devoid of any physical or mental comfort whatsoever. To his great credit, he was mentally tough enough to resist the temptation to give up his painful attempts at finding a means to overcome his fear. The worsening fever, combined with his agonizing fear of tigers, did unsettle his composure, however, nearly driving him crazy.

Once in a long while he thought of Ācariya Mun's kindness and the advice he had given, which temporarily helped to douse the fires of misery burning in his heart. As symptoms of the malaria became more and more intense, he reflected back on his earlier intention to sacrifice his life in that cave: *Previously, I made a decision to sacrifice my life here. When Ācariya Mun asked me where I was going, I immediately announced that I was going off to die in this cave. And as I hiked up here, I felt as though I was walking on air, such was my determination to brave death. So, why is it that upon reaching the cave and actually entering the jaws of death, I have now changed my mind and decided I don't want to die? Now, I'm so afraid of dying I can hardly hold my own. I'm exactly the same person I was then. I didn't exchange my heart for the heart of some coward. So why do I seem to be a new person with a cowardly attitude? In the monastery, I was prepared to die. Now that I'm actually here, I've changed my mind. Which is it going to be? Make up your mind right now — don't wait any longer. How about this? I'll go sit in meditation at the overhanging edge of a steep precipice. If my mindfulness falters, then let me fall to my death at the bottom of the ravine where the vultures and the flies can take care of my corpse. There would be no need to trouble the villagers about it. No one should have to dirty their hands handling the corpse of a useless monk — my futility might prove contagious. Then again, I could sit in meditation right in the middle of the path leading to the tiger's cave. I'll make it easy for that tiger when it goes out hunting for food. It can just sink its teeth into my useless neck and have me for a snack tonight. Which will it be? Make up your mind quickly — do it now!*

His resolve bolstered, he walked to the front of the cave and stood for a moment, awaiting inspiration. Weighing his two options, he finally decided to go with the first one: to meditate, seated precariously on the brink of the steep precipice near his cave. Any slip in mindfulness, and vultures and flies would be there to take care of his remains. That decided, he walked over and sat down, facing a deep gorge with his back to the path the tiger took to and from its cave. He began repeating "*buddho*", intensely aware that, if careless, he could die in an instant. Seated there meditating on *buddho*, he kept a vigilant watch on his mind to see which fear predominated: that of falling down the precipice, or that of being attacked by a tiger. As soon as it became apparent that fear of the precipice was the greatest, he gathered his mindfulness and focused intensively on one of his two meditation themes: either the repetition of *buddho* or the recollection of death — depending on which one arose in his mind at any one moment. Meditating thus, poised on the brink of death, his *citta* soon gathered itself into one point of focus, and then suddenly dropped down to the very base of *appanā samādhi*,[9] rapidly converging into a state of total calm. In an instant, he was oblivious to all the fiery turmoil that had engulfed his mind for so long. All that remained was the essential knowing nature of the *citta* — existing alone, by itself, in all its amazing splendor. Fear of death had utterly vanished.

The hour was ten p.m. when the monk's *citta* 'converged' dramatically into *appanā samādhi*, an experience so profound that he did not withdraw from that state until ten o'clock the next morning. Opening his eyes, he saw the sun halfway up the sky. Since it was already too late for morning almsround, he didn't bother to go to the village — he simply went without food that day. Withdrawing from *samādhi*, he was aware of a complete absence of fear. In its place was an amazing sense of courage he had never before experienced. His fever was gone as well — completely cured that night, and he never again suffered a recurrence of malaria. He was convinced that the 'therapeutic powers of Dhamma' had cured both his malaria and his fear of tigers. From that day on, his body was never again plagued by malaria, his mind never again ravaged by fear. No longer terrified of tigers, he could go anywhere, live anywhere — unperturbed

Occasionally, he wished a tiger would show up to test his mental fortitude. He imagined himself calmly walking right up to it without the least apprehension. Reflecting on the whole experience, he felt immensely gratefully to Ācariya Mun for so kindly teaching him about the corrupting power of fear. Now that he understood how his mind worked, he persistently used this coercive style of practice. Preparing to meditate, he preferred looking for the most frightening places he could find. For the remainder of his stay there he continued this training, making a special effort to seek out frightening locations for conducting his meditation. Noticing that tigers regularly used a certain path, he made a point of sitting right in the middle of it. While meditating in the cave, he resolved not to lower his mosquito net because sitting inside a lowered mosquito net gave more protection from the threat of tigers. Minus that element of fear his *citta* was reluctant to drop into the desired state of calm. Where he sat depended each time on where he felt his *citta* was most likely to rapidly 'converge' to the very base of *samādhi*.

Late one night as he sat out in the open, his *citta* refused to drop into calm despite his best efforts. He sat there frustrated for a long time until he finally thought about the huge tiger that came and went frequently in the area: *I wonder where that tiger is today. It would be nice if it came by here to help my citta drop into calm. If it passed by, I wouldn't have to struggle with my meditation like this — the citta would just instinctively drop into calm.*

Not long after thinking of his friend – perhaps after half an hour – he heard the footsteps of that huge animal walking towards its cave, as though right on cue. The time was approaching two a.m. Hearing the tiger draw nearer, he roused himself with a timely warning: *Here it comes, right now! Are you really so casual? Aren't you afraid it will sink its teeth into your neck and make a meal of you? If you don't want to be tiger food, then you better hurry up and look for a safe place to hide.*

As he thought this, he conjured in his mind an image of the tiger pouncing on him, its gaping jaws closing in around his neck. The moment he fixed his attention on this mental image, his *citta* 'converged', dropping rapidly until it reached the very base of *appanā samādhi*. Instantly all external phenomena completely vanished from his awareness – himself, the tiger, everything. What remained was serenity and tranquility – the union of *citta* and Dhamma as they melded into one essence of indescribable wonder. His *citta* rested in that sublime state for a total of eight hours – from two o'clock that night until ten o'clock the next morning. Upon withdrawing, he saw the sun was already high, so he again canceled his almsround and went without food. He then walked over to inspect the place where he heard the tiger approaching, to see if there were any signs that a tiger really had passed by. Or had his ears merely been playing tricks on him? Looking at the ground, he saw the tracks of a huge tiger, about twelve feet behind the spot where he had been sitting. The tiger's tracks continued in a straight line all the way up to its cave, never veering off to the direction where its friend was sitting in meditation. The whole incident was strange, and quite amazing.

The experience, in *appanā samādhi*, of the *citta* fully 'converging' into its true base, is an experience that varies according to the natural inclination of each individual. Some people are inclined by temperament to experience a very rapid convergence, feeling as though they are falling down a well. The internal sense faculties cease to function at that time, meaning they are totally unaware of all external sense impressions. This monk's *citta* was one such case: when it fully 'converged' in *samādhi*, all awareness of external phenomena ceased as a consequence. As the monk explained it, the moment his *citta* fully 'converged,' everything that was involved with it in any way vanished instantly. Only when he withdrew from that state did his normal awareness of things return. But, he found it difficult to attain this state unless he was under duress by some external threat. A real threat of danger forced his *citta* to 'converge' very rapidly — in a split second it reached its true base. He said this was the reason he liked to seek out frightening places.

"I find this the most convenient way to develop my meditation: practicing in places that arouse fear. I actually prefer wild mountains that have caves frequented by tigers, and tend to shy away from those that don't. As you can see: tiger-infested areas are perfectly suited to a rough character like me — that's what makes me so fond of them.

"I had other strange experiences while living in that cave. Besides realizing my goal to attain deep meditative calm, I also developed several unusual kinds of psychic awareness. For example, terrestrial *devas* came some nights to visit and converse with me. Even stranger still, when someone in the local village died I always knew about it immediately, though I'm not sure where this knowledge came from. It simply arose spontaneously in my heart. And it was invariably correct — never did I find reason to doubt it. My cave was located about five miles from the village, yet those people still insisted on coming to request my help in performing the funeral rites, which was very troublesome for me. As soon as someone died in the village I was aware of it, knowing straightaway that the next day I'd have to make another long trek to the village cemetery. And sure enough, the villagers came once again to bother me. Nothing I said could dissuade them. They told me that monks were scarce in that area, so they had no other choice but to disturb me. They believed that the deceased would benefit if a monk performed the funeral. I sympathized and felt sorry for them, so I had to go. During periods of fasting, which I found conducive to intensive meditation, I didn't want anything to interfere with my practice; but something usually did come up.

"While living in that cave I always relied on my friend the tiger to give my meditation practice a timely boost. Every other night it ventured down in search of food, as all hungry animals do. But it never showed any interest in me, even though it walked right past me on its way out. There was only one way down so it had to go that way."

This monk had the rather unusual habit of leaving his cave late at night to go sit in meditation on stone outcrops high up in the mountains. He appeared wholly unfazed by the danger from wild animals. By temperament, he preferred to wander alone through the wilds. I have included his story here because it teaches some valuable lessons. He practiced with unwavering purpose until he managed to expose the truth of his unruly mind, thus disciplining it and bringing it under his control. Things once viewed as threats, like tigers, became friends instead, assisting his practice. He managed to make use of a wild tiger — a most unpredictable creature — to inspire him in his mediation practice, thus achieving remarkable results.

ONCE ĀCARIYA MUN had settled in the monastery at Ban Nong Pheu, he was contented to encourage the community of *dhutanga* monks practicing under his tutelage. As many as twenty to thirty of them joined him there during retreat periods. Despite the increasing numbers, however, conflicts that might have caused him concern seldom arose. Each monk was determined to focus diligently on his own practice. An harmonious sense of fraternity existed among the monks who all lived together in unity of purpose. Peacefully walking together to the village for alms each morning — they were an impressive sight. A long bench had been constructed in the village where the monks sat to chant a blessing after receiving offerings of food. Later, back in the monastery, they ate together in silence, seated in rows according to seniority. Once they finished eating, each monk washed his own bowl, dried it thoroughly, replaced its cloth covering, and put it neatly away. When their morning duties were completed, they separated, each monk walking into the extensive forest surrounding the monastery to find a secluded meditation track where he concentrated on his meditation — walking or sitting, as he preferred. Remaining in the forest until the afternoon chores began at four p.m., they then returned from their meditation sites to help each other sweep the monastery grounds clean. Once they finished sweeping, they worked together to carry water from the well to fill the various water barrels — water for drinking, water for washing feet, or water for washing their alms bowls. A quick bath at the well was followed by a resumption of meditation. On nights when no meeting had been called, they continued to practice as usual until it was time to retire. Normally, Ācariya Mun called a general meeting once every seven days, though any monk desiring personal advice could see him on any day. Monks wanting to ask questions about their practice were advised to approach Ācariya Mun at a time during the day when he was free — usually just after the morning meal, in the early afternoon, at five in the afternoon, or at eight o'clock at night.

Hearing Ācariya Mun discuss Dhamma and answer questions in the quiet hours of the evening was a very pleasant experience. Then, many unusual questions were asked by disciples who came from various locations in the surrounding area to seek his advice. Some of these questions dealt with internal matters that arose in the course of a monk's meditation. Others dealt with external phenomena, such as *devas*. The monks who arrived to discuss their practice with him had varying skills and abilities in meditation. Some had unusual meditative experiences to relate. We listened eagerly, so mesmerized by his replies that none of us wanted the sessions to end. Each time we learned valuable lessons that led to practical methods for improving our meditation and thus gave us great satisfaction.

On timely occasions, Ācariya Mun recounted edifying stories about his past. He told us about his early years in lay life: how he ordained, first as a novice, then as a monk. Some of these stories were so funny they made us laugh; some made us pity him for what he had gone through; and some, the ones about his attainments, were just incredibly amazing. Living continuously with a good teacher for a long time had many distinct advantages. Following his example, his disciples gradually altered their basic attitudes and ways of behavior, adjusting their outer conduct and augmenting their inner skills little by little to match his, until eventually their characters naturally harmonized with his as much as possible. The secure environment he offered to his disciples meant that their practice was unlikely to go astray. Constant exposure to his inspirational teaching gradually allowed the essence of Dhamma to penetrate deep into their hearts. His intimidating presence promoted the kind of vigilant self-control that reinforces mindfulness and wisdom. Fear prevented his disciples from becoming complacent by forcing them to be extremely circumspect in their behavior and their thoughts. Even then, despite their best intentions, he could still catch them napping, and then expose their shortcomings for everyone else to hear. It was extremely embarrassing to have one's personal failings exposed like this; but a monk had to accept the consequences of failing to be properly circumspect.

We all experienced an indescribable sense of joy, living and practicing with Ācariya Mun. But if we held unreasonable opinions, our delight could easily turn to frustration, for those wrong views became a constant hindrance. I cannot speak for others, but I've always had a rather rough disposition, so I relied on Ācariya Mun to pound me into shape. In that way, I managed to find some breathing room when the *kilesas* began to suffocate me. Hearing him recount the various stages of his own practice, my spirit was so energized I felt I could float up and walk on the clouds. While listening to him, my whole being felt light as a wisp of cotton. But later, when I tried to duplicate this buoyancy on my own in meditation, I felt as though I was laboring under the weight of a mountain. I met nothing but heavy resistance. I became so frustrated with myself I wanted to bury my head in the ground to hide my shame — a fitting humiliation for such a vulgar character who was loath to accept advice.

I have mentioned my own coarse, callous nature here to let the reader know just how low the heart can sink when loaded down with destructive influences, and how hard it can be to pull it back up again and discipline it in the proper way. If we do not make a supreme effort now, eventually this tendency will plunge us into the depths of disaster, regardless of who we are or where we live. Effort must be used to discipline the heart. Any person who succeeds in subduing the unruly nature that has burdened his heart from time immemorial and who is thus living in total freedom — that person deserves the highest respect. The Lord Buddha and his Arahant disciples are shining examples of this achievement.

Likewise, I am absolutely convinced that Ācariya Mun was one of the Lord Buddha's present-day Arahant disciples. He was courageous and masterful in the way he lived his life, and was never in danger of succumbing to the power of the *kilesas*. Even in old age, when he could be expected to rest and take it easy, no longer needing to exert himself in meditation practice, he still did as much walking meditation as he always had — so much so that the younger monks could hardly keep up with him. Fulfilling his teaching obligations with great compassion, he never lost hope in his students. His exhortations reflected his resolute character, and he invariably preferred the rhetoric of a warrior. He delivered his talks forcefully, aiming to arouse in his disciples the strength and courage needed to completely transcend *dukkha*. He rarely compromised or made allowances for their shortcomings. He did not want to lull to sleep those very monks who already had a deplorable tendency to show weakness in their practice.

Ācariya Mun had utmost respect for all aspects of the Buddhasāsana, from the theory and practice of Dhamma to its inner realization. And this in an age when genuine disciples of the Buddha are hard to find.

He placed special emphasis on the thirteen *dhutanga* observances, which Buddhists everywhere had long since lost interest in. No one thought to restore them to the prominent position they deserve. The fact that they have now become such a significant part of a *dhutanga* monk's practice is a direct consequence of the earnest efforts that Ācariya Sao and Ācariya Mun made to revive their use in Thailand's Northeast region. Both Ācariya Sao and Ācariya Mun observed all thirteen of these ascetic practices at one time or another in their lives, although only the ones I've mentioned earlier were practiced on a daily basis. Other *dhutanga* observances, like staying in a cemetery or living out in the open at the foot of a tree, were practiced so often that these two *ācariyas* became thoroughly familiar with them. *Dhutanga* monks in the Northeast today are descendants following directly in their footsteps.

Ācariya Sao and Ācariya Mun were keenly aware of the practical value the *dhutanga* observances had for practicing monks. They clearly understood that each of these thirteen practices was an extremely effective means of closing off the outlets through which *kilesas* of *dhutanga* monks tend to flow. Without the restraining influence of ascetic practices to stem the flow from those outlets, *dhutanga* monks are 'ascetic' in name only, their *kilesas* being free to roam at will, causing considerable annoyance to everyone. With the help of the *dhutangas*, monks can rest assured that their conduct will not be offensive to others. Each *dhutanga* practice promotes a virtuous quality, while its observance reminds a *dhutanga* monk not to be careless by thinking in ways that contradict the very virtue he is trying to develop. On guard, he immediately becomes conscious of any lapses in judgment, which in turn fosters mindfulness to catch such oversights in the future. Considered in its entirety, *dhutanga* asceticism is broad in scope, each separate practice having a very distinct purpose. Provided a monk understands the true purpose of each *dhutanga* he undertakes and then observes them properly, they are easily capable of totally eliminating his *kilesas*. They are powerful enough to deal a decisive blow to every type of *kilesa* — no *kilesa* is beyond their reach.

As long as we dread the hardships involved in observing ascetic practices, then the *kilesas* have little fear of us. The hardships that the *kilesas* cause us, when there are no ascetic practices to suppress them, are somehow forgotten, opening the way for us to accuse these practices of being too difficult — or even obsolete. When our own thoughts become our enemies, the *kilesas* are secretly held in high regard; but in our rush to admire them we fail to realize this. The harmful effects of this supportive admiration are plain, and plainly infinite in scope.

The monk who truly practices any one or more of the *dhutangas* inevitably presents a pleasing, dignified appearance. His basic needs are easily taken care of. What he eats and where he sleeps are never a problem for him. He is always contented with the simple belongings he possesses. Unencumbered by emotional attachments and material possessions, he feels mentally and physically buoyant. Even lay people can benefit from undertaking some of the *dhutanga* practices, just as the monks do, since both monks and lay people are burdened with the same kinds of *kilesas*. The *dhutanga* practices are, after all, designed to counteract the *kilesas*, so people from all walks of life should try their best to make use of them for this purpose. The *dhutangas* comprise qualities of Dhamma so supremely profound that it is difficult to fully comprehend their true magnitude.

I myself do not have as comprehensive a knowledge and understanding of the *dhutanga* practices as I should, but in my own unsophisticated way I have tried my best to do justice to them. I hope you will forgive my shortcomings in this regard. In truth, the *dhutangas* are so profoundly subtle it would be virtually impossible to fully elaborate on all their outstanding qualities. They have the capacity to take someone, who is truly devoted to their practice, from the basic levels of Dhamma all the way to the highest *ariya* levels. In fact, no Dhamma attainment is beyond the scope of the *dhutangas*. As a teacher, Ācariya Mun always led his disciples in observing these ascetic practices, right until the last days of his life. Only when his strength was completely exhausted did he let go of them, along with his physical body. Clearly the *dhutangas* are essential practices for those intending to purify their hearts of all vestiges of the *kilesas* – this truth is undeniable.

I shall refrain from giving a detailed explanation here of each ascetic observance with its distinctive merits and importance. Anyone interested in looking into them can uncover these attributes for themselves. You may discover a degree of subtlety that proves to be more beneficial to you than simply reading someone else's explanation. I have been looking into these practices since my early days as a *dhutanga* monk and I continue to gain good results from them to this day. I have always considered them an essential part of my overall practice. Anyone intent on seeing an end to the *kilesas*, from the most vulgar ones to the most refined, should never overlook the *dhutanga* observances, thinking them incapable of doing the job.

His Final Illness

Ācariya Mun had already lived for five years at Ban Nong Pheu monastery when, in March of 1949 — precisely on the fourteenth day of the fourth lunar month — his body began exhibiting signs indicating the approaching end of his life. By then, he was 79 years old. On that day there appeared the first symptoms of an illness that was to worsen until it finally brought to a close his long life[10] — a day that sent tremors through Ācariya Mun's body elements and shock waves through the community of his close disciples. Initially there was a light fever, accompanied by a slight cough. But as the days passed, the symptoms steadily worsened, never showing the slightest improvement. Obviously abnormal, the constant decline in his health worried us all. But Ācariya Mun himself clearly knew that this was to be his final illness — an illness no type of medical treatment could cure. He informed his disciples of this from the very beginning and from then on never showed any interest in medicines. On the contrary, he seemed annoyed when someone brought him medicines to take. This he expressed in no uncertain terms:

"This is the illness of an old man who has reached the end of the line. No matter what kind of medicine I take, it will never be cured. All that's left is the breath in my body, biding its time, awaiting the day it finally ceases. I'm like a dead tree that's still standing: no matter how much you fertilize and water that tree, it is impossible to make it sprout and flower again. This old dead tree now stands anticipating the day it will topple over and go crashing to the ground, felled by this very same illness. I thoroughly investigated my condition long before the symptoms appeared. That is why I've been warning you all: Don't be complacent. Hurry up, intensify your efforts now while I am still alive. In that way, I can help you resolve any problems you may have in the meantime. Missing this opportunity now may cause you to waste a lot of time in the future. I will not be here much longer. Soon I shall depart this world, in keeping with the law of impermanence that follows constantly on the heels of all conditioned things without exception.

Three years ago I warned you that I would not last more than three years. What more can I say? What I've told you, I know to be inevitable. The work that the round of *saṁsāra* performs inside the minds and bodies of human beings and animals alike continues unerringly along its natural course. In just a few months time it will complete its final task within this body of mine. How can it possibly alter its appointed task?"

With each passing day his symptoms gradually worsened. Showing no interest in medicines of any kind, he was clearly annoyed when people came and urged him to try this remedy or that cure. But so many people arrived offering 'cures' that he had a hard time resisting them all. Each one touted the effectiveness of the medicine he was offering, insisting that if he took it he was sure to get better, for it had already cured many others. They all pleaded with him to try their medicines out of compassion for them. They wanted him to get better so he could continue to be of service to his many followers for a long time to come. He often warned them that medicines were useless for his illness; that only firewood for cremating the corpse was appropriate. But the more he protested, the more they beseeched him. So occasionally he yielded to their appeals and took a small dose of medicine. He was concerned that people would feel disappointed if they believed he had given up on his condition.

As news of his illness spread across the region, people began arriving from all directions to visit him at Ban Nong Pheu. Traveling from locations far and near in all kinds of weather, a steady flow of monks and laity poured in like the waters from a monsoon rain. Ban Nong Pheu was situated in a valley surrounded by thick forest some twelve to fifteen miles from the main highway between Udon Thani and Sakon Nakhon. Though people had to travel by foot to see him, they appeared undaunted by the distance and the difficulties it posed. Only the elderly, unable to make the journey on foot, hired ox carts to take them there.

By nature, Ācariya Mun always preferred to live alone quietly. Even the monks living with him were discouraged from bothering him unless absolutely necessary. Consequently, receiving large numbers of well-wishers disagreed with his natural inclination to remain aloof from such tiresome affairs. When sick, he had always been reluctant to allow even his close disciples to take care of him, though he did make certain exceptions. When he did allow it, the monks attending to his personal needs had to be very circumspect in his presence. Only monks deemed trustworthy were selected for these duties. As his health deteriorated, a discerning senior monk was appointed to oversee all arrangements for his health care. Since by nature Ācariya Mun was very thorough and meticulous, this monk had to decide what action was appropriate in each instance and then see that the other monks carefully followed this regimen. For this reason, monks attending on him were carefully chosen to ensure their behavior did not conflict with his subtle temperament.

The lay people and the monks, arriving from various locations around the region with hopes of seeing him to pay their respects, were first asked to wait until an appropriate time could be arranged. When the monk handling these matters felt the time was right, he entered Ācariya Mun's hut to inform him about the visitors. Once permission was granted, the visitors were taken to see him. After Ācariya Mun had spoken to them for awhile, they respectfully took their leave and departed. The monks at Ban Nong Pheu monastery had always arranged visits in this manner for those who came to see him. Visitors were invariably asked to wait until permission was granted; and then, they were escorted to his hut in groups at the time which he had agreed to receive them. The exceptions to this rule were senior disciples, who enjoyed a special, close relationship with him, being *ācariyas* in their own right. Once Ācariya Mun was informed of their arrival and had given his consent, the *ācariyas* went straight in to converse with him in private.

As the months passed, his condition continued to deteriorate. Although the symptoms never became very severe, he always felt unwell. His illness resembled an armed insurgency gradually escalating into a full scale war, consuming everything in its path, and leaving its victim decimated. His disciples were deeply affected. He occupied a special place at the center of their hearts, so his failing health left them all distraught. Feeling sad, even dejected, they were not so cheerful as before. Every conversation began with the topic of Ācariya Mun's illness and moved on to something else, only to return to his health again as the conversation ended.

Despite failing health, Ācariya Mun did not neglect his teaching obligations. His compassionate concern for his disciples never diminished, though he was no longer able to expound the Dhamma in such detail as before. Having finished his talk, he briefly answered questions and then promptly adjourned the meeting to return to his hut for a rest.

Incredibly though, while sitting there expounding Dhamma to the assembled monks, he showed no signs of his illness. He spoke with characteristic resoluteness in a sharp, lively fashion, his voice booming loudly as if he never had been sick. When he wanted to emphasize a point, the tempo of his voice quickened dramatically to drive the point home. He held nothing back as he spoke. His whole demeanor belied his true condition. Only after he finished speaking did we all realize how exhausted he was. So we quickly adjourned to allow him a chance to rest.

ONE EVENING SHORTLY before his illness began, on the occasion of Māgha Pūjā, the full moon day of February 1949, Ācariya Mun began expounding Dhamma to the assembled monks at eight p.m. and did not finish until midnight, speaking for a total of four hours. The power of the Dhamma he delivered that night truly amazed the whole assembly of *dhutanga* monks who were gathered for that occasion. To those listening, the entire universe appeared to have vanished without a trace, replaced in their awareness by the flow of his all-encompassing Dhamma, radiating forth in every direction. He began by paying tribute to the 1,250 Arahants who had come together spontaneously on this full moon day in the time of the Buddha.

"On this day 1,250 Arahants assembled spontaneously at the Lord Buddha's residence without prior arrangement. They were all individuals of the utmost purity, completely free of *kilesas*. The Lord Buddha himself delivered the *Pāṭimokkha* exhortation[11] that day, making the occasion a *visuddhi uposatha*; that is, an *uposatha* observed among monks who are all absolutely pure. Compare that assembly with the one gathered here today. You listen to the *Pāṭimokkha* being recited among monks who are all absolutely tainted – not one of you is completely free of *kilesas*. It is dismaying to think that, having ordained as a monk, each of you is a son of the same Buddha as those Arahant disciples.[12] Yet, in your case it is just an empty claim lacking any real substance; like a person having the name 'Goodman' who, on the contrary, is so weighed down under his own evil doings he can hardly move. In the Buddha's day, monks practiced the Dhamma truly and so became true monks with a true understanding that concealed nothing false. Today, the fame and celebrity of some monks is so great that they rival the sun and the moon, yet their actions sink to the depths of *avīci*. Where will they ever find virtue, truth, and purity? They merely accumulate a mass of *kilesas* and create the evil *kamma* that goes with them. Since monks today are not engaged in uprooting the *kilesas* from their hearts, how can *visuddhi uposatha* possibly arise? Once ordained, they are satisfied with their exalted status as Buddhist monks, taking for granted that this makes them models of virtue. But they have no idea what the true virtues of a Buddhist monk really are. If they understood the meaning of the *Pāṭimokkha* exhortation that the Lord Buddha delivered, they would know the true nature of virtue. He condensed the essential meaning of virtue into this concise statement: Refrain from all evil, develop goodness and wisdom in abundance, and purify the mind until it is bright and clear. This is the essence of the Buddha's teaching.

"Refraining from evil, what does it mean? Some people refrain from acting in evil ways but still speak in evil ways. Others may not act or speak in evil ways but still like to think in evil ways. They continue to amass evil within themselves from dawn to dusk. Waking up the next morning, they resume — amassing more evil. So it continues, day in and day out, and they are not interested in reflecting upon their actions. Convinced they are already virtuous people, they wait around expecting a state of purity to arise from virtue that exists in name only. So they never find a state of purity; instead, they find only defilement and disquiet. This is bound to happen, for anyone intent on looking for trouble is sure to find it. What else would they find? There is no shortage of such things in the conventional world we live in."

This was Ācariya Mun's way of explaining the underlying, natural principles of virtue to practicing monks in the hope that they would gain a profound insight into the Truth. He then went on to explain the way of practice that begins with *samādhi* and wisdom and ends with the ultimate attainment — absolute freedom. Discussing all areas of practice fully and openly, his exposition that day held nothing back. But, since much of what he said has already been covered in previous talks, I shall not elaborate any further here. The assembly of monks sat perfectly still the entire time he spoke, no one making the slightest sound to interrupt the cadence of his voice as he delivered this eloquent discourse.

As he finished speaking, he made a similar remark to the one he previously made at Wat Chedi Luang monastery in Chiang Mai. He said, in effect, that this talk would be the "final encore" of his old age – never would he give another such talk. His words that night were prophetic, because from that day on he never gave another profound and lengthy exposition of Dhamma. One month later his illness began, and his health steadily declined until he finally passed away.

Despite the physical difficulties he suffered as a result of that degenerative disease, he insisted on making the effort to walk to the village for almsround and continued eating only one meal a day from his alms bowl, as he always had. He did not simply abandon these practices. Eventually, when he felt that he could no longer walk the entire distance, he made an effort to walk at least halfway through the village before returning to the monastery. Seeing that so much walking caused him great difficulty, lay supporters and senior monks conferred and decided to invite him to walk only as far as the monastery gate, where offerings of food would be placed in his bowl. Had they requested him to abstain altogether from going on almsround, he would surely have demurred – so long as he was still physically able, he felt obliged to continue. So everyone had to respect his wishes. They wanted to avoid doing anything that might conflict with his resolute temperament. He continued walking to the front gate for alms until he became too weak to make it there and back. At that point, he began walking only as far as the refectory to collect alms. Only when he could no longer walk at all did he stop going for alms. Even then, he continued to eat just one meal a day, which he took in his alms bowl. The rest of us had to respect his wishes each time. We were all amazed at the endurance of this noble sage who, refusing to forsake his fighting spirit, conceded nothing to the *kilesas*.

As for the rest of us, we would probably be so dispirited at the very first sign of sickness that someone would have to carry us to the refectory to eat. It is truly disgraceful: the *kilesas* always laughing at us as we lie hopelessly on their chopping block, waiting for them to shred us to pieces like so much raw meat. What a pathetic sight! Here we are full-fledged human beings willingly putting ourselves at the mercy of the *kilesas*. All of us who carry this shame on our conscience should stop and reflect on Ācariya Mun's mode of practice. We can then adopt it to safeguard us in our struggle with these defilements. In that way, we will always remain faithful to our Buddhist principles — instead of just being the *kilesas'* whipping boys.

Eventually, Ãcariya Mun's condition became so serious that the rest of us felt obliged to undertake certain precautions. We quietly arranged for groups of three or four monks to keep a vigil every night sitting beneath his hut. We arranged this ourselves without informing him, though he may have been intuitively aware of it. We were concerned he might forbid us to do it, reasoning that it was a burden on the monks and thus an unnecessary nuisance. Every night small groups of monks took turns, sitting silently beneath his hut in continuous shifts that lasted until dawn. Each group stayed for several hours until it was replaced by the next. This routine was already well established by the beginning of the rainy season retreat that year. When it became obvious that his illness had become very debilitating, we conferred among ourselves and decided to request his permission for two monks to be allowed to sit in meditation on his verandah. With his consent, two monks were always seated on his verandah from then on, and two more were seated down below. Besides the regular shifts of monks who kept watch on him, others were quietly overseeing the whole arrangement throughout the night.

The end of the rains retreat saw an increasing number of senior disciples begin arriving from their own retreat locations to pay him their respects and help look after his needs. By that time his condition was critical, and becoming more and more unstable by the day. Eventually, he called all his disciples together one day to remind them of the proper way to handle his impending death.

"My illness has now reached its final stage. It is time to think about what will happen when I die — preparations must be made in time. As I've told you many times, I am going to die — this much is certain. My death is destined to be a major event affecting not only the general public, but animals as well. I want you to know that I do not wish to die here at Ban Nong Pheu. If I die here, it will be necessary to slaughter large numbers of farm animals in order to feed all the people coming to my funeral. I am only one dying person, but the death of this one person will in turn cause the deaths of a great many animals. Crowds of people will travel here to attend my funeral, but there's no market in this village where foodstuffs can be purchased. Since ordaining as a monk I have never for a moment considered doing harm to any animal, to say nothing of killing them. Compassion has always been the foundation of my conscious existence. I am continuously extending the spirit of loving kindness and dedicating the fruits of my merit to all living beings without exception. I do not want to see any animal lose the life it cherishes so dearly. I could never countenance having my own death become a source of enmity between myself and the world's animals.

"I want you to take me to Sakon Nakhon so I can die there. That town has a large marketplace, so my death should not affect the lives of so many animals. I have yet to die, but monks and lay people are already arriving here in a steady stream, their numbers increasing each day – clear evidence of the scale of the problem. Now think of how many people will come when I finally do die. Many people will mourn my death, but that is not my concern. I am ready for death – whenever and wherever it happens. I have no regrets about parting with my body. Having already investigated it thoroughly, I know that it is merely a combination of elements that have joined together temporarily, only to break apart again and revert back to their original elemental nature. What is there to be attached to? What I am concerned about is safeguarding the local farm animals so they won't have to perish as well. I don't want to see animal carcasses laid out for sale all up and down the roadsides here. That would be extremely regrettable. Fortunately, it's not too late to remedy the situation. I am asking that you arrange for my departure as soon as possible for the sake of all those animals that would otherwise die as a result of my death. It is my express wish that their lives be protected. Does anyone have anything to say? If so, speak up now."

Not a single person in the group spoke up. A atmosphere of quiet despair pervaded the assembly. As the Buddha said: *yampiccaṁ na labhati tampi dukkhaṁ*: not getting what one wants is truly a form of *dukkha*. Everyone realized that whether he went to Sakon Nakhon or remained at Ban Nong Pheu, in either case the situation was hopeless – he was going to die. So the meeting remained silent. There was just no way to resolve this dilemma. In the end, everyone willingly agreed to his request.

Prior to the meeting, the residents of Ban Nong Pheu village had made it known that they would feel honored to have him die there. "We will manage all the funeral arrangements ourselves. We may be quite poor here but our hearts are rich in faith and respect for Ācariya Mun. We will do everything we possibly can to arrange the funeral here.

We won't let anyone look down on us saying that the villagers of Ban Nong Pheu couldn't cremate the body of even one *ācariya* — instead, it had to be done elsewhere. We don't want that kind of reputation. Whatever happens, all of us here are ready to offer ourselves to Ācariya Mun, body and soul. He will remain our cherished refuge until the day he dies. We can't allow anyone to take him away. We will resist to the last breath any attempt to do so."

So when hearing Ācariya Mun's explanation for being taken away, their disappointment was palpable, but they felt they couldn't object. Although they venerated him so much their sadness and disappointment at hearing his reasons nearly broke their hearts, they were forced to accept his decision. They truly deserve a lot of sympathy. Their willingness to sacrifice everything in their devotion to Ācariya Mun is a gesture I will always treasure. I'm sure that all of my readers feel the same way.

Many of Ācariya Mun's most senior disciples attended the meeting, aware as he spoke that he must be moved as soon as possible. After he had announced his decision and stated his reasons, and there being no dissenting voices, the monks and laity who were present all agreed to construct a stretcher suitable to carry him on the long journey from Ban Nong Pheu to Sakon Nakhon. The next day, a large crowd of lay supporters and monks brought the stretcher to his hut, awaiting his departure. An immense sorrow overcame everyone that day. They realized they were about to lose somebody whom they so deeply cherished and revered. It was a sorrow so great that local people and monks alike could barely contain their emotions.

After the morning meal was over and everyone awaited in readiness for the journey to start, emotions began to run high in the crowd surrounding his hut as the local people, gathered to see him off, gave vent to their despair one last time. Many monks and novices swelled the crowd; they too felt the strain. The deep sadness depressing their hearts slowly welled up, and tears flowed quietly, dampening their cheeks. At that moment Ācariya Mun appeared, carried by a group of his senior disciples — a moment of further heightened emotion. As the monks carried him down the steps and placed him on the stretcher, the mixture of affection, respect, and despair that everyone had kept bottled-up inside freely poured out: men, women, monks, and novices were no longer able to hold back their flood of tears. Onlookers wept openly, expressing an unrestrained and deep sense of sorrow. I myself could not avoid getting caught up in the despondent mood pervading that sad occasion, despite the fact that I was accompanying Ācariya Mun when he left. The air filled with sounds of weeping and crying. People called out, begging Ācariya Mun, "Please get better: Don't pass away from this world leaving us forever in unbearable sadness." They were almost inconsolable at that point. In his great compassion, he sympathized with how poor their community was. This they knew; yet they couldn't help but feel terribly miserable watching the cherished treasure over whom they had faithfully kept watch for so many years slip away from them forever. He was departing now, and there was nothing they could do to prevent it.

As Ācariya Mun was carried past, the sounds of their heartfelt laments surged along the path, a tidal wave of grief inundating the hearts of those who lined the route. As he passed by, everything appeared gray and bleak, as though their lives had suddenly been snuffed out. Even the grasses and trees, though insensible to the unfolding scene before them, appeared to wither up and die in response. As Ācariya Mun left the peaceful shade of the forest sanctuary where he and his disciples had lived so contentedly — a place where so many ordinary people had come to find shelter over the years — the monastery suddenly felt deserted, even though many monks still remained. Suddenly it no longer had that enormous tree with the thick, broad foliage that had always given so much peace and comfort to all who came to shelter there. The heartrending, anguished cries of those wanting to offer their undying devotion to the *sāsana* was an immensely sad, forlorn sound indeed. They were witnessing the departure of the one man who embodied the high ideals of their unshakable religious faith.

Long after the procession had passed through the village and the sounds of inconsolable grief had faded into the distance, hundreds of monks and lay people continued to walk behind his stretcher, their long, drawn faces mirroring the somber, cheerless spirit of the occasion. Walking along in complete silence like mourners in a funeral procession of a close friend or relative, they did their best to come to terms with the heartbreak. No one spoke a word, but in their hearts they pondered long and deeply on their shattered hopes, the overwhelming feeling being that all was now lost. It seemed then as if we were taking his corpse away to dispose of it, even though he was still very much alive. The realization that all hope was now gone, that he would never return again, had fully sunk in. The more we thought about it, the sadder we became. Yet we couldn't stop thinking about it. We all walked along in a kind of melancholy daze, contemplating thoughts of despair.

I must confess to being shamefully inadequate in this regard — the whole journey I thought only of how I was about to lose my one true refuge in life. No longer would there be someone to rely on when questions arose in my practice, as they so often did. The distance from Ban Nong Pheu to the district seat of Phanna Nikhom was approximately fifteen miles; but the long hours of walking passed almost unnoticed. Walking behind him, knowing he was dying, I thought only of how much I was going to miss my teacher. I desperately wanted him to continue living at the time. His final days corresponded to a crucial stage in my own meditation practice, a time when I had many unresolved problems to work out. No matter how much I pondered this predicament, I always arrived at the same conclusion: my dependence on him would have to be terminated soon. This made the future look bleak.

His condition remained calm and stable throughout the long journey — he did not display any obvious signs of ill health. In fact, he appeared to be lying fast asleep, though of course he wasn't sleeping at all. Around midday, the procession reached a cool, shady grove of trees. We asked Ācariya Mun's permission to take a short rest for the sake of the large group of people accompanying him. He immediately asked, "Where are we now?" The moment I heard his voice I was caught off guard by a surge of affection and emotional attachment. Why was I so deeply moved by this wonderful, welcome sound? It seemed, suddenly, as though Ācariya Mun was his old self again.

Is this beloved paragon of the three worlds truly going to abandon me, a poor orphan whose heart is about to break? Will his pure heart, whose kind assistance has always helped to breathe life into my spirit, really withdraw from my life and disappear — forever? Such were my immediate feelings the moment Ācariya Mun spoke up. Some people may consider this a somewhat crazy reaction. But I have no misgivings — I willingly admit this kind of craziness. For Ācariya Mun's sake, I was so crazy I would gladly have volunteered to die in his place without the least concern for my own life. Had it been his wish, I would have happily laid down my life — no second thoughts. I was prepared at a moment's notice to sacrifice my life for his. But, alas, it was impossible for him to accept any sacrifice I might be willing to offer. The truth is that everyone in the world must inevitably travel the same route: whatever is born must die. There are no exceptions.

The journey to Sakon Nakhon was planned in two stages. The first day we walked as far as Ban Phu monastery in Phanna Nikhom district, where we were to rest for a few days, allowing Ācariya Mun a chance to recuperate before moving on to Sakon Nakhon.[13] Leaving Ban Nong Pheu at nine o'clock that morning, the procession eventually reached Ban Phu monastery shortly before dark. The journey had taken all day because we followed the more circuitous route, skirting the edge of the mountains, to make it easier for him and the many elderly men and women determined to follow him all the way. Upon arriving, we invited him to rest in a low pavilion where his needs could easily be attended. It was also a convenient place for monks and lay people to pay him their respects.

Ācariya Mun's sojourn at Ban Phu monastery dragged on for many days, his condition steadily worsening the entire time. Meanwhile, each new day brought visiting crowds of monks and lay people from the surrounding area. Some even came at night. All were eager for a chance to meet him and pay their respects. Though well aware of his illustrious reputation, most of them had never made his acquaintance. They had heard the news that he was certainly a modern-day Arahant who would soon pass away into Nibbāna. It was rumored that those who met him would be blessed with good fortune, while those that didn't would have lived their lives in vain. So they were all anxious to benefit by coming to pay him homage. They did not want to feel they had wasted their birth as human beings.

The very first morning after arriving at Ban Phu, Ācariya Mun demanded to know when he would be taken to Sakon Nakhon. He told his disciples that it was not his intention to die at Ban Phu – they must take him on to Sakon Nakhon without further delay. His senior disciples replied that they planned to wait for a short while for him to recuperate, then they would proceed to Sakon Nakhon as he requested. So Ācariya Mun let the matter drop for awhile. The next day he again asked the same question. His senior disciples repeated their reasons and he remained silent, only to bring it up again later. Time and again he demanded to know when they would take him to Sakon Nakhon. He said that, by waiting too long, he would fail to make it in time.

In the end, they asked him to extend his stay at Ban Phu monastery for a full ten days. By the time four or five days had passed, he was pressing them constantly to take him to Sakon Nakhon. Each time, his senior disciples either kept silent or repeated their previous justifications for staying. Repeatedly he pressed them, scolding them for waiting so long.

"Are you going to have me die here?! I've told you from the very beginning – I am going to die in Sakon Nakhon. My time is almost up. Get me there in a hurry! Don't wait so long!"

During the final three days, his demands to be taken to Sakon Nakhon became increasingly vociferous. During his last night there he flatly refused to lie down and sleep. Instead, he urgently called the monks to his bedside and told them unequivocally that he could not remain alive much longer. He insisted on being taken that very night to be sure of arriving in time. He then had us prop him up, sitting cross-legged in *samādhi* and facing in the direction of Sakon Nakhon. As soon as he withdrew from *samādhi*, he told us to prepare to leave – he was waiting no longer. We rushed off to call his senior disciples. They informed him that he would definitely be taken to Sakon Nakhon the next morning. Following this assurance, his sense of urgency lessened somewhat, but he still refused to go to sleep, speaking openly about how he felt:

"My time is almost up, I cannot hang on much longer. It would be better to leave tonight. In that way, I will be sure to arrive in time for that critical moment which is now fast approaching. I have no wish to shoulder the burden of this flaming mass of body elements any longer. I want to discard the body once and for all so that I needn't be concerned with this great pile of pain and suffering ever again. I am literally on the verge of death right now. Don't you monks realize that I could die at any minute? My body is completely useless now. There is no justifiable reason to keep me in this state of physical torment. All of you understand my reasons for going to Sakon Nakhon – that's why we came here in the first place. So why do you still insist on delaying my departure? Is this Sakon Nakhon? Why don't you take me there immediately? I want to go right now! What are you waiting for? What use is a corpse? It's not useful for anything, not even for making fish sauce!

"I have already told you: my body has reached its limit – it simply cannot last any longer. Isn't anyone here interested in listening to me and doing what I say? I have explicitly stated what I want you to do, still no one seems to listen. If you insist on adopting such an attitude, how will you ever discover the Truth? If here in my presence, while I'm alive, you are so stubborn, refusing to believe what I say, how will you ever manage to be good, reasonable people once I'm dead? I know what I told you to be absolutely true. I have explained the whole situation to you in a carefully considered, reasonable manner. Yet, you stubbornly refuse to comply. I am beginning to lose hope that any of you will develop the principles of sound judgment needed to uphold the *sāsana*."

Ācariya Mun was very adamant the last night at Ban Phu — he absolutely refused to sleep that whole night. I suspect he was afraid that, in his condition, he might never wake up again. At the time none of us there with him could figure out his reason for staying awake all night. Only later did the real reason occur to me.

At seven o'clock the next morning, several trucks from the provincial highway department arrived to escort Ācariya Mun to Sakon Nakhon. Mrs. Num Chuwanon, as head of the escort, invited him to ride in one of the vehicles. He readily agreed and asked only whether there were enough vehicles to carry all of the many monks who were scheduled to accompany him. He was informed that three trucks had come. If these were not sufficient to transport all the monks who wanted to go, a return trip would be made to pick up the rest. Understanding the arrangement, Ācariya Mun remained silent. After the monks had eaten their meal, a doctor injected him with a sedative so that he would not be disturbed by the bumpy ride. In those days, the roads were quite rough — full of potholes and in generally poor condition. Having received the injection, he was placed on a stretcher and carried out to one of the trucks parked at the edge of the field, there being no road into the monastery. Soon after, he began to fall asleep. The convoy of vehicles then began the trip to Sakon Nakhon, arriving there at exactly noon.

Upon arrival, he was carried down from the truck and placed, still sleeping, in a hut at Wat Suddhawat monastery. He remained asleep the entire day, not waking until about midnight. Within an hour of his waking those critical symptoms — of which he had repeatedly forewarned his seemingly deaf and blind disciples — became more and more apparent, as if to say to us all: *Now do you see? This is why I kept insisting that you hurry to bring me to Sakon Nakhon. I want to quickly rid myself of this messy heap of suffering. The symptoms are fully obvious now. If you still don't understand, then take a look. If you still don't believe what*

I was telling you, then watch carefully and consider with all your heart what you see appearing before you at this moment. Was I telling you the truth or not? Stop being so deaf, blind, and thoughtless from now on. Otherwise, you will never find the wisdom needed to save yourselves. What you are witnessing right now should inspire you to think deeply — so don't be complacent.

Bhārā have pañcakkhandā: the five *khandhas* are indeed a heavy burden. In the very early hours of the morning he began to take leave of this heavy burden — this heap of intense suffering that no truly wise person wants to encounter again in the future. The monastery was absolutely quiet that night. No one milled about to disturb the stillness. Shortly, some important *ācariyas*, like Chao Khun Dhammachedi from Wat Bodhisomphon monastery in Udon Thani, arrived at his hut, having come in great haste as soon as they heard the news. As they entered, they hurriedly sat down in a calm, composed manner, though their hearts were actually troubled by the obvious deterioration in his condition. It was a poignant reminder that he could pass away at any moment. Monks arriving to monitor his condition sat silently in three rows facing him. Important senior disciples, led by Chao Khun Dhammachedi, sat in the front, the more junior monks and novices filling the remaining rows. All sat in complete silence, their eyes fixed on Ācariya Mun. Their lower eyelids were moistened by tears they couldn't hold back — such was the intensity of their despair. They knew all hope was lost, for nothing at all could be done to change the inevitable. They felt as if their own lives were losing all meaning.

At the beginning, Ācariya Mun was lying on his right side in the 'lion's posture'. Fearing this might exhaust him, some monks gently removed the pillow supporting him so that he came to rest lying on his back. As soon as he became aware of this, he tried to shift back to his right side, but he no longer had the strength to move. As he struggled to turn on his side, some senior *ācariyas* attempted to reposition the pillow so that it again supported his back. But noticing how very weak he was, they decided to stop, fearing that it might just make matters worse. Consequently, when Ācariya Mun finally passed away he was lying neither on his back nor on his right side, but slightly propped up somewhere in between. It was simply impossible to adjust his posture further under the circumstances. His disciples, mostly monks and novices with a few lay people, sat in total despair as life slowly ebbed from his body. So apprehensive were they about his imminent death, they had almost forgotten to breathe.

As the minutes passed, his breathing gradually became softer and more refined. No one took their eyes off him for it was obvious the end was fast approaching. His breathing continued to grow weaker and weaker until it was barely discernible. A few seconds later it appeared to cease; but it ended so delicately that no one present could determine just when he passed away. His physical appearance revealed nothing abnormal — so different from the death of the ordinary person. Despite the fact that all his disciples observed his final moments with unblinking attention, not one of them was able to say with any conviction: "That was precisely the moment when Ācariya Mun finally took leave of this dismal world."

Seeing no apparent signs of life, Chao Khun Dhammachedi rather tentatively said, "I think he's passed away." At the same time he glanced down at his watch — it was exactly 2:23 a.m. So that was taken as the time of death. When death had been confirmed, the impact of his passing was reflected in the grief-stricken, tearful faces of all the monks who sat crowded around the lifeless body. There followed an anguished few moments of low coughs and soft, incoherent mutterings before the whole room sank into a mood of silent despair which is beyond the power of words to describe. Our hearts were plunged into unbearable feelings of emptiness; our bodies sitting there appeared to be mere empty shells. Several long moments of stilled silence ensued when the whole world appeared to cease momentarily while Ācariya Mun abandoned his conventional existence and entered into the domain of Ultimate Happiness where no vestige of conventional reality could disturb him ever again.

I myself very nearly died of a broken heart along with him as I sat by his side steeped in pensive sorrow. I could not manage to shake off the gloomy, somber mood that clouded my heart as he departed the world. I could do nothing to alleviate the extreme pain of the loss I felt. 'Living dead' fittingly describes my sense of hopelessness at that moment.

After a period of silence, his senior disciples had the monks neatly rearrange his bedding. They laid out his body there for the time being, with the understanding that next morning they would consult together about making further arrangements. This accomplished, the monks began filing out of his room. Though a few remained on the verandah outside the room, most of them went down below. Even though the whole area surrounding the hut was illuminated by brightly-lit lanterns, his disciples stumbled around blindly in dejection, unsure where they were going. Appearing somnolent, almost drugged, they wandered aimlessly back and forth. Several monks actually fainted at the time, as though they too were about to expire because life no longer held any meaning for them. The entire monastic community found itself in a chaotic state of confusion late that night; all were inconsolable over the terrible sense of loss they suffered. Monks milled around absent-mindedly, having no clear idea where they were going or why. Such was the power of utter despondency arising from the departure of that shining beacon which so illuminated their lives and brightened their hearts. Suddenly, all sense of comfort and security had evaporated, exposing them to the uncertainty of living on without a reliable refuge. This cold, dark constriction in their hearts left them feeling that nothing substantial remained in the entire universe, nothing they could hold to for support. Failing to consider that beings throughout the universe have always managed to find a source of refuge, at that moment they appeared to face a bleak and uncertain future, as if dire misfortune were engulfing them all. Ācariya Mun had been the one, true refuge. To him they could always confidently entrust themselves, heart and soul, without reservation.

I mean no disregard to the Buddha, Dhamma, and Sangha, but at that moment they seemed somehow very distant, making it difficult to reestablish them as a viable refuge. They did not appear to project the same affirmative presence that Ācariya Mun did; he was always close at hand and ready to help resolve our doubts and provide us with inspiration. Approaching him with pressing problems that we were unable to solve on our own, these same burning issues invariably dissolved away the moment he offered a solution. This salient recollection, so deeply engraved on my heart, profoundly affected me when he passed away. I could think of no other person capable of helping me solve my problems. Who else could I find with such compassion for me? Who else's advice could I trust? I was afraid of being left alone, depressed, and hopelessly stuck with my own store of ignorance. Gone were the easy solutions I had found while living with him. The more I thought about this dilemma, the more discouraged I became about finding a safe, painless way out on my own. In my ignorance, I saw no way forward at that moment; only misery and despair stared me in the face. Sitting there in front of his dead body, as though I myself were dead, I could think of no way to save myself and relieve my misery. I sat brooding, a living, breathing ghost, completely oblivious to time or bodily fatigue. This was the first time in my life as a monk that I felt so gloomy, frightened, and confused—and there was no one to help me, no means of extricating myself from this distress. Each time I glanced down at Ācariya Mun's still, lifeless body, tears welled up in my eyes and flowed down my cheeks. I was helpless to stop them. My chest heaved and sobbed as an uncontrollable emotion arose and lodged in my throat, nearly suffocating me.

Eventually I regained enough presence of mind to reflect inwardly, admonishing myself: *Do I really intend to die of a broken heart right now? He died free of concerns and attachments, which are matters of the kilesas. If I were to die now, I would die as a result of my concerns and attachments. That would be harmful to me. Neither my despondency nor my death is of any use to me, or to Ācariya Mun. When he was alive, he never taught us to miss him to the point of death. This kind of longing is the way of worldly people everywhere. Even though my reason for missing him is associated with Dhamma, it is still contaminated by worldly concerns, and thus hardly worthy of a Buddhist monk. Such thoughts are especially inappropriate for someone like me who has set his sights firmly on achieving the highest level of Dhamma. The Lord Buddha stated that whoever practices the Dhamma properly is, in fact, worshipping the Buddha; that whoever realizes the Dhamma, realizes the Buddha as well. It is clear that my longing is not in perfect accord with Dhamma. To be in perfect accord with Dhamma I must practice precisely what Ācariya Mun taught me. This is the correct way for me to show how much I miss him. Should I die while engaged in those harsh training methods that he recommended, I shall feel confident that my death is in harmony with the principles of Dhamma. This is the only sensible way to behave. I must not obstruct my own progress by longing for him in an unreasonable, worldly manner — I'll only harm myself.*

In this way I regained mindfulness, allowing reason a chance to intervene and forestall the maelstrom raging in my heart at the time. And so I avoided being buried alive in my own futility.

The Funeral

By midmorning, reports of Ācariya Mun's death had spread throughout the adjacent communities; senior monks and government officials of all levels had heard the news. All hurried to the monastery, anxious to pay their last respects to his body. While gathered there, they conferred with Ācariya Mun's senior disciples to reach a consensus on the most suitable way to arrange the funeral. They were determined that it be conducted in a manner reflecting his exalted status as a distinguished *ācariya*, greatly revered nationwide. At the same time, they arranged to have news of his death broadcast over the radio and printed in the newspapers so that his faithful followers would have access to the news wherever they might be.

No sooner had reports of his death begun to circulate than groups of monks and lay devotees began pouring into the monastery from all directions to pay their last respects. From the time his death was announced until the day his body was cremated, a steady flow of visitors came daily to pay their respects. People living close by came and returned home the same day. But those living some distance away had to stay in the monastery overnight — transportation being less convenient then, than it is today.

During Ācariya Mun's earlier stay at Ban Phu monastery, the people who came to see him had offered so many gifts of various kinds it was hard to keep track of them all. The amount of gift offerings he received from the faithful was extraordinary — a trend which continued until the day of his death. Like rainwater in the monsoon season, donations flowed into the monastery in a continuous stream. In his lifetime he had always been the recipient of much largess, regardless of whether he was staying near a population center or deep in the mountains. Even when staying in the remotest locations, there were invariably generous people willing to make the effort to trek through thick forest so they could offer him something special. By nature, Ācariya Mun was always generous and self-sacrificing: he gave away everything he was offered to assist others. He never thought of keeping things for himself and he never regretted his beneficence. He gave away everything he received, irrespective of what it was or how much it may have cost. In terms of actual poverty, perhaps no monk was poorer than Ācariya Mun. The combined amount of all the donations he received during his life was prodigious, but the amount he gave away in charity was equally as great, if not greater. Whatever he was given, he very soon passed on to someone in need. Even on occasions when he had nothing to give away, he thought of other ways to be of help, though he did this unobtrusively. His beneficence often provided nearby monasteries with much-needed assistance. As the result of a life of self-sacrifice, even after his death people from all over the region continuously arrived with offerings to place before his body as it lay in state at Wat Suddhawat monastery.

Prominent senior monks, in consultation with local government officials, decided that it would be best to keep Ācariya Mun's body for several months before proceeding with the cremation. Agreement was reached that the cremation should take place during the period of the waxing moon in January of 1950. With this in mind, they arranged a special casket to hold the body.

At four o'clock that afternoon, a large crowd of laity, monks, and novices came to attend the funeral bathing rites for his body. When this ceremony was completed, his body, still draped in his monk's robes, was wrapped in many layers of white cloth and placed respectfully in the special casket. The casket's entire front panel was made of glass, allowing those coming from afar, who had never before seen him, to view his body. No one was to be disappointed. The community of monks, headed by Chao Khun Dhammachedi, decided to arrange nightly sessions of *sutta* chanting to honor him, accompanied by discourses on Dhamma, which were always well attended.

All the various functions connected with Ācariya Mun's funeral were organized with the generous cooperation of the local populace. From government officials and business leaders down to the general public, all contributions were made in a spirit of geniality. Sincere in their faith, they took these responsibilities very seriously, never losing heart. From the day Ācariya Mun passed away until the time of his cremation, the people of Sakon Nakhon put forth a concerted effort to make life as convenient as possible for the monks and novices gathered there for the occasion. They worked tirelessly, with enthusiasm, to insure that this huge funeral ceremony was an unqualified success, and spared no effort or expense in the process.

In the months leading up to the cremation, hundreds of monks arrived in Sakon Nakhon wishing to pay their final respects. Most then returned home, but over one hundred remained, residing in the monastery to help coordinate all the necessary arrangements. Despite the large influx of monks, local residents never felt discouraged; the faithful were prepared to support them each day with plenty of alms food. The lines of monks receiving food every morning seemed to stretch on forever, but people remained unstinting in their generosity from the first day to the last — on not a single day was alms food in short supply. Even with the increasing demand, ample food offerings were always graciously provided to support the monks.

I witnessed the enormous sacrifices these people made during that period, so I feel obliged to record for posterity their charitable goodness and amicable cooperation. It made such a deep impression on me — I shall never forget it. I never imagined I would see so much patience, endurance, and self-sacrifice shown by one group of people. Having experienced this incredible outpouring of generosity firsthand, I want to express my admiration to the people of Sakon Nakhon: they possessed a magnanimous faith that never waned. Their grand hospitality has left me with a warm feeling of gratitude — an impression that will forever remain in my heart.

One had to sympathize with the monks and novices, staying at the monastery, who helped supervise suitable arrangements for all the people attending the funeral, and with the many lay supporters who toiled so hard, helping with the labor. Well in advance of the cremation date, monks and novices were already arriving in large numbers, while the cremation ceremony was expected to attract a crowd of well over ten thousand people. Several pavilions were constructed to house people, and as many kitchen areas as possible were set up around the grounds to accommodate the large crowd that was expected to attend this important occasion. Begun shortly after Ācariya Mun passed away, these preparations were completed just in time for his cremation.

As the day of the funeral ceremony drew near, monks and lay devotees flooded in from all directions, their numbers swelling until those charged with receiving them were hardly able to cope. The closer it came to cremation day, the greater the multitude of people pouring into the monastery. In the end, no more space could be found to accommodate the hordes of people who kept arriving. By funeral day, all the huts were full, and the whole extensive tract of forest within the monastery grounds was crowded with monks and novices who had traveled from all over the region. Most of them camped out in the woods, their white umbrella-tents visible everywhere. A total of eight hundred monks and novices were camped out inside of Wat Suddhawat alone; several hundred more found shelter in nearby monasteries. In all, well over a thousand monks and novices were present at Ācariya Mun's cremation. As for the lay devotees, it was simply impossible to count how many were camped inside the monastery grounds. Over and above that, many more people stayed outside the monastery, sleeping under trees or out in the open fields. Many more slept in town, filling up all the limited hotel space. With the entire multitude finally assembled at the funeral pyre on cremation day, it was impossible to give an accurate reckoning of their total strength. At best, one could estimate that tens of thousands were in attendance that day.

And yet, strangely, amazingly, there was very little of the kind of noise usually associated with such a crowded ceremony. Only the sound of the public address system was heard, broadcasting the religious functions being performed in connection with the cremation. Performed strictly in accordance with *kammaṭṭhāna* tradition, there were no sideshows to entertain the crowd. The quantities of food, cloth, and other items, that were offered by devotees from all over the region to help the monastery with the funeral, amounted to a small mountain of goods. Hundreds of sacks of rice were offered, while the cars of faithful donors continuously brought food of all sorts to help feed everyone. The quantity of merit-making cloth, offered in honor of Ācariya Mun, would probably have filled a weaving factory. I've never seen a weaving factory and I have no idea how big they are, but I am confident that this mountain of cloth brought by faithful followers from all over the country would have exceeded the capacity of any such factory.

I wish to apologize to the reader if this seems an exaggeration. I was somewhat carried away by a sense of pride I felt concerning the offerings of so many generous people. I never imagined that we Thai people could be so generous. But witnessing this wonderful display of munificence personally, I have continued to be amazed by it ever since. Self-sacrifice and bounteous generosity are hallmarks of the Thai people. From a global perspective, Thailand is but a small country, yet our compassionate tendency to engage in spontaneous acts of charitable giving is second to none. It is a tradition that is entirely appropriate for a country like ours with a Buddhist heritage that teaches us to have compassion for one another. On the whole, we Thais have always been a nation of warm, big-hearted people who tend to shun narrow-minded, stingy attitudes.

Nowhere was this more apparent than at Ācariya Mun's funeral, where faithful donors offered an abundance of items for general consumption. The bounty was truly extraordinary. The sizes of the enormous pots of rice and stew prepared each day were almost frightening. These pots were so big and heavy that several people were required to carry them to the pavilions where the monks gathered to eat. Due to the unusually large number of monks, many different eating places were set up to accommodate them. Most of them ate in large groups — thirty to forty monks here, fifty to sixty monks there — at locations set aside for that purpose within the grounds. Smaller groups of nine to ten monks ate together in the monks' living quarters. The vast majority of them were *kammaṭṭhāna* monks who ate directly from their alms bowls, so large quantities of dishes and eating utensils were unnecessary, making it much easier to serve so many. Sets of dishes were provided only for the relatively few, prominent administrative monks and those accompanying them.

Once the pots of rice and stew had been offered, monks served themselves in order of seniority, placing rice, stew, and assorted sweets together in their alms bowls. This was normal practice — they invariably mixed their food in that way. The religious faith of the general public and the protective power of Ācariya Mun's spiritual greatness combined to ensure that food was always plentiful.

For the duration of the funeral, there were no instances of drinking or drunken behavior, no quarreling or fighting, and no cases of theft were reported. When found, lost articles were handed over to someone in authority who announced them over the loudspeakers. If the item in question was something valuable, the announcer did not describe it. He said merely that a valuable item had been found and urged the owner to come and claim it. Having correctly identified it, the item was returned to him. If the lost article was something common, the announcer simply described what had been found so the owner could then reclaim it. If it was money, he announced only that some money had been found, but the amount and its container — such as a wallet — were not mentioned. The owner was required to supply this information as proof of ownership.

The funeral ceremonies preceding the cremation of Ācariya Mun's body lasted a total of four days and three nights. The entire event was remarkable in many respects. To begin with, despite the enormous crowds, there was very little noise; no fights or wild, drunken behavior anywhere in the area, no pickpockets, and no thefts reported. Lost valuables were promptly handed over to the authorities; all monks and novices were calm, quiet, and very well-behaved. In any gathering of such size, it is unusual to meet with even one of these favorable conditions. Having them all combined in a single event was truly remarkable indeed.

Beginning at eight o'clock each night the monks assembled to chant *suttas* in honor of Ācariya Mun. The laity then offered gifts of cloth to the monks, one of whom gave a discourse on Dhamma. Again the next morning after the meal, members of the laity began presenting traditional offerings of merit-making cloth to the monks, offerings which continued with no fixed schedule throughout most of the day. During the four-day period, there were so many faithful devotees, traveling such great distances, hoping to dedicate offerings of cloth, that it would have been impractical to restrict those offerings to scheduled times. The issue was resolved by permitting lay people who wanted to dedicate offerings of cloth to a monk, or a group of monks, to make their dedications as quickly and easily as possible. Those arriving with cloth to offer were advised to contact the announcer and specifying to him how many monks they required. Using the public address system was by far the most convenient method, since it was almost impossible to find a specific monk in such a large crowd in any other way. So if certain devotees wanted to invite a specific monk to come and receive an offering, his name was announced on the public address system. The announcer had a complete list of the names of all the monks in attendance. All visiting monks and novices were required to register their names at the announcer's booth as soon as they arrived, and an announcement to this effect was broadcast on a regular basis. This policy allowed the organizers to make an accurate estimation of the number of monks and novices attending the funeral ceremonies. It also enabled the announcer to call out their names correctly when required.

Monks walked to the nearby villages, or into town, for alms every morning. The only exception was the day of the cremation itself. On that day, the laity made a special request that the monks collect food in the immediate vicinity of the monastery. The faithful lined up in groups at various places inside and outside the monastery, placing offerings into their bowls as the monks filed past.

The ceremony began on the tenth lunar day of the third lunar month and ended at midnight on the thirteenth lunar day with the cremation of Ācariya Mun's body. The special casket containing Ācariya Mun's body was placed on an ornate funeral pyre, specially constructed for the cremation. Built on the site where the *uposatha* hall presently stands, it was a four-sided wooden structure decorated with intricately carved motifs that skilled craftsman had created for the auspicious occasion. It looked very impressive — worthy of such a distinguished *ācariya*. His remains were later collected on the morning of the fourteenth lunar day. Unfortunately, I cannot recall the day of the month according to the international calendar.[14]

To the best of my recollection, his body was placed there on the eleventh lunar day. As they prepared to move his body from the pavilion where he lay in state, the monks and the laity held a short service to ask his forgiveness for any past transgressions they might have committed. The casket containing his body was then carried solemnly to the funeral pyre, prompting a dramatic outburst of emotion among his followers as they expressed their grief once more. Watching his body pass by for the last time, the crowd looked on with long, sad faces, tearful expressions occasionally erupting in cries of anguish. It was a chaotic scene, his casket moving slowly through throngs of impassioned supporters, all mourning the loss of an exceptionally noble person who possessed such a boundless ocean of loving kindness. Many in the crowd wept openly as his body passed by. It was all they had left of him — the last vestige of conventional reality still associated with his presence in the world. He had entered the sublime, pure land of Nibbāna. Never again would he return to physical, bodily existence — the domain of tearful lamentations.

His devotees wept one last time — with affection and respect for a man whose Dhamma teaching had soothed their hearts and tempered their ignorance. Through his grace, they had gained the presence of mind needed to reflect on the merits of virtue and the failings of evil. Reminded of his great virtue, they longed to keep his body awhile longer as an object of veneration, though they knew this was now impossible. So they asked only that they be allowed this final chance to offer their tears and heartfelt emotions as tokens of their deep appreciation.

Although they may have been unfortunate in many ways, they did have the wonderful good fortune to witness for themselves the final farewell of a supreme sage, sublimely free of all *kilesas* — an extremely auspicious event that is rarely ever witnessed. Having transcended *saṁsāra's* abundant misery, he had already reached the Ultimate Happiness of Nibbāna. Even so, they continued to hope that his compassion would be with them in this hour of sorrow — a sorrow that made them weep with longing for that noble being of unbounded virtue who was so dear to their hearts. They wondered when they would ever find a way to escape Māra's net and reached the safety of Nibbāna as well. But their time was not yet ripe. All they could do was extol his extraordinary virtue and honor his magnificent achievement with their tears. Such was the overwhelming sentiment of the Buddhist faithful as they mourned the loss of the monk they so revered. Only when his body had finally been placed upon the funeral pyre did they begin to calm down and grow quiet.

At midnight the funeral pyre was lit. In anticipation, such a mass of people had crowded in around the cremation site that no one could move. Packed tightly together, they pushed and pressed against one another trying to get a better look. All had patiently waited late into the night to have one last glimpse of his body — a memory to be long cherished by everyone.

Just as the funeral pyre was lit, something unimaginably strange and wonderful occurred. As the first flames began to shoot up, a small cloud appeared in the sky and began to rain ever so gently on the burning pyre. It was the night of the full moon. Bright moonlight was shining over the surrounding area, but the cremation site was suddenly bathed in a fine, misty rain. Softly sprinkling for about fifteen minutes, the cloud then gradually faded into the clear night sky. You may wonder why I think it so strange. Normally, at that time of year, the sky is completely clear; only the stars and the moon are visible. And so it was that night, until the funeral pyre was lit, when a small cloud floated over, sprinkling a gentle shower on the whole proceeding. I clearly witnessed this amazing event — such an extraordinary spectacle I've never forgotten it. Anyone who was there that night will be able to confirm it.

Instead of the usual pile of firewood or charcoal, Ācariya Mun's funeral pyre was made with fragrant sandalwood that ardent devotees had specially ordered from across the Mekong River in Laos. Having acquired a sufficient amount, they mixed it with incense, using this as a pyre to cremate the body. The results were just as satisfactory as those obtained by using plain firewood or charcoal. From the moment the pyre was lit until the cremation of his body had been completed and his remains had been safely collected, the whole affair was supervised by officials from the monastic and lay communities.

At nine o'clock the following morning the bone remains were carefully collected from the ash.[15] Bone relics were distributed to monks representing the various provinces in attendance with the understanding that these relics would be placed in suitable public shrines in their respective locales. Fragments of bone were also handed out to members of the general public, but due to the size of the crowd, there were not nearly enough to go around. As far as I can recall, representatives from over twenty provinces took bone relics back with them that day.

When the collection and distribution of the bone relics were finally completed, something indescribably moving happened that made a profound impression on me. As soon as the officials in charge of collecting the bones had finished their work and left, a scene of total confusion ensued as men and women of all ages rushed in to collect bits and pieces of ash and charcoal to keep as objects of worship. Everybody scrambled to get a bit of this or a piece of that, combing the ground around the funeral pyre for any small memento they could find. In the end, the whole area was spotless — as if it had been scrubbed clean. Walking away, each person seemed to be floating on air, smiling, overjoyed beyond words. All clasped some small keepsake in their fists, guarding their treasure jealously, as though afraid someone might try to snatch it away at any moment. Like so many other events occurring during the course of Ācariya Mun's funeral, it was an extremely moving sight.

Later, as their last act of homage before going home, most people returned one more time to the site of the cremation — the final resting place of Ācariya Mun's body. Prostrating themselves three times, they sat quietly on the ground for a few moments in an attitude of deep reflection, expressing their sense of loss with tears and quiet sobs in a way that was heartrending to witness. As I watched those people who felt such profound gratitude for a monk of surpassing virtue, I shared with them the same painful sense of loss. When their moment of quiet reflection was over, they rose and sadly walked away, their faces stained with tears. Other faithful devotees then took their places, solemnly paying their final respects, aware that they had lost the person they so dearly revered. And so it continued for many hours that day — it was an incredibly touching scene to watch.

The key factor here is the heart: the heart is the most important thing in the world. People's hearts were the primary force behind all the events I have just described. Tens of thousands of monks and lay people attended the funeral — their motivation for going came directly from the heart. Their hearts were instinctively drawn to Ācariya Mun, for his heart was pure Dhamma — an attainment so sought-after that it induced good, moral people from all over the country to come to worship him. Although their hearts may not have amassed as much virtue as they would have liked, it was still enough to create in them a tendency toward future rebirth as human beings. This is unlike the hearts of shameless people who seem to be vying for rebirth in hell or the animal world — types of birth that result in endless suffering. Rebirth in the lower realms of existence effectively debases the heart even further. Eventually, nothing of value is left to hold on to and all hope is lost.

All matters, without exception, converge at the heart: the heart is the driving force churning out the affairs of this world and determining the direction they take. If the heart is inclined toward goodness, everything a person does will bring contentment, both now and in the future. All paths branching off from the main avenue of goodness will invariably provide comfort and security to the virtuous wayfarer. Each rebirth will be a happy, prosperous one where hopes and desires are constantly being fulfilled. One day, that accumulated virtue is bound to lead to the most cherished goal of all. Witness Ācariya Mun, whose heart was a wellspring of goodness from the beginning stages to the very highest one.

Ācariya Mun has been widely glorified for his attainment of *Parinibbāna*. The word *Parinibbāna* is used solely in connection with someone absolutely free of all *kilesas*. When the average person stops breathing, bringing his physical existence to an end, this condition is known as 'death'. But when the Lord Buddha or an Arahant dies, this is *Parinibbāna*. It is generally presumed that Ācariya Mun's death was also *Parinibbāna*, a conclusion I have no reason to dispute. I gladly yield to the verdict of all those fine people who have given him this prestigious epitaph. For many years I lived with him, listening closely to his every word, and I found nothing contradictory in his way of life or his

Dhamma teaching. In truth, his teaching so profoundly impressed me that I am convinced it was *amatadhamma*,[16] emanating from a heart of genuine purity. A heart of such pureness is by no means inherent within human beings. To experience it, one must take the heart of an ordinary human being, then cleanse it until it becomes the pure heart of an Arahant — there is no other way. This purified heart then remains *ariyacitta ariyadhamma* forever.

Saying that the heart is the most important thing in the world means that the heart is the decisive factor controlling all manifestations of good and all manifestations of evil. The heart is the principal actor, and the one ultimately held accountable for all actions. If people's hearts motivate them to act in evil ways, the entire planet can easily be destroyed as a consequence. Thus, it is essential that our hearts should receive enough proper training and care so that we can safely look after ourselves and the world we live in. Then we will live in comfort, our lives free of undue disturbance; and the world will be a pleasant place to live, without the specter of strife constantly hanging over it.

Ācariya Mun (circa 1942)

Ācariya Mahā Boowa standing before Ācariya Mun's funeral pyre, which skilled craftsman decorated with intricately carved motifs created especially for the occasion. The ornate casket is laying lengthways just above his head.

A group photograph of Ācariya Mun's *dhutanga kammaṭṭhāna*
disciples gathered in front of his ornate funeral pyre.

Chao Khun Dhammachedi standing before Ācariya Mun's
funeral pyre. His casket is laying endwise to the camera.

Ācariya Chob Thānasamo (1902-1995)

7

The Legacy

In the period following his cremation, many of the monks in Ācariya Mun's lineage remained distraught as they continued to feel the loss of their one reliable refuge in life. Like kites with their strings broken, drifting at the mercy of the winds, they wandered off in all directions. Their spirits depressed, they felt like small, helpless orphans who had lost both parents. Consequently, the circle of practicing monks in Ācariya Mun's lineage found itself quite unsettled in the immediate aftermath of his funeral. By the time they eventually began to regroup, they had all realized the harmful effects of being without a good teacher.

The passing away of an outstanding *ācariya* is never a small matter. Invariably it affects the community of practicing monks in a very serious way — shaking them like an earthquake to their very foundations. If his disciples have already established themselves firmly in the practice, possessing the mental fortitude to hold their own while helping to sustain their fellow monks, then the long-term effects will not be so adverse. Whether it's a family leader, a social leader, a business leader, a government leader, or a leader in any branch of the community of monks — the death of a good leader is always felt as a huge loss. Since it is ultimately unavoidable, those subordinates who depend on their leadership should earnestly prepare themselves for such an eventuality so that they may prosper now and in the future.

When Ācariya Mun passed away, I saw the incredibly harmful effects that such a loss can have. He was only a single individual, but vast numbers of monks and lay devotees were so grieved by his death that they appeared to be left in a state of ruin — like a building whose foundation has been damaged so that its entire structure suffers accordingly. I was shocked by this development, and worried for the future of the circle of practicing monks who could easily suffer damage without the protection of a strong teacher. If we do not make the effort to intensify our practice and get results while our teacher is still alive, upon his death we will be like the living dead, lacking firm principles of our own to hold on to.

I myself was caught woefully unprepared at that time. It was a terrible experience. I felt as if the winds of a cyclone were raging through my heart, blowing me in all directions. One storm blew in to assail me with the thought that I had been left stranded without a refuge; another blew in to fill me with doubts and left me wondering about whom I could possibly rely on now. Then a gale blew through, driving the thought that, having passed away sublimely without any concerns, he had left me behind feeling empty and lifeless to drift along hopelessly without a mainstay to which I could cling. Yet another wind buffeted me with the thought that everything would come to an end now that he was gone: Who would I stay with now that my father had died? Did this really signal my downfall? No sooner had I begun to stand on my own than my father left me. What a terrible misfortune! Another howling wind inveighed against the miserable bad luck of this poor orphan: *I am finished for sure this time, and at such a crucial juncture in my own development as well. The kilesas and Dhamma are engaged in a full-scale war, and Ācariya Mun has been my advisor, helping me to work out a battle plan. Who will have this kind of compassion for me in the future?* I had never reached such an agonizing impasse before. I felt as though I had fallen into an infernal pit of mortal despair. All hope seemed lost as I lived on without him.

Such was my troubled state of mind when Ācariya Mun passed away. That experience chastened me. Ever since then I've been loath to see other practicing monks encounter a similar agonizing experience simply because they lack the firm principles needed to stand on their own. Fearing that they will miss their rightful destiny by default, I constantly warn them of the dangers. Should they wait until the sun has already set before rushing to find a safe refuge, I'm concerned they may end up feeling as empty and lifeless as I did. Not wishing to see this happen, I caution them to hurry and intensify their efforts while the moon is still bright, their hearts still willing, and their bodies still able. Thus committed, those desiring to attain the wealth of virtue inherent within *magga*, *phala*, and Nibbāna can still manage to do so. They need not live poverty-stricken amid a world of spiritual riches.

Relics Transformed

All the people who received some of the bone fragments that were distributed after Ācariya Mun's cremation, placed them in suitable reliquaries and worshipped these relics in his stead. Everyone went their separate ways after the funeral, and nothing further was heard about this matter until some four years later when Khun Wan Khomanamun, owner of the Siriphon Phanit Store and the Suddhiphon Hotel in Nakhon Ratchasima, returned to Sakon Nakhon for a merit-making ceremony. When he presented a cloth offering at Wat Suddhawat monastery, where Ācariya Mun had passed away, the abbot gave him a piece of bone taken from Ācariya Mun's funeral pyre. Upon returning home, he decided to place it in the reliquary with the other remains of Ācariya Mun which he had received four years earlier. When he opened the container, he was astonished to find that these bone fragments, received at the cremation, had all been transformed into crystal-like relics.[1] He was so amazed at seeing them that his spirits soared. He quickly sent someone to check on another set of Ācariya Mun's remains that he kept in a reliquary at the Suddhiphon Hotel, and discovered that they too had been transformed into crystal-like relics. A small portion of the original bone remained in the form of a coarse powder, but soon that, too, underwent the same transformation. In the end, a total of 344 relics were counted in the two reliquaries belonging to Khun Wan. This was the first instance where Ācariya Mun's remains were found to have transformed into relics.

News of this miracle spread far and wide. Soon people began coming to ask him for a share of the relics. Khun Wan was a very generous person and he sympathized with their request. So, he shared the relics out among them one or two at a time. He very kindly gave me some on two occasions. On the first occasion, I received five; on the second, two, making seven altogether. As soon as I received them I publicized the fact that I had something very special. I was enormously pleased to have them, but my mouth wasn't satisfied to keep quiet about it. In the end I lost out — some women came and took them all. But, oddly enough, I was not at all disappointed that they took advantage of me. And there being nothing left to publicize, my mouth was finally satisfied.

When word got out that I had something very special, the first people who came to ask to see them were all women. When I brought out the relics, first, this woman picked one up to inspect it; then, that woman picked one up to inspect it. Before I knew it, each of them had quietly slipped the one she was holding into her pocket, asking me if she could keep it. Who would dare ask for their return at that point, and make a fool of himself twice. Since then I have never had any of Ācariya Mun's relics in my possession. Later, I heard that Khun Wan had given so many of his relics away to other devotees that he had hardly any left; so, I didn't dare to bother him again.

It is my understanding that Khun Wan's store in Nakhon Ratchasima was the first place where Ācariya Mun's bone fragments were discovered to be genuine relics. From that time on, such relics have appeared in many different places where faithful people, who received pieces of Ācariya Mun's bone, continued to worship them with special reverence. Even today, people still discover that Ācariya Mun's bone fragments have turned into relics, though the families who have them keep very quiet, fearing that others will ask for a share of these rare, priceless gems. In any case, someone who did not have an inherent spiritual connection with Ācariya Mun would find it difficult to receive one of his relics to worship. Just look at me: I received several of them but lacked the merit necessary to look after them — I had to give them to someone else to care for them in my place.

Ācariya Mun's relics possess many strange, amazing qualities. One person who owned two of them made a solemn wish that his two relics become three so that he would have one for each of the "Three Jewels": Buddha, Dhamma, and Sangha. Soon afterward a third relic materialized with the other two. Another person with two relics made the same solemn wish, but instead of increasing, the two fused into one, which greatly disappointed him. This person told me what had happened and asked my advice. I explained to him that whether one has three of Ācariya Mun's relics, or one of them, or merely a bone fragment that has yet to undergo any transformation, all are essentially relics from his body. So no one should be disappointed if two became one, for it's a miraculous occurrence just the same. What could be more amazing than that? Even the hair samples from Ācariya Mun's head — which were collected when he shaved his head each month, and which are now kept and revered by people in many different places — have undergone a transformation similar to the bone fragments. In either case, the result is the same: undergoing an essential transformation, both become relics.

People who have genuine relics of Ācariya Mun cherish them so much that they keep very quiet about it. But, if someone inquires skeptically whether Ācariya Mun's bones really did become relics, the same people will answer boldly in the affirmative. Should they then be asked whether or not they possess any, they will just smile and say they have so few they couldn't possibly give one away, thus precluding someone from asking. For this reason, it is difficult to find out these days who actually possesses Ācariya Mun's relics. Even if they were asked by a monk whom they revere, they would probably give a rather vague answer. So we must sympathize with those who venerate and treasure Ācariya Mun's relics.

AS A LIVING TEACHER, Ācariya Mun was extremely influential. He had very effective methods for alleviating the mental stress and feelings of anxiety experienced by his followers. Many people have recounted instances when they were determined to commit evil, or their minds were very hot and agitated, or they felt vengeful enough to kill someone — and the mere thought of Ācariya Mun then was enough to cause these emotions and ideas to subside immediately. It was as though he had doused their flaming hearts with cool water, allowing them to realize their misunderstandings. Their harmful thoughts had simply vanished. The sense of relief they felt made them want to prostrate before him then and there. Many lay followers have testified to this, and surely there are many more unreported cases of devotees using the power of remembering Ācariya Mun to successfully counter their wrongful intentions. Many monks, as well, have used the power of their faith in him to restrain themselves in accordance with their spiritual calling.

During his lifetime Ācariya Mun trained countless numbers of people to be good, righteous individuals. At least forty years of his life as a monk were spent engaged in teaching monks and laity from all over the country. Just think of how many monks and how many lay people must have trained under him in that forty year period. If we consider only the monks, the disciples who became accomplished in meditation and the way of practice were already numerous. These monks have in turn become *ācariyas*, teaching their own disciples how to develop firm principles for the future. All of this resulted from Ācariya Mun's pioneering efforts to pass on that knowledge and understanding to others. Without his guidance they would never have been able to find the right path, to say nothing of teaching others how to practice it.

The task of laying a firm spiritual foundation in the heart, so that it is solidly anchored in reason and propriety, is an important and difficult one — far more so than any other seemingly difficult task we've ever done. Spiritual work, like all other work, follows the lead of the heart. In truth, the primary basis for everything we do is found in the heart. The heart is both instigator and director of all affairs concerning good and evil, right and wrong. Being both arbiter and taskmaster in all moral issues, the more the heart learns about itself and its relation to matters of good, evil, right, and wrong, the better equipped it will be to sustain itself in a smooth, safe, and joyful manner. Those of us, who were aware of Ācariya Mun's profound knowledge of this subject, feel obliged to pay homage to him with unshakable faith. While he was alive, we were constantly reminded of the depth of his understanding. And although he has now passed away, we have never forgotten it. We cannot help but recollect him with a profound and boundless sense of gratitude.

Ācariya Mun was a teacher of the highest caliber when it came to developing people's hearts — a development that goes straight to the essential core of life in this world. A heart well developed in Dhamma is unlikely to suffer adverse consequences. More than that, we can state with confidence that a fully developed heart will never suffer any adverse consequences at all. All its actions will bring beneficial results. A world in which proper spiritual development keeps pace with material development is a truly progressive world where people are bound to live in peace and happiness. When the material side of the world progresses at the expense of the spiritual side, people's hearts are forever ablaze, so the world experiences strife, oppression, exploitation, and corruption on a grand scale. Such progress is equivalent to the advance of the fires of hell. If you want to know what the advancing fires of hell are like, you need only look at a world devoid of spiritual development; a world that is constantly polluted by the heart's filthy excretions. When the heart is neglected, people's behavior becomes perverse, immoral, irritating, and quite offensive. So much so that nothing of pleasure or praiseworthiness can be found in a world ruled by impropriety.

Understanding this, wise, intelligent people emphasize spiritual development over all other kinds of development—which are all merely creations of the heart anyway. Once the heart has been well developed, its overriding influence then cleanses all aspects of a person's behavior. The world thus enjoys peace and happiness following the lead of intelligent people who have developed themselves spiritually, and therefore, strive to govern society with reason, according to the principles of Dhamma.

We should be very wary of admiring or trusting the intelligence of people who lack spiritual development even if they're so clever that they can explore the sun, the moon, and the stars. Such achievements are not all that significant; especially if the intelligence in question is of the kind that is unmindful of its own misdoing and exudes poisonous elements that cause trouble in society. Applied indiscriminately, this 'clever' knowledge may well lead to behavior rivaling that of common animals that ruthlessly prey on and devour each other, believing all the while that it is a clever way to satisfy their needs. Regardless of our position in society, genuine intelligence is measured by our ability to use the principles of reason to bring prosperity to ourselves and others, and there is no need to earn a diploma to certify it. Thoughts and actions bringing peace and happiness to ourselves and others are considered the true fruits of genuine intelligence; and as such, they constitute their own certificate of recognition. We need not boast of our credentials to verify our intelligence. In fact, such certification may secretly act as a cover for immoral behavior. In that case, the means may be furtive, but the resultant disturbance to others is no secret — the troublesome problems it creates are obvious everywhere we look.

Such is the harm that arises when spiritual development is overlooked. Who can seriously believe that material development alone — driven by people whose hearts are corroded by *kilesas* and corrupted by selfish motives — will ever bring true peace and prosperity to the world? Only someone who is completely insensitive to moral issues could possibly accept this view. The difference between the actions of those who have developed themselves spiritually and those who have not is the difference between day and night. It was for this reason that the Lord Buddha did not recommend that the *samādhi* attainments be used for such psychic purposes as levitating, diving through the earth, or walking on water. He did not praise the intelligence of people acting like that. On the contrary, he praised as intelligent those who made an effort to thoroughly train themselves in the way of virtue, regardless of whether they were using *samādhi* attainments or some other means to achieve this. Such people are a blessing to themselves and to others, for a sense of contentment is the primary determinant of how pleasant our world really is. Even though the state of our health and other physical needs may be uncertain, following the fluctuating nature of *anicca*, life remains pleasant if our hearts have sufficient contentment to insure us against life becoming unbearable.

QUESTIONS HAVE ARISEN concerning the spontaneous transformation of the bone remains of Ācariya Mun and Ācariya Sao into relics. As news of this marvel spread shortly after the first relics of Ācariya Mun appeared, many people voiced doubts about why the bone remains of ordinary people could not also become relics: after all, the bones of an Arahant and the bones of an ordinary person are composed of the same body elements. Why is it that only an Arahant's bones can become relics? What's the essential difference between the two?

Briefly, my own explanation is that the heart, or the *citta*, is the fundamental, determining factor here. Although the *citta* is something common to all living beings, it varies greatly in power and quality from one person to the next. As for an Arahant, his *citta* is an *ariyacitta*; meaning that it is absolutely pure. The *citta* of the average person, on the other hand, is merely an ordinary *citta*; meaning, that it is polluted by *kilesas*. In either case, the nature of the *citta* — the master and prime mover — has a decisive impact on the condition of the physical body in which it resides. For instance, the Arahant's *citta* being pure, it may well have the power to cleanse his body elements, making them pure as well, and thus allowing his bones to transmute into relics. Although the body of an ordinary person is composed of the same types of elements, the body's master, the *citta*, is full of *kilesas*. It has no power to cleanse the body elements and purify them. Because the body elements have not been purified, the cremated bones of the average person remain unchanged, reflecting the impure nature of the *citta*. We could say that purified elements are synonymous with the *ariyacitta*, while ordinary elements are synonymous with the ordinary *citta*. The attributes of the Arahant's *citta* — and by extension, his body elements — differ significantly from those of the average person, so their bone remains are bound to differ as well.

However, I am not sure that, after death, the bones of all Arahants will automatically be transformed to relics. The *citta* of someone attaining the level of Arahant is completely purified at the moment of its attainment. The question remains: When the body of an Arahant is cremated, do the remaining bones become relics in each and every case or not? From one Arahant to another, there is a considerable difference in time between the moment when he reaches that attainment and the moment when he finally passes away. The bones of living Arahants, who maintain their body elements for a long period of time after their attainment, are very likely to become relics after death. This is due to the length of time involved. The *citta* of an Arahant maintains the body elements by means of the various life-sustaining systems present in the body, like the breath for example. At the same time, an Arahant maintains throughout his daily activities an intrinsic level of *samādhi* that steadily works to cleanse his body elements until they also become pure. This results in his bone remains becoming relics after he passes away. But I'm not convinced that the bone remains of an Arahant, who passes away shortly after his attainment, do become relics, since his body elements were not subject to the same lengthy cleansing process mentioned above.

An Arahant classified as *dandhābhiññā* is one who attains enlightenment slowly and gradually. He may well reach the Anāgāmī level, and then be stuck there for a long time before he finally reaches the level of Arahant. He must spend a lot of time investigating back and forth between *arahattamagga* and *arahattaphala* before the *citta* develops sufficient strength and skill to pass beyond. This process of investigating *arahattamagga* for the sake of attaining *arahattaphala* is in fact an effective means of cleansing the body elements. Having finally attained the level of Arahant, his bones may well become relics after he passes away. On the other hand, I am not at all sure that the bones of an Arahant, who attains enlightenment quickly — that is, *khippābhiññā* — and then passes away shortly afterward, will necessarily become relics, since his purified *citta* would have very little time to cleanse his body elements. As for the ordinary *citta* of the average person, producing a transformation from bone to relic is well beyond its capability.

NOT ONLY WERE Ācariya Mun's bone remains clearly transformed into relics, but some of these relics then underwent some amazing changes of their own. As I have already mentioned, someone who had two relics made a solemn wish that they become three and was rewarded with an extra one. Someone with two wished for a third and ended up with only one instead. Although it seems virtually impossible, such transformations actually happened.

There was another strange case where a man who had been given two relics one morning found three when he looked again that evening: in the short period between morning and evening they had increased from two to three. The man in question was a senior government official with enormous faith in Ācariya Mun. From the day he passed away until the time of his cremation, this man had been extremely helpful in nearly every aspect of the funeral arrangements. A certain senior monk, having received some relics from Khun Wan of Nakhon Ratchasima and remembering this man's kind assistance, gave him a pair as a keepsake one morning. The man felt an overwhelming sense of joy the moment he was handed that precious gift. Having nothing suitable to put them in just then, he put the relics in an empty snuff bottle for the time being. He closed the cap tightly and placed the bottle in his shirt pocket, buttoning it for good measure to insure against loss. Upon leaving the monastery that morning, he went directly to work where he spent the whole day in a bright, happy frame of mind, his thoughts returning time and again to the relics he had just received.

Arriving home that evening, he excitedly told his family that he had received something splendid, a gift he had never received before. After the whole household gathered around to see what it was, he produced a proper reliquary for holding the relics. Opening the snuff bottle to remove the relics, he saw, to his amazement, that there were three of them. This sight heightened his reverence for Ācariya Mun, and he was so overjoyed at receiving the relics that he could hardly contain himself. He boldly proclaimed to his wife and children that this was a genuine miracle — proof that Ācariya Mun was truly an Arahant. His family were somewhat skeptical, worried that, perhaps, he had miscounted them in the morning. He refused to accept this, arguing vehemently that he clearly remembered being given two relics by the senior monk that morning. He insisted that he had accepted them with great interest and respect. Even at work he had kept them in mind all day, repeating to himself "two relics, two relics", as though it was a meditation subject. How could he have forgotten how many there were? He told his family that if they still harbored any doubts, tomorrow he would take them all to ask the senior monk: then they would realize that what he said was true. But his family didn't want to wait: they were determined to go immediately. So, they all agreed to go straight away. Upon arriving at the monastery, the government official asked the senior monk how many relics he had given him that morning.

"I gave you two relics. Why do you ask? Is one missing?"

"No, none are missing. In fact, they have actually increased by one, so now I have three! The reason I ask is, when I returned home and opened the bottle to remove the relics and place them in a reliquary, there were three instead of the two I expected to see. This made me tremble with joy. I quickly told my wife and children what had happened, but no one believed me. Afraid that I had miscounted them, they insisted that I come again and ask you to make sure. Now that we know the truth, I feel even happier. Well, what do you say — do you believe me now?"

His wife smiled and said she was worried that he may have miscounted them, or that perhaps he was just kidding her. She just wanted to make sure. Since it was obviously true, she believed it; she had no intention of denying the truth. At this the senior monk smiled and explained to her what had happened:

"This morning I gave your husband two relics. He was always especially helpful to Acariya Mun and the rest of the monks. He gave us invaluable assistance from the time Acariya Mun died until his cremation was completed. I have never forgotten this, so, when I was given some relics by Khun Wan of Nakhon Ratchasima, I put a few aside to give to your husband as a keepsake since they are so hard to find nowadays. Acariya Mun is the first person I have ever encountered whose bones have changed to relics. Though such things are mentioned in the ancient texts, I had never seen the real thing with my own eyes. Now I have seen irrefutable proof. Please keep them in a suitable place and look after them well. Should they happen to vanish one day, your disappointment will be far more profound than the joy you felt when they increased in number. Don't say I didn't warn you. Acariya Mun's relics possess very miraculous properties. When they can increase in number as easily as they just have for you, they can just as easily vanish if they are not properly respected. Please keep them in a prominent, high place and pay homage to them every morning and evening. They may well bring you some unexpected good fortune. I am absolutely convinced that Ācariya Mun was a monk of the highest purity, but I don't tell people this very often for fear they may think I'm crazy. You see, people tend to easily believe in bad things, but they have difficulty believing in good ones. Consequently, it is difficult to find a good person but easy to find a bad one. By observing ourselves, we will notice that we too tend to prefer thinking in unwholesome rather than in wholesome ways."

When the senior monk finished speaking, the government official and his wife respectfully took leave of him and returned home in an exceptionally cheerful mood.

I have mentioned these strange, miraculous properties of Ācariya Mun's relics so that my readers may ponder for themselves what causes such phenomena to occur. Those searching for scientific proof to authenticate their occurrence will find empirical evidence hard to come by. Since such things are impossible for people with *kilesas* to fathom, they may not find a shred of evidence to support them. The difference between the body elements of an Arahant and those of the rest of us is clearly demonstrated by the fact that an Arahant's bones can become genuine relics. As for the body elements of people with *kilesas*: even the cremated remains of a million such people will never produce the same results. Thus it is clear that a living Arahant is a human being who is incomparably different from the rest of us. Just the fact that his heart is pure makes him stand out in a uniquely amazing way. His attainment is something that the whole world should respect and revere.

Other Mysteries

Ordinarily, people's sense of their own self-importance makes it difficult for them to believe in someone else's superiority. Nevertheless, aspiring to be good people, they feel obliged to accept what is obviously true, for refusing to accept manifestations of genuine goodness would show a kind of stupidity that defies human dignity. Take Ācariya Mun, for example. I am unaware of any monk, novice, or nun, who knew him well and understood what he taught yet remained so stubborn and conceited that they refused to accept the truth of his teaching. Moreover, they all seemed to be quite willing to sacrifice their lives for him.

The way of truth and purity, that he taught in such detail, can be compared to a discipline like mathematics: both are established in fixed principles that give precise results when followed correctly. For example, one plus one must equal two, two plus two must equal four. No matter how many multiples are calculated in this fashion, the calculations will always be correct so long as the basic rules are applied. Whether it is an adult making the calculations, or a child, if the right method is followed, then the results will inevitably be correct. No matter how many people may come along arbitrarily denying the validity of these basic principles, their truth remains the same. Such people merely display their own senseless stupidity. Likewise, principles of Truth do not depend on the whims of any particular age group, gender, or nationality. They are accepted as irrefutable natural laws. The principles of Dhamma, that the Lord Buddha and the Arahants fully realized to be true, can be proclaimed in their entirety with absolute assurance about their validity.

Ācariya Mun was one individual who fully realized the principles of Truth within himself. He could fully describe all the knowledge about internal and external phenomena that he had so clearly attained, without concern for the belief or disbelief or the praise or criticism of others. Every aspect of his internal practice — beginning with moral discipline and *samādhi*, and progressing all the way to the absolute freedom of Nibbāna — was declared openly and boldly so that his listeners could make use of that knowledge according to their own capabilities. He spoke fearlessly about the external aspects of his practice, like *devas*, *brahmas*, and various types of ghosts, leaving it up to his listeners to investigate as best they could. Besides receiving encouragement in their practice, those who shared his natural inclination to perceive such phenomena, were able to significantly broaden the scope of their knowledge, enabling themselves to deal expeditiously with the mysterious phenomena they encountered.

Some of his disciples bore witness to these phenomena, though they did not possess nearly the mastery that he did. I'll give you an example. One night Ācariya Mun received groups of *devas* late into the night, having no chance to rest. Eventually feeling very tired, he wanted to lay down for a while. When yet another group of *devas* arrived late that night, he explained to them that he was very tired from receiving several previous groups and now needed a rest. He requested that they go instead to visit one of his disciples and listen to his Dhamma discourse — which they did. When told what Ācariya Mun had said, this disciple agreed to talk with them about Dhamma for awhile, after which they left.

The next morning this monk asked Ācariya Mun about the incident: "Last night a group of *devas* came to visit me. They said that, before coming to me, they had paid you a visit to request a Dhamma teaching, but you were very tired and needed a rest, so you sent them to me instead. Is this true, or were they misleading me just so they could listen to me talk about Dhamma? Feeling somewhat skeptical, I wanted to ask you about it."

Ācariya Mun replied:

"Well, having already received several groups of *devas*, I was dead tired. Then the last group came, so I sent them to you, exactly as they said. Believe me, *devas* never lie to monks. They are not like human beings, who tend to be quite deceitful and untrustworthy. When *devas* make a promise, they always keep it; and when they make an appointment, they are always right on time. I have associated with terrestrial and celestial *devas* for a long time now and I have never heard them say anything false or deceitful. They are far more honest and virtuous than humans are. They scrupulously honor their word as if their very lives depended on it. They will severely criticize anyone who deviates from his word; and if that individual does not have a genuinely sound reason for failing to honor his commitments, they lose all respect for him.

"They have criticized me sometimes, though I had no intention of being dishonest. On certain occasions I entered into a deep state of *samādhi* prior to the appointed hour. I became absorbed there, only to find the *devas* waiting for me when I finally withdrew to a level where I could access them. When they reproached me for making them wait so long, I explained that I had been resting in *samādhi* and inadvertently failed to withdraw at the scheduled time, a reason which they accepted.

"Then there were other occasions when I reproached the *devas*. I explained to them that I am only one individual, yet tens or even hundreds of thousands of *devas* from the upper and lower realms insist on coming to visit this one monk: 'How could anyone successfully manage to receive each and every group exactly on time? There are times when my health is not so good, yet I must patiently sit there receiving visitors. You should sympathize with some of the difficulties I face. Sometimes I'm pleasantly absorbed in *samādhi*, only to get roundly criticized when I withdraw a little later than scheduled. If that's how it's going to be, I'll just keep to myself and not waste my time and energy receiving visitors. What do you say to that?' When rebuked like this, the *devas* invariably admitted their mistake and immediately asked for forgiveness.

"Those *devas* who visit me often are familiar with my way of doing things, so, they don't mind if I am a little late sometimes. It's those who have never come before that tend to mind my being late, since by nature they place such a high value on truthfulness. All *devas* from all realms, including terrestrial *devas*, are the same in this respect. Sometimes, being aware that I must withdraw from a restful state of *samādhi* to receive them, they do worry about the moral consequences of criticizing me for not keeping my word. I occasionally counter their reproaches by telling them I actually value my word more than my own life: 'The reason that I did not withdraw from *samādhi* in time to receive you was due to an obligation I have to Dhamma, which is something far more important than any promise made to a *deva*. Although *devas* and *brahmas* of the celestial realms possess nonphysical forms more refined than this human body of mine, my *citta* and my sense of truthfulness are exceedingly more subtle than those of all the *devas* and *brahmas* combined. But I am not one to talk incessantly about such things like some idiot. I mention it to you now only to remind you how important the Dhamma I maintain really is. So please consider the consequences carefully before criticizing me.'

"Once I explained my true priorities to them, the *devas* realized their mistake and felt very concerned about the moral implications of what they had done. Together they asked for my forgiveness. I made a point of assuring them that I do not feel any resentment toward any living being in the whole universe: 'I put my trust in the Dhamma of compassion and loving kindness which is devoid of all forms of malice. My every activity is governed by the Dhamma of absolute purity. *Devas*, on the other hand, possess only wholesome intentions and a sense of integrity — qualities that are not really all that amazing. The Lord Buddha and the Arahants possess an integrity that is pure because the Dhamma in their hearts is absolutely pure. No living being in the universe can possibly imagine just how supremely amazing such a state of purity is. The kind of integrity that *devas* observe is something that exists within the sphere of conventional reality. And the knowledge and the practice of it are well within the range of all living beings. The Dhamma integrity of a pure heart, however, is the exclusive property of the Buddha and the Arahants. No one who has yet to realize that attainment can possibly comprehend it or put it into practice. Whether or not I myself possess an absolutely pure level of integrity is not a matter to boast about. But please keep in mind that, in contrast to the Dhamma integrity of the Lord Buddha and the Arahants, the moral integrity that *devas* observe is neither exceptional or unique.' "

Had Ācariya Mun addressed these words to human beings instead of *devas*, the humans would probably have felt embarrassed — or something even worse. But the *devas* were keen to hear his Dhamma, and so listened with intense interest to what he said. They were able to realize the mistake they made in taking liberties with him out of their ignorance of the situation. They were more than glad to carefully guard their conduct after that. They weren't angered or offended in the least. Ācariya Mun said that such admirable behavior was truly commensurate with their lofty plane of existence.

This brief example should serve as food for thought about the mysterious phenomena existing beyond the range of the physical senses. Such phenomena are mysterious only to those unable to perceive them; they cease to be a mystery to those who can. This same principle applies to *dhammābhisamaya*.[2] So long as the Lord Buddha was the only person capable of comprehending the true nature of Dhamma, that Dhamma remained a mystery to everyone else. But once the Buddha's Arahant disciples comprehended that same Dhamma, its true nature ceased to be a mystery to them. So it is with the mysterious phenomena mentioned above: they cease to be a mystery to those who can perceive them.

At the time of the Lord Buddha, he and his Arahant disciples were the only ones capable of fully comprehending the mysterious nature of Dhamma, and the only ones capable of perceiving every type of mysterious external phenomena. Such things were not common knowledge. Many people at that time were incapable of perceiving these mysteries. At most, they had heard about such things, and, after consideration, they came to believe in them, being satisfied of their existence even though they hadn't perceived them directly. Others, who also considered the matter, refused to believe in these mysteries. This became a hindrance to their practice, preventing them from unreservedly following the Lord Buddha and his Arahant disciples. It is the same today: only those possessing an innate capacity to perceive these phenomena can uncover their mysteries; for the rest it's just hearsay. Whether we choose to believe in such things or not, there is unlikely to be any scientific evidence to prove their existence. I too might have been tempted to disbelieve, but I never found enough reason to be skeptical. So I have tried to remain impartial and simply write Ācariya Mun's story as he and his senior disciples related it to me.

Although my knowledge of these matters is not very astute, I must admit that my heart is full of immense faith and respect for Ācariya Mun. If someone whom I trusted were to come to me and suggest that I exchange my own life for that of Ācariya Mun, so he could return from the dead to teach again – pointing out that with my stupidity I could never possibly teach others the way – I would agree immediately, provided I could confirm what he said to be true. If he could guarantee that Ācariya Mun would return in exchange for my life, I would quickly arrange for my own death then and there without a second's delay. In truth, I've been quite troubled by my own stupidity for a long time now. Although no one has ever requested that I exchange my life for Ācariya Mun's return, I am constantly disappointed, that in writing his biography, I am unable to remember so many things he kindly recounted to me in such detail. Because of my poor memory, so much of what he said has been lost. I feel rather apologetic even about what I have been able to remember and write down. The little that has stuck in my memory is a bit like a pet animal that sticks to its owner, no matter what, and never runs away. In any case, what is written here can merely serve to whet the reader's appetite, as words alone cannot properly convey the mystery of these things.

In modern-day Thailand, Ācariya Mun was the person responsible for reviving an interest in experiencing these internal and external insights, though very few people could hope to perceive such mysterious phenomena nearly as well as he did. It's almost as though Ācariya Mun was practicing for the sake of sharp vision and clear understanding, while the rest of us were practicing for the sake of blind ignorance, and were thus never able to see as he did. The fact that so little has been written here about his unusual abilities is a result of my own failure to take enough interest in these matters when he explained them to us. Still, to my knowledge, none of his disciples possessing similar abilities ever contradicted what he said about them. Instead, they themselves bore witness to the existence of these mysterious things. Which should be enough of an indication to convince the rest of us, who are not sufficiently skilled in their perception, that these things do exist even though they are hidden from view. In the same way, the Lord Buddha was the first person to attain enlightenment and the first person to perceive many mysterious phenomena — attainments that his Arahant disciples were eventually able to duplicate, and bear witness to.

IN OUR PRESENT TIME, the sort of unusual phenomena that was perceptible to Ācariya Mun ceased to be mysterious to a few of his contemporaries who possessed an ability similar to his. This is evident in the case of another mysterious affair that, though quite intriguing, is likely to raise doubts among those of us who are self-confessed skeptics. While Ācariya Mun lived at Ban Nong Pheu monastery, an elderly, white-robed lay woman from the local community, who had great respect for him, came to the monastery and told him about an experience she had in meditation. As she sat in meditation late one night, her *citta* 'converged', dropping deeply into *samādhi*. Remaining absolutely still in that state for a time, she began to notice a very fine thread-like tentacle flowing out of her *citta* and away from her body. Her curiosity aroused, she followed the flow of her *citta* to find out where it had slipped away to, what it was doing, and why. In doing so she discovered that this subtle flow of consciousness was preparing to reserve a new birthplace in the womb of her own niece who lived in the same village — this despite the fact that she herself was still very much alive. This discovery shocked her, so she quickly brought her *citta* back to its base and withdrew from *samādhi*. She was greatly troubled for she knew that her niece was already one month pregnant.

The next morning she hurried off to the monastery and related the whole affair to Ācariya Mun. Listening quietly, many of the monks overheard what she said. Having never heard anything like it before, we were all puzzled by such a strange tale. I was especially interested in this affair and how Ācariya Mun would respond to the elderly lady. We sat perfectly still in breathless anticipation, all eyes on Ācariya Mun, waiting to hear his reply. He sat with eyes closed for about two minutes and then spoke to the elderly lady, telling her precisely what she should do.

"The next time your *citta* 'converges' into calm like that carefully examine the flow of your *citta*. Should you notice that the flow of your *citta* has again gone outward, then you must concentrate on severing that outward flow with intuitive wisdom. If you succeed in completely cutting it off with wisdom, it will not reappear in the future. But it's imperative that you carefully examine it and then fully concentrate on severing it with wisdom. Don't just do it halfheartedly, or else, I warn you, when you die you'll be reborn in your niece's womb. Remember well what I'm telling you. If you don't succeed in cutting off this outward flow of your *citta*, when you die you will surely be reborn in your niece's womb. I have no doubt about this."

Having received this advice, the elderly lady returned home. Two days later she came to the monastery looking bright and cheerful. It didn't require any special insight to tell from her expression that she had been successful. Ācariya Mun began questioning her the moment she sat down.

"What happened? Did you manage to prevent yourself from being reborn within your niece's womb despite being very much alive?"

"Yes, I severed that connection the very first night. As soon as my *citta* 'converged' into a state of complete calm, focusing my attention there, I saw exactly what I had seen before. So I concentrated on severing it with intuitive wisdom, just as you said, until it finally snapped apart. Again last night I examined it thoroughly and couldn't find anything—it had simply disappeared. Today I could not wait any longer. I just had to come and tell you about it."

"Well, that is a good example of how very subtle the *citta* can be. Only someone who practices meditation can become aware of such things—there is no other way. You nearly fell prey to the *kilesas*, which were preparing to shove you into your niece's womb without you being aware of it. It's a good thing you uncovered it in your meditation and managed to correct it in time."

Shortly after the flow of her aunt's *citta* to her womb had been severed, the woman's niece had a miscarriage, thus cutting that connection for good.

Soon the monks in the monastery began pondering two questions related to that incident: one to do with the rebirth of a person who has yet to die, the other to do with miscarriages. The old woman never told anyone in the village about what happened, so no one else knew about it. But having heard the whole affair as it was related to Ācariya Mun, the monks were well informed about the incident. This prompted several questions, so the monks asked Ācariya Mun for an explanation. To the question: "How could a person who has not yet died begin to take birth in a womb?", he answered as follows:

"She was merely preparing to take birth, the process had not been completed yet. It's quite common for preparations to be made before the work takes place. In this case, she was making the preparations but she had yet to finalize them. So it would be incorrect to say that a person can be reborn while she is still alive. But had she not been so perceptive, she would certainly have established a new home in her niece's womb."

To the second question: "Isn't severing the flow of the *citta*, connecting the elderly lady to her niece, tantamount to destroying a human life?", he answered as follows:

"What was there to destroy? She merely severed the flow of her *citta*. She didn't cut off the head of a living being. The true *citta* remained with that woman the whole time; it simply sent a tentacle out to latch on to her niece. As soon as she realized it and cut the outward flow of her *citta* to break that connection, that was the end of the matter."

The important point here was, Ācariya Mun did not contradict the old woman when she described how the flow of her *citta* had stolen out to reserve a place in her niece's womb. He did not dispute the truth of her experience, telling her that she was mistaken or that she should reconsider the nature of her assumptions. Instead, he responded by addressing her experience directly.

This story is very intriguing because there was in fact a good reason why her *citta* flowed out to her niece. The woman said she had always been very fond of her niece, keeping in constant touch and always doting on her. But she never suspected that anything mysterious lurked in their relationship, waiting to sneak out and cause her to be reborn as her niece's child. If Ācariya Mun had not helped to solve this problem, she would have ended up in that young woman's womb for sure.

Ācariya Mun stated that it is far beyond the average person's capabilities to fathom the *citta's* extraordinary complexity, making it very difficult for them to properly look after the *citta* and avoid jeopardizing their own well-being. Had that woman possessed no basis in *samādhi* meditation, she would have had no means of understanding the way the *citta* functions in relation to living and dying. Consequently, *samādhi* meditation is an effective means of dealing correctly with the *citta*. This is especially true at critical junctures in life when mindfulness and wisdom are extremely important aids to understanding and caring for the *citta*. When these faculties are well developed, they are able to effectively intervene and neutralize severe pain so that it does not overwhelm the heart at the time of death.

Death is an absolutely crucial time when defeat means, at the very least, a missed opportunity for the next life. For instance, someone who misses out at death may be reborn as an animal and be forced to waste time, stuck for the duration of that animal's life and suffering the agony of that lowly existence as well. If, however, the *citta* is skillful, having enough mindfulness to properly support it, then a human birth is the least one can expect. Over and above that, one may be reborn in a heavenly realm and enjoy a variety of celestial pleasures for a long time before being reborn eventually as a human being again. When reborn as a human being, the virtuous tendencies, that were developed in previous lives, are not forgotten. In this way, the power of an individual's inherent virtue increases gradually with each successive birth until the *citta* gains the strength and ability to look after itself. Dying then becomes merely a process by which an individual exchanges one bodily form for another, progressing from lower to higher, from grosser to ever more refined forms of existence — and eventually from the cycle of *saṁsāra* to the freedom of Nibbāna. This is similar to the way that the Lord Buddha and his Arahant disciples raised the quality of successive existences over many lifetimes, while steadily altering their spiritual makeup until there were no more changes to be made. Thus it is that a *citta* trained in virtue through each successive rebirth, is eventually transformed into the treasure of Nibbāna. All of which stems directly from the *citta* being trained gradually, step by step, in the way of virtue. For this reason, wise, intelligent men and women of all ages never tire of doing good deeds that redound to their spiritual credit, always enhancing their well-being now and in the future.

I FEEL I MUST APOLOGIZE to the reader for meandering so much in telling Ācariya Mun's story. I am trying very hard to present his biography in an orderly fashion, but my inherent forgetfulness has caused me to mix up the subject matter, putting first what should have come last, while putting last what should have come first. Although the story of Ācariya Mun's life has already drawn to a close, I am still tacking on afterthoughts that I failed to remember earlier on. Because of this tendency, there's still no end in sight. As you read along you'll see how unreliable I am at arranging events in their proper sequence.

ANOTHER INTRIGUING INCIDENT took place one morning at Ban Nong Pheu monastery when Ācariya Mun, rising from meditation, came out of his room and, before anyone spoke, immediately told the monks to look under his hut and tell him whether or not they could see the track of a large snake imprinted in the dirt there. He explained to them that the night before a great *nāga* had come to visit him and to listen to Dhamma. Before it left, he had asked it to leave some marks on the ground as a visible sign to show the monks in the morning. The monks informed him that they could see the track of a very large snake trailing out from underneath his hut and into the forest. There being no other tracks leading in, they could not tell how it had gotten there. The only visible track was the one going out from under his hut. The ground around his hut was swept clean so other tracks would have been easily noticed; but there were no others; only the one. Ācariya Mun told them they need not look for others because they wouldn't find them. He reiterated that the *nāga* left directly from his hut soon after he requested it to leave a mark on the ground below.

Had the monks seen the track first and then asked Ācariya Mun about it, the incident would not be so thought-provoking. The intriguing fact is that Ācariya Mun immediately broached the subject first, without being prompted; and sure enough, they then found the track of a large snake under his hut. Which means that, perceiving the *nāga* with his inner eye, he told it to leave some visible mark for the monks to see with their physical eyes, since their inner eyes were blind and they had no way to see the *nāga* when it came to visit.

Later when they had an opportunity, the monks asked Ācariya Mun whether the *nāgas* who visited him appeared in a serpent-like form or in some other form. He replied that one could never be sure with *nāgas* how they would appear.

"If they come for the purpose of listening to Dhamma, as they did last night, then they'll come in the form of a human being of a comparable social status to their own. A great *nāga* will come in the guise of a sovereign king surrounded by a royal entourage. Its comportment will be very regal in every respect; so when I discuss Dhamma with it I use royal terms of speech, just as I would with any royal personage. Its entourage resembles a delegation of government officials accompanying a crowned head of state. They all behave in a most polite, respectful manner — much more so than we humans do. They sit perfectly still when listening to Dhamma, showing no signs of restlessness. When discussing Dhamma with me, the leader always speaks on behalf of the whole group. Anyone with a question will refer it to the leader first. Then he asks me and I give a reply. Once I have answered all their questions, they all depart together."

HERE IS ANOTHER INCIDENT that we can take on faith about Ācariya Mun's extraordinary abilities, even though its true nature lies beyond our comprehension. A certain monk noticed that Ācariya Mun liked to smoke a particular brand of cigarettes,[3] so he told a lay supporter to use some money he had been offered to buy some for Ācariya Mun. The lay supporter complied; and the monk then offered them to Ācariya Mun. At first Ācariya Mun said nothing, probably because he was speaking on Dhamma at the time and did not have any opportunity to investigate the matter. But, the following morning when that monk went to see him, he ordered him to take the cigarettes away. He said that he would not smoke them since they were owned in common by many different people. The monk in question assured Ācariya Mun that the cigarettes belonged to him alone, since he had told a lay supporter to buy them with his own money the day before. He specifically had them purchased as an offering for Ācariya Mun, so they could not possibly be owned in common by many people. Ācariya Mun reiterated that he wanted them taken away. Being owned in common by many different people, the offering was not 'pure', so he did not want to smoke them.

Not daring to press the issue any further for fear of being rebuked, the monk was obliged to take back the cigarettes. He sent for the lay supporter who had purchased them for him and asked what had happened. It turned out that this layman had taken money belonging to many different monks, all of whom instructed him to buy some necessity or other. He had used the money left over from those purchases to buy the cigarettes. The monk asked him for the names of the monks whose money was involved, and then hurried off to find them. Once he explained about the mix-up with the cigarettes, each was more than happy to see them offered to Ācariya Mun. So the monk took the cigarettes and once more offered them to Ācariya Mun, confessing that he was really at fault for not questioning the layman thoroughly about the matter first. He acknowledged that Ācariya Mun was exactly right: the layman confirmed that he had taken money belonging to many different monks and put it all together to make various purchases. Since all the monks had been asked and were happy to share the offer of cigarettes to Ācariya Mun, he was offering them again. Ācariya Mun took them without saying a word and the matter was never mentioned again.

Later, that monk told some of his fellow monks how he first tried unsuccessfully to contradict Ācariya Mun, only to discover in the end that Ācariya Mun was exactly right. Some monks were puzzled as to how he could possibly have known whose money was involved in the cigarette purchase since he had never been informed about it. One monk at this informal meeting spoke up, protesting vigorously.

"Were he simply like the rest of us, obviously he wouldn't have known a thing. But it's precisely because he is so very different from us that we respect him and admire his superior wisdom. All of us gathered here under his tutelage realize that his capabilities are as different from ours as day is from night. Although I don't know much, I do know for certain that he is wiser and more knowledgeable than I am in every way. I see he is truly above reproach, which is why I have entrusted my life to him and his training methods with self-effacing humility. My heart is still full of *kilesas*, but those *kilesas* are very afraid of him, so they don't dare show their faces in his presence. I believe this is due to my willingness to surrender to him out of fear and respect, an attitude far more powerful than these vile *kilesas*, which naturally tend to oppose the teacher. Confronted by Ācariya Mun, they give up completely, not daring to display the same reckless abandon they do when I live with other teachers.

422

If we feel we cannot submit wholeheartedly to his judgment, then we do not belong here under his guidance. Should we persist in staying under those conditions, we will not benefit at all — only harm will come. What more need be said after this incident with the cigarettes."

Just an unwholesome train of thought in the middle of the night was enough to elicit a stern response from him the next morning. Meeting Ācariya Mun, the offending monk would be met by his sharp, penetrating gaze, a gaze that seemed to pierce the culprit and tear him to pieces. In a situation like that it was inadvisable to approach him or attempt to help him with his requisites, since he would strictly refuse to allow that monk to do anything for him. It was his indirect way of tormenting the monk's innate stubbornness. But it is strange how a monk initially felt quite chastened, yet somehow the effect didn't last long. He felt chastened at the moment he was stung by a severe reprimand; but later, when Ācariya Mun spoke to him in a normal tone of voice he would let down his guard and make the same mistake again. Despite having no intention of thinking in ways that were harmful to himself, he was simply unable to keep up with his own restive thoughts, which tended to jump from one thing to another quicker than a horde of wild monkeys. Later on, when the same monk went to see Ācariya Mun again, he could sense immediately that he was not welcome — just the look in Ācariya Mun's eyes was enough to make him extremely wary. Even with that, he had yet to fully learn his lesson. After a while, if the dangers of his way of thinking were not brought home again to him, he would inadvertently begin to befriend those harmful thoughts once more, entertaining them as if they were actually something worthwhile. That is why I say that, despite feeling quite chastened, somehow the effect didn't last long. When he not only felt chastened but also remained very conscious of the fear of revisiting those thoughts, then the positive effects were long-lasting. His mind remained cool, calm, and peaceful throughout. The next time he went to see Ācariya Mun, he needn't be so fearful about being taken to task.

My own mind tended to react in a very similar fashion. Being unable to rely on myself alone, I could not allow myself to stray far from my teacher. Living with him I was always fearful and on guard, which prevented my thoughts from deviating from the path of practice.

Becoming quickly aware when my mind did stray, I was able to pull it back in time to avoid harmful consequences.

I am absolutely convinced that Ācariya Mun could read my thoughts. Whether or not he could read other people's thoughts doesn't concern me so much. What does concerns me is how he used that ability to mitigate my own stubborn tendencies and teach me a good lesson. There was a time, when I first went to stay with him, that I thought, rather bizarrely: *They say that Ācariya Mun can read other people's thoughts, that he knows everything we're thinking. Can this really be true? If it is true, then he needn't take an interest in everything I'm thinking — I just want to know if he's aware of what I'm thinking right now. That would be enough. If he does know what I'm thinking at this moment, I will prostrate myself before him. That's all I ask of him.*

Coming face to face with him that evening I could hardly sit still. As his eyes glared directly at me without blinking, I felt in my heart that he was about to shout and point straight at me. When he began speaking to the assembled monks, I was so worried about being singled out and scolded for stubbornly testing him, that I had a hard time paying attention. Before long his voice began cracking like a whip as it rained down blows all around me, brushing past and narrowly missing me time and again until finally the whip lashed into the very core of my being. I became flushed as my body shook uncontrollably. The more my fear mounted, the more agitated I became until all traces of contentment vanished from my heart. While I sat there, his voice kept whipping and lashing at my heart, his words hitting home time and time again until by the end of his talk I could no longer bear the pressure. My heart gave in to him, thinking: *I thought as I did simply because I wanted to know if you could truly read other people's thoughts. I had no intention of disparaging your other virtuous qualities. I now acknowledge that you are a true master in every respect, so I wish to entrust my life to you until the day I die. Please have compassion for me and assist me with your teaching. Please don't become fed up with me because of this one incident.*

Once my heart completely surrendered to him, the fiery tone in his voice began to subside. Finally he concluded by elucidating a basic principle.

"Right and wrong both exist within yourself. Why don't you take an interest in looking there? What's the point in meddling in the rights and wrongs of others? Is this the type of thinking that will make you a good, skillful person? Even though you may find out how good or skillful someone else is, if you yourself are neither good nor skillful, then you will never be successful. If you want to know how good other people are, first you must thoroughly examine yourself; then, knowledge about others will come on its own. There is no need to test them to find out. Good, skillful people do not have to resort to such testing. A good person who is truly skillful in Dhamma can know about others without having to test them."

Ācariya Mun ended his talk to the monks on this note. I almost fainted at the time, sitting there soaked with sweat. Surrendering to him completely that night, I learned a lesson I've never forgotten — never again did I dare to test him out. Had I been as severely chastened about matters concerning my own practice as I was that night about matters concerning Ācariya Mun, then I would probably have transcended *dukkha* long ago. But, alas, I have never been able to chasten myself to such good effect, which really rankles me sometimes.

This was another issue that the monks discussed secretly among themselves at their informal meeting, which I also attended. Since this incident involved me personally, I've included it here with the story about the cigarettes to highlight the principle that the truth about the nature of Truth exists all around us everywhere, at all times — *akāliko*. All that's required is that we practice sincerely until we attain the Truth; then we will surely understand the nature of that Truth, the fullest extent of our understanding being conditioned only by the natural limitations of our inherent abilities. This includes the intrinsic truths, or *saccadhamma*, as well as all the various forms of extrinsic knowledge. Keep in mind also that people differ in the type and degree of the inherent good qualities they have developed through successive existences, as well as the spiritual goals they have variously set for themselves. But the primary results of *magga*, *phala*, and Nibbāna do not differ. These results are the same for everyone who attains them.

The Adventures of Ācariya Chob

Ācariya Mun was a teacher whose unique mode of practice will never be forgotten by those of us who were closely associated with him. Many such senior disciples of his are still alive today. Each *ācariya* differs somewhat in his inherent virtuous qualities, his specific mode of practice, and the special kinds of knowledge and understanding he has attained as a result. Earlier on I mentioned some of these *ācariyas* by name; but there are many others whose names were not identified. Nonetheless, it was always my intention to identify one of his senior disciples in particular, once the story of Ācariya Mun's life was completed, so that the reader could learn something of the way he practiced, the experiences he encountered, and the insights he gained. Ācariya Mun's disciples followed in his footsteps much in the same manner that the Lord Buddha's Arahant disciples followed in his, experiencing many difficulties along the way before ultimately attaining the same knowledge and understanding that their teacher had before them. The extent to which these monks met with spine-tingling, frightening situations in their practice environment depended largely on the nature of the places where they lived and traveled.

This brings me to one senior disciple of Ācariya Mun for whom I have a great amount of respect. Since this *ācariya's dhutanga* experiences are quite different from most of his contemporaries, I would like to present here some episodes from his practice as evidence of the possibility that some of the unusual external phenomena commonly reported at the time of the Buddha may still exist today. Certain incidents in the life of the Buddha — like the elephant who gave him protection and the monkey who offered him honeycomb — may have their modern-day parallels in some of this *ācariya's* experiences. To demonstrate the authenticity of the episodes I'm about to relate, I shall identify him by name. He is Ācariya Chob[4] who, having been ordained as a monk for many years, is now about 70 years old. He has always preferred living in remote forest and mountain areas and still does so to this day. Since he likes to trek through such wilderness areas at night, he's constantly encountering nocturnal creatures like wild tigers.

Leaving Lomsak in Phetchabun province one afternoon, he started trekking north toward Lampang in the province of Chiang Mai. As he was about to enter a large tract of forest, he met with some local villagers who advised him, with obvious concern, to spend the night near their village and then continue on the next morning. They warned him that the forest he was about to enter was vast, so there was no way someone entering it in the afternoon could get through to the other side before dark. Those who ended up stranded in this forest after dark invariably became food for the huge tigers that roamed there at night. Since it was already afternoon, he had no chance to hike through it in time. Once darkness fell, the tigers began roaming around looking for something to eat, and they considered any person that they happened on as just another source of food. Since no one ever escaped from them alive, the villagers were fearful that Ācariya Chob would meet the same fate. It was already well after noon, so they did not want him to enter the forest. They told him that a notice had been posted, warning travelers about this 'forest of *yakkhas*' to keep them from being eaten by those monsters. Being curious, Ācariya Chob asked what *yakkhas* they were talking about. He had read old accounts about such creatures but had never actually seen one. They told him that it was just their way of referring to those huge, striped tigers who devoured anyone failing to make it through the forest by nightfall. They invited him to return with them to their village and spend the night there. He could then have a meal the next morning and continue on his journey.

Telling them that he intended to continue walking anyway, Ācariya Chob refused to return to the village. Concerned for his safety, they insisted that, no matter how fast he walked, by having started this late in the day he could not possibly reach the other side before nightfall and would end up stranded in the middle of that vast forest. But, determined to press ahead, he refused to be deterred. They asked him if he was afraid of tigers. He acknowledged that he was but said it was irrelevant: he intended to go in any case. They insisted that the tigers there never ran away from people. If he encountered one, he was sure to lose his life. If he wanted to avoid being attacked by man-eating tigers, he should wait until morning to proceed further. He replied that should his *kamma* dictate that he was destined to be eaten by tigers, then that's the way it would be. If, however, he was destined to continue living, then the tigers wouldn't trouble him.

Taking leave of the villagers, Ācariya Chob resumed his journey, feeling no qualms about dying. No sooner had he begun to enter the forest than he noticed that both sides of the trail he was on were covered with claw prints, where tigers had been scratching in the earth. He saw piles of tiger scat scattered all along the trail — some of it old, some of it quite fresh. As he walked along doing meditation practice, he observed these telltale signs, but he wasn't afraid. By the time he had reached the very middle of the forest, darkness had closed in all around him.

Suddenly, he heard the roar of a huge tiger coming up behind him, followed by the roar of another huge tiger moving toward him, both calling out to each other as they quickly closed in on him. The roaring sounds from both directions grew closer and louder until suddenly both tigers emerged from the darkness at the same moment — one, merely six feet in front of him and the other a mere six feet behind. The sound of their roars had become deafening. Seeing the gravity of the situation, Ācariya Chob stood transfixed in the middle of the trail. He saw that the tiger in front of him was crouched and ready to pounce. Glancing behind him, he saw that the tiger there, too, was crouched and ready to pounce. Fear arose in him then, for he was sure that this signaled the end of his life. Petrified with fear, he stood stock-still, rooted to the spot. But his mindfulness remained strong, so he concentrated his mind intently, and that prevented him from panicking. Even though he might be killed by those tigers, he would not allow his mind to falter. With that resolve, he turned the focus of his attention away from the tigers and back within himself, thus excluding everything external from his awareness. At that moment, his *citta* 'converged', dropping quickly into a deep state of *samādhi*. As this occurred, the knowledge arose in him that the tigers could not possibly harm him. After that, everything in the world simply vanished, including himself and the tigers. Experiencing no physical sensations whatsoever, he was totally unaware of what then happened to his body. All awareness of the external world, including his physical presence, had utterly disappeared. Which meant that awareness of the tigers had also disappeared. His *citta* had 'converged' completely, dropping to the very base of *samādhi*, and many hours passed before it withdrew from that state.

When his *citta* finally withdrew, he found that he was still standing in the same position as before. His umbrella and alms bowl were still slung over his shoulder, and in one hand he still carried a candle lantern, which had long since gone out. So he lit another candle and looked around for the tigers; but they were nowhere to be found. He had no idea where they had disappeared to.

Withdrawing from *samādhi* that night, he felt no fear whatsoever. His heart was full of such remarkable courage that even if hundreds of tigers appeared at that moment, he would have remained completely unperturbed; for, he had seen with absolute clarity the extraordinary power of the *citta*. He felt amazed to have escaped the gaping jaws of those two tigers – a sense of amazement defying description. Standing there alone in the forest, Ācariya Chob was suddenly overcome by a feeling of compassionate affection for the two tigers. In his mind they became friends who, having provided him with a lesson in Dhamma, then miraculously disappeared. He no longer feared them – in fact, he actually missed them.

Ācariya Chob described both tigers as being enormous: each was about the size of a racehorse, though its body length well exceeded that of a horse. Their heads would easily have measured sixteen inches from ear to ear. He had never in his life seen tigers that were so grotesquely large. Consequently, when he first saw them he stood petrified, stiff as a corpse. Fortunately, his mindfulness remained strong throughout. Later, after his *citta* had withdrawn from *samādhi*, he felt joyful and serene. He knew then that he could go wherever he wished without fearing anything in the world. Believing wholeheartedly that the *citta*, when fully integrated with Dhamma, reigns supreme in the universe, he was convinced that nothing could possibly harm him.

With this serene Dhamma filling his heart, he resumed his trek through the forest, practicing walking meditation as he hiked along. His two tiger friends were still fresh in his mind and he often thought about them. He felt that, were he to see them again, he could easily walk up and playfully stroke their backs as if they were pets, though it's questionable whether they would ever allow it.

Ācariya Chob walked the rest of that night in peace and solitude, buoyed by a joyful heart. When day finally broke, he still had not reached the end of the forest. It wasn't until nine o'clock that morning that he emerged from the forest to arrive at a village settlement. Putting down his belongings, he put on his outer robes and walked through the village for alms. When the inhabitants saw him entering the village with his alms bowl, they called out to one another to come and offer him food. Having placed food in his bowl, some of them followed him back to where he had left his belongings and asked where he had come from. These being forest people who knew the ways of the forest, when they saw him emerging from that vast wilderness at an unusual hour, they wanted to questioned him about it. He told them that, having begun at the southern end, he trekked all night through the forest without sleeping and now intended to continue wandering north. Astounded by this statement, they wanted to know how it was possible, for it was common knowledge that passing through there at night meant almost certain death in the jaws of a tiger. How had he managed to avoid the tigers? Had he come across no tigers during the night? Ācariya Chob admitted he had met some tigers, but said he hadn't been bothered by them. The villagers were reluctant to believe him because the ferocious man-eating tigers roaming that forest were renowned for waiting to ambush anyone caught there overnight. Only after he had explained the actual circumstances of his encounter with the tigers did they finally believe him, realizing that his miraculous powers were a special case, and not applicable to ordinary people.

Whether it is the spiritual path of the heart or the physical path through the forest, ignorance of the path we are on, the distances that must be traveled, and the potential dangers along the way are all obstacles to our progress. So we must depend on a knowledgeable guide to ensure our safety. We, who are journeying along the path toward safe, happy, prosperous circumstances now and in the future, should always keep this in mind. Just because we've always thought and acted in a certain way, we must not carelessly assume that it is necessarily the right way. In truth, our habitual ways of thinking and acting usually tend to be mistaken, continuously leading most of us down the wrong path.

During his life as a *dhutanga* monk, Ācariya Chob had many close encounters with wild animals. Once while wandering through Burma,[5] he stopped to do his practice in a cave frequented by tigers. Although these huge beasts roamed freely through the area while he lived there, they never harmed him. So he never dreamed that one would actually come looking for him. But then one afternoon at about five o'clock, as he was getting up from his meditation, his eyes glanced up to the mouth of the cave to see a huge, striped tiger approaching the entrance. It was an enormous animal and very frightening-looking; but Ācariya Chob remained unperturbed — probably because he was so accustomed to seeing these creatures wherever he went. Peering into the cave, the tiger spied him just as he was looking up at it. Instead of showing alarm at the sight of him or roaring out in a terrifying manner, it just stood there passively, as though it were a house pet. It showed no signs of fear and made no threatening gestures. Looking casually about, the tiger leapt onto a large, flat rock at the entrance to the cave, about eighteen feet from where Ācariya Chob stood. Sitting nonchalantly, licking its paws, it seemed uninterested in him, though it knew perfectly well he was in the cave. It sat there calmly with the air of a pet dog sitting in front of the house. Growing tired, it flopped down, stretched out its legs, and lay there comfortably just like a pet dog, continuing to lick itself as though feeling right at home.

Since Ācariya Chob's meditation track was right in front of the cave, he didn't dare go out and walk there — the proximity of the huge tiger made him feel a bit nervous. His uneasiness was compounded by the fact that he had never before seen a wild tiger behave like a household pet in this way. So he continued his sitting meditation on a small bamboo platform inside the cave, though with no sense of fear that the tiger might try to harm him there. Once in a long while it casually glanced at him in the nonchalant manner of an old friend, while lying contentedly with no evident intention of moving. Ācariya Chob expected it to eventually wander off, but it showed no interest in going anywhere.

At first, Ācariya Chob was sitting outside his mosquito net; but once darkness fell he moved inside the net and lit a candle. The tiger remained impassive as the candlelight illuminated the cave. It continued lying contentedly on the rock until late into the night, when Ācariya Chob finally lay down to take a rest. Awaking at about three a.m., he lit a candle only to find the tiger reclining impassively as before. After washing his face, he sat in meditation until the first light of dawn; then he rose from his seat and put away his mosquito net. Glancing up, he saw the tiger still stretched out comfortably, looking like some oversized pet dog in front of its master's house. Eventually, the time for his daily almsround arrived. The only way out of the cave went straight past the tiger. He wondered what its reaction would be when he walked by. As he put on his robes he noticed the tiger looking at him with soft, gentle eyes like a dog looking wistfully at its master. Since he had no other alternative, he would have to pass within several feet of it on his way out. When he was ready, he approached the mouth of the cave and began speaking to the tiger:

"It's now time for my morning almsround. Like all other creatures in this world, I am hungry and need to fill my stomach. If it's okay with you, I'll go out and get some food. Please be kind enough to let me pass by. If you want to stay on here, that's fine with me. Or, if you prefer to go off searching for something to eat, that's all right too."

The tiger lay there listening to him with its head cocked like a dog listening to the voice of its master. As Ācariya Chob walked past, it watched him with a soft, gentle gaze as if to say: Go ahead, there's no need to be afraid. I've only come here to protect you from danger.

Ācariya Chob walked down to the local village for his almsround, but he didn't tell anyone about the tiger for fear they might try to kill it. Returning to the cave he looked at the place where the tiger had been, but there was no longer any sign of it. He had no idea where it had gone. During the remainder of his stay in that cave, it never came to visit him again.

Ācariya Chob suspected that the tiger was no ordinary forest creature but rather a creation of the *devas*,[6] which is why it appeared so tame and unthreatening the entire time it was with him. He felt a lot of affection for it and so missed its presence for many days thereafter. He thought it might return from time to time to see him, but it never did. Although he heard the sounds of tigers roaring every night, he couldn't tell whether his friend was among them. In any case, the whole forest was teeming with tigers. A faint-hearted person could never have lived there, but he was not affected by such dangers. In fact, the tame-looking tiger, who kept watch over him all night, made him feel more affection than fear. Ācariya Chob said that experience increased his belief in Dhamma in quite a special way.

ĀCARIYA CHOB SPENT five years living in Burma, where he learned to speak Burmese as fluently as if it were his own language. The reason he eventually returned to Thailand concerned the Second World War. The English and the Japanese were fighting each other all up and down the countryside — in the towns, the villages, and even in the mountains. During that period, the English accused the Thai people of collaborating with the Japanese.[7] Consequently, they searched for Thais in Burma, hunting them down with a vengeance. They summarily executed any Thai they found inside Burma, regardless of whether it was a man, a women, or a monk — no exceptions were made.

The villagers that Ācariya Chob depended on for his daily alms loved and respected him; so when they saw the English soldiers being very meddlesome, they became concerned for his safety. They hurriedly took him deep into the mountains and hid him in a place where they decided the English would not be able to find him. But eventually a contingent of English soldiers did come across him there, just as he was giving a blessing to a group of villagers. The villagers were crestfallen. Questioned by the soldiers, Ācariya Chob told them that he had been living in Burma for a long time and was never involved in politics. He said that being a monk, he knew nothing about such matters. The villagers spoke up in his defense to say that, unlike lay people, monks had nothing to do with the war, so it would be wrong to try to involve him in any way. They warned the soldiers that, should they take any action against him, it would amount to hurting the feelings of the Burmese people who had done nothing wrong. It would unnecessarily damage relations with the local population, which would be a grave mistake. They assured the soldiers that he had been living there since long before the war began and knew nothing about international affairs. Even though their country was now in a state of war, the Burmese people did not view this monk as a threat of any kind. Thus, if the soldiers were to harm him, it would be tantamount to harming the whole of the Burmese nation. The Burmese people could never condone such an action.

The contingent of English soldiers stood talking among themselves about what to do with Ācariya Chob. After discussing his case for about half an hour, they told the villagers to quickly take him away to another location, for if another army patrol came and spotted him, there could be trouble. Should their pleas be rejected the next time, his life might well be in danger. While the soldiers were viewing him as an enemy, Ācariya Chob sat quietly, extending forth thoughts of loving kindness and recollecting the virtues of the Buddha, the Dhamma, and the Sangha.

When the soldiers had gone, the villagers took him deeper into the mountains, telling him not to come down to the village for almsround. Instead, each morning they secretly brought food for him to eat. From that day on, patrols of English troops regularly came to bother the villagers. Soon patrols were coming daily to ask the whereabouts of the Thai monk, and it became increasingly obvious that he would be killed if they found him. As the situation worsened, the villagers became more and more concerned for his safety. Finally, they decided to send him back to Thailand by way of a remote forest trail that passed through thick mountainous terrain. This trail was known to be safe from incursions by English patrols. They gave him detailed instructions on how to proceed, warning him to stick to the trail no matter what happened. Even if he found the trail overgrown in places, he was not to attempt a different route. It was an old footpath used for generations by the hill tribes that eventually led all the way to the Thai border.

Once he had these instructions, he began walking. He walked all day and all night without sleeping or eating, drinking only water. With great difficulty he made his way through this dense wilderness region teeming with all manner of wild animals. Everywhere he looked he saw tiger and elephant tracks. He feared he would never survive his flight from Burma; he was constantly worried that he might make one wrong turn on the trail and end up hopelessly lost in that vast wilderness.

On the morning of the fourth day of his trek to the Thai border, something incredibly amazing happened to Ācariya Chob. Please reserve judgment on this incident until you have read the whole story. As he crested the top of a mountain ridge, he was so extremely hungry and exhausted that he thought he couldn't possibly go on. By that time he had been walking for three days and three nights without any sleep or food. The only breaks he had taken were short periods of rest to alleviate the physical stress of such an arduous journey. While dragging his enfeebled body over the ridge, a thought arose in his mind: *I have walked the entire distance to this point risking my life with every breath I take, yet somehow I'm still alive. Since starting out I've yet to see a single human habitation where I could request alms food to sustain my life. Am I now going to die needlessly for lack of a single meal? I've suffered enormous hardships on this trip — at no other time in my life have I suffered so much. Is it all going to be in vain? Have I escaped war, a sphere of death everyone fears, only to die of starvation and the hardships of this trek? If, as the Lord Buddha declared, there really are devas in the upper realms, possessing divine eyes and ears that can truly perceive at great distances, can't they see this monk who is about ready to die at any moment? I do believe what the Lord Buddha said. But are the devas, who have received kind assistance from so many monks, from the Buddha's time until the present day, really so heartless as this? If devas are not in fact hardhearted, then let them demonstrate their kindness to this dying monk so that their pure, celestial qualities can be admired.*

No sooner had this thought occurred to Ācariya Chob than something incredibly strange and amazing happened. It was almost impossible to believe. As he staggered along that remote mountain trail, he saw an elegantly dressed gentleman, who bore no resemblance to the hill tribes people of that region, quietly sitting at the side of the path, holding a tray of food offerings up to his head. It seemed impossible! Ācariya Chob was so flabbergasted by what he saw that he got goose flesh and his hair stood on end. He forgot all about being hungry and exhausted. He was wholly astounded to see a kind-looking gentleman sitting beside the path about twenty-five feet ahead waiting to offer him food. As he approached, the gentleman spoke to him:

"Please, sir, rest here awhile and eat something to relieve your hunger and fatigue. Once you've regained your strength, you can continue on. You're sure to reach the other side of this vast wilderness some time today."

Ācariya Chob stopped, put down what few requisites he was carrying, and prepared his alms bowl to receive the food that the gentleman was offering. He then stepped forward and accepted the food. To his amazement, as soon as the food items were placed in his bowl, a sweet fragrance seemed to permeate the whole surrounding forest. The amount of food he was offered by the gentleman was exactly the right amount to satisfy his needs. And it had an exquisite taste that was absolutely indescribable. This might seem like an extravagant exaggeration, but the truth of what his senses perceived at that moment was so amazing as to be virtually impossible to describe.

When the gentleman finished putting food in his bowl, Ācariya Chob asked him where his house was located. He said that he had been walking for three nights and four days now but had yet to see a single human habitation. The gentleman pointed vaguely upward, saying his house was over there. Ācariya Chob asked what had prompted him to prepare food and then wait along that trail to offer it to a monk. How had he known in the first place that there would be a monk coming to receive it? The gentleman smiled slightly, but didn't speak. Ācariya Chob gave him a blessing, after which the gentleman told him that he would have to leave since his house was some distance away. He appeared to be quite different from the average person in that he was remarkably dignified while speaking very little. He looked to be a middle-aged man of medium height with a radiant complexion and behavior that was impeccably self-composed. Having taken his leave, he stood up and began to walk away. As he was obviously an unusual man, Ācariya Chob observed him carefully. He walked about twenty-five feet, stepped behind a tree, and disappeared from sight. Ācariya Chob stared at the tree waiting for him to reappear on the other side, but he never did. This was even more puzzling; so he stood up and walked over to the tree to have a closer look — but no one was there. Had someone been in that area, he would definitely have seen him. But looking around in all directions he saw no one. The strange circumstances of the man's disappearance surprised him all the more.

Still puzzled, Ācariya Chob walked back and began to eat his food. Tasting the various foods he had been given, he found them to be unlike the human cuisine that he was used to eating. All the food was wonderfully fragrant and flavorful, and perfectly suited to his bodily needs in every possible way. He had never eaten anything like it. The food's exquisite taste permeated throughout every pore in his body which had so long been oppressed by hunger and fatigue. In the end, he wasn't sure if it was his extreme hunger that made it taste so good or the celestial nature of the food itself. He ate every last morsel of what was offered, and it turned out to be exactly the right amount to fill his stomach. Had there been even a little extra, he would have been unable to finish it.

Having eaten, he set off again feeling incredibly robust and radiant, not at all like the person who was at death's door a short while before. Walking along he became so absorbed in thinking about the mysterious gentleman that he forgot about the rigors of the journey, the distance he had to walk, and whether or not he was on the right trail. As evening fell, he emerged from the other side of that vast wilderness just as the mysterious gentleman had predicted. He crossed the border into Thailand with the same feeling of joy that he had been experiencing all day. The mental and physical distress that had tormented him earlier in his journey had disappeared after his morning repast. When he finally crossed into Thailand, the land of his birth, he knew for certain that he was going to live.

He said that the strange gentleman he met was surely a devic being and not one of the local inhabitants. Think about it: From the point where he met that gentleman to the point where he entered Thailand, he encountered not a single human habitation. The whole affair was very puzzling. Ordinarily, one would expect to meet with at least a small settlement of some sort along the whole of that route through Burma.

As it turned out, his evasion of the army patrols had been so successful that he had encountered neither people nor food. It had been so successful that he had nearly starved to death.

Ācariya Chob said that his almost miraculous escape from death in that vast wilderness caused him to suspect the involvement of divine intervention. Although the wilderness he passed through teemed with dangerous wild animals like tigers, elephants, bears, and snakes, he never encountered them. The only animals he came across were harmless ones. Normally, someone trekking through such a wilderness would encounter dangerous wild animals daily, especially tigers and elephants. And there was a very strong possibility that that person might be killed by one of those savage beasts. Surely his own safe passage can be attributed to the miraculous properties of Dhamma, or miraculous intervention by the *devas,* or both. The villagers who helped him escape were very concerned that he would not survive the threat posed by dangerous wild animals, but there had been no other choice. Had he remained in Burma, the threat posed by the war and the English soldiers was even more imminent. So opting for the lesser of two evils, they had helped him escape from the land of bloodthirsty people, hoping that he would survive the savage beasts and enjoy a long life. Which is why he was forced to make the perilous trek that nearly cost him his life.

Please contemplate these mysterious happenings for yourself. I have recorded the stories just as I heard them. But being reluctant to pass judgment on them alone, I would prefer that you come to your own conclusions. Still, I cannot help but feel amazed that something so seemingly impossible actually occurred. Due to the rigorous nature of Ācariya Chob's *dhutanga kammaṭṭhāna* lifestyle, he has had many other similar experiences, for he always prefers living and practicing in remote wilderness areas. Since he lives deep in the forest, few people dare to go visit him, so his involvement with society is very limited.

Conclusion

Practicing monks in the lineage of Ācariya Mun tend to prefer living in mountains and forests. Leading the way in this lifestyle himself, Ācariya Mun encouraged all his disciples to do the same. By nature, he was fond of praising the virtues of life in the wilds. He said the reason he preferred such places was that knowledge and understanding of Dhamma was much more likely to arise while he lived in remote forest areas than while staying in congested ones. Crowded, congested places are hardly conducive to calm and contentment in the practice of Dhamma. Even the Dhamma that his disciples are teaching today was earned practicing at the threshold of death in that same wilderness environment.

In the physical sense, Ācariya Mun died many years ago. Nevertheless, disciples of his who naturally possess the meditative ability to perceive such phenomena still regularly experience visual images of him arising spontaneously in their meditation, just as if he were still alive. Should one of them experience a problem in his practice, a visual image of Ācariya Mun will appear to him while he is meditating, demonstrating effective ways to solve the problem. He appears to be sitting there in person giving advice, much in the same way that past Arahants came and instructed him on the various occasions I mentioned earlier. When a monk, whose practice has reached a certain level, finds a specific problem that he cannot solve himself, a visual image of Ācariya Mun appears and advises him on that very question, and then disappears on its own. After that, the monk takes the teaching that Ācariya Mun has given him, analyzes it carefully and uses it to the best of his ability. And thus he gains new insights in his meditation practice.

Those monks who are naturally inclined to perceive external phenomena possess the necessary psychic ability to receive such advice on their practice. This is known as 'listening to Dhamma by way of *nimittas* appearing in meditation'. That is, the teacher presents his teaching in the form of a *nimitta*, while the disciple understands that teaching as he perceives the *nimitta*. This may seem rather mysterious to those who have never heard about it or experienced it for themselves. Some people may reject such psychic communication out of hand as being sheer nonsense; but in truth, it does occur. Practicing monks having a natural psychic inclination perceive various external phenomena in the same manner. However, this talent is not shared by all practicing monks. Rather, individuals possessing this capability are special cases, meaning they have previously developed the specific virtuous qualities suited to such psychic achievements. For instance, the Buddha and the Arahants appeared in Ācariya Mun's meditation as *nimittas*, so he was able to hear their teachings in that way. Similarly, disciples of Ācariya Mun, who possessed similar psychic tendencies, were able to perceive *nimittas* of him, or of the Buddhas and the Arahants, and so hear their teachings. In principle, it can be compared to the *nimitta* that the Lord Buddha used to teach his mother when she resided in the *Tāvatiṁsa* heavenly realm. But the Lord Buddha constitutes a very exceptional case, one which people consent to believe in far more readily than that of someone less exalted, even though both share the same causal basis — which makes it difficult to further elaborate on this matter.

Being reluctant to write any more on this subject, I leave it up to those practicing meditation to discover this knowledge for themselves — *paccattaṁ* — which is better than relying on someone else's explanation, and far more certain as well. I am wholly convinced of this. No matter what is being discussed, without having the ability to perceive such things directly with our own senses, we will be reluctant to simply rely on another person's description of them. Although that person may provide us with accurate information, there will always be certain aspects that we are bound to doubt or take exception to, notwithstanding the fact that the person is compassionately explaining the matter to us with a pure heart. The problem is: we ordinary people are not pure ourselves so we tend to balk at what we hear, hesitant to accept someone else's judgment. So it is better that we experience these things for ourselves. Only then can we truly accept their validity. Then we needn't annoy others with our remonstrations. As the Buddha said: *All of us must accept the consequences of our own actions. We shoulder the burden of pain and suffering and enjoy the fruits of happiness that we have created for ourselves.* This is absolutely right and beautifully simple too.

THE STORY OF ĀCARIYA MUN is a splendid story. Beginning from the time he was still in lay life, he demonstrated the characteristics of a true sage. Always conducting himself in a safe, steady manner, he was never known to have caused any disgrace or undue trouble to his parents or relatives. Having ordained as a monk, he strove relentlessly to develop firm principles within himself and so became a spiritual refuge to monks, novices, and lay people for the rest of his long life. He was a man whose life was a bright, shining example from beginning to end – a life of virtue that should definitely be considered an excellent model for people in this day and age. His meditation methods were extremely rigorous, his spiritual development of the highest caliber. The *kilesas* never had a chance to overrun his heart, for he systematically destroyed them until not a single one remained. So much so that he was acknowledged by his close disciples and those revering him to be a present-day Arahant.

The spiritual benefits that he bestowed upon the world were always in line with the principles of mindfulness and wisdom – from the initial stages of practice to the very highest level, his teaching never deviated from the true way of Dhamma. Internally, he was very astute at judging the character and temperament of his students. Externally, he was very clever in the way he gave assistance to people in every strata of society, from simple hill tribes people to urban intellectuals. Even when nearing death, he did not abandon his natural compassion for others. When a student with a problem in his practice went to seek assistance, he kindly made an effort to discuss the issue until all doubts had been allayed. All his disciples received some piece of farewell advice from him to carry in their hearts forever. Having been fortunate enough to meet such a supreme individual and having wholeheartedly accepted him as their one true refuge, they were confident that they had not lived their lives in vain. Many of his senior disciples were able to establish themselves firmly in the principles of Dhamma. By virtue of their own spiritual development, they also became *ācariyas* passing on the teaching to their students, thus assuring that the Supreme Noble wealth of the Lord Buddha does not disappear. Many of his more junior disciples are still alive today serving as a strong base for the *sāsana* into the foreseeable future. Though they may not openly demonstrate it, many of them possess excellent Dhamma credentials. Every one of these monks was inspired by the magic quality of Ācariya Mun's compassionate teaching.

As a teacher, Ācariya Mun was unrivaled in his ability to help develop the spiritual potential of members of the lay community, enabling them to grasp the significance of Dhamma and the basic moral principles of cause and effect, which are universal principles governing the world. Spiritual development means developing the one factor that is absolutely central to the well-being of the world. The world comes to ruin only if people's spiritual values come to ruin first. When spiritual values deteriorate, then everything people do becomes just another means of destroying the world and subverting Dhamma. When people's hearts are well trained in spiritual values, their speech and actions become an effective means of promoting the world's prosperity; so inevitably Dhamma flourishes as well. How could people who have sincerely developed the way of Dhamma in their hearts possibly turn around and act ruinously, showing no compunction? Such behavior would be unnatural to them — unless of course they simply memorize the principles of Dhamma, reciting them by heart without ever making an effort to develop those spiritual values within their hearts.

Ācariya Mun invariably made a deep impression on the people who met him. Those who sincerely respected him were willing to offer their lives to him — unconditionally. Whether it be matters of good or matters of evil, once such concerns are embraced and taken to heart they then exert a powerful influence on that person, one no other force in the world can match. Were this not the case, people would not have the self-assurance to act upon their intentions — be they good, or evil. It is precisely because they take such matters to heart that they can act boldly upon them. Having assumed this attitude, the outcome becomes inevitable.

This was especially evident among practicing monks who revered Ācariya Mun. By taking the Dhamma that he taught to heart, those monks became uncompromising in their respect for him. The power of their belief in him was so strong that they would even dare to sacrifice their precious lives for him. But although they could have given their lives without difficulty, their strong faith in him was never sacrificed. It was this extraordinary magnetic quality he possessed that so attracted people and engendered such veneration in them, both during his lifetime and after he passed away.

As for myself, well, I have always been a rather hopeless individual, so my sentiments are very different from most people's. Although over twenty years has elapsed since his death, to me it feels as if Ācariya Mun passed away only yesterday. And though his body died at that time, his *citta* seems never to have passed away. I feel he is always here with me, helping me continually.

AS A CONCLUDING CHAPTER to his biography, I would like to present a representative sample of the teachings Ācariya Mun gave, beginning with comments he made at the onset of his final illness and ending with his last instructions to the monks — teachings which have continued to make a profound impression on me ever since. The Dhamma he presented to the monks at the start of his illness took the form of a warning to them that the illness had begun a process of uprooting the very source of his physical existence, including all his bodily functions, which were destined to steadily deteriorate, break down, and finally fail altogether. He began:

"I have been investigating matters concerning the life and death of this body for nearly sixty years now and I have found nothing in the physical *khandha* that is worthy of the least attachment or that would cause me to regret its passing away. I ceased to have doubts about such things the moment I realized Dhamma's Supreme Truth. Whether they exist inside of the body or outside of it, all material substances are composed of the same physical elements. They gradually break down and decompose with each passing day, and thus are always reverting back to their fundamental natural state. Although we imagine the body belonging to us, in truth it is just a conglomeration of physical elements that are commonly found everywhere on this earth.

"What most concerns me now is my students who have come here from all over the country. I worry that you will not have gained a firm basis of Dhamma in your hearts before I pass away. That is why I have always warned you against being complacent about the *kilesas*, which are the source of an endless procession of births and deaths. Never assume that the *kilesas* are insignificant, or somehow harmless, and thus fail to tackle them seriously while the time is still right. Once death overtakes you, it will be impossible to take any action against them. Don't say I didn't warn you!

"Every human being and animal on this planet suffers *dukkha* as a matter of course. Don't misunderstand the cause of this suffering: it is caused by those very *kilesas* that you seem to think are so insignificant and harmless. I have examined the origins of birth, death and suffering with all the mindfulness and wisdom at my disposal. Only one cause induces the hearts of living beings to seek a place in the realm of birth and death experiencing various degrees of pain and suffering, and that cause is the *kilesas* that people everywhere overlook. In truth, they are the principal instigators. All of you who have *kilesas* ruling over your hearts, what is your attitude? Do you also consider them unimportant? If so, then no matter how long you live under my guidance, you will always be like the ladle in a pot of delicious stew. If you want to be able to taste the flavor of that stew, then you must listen with keen interest to the Dhamma that I teach you and fully take it to heart. Don't act like ladles and obstruct my teaching by failing to appreciate its value. Otherwise, you will live and die having nothing of value to show for it. Which is worse than being animals, whose flesh and skins are at least of some value when they die. Heedless people are always worthless — alive or dead.

"Since this illness began, I have reminded you constantly that I am slowly dying, day by day. When a person transcends *dukkha* he is perfectly satisfied in every respect, and so he dies free of all concerns. Forever unblemished, he has nothing further to attain, for nothing is missing from his sense of perfect satisfaction. But someone who dies while under the influence of the *kilesas*, which are never satisfied, will find the same sense of dissatisfaction clinging to his heart wherever he is reborn. The stronger the influence of the *kilesas*, the more intense the *dukkha* he will suffer. Don't imagine this or that realm of existence will be a pleasant, joyful place to be reborn in when you die. Such thoughts are merely an indication that craving and dissatisfaction are disturbing your hearts before you've even died. Which means you are still unwilling to view the *kilesas* as enemies that constantly stir up trouble in your hearts. With that attitude, where will you ever find happiness and contentment? If you cannot rid yourself of the desire to be reborn in the future, then I am at a loss as to how I can help you.

"Monks who have yet to develop the calm and concentration of *samādhi* within themselves should not expect to find peace and contentment in the world; instead, they will encounter only the frustration that is hidden inside their agitated hearts. You must hurry to remedy this situation now by developing an effective means to counter such agitation. By being diligent, courageous, and persevering in your struggle with the *kilesas* — which are always antagonistic to Dhamma — you will soon discover the peaceful nature of genuine tranquillity arising in your hearts. With persistence, results will come quickly; especially when compared with the endless amount of time you have spent wandering through *saṁsāra* from one type of existence to another.

"The teachings of the Lord Buddha are all designed for the purpose of helping those who believe what he taught to gradually transcend *dukkha*, step by step, until they finally reach the stage where they will never again return to this world of repeated birth and death. Those who desire not to return to birth must analyze every aspect of existence in the entire universe, from the grossest to the most subtle, in terms of the three basic characteristics of all existence — *anicca, dukkha,* and *anattā* — and use wisdom to thoroughly investigate each aspect until all doubts have been eliminated. Once that happens, even strong attachments[8] that are difficult to break will evaporate and disappear in the blink of an eye. All that's needed to cut through those oppressive doubts is wisdom that is sharp and incisive. In all the three worlds of existence there is no more effective, up-to-date means for confronting the *kilesas* than the combination of mindfulness and wisdom. The Lord Buddha and all the Arahants employed mindfulness and wisdom to counteract every kind of *kilesa* — no other means was used. The Lord Buddha himself endorsed the unrivaled supremacy of mindfulness and wisdom as weapons for combating the *kilesas*. This is not meant to belittle the value of other spiritual qualities, but they perform an auxiliary role — like provisions of food used to support and maintain the fighting strength of soldiers in battle. It is the soldiers and their weapons, however, that are indispensable to the war effort. Soldiers in this case means your absolute determination to never retreat in the face of the *kilesas* and thus slide back into the mire of birth and death where these defilements can ridicule you once more. The premier weapons of choice are mindfulness and wisdom. Being effective at every level of combat, they should always remain close at hand.

"The points in the course of your practice where the *citta* gets stuck, are the points you must examine fearlessly without concern that the intensity of your efforts to dismantle the cycle of rebirth will somehow prove fatal. When you face the moment of death, I want you to die victorious. Don't allow yourself to die defeated or else you will continue to suffer for a long time to come. You must make every effort to fight on until *samsāra* becomes a completely deserted place. Try it! Is it really possible that *samsāra* will become deserted, due to lack of deluded people taking birth there, simply because you put forth effort in your practice? Why are you so worried about returning to occupy a place in *samsāra*? You haven't even died, yet every thought arising in your mind is directed toward reserving a future existence for yourself. Why is that? Whenever you reduce your efforts in practice, you are automatically working hard to reserve a place in the continuing cycle of birth and death. Consequently, birth and death are always bound up with your heart and your heart is always bound up with *dukkha*.

"I have made every effort to teach you the way of Dhamma, candidly revealing everything that you should know about the Four Noble Truths and the Four Foundations of Mindfulness. I have withheld only certain aspects of Dhamma dealing with specific kinds of psychic perception that are not directly connected with enlightenment, such as those special insights that I have alluded to from time to time. I am always glad to listen to anyone who experiences such perceptions and assist them in any way I can. Once I have died, it will be very difficult to find someone who can advise you on these matters. You must keep in mind that the practice of Dhamma differs considerably from the theory of Dhamma.[9] Those who have not actually attained *samādhi* and *paññā*, or *magga*, *phala*, and Nibbāna, cannot possibly teach others the correct way to reach these attainments."

Ācariya Mun concluded his *pacchima ovāda*[10] by emphasizing the importance of *sankhāradhamma*, just as the Lord Buddha had done in his final instructions to the community of monks prior to his *Parinibbāna*. Ācariya Mun began by paraphrasing the Buddha's instructions: *Monks, heed my words. All sankhāra dhammas are subject to change. They arise, evolve, decay, and then pass away, so you should always remain diligent in your practice.* He then explained the essential meaning of this passage.

"The word 'sankhāra' in the Lord Buddha's *pacchima ovāda* refers to the highest Dhamma. He gathered together all conditioned things in the word 'sankhāra', but he wished at that time to emphasize the internal *sankhāras* above all others.[11] He wanted the monks to see that these *sankhāras* are important because they are *samudaya* — the cause of *dukkha*. They are the factors that disturb the *citta*, causing it to languish in a state of delusion where it never experiences a tranquil, independent existence. If we investigate such *sankhāras* — being all of our thoughts and concepts from the most vulgar to the most refined — until we fully comprehend their true nature, they will then come to an end. When *sankhāras* come to an end, nothing remains to disturb the *citta*. Although thoughts and ideas do still arise to some extent, they merely follow the natural inclination of the *khandhas* — *khandhas* that are now pure and unadulterated. They no longer conceal any form of *kilesa*,

445

taṇhā, or *avijjā*. Comparing it to sleep, it is equivalent to a deep, dreamless sleep. In this case, the *citta* is referred to a '*vūpasama citta*'; that is, a tranquil *citta* completely devoid of all remnants of the *kilesas*. The *citta* of the Lord Buddha and those of all the Arahants were of just such a nature, so they harbored no aspirations to attain anything further. The moment the *kilesas* are extinguished within the *citta*, a state of purity arises in their place. This is called *sa-upādisesa-nibbāna*.[12] That is the precise moment when the attainment of Arahant occurs – an absolutely amazing pure essence of mind for which no comparison can be found in all the three worlds of existence."

Upon reaching this point, Ācariya Mun stopped speaking and retired to rest. From that day onward he never gave another discourse to the monks, which is why I have called it his *pacchima ovāda*. It is a very fitting note on which to conclude his biography.

As THE AUTHOR, I have done my utmost to write a thorough and accurate account of Ācariya Mun's life. I feel it to be a once-in-a-lifetime endeavor. I have written down the whole story as meticulously and as eloquently as I possibly could. Should there be any inaccuracies in what I've written, I trust you will forgive my shortcomings. I have spent a considerable amount of time attempting to record the story of his life from beginning to end. But even if I were to continue writing for another three years, I could never encompass it all. Although I would like to write as much as possible for the sake of my readers who never had a chance to meet him, my ability to recollect and transcribe the events comprising Ācariya Mun's life has now been exhausted. Still, many people may now read his biography, learning how he practiced and trained himself from the day of his ordination to the day he passed away. At least the story of his life is available to the interested reader, even though it is by no means a complete picture of Ācariya Mun and his extraordinary achievements.

In compiling this biography, I have tried very hard to select only those aspects of his life and teaching that I felt would be of greatest benefit to the average reader. At the same time, I have omitted any aspect that I felt would serve no definite purpose. Of the relevant material which was collected to write this book, approximately seventy percent has been included in the text you've just read. That much

I felt was neither too deep nor too confusing for the reader's understanding. The remaining thirty percent was excluded because I felt those aspects of Ācariya Mun's life and teaching would be difficult to present in a way that's easy to read and understand. I was concerned they wouldn't benefit the reader enough to justify their inclusion. Thus they were omitted, though often with some reluctance. Even then, I'm not wholly comfortable with some of the things I have included in the book, though they do faithfully represent the truth of what Ācariya Mun said. I managed to resist the urge to exclude them, however; yet, I could not bring myself to write about certain other matters, and for this reason they were left out.

Ācariya Mun's story, with all its many remarkable facets, tells of a truly beautiful life that is full of subtlety and grace. It would certainly be difficult finding someone to equal him nowadays. If his life were fully narrated in every detail, then it probably would not differ significantly from the lives of those Arahants who attained such mastery in the time of the Buddha. Listening to him explain various aspects of Dhamma, including the countless variety of external phenomena he contacted, I was truly amazed by his incredible mastery. When he proclaimed that impressive Dhamma for us to hear, it seemed as though he was speaking on behalf of the Lord Buddha and his gifted Arahant disciples. We could almost picture the Buddha and his disciples sitting right in front of us and bathing our hearts with the pure waters of Dhamma.

Were I to attempt to describe each and every facet of Ācariya Mun's knowledge and understanding, I would feel ashamed of my own inadequacies in this regard — ashamed of being a forest monk in appearance only, a phony who has somehow encroached upon the *sāsana*. Through my own ignorance I might inadvertently damage his excellent reputation, which should be preserved at all costs. Although I stated at the beginning of the book that I intended to write in the style of the Venerable Ācariyas of antiquity, who transcribed the lives of the Lord Buddha and his Arahant disciples, I can't help feeling embarrassed that I am not so gifted as they were. Nevertheless, I have done the best I could. Should this somewhat imperfect biography fall short of your expectations, please be so kind as to forgive my shortcomings.

It is appropriate now to bring this biography to a close. If the account I have written contains any inaccuracies or misrepresentations, I respectfully ask forgiveness of Ācariya Mun who, like a loving father, gave birth to my faith in Dhamma. May the power of his all-encompassing love and compassion always bring peace and happiness to people everywhere. May you all have sufficient faith and resources of merit to follow in his footsteps, practicing the Dhamma that he taught to your ultimate satisfaction. May Thailand enjoy continual, uninterrupted prosperity and remain free of enemies and natural disasters. And may the Thai people remain untroubled by misfortune and hardship, forever experiencing happiness and contentment in harmony with the Buddhasāsana.

Should my presentation of Ācariya Mun's life be deemed inappropriate in any way, either in terms of the subject matter or the style in which it was written, I do sincerely apologize. I hope you will make allowances for my forest background, for it's difficult to transform the natural character of a forest monk into something eloquent and sophisticated. Though I have attempted to present every aspect of Ācariya Mun's life in a suitable, accurate fashion, I must confess that my own disorderly tendencies are hopelessly incurable. In writing a book of this nature, there will inevitably be some inconsistencies that may confuse the reader — which is why I have been at pains to stress my shortcomings.

Before the life history of Ācariya Mun could come to a successful conclusion in my own mind, I had to carefully contemplate the whole matter for a long time. This prompted me to go around recording the recollections of many *ācariyas* who have lived with him at various times in the past. To this I added my own memories of what he told me about his life. It took me many years to gather all the strands of his story and weave them into a creditable whole. Be that as it may, my often confusing style of writing, plus the fact that so many events appear out of sequence, will probably confound the reader.

I accept full responsibility for everything in this biography. As I feel somewhat guilty about my own incompetence in this endeavor, I shall be glad to entertain your critical comments. At the same time, I shall be pleased to receive any complimentary remarks with the satisfaction of knowing that this book has been of some small benefit to those who read it. May all the merit gained from this work be fully credited to the readers and to those who helped to make the book possible. Should I deserve a portion by virtue of being the author, I ask to share it with every one of you who venerate the memory of Ācariya Mun. May we all share this merit equally.

Finally, may the Supreme Merit of the Buddha, the Dhamma, and the Sangha — plus the great virtue of Ācariya Mun and whatever virtue I may possess — may everything sacred in the world watch over and protect all my readers as well as the editors of Srisapada Publishing. The folks at Srisapada worked tirelessly in their efforts to bring this biography to fruition, struggling to print a manuscript that was sent to them in numerous installments. Never once did they complain about the difficulties and inconveniences associated with this project or with any of the other issues on which I requested their assistance. May they all be free of sickness and misfortune, enjoying only prosperity and contentment now and in the future. And may their aspirations in the sphere of Dhamma be fulfilled to their ultimate satisfaction.

October 1971

Appendix I

Answering the Skeptics

After his biography of Ācariya Mun first appeared, Ācariya Mahā Boowa received many inquiries and much skepticism concerning certain aspects of Ācariya Mun's life and practice. Most notably, he encountered criticism that, in principle, some episodes appear to contradict specific long-held views about the mind's pure essence and the existential nature of the fully-enlightened Arahant. Ācariya Mahā Boowa was quick to point out that the truth of Ācariya Mun's profound and mysterious inner knowledge lies beyond the average person's ability to grasp with the intellect or define in a theory. In this context, he included those students of the Pāli scriptures who, believing that the written texts comprise the sum total of all aspects of Dhamma, assert that scriptural doctrine and convention are the only legitimate criteria for authenticating all of the countless experiences known to Buddhist practitioners over the ages. In order to address this issue, Ācariya Mahā Boowa included an addendum to subsequent editions of the biography. The following is a summary of his remarks:

Ācariya Mun often told his disciples how he daily experienced such an incredible variety of Dhamma within his heart that it would be impossible to enumerate all of the things that were revealed to him. He was constantly aware of things that he could never have imagined to exist. The extent of his own experiences left him in no doubt that the aspects of Dhamma that the Lord Buddha and his Arahant disciples witnessed, from the moment they attained full enlightenment until the day they passed away, were simply incalculable. Obviously, they must have been numerous beyond reckoning.

Ācariya Mun stated that the Dhamma inscribed in the Pāli Canon is analogous to the amount of water in a small jar; whereas the Dhamma that is not elucidated in the scriptures is comparable to the immense volume of water contained in all the great oceans. He felt it was a shame that no one thought to formally transcribe the Buddha's teachings until many hundreds of years after his death, and the deaths of his fully-accomplished disciples. For the most part, the nature and emphasis of the Dhamma that was eventually written down was dictated by the particular attitudes and opinions of those individuals who compiled the texts. For this reason, it remains uncertain to what extent the compilations that have been passed down to us are always an entirely accurate reflection of what the Buddha actually taught.

Ācariya Mun frequently declared to his disciples: "Personally, I feel that the Dhamma which issued directly from the Buddha's own lips, and thus emanated from his pure heart, must have been absolutely amazing because it possessed an extraordinary power to inspire large numbers of his audience to realize the paths and fruits of his teaching with apparent ease. Such genuine, living Dhamma, whether spoken by the Buddha or by one of his Arahant disciples, had the power to transform those who listened, allowing them to clearly understand his profoundest meaning in a way that went straight to the heart. As for the *Tipiṭika*, we study and memorize its contents all the time. But has anyone attained Nibbāna while learning the texts, or while listening to recitations of the suttas? By saying this, I do not mean to imply that the scriptures are without benefit. But, when compared with the Dhamma that issued directly from the Buddha's lips, it is obvious to me which had the greater value, and the greater impact.

"Consider my words carefully, those of you who believe that I am advocating some false, ignoble truth. I myself wholeheartedly believe that Dhamma coming from the Buddha's own lips is Dhamma that forcibly uproots every type of kilesa from the hearts of his listeners — then and there on the spot, and to their total satisfaction. This is the same Dhamma that the Lord Buddha used so effectively to root out the kilesas of living beings everywhere. It was an exceptionally powerful teaching that reverberated throughout the three worlds of existence. So, I have no intention of encouraging the Buddhist faithful to become opinionated bookworms vainly chewing at pages of scripture simply because they insist on holding tenaciously to the Dhamma they have learned by rote, and thus cannot be bothered to investigate the supreme Noble Truths that are an integral part of their very own being. I fear that they will mistakenly appropriate the great wealth of the Lord Buddha as their own personal property, believing that, because they have learned his Dhamma teaching, they are therefore sufficiently wise; even though the kilesas that are piled as high as a mountain and filling their hearts have not diminished in the least.

"You should develop mindfulness to safeguard yourselves. Don't be useless scholars learning to no good purpose and so dying in vain because you possess no Dhamma that is truly your own to take with you. It is not my intention to in any way disparage the Dhamma teachings of the Lord Buddha. By its very nature, Dhamma is always Dhamma, whether it be the Dhamma existing within the heart or external aspects of Dhamma like the Pāli scriptures. Still, the Dhamma that the Buddha delivered directly from his heart enabled large numbers of those present to attain enlightenment every time he spoke. Now contrast that living Dhamma with the Dhamma teachings transcribed in the Pāli scriptures. We can be certain that the Dhamma in the Lord Buddha's heart was absolutely pure. But, since the Buddha's teachings were written down only long after he and his Arahant disciples passed into total Nibbāna, who knows, it may well be that some of the transcribers' own concepts and theories became assimilated into the texts as well, reducing the value and sacredness of those particular aspects accordingly."

Such was the essence of Ācariya Mun's discourse. As to the criticism that the Pāli Canon contains no evidence to support Ācariya Mun's assertion that deceased Arahants came to discuss Dhamma with him and demonstrate their manner of attaining total Nibbāna: If we accept that the *Tipiṭika* does not hold a complete monopoly on Dhamma, then surely those who practice the Buddha's teaching correctly are entitled to know for themselves all those aspects of Dhamma that fall within the range of their own natural abilities, regardless of whether they are mentioned in the scriptures or not. Consider the Lord Buddha and his Arahant disciples, for instance. They knew and thoroughly understood Dhamma long before the Pāli Canon appeared. If these Noble individuals are truly the genuine refuge that the world believes them to be, it is clear that they achieved that exalted status at a time when there were no scriptures to define the parameters of Dhamma. On the other hand, should their achievements thereby be deemed false, then the whole body of the Pāli Canon must perforce be false as well. So please decide for yourselves whether you prefer to take the Buddha, Dhamma and Sangha as your heartfelt refuge, or whether you want to take refuge in what you chance to read and what you imagine to be true. But those who choose to be indiscriminate in what they eat should beware lest a bone get stuck in their throat....

Appendix II

Citta – The Mind's Essential Knowing Nature.

The following comments about the nature of the *citta* have been excerpted from several discourses given by Ācariya Mahā Boowa.

Of foremost importance is the *citta*, the mind's essential knowing nature. It consists of pure and simple awareness: the *citta* simply knows. Awareness of good and evil, and the critical judgements that result, are merely activities of the *citta*. At times, these activities may manifest as mindfulness; at other times, wisdom. But the true *citta* does not exhibit any activities or manifest any conditions at all. It only knows. Those activities that arise in the *citta*, such as awareness of good and evil, or happiness and suffering, or praise and blame, are all conditions of the consciousness that flows out from the *citta*. Since it represents activities and conditions of the *citta* that are, by their very nature, constantly arising and ceasing, this sort of consciousness is always unstable and unreliable.

The conscious acknowledgement of phenomena as they arise and cease is called *viññāṇa*. For instance, *viññāṇa* acknowledges and registers the sense impressions that are produced when sights, sounds, smells, tastes, and tactile sensations contact the eyes, ears, nose, tongue, and body respectively. Each such contact between an external sense sphere and its corresponding internal base gives rise to a specific consciousness that registers the moment at which each interaction takes place, and then promptly ceases at the same moment that the contact passes. *Viññāṇa*, therefore, is consciousness as a condition of the *citta*. *Sankhāra*, or thoughts and imagination, is also a condition of the *citta*. Once the *citta* has given expression to these conditions, they tend to proliferate without limit. On the other hand, when no conditions arise at all, only the *citta's* inherent quality of knowing is apparent.

Still, the essential knowing of the average person's mind is very different from the essential knowing of an Arahant. The average person's knowing nature is contaminated from within. Arahants, being *khīnāsava*, are free of all contamination. Their knowing is a pure and simple awareness without any adulteration. Pure awareness, devoid of all contaminants, is supreme awareness: a truly amazing quality of knowing that bestows perfect happiness, as befits the Arahant's state of absolute purity. This Supreme Happiness always remains constant. It never changes or varies like conditioned phenomena of the world, which are always burdened with *anicca*, *dukkha*, and *anattā*. Such mundane characteristics cannot possibly enter into the *citta* of someone who has cleansed it until it is absolutely pure.

The *citta* forms the very foundation of *samsāra*; it is the essence of being that wanders from birth to birth. It is the instigator of the cycle of existence and the prime mover in the round of repeated birth and death. *Samsāra* is said to be a cycle because death and rebirth recur regularly according to the immutable law of *kamma*. The *citta* is governed by *kamma*, so it is obliged to revolve perpetually in this cycle following *kamma's* dictates. As long as the *citta* remains under the jurisdiction of *kamma*, this will always be the case. The *citta* of the Arahant is the sole exception, for his *citta* has completely transcended *kamma's* domain. Since he has also transcended all conventional connections, not a single aspect of relative, conventional reality can possibly become involved with the Arahant's *citta*. At the level of Arahant, the *citta* has absolutely no involvement with anything.

Once the *citta* is totally pure, it simply knows according to its own inherent nature. It is here that the *citta* reaches it culmination; it attains perfection at the level of absolute purity. Here the continuous migration from one birth to the next finally comes to an end. Here the perpetual journey from the higher realms of existence to the lower ones and back again, through the repetitive cycle of birth, ageing, sickness, and death, totally ceases. Why does it cease here? Because those hidden, defiling elements that normally permeate the *citta* and cause it to spin around have been completely eliminated. All that remains is the pure *citta*, which will never again experience birth and death.

Rebirth is inevitable, however, for the *citta* that has yet to reach that level of purity. One may be tempted to deny that rebirth follows death, or one may doggedly hold to the nihilistic viewpoint that rejects all possibility of life after death, but such convictions cannot alter the truth. One's essential knowing nature is not governed by speculation; nor is it influenced by people's views and opinions. Its preeminence within one's own being, coupled with the supreme authority of *kamma*, completely override all speculative considerations.

As a consequence, all living beings are compelled to move from one life to the next, experiencing both gross incarnations, like the creatures of land, sea and air, and the more refined incarnations of ghosts, *devas* and *brahmas*. Although the later are so ethereal as to be invisible to the human eye, the *citta* has no difficulty taking birth in their realms. The appropriate *kamma* is all that is required. *Kamma* is the determining factor; it is the power that propels the *citta* on its ceaseless journey in *saṁsāra*.

The *citta* is something so extremely subtle that it is difficult to comprehend what actually constitutes the *citta*. It is only when the *citta* attains a state of meditative calm that its true nature becomes apparent. Even experienced meditators who are intent on understanding the *citta* are unable to know its true nature until they have attained the meditative calm of *samādhi*.

Even though the *citta* resides within the body, we are nevertheless unable to detect it. That's how very subtle it is. Because it is dispersed throughout the physical body, we cannot tell which part or which aspect is actually the true *citta*. It is so subtle that only the practice of meditation can detect its presence and differentiate it from all the other aspects associated with the body. Through the practice of meditation we can separate them out, seeing that the body is one thing and the *citta* is another. This is one level of separation, the level of the *citta* that is experienced in *samādhi*, but its duration is limited to the time spent practicing *samādhi*.

At the next level, the *citta* can totally separate itself from the physical body, but it cannot yet disengage from the mental components of personality: *vedanā, saññā, sankhāra,* and *viññāna.* When the *citta* reaches this level, one can use wisdom to separate out the body and eventually become detached forever from the belief that one's body is oneself, but one is still unable to separate the mental factors of feeling, memory, thoughts, and consciousness from the *citta.* By using wisdom to investigate further, these mental factors can also be detached from the *citta.* We then see clearly for ourselves — *sanditthiko* — that all five *khandhas* are realities separate from the *citta.* This is the third level of separation.

At the final level, our attention turns to the original cause of all delusion, that extremely subtle pervasion of ignorance we call *avijjā.* We know *avijja's* name, but we fail to realize that it is concealed there within the *citta.* In fact, it permeates the *citta* like an insidious poison. We cannot see it yet, but it's there. At this stage, we must rely on the superior strength of our mindfulness, wisdom, and perseverance to extract the poison. Eventually, by employing the full power of mindfulness and wisdom, even *avijjā* can be separated from the *citta.*

When everything permeating the *citta* has finally been removed, we have reached the ultimate stage. Separation at this level is a permanent and total disengagement that requires no further effort to maintain. This is true freedom for the *citta.* When the body suffers illness, we know clearly that only the physical elements are affected, so we are not concerned or upset by the symptoms. Ordinarily, bodily discomfort causes mental stress. But once the *citta* is truly free, one remains supremely happy even amid intense physical suffering. The body and the pain are known to be phenomena separate from the *citta,* so the *citta* does not participate in the distress. Having relinquished them unequivocally, body and feelings can never again intermix with the *citta.* This is the *citta's* absolute freedom.

* * ❋ * *

Being intrinsically bright and clear, the *citta* is always ready to make contact with everything of every nature. Although all conditioned phenomena without exception are governed by the three universal laws of *anicca, dukkha,* and *anattā,* the *citta's* true nature is not subject to these laws. The *citta* is conditioned by *anicca, dukkha,* and *anattā* only because things that are subject to these laws come spinning in to become involved with the *citta* and so cause it to spin along with them. However, though it spins in unison with conditioned phenomena, the *citta* never disintegrates or falls apart. It spins following the influence of those forces which have the power to make it spin, but the true power of the *citta's* own nature is that it knows and does not die. This deathlessness is a quality that lies beyond disintegration. Being beyond disintegration, it also lies beyond the range of *anicca, dukkha,* and *anattā* and the universal laws of nature. But we remain unaware of this truth because the conventional realities that involve themselves with the *citta* have completely surrounded it, making the *citta's* nature thoroughly conform to theirs.

Birth and death have always been conditions of the *citta* that is infected by *kilesas.* But, since *kilesas* themselves are the cause of our ignorance, we are unaware of this truth. Birth and death are problems arising from the *kilesas.* Our real problem, our one fundamental problem — which is also the *citta's* fundamental problem — is that we lack the power needed to be our own true self. Instead, we have always taken counterfeit things to be the essence of who we really are, so that the *citta's* behavior is never in harmony with its true nature. Rather, it expresses itself through the *kilesas'* cunning deceits, which cause it to feel anxious and frightened of virtually everything. It dreads living, and dreads dying. Whatever happens — slight pain, severe pain — it becomes afraid. It's perturbed by even the smallest disturbances. As a result, the *citta* is forever full of worries and fears. And although fear and worry are not intrinsic to the *citta,* they still manage to produce apprehension there.

When the *citta* has been cleansed so that it is absolutely pure and free of all involvement, only then will we see a *citta* devoid of all fear. Then, neither fear nor courage appear, only the *citta's* true nature, existing naturally alone on its own, forever independent of time and space. Only that appears — nothing else. This is the genuine *citta.*

The term "genuine *citta*" refers solely to the absolute purity, or the *sa-upādisesa-nibbāna,* of the Arahant. Nothing else can wholeheartedly and without reservations be called the "genuine *citta*". I myself would be embarrassed to use the term in any other way.

The term "original *citta*" means the original nature of the *citta* that spins endlessly through the cycle of rebirth. The Buddha indicated this when he said: "Monks, the original *citta* is intrinsically bright and clear, but it becomes defiled by the commingling of the *kilesas* that come passing through."

In this sense, "original *citta*" refers to the origin of conventional reality (*sammuti*), not the origin of Absolute Purity (*parisuddhi*). When referring to the original citta, the Buddha stated: "*Pabhassaramidaṁ cittaṁ bhikkhave.*" *Pabhassara* means radiant, it does not mean pure. His reasoning is absolutely correct; it is impossible to argue against it. Had the Buddha equated the original *citta* with the pure *citta*, one could immediately object: "If the *citta* was originally pure, why then should it be born at all?" The Arahant, who has purified his *citta*, is one who never comes to birth again. If his *citta* were originally pure, why then would he need to purify it? This would be the obvious objection: What reason would there be to purify it? The radiant *citta*, on the other hand, can be purified because its radiance is nothing other than the essential, true nature of *avijjā*. Meditators will realize this truth clearly for themselves at the moment when the *citta* transcends this radiance to reach Absolute Freedom (*vimutti*). Then, the radiance will no longer appear in the *citta*. At this very point, one realizes the supreme truth about the *citta*.

* * ✳ * *

Once the *citta* has become so well-cleansed that it is always bright and clear, then when we are in a quiet place, surrounded by complete silence — as in the still of the night — even though the *citta* has not 'converged' in *samādhi*, the focal point of its awareness is so exceedingly delicate and refined as to be indescribable. This subtle awareness manifests as a radiance that extends forth in all directions around us. We are unconscious of sights, sounds, odors, tastes, and tactile sensations, despite the fact that the *citta* has not entered *samādhi*. Instead, it is actually experiencing its own firm foundation, the very basis of the *citta* that has been well-cleansed to the point where a mesmerizing, majestic quality of knowing is its most prominent feature.

Seeming to exist independent of the physical body, this kind of extremely refined awareness stands out exclusively within the *citta*. Due to the subtle and pronounced nature of the *citta* at this stage, its knowing nature completely predominates. No images or visions appear there at all. It is an awareness that stands out exclusively on its own. This is one aspect of the *citta*.

Another aspect is seen when this well-cleansed *citta* enters meditative calm, not thinking or imagining anything. Ceasing all activity, all movement, it simply rests for awhile. All thought and imagination within the *citta* come to a complete halt. This is called "the *citta* entering a state of total calm." Then, the *citta's* essential knowing nature is all that remains. Except for this very refined awareness — an awareness that seems to blanket the entire cosmos — absolutely nothing else appears. For unlike a beam of light, whose range is limited, reaching either near or far depending on the strength of the light, the flow of the *citta* has no limits, no "near" or "far". For instance, the brightness of an electric light depends on its wattage. If the wattage is high, it shines a long distance; if low, a short distance. But the flow of the *citta* is very different. Distance is not a factor. To be precise, the *citta* is beyond the conditions of time and space, which allows it to blanket everything. Far is like near, for concepts of space do not apply. All that appears is a very refined awareness suffusing everything throughout the entire universe. The whole world seems to be filled by this subtle quality of knowing, as though nothing else exists, though things still exist in the world as they always have. The all-encompassing flow of the *citta* that has been cleansed of the things that cloud and obscure it, this is the *citta's* true power.

The *citta* that is absolutely pure is even more difficult to describe. Since it is something that defies definition, I don't know how I could characterize it. It cannot be expressed in the same way that conventional things in general can be, simply because it is not a conventional phenomenon. It is the sole province of those who have transcended all aspects of conventional reality, and thus realize within themselves that non-conventional nature. For this reason, words cannot describe it.

* * * * *

Why do we speak of a "conventional" *citta* and an "absolutely pure" *citta?* Are they actually two different *cittas?* Not at all. It remains the same *citta.* When it is controlled by conventional realities, such as *kilesas* and *āsavas,* that is one condition of the *citta.* But when the faculty of wisdom has scrubbed it clean until this condition has totally disintegrated, the true *citta,* the true Dhamma, the one that can stand the test, will not disintegrate and disappear along with it. Only the conditions of *anicca, dukkha* and *anattā,* which infiltrate the *citta,* actually disappear.

No matter how subtle the *kilesas* may be, they are still conditioned by *anicca, dukkha,* and *anattā,* and therefore, must be conventional phenomena. Once these things have completely disintegrated, the true *citta,* the one that has transcended conventional reality, becomes fully apparent. This is called the *citta's* Absolute Freedom, or the *citta's* Absolute Purity. All connections continuing from the *citta's* previous condition have been severed forever. Now utterly pure, the *citta's* essential knowing nature remains alone on its own.

We cannot say where in the body this essential knowing nature is centered. Previously, with the conventional *citta,* it formed a prominent point that we could clearly see and know. For example, in *samādhi* we knew that it was centered in the middle of the chest because the knowing quality of our awareness stood out prominently there. The calm, the brightness, and the radiance appeared to emanate conspicuously from that point. We could see this for ourselves. All meditators whose level of calm has reached the very base of *samādhi* realize that the center of "what knows" stands out prominently in the region of the heart. They will not argue that it is centered in the brain, as those who have no experience in the practice of *samādhi* are always claiming.

But when the same *citta* has been cleansed until it is pure, that center then disappears. One can no longer say that the *citta* is located above or below, or that it is situated at any specific point in the body. It is now pure awareness, a knowing quality that is so subtle and refined that it transcends all conventional designations whatsoever. Still, in saying that it is "exceedingly refined", we are obliged to use a conventional figure of speech that cannot possibly express the truth; for, of course, the notion of extreme refinement is itself a convention. Since this refined awareness does not have a point or a center, it is impossible to specifically locate its position. There is only that essential knowing, with absolutely nothing infiltrating it. Although it still exists amid the same *khandhas* with which it used to intermix, it no longer shares any common characteristics with them. It is a world apart. Only then do we know clearly that the body, the *khandhas,* and the *citta* are all distinct and separate realities.

Acknowledgements

I would like to acknowledge a special debt of gratitude I owe to Bhikkhu Khemasanto, who worked for several years to prepare a translation of this biography that was eventually entrusted to me for editing and revisions. After careful comparison with the original Thai text, I decided to begin from scratch and to translate the entire book myself. Bhikkhu Khemasanto's efforts did, however, prove to be a useful source of reference. I am also indebted to Bhikkhu Piyadhammo who, having managed to decipher my often jumbled handwriting, worked tirelessly to type and format the entire manuscript. And a special thanks must go to Swe Thant, without whose careful copy-editing and timely prompting the book would be far less polished than it is at present. I am also extremely grateful to Mr. Chaleo Yuvittaya who generously sponsored the entire second printing of this book and also helped to distribute it around the world as a gift of Dhamma. May he and all who read this book be blessed with faith in Ācariya Mun, his life, and his teachings.

Notes

1. The Early Years

1. The minimum age for full ordination as a Buddhist monk is 20 years. However, boys under that age are allowed to ordain as sāmaṇeras (novices). Novices shave their heads, wear the yellow robes, and observe the ten basic precepts.

2. The year 2436 B. E., according to the traditional Thai calendar.

3. An *upajjhāya* is the preceptor who presides over a *bhikkhu's* ordination. The *kammavācariya* and *anusāsanācariya* are a new *bhikkhu's* announcing teacher and instructing teacher respectively.

4. The name Bhūridatta is found in one of the Buddha's previous births, the last ten of which were spent perfecting the ten *pāramī* (perfections of virtue). In his fifth to last birth the Bodhisatta was born as a Great *Nāga*, or Serpent King, with the name Bhūridatta (meaning: Gift of the Earth). Weary of life in the subterranean world of *nāgas*, he rose to the earth's surface where he was captured by a snake charmer who saw an opportunity to become rich and famous by making the majestic *nāga* perform feats in front of the regional monarch. Though he could have used his mystical powers to annihilate the snake charmer in an instant, the *nāga* Bhūridatta, who cherished his moral virtue above all else, did what his "master" ordered, and endured the humiliation. In this way, he developed the *Khanti Pāramī* (The Virtue of Forbearance) to ultimate perfection.

    Its association with the Bodhisatta makes the name Bhūridatta very auspicious, which is probably the reason that Ācariya Mun's preceptor chose it.

    The word *bhūri* is also equated with *paññā* (wisdom), according to some Pāli commentaries. As such, Bhūridatta might be rendered as "A Gift of Wisdom".

5. *Jāti* tree is a type of deciduous hardwood indigenous to the highland forests of Thailand's northeast region. The simile in Ācariya Mun's dream hinges on the word "*jāti*", which is also the Pāli word for "birth".

6. A *Tipiṭaka* cabinet is a bookcase that is specially designed to house a full printed set of the Buddhist Canon, comprising a total of some 50 volumes.

7. The *dhutangas* are a set of 13 specialized ascetic practices that Buddhist monks voluntarily undertake. These *dhutanga* observances are explained in detail in the next chapter.

8. The outer, upper, and lower robes of a Buddhist monk are the *sanghāṭi*, *uttarāsanga*, and *antaravāsaka* respectively.

9. *Kilesa* is a term that is crucial to understanding the aim of Buddhist practice because it highlights the mind's basic obstacle and thus indicates what needs to be surmounted in order to make progress along the spiritual path. *Kilesas*, or mental defilements, are negative psychological and emotional forces within the hearts and minds of all living beings. They are of three basic types: greed, hatred, and delusion.

All are pollutants that contaminate the way people think, speak, and act and thus corrupt from within the very intention and purpose of their existence, binding them (through the inevitable consequences of such actions) ever more firmly to the perpetual cycle of rebirth. Their manifestations are many and varied. They include passion, jealousy, envy, conceit, vanity, pride, stinginess, arrogance, anger, resentment, etc., plus all sorts of more subtle variations that invariably produce unwholesome and harmful states of mind that are responsible for so much human misery. *Kilesa*-driven mental states interact and combine to create patterns of conduct that perpetuate people's suffering and give rise to all of the world's disharmony.

10. The *citta* is the mind's essential knowing nature, the fundamental quality of knowing that underlies all sentient existence. In association with a physical body, it is referred to as "mind" or "heart". Normally, the "knowing nature" of the *citta* is timeless, boundless, and radiant, but its true nature is obscured from within by mental defilements (*kilesa*). Through the power of fundamental ignorance (*avijjā*), its currents "flow out" to manifest as feelings (*vedanā*), memory (*saññā*), thoughts (*sankhāra*), and consciousness (*viññāṇa*). *But, the true nature of the citta simply "knows". It does not arise or pass away; it is never born and never dies.*

In this book the *citta* is often referred to as the heart; the two are synonymous. The heart forms the core within the body. It is the center, the substance, the primary essence within the body. It is the basic foundation. Conditions that arise from the *citta*, such as thoughts, arise there. Goodness, evil, happiness, and suffering all come together in the heart.

There is a strong tendency to think that consciousness results purely from complex interactions within the human brain, and that when the brain dies, consciousness ceases. This mechanistic view is wholly mistaken. While there is evidence that certain parts of the brain can be identified with certain mental functions, that does not mean that the brain produces consciousness. In essence, the brain is a complex processing organ. It receives and processes incoming data impulses that inform about feelings, memory, thoughts, and consciousness, but it does not generate these mental functions; nor does it generate conscious awareness. That is entirely the province of the *citta*. (for a more detailed discussion see Appendix II) (also see Glossary)

11. When the *citta* (mind) gathers all of its outflowing currents into one point, this is known as the *citta* 'converging'. Under the power of the *kilesas*, currents of consciousness flow from the *citta* into its various manifestations (feelings, memory, thoughts, and consciousness) and through them into the sense media (sights, sounds, smells, tastes, and tactile sensations). The practice of *samādhi* meditation is a method for concentrating these diverse currents into one focal point, thus centering the *citta* into a condition of complete stillness and calm. This does not mean that the mind is straining to concentrate on one point, but rather that it is concentrated in the sense that everything has "come together to center in one place." In this way, the *citta* becomes fully absorbed within itself. The resulting experience is a feeling of pure and harmonious being that is so wondrous as to be indescribable.

12. An *uggaha nimitta* is an image that arises spontaneously in the course of meditation.

13. A home-made umbrella that serves as a tent-like shelter when suspended from the branch of a tree. A specially sewn sheet of cloth is hung around the outside edge of the open umbrella, extending down to the ground and forming a cylindrical inner space where a monk can sit in meditation or lie down to rest with adequate protection from mosquitoes and other insects, and, to some extent, the wind and rain.

14. *Sāmīcikamma.*

15. *Dukkha* is the condition of fundamental discontent that is inherent within the very nature of all sentient existence. Depending on its degree of severity, *dukkha* is experienced as pain and discomfort, discontent and unhappiness, or suffering and misery. Essentially, it is the underlying sense of dissatisfaction that ultimately undermines even the most pleasant experiences, for everything in the phenomenal world is subject to change and therefore unreliable. Thus all of saṁsāric existence is characterized by *dukkha*. The wish to relieve this unsatisfactory condition constitutes the starting point of Buddhist practice. Eliminating its causes (the *kilesas*), and thus transcending *dukkha*, is the primary aim of a Buddhist monk.

16. *Paccavekkhaṇa: Paṭisankhā yoniso...*etc. A monk is taught to wisely reflect on his requisites, such as food, not as ends in themselves, but as tools in the training of the mind; and to develop an attitude of contentment with whatever he receives. He is taught to contemplate food as follows:

> "Reflecting appropriately, he uses alms food, not playfully, or for intoxication, not for putting on weight, or for beautification; but simply for the survival and continuance of the body, for ending its afflictions, and for supporting the spiritual life, thinking, 'Thus will I destroy old feeling (of hunger) and not create new feelings (from overeating). I will maintain myself, be blameless, and live in comfort'."

17. *Paṭikkūla.* This is a reference to the inherently disgusting, repulsive nature of all food. Once chewed in the mouth, even the most eye-appealing dishes become a disgusting mess. Even more so is the food in the stomach, which is being digested and broken down into its constituent elements. This is the true nature of food.

18. Ācariya Sao Kantasīlo (1859-1942) was a native of Ubon Ratchathani province. As Ācariya Mun's teacher, he introduced him to the *dhutanga kammaṭṭhāna* way of life. Between rainy season retreats, Ācariya Mun went wandering with Ācariya Sao, searching out forest sanctuaries suitable for meditation. Together they have been credited with reviving the *dhutanga* lifestyle of the wandering ascetic in the Northeast region of Thailand.

19. A Paccekabuddha, or Private Buddha, is one who, like a Buddha, has attained Enlightenment without the benefit of a teacher, but who lacks the capacity to effectively teach others. Therefore, he does not proclaim this truth to the world. A Paccekabuddha is described as someone who is frugal of speech and who cherishes solitude.

20. *Upacāra samādhi*, or access concentration, is the intermediate level of *samādhi* which precedes the complete stillness of full absorption (*appanā samādhi*). At this level, the *citta* may actively engage with a variety of internal and external phenomena without losing its fundamental inward focus.

21. Chao Khun Upāli (Jan Sirichando, 1856-1932) was born at a village in Ubon Ratchathani province not far from Ācariya Mun's native village. Ordained a monk in 1878, he was later appointed administrative head of the Sangha for the Northeast region. In 1904 he became the abbot of Wat Boromaniwat Monastery in Bangkok. Chao Khun Upāli was a renowned Buddhist scholar who always endeavored to put the theory of Dhamma into practice. Due to a close personal rapport and a respect for his wise counsel, Ācariya Mun considered him a mentor and always sought him out when he traveled to Bangkok.

22. This is a reference to the *saññā khandha*: one of the mental components of personality which is associated with the function of memory; for instance, recognition, association, and interpretation. *Saññā* both recognizes the known and gives meaning and significance to all of one's personal perceptions. Through recollection of past experience, the function of memory gives things specific meanings and then falls for its own interpretations of them, causing one to become either sad or glad about what one perceives.

23. This is a reference to the *sankhāra khandha*: one of the mental components of personality which is associated with thought and imagination. *Sankhāra* are the thoughts that constantly form in the mind and conceptualize about one's personal perceptions. *Sankhāra* creates these ideas and then hands them on to *saññā*, which interprets and elaborates on them, making assumptions about their significance.

24. Terrestrial or *rukkha devas* are a special class of nonhuman beings who inhabit a realm of sensuous existence immediately above the human realm. Also known as *bhumma devas* because of their natural affinity with the earth, these beings normally "inhabit" the uppermost foliage of large trees, a group or "family" of them often living together in a cluster in one tree. Birth in this realm is a consequence of certain kinds of wholesome, meritorious actions, combined with a strong attachment to the earth plane.

Although their existence has a substantive, physical base (the earth), the bodies of these *devas* have no gross material characteristics. A *rukkha deva* is composed of ethereal light, which is beyond the range of the human senses but clearly visible to the divine eye of the meditator. It seems that the majority of *devas* who visited Ācariya Mun during his career as a wandering monk were from this terrestrial realm, for remote wilderness areas have always been their preferred habitat.

25. A *sāvaka* is a direct disciple of the Lord Buddha who hears the Buddha's teaching and declares him to be his teacher.

26. *Samādhi nimitta* is a sensory image that appears in the *citta* at the level of *upacāra samādhi* (access concentration). The message, in the case of the *sāvaka* Arahants, is communicated telepathically by means of the heart's own universal

language: a direct, non-verbal communication in which the essence of the meaning appears unambiguously in its entirety, allowing no room for misunderstanding or misconception to occur. Unobscured by conjecture or interpretation, the "listener" intuitively "knows" the whole meaning as it is conveyed.

27. A *samaṇa* is a contemplative who abandons the conventional obligations of social life in order to follow a life of spiritual striving. At the time of the Buddha, a *samaṇa* was considered to embody the ideal of the wandering ascetic.

28. An Anāgāmī, or Non-returner, is a person who has abandoned the five lower fetters that bind the mind to the cycle of rebirth, and who after death will appear in one of the worlds called the Pure Abodes, to eventually attain Nibbāna and thus never again to return to this world.

The five lower fetters are: 1) personality view (*sakkāyadiṭṭhi*) 2) skeptical doubt (*vicikicchā*) 3) wrong attitude toward precepts and vows (*sīlabbataparāmāsa*) 4) sensual desire (*kāmarāga*) 5) aversion (*paṭigha*)

29. *Paṭiccasamuppāda*, or Dependent Origination, is a concise statement of how fundamental ignorance (*avijjā*) conditions the rise of the whole cycle of repeated existence.

2. The Middle Years

1. Ācariya Singh Khantayākhamo (1888-1961). Ordained in 1909, Ācariya Singh first met Ācariya Mun in 1919 at Wat Burapha in Ubon Ratchathani. Ācariya Singh was studying the Buddhist scriptures at a nearby monastery at the time. He was so impressed by the clarity of Ācariya Mun's discourses and the serenity of his manner that he left his academic studies to go wandering *dhutanga* with Ācariya Mun. He later became a central figure helping to establish the *dhutanga* way of life among monks in the provinces of Khon Kaen and Nakhon Ratchasima.

2. Ācariya Mahā Pin Paññāphalo (1892-1946). Ordained in 1912, Ācariya Mahā Pin spent the first 10 years of his monastic career studying the Buddhist scriptures in Bangkok, eventually earning a degree (Mahā) in Pāli studies. In 1922 he returned to Ubon Ratchathani where his brother, Ācariya Singh, convinced him to try the *dhutanga* lifestyle. Ācariya Mahā Pin was the first scholastic monk of Mahā grade to become a disciple of Ācariya Mun.

3. Ācariya Thet Thesarangsī (1902-1994). Having ordained as a novice at the age of 18 with the help of Ācariya Singh, Ācariya Thet took higher ordination in 1922. After living and practicing with Ācariya Singh for many years, in 1933 Ācariya Thet traveled to Chiang Mai in search of Ācariya Mun. He wandered and practiced meditation with Ācariya Mun and other *dhutanga* monks for 5 years before returning to settle in the Northeast.

4. Ācariya Fan Ajāro (1898-1977). Having initially ordained as a novice, then as a monk, Ācariya Fan first met Ācariya Mun in 1920 when the latter came to stay near his home village in Sakon Nakhon. Ācariya Mun's clear articulation of the Dhamma impressed him, inspiring him to follow the *dhutanga* way of life. In 1926 he followed Ācariya Mun to Ubon Ratchathani where he helped to establish several forest monasteries in the succeeding years. After a life of extensive wandering, Ācariya Fan eventually settled at a monastery in his home district in Sakon Nakhon.

5. Ācariya Khao Anālayo (1888-1983). Ordained in Ubon Ratchathani at the age of 31, having already had a wife and family, Ācariya Khao wandered over much of the Northeast in search of Ācariya Mun, whom he eventually met up with in Nong Khai province. He later followed Ācariya Mun to Chiang Mai and spent many years with him there. In his frequent encounters with wild animals, Ācariya Khao was known to have a special affinity for elephants.

6. *Yakkhas* (ogres) are a special class of powerful nonhuman beings who often have cruel and murderous temperaments.

7. Wat Pa Baan Taad, the author's forest monastery in Udon Thani province, was established in 1955.

8. The Four Foundations of Mindfulness are: 1) body (*rūpa*) 2) feelings (*vedanā*) 3) states of mind (*citta*) 4) mental phenomena (dhamma).

9. The Four Noble Truths are: 1) suffering (*dukkha*) 2) the cause of suffering (*samudaya*) 3) the cessation of suffering (*nirodha*) 4) the path leading to the cessation of suffering (*magga*).

10. "When we are taught to visit a cemetery, we should never neglect the inner cemetery. Even if we visit a cemetery outside, the purpose is to reflect inwardly on the inner cemetery — our own body. Dried corpses, fresh corpses, raw corpses, cooked corpses, all kinds of corpses are gathered together in this body, but I've never heard the place where they are barbecued, roasted, and stewed called a crematorium. Instead it's called a kitchen. But actually, that's what it is, a crematorium for animals. And they are all buried here in this stomach, this grave. If we look at ourselves in all fairness, with impartiality, we see that we are a burial ground for all kinds of animals — yes, us! — because we're filled with corpses old and new. Once we have contemplated in this way, if we don't feel disenchanted, if we don't feel disengaged, what will we feel? — for that's the way the truth actually is."

— comments by Ācariya Mahā Boowa

11. Māra represents the personification of evil and temptation, and by extension, a personification of the insidious hold which the senses have on the mind. Ensnared by Māra one remains lost in the world and fails to find the path that leads to the cessation of suffering.

12. In the past, cemeteries were not like they are today. An open stretch of ground well outside the village was set aside for disposing of the dead. Corpses were cremated out in the open on pyres made of firewood, and the charred skeletal remains were left scattered around the area.

13. This is a reference to the *saññā khandha*, one of the mental components of personality which is associated with the function of memory; as for instance, recognition, association, and interpretation. When thoughts (*sankhāra*) are formed in the mind, *saññā* immediately defines and then interprets them from various angles. This is where one gets deluded. The mind falls for its own assumptions — its own shadows — which paint pictures that constantly delight or upset it. The mind is deceived by its own shadows (*saññā*) into feeling happy or sad, frightened or worried. Such emotional turmoil is caused simply by the mind painting pictures to delude itself.

Because the monk in this story had the idea of ghosts firmly fixed in his mind, his perceptions were then instinctively interpreted in that way. He assumed an external threat, but in fact was haunted by the shadows lurking in his own mind.

14. A monk's 8 basic requisites are: his three principal robes, alms bowl, belt, razor, needle, and water filter.

15. The *Pāṭimokkha* is the basic code of monastic discipline. It comprises 227 rules of conduct and is usually recited rule by rule before an assembly of monks once every fortnight.

16. The First Sangha Council was held during the rainy season retreat immediately following the Lord Buddha's *Parinibbāna* for the purpose of officially codifying the entire body of his teachings. All of the 500 monks scheduled to attend were fully-enlightened Arahants — except the Venerable Ananda. Before his passing away, the Buddha had predicted that Venerable Ananda, his personal attendant, would attain full enlightenment in time to participate in the First Council, which he did — on the very morning the council was scheduled to convene.

17. "Fundamental ignorance (*avijjā*) conditions the arising of conditioned phenomena (*sankhāra*)... such is the origin of this entire mass of suffering (*dukkha*)." This is an abbreviated sequence of the factors of Dependent Origination (*paṭiccasamuppāda*), progressing from cause to effect.

18. "With the remainderless fading and cessation of fundamental ignorance (*avijjā*) comes the cessation of conditioned phenomena (*sankhāra*)... such is the cessation of this entire mass of suffering (*dukkha*)." This is an abbreviated sequence of the cessation of those factors.

19. *Rāgataṇhā* is usually translated as "sexual desire" or "lust". Predicted on the belief that the body is oneself and that happiness can be achieved for oneself through bodily sensations, *rāgataṇhā* is the desire, even craving, to seek pleasure and self-gratification by means of the physical body. With this mental defilement as the driving force, most people attempt to overcome discontent and find fulfillment using physical stimulation as the primary means. If such craving is allowed a free rein, it easily becomes a preoccupation that gives rise to even more craving, leaving the heart forever hungry and dissatisfied. For lust is a hunger that no amount of gluttony can satiate. The harder one tries to find satisfaction in this way, the more one suffers the consequences. This deep-rooted sexual drive is the main fetter binding living beings to the Sensuous World (*Kāma-loka*).

But, as Ācariya Mun points out here, *rāgataṇhā* also has another more sinister side, for passionate intentions can easily become aggressive and violent. Thus, united in a passion for physical stimulation, the *kilesas* of greed and aversion join forces in the guise of *rāgataṇhā*, which strives to assuage its insatiable hunger by dominating and exploiting others. In this way, passion for sex and lust for power are two aspects of the same fundamental craving. The thirst for war and murder, the thirst for torture and all forms of abuse, all have their roots in *rāgataṇhā*. As such, *rāgataṇhā* is a primary factor governing birth in the sub-human realms (demons, ghosts, animals, and hells).

20. The sphere of conventional reality (*sammuti*) includes all conditioned phenomena without exception. That is, all phenomena characterized by being impermanent (*anicca*), bound up with suffering (*dukkha*), and not-self (*anattā*) are relative, conventional realities. Only Nibbāna is completely beyond the sphere of conventional reality.

21. *Sugato*, meaning "well-gone" or "gone to a good destination", is a frequently used epithet for the Buddha.

22. *Sādhu*, meaning "it is well", is an exclamation expressing appreciation or approval.

23. *Samādhi's* access level is *upacāra samādhi*. It is the level that precedes the complete stillness of full absorption (*appanā samādhi*). At this level the *citta* may engage with external phenomena, such as *devas*, without losing its fundamental inward focus.

24. "The Venerable Ācariya Mun taught that all hearts share the same language. Regardless of one's language or nationality, the heart has nothing but simple awareness, which is why he said that all hearts have the same language. When a thought arises, we understand it; but in translating it into words, it must become this or that language, so we don't really understand one another. The feelings within the heart, however, are the same for everyone. This is why Dhamma fits the heart perfectly, for Dhamma is not any particular language. Dhamma is the language of the heart."
— comments by Ācariya Mahā Boowa

25. The attainment of Nibbāna is the ultimate goal of the holy life (*brahmacāriya*).

26. The Pāli word *vāsanā*, variously translated as "inherent virtuous tendencies" or "resources of merit", refers to virtues developed in past lives which then become part of an individual's ongoing spiritual legacy that is experienced in the present life.

It is a common belief among Buddhists that those who feel a strong inclination to ordain as monks and practice meditation must have cultivated Buddhist practices in their previous lives, and therefore have available to them a store of accumulated virtue that they can fall back on. Some rely on these presumed inherent tendencies to ensure their continued progress.

Ācariya Mun is insisting here that only diligent effort at the practice in a suitable environment can truly ensure spiritual progress.

27. "As for Dhamma, which is the path that the Lord Buddha taught us to follow, its basis is faith (*saddhā*) — in other words, faith that following the path will bring us good results — and diligent effort (*viriya*) to make us persistent in our attempt to earnestly follow that path. Mindfulness (*sati*) is what guides our efforts along the path.

Concentration (*samādhi*) is firmness of the heart as it progresses along the path, in addition to being food for the journey—in other words, the spiritual peace and happiness that we enjoy along the way before we reach the goal. And wisdom (*paññā*) is the circumspection needed to follow the path step by step from beginning to end. All of these qualities support us and encourage us to stay on the right path. When we have these five qualities—faith, diligent effort, mindfulness, concentration and wisdom— constantly with us, there is no doubt that the right results will clearly appear as our reward, in line with our strength and abilities. If we develop these five qualities so that they are powerful within our hearts, then the results that the Lord Buddha declared to be lying at the end of the path—release from suffering and Nibbāna—will not be able to elude us, for all of these qualities aim at just those results."

—comments by Ācariya Mahā Boowa

28. Generosity (*dāna*), moral virtue (*sīla*), and meditative development (*bhāvanā*) are the three basic categories of meritorious activity taught by the Buddha.

29. Mindfulness of breathing (*ānāpānasati*) is practiced by focusing one's attention on the in-and-out breaths at the spot where the sensation of the breath passing in and out appears most prominent. One is mindful each time the breath comes in and each time it goes out until one gradually becomes absorbed in the subtle feeling of the breath to the exclusion of everything else.

30. "*Buddho*", "*dhammo*", "*sangho*" are meditation-words used to hold the mind's attention. When focusing on the repetition of "*buddho*", for example, one mentally repeats the word "*buddho*" continuously while meditating. Simply be aware of each repetition of "*buddho, buddho, buddho*" to the exclusion of all else. Once it becomes continuous, this simple repetition will produce results of peace and calm in the heart.

31. This is a contemplation on the nature of the human body. Using *kesā* (hair of the head), *lomā* (hair of the body), *nakkhā* (nails), *dantā* (teeth), and *taco* (skin) as its most visible aspects, one analyzes the body according to its constituent parts (of which 32 body parts are traditionally cited). Each part is analyzed in turn, back and forth, until one specific part captures one's interest. Then one focuses exclusively on an investigation into that body part's true nature.

32. Meditation on death (*maraṇānussati*) is a reflection on the nature of death and its implications for oneself. One contemplates how all beings on this earth are subject to death: having been born, we get old and sick and then we die; and one sees that it is a completely natural process. One realizes that nobody knows when, where, or under what circumstances death will occur, or what kind of fate one can expect after death; and that life is very short and one's time here is limited, so one should make the most of it. Continuous contemplation of death inspires diligence in the way of practice, while developing detachment toward the affairs of the world.

33. *Paracittavijjā*, also known as *ceto-pariya-ñāna*, is knowledge of the hearts and minds of others; in other words, thought-reading and telepathy.

34. In momentary (*khaṇika*) *samādhi* the *citta* 'converges' into a still calm state for only a moment before withdrawing on its own. This is the initial stage of *samādhi*.

In access (*upacāra*) *samādhi* the *citta* 'converges' into a prolonged state of calm and stillness which is at the same time a state of enhanced awareness concerning internal and external phenomena that make contact with the internal and external sense bases. At the access level, normal thought processes (the inner dialogue) are temporarily suspended, while powers of perception are heightened. This is the intermediate stage of *samādhi*.

In full-absorption (*appanā*) *samādhi* the *citta* completely 'converges' into the very base of *samādhi*. Perceptions of body and mind totally disappear from awareness at that time, leaving only the "knowing nature" of the *citta* alone on its own. Clear, bright, and expansive, the *citta* simply "knows". There is no object, no duality, just "knowing". This is the advanced stage of *samādhi*.

35. This is the ultimate stage of body contemplation (*kāyagatāsati*) where both the body's attractive aspects (*subha*) and its repulsive aspects (*asubha*) are fully comprehended for what they really are and successfully surpassed. This happens with the clear realization that both attractiveness and repulsiveness are a matter of the *citta* deceiving itself.

36. An *upāsikā* is a female devotee who wears white robes and strictly follows the standard 8 precepts. She is the modern-day equivalent of a Buddhist nun.

3. A Heart Released

1. Chao Khun Upāli (Jan Sirichando, 1856-1932) The abbot of Wat Boromaniwat Monastery in Bangkok, Chao Khun Upāli was a renown Buddhist scholar who always strove to put the theory of Dhamma into practice. Due to a close personal rapport and a respect for his wise counsel, Ācariya Mun considered him a mentor and always sought him out whenever he traveled to Bangkok.

2. The *nāma khandhas* are the four mental components of personality: feelings (*vedanā*), memory (*saññā*), thoughts (*sankhāra*), and consciousness (*viññāṇa*). They are all simply natural phenomena that continuously arise and pass away. Since no substantial and continuous self-entity can be found anywhere in these mental phenomena, they are said to be *anattā* (not-self).

3. A theoretical understanding acquired from memory (*saññā*) greatly differs from a genuine understanding based on wisdom (*paññā*). In this context, *saññā* means the knowledge gained from studying the theories and commentaries pertaining to Buddhist practice, that is, academic learning. On its own, such intellectual comprehension is quite inadequate, for it relies on views and opinions, which lead to speculation and guesswork. One can remember names and descriptions of all the factors of Dhamma, for instance, but one cannot discover the truth of those factors within oneself.

Paññā, on the other hand, is a clear intuitive insight gained by directly probing, investigating, and analyzing the various factors that arise during meditation in light of principles of reason until their cause-and-effect relationships become clearly apparent. Such intuitive understanding, while not at odds with the theory of Dhamma, carries with it the certainty of direct personal experience, which can confidently be applied to help solve the next set of problems that arises in meditation practice.

4. *Sandiṭṭhiko* means self-evident; immediately apparent; visible here and now. It is a traditional epithet for the Dhamma.

5. Literally, "a pool of understanding" (Thai: *Nong Aw*. The Thai word *aw* is an oral inflection used to signify that one has just awakened to a true understanding of a certain matter, as in "Ah! So this is how it is!"). In Ācariya Mun's case, it might be phrased "Ah! So this is how the Buddha attained enlightenment!"

6. *Paṭiccasamuppāda* (referred to in the text as *paccayakāra*) is Dependent Origination: a concise statement of how fundamental ignorance (*avijjā*) conditions the rise of the whole cycle of repeated existence.

7. *Visuddhidhamma*, meaning "Dhamma of Absolute Purity", is a synonym for Nibbāna.

8. *Sukhavihāra-dhamma* (or *diṭṭhadhamma sukhavihāra*). Of an Arahant: Living happily, at ease in the sensory world until he finally passes away.

9. The *vaṭṭa-cakka* is the cycle of rebirth, which "spins" around continuously like a "wheel". With the destruction of the *vaṭṭa-cakka*, the *vivaṭṭa-citta* (the *citta* that has stopped "spinning") is fully realized.

10. *Vimuttidhamma*, meaning "Dhamma of Absolute Freedom", is another synonym for Nibbāna.

11. The 5 *khandhas* , or aggregates (body, feelings, memory, thoughts, and consciousness), are the physical and mental components of personality and of sensory experience in general. Normally, the *khandhas* are the "tools" that the *kilesas* use to construct and maintain the world of *saṁsāra*. Once the *kilesas* have been eliminated, the *khandhas* continue to function naturally, as they always have. However, since the defiling influences of the *kilesas* are no longer present to dictate their activities, they then work solely at the command of Dhamma. The 5 *khandhas* remain components of an Arahant's personality for as long as he lives; when he finally passes away, his *citta* no longer has any connection with the 5 *khandhas* .

12. *Yathādīpo ca nibbuto* means "extinguished like the flame of a lamp." This is a reference to the Nibbāna of an Arahant after his passing away. Another analogy compares it to an extinguished fire whose embers are cold.

13. Here Ācariya Mun contrasts relative, conventional reality (*sammuti*) with Absolute Freedom (*vimutti*).

The *citta*, the mind's essential knowing nature, has been dominated by fundamental ignorance (*avijjā*) since time immemorial. This fundamental ignorance has created within the *citta* a center or focal point of the knower. The existence of that false center engenders an individual perspective which is the nucleus of self-identity. This "self" forms perceptions of duality (the knower and the known) and from there awareness flows out to produce the world of the 5 *khandhas* and of all sensory experience, which in turn reinforce the knower's sense of individuality. It all begins with the currents of the *citta*, which flow out to create the entire sensory world, the world of conditioned phenomena. Because of this, it is said that all physical and mental phenomena are relative, conventional realities (*sammuti*). They exist only relative to the knower, the one who perceives them. As such they are merely conventions that the *citta* has brought into being and given a subjective identity to in order to experience its own manifestations. In turn, these manifestations become incorporated into the *citta's* sense of its own identity. Thus the known becomes indistinguishable from the knower, and duality comes full circle, trapping the *citta* in a web of self-delusion. The *citta* is reduced to depending on its manifestations to assess the nature of its own existence.

When fundamental ignorance has been destroyed, the focal point of the knower disintegrates, which causes the "self" perspective to disappear from the *citta* altogether. With the disappearance of self-identity, all manifestations of the *citta*, all relative, conventional realities, are divested of their power to deceive and no longer appear within the *citta*. Although they do continue to play a role, in the form of the 5 *khandhas* , as long as the Arahant remains alive, they are no longer incorporated into the *citta's* identity and have no part in conditioning its outlook. This is called *vimutti* — absolute freedom from all conditions. No conditions whatsoever exist for this freedom.

14. *Nong Aw*. Literally, "a pool of understanding". (see Note #5 of this section)

15. A *visuddhi-deva* is a being made divine by the purity of his attainment, that is, an Arahant.

16. Dhammapada verse 354:

> The gift of Dhamma surpasses all gifts,
> The taste of Dhamma surpasses all tastes,
> Delight in Dhamma transcends all delights,
> Freedom from craving ends all suffering.

17. Spiritual partner. Literally, "one's partner in developing the spiritual perfections (*pāramī*)".

Most living beings have an individual, usually of the opposite sex, with whom they have maintained an intimate, personal relationship spanning countless lifetimes over many eons of existence. Life after life, those couples who share a deep spiritual commitment will reconnect and renew their relationship, assisting each other to develop one or another aspect of spiritual perfection. Such a devoted companion is considered to be essential for the eons-long quest to become a fully-enlightened Buddha, as Gautama Buddha's own story illustrates:

In a past eon of the world, as a forest-dwelling ascetic named Sumedha, he threw himself at the feet of an earlier Buddha, Dīpankara, and resolved to become a Buddha himself in the future. As he made this vow, a young woman bearing incense and flowers stepped forth joyously to congratulate him. He immediately rejected her support, saying that as a forest-dwelling ascetic he was determined to live alone. Dīpankara

Buddha then cautioned the young ascetic, telling him that every aspirant to Buddhahood had a spiritual companion (*pāda-paricārika*) who was his inseparable partner throughout the long, arduous journey to perfection. After that, through countless lives, the Bodhisatta and his spiritual partner labored and sacrificed together for the benefit of other living beings as they traveled the Path of Awakening.

18. Knowledge of wisdom (*paññāñāṇa*). This is a reference to the sixth and last of the "special knowledges" (*abhiññā*): knowledge of the total extinction of the *citta's* "outflows" (*āsavakhayañāṇa*), and signifies the attainment of Nibbāna.

19. The *brahmavihāras* are the four "sublime" or "divine" abodes that are developed through the practices of loving kindness (*mettā*), compassion (*karuṇā*), appreciative joy (*muditā*) and equanimity (*upekkhā*). Meditation on these four spiritual qualities is particularly beneficial as an antidote to hatred and anger.

20. All four *brahmavihāras* — loving kindness, compassion, appreciative joy, and equanimity are included in this statement.

21. Originally, *sāvaka* meant a direct disciple of the Buddha — one who attained enlightenment after hearing the Buddha teach. In Ācariya Mun's case, he renounced his previous determination to become a Buddha in the future in order to practice the existent teaching of a Buddha and thus become an enlightened "disciple" instead.

22. The *āsavas* are mental pollutants that "flow out" from the mind to create a "flood" of repetitive birth and death cycles.

23. The minimum age for ordaining as a Buddhist monk is 20 years. However, boys under that age are allowed to ordain as novices (*sāmaṇera*). Novices shave their heads, wear the yellow robes, and observe ten basic precepts. Although no specific minimum age for novices is mentioned in the scriptures, traditionally in Thailand boys as young as seven are accepted. This tradition follows the story of the Lord Buddha's son, Rāhula, who was allowed to become a novice at the age of seven.

24. Literally, *vaṭṭa-dukkha*, the pain and suffering experienced in the round of *saṁsāra*.

25. For relative, conventional realities (*sammuti*) see Note #13 of this section.

26. *Anupādisesa-nibbāna*, meaning "Nibbāna without any remaining physical or mental components of personality (i. e. the 5 *khandhas*) ", is the total Nibbāna of the Arahant after he has passed away.

27. A *nimitta* is a mental sign, image, or vision that arises spontaneously in the *citta*.

28. In light of widely-held views about Nibbāna, one would do well to keep in mind that the unconditioned (*asankhata*) nature of Nibbāna naturally implies that absolutely no conditions or limitations whatsoever can be attributed to Nibbāna. To believe that, having passed away, the Buddhas and the Arahants are completely beyond any possibility of interacting with the world is to place conditions on the Unconditioned. (see Appendix I, page 451)

29. *Sammodaniyadhamma* literally means, "the courtesy of exchanging friendly greetings".

30. *Sāmīcikamma*

31. *Visuddhidhamma*, meaning "Dhamma of Absolute Purity", is a synonym for Nibbāna.

32. Seniority within the Sangha is based on the date of a monk's ordination and the number of consecutive rainy season retreats he has spent in the robes.

33. Heartwood from the jackfruit tree, a fruit tree indigenous to much of South and Southeast Asia, is boiled to bring out the yellowish-brown color, which is then used to dye a monk's robes.

4. The Chiang Mai Years

1. Sundara Samudda was an Arahant at the time of the Buddha who thwarted a courtesan's seductions and attained Enlightenment. Tradition has it that he floated up and out a window in the top of her house to escape her advances. (Theragātha VII.1)

2. That is to say, penetrating realization of the Path to Enlightenment (*maggañāṇa*) had destroyed the king (*avijjā*) of the *citta* caught in the perpetual cycle of rebirth (*vaṭṭa-citta*).

3. Thai-style kick boxing is a sport where the feet, knees, and elbows, as well as the fists, are used to fight and subdue an opponent.

4. That is, Ācariya Mun used both *samādhi nimittas* and his ability to read other's thoughts (*paracittavijjā*) to equally good effect in teaching his students.

5. This passage refers to *nirodhasamāpatti*, also called *saññā-vedayitanirodha* (the cessation of consciousness and feeling), the highest and most profound of all the *samādhi* attainments.

All conditioned phenomena are, by their very nature, conventional realities (*sammuti*). Since *anicca* (constant change), *dukkha* (unsatisfactoriness), and *anattā* (not-self) are the basic characteristics inherent in all conditioned phenomena, *anicca*, *dukkha*, and *anattā* are therefore part and parcel of the nature of all conventional realities (see Note #13, page 477). Upon the attainment of *nirodhasamāpatti*, all such phenomena, including the 5 *khandhas* and the sense bases, temporarily cease to appear within the knowing nature of the *citta* which has reached that attainment.

6. The terms *vimutti-citta* and *visuddhi-citta* (the absolutely free and absolutely pure *citta*) are synonymous with the Arahant, who has completely transcended every aspect of conventional reality (*sammuti*).

7. A specially sewn sheet of cloth was hung around the outside edge of the open umbrella, which extended down to the ground forming a cylindrical inner space where a monk could sit or lie down and receive some moderate protection from the wind and rain.

8. That is, Ācariya Mun was a *visuddhi puggala* (pure one) and a *puññakkhettaṁ lokassa* (a field of merit for the world), both traditional epithets for the Arahant.

9. *Sugato*, meaning "well-gone" or "gone to a good destination", is a traditional epithet for the Buddha.

10. Ācariya Fan Ajāro was the monk visited by the author on that occasion.

11. *Puthujjana* is the ordinary worldly person who lacks any special Dhamma attainment.

12. *Conquer anger with lack of anger* is taken from Dhammapada verse 223:

> Conquer anger with lack of anger,
> Conquer evil with good.
> Overcome stinginess by being generous,
> And lies by telling the truth.

13. This story was related to the author by Ācariya Mahā Thong Sak himself.

14. Ācariya Mun was referring to the image of the calf lodged under its mother's neck: it appeared as though it was trying to carry her on its back.

15. *Maw lam*, also known as "folk opera", was a popular form of village entertainment in the Northeast region of Thailand. *Maw lam* takes the form of a contest in extemporaneous rhyming, usually performed on a public stage between a man and a woman, in which the battle of wits can become quite fierce. Much use is made of word play: riddles, puns, innuendoes, metaphors, and simply playing with the sounds of words. The verses are made up as the singers go along, and the winner is the one who comes up with the most humorous verses, thus making the other one look foolish.

16. He was the same Chao Khun Upāli who later became a senior administrative monk and a renowned Buddhist scholar. He was the "mentor" whom Ācariya Mun always sought out when he traveled to Bangkok. As a youth his name was "Jan". (see Note #21, page 470)

17. By then it was nighttime, and the local people were instinctively reluctant to walk long distances alone at night for fear of tigers and ghosts.

18. The *Vessantara Jātaka* is one of the more popular of the *Jātaka* tales, which recount stories of the previous births of the Buddha. In this *Jātaka*, Sakka, in the guise of an old brahmin, asked Lord Vessantara for that which was most precious to him, his wife, in order to test his joyful generosity.

19. *Mettā appamaññā brahmavihāra* is the spiritual practice of focusing the mind to "dwell in a state of boundless loving kindness".

20. A *stupa* (*cetiya*) is a dome-shaped monument that usually houses the remains of a revered Buddhist monk; though some are built by the Buddhist faithful to act as memorial shrines.

21. Traditional Buddhist meditation contains two different but complementary aspects, namely, calm (*samatha*) and insight (*vipassanā*), which are suited to the development of deep states of concentration (*samādhi*) and wisdom (*paññā*) respectively.

The Arahant, having already developed meditative calm and insight to perfection, uses them as a means of living at ease in the sensory world (*sukhavihāra-dhamma*) until he passes away.

22. Literally, the *vimutti-citta*.

23. There is virtually unanimous agreement in Thailand that the author, Ācariya Mahā Boowa, is one of those auspicious monks. There is debate as to who the other one might be.

24. This is a reference to the *Duddubha Jātaka* (No.322) in which a rabbit in the forest, having heard a loud thud caused by a fruit striking a palm leaf, imagined that the sky was collapsing and ran panic-stricken, spreading this false news to the other animals. Those animals in turn stampeded, thus placing themselves in great danger by believing in unfounded rumors instead of trying to find out the truth for themselves.

25. Literally, *vatta-dukkha*.

26. For Paccekabuddha see Note #19, page 469

27. *Nāgas* are a special class of nonhuman beings comprising all kinds of serpents. Included in this category are snakes, deities associated with bodies of water, and spirits of earth and the realm beneath it. As such, *nāgas* represent the vital potential of falling rain and flowing water. They are a class of beings whose primary role is that of protector and benefactor, though, like all beings with *kilesas*, they may be temperamental, as the following story illustrates. It is said that *nāgas* can change their form at will. In the ancient texts there are many stories of *nāgas* presenting themselves in human guise. *Nāgas* were known to have great respect for the Buddha and his disciples.

28. Ācariya Mun explained that the *nāga* had sprayed those monks with its venom, thus causing various unpleasant symptoms to arise until they could no longer bear the discomfort and fled.

29. *Anupādisesa-nibbāna*, meaning "Nibbāna without any remaining physical or mental components of personality (i. e. the 5 *khandhas*)", is the total Nibbāna of the Arahant after he has passed away.

30. Lion's posture: The Buddha slept on his right side with his right hand under his head, his legs flush, and one foot slightly overlapping the other. When he lay down for the final time to enter *Parinibbāna*, he assumed the same "lion's posture".

31. Mahā is a Pāli word meaning "great". In Thailand, it is an honorary title given to a monk who has earned a degree in Pāli studies, as the monk in question had done.

32. The *kammatthāna* referred to here are the five most visible parts of the human body—hair of the head, hair of the body, nails, teeth and skin—which are recommended to a newly-ordained monk, by his preceptor, as essential objects of meditation.

33. *Paracittavijjā*, also known as *ceto-pariya-ñāna*, is knowledge of the hearts and minds of others, in other words, thought-reading and telepathy.

34. This is a reference to the ancient Thai art of magic, which uses tattoos and incantations to prevent bullets, swords, and knives from penetrating a person's body.

35. Visākha is the ancient name for the sixth lunar month, which occurs in May. According to tradition, the Buddha's birth, Enlightenment, and *Parinibbāna* each took place on the full-moon night in the month of Visākha. Visākha Pūjā (or Vesak) is a festival day commemorating these events that is celebrated annually throughout the world of Theravāda Buddhism.

5. Unusual Questions, Enlightening Answers

1. The elder in question was the Venerable Chao Khun Upāli. (see Note #21, page 470)

2. "Oneself is one's own refuge" (*attāhi attano nātho*) is taken from Dhammapada verse 160:

> Oneself is one's own refuge,
> For who else could one's refuge be?
> Having trained oneself well,
> One obtains a refuge hard to gain.

3. *Pubbenivāsa*. Literally, one's previous state of existence (in a former life).

4. That is, concentration, wisdom, absolute freedom, and perfect realization of absolute freedom.

5. The Four Roads to Spiritual Power (*iddhipāda*) are: intention (*chanda*), effort (*viriya*), contemplation (*citta*), and analysis (*vimaṁsa*).

6. The term *sāvakasangha* refers to the *ariyasangha* and denotes all of those followers of the Buddha who have attained at least Stream-entry (Sotāpanna), the first of the transcendent Noble Paths (*Ariya-magga*). Such individuals are sure to "practice well (*supaṭipanno*), straightly (*uju*), rightly (*ñāya*), and properly (*sāmīci*)".

7. Ācariya Mun died in November of the year 2492 of the Buddhist Era, approximately twenty years before this biography was written.

8. The Bodhi Tree, or Tree of Awakening, was the tree under which the Buddha was seated when he attained Enlightenment. It was an Indian pipal tree (*ficus religiosa*).

9. All of these *ācariyas* have now passed away.

10. Stream-enterer (Sotāpanna), Once-returner (Sakadāgāmī), and Non-returner (Anāgāmī): the first three stages of the Noble Path to Nibbāna, which culminate in the fourth or Arahant stage.

6. The Final Years

1. When Ācariya Mun's biography was written, only three photographs of him were known to exist. In the intervening years, several more photographs were discovered, bringing to nine the number of pictures of Ācariya Mun now in circulation. Most of them are reproduced in this book.

2. This is said with tongue in cheek, since in the Thai system of Buddhist scholarship the ninth grade of Pāli studies is the highest level of achievement.

3. The *Pāṭimokkha* is the basic code of monastic discipline. It comprises 227 rules of conduct and is usually recited rule by rule before an assembly of monks every fortnight.

4. *Ti-lakkhaṇa* are the three fundamental characteristics inherent in all conditioned phenomena, that is, they are inherently impermanent and unstable (*anicca*), bound up with pain and suffering (*dukkha*), and devoid of anything which can be identified as "self" (*anattā*).

5. *Rāgataṇhā* (see Note #19, page 473)

6. That is, the Four Foundations of Mindfulness or *Satipaṭṭhāna*: *rūpa* (body), *vedanā* (feelings), *citta* (mental states), and *dhamma* (mental phenomena).

7. *Kho nu hāso kim ānando* ("why all this laughter, why all the joy") is taken from Dhammapada verse 146:

> Why all this laughter, why all the joy,
> When the world is always burning?
> Since you are shrouded in darkness,
> Why not seek the light?

8. The *suddhāvāsa*, or Pure Abodes, are the five highest realms of the *brahma* world. After death, an Anāgāmī will be reborn in one of the Pure Abodes, there to attain Nibbāna, and thus never to return to this world again.

9. *Appanā samādhi*, or "full absorption", is a state into which the *citta* 'converges', or 'drops', once it has become fully integrated with the object of meditation. Upon reaching the *appanā* or base level of *samādhi*, the meditation object and awareness of body, mind, and environment all disappear. (see Note #33, page 475)

10. Ācariya Mun was diagnosed as having pulmonary tuberculosis. He died on November 10, 1949.

11. *Ovāda Pāṭimokkha*

12. Literally, *sākyaputta*, which means "son of the Sakyan", the Buddha having been a native of the Sakyan Republic. *Sākyaputta* is an epithet for Buddhist monks.

13. The distance they walked from Ban Nong Pheu to Ban Phu was approximately 12 miles.

14. The date of Ācariya Mun's cremation was January 31, 1950.

15. Once the body of a revered monk has been cremated, the charred pieces of bone that survive the fire are collected. The extreme heat of the fire usually causes the larger bone segments to disintegrate and break up, leaving many small, often porous, fragments. Such bone fragments, usually burned to an ashen white color by the fire, are kept and treasured as 'relics' by the Buddhist faithful.

16. *Amatadhamma* means "the Deathless Dhamma" and is a synonym for Nibbāna, which is the final liberation from the cycle of rebirths, and therefore also freedom from ever-repeated deaths.

7. The Legacy

1. The bodily relics (*sarira-dhatu*) left behind after death by an Arahant are one of the ineffable mysteries of the mind's pure essence, a phenomena so miraculous that it appears to transcend the laws of modern science. Due to the extreme heat of the fire, bone fragments collected after an Arahant's cremation are usually porous in nature. Kept with great reverence and venerated by the faithful, over a period of years — or sometimes even months — the physical elements in each piece of bone somehow amalgamate into dense, hard, crystalline pebbles of various hues of translucency and opacity. (see color photo at the beginning of this book)

As Ācariya Mahā Boowa explains it, this transformation from bone to relic is a result of the cleansing effect that the pure *citta* of the Arahant has on his body elements. Such relics are cherished as rare gems by the Buddhist faithful. Having a supernatural, spiritual potency, they bless those who possess them with good fortune, even seeming miracles, in direct proportion to the strength of faith and virtue which their owners maintain in their hearts.

2. *Dhammabhisamaya* means "full comprehension of Dhamma".

3. In his old age, Ācariya Mun smoked four cigarettes each day. He smoked one after his morning meal, one in the early afternoon, one at about 5 p.m., and a final one at about 8 p.m. He preferred to smoke Cock Brand cigarettes, which were the ones purchased for him on that occasion.

4. Ācariya Chob Thānasamo (1902-1995). Born in the northeastern province of Loei, Ācariya Chob left home at the age of 15 to follow a *dhutanga* monk on his wanderings. Ordained initially as a novice and later as a monk, he first met Ācariya Mun in 1928 in Nakhon Phanom province. Ācariya Chob mostly lived a very reclusive life in inaccessible locations where he had many memorable encounters with wild animals and various classes of nonhuman beings.

5. Burma shares a long common border with Thailand.

6. Either a *deva* assuming the bodily form of a tiger, or possibly, a *deva* using its superior psychic power to mesmerize a real, flesh-and-blood tiger to make it behave in a docile manner.

7. At that time Thailand was effectively under the control of the Japanese Imperial Army, which had established a puppet regime in the country.

8. Literally, *upadana*.

9. For a related discussion of the practice of Dhamma (*patipatti*) as opposed to theoretical knowledge of Dhamma obtained through reading, study, and learning (*pariyatti*), see Note #3, page 476.

10. The Buddha's *pacchima ovada* was the "final instruction" he imparted to his disciples just prior to his *Parinibbana*. He declared to them: "All conditioned phenomena are subject to disintegration. Strive diligently to attain the goal." (*Vayadhamma sankhara appamadena sampadetha*)

11. "In this teaching, the Buddha's "final instructions", how should we understand the word *sankhāra?* What kind of phenomena does it refer to? We could take it as referring to external phenomena, or internal phenomena, and we wouldn't be wrong in either case. But at that moment, we can be fairly certain that his final instructions at that final hour were for practicing monks with high levels of spiritual attainment, from Arahant on down. So I would think that the main point the Buddha was emphasizing then was the internal, mental phenomena which form thoughts in the mind and so disrupt the mind at all times. He taught that the arising and ceasing of these mental phenomena should be investigated with diligence—in other words, they should be constantly investigated using mindfulness and wisdom. These phenomena encompass the entire cosmos!

"We could, if we wanted, interpret the word *sankhāra* to mean external phenomena—trees, mountains, animals, people—but that would not be consistent with the spiritual level of the monks gathered there. Nor would it be keeping with the occasion: the Buddha's last moments before his *Parinibbāna* when he gave this exhortation to the Sangha—the ultimate teaching at his final hour.

"Thus the Buddha's final exhortation concerning conditioned phenomena, given as he was preparing to enter *Parinibbāna*, must refer to those phenomena which arise exclusively within the heart. Once we have clearly understood these inner phenomena, how could we help but understand their basis, what they arise from? For to do that we must penetrate into the well-spring of the cycle of rebirth—the *avijjā-citta*. This is the way we discover the crucial point. Those disciples of the Buddha who had already reached that level had to know this. Those who were approaching it in stages, but had yet to fully realize it, still knew this clearly because they were already investigating the matter. Thus the Buddha's final instructions to them, which were given in the middle of such a momentous event."

—comments by Ācariya Mahā Boowa

12. *Sa-upādisesa-nibbāna,* meaning "Nibbāna with the physical and mental components of personality (i. e., the 5 *khandhas*) still remaining", is the Nibbāna experienced by the Arahant during his lifetime.

Glossary

ācariya: Teacher, mentor; also used as a term of respect when referring to a senior monk. When capitalized, Ācariya is the respectful title given to a teacher by his disciples, as in Ācariya Mun and Ācariya Sao.

akāliko: Timeless, not conditioned by time or season; existing beyond time and space. *Akāliko* is a traditional epithet for Dhamma.

Anāgāmī: Non-returner. An Anāgāmī is a person who has abandoned the five lower fetters that bind the mind to the cycle of rebirth, and who after death will appear in one of the worlds called the Pure Abodes, to eventually attain Nibbāna and thus never again to return to this world.

anattā: Not-self; the truth that all phenomena are devoid of anything that can be identified as "self". This means that none of the physical and mental components of personality (the 5 *khandhas*) make up an entity, either individual or collective, nor can a self-entity be found anywhere within the heart (*citta*). Therefore, what is experienced as being an abiding self is no more than a phantom personality born of ignorance and delusion — inherently transient, unstable, and bound up with suffering.

anicca: The unstable, impermanent, transient nature of all phenomena in all realms of existence. In other words, all things arise and cease, are subject to change, and will become otherwise, making them all inherently unsatisfactory and bound to cause suffering.

appanā: Full-absorption *samādhi*. In *appanā samādhi* the *citta* completely 'converges' to the very base of *samādhi*. Perceptions of body and mind totally disappear from awareness at that time, leaving only the essential "knowing nature" of the *citta* alone on its own. Clear, bright, and expansive, the *citta* simply "knows". There is no object, no duality, just "knowing". The previous sense of dividedness is replaced by a wholly unified mental state, and a feeling of pure and harmonious being that is so wondrous as to be indescribable. This is the advanced stage of *samādhi*.

Arahant: A "fully enlightened one" or "pure one". A person who, by following the Buddha's Path to Freedom, has totally eradicated his mental defilements (*kilesas*) and thus possesses the certainty that all traces of ignorance and delusion have been conclusively destroyed, never to arise in his heart again in the future. Having completely severed the fetters that once bound him to the cycle of repeated birth and death, he is no longer destined for future rebirth. Thus, the Arahant is the individual who has attained Nibbāna; and though the physical and mental components of personality (*khandhas*) remain intact until his death, his *citta* — being free of all defiling elements whatsoever — is absolutely pure. At death, body and mind disintegrate, leaving only the unconditioned, absolutely pure nature of the *citta* — which is wholly beyond conventional description.

avijjā: Fundamental ignorance. This ignorance is the central factor in the delusion about the true nature of oneself and therefore the essential factor binding living beings to the cycle of rebirth. *Avijjā* exists entirely within the *citta* (the one who knows). Being an integral part of the *citta's* conscious perspective since time-without beginning, it has usurped the *citta's* "knowing nature" and distorted its intrinsic quality of simply "knowing" by creating the false duality of the "knower" and the "known". From this individual viewpoint spring right and wrong, good and evil, heaven and hell, and the whole mass of suffering that comprises the world of *saṁsāra*. Thus *avijjā* is the seed of being and birth, the very nucleus of all existence. It is also the well-spring from which all other mental defilements arise.

Far from appearing dark and menacing, *avijjā* is the epitome of all the mental and spiritual virtues that living beings hold in the very highest esteem. This is its beguiling allure, the reason why living beings cannot see it for what it actually is — the great lord and master of birth and death. Appearing at first to be the ultimate in virtue and happiness, the *citta's* true abiding sanctuary, when wisdom finally penetrates to its core and exposes its fundamental deception, *avijjā* promptly dissipates, revealing the pure, unblemished *citta*, the true Supreme Happiness, Nibbāna.

bhikkhu: A Buddhist monk; a male member of the Buddhist Sangha who has gone forth into homelessness and received the higher ordination. In Theravāda countries today, *bhikkhus* form the nucleus of the Buddhist community. Living entirely off donations of food and other basic requisites, their monastic lifestyle is based on the principles of poverty, celibacy, virtue, and meditation.

bodhi: Awakening; enlightenment; transcendent wisdom. *Bodhi* is equated with perfection of insight into the Four Noble Truths and the realization of Nibbāna, the cessation of all suffering.

brahma (brahmā): Celestial beings who inhabit the first three realms of the Fine Material World. Beings reborn into those sublime realms are said to have some experience with the meditative absorptions (*jhāna*). Consequently, *brahmas* have extremely refined bodies composed of pure light and experience extremely refined degrees of mental pleasure. When the good *kamma* that sent them to those realms is finally exhausted, these beings pass away and are reborn again somewhere else, in a realm of existence suitable to their remaining *kamma*.

Buddhasāsana: The Teachings of the Lord Buddha and, by extension, the Buddhist religion in general (see *sāsana*).

buddho: Supremely enlightened. A traditional epithet for the Buddha, *buddho* is a preparatory meditation-word (*parikamma*) that is repeated mentally while reflecting on the Buddha's special qualities. In its simplest form, one focuses attention exclusively on the repetition of "*buddho*", continuously thinking the word "*buddho*" while in meditation. One should simply be aware of each repetition of "*buddho, buddho, buddho*" to the exclusion of all else. Once it becomes continuous, this simple repetition will produce results of peace and calm in the heart.

citta: The *citta* is the mind's essential knowing nature, the fundamental quality of knowing that underlies all sentient existence. When associated with a physical body, it is referred to as "mind" or "heart". Being corrupted by the defiling influence of fundamental ignorance (*avijjā*), its currents "flow out" to manifest as feelings (*vedanā*), memory (*saññā*), thoughts (*sankhāra*), and consciousness (*viññāṇa*), thus embroiling the *citta* in a web of self-deception. It is deceived about its own true nature. *The true nature of the citta is that it simply "knows". There is no subject, no object, no duality; it simply knows. The citta does not arise or pass away; it is never born and never dies.*

Normally, the "knowing nature" of the *citta* is timeless, boundless, and radiant, but this true nature is obscured by the defilements (*kilesa*) within it. Through the power of fundamental ignorance, a focal point of the "knower" is created from which that knowing nature views the world outside. The establishment of that false center creates a "self" from whose perspective consciousness flows out to perceive the duality of the "knower" and the "known". Thus the *citta* becomes entangled with things that are born, become ill, grow old, and die, and therefore, deeply involved it in a whole mass of suffering.

In this book the *citta* is often referred to as the heart; the two are synonymous. The heart forms the core within the body. It is the center, the substance, the primary essence within the body. It is the basic foundation. Conditions that arise from the *citta*, such as thoughts, arise there. Goodness, evil, happiness, and suffering all come together in the heart.

Samādhi meditation provides confirmation of the heart's significance. When the *citta* gathers all of its outflowing currents into one point, the calm, still state of *samādhi* arises. From the meditator's perspective, that experience is centered in the middle of the chest. The stillness, the brightness, and the awareness of this experience appear to emanate prominently from the region of the heart. The knowing nature of the *citta* is pronounced right there. Thus, the true seat of consciousness is in the heart; and it is wise, therefore, to avoid thinking of the "mind" as essentially cerebral and located in the head.

There is a strong tendency to think that consciousness results purely from complex interactions within the human brain, and that when the brain dies, consciousness ceases. This mechanistic view is wholly mistaken. While there is evidence that certain parts of the brain can be identified with certain mental functions, that does not mean that the brain produces consciousness. In essence, the brain is a complex processing organ. It receives and processes incoming data impulses that inform about feelings, memory, thoughts, and consciousness, but it does not generate these mental functions; nor does it generate conscious awareness. That is entirely the province of the *citta*. (for a more detailed discussion see Appendix II, page 455)

'converge': When the *citta* gathers all of its outflowing currents into one point, this is known as the *citta* 'converging'. The practice of *samādhi* meditation is a method for concentrating all of these diverse currents into one focal point, thus centering the *citta* into a condition of complete stillness and calm.

deva: Literally, "shining one"; an inhabitant of one of the celestial realms of sensual bliss, which are located immediately above the human realm. With bodies composed entirely of ethereal light, *devas* exist in a spiritual dimension that lies beyond the range of normal sense faculties. These beings are usually associated with such qualities as splendor, mobility, beauty, goodness, and radiance. The upper and lower celestial *devas* referred to by Ācariya Mun are the *brahmas* and the upper Sensual World *devas* respectively. On a still lower level are the terrestrial *devas* who, having an affinity for the earth, inhabit a realm of existence located just above the human realm and just below the celestial realms.

devarāja: King of the *devas*. This is a reference to Sakka, a preeminent follower of the Buddha who presides over the *Tāvatiṁsa* celestial realm.

Dhamma (skt. Dharma): Supreme Truth; the basic principles of that Truth; transcendent spiritual qualities; the Buddha's Teaching. First and foremost, Dhamma is the quintessential nature of perfect harmony existing in and of itself, independent of all phenomena, yet permeating every aspect of sentient existence. Dhamma is the right natural order of things that forms the underlying basis for all existence, though it is not dependent on or conditioned by any form of existence. Ultimately, Dhamma is the sum of those transcendent qualities, such as detachment, loving kindness and wisdom, the spiritual perfection of which brings the mind into harmony with the Supreme Truth. By further extension, Dhamma encompasses the basic principles that are the essence of the Buddha's Teaching, including the patterns of behavior that should be practiced so as to harmonize oneself with the right natural order of things.

dhammā: Elemental factors of experience; the intrinsic essence of something; mental phenomena.

dhutanga: Ascetic practices. The *dhutangas* are a set of 13 specialized ascetic practices that Buddhist monks voluntarily undertake. Their purpose in each case is to counteract specific mental defilements (*kilesas*). They are: 1) Wearing only robes made from discarded cloth; 2) Wearing only the three principle robes and no others; 3) Going on almsround everyday without fail; 4) Not omitting any house on almsround; 5) Eating only one meal per day; 6) Eating all food directly from the alms bowl; 7) Refusing to accept food offered after the almsround; 8) Living in the forest; 9) Dwelling at the foot of a tree; 10) Living in the open — not at the foot of a tree or under a roof; 11) Living in a cemetery; 12) Being satisfied with whichever bed or resting place is available; 13) The sitter's practice; that is to say, sitting, standing or walking, but never lying down.

dukkha: Suffering, pain, discontent; the unsatisfactory nature of all phenomena. *Dukkha* is the condition of fundamental discontent that is inherent within the very nature of all sentient existence. Essentially, it is the underlying sense of dissatisfaction that ultimately undermines even the most pleasant experiences, for everything in the phenomenal world is subject to change and therefore unreliable. Thus, all of samsāric existence is characterized by *dukkha*.

garuḍa: A special class of nonhuman beings characterized by features that appear part bird and part human. *Garuḍas* are the archenemies of all classes of serpents, especially *nāgas*.

kamma (skt. karma): One's intentional actions of body, speech, and mind that result in birth and future existence. These actions carry with them a specific moral content – good, bad, or neutral – and leave in the ongoing continuum of consciousness a potential to engender corresponding results in the future. Buddhism holds that all unenlightened beings are bound to be born, live, die, and be reborn again and again in a variety of worlds and circumstances, a perpetual cycle of existence that is driven by the nature of their *kamma* and the inevitable manifestation of its consequences.

kammaṭṭhāna: Literally, "basis of work", *kammaṭṭhāna* refers to the "occupation" of a practicing Buddhist monk: namely, the contemplation of certain meditation themes that are conducive to uprooting the defiling forces of greed, hatred, and delusion from his mind . In the ordination procedure, a new monk is taught the 5 basic *kammaṭṭhāna* that lay the groundwork for contemplation of the body: hair of the head, hair of the body, nails, teeth, and skin. By extension, *kammaṭṭhāna* includes all 40 of the classical Buddhist meditation subjects. The term *kammaṭṭhāna* is most often used to identify the particular Thai forest tradition and lineage that was founded by Ācariya Sao and Ācariya Mun.

khandha: Literally, "group" or "aggregate". In the plural, *khandhas* refer to the five physical and mental components of personality (body, feelings, memory, thoughts, consciousness) and to sensory experience in general (sights, sounds, smells, tastes, tactile sensations). Also known as "aggregates of attachment" because they are the objects of a craving for personal existence, they are, in fact, simply classes of natural phenomena that continuously arise and cease and are devoid of any enduring self-identity whatsoever.

kilesa: Mental defilement. *Kilesa* are negative psychological and emotional forces existing within the hearts and minds of all living beings. These defilements are of three basic types: greed, hatred, and delusion. All of them are ingenerate pollutants that contaminate the way people think, speak and act, and thus corrupt from within the very intention and purpose of their existence, binding them (through the inevitable consequences of their actions) ever more firmly to the perpetual cycle of rebirth. Their manifestations are many and varied. They include passion, jealousy, envy, conceit, vanity, pride, stinginess, arrogance, anger, resentment, etc., plus all sorts of more subtle variations that invariably produce the unwholesome and harmful states of mind which are responsible for so much human misery. These various *kilesa*-driven mental states interact and combine to create patterns of conduct that perpetuate people's suffering and give rise to all of the world's disharmony.

magga, phala, and Nibbāna: The Transcendent Paths, their Fruition, and Nibbāna. As used by Ācariya Mun, the expression *magga, phala*, and Nibbāna refers to the transcendent nature of the Buddhist path of practice and its primary aim of leading one, stage by stage, through successive levels of spiritual liberation until one ultimately reaches the absolute freedom of Nibbāna.

mahāsati and *mahāpaññā*: Supreme-mindfulness and supreme-wisdom. Mindfulness (*sati*) is the faculty of being keenly attentive to whatever arises within one's field of awareness. Wisdom (*paññā*) is the faculty of intuitive insight that probes, examines, and analyzes the nature of phenomena as mindfulness becomes aware of them. Supreme-mindfulness and supreme-wisdom are these two faculties developed to an advanced level of proficiency characterized by heightened alertness, quickness, and agility, combined with incisive powers of reasoning. Constantly working in unison, without a moment's lapse in concentration, *mahāsati* and *mahāpaññā* are said to be capable of automatically tracking and penetrating to the truth of all phenomena as they arise and cease. Being the only mental faculties capable of investigating the increasingly more subtle defilements at the highest stage of the Transcendent Path (*arahattamagga*), their development is a prerequisite for reaching this level of practice and thus for attaining the ultimate goal, Nibbāna.

mindfulness (*sati*): Attentiveness; the ability to keep one's attention deliberately fixed on whatever one chooses to observe. In all forms of meditation, this means an uninterrupted span of attention focused directly on the chosen object of meditation or on the unfolding process of occurring phenomena that is the subject of investigation. Mindfulness is the one faculty that's essential to every type of meditation. Without it the mind will invariably falter and fail to achieve its objectives.

nāga: A special class of nonhuman beings comprising all kinds of serpents. *Nāgas* include snakes, deities associated with bodies of water, and spirits of the earth and the realm beneath it. As such, they represent the vital potential of falling rain and flowing water. *Nāgas* are a class of beings whose primary role is that of protector and benefactor. They are said to be able to change their formal appearance at will. In the ancient texts there are many stories of *nāgas* presenting themselves in human guise. *Nāgas* were known to have great respect for the Buddha and his disciples.

nāma: Mental phenomena. *Nāma* refers to the mental components of personality (*nāma khandha*), which include feelings, memory, thoughts, and consciousness.

Nibbāna (skt. Nirvana): Literally meaning "extinguished", Nibbāna is compared to a lamp or a fire going out. That is to say, the threefold fire of greed, hatred and delusion goes out in the heart due to lack of fuel. The extinguishing of this fire frees the mind from everything that binds it to the cycle of rebirth and the suffering experienced therein. Nibbāna is Absolute Freedom, the Supreme Happiness. As such, it is the ultimate goal of the Buddhist training. It is said to be Unborn, Deathless, and Unconditioned, but being totally detached from all traces of conventional reality, a description of what Nibbāna is, or is not, lies wholly beyond the range of conventional figures of speech.

nimitta: Mental image; vision. A *samādhi nimitta* is an image that arises spontaneously during the course of meditation. *Nimittas* may take the form of extrasensory perceptions, visualizations, symbolic representations of reality, or prophetic dreams.

Pāli: An ancient variant of Sanskrit, Pāli is the literary language of the early Buddhists and the language in which the texts of the original Buddhist Canon are preserved. Most of the terms that have been italicized in this book are Pāli words.

paññā: wisdom; intuitive insight. (see wisdom)

Parinibbāna: Total Nibbāna. That is to say, the total extinction of the physical and mental components of personality (the 5 *khandhas*), and with their disintegration the ending of all traces of existence in the phenomenal world and thus total release from the misery of *saṁsāra. Parinibbāna* is the Nibbāna that occurs at the death of an Arahant. It is most frequently used to refer to the passing away of the Lord Buddha.

paṭiccasamuppāda: Dependent Origination. *Paṭiccasamuppāda* is a concise statement of how fundamental ignorance (*avijjā*) conditions the rise of the whole cycle of repeated existence.

Pāṭimokkha: The Buddhist monk's basic code of discipline. It comprises 227 rules of conduct and is usually recited rule by rule before an assembly of monks once every fortnight.

rāgataṇhā: Sexual desire; lust. Predicated on a belief that the body is oneself and that happiness can be achieved for oneself through bodily sensations, *rāgataṇhā* is the desire, even craving, to seek pleasure and self-gratification by means of the physical body. With this mental defilement as the driving force, people attempt to overcome discontent and find fulfillment using physical stimulation as the primary means. If such craving is allowed a free rein, it easily becomes a preoccupation that gives rise to even more craving, leaving the heart forever hungry and dissatisfied.

rainy season retreat (*vassa*): The annual three-month-long meditation retreat observed by Buddhist monks in the Theravādin tradition. The retreat is always held during the Asian monsoon season and stretches from the full moon day of July to the full moon day of October. In the *dhutanga* forest tradition of Ācariya Mun, the retreat accentuates a lifestyle of renunciation, strict ascetic practices, and intensive meditation.

rūpa: The body, and physical phenomena in general. When opposed to *nāma* (mental phenomena), *rūpa* is the strictly physical component of personality.

saddhā: Faith; conviction. Faith in the Buddha, or one's teacher, that gives one the confidence and willingness to put his teachings into practice. A reasoned faith, rooted in understanding, *saddhā* gains strength with each successive attainment along the path of Dhamma.

sādhu: "It is well." Commonly used in Buddhist circles, *sādhu* is an exclamation expressing appreciation, assent, or approval.

Sakka: Known as "king of *devas*", Sakka is a preeminent follower of the Buddha who presides over the *Tāvatiṁsa* heavenly realm.

samādhi: Meditative calm and concentration. *Samādhi* is experienced by practicing various meditation techniques that are designed to calm the mind's emotional turbulence and mental distraction by fixing it firmly on a single object of attention and mindfully holding it there until the mind becomes fully absorbed in that single preoccupation to the exclusion of everything else, and thus wholly integrated within a simple, unified state of awareness. By concentrating one's attention on just one object, distracting thoughts and currents of the mind that would normally flow out into the sensory environment are gradually gathered into one inner point of focus, one still, calm, concentrated state called *samādhi*. This does not mean that the mind is striving to concentrate on one point (an outward focus), but rather that by assiduously following the method with mindful attention, the mind naturally, on its own accord, converges into a unified state of awareness. The resulting experience is a feeling of pure and harmonious being that is so wondrous as to be indescribable. Upon withdrawing from *samādhi*, this calm, concentrated mental focus then serves as a basis for successfully pursuing investigative techniques to develop wisdom and gain insight into the true nature of all phenomena.

    Samādhi has many levels and classifications. For one such classification see Note #34, page 475.

samaṇa: A contemplative who abandons the conventional obligations of social life in order to follow a life of spiritual striving. At the time of the Buddha, a *samaṇa* was considered to embody the ideal of the wandering ascetic.

saṁsāra: The round of rebirth without beginning, in which all living beings revolve. *Saṁsāra* is the name given to the continuous process of being born, getting sick, growing old, and dying—an uninterrupted succession of births, deaths, and rebirths. It encompasses the entire universe of sentient existence, from the grossest beings to the most refined, from the highest realms of the Immaterial World to the lowest realms of hell. All existence within this cycle is subject to change, inherently unstable, and burdened with pain and suffering, with each state of existence being determined by a being's intentional actions of body, speech, and mind (*kamma*). The attainment of Nibbāna marks the complete transcendence of the world of *saṁsāra*.

Sangha: The community of the Buddha's disciples. On the conventional level, this means the Buddhist monastic order. On the ideal level, it refers to those of the Buddha's followers, whether lay or ordained, who have attained at least the first of the four Transcendent Paths culminating in Arahantship.

sankhāra: As a general term, *sankhāra* refers to all forces that form or condition things in the phenomenal world of mind and matter, and to those formed or conditioned phenomena that result. As the fourth component of personality (*sankhāra khandha*) it refers to thought and imagination; that is, the thoughts that constantly form in the mind and conceptualize about one's personal perceptions. *Sankhāra* creates these ideas and then hands them on to *saññā*, which interprets and elaborates on them, making assumptions about their significance.

saññā: Memory; recognition of physical and mental phenomena as they arise. As the third component of personality, *saññā khandha* is associated with the function of memory; for instance, recognition, association, and interpretation. *Saññā* both recognizes the known and gives meaning and significance to all of one's personal perceptions. Through recollection of past experience, the function of memory gives things specific meanings and then falls for its own interpretation of them, causing one to become either sad or glad about what one perceives.

sāsana: The teaching of the Buddha and, by extension, the Buddhist religion in general. The Buddhist spiritual path is inevitably a multidimensional one where all legitimate wholesome practices, from generosity to virtuous conduct to transcendent meditation, are essential aspects of the way leading toward the ultimate goal, the cessation of suffering. The term *sāsana* usually refers to this aggregate of the Buddha's teaching, its practices, and its realization.

sāvaka: A direct disciple of the Lord Buddha who hears the Buddha's teaching and declares him to be his teacher.

sugato: "Well-gone" or "gone to a good destination"; a traditional epithet for the Buddha.

sutta: A discourse or sermon spoken by the Buddha. After the Buddha's death, the *suttas* he delivered to his disciples were passed down in the Pāli language according to a well-established oral tradition. They were finally committed to written form in Sri Lanka around 100 BCE and form the basis for the Buddha's teachings that we have today.

Tathāgata: "One thus gone." One of the epithets a Buddha uses when referring to himself.

Tāvatiṁsa: "The Thirty-three." A realm of heavenly beings (*devas*) in the Sensuous World where Sakka is the presiding deity.

terrestrial *devas*: A special class of nonhuman beings who inhabit a realm of sensuous existence immediately above the human realm. Also known as *rukkha* or *bhumma devas* because of their natural affinity with the earth, these beings normally "inhabit" the uppermost foliage of large trees, a group or "family" of them often living together in a cluster in one tree. Birth in this realm takes place as a consequence of certain kinds of wholesome, meritorious actions, combined with a strong attachment to the earth plane. It seems that the majority of *devas* who visited Ācariya Mun during his career as a wandering monk were from the terrestrial realm, for remote wilderness areas have always been their preferred habitat.

Theravāda: "Doctrine of the Elders". Handed down to us in the Pāli language, it is the oldest form of the Buddha's teachings. Theravāda is the only one of the early schools of Buddhism to have survived into the present. It is currently the dominant form of Buddhism in Thailand, Sri Lanka, and Burma.

three worlds of existence: The Sensuous World (*Kāma-loka*), The Fine Material World (*Rūpa-loka*), and the Immaterial World (*Arūpa-loka*), which together comprise the entire universe of sentient existence. (for a graphic illustration

of Buddhist cosmology see <u>The Thirty-One Planes of Existence</u> at
www.accesstoinsight.org)

vimutti: Absolute Freedom, that is, freedom from the fabrications and conventions
of the mind. *Vimutti* is a synonym for Nibbāna.

viññāṇa: Consciousness; simple cognizance. As the fifth component of personality,
viññāṇa khandha simply registers sense data, feelings, and mental impressions as
they occur. For instance, when visual images make contact with the eye, or when
thoughts occur in the mind, consciousness of them arises simultaneously. When
that object subsequently ceases, so too does the consciousness that took note of it.

vipassanā: Clear intuitive insight. Aided by a clear, quiet state of meditative calm,
vipassanā is spontaneous insight into physical and mental phenomena, as they arise
and cease, that sees them for what they really are: inherently impermanent and
unstable, bound up with pain and suffering, and devoid of anything that can be
identified as "self".

visuddhi: Perfect purity of mind. The pure nature of a mind that has completely
transcended all mental defilements. That is, the state of Absolute Purity experienced
by an Arahant.

wisdom (*paññā*): The term wisdom denotes an active, incisive application of the
principles of cause and effect for the purpose of probing, examining, and analyzing
physical and mental phenomena, as they arise and cease, so as to see them for
what they really are: inherently impermanent and unstable, bound up with pain
and suffering, and devoid of anything that can be identified as "self". As it is used
in Buddhism, wisdom implies much more than just sound judgement. Wisdom is
a faculty that searches, probes, compares, and investigates the workings of body
and mind in light of the fundamental principles of truth in order to gain a decisive
advantage over the defiling elements (*kilesas*) that obscure their true nature and
the true nature of the one who knows them.

Although inductive reasoning is initially very much a part of the practice of
wisdom, insights based solely on it are still superficial. As the faculty of wisdom
develops and becomes more introspective, its skills become increasingly more subtle,
while its insights become more intuitive in nature. Only when meditative insight
penetrates deeply can the root causes of the mind's discontent be truly exposed,
uprooted, and destroyed.

In general, wisdom is the proactive complement to the quiescence of *samādhi*.
Both work together in tandem to ensure that the task of eradicating the *kilesas* is
accomplished with maximum efficiency. Both are essential aspects of the path
leading to the cessation of all suffering.

yakkha: Ogres. A special class of powerful nonhuman beings who often have cruel
and murderous temperaments.

About the Translator

Bhikkhu Sīlaratano was born Richard E. Byrd, Jr. at Winchester, Virginia in 1948. He began his life as a Buddhist monk in 1975 in Bangalore, India where he ordained as a novice monk with Ven. Buddharakkhita Thera. While still a novice he moved to Sri Lanka, taking full bhikkhu ordination at Sri Vajiragnana Dharmayatanaya in Maharagama in June of 1976. In early 1977 Bhikkhu Sīlaratano traveled to Thailand, where he was ordained into the Dhammayutha Nikāya at Wat Bovornives Vihāra in Bangkok on April 21, 1977. He soon moved to Baan Taad Forest Monastery in Udon Thani province, where he has been living and practicing under the tutelage of Ven. Ācariya Mahā Boowa Ñāṇasampanno and his senior disciples ever since. Bhikkhu Sīlaratano's other books include *Arahattamagga Arahattaphala — The Path to Arahantship* and *Mae Chee Kaew — Her Journey to Spiritual Awakening & Enlightenment*.

Other Forest Dhamma Books Publications: